THE LEGITIMACY OF INTERNATIONAL TRADE COURTS AND TRIBUNALS

The recent rise of international trade courts and tribunals deserves systemic study and in-depth analysis. This volume gathers contributions from experts specialized in different regional adjudicators of trade disputes and scrutinizes their operations in the light of the often-debated legitimacy issues. It not only looks into prominent adjudicators that have played a significant role for global and regional integration, but it also includes the newly established and/or less-known judicial actors. Critical topics covered range from procedures and legal techniques during the adjudication process to the pre- and postadjudication matters in relation to forum selection and decision implementation. The volume features cross-cutting interdisciplinary discussions among academics and practitioners, lawyers, philosophers, and political scientists. In addition to fulfilling the research vacuum, it aims to address the challenges and opportunities faced in international trade adjudication.

ROBERT HOWSE is the Lloyd C. Nelson Professor of International Law at NYU School of Law, New York, USA.

HÉLÈNE RUIZ-FABRI is Director of the Max Planck Institute Luxembourg for Procedural Law, and Head of the Department of International Law and Dispute Resolution.

GEIR ULFSTEIN is Professor of International Law in the Department of Public and International Law and Co-director of PluriCourts, the Centre for the Study of the Legitimate Roles of the Judiciary in the Global Order, at the University of Oslo, Norway.

MICHELLE Q. ZANG is a postdoctoral research fellow at PluriCourts, the Centre for the Study of the Legitimate Roles of the Judiciary in the Global Order, at the University of Oslo, Norway.

STUDIES ON INTERNATIONAL COURTS AND TRIBUNALS

General Editors
Andreas Follesdal, University of Oslo
Geir Ulfstein, University of Oslo

Studies on International Courts and Tribunals contains theoretical and interdisciplinary scholarship on legal aspects as well as the legitimacy and effectiveness of international courts and tribunals.

Other books in the series:

Mads Andenas and Eirik Bjorge (eds.) *A Farewell to Fragmentation: Reassertion and Convergence in International Law*

Cecilia M. Bailliet and Nobuo Hayashi (eds.) *The Legitimacy of International Criminal Tribunals*

Amrei Müller with Hege Elisabeth Kjos (eds.) *Judicial Dialogue and Human Rights*

Nienke Grossman, Harlan Grant Cohen, Andreas Follesdal and Geir Ulfstein (eds.) *Legitimacy and International Courts*

Robert Howse, Hélène Ruiz-Fabri, Geir Ulfstein and Michelle Q. Zang (eds.) *The Legitimacy of International Trade Courts and Tribunals*

Marlene Wind (ed.) *International Courts and Domestic Politics*

THE LEGITIMACY OF INTERNATIONAL TRADE COURTS AND TRIBUNALS

Edited by

ROBERT HOWSE

New York University

HÉLÈNE RUIZ-FABRI

Max Planck Institute Luxembourg for International, European and Regulatory Procedural Law

GEIR ULFSTEIN

University of Oslo

MICHELLE Q. ZANG

University of Oslo

CAMBRIDGE
UNIVERSITY PRESS

CAMBRIDGE
UNIVERSITY PRESS

University Printing House, Cambridge CB2 8BS, United Kingdom

One Liberty Plaza, 20th Floor, New York, NY 10006, USA

477 Williamstown Road, Port Melbourne, VIC 3207, Australia

314–321, 3rd Floor, Plot 3, Splendor Forum, Jasola District Centre, New Delhi – 110025, India

79 Anson Road, #06–04/06, Singapore 079906

Cambridge University Press is part of the University of Cambridge.

It furthers the University's mission by disseminating knowledge in the pursuit of education, learning, and research at the highest international levels of excellence.

www.cambridge.org
Information on this title: www.cambridge.org/9781108424479
DOI: 10.1017/9781108335690

First published 2018

Printed in the United Kingdom by Clays, St Ives plc

A catalogue record for this publication is available from the British Library.

Library of Congress Cataloging-in-Publication Data
Names: Howse, Robert, 1958–, editor.
Title: The legitimacy of international trade courts and tribunals / edited by Robert Howse and others.
Description: New York : Cambridge University Press, 2018. |
Series: Studies on international courts and tribunals
Identifiers: LCCN 2017041377 | ISBN 9781108424479 (Hardback)
Subjects: LCSH: Commercial courts. | Foreign trade regulation.
Classification: LCC K1008 .L44 2018 | DDC 343.08/70269–dc23
LC record available at https://lccn.loc.gov/2017041377

ISBN 978-1-108-42447-9 Hardback

CONTENTS

List of Contributors vii

PART I International Trade Courts and Tribunals 1

1 **Introduction** 3
ROBERT HOWSE, HÉLÈNE RUIZ-FABRI, GEIR ULFSTEIN, AND MICHELLE Q. ZANG

2 **The WTO Adjudicating Bodies** 20
RETO MALACRIDA AND GABRIELLE MARCEAU

3 **The Court of Justice of the European Union** 70
P. J. KUIJPER

4 **The EFTA Court** 138
HALVARD HAUKELAND FREDRIKSEN

5 **The United States Court of International Trade** 182
DONALD C. POGUE

6 **The Federal Courts of Canada** 202
MAUREEN IRISH

7 **The Case of MERCOSUR** 227
PAULA WOJCIKIEWICZ ALMEIDA

8 **The Andean Court of Justice** 255
MIGUEL ANTONIO VILLAMIZAR

9 **The Case of the Economic Court of the CIS** 286
RILKA DRAGNEVA

10 **The COMESA Court of Justice** 314
JAMES THUO GATHII

11 The WAEMU Court of Justice 349

OUSSENI ILLY

12 The ASEAN Trade Dispute Settlement Mechanism 365

MICHAEL EWING-CHOW AND RANYTA YUSRAN

PART II Cross-Cutting Studies 403

13 A Comparative Analysis of Formal Independence 405

THERESA SQUATRITO

14 Judicial Interaction of International Trade Courts and Tribunals 432

MICHELLE Q. ZANG

15 Access to Trade Tribunals – Comparative Perspectives 454

OLE KRISTIAN FAUCHALD

16 Toward a More Just WTO: Which Justice, Whose Interpretation? 479

ANDREAS FOLLESDAL

17 Conclusions 503

ROBERT HOWSE, HÉLÈNE RUIZ-FABRI, GEIR ULFSTEIN, AND MICHELLE Q. ZANG

Index 511

CONTRIBUTORS

RILKA DRAGNEVA is Professor of International Legal Studies at the University of Birmingham, UK. Her current research interests center on the legal regime of Eurasian economic integration and its overlap with European Union (EU) external policy in the EU–Russia shared neighborhood. One of her recent principal publications is *Eurasian Economic Integration: Law, Policy and Politics* (2013). Dragneva-Lewers is also actively engaged in policy advice in relation to these matters and has extensive experience in technical assistance and consultancy in the field of legal reform and rule of law postcommunism.

MICHAEL EWING-CHOW is Associate Professor and WTO Chair at the Faculty of Law, National University of Singapore (NUS), Singapore, as well as Head of Trade/Investment Law and Policy at the Centre for International Law, NUS. He has a First Class Honors degree in law from NUS and a master's degree from Harvard Law School. Michael worked in Allen & Gledhill before joining NUS, where he started the first World Trade Law course in Singapore and was involved in the negotiations for some of Singapore's early free trade agreements (FTAs). For his work, he was awarded the Social Entrepreneur of the Year 2007. He has received several Teaching Excellence Awards and was awarded the Inspiring Mentor Award in 2009.

OLE KRISTIAN FAUCHALD is Professor of International Law at the Department of Public and International Law, University of Oslo, Norway, and coordinator of PluriCourts – Centre of Excellence for the Study of the Legitimate Roles of the Judiciary in the Global Order in Oslo, Norway. Fauchald has published in different areas of international law, including international investment law, international trade law, international environmental law, and international human rights. He is also part of the Research Group on Internationalisation of Law and the

Research Group on Natural Resources Law, both part of the Faculty of Law, University of Oslo.

ANDREAS FOLLESDAL, Ph.D., is Professor of Political Philosophy at the Faculty of Law, University of Oslo, Norway, and Co-Director of PluriCourts – Centre of Excellence for the Study of the Legitimate Roles of the Judiciary in the Global Order in Oslo, Norway. He holds a Ph.D. in philosophy from Harvard University and publishes in the field of political philosophy, mainly on issues of international political theory, globalization/Europeanization, human rights, and socially responsible investing.

JAMES THUO GATHII is Professor of Law and the Wing-Tat Lee Chair in International Law at Loyola University Chicago School of Law, Illinois, USA, since July 2012. He is on the Board of Editors of the *American Journal of International Law* and is an independent expert of the Working Group on Extractive Industries, Environment, and Human Rights Violations in Africa formed by the African Commission on Human and Peoples' Rights. His research and teaching interests are in public international law, international trade law, and third world approaches to international law and human rights.

HALVARD HAUKELAND FREDRIKSEN is Professor of EU and EEA law at the Faculty of Law, University of Bergen, Norway, and an associate of Bergen Centre of Competition Law and Economics. Besides his Norwegian law degree (2003) he holds the degrees Mag.iur. (2005) and Dr.iur. (2009) from the University of Göttingen in Germany and Ph.D. (2013) from the University of Bergen in Norway.

MAUREEN IRISH is Professor of Law at the Faculty of Law, University of Windsor, Ontario, Canada. She holds B.A. and LL.B. degrees from the University of Toronto, Canada, and LL.M. and D.C.L. degrees from McGill University, Canada. Professor Irish teaches international economic law, international business transactions, transportation law, and private international law (conflicts). She is the author of *Customs Valuation in Canada* (1985), as well as editor or coeditor of various publications with regard to economic law. She has served on dispute settlement panels under the Canada–United States Free Trade Agreement and the North American Free Trade Agreement.

P. J. KUIJPER is Professor of Law of International (economic) Organizations in the University of Amsterdam, the Netherlands since 2007. Before that, he had a long career in international organizations, first as the director of the Legal Affairs Division of the WTO Secretariat (1999–2002) and next as the director of the Division for External Relations and International Trade in the Legal Service of the European Commission (2002–2007). His main research interests are the comparative approach to international organizations; European Union (EU) institutional law, in particular foreign relations law (including trade policy); WTO law; and relations between EU law, WTO law, and general international law.

RETO MALACRIDA, Ph.D., is Counsellor (senior dispute settlement lawyer) in the Legal Affairs Division of the WTO Secretariat since 1999 and a part-time lecturer at the University of St. Gallen, Switzerland.

GABRIELLE MARCEAU is a counsellor in the Legal Affairs Division of the WTO Secretariat since 11 September 1994. Gabrielle Marceau is also Associate Professor at the Law Faculty of the University of Geneva, Switzerland, and has previously been Visiting Professor at the Graduate Institute in Geneva, the Sorbonne in Paris, Monash University in Melbourne, Australia, the World Trade Institute in Bern, Switzerland, and others. Professor Marceau is President of the Society of International Economic Law and is also involved with other associations and groups promoting international law.

OUSSENI ILLY is currently Assistant Professor of International Law at the University Ouaga II, Ouagadougou, Burkina Faso. He is also the cofounder and executive director of the African Centre of International Trade and Development (www.cacid.net), an independent and nonprofit think tank on Africa and international trade based in Burkina Faso. Illy holds a master of public law from the University of Ouagadougou, Burkina Faso, and a Ph.D. in international trade law from the University of Geneva, Switzerland.

DONALD C. POGUE was appointed as a judge to the U.S. Court of International Trade (CIT) in 1995 and has obtained senior status as of July 1, 2014. Prior to his appointment to the CIT, he served as Judge in Connecticut's Superior Court and was Chairman of Connecticut's

Commission on Hospitals and Health Care. He was also a partner of the law firm Kestell, Pogue, & Gould. Judge Pogue is a magna cum laude, Phi Beta Kappa graduate of Dartmouth College, Hanover, New Hampshire, and holds a J.D. degree from Yale Law School and a master's of philosophy from Yale University, New Haven, Connecticut.

THERESA SQUATRITO is a lecturer in International Relations at the University of Liverpool. She received her Ph.D. from the University of Washington, Seattle, USA, in political science, where she was a fellow with the Comparative Law and Society Studies Center. She is a former postdoctoral research fellow of the PluriCourts – Centre of Excellence for the Study of the Legitimate Roles of the Judiciary in the Global Order at the University of Oslo, Norway. Before that, she was a postdoc at Stockholm University, Sweden, on the Transdemos research program, which explores transnational actors in relation to questions on global democratic governance. She has published on topics related to international organizations and international law, as well as transnational actors.

MIGUEL ANTONIO VILLAMIZAR is a dispute settlement lawyer in the Legal Affairs Division of the WTO Secretariat, which he joined on October 1, 2013. He obtained his LL.B. and LL.M. degrees from the University of Los Andes, Bogotá, Colombia, in 2005 and 2009, respectively. Between 2005 and 2011, Miguel worked in different law firms in Colombia and served the Colombian government in the Bureau of International Legal Affairs of the Ministry of Trade Industry and Tourism. He has lectured on public international law, international economic law, and comparative law at University of Los Andes, Bogotá, Colombia and Francisco Marroquín University, Guatemala.

PAULA WOJCIKIEWICZ ALMEIDA is Professor of International Law, Getulio Vargas Foundation Law School in Rio de Janeiro (since 2008). Jean Monnet Chair, sponsored by the European Commission at the Getulio Vargas Foundation Law School. Associate Researcher at the Institute of International and European Law at the Sorbonne (IREDIES). Professor of International Law of the Masters in International Relations of the Faculty of Social Sciences, Getulio Vargas Foundation in Rio de Janeiro. Qualified as 'maître des conferences' in Public Law (France, CNU). Doctorate with honors *summa cum laude* in International and European

Law at the *Université Paris 1 Panthéon-Sorbonne*. Masters of Law (Master II Recherche – former DEA) in Public International and European Law – Université Paris XI, Faculté Jean Monnet. Post-doctoral visiting scholar at the Max Planck Institute for Comparative Public Law and International Law. Professor Almeida is also Chair of the Interest Group on International Courts and Tribunals of the Latin American Society of International Law.

RANYTA YUSRAN is a Research Fellow at the Centre for International Law (CIL), NUS, Singapore. Her research interests at CIL include Treaty Law and Practice, ASEAN Law and Policy, and International Dispute Settlement. She obtained her LL.B. in Public International Law from University of Indonesia, Depok, Indonesia, and her LL.M. in International Human Rights from Lund University, Sweden.

PART I

International Trade Courts and Tribunals

1

Introduction

ROBERT HOWSE, HÉLÈNE RUIZ-FABRI, GEIR ULFSTEIN AND MICHELLE Q. ZANG

Since the end of World War II, there has been an expansion of free trade agreements (FTAs) in both numerical and geographical terms. In the period from 1948 to 1994, the General Agreement on Tariffs and Trade (GATT) received 124 notifications of regional trade agreements (RTAs), and since the creation of the World Trade Organization (WTO) in 1995, over 400 additional arrangements covering trade in goods or services have been notified. At present, negotiations of new RTAs continue to rise and the most recent development of FTAs has been the so-called plurilateral negotiations among several countries across or within certain regions. This includes negotiations in the Asia–Pacific Region for a Trans-Pacific Partnership (TPP) Agreement, the Transatlantic Trade Investment Partnership (TTIP), the Regional Comprehensive Partnership Agreement in Asia, the Pacific Alliance in Latin America and the Tripartite Agreement in Africa.

At first glance, the legal system in international trade is confusing. There is the multilateral system of the WTO, a large number of regional, plurilateral regimes, together with myriad bilateral agreements. On the enforcement front, almost every regime has established its own mechanism for dispute settlement. In other words, in parallel with, and as a result of, the expansion of FTAs, recent decades also witness the rise of fora where trade disputes are adjudicated.

There is a clear trend in the choice of the dispute settlement mechanism: more and more FTAs have abandoned the political model of diplomatic negotiations and moved toward a third-party adjudication system, in the form of ad hoc panels, a permanent judiciary or a combination of both. Sixty-five per cent of existing trade dispute settlement mechanisms (DSMs) have adopted a 'quasi-judicial model' that provides for ad hoc adjudicatory procedures. Under this model, the panels are established for purpose of resolving the specific dispute and dissolved once it has issued a decision. Although the vast majority of quasi-judicial mechanisms provide for a single instance of binding third-party adjudication, some, being inspired by the WTO dispute settlement system, further include an appellate organ, e.g. the Association of Southeast Asian Nations (ASEAN) and the Southern Common Market in Latin-America (MERCOSUR). A small group of FTAs opt for the judicial model, which consists of the establishment of a permanent judiciary. In most cases, the jurisdiction of the court as such goes beyond just trade disputes and extends to a range of matters related to regional integration. The most well-known example is the Court of Justice of the European Union (CJEU).

As a result of the shift away from politically oriented approaches toward more sophisticated legalistic proceedings, trade dispute settlement is emerging and becoming a major branch of international adjudication.[1] The impact of international adjudication on the development of the trade regime cannot be overstated. Important examples include the CJEU and the WTO Appellate Body. The former has been a major driving force of the constitutionalization process of the European Union,[2] while at the WTO the approximately 500 disputes initiated over the last 20 years reveal the solid confidence members have placed in the dispute settlement system, which has been long regarded as the 'jewel in the crown'.

1 The Legitimacy Debate

International trade courts and tribunals (ITCs) have, like other parts of the international judiciary, come under increasing scrutiny over their functioning and operation. A large number of legitimacy issues have been raised in relation to international trade adjudication. Views and claims have been presented from a range of actors; inter alia, scholars, practitioners, NGOs and government officials. They point to the institutional and procedural features of the dispute settlement system, as well as the style of their adjudicating methods and the quality of legal reasoning, as the outcome of adjudication has affected a large group of stakeholders.

[1] By the end of 2014, the WTO had registered 474 disputes since its establishment in 1995, and NAFTA panels have delivered 75 decisions in the last two decades.

[2] J. H. H. Weiler, The transformation of Europe. *Yale Law Journal*, 100 (1991), 2403–83; J. H. H. Weiler, *The Constitution of Europe: 'Do the New Clothes Have an Emperor?' and Other Essays on European Integration* (Cambridge, UK: Cambridge University Press, 1999).

The term *legitimacy* has been used with a variety of meanings in the context of international law and global governance.[3] At the core, legitimacy is a question of whether the power or the authority to rule by an institution, in our case, international trade courts and tribunals, can be properly justified. Legitimacy can be understood in both normative and sociological terms. In the normative sense, the legitimacy of an institution depends on whether the institution fulfils certain defined standards when executing its mandates. Unlike the normative concept, sociological legitimacy does not make a normative commitment to any defined standards. It is an empirical concept, which concerns the extent to which external actors outside the institution are convinced by the authority of the relevant institution. In other words, sociological legitimacy underlines actual perceptions rather than predetermined standards. Our research focuses primarily on the normative legitimacy. Rather than investigating the perceptions of outside actors, we will explore the legitimacy concerns arising from the existing institutional structures and adjudicative practices.

The fundamental basis for the legitimacy of ITCs is the consent of sovereign states to their delegated powers. States' consent, in the form of ratification of or, accession to the constituent legal instrument, establishes the initial capital of legitimacy that is a structural asset held by the international courts. However, this legitimacy capital is also dependent on several other factors, such as the procedure and practice of the judicial mechanism. Furthermore, the legitimacy may fluctuate over time in response to how the delegated power is exercised. In other words, in addition to the original consent from the states, a number of elements are involved in the evaluation of the overall legitimacy of the adjudicator concerned.

The first element is the institutional arrangements of the courts and tribunals. The most outstanding feature of international trade adjudication is the high number of fora for dispute resolution and the institutional choice between the judicial model and the quasi-judicial model

[3] See, for example, D. Bodansky, Legitimacy in international law and international relations. In, J. L. Dunoff and M. A. Pollack, eds., *Interdisciplinary Perspectives on International Law and International Relations: The State of the Art* (Cambridge, UK: Cambridge University Press, 2013), pp. 321–45; A. Buchanan and R. O. Keohane, The legitimacy of global governance institutions. *Ethics and International Affairs*, 20 (2006), 405–37; A. Von Bogdandy and I. Venzke (eds.), *In Whose Name? A Public Law Theory of International Adjudication* (Oxford, UK: Oxford University Press, 2014); N. Grossman, The normative legitimacy of international courts. *Temple Law Review*, 61 (2012), 61–106.

mentioned earlier. Therefore, the legitimacy assessment, as well as the standards involved, varies substantively depending on the structure and settings of the adjudicator.

The second aspect refers to procedure-related issues. In comparing judicial and quasi-judicial models, there are significant differences among ITCs on the selection of judges, the involvement of nonstate parties and the extent of proceeding transparency. It is thus of interest to explore the procedural impact on the adjudicator's overall legitimacy.

The third legitimating factor concerns judicial behaviour in the form of the style of legal interpretation and of fact-finding. It depends on the mandate of the court, evolves within the institutional and procedural framework and affects the outcome of the dispute.

Fourth, the output of the ITCs through decisions or judgments also plays a significant role in the legitimacy assessment. The output might be viewed in light of the effectiveness of the adjudicator in promoting the intended objectives stipulated in its mandate, as agreed among the state parties on its establishment. It can also be assessed in terms of the actual performance of the adjudicator, particularly as regards the de facto influence of the decision that goes beyond its stated mandate.

Finally, a distinction should be made between the internal and external legitimacy of international adjudicators.[4] Although internal legitimacy underlines the institutional and operational aspects of the adjudicator itself, external legitimacy focuses on the 'universe' outside the adjudicator. In particular, external legitimacy means the influence the adjudicator has on the norms, institutions and regime that the adjudicator is embedded in; it might even go beyond the regime with extended impact on other trade courts and national courts. The internal legitimacy of an international adjudicator may serve as a prerequisite for external legitimization, being an intermediate goal instead of an end in itself.[5]

Insofar as this book is concerned, the legitimacy assessment focuses on whether the ITCs are living up to the reasons and mandates for their establishment; it is a question of degree with the possibility of eroding and/ or increasing legitimacy. Our research scope is broadly defined, including

[4] J. H. H. Weiler, The rule of lawyers and the ethos of diplomats: Reflections on the internal and external legitimacy of WTO dispute settlement. *Journal of World Trade*, 35 (2) (2001), 191–207.

[5] Y. Shany, Assessing the effectiveness of international courts: A goal-based approach. *American Journal of International Law*, 106 (2) (2012), 225–70, at 137.

institutional settings and establishment, the procedures, judicial practice in legal interpretation, fact finding and rule application, enforcement of and compliance with their decisions, as well as the influence of specific decision or the adjudicator in general.

2 Research Questions

This book is divided in two parts. The first part consists of studies of selected ITCs. Based on their functioning and operation, the examination of each court and tribunal attempts to address all the research questions listed next. The seven specific research questions cover a number of issues that are closely linked to the legitimating elements outlined in the previous section, presenting a collection of legitimacy concerns raised by both practitioners and scholars. Admittedly, certain questions may not be applicable for a given tribunal, or some other tribunals are facing legitimacy challenges that are not listed. There is thus also need for context-specific assessments, in addition to our guiding questions.

2.1 Selection and Composition of the Adjudicators

This question focuses on the selection criteria and procedure, as well as the resulting composition, of the judges, panelists and arbitrators that are adjudicating trade disputes. Examples of the specific matter to be addressed include the role and involvement of different stakeholders during the selection process, e.g. sovereign states, nongovernmental bodies and civil society; and the impact that the composition of adjudicators have on the functioning of the tribunal. The selection and composition of adjudicators are directly linked to a number of legitimacy concerns, and one much-debated issue refers to the independence of the courts and tribunals.

2.2 Procedural Rules

Procedural rules here are broadly defined, covering all rules governing the relevant processes of adjudication by courts and tribunals. They may have substantial impact on the overall legitimacy of the adjudicator concerned, for example, by determining which group is able to bring a dispute to the tribunal. The issue of standing is linked to the broader debate of the access to the tribunal, the participation of civil society and rights and obligations of third parties. Procedural rules are also often relevant in the transparency debate, enquiring the extent of openness of the proceedings, information disclosure and the decision-making process.

2.3 Fact-Finding

The process of fact-finding establishes the case-specific background and context the relevant law and its interpretation apply to. This process involves a number of specific issues, ranging from the allocation of burden of proof and standards of review, to rules on evidence and information from nondisputing parties.

2.4 Interpretative Approaches

One major adjudicative function of trade courts is to provide legal interpretation of the applicable rule of law. An adjudicator normally establishes, or attempts to establish, consistent interpretative approaches. ITCs also develop, through their case law, specific techniques, e.g. concerning a textual or dynamic interpretation, and the role of precedence and reference to other courts and tribunals. The interpretative methodology mirrors the attitude of the adjudicator on many critical legitimacy questions, e.g. interface between trade and environment or human rights and the preservation of domestic regulatory space for sensitive policies.

2.5 Forum Shopping

As a result of the proliferation of trade agreements, there is usually more than one forum that has jurisdiction in a trade dispute between specific parties. The applicant's preference in the choice of forum is linked to many factors, inter alia, the expenses incurred in both economic and political terms, the duration of the proceedings and the subsequent enforcement of the decision. The very existence of forum shopping is a 'luxury problem' definitely better than no forum for resolution, and a healthy level of competition among tribunals may also improve the quality of rulings and the expediency of proceedings. However, the reality of jurisdictional overlap and the phenomenon of parallel litigations have raised the risk of inconsistent judicial decisions and fragmented legal interpretation that might ultimately render a dispute concerned unsolved and general trade law inconsistent or contradictory.

2.6 *Implementation and Interaction with National Courts*

Most ITCs are linked to distinct mechanisms for implementation. Questions then arise on whether such mechanisms further guarantees, increases or decreases, the credibility and legitimacy of the rulings, as well as that of the system as a whole.

Domestic implementation of decisions from an international tribunal may, to a certain extent, be considered a national 'screening' process. The approach and attitude engaged in by different domestic bodies, of administrative, legislative or judicial nature, may reveal their perception of the legitimacy of the ruling as well as of the tribunal delivering it. Such domestic perceptions are usually reflected in approaches like direct/indirect effect of international rulings, together with relevant principles on the relationship between international and domestic law, such as consistent interpretation.

2.7 *Tribunal-Specific Legitimacy Concerns*

We recognize that ITCs are embedded in varying legal regimes and local political climate. The functioning of a given adjudicator reflects social, political, economic and cultural realities. Any legitimacy assessment therefore has to be grounded on an elaborate understanding of the system and environment within which the adjudicator is established and operate.

The second part of the volume includes cross-cutting studies that aim to provide legitimacy assessment of international trade adjudication across the board. This part is interdisciplinary in nature, including not only research by legal scholars but also contributions from political scientists and political philosophers. The chapters in this part address specific issues of judicial independence, interaction and access to courts, and it also provides a philosophical analysis in the light of global justice theory.

3 Selection of Trade Courts and Tribunals

The preceding research questions require case-by-case assessment of each court and tribunal, as opposed to a collective evaluation across the board. For that purpose, we selected 11 trade courts and tribunals as the research subjects in the first part of the volume.

As mentioned earlier, a majority of the contemporary mechanism for trade disputes has adopted the quasi-judicial model or judicial model or a combination of both. While the quasi-judicial model refers to an ad hoc adjudicatory system, the judicial model takes the form of a permanent body of a judicial nature. What they have in common is the automatic right of referral of a dispute to third-party adjudication. Therefore, during our selection process, one important selection criterion was that the adjudicator must have certain judicial features, either as a permanent court or, for those following the quasi-judicial model, with an appeal body functioning similar to court. We therefore did not include dispute settlement mechanisms that are pure ad hoc in nature, e.g. North American Free Trade Agreement. We also took into account the geographic distribution of our research subjects, striving to cover several different regions of the globe. Furthermore, we placed great emphasis on trade courts and tribunals that are understudied. Last but not least, we also included two domestic judiciaries, examining their functioning and performance in trade dispute resolution, as well as their interaction with relevant international adjudicators.

The selected ITCs are as follows:

3.1 *The World Trade Organization Dispute Settlement System*

Dispute settlement is a central pillar of the multilateral trading system and of the WTO's contribution to the stability of the global economy. As the only multilateral forum for trade disputes, the WTO consists of ad hoc panels and the permanent Appellate Body and deals with interstate disputes over the application and interpretation of WTO rules pursuant to the procedures and requirements provided in the WTO Dispute Settlement Understanding. On the one hand, through the record of nearly 500 disputes over the last 20 years, member states have shown their solid confidence in the system, which is thus considered the most influential adjudicator of international trade disputes. On the other hand, different aspects of its legitimacy are continuously discussed, which is the focus of our research.

3.2 *The Court of Justice of the European Union*

The Court of Justice of the European Union (CJEU) in Luxembourg encompasses three distinct courts, i.e. the Court of Justice, the General Court, and the Civil Service Tribunal, which exercise the judicial functions of the European Union and aim to achieve greater political and economic integration among EU member states. Originally established in 1952 as the Court of Justice of the European Coal and Steel Communities, CJEU currently holds jurisdiction to review the legality of institutional actions by the European Union, ensure that member states comply with their obligations under EU law and interpret EU law at the request of the national courts and tribunals. Nowadays, as one of the most active and influential international adjudicators, the CJEU has been widely recognized for its contribution in the formation of the EU internal market and achieving of intra-EU free movement of goods and services. Its institutional design and practical functioning provide significant inspiration for, and influence on, the establishment of a number of regional courts.

3.3 The European Free Trade Association Court

The European Free Trade Association (EFTA) Court is a rather exceptional judicial body created by the equally exceptional Agreement on the European Economic Area (EEA) between the EU member states and certain EFTA states, i.e. Iceland, Norway and Liechtenstein. The Court is not an institution of the EFTA but rather an independent organisation under public international law established by those three EFTA states. The EFTA Court has jurisdiction with regard to EFTA states that are parties to the EEA Agreement and is mainly competent to deal with infringement actions brought by the EFTA Surveillance Authority against an EFTA state with regard to the implementation, application or interpretation of EEA law rules, giving advisory opinions to courts in EFTA states on the interpretation of EEA rules, and dealing with appeals concerning decisions taken by the EFTA Surveillance Authority. Together with the study on the CJEU, the examination of the EFTA Court will provide a broad picture of the functioning and performance of European adjudicators and their influence on Europe's economic integration and cooperation.

3.4 The Economic Court of the Commonwealth of Independent States

The Economic Court of the Commonwealth of Independent States (ECCIS) is not only the oldest regional court in the post-Soviet region, but it also acts as the sole regional adjudicator with jurisdiction over trade matters. Having come into being more than 20 years ago, the ECCIS was originally mentioned in the 1991 agreement between Belarus, the Russian Federation and Ukraine. The Court is empowered to settle disputes concerning the fulfilment of economic commitments within the framework of the Commonwealth of Independent States (CIS), to interpret provisions of international agreements and the CIS acts related to the economic issues and to settle other disputes related to the CIS participating states. The complexity and sensitivity of the regional political climate not only leaves in question the influence and impact the ECCIS is able to generate on economic integration; they also cast considerate uncertainty on the overall legitimacy of the adjudicator.

3.5 The Association of Southeast Asian Nations Dispute Settlement System

Since its founding, ASEAN's primary purpose has been to promote peace and stability in Southeast Asia. However, peaceful settlement of disputes was not referred to in the founding ASEAN Declaration of 1967. As ASEAN's institutions developed, the creation of formal mechanisms for dispute settlement has been incremental. The earliest mention of dispute settlement in an ASEAN agreement was in the 1971 Declaration on the Zone of Peace, Freedom and Neutrality and the 1976 Declaration of ASEAN Concord. On this basis, ASEAN has developed three key mechanisms for dispute settlement: the 1976 Treaty of Amity and Cooperation, the 1996 Protocol on Dispute Settlement Mechanism and subsequently the 2004 Protocol for Enhanced Dispute Settlement Mechanism for disputes relating to ASEAN economic agreements, and the provisions of the 2007 ASEAN Charter that serve as an overarching framework for dispute settlement in ASEAN.

Despite its nonuse in solving trade disputes, the ASEAN dispute settlement mechanism nevertheless stands as one significant forum in Asia, which otherwise presents a general lack of international adjudicators for trade disputes. Therefore, its performance, functioning and legitimacy are explored, taking into account elements such as local culture, legal tradition and political climate.

3.6 The Andean Community Court of Justice and the Southern Common Market in Latin-America Dispute Settlement System

In Latin America, the most important dispute settlement mechanisms are established under the Andean Community and MERCOSUR, which represent two different models of trade adjudication in the region. While the former adopted the judicial model based on the design of the CJEU, the latter is built on the general structure of the WTO dispute settlement.

The Andean Community Court of Justice was created on 28 May 1979 and began operating in January 1984. It was part of the institutional setting of the 'Cartagena Agreement', a scheme created to achieve subregional integration between countries from the Andean region of South America. It is charged with settling disputes between Andean Community member states that arise under Community law. Over thirty years after its creation, the Court has been recognized as one of the most active international tribunals.

The MERCOSUR dispute settlement system is evolving in line with the political and economic conditions of its members. Starting from a system based on consultation and negotiation, MERCOSUR dispute settlement gradually evolved into a WTO-type interstate adjudicatory mechanism, which further offers access for private parties. The system applies to conflicts between members with regard to the interpretation, application or noncompliance of legal norms of MERCOSUR and to complaints presented by private parties against members on the application of legal or administrative measures that are restrictive, are discriminatory or create unfair competition, in violation of the legal provisions of MERCOSUR.

3.7 The Common Market for Eastern and Southern Africa Court of Justice and the Western African Economic and Monetary Union Court of Justice

There is a significant lack of scholarship on African subregional courts and tribunals. We therefore included chapters examining two of the most understudied adjudicators in the region, namely, the Common Market for Eastern and Southern Africa (COMESA) Court of Justice and the Western African Economic and Monetary Union (WAEMU) Court of Justice.

The Preferential Trade Area for Eastern and Southern Africa (PTA), established in 1981, became COMESA in 1993 with the aim of developing into a common market and eventually into an economic community. COMESA was established primarily as a vehicle for trade and economic development, and its objectives are economically orientated. The Court of Justice was established as the major judicial organ of COMESA in 1994. It is composed of seven judges and aims to ensure economic integration by bringing justice to the common market. Its major function is to ensure adherence to law in the interpretation and application of the COMESA Treaty as well as to adjudicate on all matters referred to it pursuant to the COMESA Treaty.

Founded primarily for the purpose of promoting economic integration between its members, WAEMU is an attempt by the West African countries to go beyond the monetary union that they inherited from their former colonial powers and to establish a fully fledged economic and political union. As one of the pillars sustaining the integration process, the Court of Justice functions as the juridical arm of WAEMU with automatic jurisdiction over all member states of the Union; and bears the fundamental mission to ensure the observance of the WAEMU law by Member States, both in terms of implementation and interpretation.

3.8 The Federal Court of Canada and the U.S. Court of International Trade

Last but not least, we also include in our volume two domestic courts with nationwide jurisdiction over certain international trade cases. We selected the domestic judiciaries of two of the most active actors in international trade and frequent users of international trade courts and tribunals, namely, the U.S. Court of International Trade (USCIT) and the Federal Court of Canada. Both courts are granted jurisdiction to review federal agencies' decisions on certain trade measures. They have developed a rich jurisprudence on domestic trade matters, as well as cross-jurisdictional interaction with relevant international adjudicators in trade dispute resolutions.

4 Overview of the Book

As mentioned earlier, the first part of the book examines eleven trade courts and tribunals. Based on the defined research questions, a range of legitimacy issues and concerns have emerged. The following section will provide a brief overview of each chapter.

In Chapter 2, on the WTO dispute settlement system, Marceau and Malacrida first introduce the insider–outsider dimension of the legitimacy of WTO adjudication, the only global trade dispute settlement mechanism, reminding us of the legitimacy concerns being shared by both groups, and more important, those diverging from each other. Starting from this observation and based on current practice and existing jurisprudence, the analysis in this chapter discusses selection of members of WTO panels and the Appellate Body, procedural issues, fact-finding and standards of review, interpretative approaches, forum shopping, implementation of findings and interaction with domestic courts, and WTO-specific legitimacy concerns.

As one of the most well-known and active regional courts, CJEU has effectively established the judicial module of international trade adjudication. The contribution of CJEU goes far beyond resolution of trade disputes; it has been long perceived as the driving force of the EU integration process. Its contribution also exceeds the geographic limit inherent in its jurisdiction leading to its recognition as a leading international adjudicator. Kuijper undertakes an extensive examination of the relevant legitimacy issues raised by the CJEU and its practice in Chapter 3.

At the time of the EEA negotiations, few commentators thought that the political compromises found would prove workable in terms of the demanding objective of homogeneity between the EEA and the European Union. However, as argued by Haukeland Fredriksen in Chapter 4, the fact that the EEA Agreement in 2014 celebrated its twentieth anniversary suffices to demonstrate that the EFTA Court has proven the sceptics wrong. Through dynamic interpretation of the EEA Agreement, the EFTA Court has managed – by and large – to achieve and maintain homogeneity between the two legal systems, and it has gained a reputation as an independent guarantor for the fulfilment of EEA obligations and even established itself as a fairly regular dialogue partner of the CJEU.

The USCIT is widely perceived as the modern-day framework for judicial review of U.S. administrative agency decision making in trade-related cases. As shown in Chapter 5 by Pogue, adjudication activities of USCIT are based on domestic legal traditions and principles, while, to a varying extent, influenced by decisions made by certain ICTs. The coexistence of not only multiple international tribunals, but also national and transnational adjudicators, adds another layer of complication for the adjudication system. The author argues that USCIT may make a process-based legitimacy claim based on the independence, transparency and accountability of its decision making and a substantive legitimacy claim founded on the rules-based nature of its decisions.

In Chapter 6, Irish discusses aspects of Canadian law and the Federal Courts of Canada with exclusive focus on international trade and economic law. She addresses domestic questions such as deference to domestic administrative agencies and the appropriate role for judicial review by courts. At the international front, the chapter speaks to the relationship between domestic and regional adjudicators, as well as that between international law and domestic courts. The argument presented is that just as views on the proper role for judges have influenced the development of Canadian administrative law, so too have similar legitimacy concerns affected current doctrinal controversies over the relationship between Canadian domestic courts and public international law.

The Andean Community and MERCOSUR present two different models of trade adjudication in Latin America. While the former adopted the judicial model based on the design of CJEU, the latter goes in line with a WTO-type mechanism with certain modifications. Chapter 7, by Almeida, assesses the legitimacy of the MERCOSUR dispute settlement mechanism, combining 'normative legitimacy' and 'democratic legitimacy' in response to the defined research questions. She relies on several interviews with officials and former officials of MERCOSUR, as well as with arbitrators from the Permanent Review Court.

The existing literature has mainly focused on how the Andean Court of Justice has become a specialized intellectual property tribunal.[6] This is a striking finding when one looks at the wide array of areas where there is secondary Andean law in place. Villamizar, in Chapter 8, develops the current debate by arguing that the Court has gone beyond the function as an 'IP court' and seems to be in the process of broadening the scope of its work. The discussion particularly deals with certain legitimacy concerns arising from the existing adjudicatory practice, inter alia, the involvement and interaction with domestic IP agencies, the adaption of the Court's interpretative approach and the future role of the Court in light of regional integration.

In Chapter 9, Dragneva-Lewers argues that the existence and role of the ECCIS is closely affected by the nature and fate of the regional organisation within which it was embedded. Research has shown in detail how the design, operation and legitimacy of the ECCIS are influenced by the post-Soviet regional integration dynamics. Despite a strong political preference for consensual modes of dispute settlement and limited use in trade cases, the ECCIS has built a body of interpretative opinions.

Generally speaking, African subregional courts present a paradox: They are established to ensure rule-based economic integration, but they

[6] L. R. Helfer, K. J. Alter, and F. Guerzovich, Islands of effective international adjudication: Constructing an intellectual property rule of law in the Andean community. *American Society of International Law*, 103 (2009), 1.

have overwhelmingly decided disputes in fields other than trade, e.g. human rights and administrative cases. Chapter 10 on the COMESA Court of Justice is mainly based on an examination of the cases delivered by the Court, while being supplemented by an interview with the president of the Court in 2013. This chapter compares and contrasts the reasons underlying the COMESA Court of Justice's trajectory in becoming an administrative tribunal for COMESA employees, with how other African subregional courts and tribunals became human rights-oriented. According to Gathii, three key elements account for development of the COMESA court: the timing and mobilized constituencies, the location of the court and the interpretive approach employed by the court.

As one of the subregional courts in Africa, the WAEMU Court of Justice, discussed in Chapter 11, has not been very active: in almost 20 years of functioning, it has only rendered 37 decisions with less than three decisions per year. Furthermore, similar to the situation at the COMESA Court of Justice, the majority of the decisions concern administrative and staff cases. Both the inactive status of operation and the deviation from core mission as a trade court raise questions regarding the legitimacy of the Court. It is also because of the political climate within the region that the Commission refrains from bringing cases against member states, and these states also refrain from doing so against each other. According to Illy, instead of contesting the deviation from the mandate of the Court as a trade adjudicator, pressing efforts should focus on the institutional reform. In particular, reform should be oriented toward opening the Court to natural and legal persons on infringement actions while avoiding extending jurisdiction to human rights issues.

Chapter 12 by Ewing-Chow and Yusran approaches the legitimacy question by exploring the reasons why the ASEAN dispute settlement mechanism has never been used so far. The authors take into account three specific elements, namely, the 'ASEAN Way' of dispute management, a preference for extra-ASEAN dispute settlement mechanism, and the lack of capacity of ASEAN organs. The authors provide an in-depth an analysis with respect to the local political and cultural climate and its significance for ASEAN dispute settlement.

The second part of the volume consists of four chapters of cross-cutting studies.

Squatrito assesses in Chapter 13 the independence of courts and tribunals on the basis of formal rules governing the selection and tenure of judges, the eligibility criteria for judges, court resources, rules of procedure, recusals and limits on activities incompatible with judicial office, the confidentiality of deliberations, a judicial oath to independence, and privileges and immunities granted to judges. While formal independence cannot completely account for if and how international courts actually behave independently, it is suggested that formal safeguards can play a role in judicial behavior. By comparing sixteen permanent international trade courts or tribunals, the chapter informs our discussions of their legitimacy and reveals the extent to which ICTs vary in their formal independence.

Recent decades witness an emerging phenomenon of judicial interaction between trade courts and tribunals. According to Zang, this is reflected in the reference, deliberation and comparison, conducted by one adjudicator, of decisions and practice of another adjudicator. Chapter 14 reveals a WTO-centric network of interaction in international trade adjudication: While non-WTO adjudicators are making proactive input in judicial cross-fertilization, WTO panels and the Appellate Body have not disclosed equally strong willingness to participate in a 'judicial dialogue' across different trade courts. However, there remain a number of critical questions unanswered as for the role and influence of regional trade courts and tribunals in the WTO dispute settlement. Given the significant role of judicial interaction in a court's legitimacy strategy, this chapter calls for a cautious approach from the adjudicators involved, but with a comprehensive systemic vision.

Chapter 15 by Fauchald offers a comparative study on the access to different ICTs. He explores the formal opportunity to initiate cases at, as well as the actual recourse to, the courts. The chapter scrutinises the discrepancies between stakeholders' rights, duties and interests under the trade regime, on the one hand, and their access to trade courts, on the other. It further analyses the potential reasons for variations in the development trajectories of each court.

In Chapter 16, Follesdal deals with the accusation against ICTs that they maintain distributive injustice. The chapter focuses on the influence that ICTs have on the global basic institutional structure, the normative standards of justice that should be applied by the courts and tribunals, and the link between judicial interpretation by the judges, on the one hand, and global distributive justice, on the other. According to the author, although it is not obvious that the members of such adjudicating bodies are especially well equipped to promote global distributive justice by their decisions, it is not clear that any institution is better situated than the current crop of adjudicators, given the state-orientated nature of the global trading system.

The book ends with a Conclusions chapter summing up and reflecting on the findings on the legitimacy issues discussed in the different chapters and asks whether we are able to identify common design features and practices of the ICTs resulting in perceived legitimacy deficits, or whether the perceptions and use of the ICTs rather are dependent on the political context in which they operate.

2

The WTO Adjudicating Bodies

RETO MALACRIDA AND GABRIELLE MARCEAU*

1 Legitimacy in the WTO Context

1.1 Insider–Outsider Model

The WTO is an intergovernmental international organization whose members are states or separate customs territories possessing autonomy in the conduct of their external economic relations. Its more than 160 members are highly heterogeneous in terms of their populations, legal and political systems and level of economic development, and they make decisions by consensus.[1] Stakeholders outside the WTO that are neither observer governments nor international intergovernmental organizations are commonly referred to as members of civil society. This no less heterogeneous group covers a wide spectrum of individuals or entities, including economic operators engaging in or affected by trade, consumers, citizens and nongovernmental public interest organizations (NGOs). WTO members (members) will be referred to in this chapter as 'insiders' and members of civil society as 'outsiders'.

In considering the legitimacy of WTO adjudicating bodies and WTO adjudication, it is essential to recognize the insider–outsider dimension and bear in mind that there could be legitimacy concerns that are shared by both groups and others that are central to one group, but not shared by the other. Indeed, one and the same attribute of the WTO dispute settlement mechanism (DSM) may very well be perceived as legitimacy-enhancing by insiders and legitimacy-detracting by outsiders or vice versa. Any assessment of the legitimacy of WTO adjudication cannot therefore

* Information contained in this chapter is up to date as of June 2015. The opinions expressed in this text are those of the authors only and do not bind the WTO Members or the WTO Secretariat.

[1] Article IX:1 of the Marrakesh Agreement Establishing the World Trade Organization, Marrakesh, 15 April 1994, in force 1 January 1995, 1867 U.N.T.S. 154, 33 I.L.M. 1144 (1994) ('WTO Agreement').

escape the question, 'Legitimate to whom?' The situation is further complicated by the fact that insiders and outsiders are each highly fragmented in terms of their legitimacy outlook. Taking the insider group as an example, what attributes are deemed critical may vary from member to member and even from dispute to dispute, depending, for instance on whether the member is a developed or developing country and/or a small or large trading power, and whether it is the complaining or responding member in a dispute.[2]

From an insider perspective, it could, of course, be argued that the WTO creates rights for and imposes obligations on members, not outsiders. Seen in this light, the legitimacy concerns that matter are those on which members collectively (or at least members that are parties to a dispute) are in agreement and about which they are prepared to do something. However, the WTO does not operate in a political vacuum, and it depends on the support of outsiders, especially when it comes to implementing the results of multilateral trade negotiations or WTO dispute settlement proceedings. Moreover, while members should represent the interests of their own civil society, the representation they do provide may not always meet the expectations of all members of civil society, and some public interests may be global and lack effective representation at the level of individual members. It may therefore be in the interest of WTO insiders to pay heed to legitimacy issues raised by outsiders even in the absence of a WTO obligation to do so. That is not to say, however, that just because a legitimacy concern is raised by an outsider (say, a Western nongovernmental public interest organization), that concern should be taken up by members. Taking steps to alleviate that concern might, in the view of some insiders, undermine the legitimacy of WTO adjudication. Or there may be equally valid competing concerns that have been identified by insiders (e.g. developing country members) and that remain to be addressed.

With these introductory observations in mind, this chapter now proceeds to address a series of legitimacy-related aspects of WTO adjudication. The aspects to be considered are (1) the selection of the members of WTO adjudicating bodies and their independence (section 2), (2) relevant procedural rules (section 3), (3) fact-finding and standards of review (section 4), (4) the WTO adjudicating bodies' interpretative approach (section 5), (5) forum shopping (section 6), (6) implementation

2 C. Creamer and Z. Godzimirska, *The Rhetoric of Legitimacy: Mapping Members' Expressed Views on the WTO Dispute Settlement Mechanism* (2015) iCourts Working Paper Series, No. 16, 19, 25 and 45–7.

of adverse WTO rulings and interaction with national courts (section 7), and (7) WTO-specific legitimacy concerns (section 8).

2 Selection of the Members of WTO Adjudicating Bodies and Their Independence

2.1 WTO Adjudicating Bodies

Proceedings in disputes arising under a covered WTO agreement and concerning violation or nonviolation complaints take place before WTO dispute settlement panels (panels) at first instance. Appeals from the legal findings and conclusions of panels lie to the WTO Appellate Body (AB), as a matter of right. The AB's findings and conclusions are final, although they bind the parties to a dispute – the parties being members – only once the AB report and the accompanying panel report have been adopted by the WTO Dispute Settlement Body (DSB). The DSB is duty-bound to adopt these reports, except if it decides by consensus – and thus with the agreement of the disputing parties – that they should not be adopted (Article 17.14).

Owing to space constraints, this section focuses on original and compliance panel proceedings conducted under Articles 12 or 21.5 of the WTO Dispute Settlement Understanding (DSU)[3] and appellate review proceedings before the AB under Article 17. It does not discuss proceedings before other WTO adjudicating bodies, specifically those conducted by a WTO arbitrator under Articles 21.3 (on the determination of the reasonable period of time for implementing an adverse WTO ruling), 22.6 and 22.7 (on the determination of a level of suspension of concessions or other obligations that is equivalent to the level of nullification or impairment), or 25 (on ad hoc arbitration by mutual agreement of the parties).

2.2 Selection of Panellists

Panellists are selected on an ad hoc basis in each dispute, once the DSB has established a panel. Only the parties, the WTO Secretariat, the WTO Director-General (DG) and the chairpersons of WTO committees relevant to each dispute have an actual or potential role in the process of panel selection. Panels are composed of three individuals comprising a

[3] Unless otherwise indicated, references to article numbers will be to articles of the DSU.

chair and two members, although it is possible for the parties exceptionally to agree on a panel composed of five members (Article 8.5), which has never happened. Panellists serve for the duration of the original panel proceedings and, subsequently, if there are compliance panel proceedings and the original members of the panel are available, the same panellists will serve again for the duration of these further proceedings (Article 21.5). This transitory existence of panels has the advantage that it opens the way to selecting panellists with specialized expertise. From a legitimacy perspective, panels with the necessary expertise are better equipped to render factual findings that are sound and have credibility in epistemic communities.

The DSU contemplates that the parties to a dispute initially take 20 days to try to agree on the panellists. Absent an agreement, either party may request the DG to determine the composition of the panel. The DG is required to appoint the panellists within ten days of receiving a request (Article 8.7). This system guarantees that whenever a party wishes to see the composition of a panel settled, this will be promptly done. Most parties do not seek to have a panel composed within the minimum time-period, thus revealing a preference for a composition by agreement.

At the pre-DG stage, the parties typically seek the assistance of the WTO Secretariat in proposing possible panellists for the parties' consideration. The Secretariat is required to put forward such proposals of candidates (Article 8.6). To facilitate this, the Secretariat can draw on an official WTO indicative list of qualified individuals. Individuals may be included on the list at the suggestion of any member and following approval by the DSB (Article 8.4). The Secretariat makes proposals of possible panellists after seeking the parties' preferences regarding the desired profiles of candidates (e.g. academic background, subject-matter expertise, dispute settlement expertise). In practice, there are often several consecutive proposals before a panel is composed by agreement or a party requests DG appointment of panellists. The parties may oppose individuals proposed by the Secretariat only 'for compelling reasons' (Article 8.6). This requirement is difficult to enforce strictly, as the parties may have conflicting views on what is a compelling reason, and the Secretariat does not have a recognized adjudicator's role in this respect. But the right of either party to seek DG-appointment of panellists serves to dissuade responding parties from rejecting proposals to delay the start of panel proceedings.

More often than not, the composition of a panel has to be settled by recourse to the DG. Even then, however, the pre-DG stage frequently ends with the parties agreeing on one or two panellists, and whenever possible DGs have appointed individuals on whom the parties could agree. The DG must consult with the parties so that they can share their preferences regarding the profiles of the panellists to be appointed and confirm any agreement on certain individuals. Although the DG need not, and does not, seek the parties' agreement on his appointees, the DG must consult with the chairpersons of the relevant WTO committees before proceeding to appoint the panellists (Article 8.7). The committees' chairs can thus give neutral feedback on the proposed appointees and help to ensure that DG-appointed panels have adequate sectoral expertise. In practice, DGs have been at pains to meet the parties' sometimes contradictory preferences as much as possible and have also sought to advance systemic interests, such as increasing the number of individuals with prior experience as panellists and members that have provided panellists.[4]

Panellists must be 'well-qualified governmental and/or non-governmental individuals' (Article 8.1). In practice, panellists tend to be current or former governmental trade experts from uninvolved members, both capital-based ones and Geneva-based representatives to the WTO, private legal practitioners, academics, officials of international organizations or former Secretariat staff. The majority of panellists are governmental, which is perhaps to be expected, considering that the DSM was created to preserve the rights of Members (Article 3.2) and that it is relatively easier to develop WTO expertise and gain practical experience as a trade official than in the private sector.

Panellists must also be independent and impartial (Article 8.2). This is ensured first and foremost through the careful selection of panellists and the WTO's rules of conduct that require the disclosure of certain information (e.g. financial interests, publications) and rule out panellists who have a direct or indirect conflict of interests.[5] Under a special and confidential challenge procedure set forth in the rules of conduct, it is also possible for a party to seek, and in justified cases obtain, the resignation of a panellist.[6] In addition, members must allow panellists to serve in their individual capacities and not as representatives of their

[4] To date, 40 of the WTO's 161 members have had one or more of their nationals serve on panels.

[5] Rules II and VI of the Rules of Conduct for the Understanding on Rules and Procedures Governing the Settlement of Disputes ('Rules of Conduct'), WT/DSB/RC/1, 11 December 1996.

[6] Rule VIII of the Rules of Conduct. There has so far been no case where the Chair of the DSB had to take steps pursuant to Rule VIII to formally disqualify a panellist from continuing to serve on a panel.

government or any organization.[7] Members must therefore not give panellists instructions or otherwise influence their work as panellists (Article 8.9). But the DSU goes still further. Even if an individual's independence or impartiality is not in doubt, nationals of parties or third parties[8] are excluded from serving on panels, unless the parties agree otherwise (Article 8.3). It is very exceptional for parties to accept nationals of another party. In contrast, parties are frequently open to considering nationals from third parties. This applies in particular to nongovernmental candidates and to the pre-DG stage, where candidates can be reviewed and rejected for compelling reasons. Also significant from a legitimacy perspective is the right of a developing country party to have the panel include at least one panellist from another developing country member (Article 8.10). This provision is routinely invoked by developing country members. Moreover, it is not uncommon for developing country nationals to serve on panels that adjudicate disputes between developed country members.[9]

2.3 *Selection of AB Members*

Unlike a panel, the AB is a standing adjudicating body composed of seven members who serve for fixed terms of four years, with the possibility of reappointment for one additional term.[10] Vacancies are filled as and when they arise. Individual appeals are heard by AB divisions comprising three members, with the members being assigned on the basis of rotation and using a method designed to produce random, unpredictable results and opportunities for all members to serve irrespective of their nationality (Article 17.1; Rule 6(2) of the AB's Working Procedures). Although not specifically mandated by the DSU, each AB division hearing an appeal must exchange views with the other AB members before finalizing its AB report (Rule 4(3) of the AB's Working Procedures). This is done with a view to fostering collegiality among AB members and consistent AB decision making.

[7] As members are expected to allow their officials to serve on panels and continue paying their government salary, governmental panellists do not receive an honorarium from the WTO.

[8] For an explanation of the concept of 'third parties', see section 3.1.2.

[9] For more information, see also R. Malacrida, 'WTO Panel Composition: Searching Far and Wide for Administrators of World Trade Justice' in G. Marceau, *The History of Law and Lawyers in the GATT/WTO: The Development of the Rule of Law in the Multilateral Trading System* (Cambridge University Press, 2015), pp. 311–333.

[10] Although AB members must be available at all times and on short notice, being an AB member is not a full-time position.

AB members are appointed by the DSB, which makes decisions by consensus (Article 2.4). Any member can nominate one or more candidates. To assist the DSB, a selection committee is formed with the mandate to come up with a recommendation. The committee consists of the DG and the chairpersons of the WTO General Council, the DSB, and the WTO Councils for Trade in Goods, Trade in Services and TRIPS.[11] Prior to making its recommendation, the committee interviews the candidates and meets with members individually or receives their views in writing. Only a minority of members tend to provide input.[12] Individual members usually also invite candidates for interviews. Whereas an established appointment procedure is thus in place, unlike for panels, timely appointments to the AB are not guaranteed owing to the positive consensus requirement.[13]

AB members must be persons of recognized authority and have 'demonstrated expertise in law, international trade and the subject matter of the covered agreements generally' (Article 17.3). In practice, most AB members have been former or current government officials prior to joining the AB. The remaining AB members have tended to be academics and/or private legal practitioners.

Regarding their independence and impartiality, like panellists, AB members are subject to the WTO's rules of conduct and consequently may not hear appeals if they have a direct or indirect conflict of interests. In addition, and unlike panellists, AB members may not be affiliated with any government during their term of office, which is why AB members can hear appeals even if they are nationals of a party or third party (Article 17.3). Nonetheless, AB members in practice need the continued

[11] WTO, Establishment of the Appellate Body – Recommendations by the Preparatory Committee for the WTO approved by the Dispute Settlement Body on 10 February 1995, WT/DSB/1, para. 13, 19 June 1995.

[12] Similarly, however, only a minority of members have participated in WTO dispute settlement proceedings as parties or third parties.

[13] In one appointment process, Chinese Taipei initially blocked the appointment of several new AB members recommended by the selection committee, apparently over concerns about the impartiality of one candidate. Chinese Taipei lifted its opposition after intensive consultations. 'DSB appoints Appellate Body 'judges' and establishes panel on China's market restrictions for cultural goods', WTO news items, 27 November 2007; Jonathan Lynn, 'Taiwan blocks appointment of Chinese judge at WTO', Reuters U.S. edition, 19 November 2007. In another process, members' inability to reach a consensus on a single candidate resulted in a vacancy on the AB remaining unfilled for more than nine months. 'WTO appoints new Appellate Body member', WTO press release, 30 September 2014.

support of their government if they wish to be reappointed for a second term.[14]

Although nationals of any member can serve on the AB, the DSB must see to it that the AB's composition is 'broadly representative of membership in the WTO' (Article 17.3). There are, however, no formal quotas for specific members, world regions or developing country members. Notwithstanding this, the regions of North America, Latin America, Europe, Africa and Asia have each had at least one AB member since 1995. The only members that have had one of their nationals continuously serve on the AB since 1995 are the European Union and the United States.

2.4 *Summary Observations*

The 'democratic' legitimacy of AB members derives directly from members meeting as the DSB, and the DSB makes appointment decisions by consensus. This means that no member can impose its preferences on another member.

In the case of panels on whose composition the parties have agreed, the legitimacy is even greater, certainly from the parties' perspectives. As mentioned, however, the composition of a majority of panels is determined by the DG, although this does not rule out that the parties have agreed on one or two of the panellists appointed. For panellists appointed by the DG, there is no right of veto, which means that a panellist can be appointed even though a party would oppose that individual, were it given the opportunity. Nonetheless, the DG is only the decision maker of last resort – in situations where the parties are unable to agree on the panel's composition – and the DSB could not perform this function reliably and expeditiously.

Moreover, as DGs are appointed by members, and their legitimacy thus derives directly from members, the legitimacy of DG-appointed panels also derives from members, if indirectly.

[14] In fact, when an incumbent AB member from the United States informed the DSB that she was not 'requesting the DSB to consider her for reappointment' ('WTO appoints two new Appellate Body members', WTO press release, 18 November 2011) and a different AB member from the United States was appointed to succeed her, concerns were raised about the independence of AB members following speculation that the United States might have withheld its support because of decisions of the incumbent member or those of other members whose reappointment the United States did not wish to block. Gary Clyde Hufbauer, 'WTO Judicial Appointments: Bad Omen for the Trading System', 13 June 2011, available at: http://blogs.piie.com/realtime/?p=2209.

As concerns possible misgivings from an insider perspective, these may include the fact that an incumbent AB member seeking a second term effectively needs to secure the support of his or her government to be reappointed. The uncertainty surrounding reappointment could conceivably detract from the independence of individual AB members seeking reappointment. From an outsider perspective, some have questioned the lack of direct public participation in the process leading to the selection of panellists and AB members and the lack of a link between WTO adjudicating bodies to the citizens affected by their decisions.[15] The latter point could lead, inter alia, to a call for selecting more non-governmental individuals as panellists and AB members.

3 Relevant Procedural Rules

3.1 Participation in Panel and AB Proceedings

3.1.1 Right to Complain (Locus Standi)

Only WTO members, which comprise states or separate customs territories with autonomy in the matters covered by the WTO Agreement, have the right to bring a complaint before a panel.[16] The option of filing an appeal with the AB is likewise given solely to members, and then only to the parties to a dispute (Article 17.4).[17] Whereas natural persons or legal persons that are not members have no right to complain, members may – and frequently do – represent and espouse such persons' interests by filing a complaint in the member's name.[18]

Members enjoy liberal access to WTO adjudication. To bring a complaint, a member must 'consider that any benefits accruing to it directly or indirectly under the covered agreements are being impaired by measures taken by another Member' (Article 3.3; see also Articles XXIII:1 of the GATT 1994, XXIII:1 of the GATS and Article 64.1 of the TRIPS

[15] K. N. Schefer, 'Independent and impartial? Re-thinking the adjudication of trade and investment disputes', posted on 2 May 2014. Available at: opendemocracy.net/open-globalrights-blog/krista-nadakavukaren-schefer/independent-andimpartial-rethinking-adjudication.

[16] Appellate Body Report, *US – Shrimp*, para. 101.

[17] Appellate Body Report, *US – Lead and Bismuth II*, para. 41.

[18] Several members have introduced special domestic administrative procedures that give natural or legal person the opportunity to formally petition the government to bring a complaint against another WTO Member. See, e.g. Gregory C. Shaffer, *Defending Interests: Public-private Partnerships in WTO Litigation* (Washington: Brookings Institution, 2006), p. 84.

Agreement). Although the AB has opined that the DSU neither explicitly nor by implication contains a requirement to establish a 'legal interest' to bring a complaint, it has nonetheless proceeded to examine whether a complaining member had a 'sufficient justification' to do so. According to the AB, such a justification can be derived from, for instance, a potential export interest of the complaining member or a potential impact of the responding member's impugned measure on the relevant domestic market of the complaining member.[19] A notable exception to the rule of liberal access to WTO adjudication relates to complaints against least developed country (LDC) WTO members.[20] The DSU directs potential complaining members to 'exercise due restraint' in bringing complaints against such members (Article 24.1).[21]

The DSU provides for no specific procedure under which a responding party could seek the early dismissal by a panel of a frivolous or vexatious complaint. Although Article 3.7 directs a potential complaining member to judge whether it 'would be fruitful' to bring a complaint, the AB has interpreted this provision to indicate that a member 'is expected to be largely self-regulating in deciding whether any such action would be "fruitful"'.[22] In practice, the broad discretion that Article 3.7 leaves complaining members does not appear to have generated major concerns on the part of responding parties, and the AB has clarified that in some situations a panel may need to scrutinize a complaining member's right to have recourse to WTO dispute settlement.[23] This is probably due in large part to the careful diplomatic screening that precedes a complaining member's decision to bring a complaint, which in turn may reflect a possible concern about triggering a tit-for-tat complaint by the responding member.

3.1.2 Third-Party Participation

'Third parties' under the DSU are nondisputing party WTO members that have a substantial interest in a matter before a panel and have duly notified their interest to participate as third parties – in effect, intervening members – in panel proceedings. Thus, only members with a

[19] Appellate Body Report, *EC – Bananas III*, paras. 132–8.

[20] LDC WTO members are a subset of the large group of WTO developing country members. There are over 30 LDC WTO members.

[21] There has so far been no complaint against an LDC WTO member that was brought before a panel.

[22] Appellate Body Report, *EC – Bananas III*, para. 135.

[23] Appellate Body Report, *Peru – Agricultural Products*, para. 5.19.

substantial interest have a right to participate as third parties in panel or AB proceedings (Articles 10.2 and 17.4). Under the DSU, only members that have reserved their right to participate as a third party in the panel proceedings could be accepted as new third parties at the appellate review stage. The concept of 'substantial interest' has been interpreted more broadly than the concept of 'substantial trade interest' (which is used in Article 4.11) to include also systemic interest and is generally considered to constitute a low access threshold. In practice, panel proceedings without third parties are few and far between.

Third parties cannot put forward claims of their own.[24] However, they have a right to express their views on the matter before a panel on the basis of material submitted to the panel prior to the first substantive meeting of the panel with the parties (Article 10.3). This limitation of participatory rights is tempered by the fact that there is no bar to a third party subsequently bringing its own complaint against the same responding member (Article 10.4). Moreover, the AB has confirmed that panels can – and accordingly sometimes do – 'grant additional participatory rights to third parties in particular cases' in a manner consistent with DSU provisions and due process requirements.[25]

3.1.3 Amicus Curiae Submissions

In the WTO adjudication context, an amicus curiae submission is a – typically unsolicited – written communication addressing the matter before a panel or the AB, submitted by a person or entity, whether governmental or nongovernmental, that is neither a party nor a third party. Moreover, whereas experts consulted by a panel are subject to the WTO rules of conduct that seek to ensure their independence and impartiality, that is not the case for amici curiae.

The AB has determined that a panel 'has the authority either to accept and consider or to reject information submitted to it, whether requested by a panel or not'. According to the AB, this authority derives from Articles 12 (on panel procedures) and 13 (on the right of panels to 'seek' information from 'any individual or body').[26] The AB likewise considers, in respect of its own authority, that 'as long as we act consistently with

[24] Appellate Body Report, *Chile – Price Band System*, para. 163.
[25] Appellate Body Report, *US – FSC (Article 21.5 – EC)*, para. 243.
[26] Appellate Body Report, *US – Shrimp*, paras. 108 and 110. Appellate Body Report, *EC – Sardines*, para. 167.

the provisions of the DSU [which the AB said did not explicitly prohibit acceptance and consideration of amicus curiae submissions] and the covered agreements, we have the legal authority to decide whether or not to accept and consider any information [including amicus curiae submissions] that we believe is pertinent and useful in an appeal.'[27] The AB held that WTO members may also file amicus curiae submissions, even if they have not reserved their right to participate in a panel proceeding as a third party. The AB underscored in this connection that the key difference between third parties and amici curiae is that the latter have no right to have their views accepted and considered by a WTO adjudicating body.[28]

In *EC – Asbestos*, the AB, after consulting the parties and third parties, put in place an additional procedure, for the purpose of that appeal only, to deal with amicus curiae submissions that it anticipated receiving in that appeal. Under that procedure, any person or entity wishing to file such a submission had to apply for leave to file it by a specified deadline. The procedure was posted on the WTO website by the WTO Secretariat.[29] This procedure prompted the convening of a special meeting of the WTO's highest body (the General Council) and a statement by its Chair that the AB should 'exercise extreme caution in future cases until Members had considered what rules were needed'.[30] In the absence of an agreed result of these considerations, the AB and panels have continued to follow the AB's jurisprudence concerning amicus curiae submissions, although they have refrained from putting in place the kind of procedure that was used in the appeal in *EC – Asbestos*. In practice, WTO adjudicating bodies more often than not find it unnecessary to rely on amicus curiae submissions in rendering their decisions, which probably reflects the fact that party and third-party submissions tend to be detailed and extensive, and amicus curiae submissions may not dovetail with the precise issues under consideration.

[27] Appellate Body Report, *US – Lead and Bismuth II*, paras. 39 and 42.
[28] Appellate Body Report, *EC – Sardines*, paras. 164 and 166.
[29] Appellate Body Report, *EC – Asbestos*, paras. 51 and 52.
[30] Many delegations saw the posting of the ad hoc procedure on the website as an invitation to submit amicus curiae submissions. Most delegations also expressed the view that because there was no specific provision regarding such submissions, they should not be accepted under the DSU as it stood, and that there was a need to consider whether it would be possible to put in place clear rules for such submissions. See WTO document WT/GC/M/60, dated 23 January 2001, paras. 114, 117 and 119–20.

3.2 *Internal and External Transparency*

3.2.1 Principle of Confidentiality

The parties, third parties, WTO adjudicators and their WTO Secretariat and outside expert advisors must maintain the confidentiality of the statements made and the information provided during panel and AB proceedings. Moreover, the deliberations of WTO adjudicators are held without the presence of the parties or third parties (Articles 14 and 17.10).

3.2.2 Document Disclosure

Final panel reports and AB reports and other key documents[31] relating to panel and AB proceedings are promptly published on the WTO website.[32] Furthermore, a party may disclose its own positions during the course of the proceedings[33] and a nonconfidential summary of information contained in the written submissions of another party, which that party is required to provide upon request (Article 18.2). There is additional transparency for members participating in WTO adjudication proceedings as third parties. They receive some or all of the parties' and other third parties' written statements and other information.[34]

3.2.3 Panel Meetings and AB Hearings

Panels and the AB meet in closed session (e.g. para. 2 of the Working Procedures in Appendix 3 of the DSU). At the panel level, there is limited transparency for third parties in that they can attend a special third-party session of the first substantive meeting of the panel, but not the entire first substantive meeting, let alone the second substantive meeting. As explained, though, greater access has sometimes been granted in response to justified requests for enhanced third-party rights. On appeal, third parties can follow the entire oral AB hearing. It should also be noted that third parties have

[31] E.g. the initial complaint; the request for establishment of a panel, which defines the jurisdiction of a panel and gives definitive notice of the claims being raised; the Secretariat note about the composition of a panel and the third parties; sometimes preliminary rulings circulated at an early stage; the notices of appeal and other appeal; and notes about any DSB action with regard to the adoption of the report(s).

[32] Available at: www.wto.org/english/tratop_e/dispu_e/dispu_e.htm.

[33] Several members do this systematically and even disclose entire, full-text submissions on their official government websites.

[34] As explained, at the panel level, third parties are entitled to receive materials submitted prior to the first substantive meeting of the panel.

been allowed to attend third-party sessions of panel meetings or AB hearings even when they provide no written or oral input themselves.[35]

Panels and the AB have gone further in the direction of transparency in proceedings where the parties made a joint request to that effect. In those proceedings, they have consistently permitted the public observation of all or part of panel meetings and oral AB hearings via simultaneous or delayed CCTV broadcast to a separate room on WTO premises.[36] Public observation promotes greater transparency both internally (for WTO members that are neither parties nor third parties) and externally (for civil society and WTO observer governments and international organizations). According to the AB, WTO adjudicating bodies have the power to control the conduct of meetings, which in the AB's view includes the power to authorize joint requests by parties to forego the confidentiality of their own oral communications. This is subject to the proviso that such authorization not adversely affect the rights of third parties (including their right to maintain the confidentiality of their oral communications) or the integrity of the adjudicative process.[37]

3.3 *Other Procedural Protections*

WTO adjudicators must apply the DSU in a manner ensuring fair and orderly proceedings and promoting the prompt and effective resolution of disputes.[38] Furthermore, parties and third parties may be represented before WTO adjudicating bodies by nongovernmental legal counsel or other experts advising the relevant party or third party, provided they assume the responsibility for relevant conduct of such individuals.[39] The DSU also ensures a substantial degree of party control. In particular, WTO adjudicating bodies must not address claims that have not been properly put before them,[40] and the parties can pursue settlement talks

[35] The AB has referred to such participants as 'passive observers'. E.g., Appellate Body Report, *Argentina – Footwear (EC)*, para. 7.

[36] Since 2005, public observation has been requested and permitted in 24 panel hearings and 12 AB hearings.

[37] See, e.g., Appellate Body Report, *US – Continued Suspension / Canada – Continued Suspension*, Annex IV, paras. 7 and 10.

[38] Appellate Body Reports, *India – Patents (US)*, para. 94; *US – Stainless Steel (Mexico)*, para. 164; and *US – FSC*, para. 166.

[39] Appellate Body Reports, *EC – Bananas III*, para. 10; and *Thailand – H-Beams*, para. 74.

[40] Appellate Body Reports, *India – Patents (US)*, para. 92; and *US – Large Civil Aircraft (2nd complaint)*, para. 682.

and reach a mutually agreed solution even during panel or AB proceedings (see, e.g., Articles 12.7 and 12.12 and Rule 30 of the AB's Working Procedures).

3.4 *Summary Observations*

The liberal and prompt access to WTO adjudication that the DSU guarantees can, at least in politically controversial disputes, prove itself to be a double-edged sword. While the complaining member will likely regard such access as a legitimacy-enhancing feature, the responding member may consider that the lack of effective multilateral access-screening can lead to premature recourse to, and overreliance on, WTO adjudication in politically controversial disputes. Recourse to WTO adjudication in such disputes may also undermine the legitimacy of the DSM in the eyes of interested outsiders.

As mentioned, WTO members' dispute settlement activity has required WTO adjudicating bodies to deal with procedural situations not explicitly provided for in the DSU, notably requests by parties to hold open meetings and grant enhanced third-party rights as well as unsolicited amicus curiae submissions. WTO adjudicating bodies have played an enabling role in all three situations. Insiders have viewed this role quite differently in legitimacy terms in each of the three situations at issue, with open meetings generating the least criticism and amicus curiae submissions the most. The reason for this may lie in the following differences. In the case of joint requests for open meetings, there are consenting parties that give up rights (confidentiality protection). When enhanced third-party rights are granted, this is not infrequently done over the objections of a party. Thus, granting a third party additional rights can result in a redistribution of rights between members. In effect, one member, the third party, wins (enhanced third-party participation) what another member, the opposing party, loses (limited third-party participation). Amicus curiae submissions have also been accepted despite objections from parties, and this, too, involves a redistribution of rights. Only this time the redistribution occurs not between WTO members, but between disputing parties, inasmuch as acceptance by one of them of amicus curiae submissions means that the other disputing party can no longer determine itself which outsider views and interests are represented before a WTO adjudicating body.

From an outsider perspective, WTO adjudication suffers from a legitimacy deficit inasmuch as (i) meetings are not automatically open for public observation[41] and (ii) WTO adjudicating bodies are not required to accept and, where relevant, consider amicus curiae submissions, and members have not put in place rules to formalize, facilitate and encourage the filing of such submissions.[42] As noted, there is no consensus among members regarding the appropriateness of creating such rules.

4 Fact-Finding and Standards of Review

4.1 Allocation of Fact-Finding Power

The DSU assigns to panels the role of triers of fact, directing them in its Article 11 to make an objective assessment of the facts of a case. The facts of the case are to be presented to a panel by the parties by submitting supporting evidence, which they are expected to do at an early stage in panel proceedings.[43] The DSU does not confer a fact-finding mandate on the AB. But it also does not give the AB the power to remand a case to the panel for further proceedings when the AB disagrees with a panel's legal findings and conclusions. Mindful of this legal framework, the AB has held that, in principle and if so requested by a party, it has the power to complete a panel's inadequate legal analysis with a view to facilitating the prompt settlement and effective resolution of the dispute, as contemplated by Articles 3.3 and 21.1.[44] The AB's additional legal analysis in such cases may need to be supported by factual findings. As the AB has no fact-finding mandate of its own, it completes a panel's analysis only if nonappealed or upheld factual findings of the panel or undisputed facts on the panel record allow it to do so. Even then, however, the AB may decline to complete the analysis, for instance if the legal issues are complex and have not been sufficiently explored, such that it might affect the due process rights of the parties, were the AB to arrive at its own conclusion on these issues.[45]

41 Perhaps ironically, in those instances where panels or the AB allowed public observation of meetings, attendance numbers have not been very high. Peter Van Den Bossche, 'Non-governmental organizations and the WTO: Limits to involvement?' in Debra P. Steger (ed.), *Redesigning the World Trade Organization for the Twenty-First Century* (Ottawa: Wilfrid Laurier University Press, 2010), p. 329.

42 CUTS Centre for International Trade, Economics & Environment, 'Amicus Curiae Brief – Should the WTO Remain Friendless?', Briefing Paper No. 1/2002, 6.

43 Appellate Body Reports, *US – Large Civil Aircraft (2nd complaint)*, para. 1139; *EC – Fasteners (China)*, para. 566; and *Thailand – Cigarettes (Philippines)*, para. 149.

44 Appellate Body Report, *Canada – Periodicals*, p. 24.

45 Appellate Body Reports, *EC – Export Subsidies on Sugar*, para. 337; and *Canada – Renewable Energy / Canada – Feed-in Tariff Program*, para. 5.224.

4.2 Allocation of the Burden of Proof

The DSU is silent regarding the allocation of the burden of proof to the parties. Referring to a 'canon of evidence'[46] widely applied in international proceedings, the AB has determined, however, that:

> [A]s a general matter, the burden of proof rests upon the complaining Member. That Member must make out a *prima facie* case by presenting sufficient evidence to raise a presumption in favour of its claim. If the complaining Member succeeds, the responding Member may then seek to rebut this presumption. Therefore, under the usual allocation of the burden of proof, a responding Member's measure will be treated as WTO-*consistent*, until sufficient evidence is presented to prove the contrary.[47]

In some cases, the burden of proof nevertheless rests on the responding party. When a party invokes an exception to a WTO obligation in an attempt to justify a measure that the complaining party has alleged or proven to be in breach of that obligation, the responding party in effect advances an affirmative claim in its defence. Consequently, the burden of raising the defence and making out a prima facie case in support of it rests with the responding party.[48] Although this is sound legal logic, it may raise a concern from a legitimacy perspective because the responding party is made to bear the risk of being unable to persuade WTO adjudicators of the merits of its defence, with the consequence that the challenged measure may be found to be WTO-inconsistent. However, WTO adjudicators have been sensitive to this concern when determining what a responding party is required to show.[49]

[46] Appellate Body Report, *US – Wool Shirts and Blouses*, p. 14.

[47] Appellate Body Report, *Canada – Dairy* (*Article 21.5 – New Zealand and US II*), para. 66. A prima facie case or defence is one which, in the absence of effective refutation, requires a panel, as a matter of law, to rule in favour of the party presenting the prima facie case or defence. Appellate Body Report, *EC – Hormones*, para. 104. According to the AB, the nature and scope of arguments and evidence required can vary depending on the measure and provision at issue and even from case to case. Appellate Body Report, *Chile – Price Band System* (*Article 21.5 – Argentina*), para. 134.

[48] Appellate Body Report, *US – Gambling*, paras. 282 and 323.

[49] For instance, in the context of Article XIV(a) of the GATS, although it is for the responding party to show that a measure is 'necessary' to protect public morals or order, the AB has found that the responding party need not show, initially, that there are no reasonably available alternative measures that could achieve the same objective. Appellate Body Report, *US – Gambling*, para. 309.

In keeping with the established allocation of the burden of proof, a panel must not itself raise claims or defences, nor may it make a prima facie case or defence for a party who bears that burden.[50] A panel is also not required to conduct its own fact-finding exercise or to fill in gaps in the parties' arguments.[51] Although a panel has the authority under Article 13 to seek information or advice from any source, whether individuals or entities, including to gain a better understanding of the evidence and arguments before it,[52] that authority cannot be used to obtain information necessary to rule in favour of a party that has not made out a prima facie case or defence.[53] Similar considerations would constrain a panel in its use of information received from other nonparty sources – third parties or amici curiae – except, perhaps, in cases where a party elects to make such information an integral part of its position.[54] However, in cases where party A cannot meet its burden of adducing all necessary evidence in support of a claim or defence, e.g. because the evidence is in the exclusive possession of party B or a third party and party A has duly sought to obtain that evidence, it has the option of enlisting the assistance of the panel. It can notably request the panel to use its investigative authority under Article 13 to seek the necessary information from party B.[55] If party B nonetheless refuses to provide such information, the panel may be entitled to draw adverse inferences from such refusal.[56]

On request, panels and the AB have on occasion adopted special working procedures to provide enhanced confidentiality protection to information deemed particularly sensitive, such as business confidential information. The AB observed in this respect that if such information could not be adequately protected (e.g. by limiting access to a limited number of designated persons or not disclosing such information in the public version of a panel or AB report), the party that has access to it might in practice be unable to provide it to a panel, which could

[50] Appellate Body Reports, *Chile – Price Band System*, para. 173; *US – Shrimp (Thailand) / US – Customs Bond Directive*, para. 300; and *Japan – Agricultural Products II*, para. 129.

[51] Appellate Body Report, *US – Carbon Steel*, para. 153.

[52] Article 11.2 of the SPS Agreement explicitly provides that in a dispute involving scientific or technical issues, a panel 'should' seek advice from experts chosen by the panel in consultation with the parties.

[53] Appellate Body Report, *Japan – Agricultural Products II*, para. 129.

[54] Appellate Body Report, *US – Shrimp*, para. 89.

[55] Appellate Body Report, *US – Large Civil Aircraft (2nd complaint)*, paras. 1139–40.

[56] Appellate Body Report, *Canada – Aircraft*, para. 203.

compromise that party's ability to sustain a claim or defence. However, it remains for a panel or the AB to decide whether to accede to a request for confidentiality protection that goes beyond the protection that is explicitly contemplated in the DSU, and if so, what special arrangements are to be made.[57]

4.3 *Rules of Evidence*

A panel may, in principle, receive and consider evidence from: the parties, third parties, amici curiae, technical or scientific experts appointed by the panel or any other relevant source from which the panel seeks information. The DSU does not lay down any formal rules of evidence. Regarding what constitutes admissible evidence, essentially two grounds for exclusion have been recognized in the jurisprudence. First, a panel can refuse to admit evidence that has been unseasonably submitted.[58] Second, a panel can in certain circumstances remove evidence submitted by a party from the record if the evidence contains classified information of the other party.[59] As concerns the assessment of the relevance and probative value of the evidence received, including expert testimony, the AB has established that this is a task to be performed by panels, and that because panels are the designated triers of fact, they enjoy a considerable margin of discretion in performing that task.[60] A panel does not exceed the bounds of its discretion in appreciating the evidence so long as a panel considers all evidence in the panel record, in its totality; engages with evidence that on its face appears to be favourable to the case of one or other party and assesses its significance; does not distort that evidence; treats the evidence submitted by the parties even-handedly; and there is sufficient evidence and the panel bases its factual findings on it.[61]

[57] Appellate Body Report, *EC and certain member States – Large Civil Aircraft*, Annex III, paras. 12 and 15.

[58] Appellate Body Reports, *Argentina – Textiles and Apparel*, para. 80; and *EC – Sardines*, para. 301.

[59] Documents WT/DS400/6 and WT/DS401/7, para. 2.1.

[60] Appellate Body Reports, *EC – Hormones*, para. 132; *EC – Asbestos*, para. 161; *Korea – Dairy*, para. 137; and *Brazil – Retreaded Tyres*, para. 202.

[61] Appellate Body Reports, *US – Continued Zeroing*, para. 331; *US – Zeroing (Japan)*, para. 82; *Australia – Apples*, para. 270; and *EC – Fasteners (China)*, para. 441.

4.4 Standards of Review

The general standard of review to be applied by a panel is set forth in Article 11.[62] It provides that 'a panel should make an objective assessment of the matter before it, including an objective assessment of the facts of the case and the applicability of and conformity with the relevant covered agreements.'[63] Turning first to the requirement that a panel should make an objective assessment of the 'facts of the case', the AB has clarified that in order to ensure a correct application of Article 11, a panel needs to be mindful of the specific WTO provision at issue.[64] More particularly, a panel needs to ascertain whether the WTO provision under which it conducts its analysis contemplates that the panel should act as an initial trier of fact that can make its own factual findings or merely as a reviewer of a fact-based determination to be ultimately made by a domestic authority.[65] The latter role of a panel is typical of disputes involving antidumping, countervailing duty or safeguard measures, but is also engaged, for instance, in disputes concerning the Agreement on Sanitary or Phytosanitary Measures and arising from the conclusions of a member's risk assessment.[66]

The panel's task varies depending on its role. In cases where a panel acts as an initial trier of fact, the panel is charged with determining the facts of the case and arriving at factual findings.[67] A panel's factual findings are in principle not subject to review by the AB (Article 17.6). The AB can, however, review the objectivity of a panel's assessment of the facts under Article 11, including its appreciation of evidence.[68] According to the AB, Article 11 requires that in acting as an initial trier of fact, a panel:

> 'consider all the evidence presented to it, assess its credibility, determine its weight, and ensure that its factual findings have a proper basis in that evidence.' At the same time, panels 'are not required to accord to factual

[62] Appellate Body Report, *Argentina – Footwear (EC)*, para. 118.
[63] As Article 11 also covers how a panel should examine the legal interpretations advanced by members or underlying their authorities' legal determinations, this matter is discussed in the present section rather than Section 5, which deals with interpretative approaches.
[64] Appellate Body Reports, *US – Softwood Lumber VI (Article 21.5 – Canada)*, para. 92; and *Australia – Apples*, para. 355.
[65] Appellate Body Report, *US – Upland Cotton*, para. 458.
[66] Appellate Body Reports, *US – Continued Suspension / Canada – Continued Suspension*, para. 590.
[67] Appellate Body Report, *Korea – Dairy*, para. 137.
[68] Appellate Body Report, *China – GOES*, para. 183.

> evidence of the parties the same meaning and weight as do the parties'. In this respect, 'the Appellate Body will not "interfere lightly" with a panel's fact-finding authority, and will not "base a finding of inconsistency under Article 11 simply on the conclusion that [it] might have reached a different factual finding".' Instead, for a claim under Article 11 to succeed, the Appellate Body must be satisfied that the panel has exceeded its authority as the initial trier of facts. As the initial trier of facts, a panel must provide 'reasoned and adequate explanations and coherent reasoning', and must base its finding on a sufficient evidentiary basis. Moreover, a participant claiming that a panel disregarded certain evidence must explain why the evidence is so material to its case that the panel's failure to address such evidence has a bearing on the objectivity of the panel's factual assessment.[69]

In cases where a panel acts as a reviewer of fact-based determinations to be properly made by domestic authorities (i.e. their factual findings and the ultimate legal conclusions drawn from the facts found), the AB has opined that the 'objective assessment' to be undertaken by a panel calls for an approach that falls between the polar opposites of total deference by the panel to the domestic authority's determination and a complete lack of any deference, that is to say, de novo review by the panel. In support of this view, the AB has reasoned that:

> [m]any panels have in the past refused to undertake *de novo* review, wisely, since under current practice and systems, they are ... poorly suited to engage in such a review. On the other hand, 'total deference to the findings of national authorities' ... 'could not ensure an "objective assessment" as foreseen by Article 11'.[70]

More specifically, the AB has cautioned panels that they have a limited mandate when acting as reviewers of fact-based determinations of domestic authorities.[71] A panel's task is to review a member's determinations, and not to make their own determinations by substituting their judgement for that of the relevant domestic authority. According to the AB, it is not the role of a panel to evaluate whether the relevant determinations are correct. Rather, a panel is to assess: (i) whether a domestic authority's determinations find sufficient support in positive evidence that the authority has relied on (scrutiny of the evidentiary basis) and (ii)

69 Appellate Body Report, *US – Tuna II (Mexico)*, para. 254 (footnotes omitted).

70 Appellate Body Report, *EC – Hormones*, para. 117 (footnotes omitted).

71 According to the AB, the precise standard of review to be applied is also a function of the substantive provision of the covered agreement at issue. Appellate Body Report, *US – Countervailing Duty Investigation on DRAMS*, para. 184.

whether the explanations provided in support of the determinations are reasoned and adequate in the light of the evidence before the authority and plausible alternative explanations, and whether the reasoning is objective and coherent (scrutiny of the reasoning regarding how the evidence support the determinations made).[72] However, a panel must go beyond merely examining whether a domestic authority's ultimate determinations appear to be plausible or reasonable in the abstract. A panel's analysis of relevant determinations must be 'critical and searching' and sufficiently rigorous, while also paying due regard to the analytical approach chosen by the domestic authority.[73]

So far as concerns another important aspect of the standard of review set forth in Article 11 of the DSU – the review by a panel of legal interpretations advanced by members before the panel or underlying their authorities' legal determinations – the AB has clarified that a panel cannot make an 'objective assessment' of such interpretations as required by Article 11, unless its assessment follows the customary rules of interpretation of public international law, as envisaged in Article 3.2.[74] This suggests that a panel must apply these customary rules and reach its own conclusions as to the interpretation to be adopted.

A special standard of review is set out in Article 17.6 of the Anti-Dumping Agreement for disputes arising under that agreement.[75] The AB has found that Article 17.6 does not replace Article 11 of the DSU and that the standard of review applicable in disputes under the Anti-Dumping Agreement is, therefore, set forth in both Article 11 and Article 17.6.[76] Article 17.6, which imposes 'limiting obligations'[77] on a panel, provides in relevant part that:

(i) in its assessment of the facts of the matter, the panel shall determine whether the [investigating] authorities' establishment of the facts was proper and whether their evaluation of those facts was unbiased and objective. If the establishment of the facts was proper and the

72 Appellate Body Reports, *US – Continued Suspension / Canada – Continued Suspension*, paras. 590–1; and *US – Softwood Lumber VI (Article 21.5 – Canada)*, para. 97.

73 Appellate Body Reports, *US – Softwood Lumber VI (Article 21.5 – Canada)*, paras. 93, 99 and 113; and *US – Anti-Dumping and Countervailing Duties (China)*, para. 526.

74 Appellate Body Report, *EC – Hormones*, para. 118.

75 Appellate Body Reports, *EC – Hormones*, para. 114; *US – Lead and Bismuth II*, para. 49, and *Argentina – Footwear*, para. 118.

76 Appellate Body Reports, *US – Hot-Rolled Steel*, paras. 55 and 62; and *US – Stainless Steel (Mexico)*, para. 76.

77 Appellate Body Report, *Thailand – H-Beam*, para. 114.

evaluation was unbiased and objective, even though the panel might have reached a different conclusion, the evaluation shall not be overturned;

(ii) the panel shall interpret the relevant provisions of the [Anti-Dumping] Agreement in accordance with customary rules of interpretation of public international law. Where the panel finds that a relevant provision of the Agreement admits of more than one permissible interpretation, the panel shall find the authorities' measure to be in conformity with the Agreement if it rests upon one of those permissible interpretations.

According to the AB, under Article 17.6(i), a panel may only review domestic authorities' fact-finding and must not, itself, engage in any independent fact-finding.[78] At the same time, the reference in Article 17.6(i) to a panel's '*assessment* of the facts' (emphasis added) indicates, in the AB's view, that a panel must undertake an 'active' review of the facts determined by a domestic authority.[79] In relation to Article 17.6(ii), the AB has held that in reviewing a domestic authority's interpretation of the Anti-Dumping Agreement, a panel must bear in mind that there could be more than one permissible interpretation.[80] At the same time, the AB has yet to identify a provision of the Anti-Dumping Agreement that permits an interpretation other than the one it has found to be appropriate after applying the customary rules of interpretation.

4.5 *Summary Observations*

From an insider perspective, relevant legitimacy-related debate has revolved mainly around evidence gathering and the proper standard of review to be applied by panels. Particularly for resource-constrained complaining members, it can be difficult, depending on the legal and political system of the responding member, to gather the quantum and type of evidence needed to make out a prima facie case, which can impede access to WTO adjudication. As to the proper standard of review, members' views about the appropriate level of WTO scrutiny of domestic authorities' fact-based determinations are perhaps inevitably shaped by whether members find themselves on the importing or the exporting side of a

[78] Appellate Body Report, *Mexico – Corn-Syrup (Article 21.5 – US)*, para. 84.
[79] Appellate Body Report, *US – Hot-Rolled Steel*, para. 55.
[80] Appellate Body Report, *US – Stainless Steel (Mexico)*, para. 76.

dispute, with the consequence that there is a wide spectrum of opinion among the WTO membership regarding the appropriate level of scrutiny. Perhaps this is one reason why the AB has staked out a middle-ground position and has directed that a panel should neither step into the shoes of a domestic authority charged with making fact-based determinations nor passively accept its determinations.[81] As concerns the review of a domestic authority's legal interpretation, AB reports addressing this matter have at times attracted criticism, notably in disputes under the Anti-Dumping Agreement. One member in particular has expressed the view that the AB has construed Article 17.6(ii) of the Anti-Dumping Agreement in an overly narrow manner.[82]

As is the case with WTO members, there is no uniformity of opinion among outsiders regarding how intensely panels should review domestic authorities' determinations, with exporting companies affected by these determinations and citizens protected by them taking opposing views. From an outsider perspective, a panel's own fact-finding may also present possible legitimacy issues if important evidence is believed not to have been put before a panel. This has led to calls for panels to assume more of an inquisitorial role in some fact-finding situations. For instance, the suggestion has been ventilated that panels should actively seek information from any relevant source(s) to ascertain and take into account the interests of affected citizens and other relevant national or international public interests, unless panels have been adequately briefed in this regard by the parties.[83]

5 Interpretative Approaches

5.1 'Interpretation' by Members versus 'Clarification' through Adjudication

Only WTO members are entitled to formally 'interpret' the provisions of the WTO-covered agreements ('covered agreements'). Article IX:2 of the WTO Agreement states that '[t]he Ministerial Conference and the General Council shall have the exclusive authority to adopt interpretations of this Agreement and of the Multilateral Trade Agreements.' However,

[81] Appellate Body Report, *US – Softwood Lumber VI (Article 21.5 – Canada)*, para. 93.

[82] Dispute Settlement Body, Minutes of Meeting (19 February 2009), WT/DSB/M/256, 14 November 2008, Item 3, paras. 9–11.

[83] In this general direction, see footnote 14.

Article 3.2 equips WTO adjudicating bodies with the authority to provide 'clarification' on the rights and obligations of the members as formulated in the covered agreements. WTO adjudicating bodies rely on the customary rules of interpretation of public international law for clarifying the existing provisions of the covered agreements. Additionally, Article 17.6 validates the authority of panels to develop legal interpretations because appeals to the AB are possible only on legal issues developed by panels. For the power of formal (authoritative) interpretation of the covered agreements resides with members,[84] the binding nature of WTO adjudicating bodies' interpretation is formally limited to the parties and to the subject matter of a particular dispute.[85] Moreover, Article 3.2 also mandates that the recommendations and rulings of the DSB, which include the interpretations of WTO adjudicating bodies, cannot add to or diminish the rights and obligations of members provided in the covered agreements. Note that Article 3.1 states that the 'GATT principles on management of a dispute' continue to apply to a WTO dispute. Thus, these principles may serve as a basis for such 'clarification' by WTO adjudicating bodies.[86]

5.2 *General Rules of Treaty Interpretation Used by WTO Adjudicating Bodies*

Panels and the AB base their interpretation, inter alia, on Articles 31, 32 and 33 of the VCLT, which codify many of the customary rules of interpretation of public international law. Article 3.2 does not explicitly refer to these Articles of the VCLT, but panels and the AB have identified these Articles as the starting point of their interpretation of the WTO provisions.[87] With respect to Article 31(1) of the VCLT, panels and the AB have refrained from creating any hierarchical order between the tools provided by the said Article and have viewed them as a holistic rule of interpretation.[88] Article 31(2) of the VCLT provides for what can be

[84] Article XI:2 of the WTO Agreement.

[85] Article 3.9, Dispute Settlement Rules: Understanding on Rules and Procedures Governing the Settlement of Disputes, WTO Agreement, Annex 2.

[86] G. Marceau, 'Balance and coherence by the WTO appellate body: Who could do better?' in Giorgio Sacerdoti, Alan Yanovich, and Jan Bohanes (eds.), *The WTO at 10: The Role of the Dispute Settlement System* (Cambridge University Press, 2006), pp. 326–47.

[87] Appellate Body Report, *US – Gasoline*, p. 17.

[88] I. Van Damme, 'Treaty interpretation by the WTO appellate body', *European Journal of International Law*, 21, 3 (2010), 627–8.

considered the context, and Article 31(3) states that any subsequent agreement or practice between the parties or any relevant rule of international law may be considered along with the context for the purpose of interpretation. Article 32 of the VCLT reduces the negotiating history of an agreement or the historical context of a provision to a subsidiary tool of interpretation. WTO adjudicating bodies may have recourse to these supplementary means of interpretation to confirm the interpretation of a provision reached in accordance with the ordinary meaning, context, object and purpose, or to determine its meaning if the application of Article 31 VCLT leads to an interpretation that is ambiguous, obscure, manifestly absurd or unreasonable. The covered agreements are authentic in English, French and Spanish. WTO jurisprudence shows that WTO adjudicating bodies have resorted to the texts in these three languages in case of ambiguity.[89] As mentioned, WTO adjudicating bodies also refer to other customary rules of interpretation that are not necessarily codified in Articles 31–33 of the VCLT. Some of them are discussed hereafter.

5.2.1 Principle of Effectiveness

Panels and the AB have viewed the principle of effectiveness as a corollary of the general rule of interpretation set out in Article 31(1) of the VCLT.[90] The AB in *US – Gasoline* noted that '. . . interpretation must give meaning and effect to all the terms of the treaty.' An interpreter is not free to adopt a reading that would result in reducing whole clauses or paragraphs of a treaty to 'redundancy or inutility'. The panel in *Turkey – Textiles* suggested that, because members have a right under Article XXIV of the GATT 1994 to form regional trade agreements ('RTAs'), the interpretation of the other WTO provisions should be such as to ensure that this right does not become a 'redundancy or inutility'.[91] The AB has used the 'principle of effectiveness' to interpret the provisions of Article XX of the GATT 1994 to provide WTO members with the fundamental right to invoke nontrade concerns and has insisted that the provisions of Article XX of the GATT 1994 are equal in value and importance to the market access rights of members.

[89] Appellate Body Reports, *US – Softwood Lumber*, paras. 87–9; *EC – Tariff Preferences*, para. 147; and *US – Upland Cotton*, paras. 447–8.

[90] Appellate Body Report, *US – Gasoline*, p. 11.

[91] Panel Report, *Turkey – Textiles*, paras. 9.96 and 9.103, recalling the Appellate Body's wording in *US – Gasoline*.

5.2.2 Principle of Harmonious Interpretation within the WTO Single Undertaking

The WTO Agreement is a single undertaking under which all members are bound by the same WTO provisions. The single undertaking principle has almost become a WTO-specific principle of interpretation, relevant to the internal relationship between the covered agreements and their provisions. This principle implies that all the WTO provisions are simultaneously and cumulatively applicable, and that they should all be interpreted harmoniously within the WTO framework, viewed as an integrated whole. The AB in *Korea – Dairy* observed that any treaty interpreter must 'read all applicable provisions of a treaty in a way that gives meaning to all of them, harmoniously'.[92] The AB in *Korea – Dairy* also noted:

> We agree with the statement of the Panel that: It is now well established that the WTO Agreement is a 'Single Undertaking' and therefore all WTO obligations are generally cumulative and Members must comply with all of them simultaneously. . .[93]
>
> In light of the interpretive principle of effectiveness, it is the duty of any treaty interpreter to 'read all applicable provisions of a treaty in a way that gives meaning to all of them, harmoniously'.[94] An important corollary of this principle is that a treaty should be interpreted as a whole, and, in particular, its sections and parts should be read as a whole.[95]

This statement implies that the covered agreements 'must *a fortiori* be read as representing an inseparable package of rights and disciplines which have to be considered in conjunction'.[96] This harmonious interpretation pursuant to the single undertaking approach has influenced the definition of 'when two WTO provisions are considered to be "in conflict"'.

Thus, in *Guatemala – Cement*, the AB favoured a narrow interpretation of internal 'conflict' and insisted on a cumulative and harmonious interpretation of the WTO provisions. Then in *EC – Banana III*, this definition has been broadened to include a situation where one provision allows for an explicit right while another provision prohibits it. In *US – Upland*

[92] Appellate Body Report, *Korea – Dairy*, para. 81. [93] Ibid., para. 74.

[94] [Original Footnote] 'We *have* emphasized this in Appellate Body Report, *Argentina – Footwear (EC)*, para. 81. See also Appellate Body Report, *United States – Gasoline*, p. 23; and Appellate Body Report, *India – Patents*, para. 45.'

[95] Appellate Body Report, *Korea – Dairy*, para. 81.

[96] Appellate Body Report, *Argentina – Footwear (EC)*, para. 81.

Cotton, the AB expanded the definition of a 'conflict' by listing at least three potential conflicts, between the AoA and the ASCM, wherein the AoA would prevail pursuant to its Article 21.1. These situations included, first, an explicit carve-out from the ASCM; second, a situation wherein a member could not comply with obligations under both agreements simultaneously; and third, when the AoA expressly authorized a measure prohibited under the ASCM.[97] For example, with respect to the prohibition against local content subsidies of Article 3.1(b) of the ASCM, the provisions of the AoA, as cited by the United States in that dispute, were found not to specifically exclude the application of the ASCM prohibition. Therefore, no conflict existed between the provisions of the two agreements, both applied cumulatively as parts of the same treaty, and the ASCM's prohibition applied to the US measure at issue.[98]

5.2.3 Principle of *in Dubio Mitius*

The AB in *EC – Hormones* referred to the principle *in dubio mitius* as a tool of interpretation. The AB observed that '[w]e cannot lightly assume that sovereign states intended to impose upon themselves the more onerous, rather than the less burdensome, obligation by mandating *conformity* or *compliance with* such standards, guidelines and recommendations.'[99] The AB in *EC – Hormones* also bestowed the status of 'supplementary means of interpretation ... as widely recognised in international law' upon the principle of *in dubio mitius*.[100]

In *China – Intellectual Property Rights*, China argued that the United States should carry a significantly higher burden of proof on a claim concerning domestic criminal law matters, and that the Panel should treat 'sovereign jurisdiction over police powers' as a powerful default norm, and departure from which can be authorized only in light of explicit and unequivocal consent of State parties. The Panel stated that 'concerns regarding sovereignty' may be expected 'to find reflection in

97 Appellate Body Report, *US – Upland Cotton*, para. 532.

98 Ibid., paras. 546 and 549–50. See for further discussion, G. Marceau and J. P. Trachtman, 'A map of the World Trade Organization law of domestic regulation of goods: The technical barriers to trade agreement, the sanitary and phytosanitary measures agreement, and the general agreement on tariffs and trade', *Journal of World Trade*, 48, 2 (2014), 426.

99 Appellate Body Report, *EC – Hormones*, para. 165.

100 Ibid., footnote 154: 'The interpretative principle of *in dubio mitius*, widely recognized in international law as a "supplementary means of interpretation ..."'.

the text and scope of treaty obligations'.[101] 'The customary rules of treaty interpretation oblige the treaty interpreter to take these limitations and flexibilities into account in interpreting the relevant provision.'[102] However, later, in *China – Publications and Audiovisual Products*, the AB, in response to invocation of this principle by China, stated that 'even if the principle of *in dubio mitius* were relevant in WTO dispute settlement', there was no scope for its application in that dispute.[103]

It is to be noted that it is the parties to the dispute that have insisted on giving deference to the 'sovereignty of Members' or invoked the so-called principle of '*in dubio mitius*'.[104] WTO adjudicating bodies have struck a balance between the 'sovereignty of the Members' and the commitments made by them, as sovereign states, in accepting the covered agreements. This balance between the two is the essence of legitimacy, and WTO adjudicating bodies play an instrumental role in maintaining it. The Panel in *China – Rare Earth* noted that:

> [A] State's sovereignty is also expressed in its decision to ratify an international treaty and accept the benefits and obligations that such ratification entails. In becoming a WTO Member, China has of course not forfeited permanent sovereignty over its natural resources, which it enjoys as a natural corollary of its statehood. Nor… has China or any other WTO Member 'given up' its right to adopt export quotas or any other measure in pursuit of conservation. China has, however, agreed to exercise its rights in conformity with WTO rules, and to respect WTO provisions when developing and implementing policies to conserve exhaustible natural resources.[105]

5.2.4 Principle of *Lex Specialis*

WTO adjudicating bodies have also applied the principle of *lex specialis*, which is considered by some as a customary rule of interpretation, although not codified in the VCLT, providing which provision is to be interpreted and applied first.[106] *Lex Specialis* can also be seen as a rule about 'conflict' providing that in case of conflict only the most specific is to be applied. The General Interpretative Note to Annex 1A provides that

[101] Panel Report, *China – Intellectual Property Rights*, para. 7.501. [102] Ibid.
[103] Appellate Body Report, *China – Publications and Audiovisual Products*, para. 411.
[104] Appellate Body Reports, *Korea – Alcohol*, paras. 5, 12, 47 and 78; *Chile – Price Band*, para. 110; and *US – Line Pipe Safeguards*, para. 20.
[105] Panel Report, *China – Rare Earths*, para. 7.270
[106] Marceau and Trachtman, 'A map of the World Trade Organization law', p. 426.

in the event of conflict between a provision of the GATT 1994 and a provision of another agreement in Annex 1A to the WTO Agreement, the provision of the other agreement shall prevail to the extent of the conflict. This rule of conflict provides that only the most specific provision will apply. The AB applied this principle of *lex specialis*, as a principle of interpretation, in *EC – Bananas III*, wherein it noted that in case the GATT 1994 and another multilateral WTO agreement in Annex 1A to the WTO Agreement can be applied to a measure, then the impugned measure should be examined first on the basis of the Agreement that 'deals specifically, and in detail', with a measure of that type.[107] This principle of interpretation has been used to identify the set of provisions in the covered agreements that are more specific and have to be examined first.[108] However, this *lex specialis* principle does not exclude the applicability of a less specific provision.[109]

5.2.5 Principle of Evolutionary Interpretation

WTO adjudicating bodies have relied on the principle of evolutionary interpretation to give more contemporary meaning to terms used in GATT 1994 provisions that were first agreed in 1947.[110] In *US – Shrimp*, while interpreting the term 'exhaustible natural resources', the AB referred to non-WTO sources of international law for confirming that the term had evolved.[111] The Panel in *China – Audio-visual Products* took the same approach to interpret the term 'public morals' in Article XX(a) of the GATT 1994:

> '[T]he term "public morals" denotes standards of right and wrong conduct maintained by or on behalf of a community or nation'... 'the content of these concepts for Members can vary in time and space, depending upon a range of factors, including prevailing social, cultural, ethical and religious values ... Members, in applying this and other similar societal concepts, should be given some scope to define and apply

[107] Appellate Body Report, *EC – Bananas III*, paras. 155 and 204.
[108] Panel Reports, *Australia – Salmon*, para. 8.39 and *EC – Hormones*, para. 8.45.
[109] The other general rules of the covered agreements may be examined after analysing the measure under the specific provisions. See Marceau and Trachtman, 'A map of the World Trade Organization Law', p. 428.
[110] G. Marceau, 'The WTO Dispute Settlement and Human Rights', *European Journal of International Law*, 13 (2002), 784.
[111] Appellate Body Report, *US – Shrimp*, paras. 130–1.
[112] Panel Report, *China – Publications and Audiovisual*, para. 7.759.

> for themselves the concepts of "public morals" ... in their respective territories, according to their own systems and scales of values.[112]

Thus, such cultural independence was considered a concept the meaning of which can evolve over time.

5.3 *Specific Interpretative Techniques*

5.3.1 Cross-Referencing

It is a technique of holistic interpretation and effective interpretation so as to ensure that a term is interpreted in context and in light of the object and purpose of the treaty.[113] It adds to the security and predictability of the WTO system as envisaged under Article 3.2. In *US – Shrimp*, the AB in conducting an analysis under Article XX(g) of the GATT 1994 noted that '... the specific language [sustainable development] of the preamble to the WTO Agreement, which, we have said, gives colour, texture and shading to the rights and obligations of Members under the *WTO Agreement*, generally, and under the GATT 1994, in particular.'[114] Thus, the AB has also relied on this technique to confirm the meaning or lend support to its interpretation of a term.

5.3.2 Reference to Prior Panel and AB Reports

The WTO adjudicating bodies have consistently upheld the strong persuasive powers of their previous decisions. In *Japan – Alcoholic Beverages II*, the AB found that: '[a]dopted panel reports ... create legitimate expectations among WTO Members, and, therefore, should be taken into account where they are relevant to any dispute.'[115] This rule implies that panels should follow their previous reasoning unless they give good reasons for departing from the previous jurisprudence.[116] The AB in *US – Stainless Steel (Mexico)*, after noting that AB reports are legally binding only on the parties, observed: 'This, however, does not mean that the subsequent panels are free to disregard the legal interpretations and

112 Panel Report, *China – Publications and Audiovisual*, para. 7.759.

113 I. Van Damme, 'Treaty interpretation by the WTO appellate body', *European Journal of International Law*, 21, 3 (2010), 627–8.

114 Appellate Body Report, *US – Shrimp*, para. 13.

115 Appellate Body Report, *Japan – Alcoholic Beverages II*, p. 14.

116 R. Howse, 'Adjudicative legitimacy and treaty interpretation in international trade law: The early years of WTO Jurisprudence' in Robert Howse, *The WTO System: Law, Politics & Legitimacy* (London: Cameron May, 2007), p. 238.

the *ratio decidendi* contained in previous AB reports that have been adopted by the DSB.'[117] In *US – Shrimp (Article 21.5 - Malaysia)*, the AB clarified that the same reasoning applies to the adopted AB reports as well.[118] In *US – Oil Country Tubular Goods Sunset Reviews*, the AB noted that '... following the AB's conclusions in earlier disputes is not only appropriate, but is what would be expected from panels, especially where the issues are the same.'[119] Thus, it has been argued that WTO adjudicating bodies' practice amounts to de facto stare decisis.[120] This rule is not formulated in the DSU, but the practice of panels and the AB to refer to and rely on their previous decisions finds a basis in Article 3.2, which indicates that the DSM aims at providing security and predictability to the multilateral trading system.

5.3.3 Reference to Other Tribunals

The AB has been viewed as being open to other sources of international law.[121] The AB, in its first dispute, noted that the covered agreements cannot be interpreted in 'clinical isolation' from public international law.[122] For instance, in order to resolve the issue of participation of private counsel in meetings of WTO adjudicating bodies, in the *EC – Bananas III* dispute, the AB took note of the practice of other international tribunals in arriving at its decision.[123] This is consistent with the fact that multiple institutions occupy the same governance space, and they may compete or cooperate for optimal public decision making.[124] The WTO adjudicating bodies have referred to the decisions of other tribunals to enhance the legitimacy of their own decisions.[125]

117 Appellate Body Report, *United States – Stainless Steel (Mexico)*, para. 158.

118 Appellate Body Report, *US – Shrimp Article 21.5*, paras. 107–9.

119 Appellate Body Report, *United States – Anti Dumping Measures on Oil Country Tubular Goods*, para. 188.

120 R. Bhala, 'The precedent setters: *De facto stare decisis* in WTO adjudication (Part Two of Trilogy)', *Journal of Transnational Law and Policy*, 9, 1(1999), 9.

121 J. Pauwelyn and M. Elsig, 'The politics of treaty interpretation: Variations and explanations across international tribunals' in J. L. Dunoff and M. A. Pollack (eds.), *Interdisciplinary Perspectives on International Law and International Relations: The State of the Art* (Cambridge University Press, 2013), pp. 459–60.

122 Appellate Body Report, *US – Gasoline*, p. 16.

123 Appellate Body Report, *EC – Bananas III*, para 10.

124 D. C. Etsy, 'The World Trade Organization's legitimacy crisis', 433 *Yale Faculty Scholarship Series Paper* 18 (2002).

125 Appellate Body Report, *US – Shrimp*, para. 130.

5.4 *Summary Observations*

A plain reading of the text of one of the covered agreements does not necessarily provide the precise scope of the rights and obligations of WTO members. The covered agreements are a result of multilateral negotiations that synthesize the diverging positions of members and also accommodate the needs of different constituents around a negotiating table. Thus, the provisions of the covered agreements are often susceptible to varied interpretations. The WTO adjudicating bodies, while interpreting the covered agreements for resolving a dispute, ground their decisions in the text of the treaty, as the text gives expression to the intentions of the parties. This approach seems to have enhanced the legitimacy of their decisions for insiders, but it has been questioned by outsiders on account of not being as integrative as envisaged by the VCLT.[126] In case of a dispute, WTO adjudicating bodies maintain an overall balance between the policy space of the member imposing the restriction and the market access rights of the other members. In light of the same, these bodies have employed the 'principle of effectiveness' which has arguably enhanced the legitimacy of the WTO for the insiders as the principle also gives effect to the terms of the treaty, which contain exceptions to WTO obligations contained in the covered agreements. In WTO jurisprudence, these exceptions have been interpreted to ensure that members can effectively benefit from the exceptions to protect their nontrade concerns. However, this could undermine WTO's external legitimacy in case these legal interpretations depart from the views of the outsiders and only resound with the views of the insiders.[127]

The WTO adjudicating bodies have preferred a narrow definition of what is a 'conflict', and this reduces the occasions where one negotiated provision is set aside by an adjudicator in favour of another provision. Such an exclusion of a treaty provision by an adjudicator while interpreting provisions of the covered agreements could negatively affect the legitimacy of the DSM, whereas finding a way to apply all provisions in a harmonious manner will improve the legitimacy of the system. Moreover, the harmonious interpretation approach fosters the internal coherence of WTO rules and increases the legitimacy of the WTO adjudication. The legitimacy of the evolutionary approach adopted by WTO adjudicating bodies has been

[126] D. A. Irwin and J. J. H. Weiler, 'Measures affecting the cross-border supply of gambling and betting services (DS 285)', *World Trade Review* 7 (2008) 94.

[127] S. Cho, *The Social Foundations of World Trade: Norms, Community and Constitution* (Cambridge University Press, 2015) p. 225

questioned notably by insiders, but it can be argued that Article 31(3) (c) of the VCLT incorporates the principle of evolutionary interpretation.[128] Panels and the AB exhibit a propensity for adopting certain interpretative techniques in the application of general rules of interpretation', or in pursuance of their mandate under the DSU. Some specific techniques such as cross-referencing, reference to prior panel/AB reports, and reference to other tribunals have been employed by the WTO adjudicating bodies with the intent to increase the legitimacy of its decisions. These techniques, on more occasions than one, have enhanced the internal coherence of the covered agreements and strengthened the legitimacy of the decisions of the DSM amongst both insiders and outsiders.

6 Forum Shopping

6.1 Jurisdictional Conflict or Overlap

A jurisdictional conflict or an overlap in the settlement of a dispute may be defined as those situations where the same dispute or related aspects of the same dispute between the same parties could be brought to two distinct fora or two different DSMs.[129] In disputes between WTO members that are also parties to an RTA, there are various scenarios in which overlaps of jurisdiction could occur. A large number of RTAs provide for either a 'choice of forum' clause or an 'exclusive forum' clause. The problem of 'forum-shopping' can exist where the complaining party would have a choice between two different jurisdictions on the same facts, and an overlap and jurisdictional clash with the WTO is inevitable, given the quasi-automatic access and compulsory nature of the WTO-DSM.[130]

6.2 Dispute Resolution under RTAs versus WTO

The dispute settlement provisions under RTAs typically have the following features: they '(i) [are] state-to-state; (ii) require consultations

[128] G. Marceau, 'A call for coherence in international law: Praises for the prohibition against "clinical isolation" in WTO dispute settlement', *Journal of World Trade*, 33, 5 (1999) 121.

[129] K. Kwak and G. Marceau, 'Overlaps and conflicts of jurisdiction between the World Trade Organization and regional trade agreements' in L. Bartels and F. Ortino (eds.), *Regional Trade Agreements and the WTO Legal System* (Oxford University Press, 2006), p. 85.

[130] G. Marceau, 'Consultations and the panel process in the WTO dispute settlement system' in R. Yerxa and B. Wilson (eds.), *Key Issues in WTO Dispute Settlement: The First Ten Year* (Cambridge University Press, 2005), p. 30.

before members litigate; (iii) offer optional access to good offices, mediation, and conciliation; (iv) provide access to formal arbitration if consultations are unsuccessful; and (v) use the suspension of concession as an enforcement mechanism.'[131] Pursuant to Article 23, the WTO has exclusive jurisdiction in case of violations of rights and obligations of the members under the covered agreements. The DSU entitles any member to initiate WTO dispute settlement proceedings by simply alleging that a measure attributable to another member affects or impairs its trade benefits arising under a covered agreement.[132] So the WTO has jurisdiction over disputes dealing with measures having the potential of affecting trade in an adverse manner even if such disputes could also be handled in other fora. An overlap of jurisdiction between an RTA-DSM and the WTO-DSM may occur when: (i) an RTA provides for exclusive jurisdiction over a matter or (ii) an RTA 'offers' jurisdiction, on a permissive basis, for dealing with the same matter or a related one over which the WTO has exclusive jurisdiction; and the dispute concerns matters that fall within the scope of a WTO covered agreement.[133]

The WTO faced the issue of a conflict of jurisdiction in *Mexico – Soft Drinks*. The dispute could have been addressed both under Chapter 20 of the NAFTA and the DSU. The responding party in that dispute agreed that the WTO Panel had jurisdiction over the dispute but claimed that the Panel should have declined to exercise its jurisdiction.[134] The AB ruled that Articles 3, 7, 11, 19 and 23 require panels to exercise their jurisdiction.[135] The AB also noted that a 'decision by a panel to decline to exercise validly established jurisdiction would seem to "diminish" the rights of a complaining member to "seek the redress of a violation of obligations"....'[136] Importantly, however, the AB expressed 'no view as to whether there may be circumstances in which legal impediments could exist that would preclude a panel from ruling on the merits of the claims that are before it'.[137] Also, the AB did not rule on whether invocation of the exclusion clause provided for would constitute 'a legal impediment to the exercise of a panel's jurisdiction...'.[138] The AB also clarified that its authority was limited to

[131] A. E. Appleton, 'Forum selection in trade litigation; ICTSD programme on international trade law', *International Centre for Trade and Sustainable Development, Geneva*, Issue Paper No. 12 (2013), 26.
[132] Kwak and Marceau, 'Overlaps and conflicts', 85. [133] Ibid.
[134] Appellate Body Report, *Mexico – Soft Drinks*, para. 42. [135] Ibid., paras. 48–53.
[136] Ibid., para. 53. [137] Ibid., para. 54. [138] Ibid.

interpreting the WTO agreements, and it was in no position to adjudicate on obligations arising from the NAFTA.[139]

In *Peru – Agriculture Products* the AB went further and added that '... the references in paragraph 4 [of Article XXIV] to facilitating trade and closer integration are not consistent with an interpretation of Article XXIV as a broad defence for measures in FTAs that roll back on Members' rights and obligations under the WTO covered agreements.'[140] This statement reinforced the AB's prior statement that it did not believe that Guatemala had violated Article 3.8 of the DSU on good faith when it challenged Peru for adopting a measure authorized by the FTA but prohibited by the WTO Agreement. The right for WTO members to initiate a WTO dispute seems to be inviolable. The AB thus emphasized that RTAs are not the agreements where WTO members can act inconsistently with WTO provisions; indeed RTA measures inconsistent with WTO can be justified in a RTA only when such RTAs are consistent with GATT Article XXIV, as interpreted in the *Turkey – Textiles* AB Report. Although not yet in force and independent of the relevant dispute clause in that *Peru – Guatemala* RTA, the AB expressed 'reservations' as to whether an FTA that includes provisions contrary to specific WTO provisions 'could be used under Article 31 (3) of the Vienna Convention in establishing the *common* intention of WTO Members' about the provisions for which the FTA is contrary of the parallel WTO provisions. It observed that '... such an approach would suggest that WTO provisions can be interpreted differently, depending on the Members to which they apply and on their rights and obligations under an FTA to which they are parties.'[141]

In the *Argentina – Poultry* dispute, which involved a subject matter that had been ruled upon by a MERCOSUR ad hoc Tribunal, Argentina requested the Panel to 'refrain from ruling on the Brazilian claim' and invoked the principles of 'good faith' and 'estoppel' in support of its claims.[142] Argentina also added that, in case the Panel nevertheless chose to proceed, it should align its ruling with the decision of the MERCOSUR tribunal.[143] The Panel rejected Argentina's arguments and found 'no evidence on the record that Brazil made an express statement that it would not bring WTO dispute settlement proceedings in respect of measures previously challenged through the MERCOSUR'.[144] The Panel

[139] Ibid., para. 56. [140] Appellate Body Report, *Peru – Agricultural Products*, para. 5.116.
[141] Appellate Body Report, *Peru – Agricultural Products*, para. 5.106
[142] Panel Report, *Argentina – Poultry*, paras. 7.17– 7.18. [143] Ibid., para. 7.17.
[144] Ibid., para. 7.38.

also noted that nothing in Article 3.2 of the DSU suggests that a panel has to follow the rulings of the MERCOSUR or any RTA.[145] In *Brazil – Retreaded Tyres*, which concerned an import restriction on retreaded tyres, the AB had to decide whether the exemption from Brazil's import restriction benefitting tyre imports from MERCOSUR countries, in view of a decision by a MERCOSUR arbitral tribunal, was justified under Article XX of the GATT 1994. The AB held that Brazil's MERCOSUR exemption introduced as a result of the MERCOSUR tribunal's ruling bore no relationship to the claimed objective of the ban on tyres for the protection of health and the conservation of the environment, and the exemption even went against that objective.[146]

6.3 *Economic and Political Costs of RTA versus WTO Dispute Settlement Proceedings*

Few RTAs have a permanent institution to deal with disputes, whereas many others establish the dispute settlement tribunals on an ad hoc basis.[147] The financial costs of the tribunals that are established on ad hoc basis are usually borne by the parties involved in the dispute, thereby making it an additional expenditure, as they are already contributing to the budget of the WTO. The proceedings at the WTO, although formally free of charge, also impose costs on the disputing parties – such as the salary of staff involved, or the fees for private lawyers hired. There are organisations like the Advisory Centre on WTO Law (ACWL), which advises its developing country members and least-developed country members (LDCs) on all issues relating to WTO law for lower fees than those that would be charged by private specialized law firms. In many disputes, developing-country members have, therefore, called upon the services of the ACWL to represent their governments in WTO dispute settlement proceedings.[148] The political costs of proceedings may also dissuade members from pursuing a dispute in one or other forum. The political cost is usually assessed in terms of the possibility of a souring of diplomatic relations with the responding party.[149]

[145] Ibid., para. 7.41. [146] Appellate Body Report, *Brazil – Retreaded Tyres*, para. 228.

[147] C. Chase, A. Yanovich, J.-A. Crawford, and P. Ugaz, 'Mapping of dispute settlement mechanisms in regional trade agreements – innovative or variations on a theme?', *WTO Staff Working Paper ERSD-2013-07* (2013), p. 45.

[148] Approximately 43 disputes till April 2015, available at www.acwl.ch/e/disputes/WTO_disputes.html.

[149] P.-L. Chang, 'The evolution and utilization of the GATT/WTO dispute settlement mechanism' in J. C. Hartigan (ed.), *Trade Disputes and the Dispute Settlement*

6.4 *Duration of WTO Dispute Settlement Proceedings*

WTO adjudication is remarkably efficient in comparison to other dispute settlement mechanisms. Articles 12.8 and 12.9 stipulate periods of six to nine months for panel proceedings, and Article 20 prescribes a period of nine to twelve months from the establishment of a panel to the adoption by the DSB of the panel the AB's report. The average actual duration for panel proceedings is twelve months, excluding the time that is expended in composing a panel and translating the adopted reports. However, important resource constraints on the WTO support staff have recently led to delays in the start of panel proceedings. Article 17.5 mandates the AB to complete appellate review proceedings within a period of sixty to ninety days, which can be extended in consultation with the parties involved in a dispute. The AB has generally been able to follow these deadlines, although in view of the high caseload in recent years the AB has sometimes required more time to complete its work.

6.5 *Legitimacy-Enhancing Elements of the DSM versus RTA-DSMs*

The rise in the number of disputes heard before WTO adjudicating bodies might be taken as an indication of the legitimacy of WTO adjudicators and WTO adjudication. This confidence in WTO adjudication may stem from the efficacy and automaticity of WTO dispute settlement proceedings and the jurisprudence developed over the past twenty years, which strengthens the rule of law. There is so far no comparable body of jurisprudence in any other regional forum. The WTO's DSM has been tried and tested for many years, and members and WTO adjudicators have gained considerable experience using it. Additionally, the DSU provides for a standing appellate body, and this possibility of appeal to another adjudicator does not exist in the DSMs of the majority of RTAs. Moreover, the WTO Secretariat and its staff serve as an institutional memory for panels, maintains continuity and consistency between panels and AB and provides legal support to the panels and the AB.[150] A vast majority of RTA tribunals are composed on an ad hoc basis, and they do

Understanding of the WTO: An Interdisciplinary Assessment (United Kingdom: Emerald Publishing Group Limited, 2009), p. 95.

150 WTO, *A Handbook on the WTO Dispute Settlement System: A WTO Secretariat Publication Prepared for Publication by the Legal Affairs and the Appellate Body* (Cambridge University Press, 2004), p. 22.

not get the support that can be provided by a permanent staff. Furthermore, the WTO-DSM also provides the possibility of forming coalitions with other complaining parties or third parties, which can substantially lower costs. Finally, the fact that implementation of an adverse DSB ruling by the losing party and any authorized retaliation against a losing party occurs under multilateral surveillance also adds to the legitimacy of the WTO-DSM.

6.6 *Summary Observations*

An increase in RTAs with a built-in DSM has presented opportunities to the members of the WTO to go 'forum shopping' for settling their disputes. The reasons for a potential complaining member's choice of forum range from the jurisdictional conflict between the WTO and an RTA, the cost-benefit analysis carried out in terms of economic, as well political costs, to the effectiveness of a specific DSM, which includes variables, such as the duration of the proceedings and the implementation mechanism. The premise underlying the choice-making process of a complainant is the legitimacy of the mechanism. As shown in the preceding discussion, the decision of a party to opt for an RTA's DSM or the WTO's DSM is affected by an overlap of jurisdictions between different fora, but WTO members continue to place more reliance on WTO adjudication than adjudication under the DSMs of RTAs. The WTO's DSM has the benefit that it allows other WTO members to participate in dispute settlement proceedings between two members and support the claims of the complaining member either as a cocomplaining party or a third party. This aspect provides the complaining member with political cover, and a coalition approach is often viewed as a safer economic and political approach. As discussed earlier, the dispute settlement proceedings take place within a tight time frame. However, it is alleged by some that these time frames are not generally adhered to by panels. These allegations can affect the perceived legitimacy of the system amongst both insiders and outsiders. Nevertheless, the WTO disputes on average run significantly faster than disputes in many other regional fora. The views expressed by the United States and the European Union, two of the most active users of the WTO's DSM, in the DSB meetings are supportive of the DSM.[151]

[151] Creamer and Godzimirska, *The Rhetoric of Legitimacy*, p. 16.

7 Implementation and Interaction with National Courts

7.1 Implementation Framework

In the WTO-DSM, the only remedy in case of a successful complaint is full implementation of the DSB recommendations, i.e. the losing member must bring the challenged measure into full conformity with the ruling of the panel and/or the AB, as appropriate (Article 19). All other compensatory measures taken by the losing member until full implementation of the DSB recommendations are for use as temporary remedies. The membership and the WTO adjudicator remain involved even after the DSB adopts the ruling (Articles 21 and 22) in order to monitor compliance. The percentage of compliance with the DSB recommendations is overall believed to be about 90 per cent for those disputes where implementing action is required. The DSB also monitors dispute review proceedings, compensation and retaliation for ensuring rigorous compliance by the losing party (Articles 21 and 22).

7.2 Time Frame for Implementation of WTO Dispute Settlement Rulings

After the adoption of any panel and AB report, if immediate compliance is not possible, a 'reasonable period of time' ('RPT') for complying with the DSB rulings and recommendations can be agreed upon by the parties, or it can be granted to the losing member following binding arbitration proceedings (Article 21.3). The procedures on implementation give due regard to the special needs of the developing members (Article 21.2), and the WTO rulings also underscore the importance of the developmental status of a member in determining the RTP. In practice, the RPT determined by arbitration has tended to vary between eight and fifteen months.

7.3 Surveillance of Implementation of WTO Dispute Settlement Rulings

The issue of implementation of rulings of adopted panel and AB reports remains under the surveillance of the DSB. Any member can enquire about the implementation of the rulings once the dispute is placed on the DSB agenda six months following the date of determination of the RPT. In order to facilitate exchanges between members, the losing member is obliged to circulate a status report ten days before each DSB meeting

(Article 21.6). The system exhibits particular sensitivity if the issue is raised by a developing country member (Article 21.7) or in case the dispute was brought by a developing country member (Article 21.8).[152] The DSB surveillance system can be useful for its potential to impose reputational costs with multilateral consequences on the noncomplying member.[153] In case of noncompliance by the losing member, countermeasures are automatically authorised by the DSB when requested, subject to a request by the noncomplying member for arbitration of their level. DSB surveillance continues for the entire period during which the countermeasures are imposed. Once imposed, countermeasures are lifted only upon full compliance by the losing member (Article 22.8). Overall, the surveillance mechanism is one of the facets that may lead members to bring complaints to the WTO rather than other available fora.[154]

7.4 Compliance Review – Article 21.5 of the DSU

At the expiry of the RPT, if parties disagree on whether the losing member fully implemented the DSB recommendations, the parties have the option of resorting to the original panel to determine the WTO-consistency of the implementing measure (Article 21.5). This review process is an extension of the surveillance mechanism.[155] It is prohibited for a member to make a unilateral determination of WTO-consistency or WTO-inconsistency of a measure adopted by another member at any stage during a dispute settlement proceeding.[156] The compliance review-process has not had to be used routinely by members, as the rate of implementation of DSB rulings is high. A compliance review panel is required to circulate a compliance report expeditiously; however, the

[152] B. Mercurio, 'Improving dispute settlement in the World Trade Organization: The dispute settlement understanding review – making it work?' *Journal of World Trade*, 38, 5 (2004), 835.

[153] W. J. Davey, 'Dispute settlement in the WTO and RTAs: A comment' in L. Bartels and F. Ortino (eds.), *Regional Trade Agreements and the WTO Legal System* (Oxford University Press, 2006), p. 343.

[154] Chase, Yanovich, Crawford, and Ugaz, 'Mapping of dispute settlement mechanism', p. 49.

[155] Jason E. Kearns and Steve Charnovitz, 'Adjudicating compliance in the WTO: A review of DSU Article 21.5', *Journal of International Economic Law*, 5, 2 (2002) 334–5.

[156] R. E. Hudec, 'Broadening the scope of remedies in the WTO dispute settlement' in Friedl Weiss (ed.), *Improving WTO Dispute Settlement Procedures: Issues & Lessons from the Practice of Other International Courts and Tribunals* (London: Cameron May, 2000), pp. 393–4.

average actual duration of compliance proceedings is closer to that of original panels.[157] This can detract from the legitimacy of the process particularly for both insiders and outsiders, but corresponds to the reality where implementing measure are often much more complex than the original measure. Thus, the time frame has been referred to as being unrealistic.[158]

7.5 *Compensation or Retaliation: Built-in Mechanisms*

The winning member maintains its fundamental right to impose countermeasures against the losing member in case the latter fails to bring its measure into conformity; the winning member can also seek compensation first and request retaliation only if satisfactory compensation is not agreed upon (Articles 22.2 and 22.6). The process of authorizing retaliation is quasi-automatic as the DSB authorization is provided through reverse consensus. The objective of retaliation is to induce the noncomplying party to bring its measure into conformity with its WTO obligations.[159] The countermeasures should be imposed first in the sector where the dispute takes place, and if that is not 'practicable' or 'effective', then the winning party can impose cross-retaliation, which gives the flexibility of designing countermeasures that target another sector or under another covered agreement (Article 22.3) than the one in which the original dispute arose. Under cross-retaliation, the idea is to target those sectors that have the potential of generating sufficient domestic pressure on the losing member to comply with the rulings.[160] The level of retaliation (or suspension of concessions) to be authorized must be equivalent to the nullification or impairment determined by the DSB (Article 22.4). If the losing member is of the view that the level of suspension proposed by the winning member is not equivalent to the level of nullification or impairment, or that the principles of suspension as specified in Article 22.3 have not been followed, it may request that the matter be referred to arbitration. The countermeasures impose a

[157] P. Van den Bossche and W. Zdouc, *The Law and Policy of the World Trade Organization: Text, Cases and Materials*, 3rd ed. (Cambridge University Press, 2013), p. 293.

[158] Ibid.

[159] B. P. McGivern, 'Seeking compliance with WTO Rulings: Theory, practice and alternatives', *The International Lawyer*, 36, 1 (2002), 144.

[160] T. Cottier, 'Dispute settlement in the World Trade Organization: Characteristics and structural implications for the European Union', *Common Market Law Review*, 35 (1998), 340.

temporary (Article 22.1) cost on the noncomplying member to bring its measure into conformity. The issue of sequencing (whether in cases where there is a disagreement by the parties over whether the responding member has implemented a DSB ruling, the winning party can impose retaliation before a compliance review process has reached its conclusion) could pose a challenge to the efficacy of these countermeasures, though it has been largely defused through a practice whereby the members concerned conclude bilateral sequencing agreements, which itself confirms the conviction of the members in the legitimacy of the dispute settlement system.[161]

7.6 Implementation of WTO Rulings by the Domestic Courts

The WTO rulings can be incorporated in the domestic legal framework by domestic courts either by the direct application of the rulings or through the principle of consistent interpretation. In certain jurisdictions, the domestic courts have been reluctant in giving direct effect to the WTO rulings for a variety of reasons. First, the WTO dispute settlement system is presumed to be partly diplomatic; second, a unilateral conferral of direct effect to the WTO rulings could be seen as curtailing the sovereignty of a member in comparison to that of its trading partners; third, such a subscription has the potential of jeopardising the member's legal order.[162] Thus, it is arguable that the implementation of the WTO rulings by the domestic courts of members or the lack thereof serves as a benchmark for gauging the legitimacy of the WTO rulings. The ECJ has relied on the WTO rulings for the interpretation of the EC law transposing a WTO covered agreement.[163] And US courts have acknowledged the position of the WTO rulings as persuasive and useful for informing their decisions.[164] The decision of the Supreme Court of Brazil in *Retreaded Tires Case*[165] gave due consideration to

[161] The issue of sequencing arises from a lack of clarity in the DSU's text as to the order in which the two options, i.e. authorization to retaliate or the initiation of proceedings under a special implementation panel, should be exercised in case a member believes that the defaulting party has failed to fully comply with the DSB rulings.

[162] M. Bronckers, 'The relationship of The EC Courts with other international tribunals: Non-committal, respectful or submissive?' *Common Market Law Review*, 44 (2007), 612–13.

[163] Case C-245/02, *Anheuser-Busch v. Budvar*, [2004] ECR I-10989, para. 49.

[164] *NSK Ltd. v. United States*, 358 F.Supp.2d 1276, 1288 (Ct. Int'l Trade 2005); and *Hyundai Electronics Co. v. United States*, 53 F.Supp.2d 1334, 1343 (Ct. Int'l Trade 1999).

[165] Supremo Tribunal Federal, Argüição de Descumprimento de Preceito Fundamental 101-DF, Justice Rapporteur Carmen Lúcia, Decision on 24 June 2009.

the international obligations cast on Brazil as a result of the WTO reports in *Brazil – Retreaded Tyres.*[166]

7.7 Summary Observations

Like any other dispute resolution forum, the efficacy and legitimacy of the WTO-DSM are measured by its implementation record. As discussed earlier, the implementation record of the WTO rulings is impressive, which enhances its legitimacy appeal amongst the insiders as well as the outsiders. The existing implementation procedures of the DSU seem to be appreciated by the insiders as the negotiations on improvements and clarifications to the DSU, in accordance with paragraph 30 of the Doha Ministerial Declaration, tabled few proposals targeting the implementation of the DSB rulings. The tight timelines for the implementation of WTO rulings increase the appeal to insiders and outsiders alike. However, certain requirements of the surveillance process, such as the submission of the 'status reports', have been referred to as lax as they do not provide adequate checks and sanctions for ensuring prompt compliance.[167] At the same time, the same requirement increases transparency, as the losing party provides for status reports at regular intervals.[168] The surveillance process further supports the legitimacy of the rulings for insiders but to outsiders this process falls short because the status reports are not public.[169] The option of countermeasures increases the credibility of the DSM from the perspective of insiders, but these countermeasures are questioned by outsiders, who favour financial compensation. Some argue that an effective use of these rulings by the domestic courts is required for confirming the legitimacy of the process. As noted earlier, the domestic courts in several jurisdictions have constructively engaged with the WTO rulings by having recourse to consistent interpretation, while refraining from explicitly acknowledging their interpretative authority. This dialogue signals their confidence in the dispute settlement system.

166 Appellate Body Report, *Brazil – Retreaded Tyres.*

167 Chairman's text, Special Session of the Dispute Settlement Body, JOB (03)/91/Rev.1, 28 May 2003 in Ernst-Ulrich Petersman, 'Multi-level judicial trade governance without justice? On the role of domestic courts in the WTO legal and dispute settlement system', *European University Institute Working Papers*, Law No. 44 (2006), 14.

168 Mercurio, 'Improving dispute settlement in the World Trade Organization', 835.

169 W. J. Davey, 'Dispute settlement in the WTO and RTAs', p. 343.

8 WTO-Specific Legitimacy Concerns

8.1 Institutional Structure

8.1.1 Nomenclature

WTO adjudicating bodies such as panels and the AB are not referred to as courts in the WTO legal texts or elsewhere in the WTO system.[170] However, the WTO strengthens its accountability as a court by a strict adherence to the rule of law in instances such as the interpretation and enforcement of the WTO rules between all WTO members; and the multilateral monitoring and surveillance by the membership of the disputing parties' implementation of DSB recommendations.[171] Further, the automaticity of the WTO's jurisdiction over disputes arising from the covered agreements, the possibility to appeal against findings and conclusions of a panel, the possibility of retaliation in case of noncompliance, all endorse the judicial nature of the dispute settlement process of the WTO.

8.1.2 Reverse Consensus

The DSB takes decisions for the establishment of panels, adoption of panel and AB reports and authorizes retaliation through reverse consensus (Articles 6.1, 16.4, 17.14 and 22.6). During the GATT era, panel reports were adopted by positive consensus, which resulted in a possibility of blocking adoption of the ruling by the losing member.[172] In the WTO system, a losing member delay reject the adoption of a panel report by an appeal, but in practice it cannot prevent the adoption of the AB's report. A report can only be denied adoption if all members present at the DSB meeting, including the winning member, consent to its rejection (Article 17(14)). Thus, the reverse consensus rule has effectively resolved the GATT's problem of nonadoption of reports. However, the DSM has a review mechanism – the AB – which has been set up to guard against the risk of 'bad' reports.[173] For instance, the AB in *US – Wool Shirts and*

[170] J. H. H. Weiler, 'The rule of lawyers and the ethos of diplomats: Reflections on the internal and external legitimacy of WTO' in P. C. Mavroidis and A. O. Sykes (eds.), *The WTO and International Trade Law Dispute Settlement* (United Kingdom: Elgar Publishing, 2005), p. 201.

[171] J. Hillman, 'An emerging international rule of law? – The WTO dispute settlement system's role', *Ottawa Law Review*, 42 (2010–11), 2280.

[172] Howse, 'Adjudicative legitimacy and treaty interpretation in international trade law', p. 215.

[173] P. Van den Bossche, 'The making of the "World Trade Court": The origins and development of the appellate body of the World Trade Organization' in R. Yerxa and

Blouses discussed Article 3.2 of the DSU and observed that the aim of dispute settlement is not:

> ... to encourage either panels or the Appellate Body to 'make law' by clarifying existing provisions of the *WTO Agreement* outside the context of resolving a particular dispute. A panel need only address those claims which must be addressed in order to resolve the matter in issue in the dispute.[174]

Thus, the requirement is for WTO adjudicating bodies to resolve disputes within the four corners of the WTO Agreement as it stands.

8.2 Political Sensitiveness

The WTO-DSM is a government-to-government mechanism, and panels and the AB may be called on to pass on the limitations imposed by WTO rules on national regulatory autonomy.[175] Thus, WTO adjudicating bodies are mindful of the broader political context in finding solutions to disputes.[176] WTO adjudicating bodies sometimes exercise judicial economy with the intent of limiting the impact of a ruling in areas that are not considered essential for settling a dispute; they also exercise restraint in borrowing legal norms from outside the WTO legal texts and avoid engaging in the exercise of filling gaps in WTO rules.[177] There is a tacit understanding that the resolution of disputes at the WTO demands sensitivity to the broader political context.[178] The analysis of multifaceted disputes such as *Shrimp-Turtle* and *Brazil – Retreaded Tyres* have shown that balancing can be important when dealing with linkage disputes but the WTO dispute settlement system, given its stature, should indulge in this balancing act in a limited way.[179]

B. Wilson (eds.), *Key Issues in WTO Dispute Settlement: The First Ten Year* (Cambridge University Press, 2005), p. 64

174 Appellate Body Report, *US – Wool Shirts and Blouses*, p. 19.

175 G. Marceau and J. Trachtman, 'A map of the World Trade Organization law of domestic regulation of goods: The technical barriers to trade agreement, the sanitary and phytosanitary measures agreement, and the general agreement on tariffs and trade', *Journal of World Trade*, 35 (2001), 851.

176 G. Goh and D. Morgan, 'Political considerations and pragmatic outcomes in WTO Dispute Rulings', *UNSW Law Journal*, 30, 2 (2007), 486.

177 See in general, Appellate Body Report, *EC – Hormones*.

178 R. Howse, 'Adjudicative legitimacy and treaty interpretation in international trade law: The EARLY YEARS of WTO jurisprudence' in J. H. H. Weiler, *EU, WTO and NAFTA: Towards a Common Law of Economic Integration?* (Oxford: Oxford University Press, 2000), p. 62.

179 K. Kuloveski, *The WTO Dispute Settlement System: Challenges of the Environment, Legitimacy and Fragmentation* (The Netherlands: Kluwer Law International 2011), p. 185.

8.3 Procedural Proceedings

8.3.1 Preliminary Rulings

A practice has developed whereby responding parties raise preliminary objections and ask panels for preliminary rulings on issues such as such as the terms of reference of a panel, their jurisdiction, the function of panels and the formalities for their establishment. There are no specific provisions dealing with such preliminary rulings in the DSU. This may give rise to concerns related to the content of the claims put forward, the timing of addressing the preliminary rulings, the level of transparency, and third-party rights. Moreover, the usage of preliminary ruling procedures in the absence of any guidance can have systemic implications, such as harming the efficiency of panel proceedings, limiting the third-party rights and transparency for systemic issues.

8.3.2 Interim Review

The draft findings and conclusions of a panel report are submitted to the parties to a dispute for their review (Article 15). This unique feature gives an opportunity to the parties to examine the accuracy of their arguments, which is summarized in the factual part of the report and also the findings and conclusions. It can help to eliminate errors in panel reports.[180] Some argue that in light of the delays in WTO dispute settlement proceedings, eliminating such a procedural step could be an avenue to save time. Others favour such review stage and would like to introduce it at the appeal stage.

8.3.3 Provisional Measures (Interim Relief)

The WTO-DSM does not provide for any provisional measures (interim relief). The WTO adjudicating bodies were supposed to operate under strict time frames (Articles 12(8) and (9), 17(5), 20 and 21(4)).[181] However, the WTO-DSM has now become a victim of its own success, and many cases cannot be handled within the prescribed time limits because of the lack of availability of WTO Secretariat support, which is a fundamental characteristic of the WTO-DSM. This is why, especially for time-sensitive disputes and in light of the fact that the WTO does not provide

[180] T. Cottier, 'Dispute settlement in the World Trade Organization: Characteristics and structural implications for the European Union, in Thomas Cottier (ed.), *The Challenge of WTO Law: Collected Essays* (London: Cameron May, 2007), p. 24.

[181] T. Cottier, 'Dispute settlement in the World Trade Organization: Characteristics and structural implications for the European Union', *Common Market Law Review*, 35 (1997), 341.

for any retroactive remedies, many experts are suggesting that it could be good to have interim measures. However, it is not clear that if provisional measures were provided for, the members to which they are directed would comply. Indeed, certain measures being challenged are claimed to serve legitimate domestic policy purposes, and an injunction issued by a panel to suspend such a measure for the duration of a WTO dispute settlement proceeding could put a risk human health or the environment.

8.4 *Summary Observations*

There has been a legal paradigm shift of the DSM from the GATT 1947 to the WTO,[182] but it remains a mix of institutional setup and practices, which at times are appealing for insiders and concerning for outsiders and vice versa. The DSM as it exists today is a hybrid of 'diplomatic' and 'judicial' models, which has led to a number of legitimacy concerns.[183] It has been pointed out that the technocratic nomenclature of WTO adjudicating bodies ('panels', 'Appellate Body' and 'arbitrator') undermines the external legitimacy of the system.[184] It must be noted that the DSB comprises the WTO membership, and it is ultimately responsible for the functioning of the DSM. Also, it is the WTO membership that is sensitive to questions of nomenclature.[185] Reverse consensus has solved the issue of nonadoption of adjudication reports, but it may pose a threat to the internal legitimacy of the system in case of judicial activism by the adjudicating bodies of the WTO.[186] As discussed earlier, the WTO adjudicating bodies seem to adopt certain judicial techniques to give due deference to the broader political context, which increases the legitimacy of the system only for insiders. Moreover, in some instances, such as in *US – Shrimp*, the AB reinforced the status of the DSM in international law and in the eyes of outsiders. The absence of specific provisions on preliminary rulings has been a concern for some

[182] R. E. Hudec, 'The new WTO dispute settlement procedure: An overview of the first three years', *Minnesota Journal of Global Trade*, 8 (1999).

[183] D. P. Steger, 'The challenges to the legitimacy of the WTO' in S. Charnovitz, D. P. Steger, and P. Van den Bossche (eds.), *Law in the Service of Human Dignity: Essays in Honour of Florentino Feliciano* (Cambridge University Press, 2005), p. 203.

[184] Weiler, 'The rule of lawyers and the ethos of diplomats', p. 201.

[185] L. Boulle, *The Law of Globalization: An Introduction* (The Netherlands: Kluwer Law International 2009), p. 198.

[186] W. Guan, 'Consensus yet not consented: A critique of the WTO decision-making by consensus', *Journal of International Economic Law*, 17, 1 (2014), 88.

insiders.[187] There is indeed a need to discipline the preliminary rulings. Insiders and outsiders have also raised issues with the selection of the panel's experts, which are crucial for the legitimacy of the WTO-DSM. The DSM has been cherished as the 'jewel in the crown of the WTO', but increasing delays in panel and AB proceedings pose a challenge to the legitimacy of the system.

9 Conclusion

As is clear from this chapter, WTO adjudication has various built-in features, and WTO adjudicators have developed a number of practices, that enhance the legitimacy of the WTO dispute settlement system. Indeed, as one WTO adjudicator has noted, the system '[h]as been developed carefully and without excess, but certainly it is cumulatively significant and has had a major stabilizing effect on the system as a whole and in that sense, it has been successful. It is utilized significantly and its outcomes are generally adhered to'.[188]

Nevertheless, the system has not remained free of legitimacy-based criticism. Both WTO insiders (members) and WTO outsiders (civil society) have raised a number of specific legitimacy concerns in response to particular outcomes of WTO adjudicative proceedings or certain features of such proceedings. These criticisms tend to be directed at different aspects of WTO adjudication, depending on whether they originate with insiders or outsiders.

This presents a quandary for WTO adjudicators. First, outsiders by definition 'critiqu[e] legal rules from outside the system that produced those legal rules'.[189] Yet those legal rules, which in the case of the WTO have been created by WTO members, bind WTO adjudicating bodies. WTO adjudicators can therefore enhance the legitimacy of WTO adjudication only within the framework established by those rules and to the extent that those rules do not prevent steps deemed appropriates. Second,

[187] Dispute Settlement Body, Minutes of Meeting (28 January 2013), WT/DSB/M/328, 22 March 2013.

[188] D. Unterhalter, 'What makes the WTO dispute settlement procedure particular: Lessons to be learned for the settlement of international disputes in general?' in R. Wolfrum and I. Gätzschmann (eds.), *International Dispute Settlement: Room for Innovations?*, Series: Beiträge zum ausländischen und öffentlichen Recht und Völkerrecht, vol. 239 (Berlin: Springer-Verlag, 2013), p. 11.

[189] J. P. Trachtman, 'The WTO, legitimacy and development' *Trade Law & Development*, 4, 1 (2012), 12.

even where no rule stands in the way, additional steps by WTO adjudicating bodies toward, for example, greater transparency might very well mitigate perceived legitimacy problems from an outsider perspective, but raise legitimacy concerns for a subset of insiders.

Any debate about the legitimacy of WTO adjudication and WTO adjudicating bodies needs to recognize this catch-22. As indicated at the beginning of this chapter, the question 'Legitimate to whom?' is central to that debate. Indeed, quite often legitimacy-based criticism of the WTO system does not so much manifest a disagreement between WTO adjudicating bodies, on the one hand, and WTO insiders or outsiders, on the other hand. Instead, such criticism may at its core reflect a disagreement between WTO insiders and outsiders, with WTO adjudicating bodies getting caught in the crossfire. That disagreement between WTO insiders and outsiders being one of policy and even philosophy, it is not a disagreement that WTO adjudicators are well suited to resolve, even if they had the necessary legal wiggle room.

3

The Court of Justice of the European Union

P. J. KUIJPER*

1 Introduction

The Court of Justice of the European Union (CJEU) is one of the institutions of the European Union, mentioned among the other institutions, such as the European Council, the Council (of Ministers), the Parliament and the Court of Auditors, in Article 13 of the Treaty on European Union (TEU[1]). Its fundamental task is to ensure 'that in the interpretation and application of the Treaties the law is observed', according to Article 19 TEU, which also lays down in brief the Court's structure, composition and jurisdiction. Articles 251–281 of the Treaty on the Functioning of the European Union (TFEU[2]) develop the three elements mentioned in Article 19 and list the different actions to which the CJEU is open and the means of enforcement of its judgements. The Statute of the CJEU gives further details on the position of the judges and Advocates General (AG) of the Court of Justice (CoJ) and the General Court (GC), the way in which these courts are organized and conduct their business. The Statute is one of the Protocols attached to the TFEU and as such has treaty rank, but its provisions, except Title 1 on the status, nomination, obligations and loss of office of judges and Article 64, the provision on the language regime of the CJEU, can be modified by normal legislative procedure, that is to say by Council and Parliament acting together, on a proposal of the CoJ after consultation of the Commission or on a proposal of the Commission, after consultation of the CoJ (Article 281 TFEU). In some instances, the TFEU

* Professor at the Faculty of Law, University of Amsterdam, former principal legal adviser/director of the Commission Legal Service. I am much indebted to Chris Timmermans for critical remarks on an earlier draft of this chapter and to the editors of this volume for their pressure with a view to reducing its length.

1 Consolidated version of the Treaty on European Union, OJ C 326/01, 26 October 2012, pp. 13–47.

2 Consolidated version of the Treaty on the Functioning of the European Union, OJ C 326/01, 26 October 2012, pp. 47–390.

provides for special decision-making rules where the CJEU is concerned. Thus the Council may unanimously increase the number of Advocates-General (8) of the CoJ laid down in Article 252 TFEU at the request of the Court,[3] and the Council must approve the Rules of Procedure of the CoJ, the GC and any specialised court.[4]

The CJEU consists of the Court of Justice (CoJ), the General Court (GC) and may also include specialized courts. The first two are mentioned explicitly in Article 19 TEU; specialized courts have to be created by the colegislators according to the same procedure as provided for the amendment of the Statute of the Court. Such specialized courts are created for hearing at first instance specific categories of cases, which may be defined by the type of action under which they are brought or by the area of Union law that they cover. They are 'attached' to the GC, and appeal from their judgements lies with the GC and is limited to points of law (Article 257 TFEU).[5] The only specialized court ever created under these provisions is the EU Civil Service Tribunal (EUCST)[6], which has been abolished as a consequence of the transfer on 1 September 2016 to the General Court of the jurisdiction over disputes between the European civil servants and the institutions for which they work.[7]

The elements that influence the legitimacy of the CJEU and its case law will be approached according to the general schedule of analysis used in this book. The analysis will focus on the CoJ and the GC with emphasis on the first. The EUCST will only sporadically be referred to.

2 Selection of Judges and Functioning of the Court

2.1 Composition, Qualifications and Length of Mandate

The CoJ consists of one judge for each member state and therefore presently has 28 judges. It shall be assisted by Advocates-General

[3] See Article 252 TFEU, second sentence.

[4] See Articles 253, fifth alinea, 254 TFEU, fifth alinea and 257, fifth alinea; the latter two provisions also require that the GC and any specialized court make their Rules of Procedure in agreement with the CoJ.

[5] In cases where there is a serious risk that the unity and consistency of Union law may be affected, there may be further review of the GC's judgement on appeal by the CoJ, see Article 256(2).

[6] Annex I to the Statute of the Court of Justice of the European Union, Council Decision 2004/752/EC establishing the European Civil Service Court, OJ 2004 No. L333/7.

[7] Regulation (EU, Euratom) 2016/1192 of the European Parliament and of the Council of 6 July 2016, OJ 2016 No. L200/137, Articles 1 and 2.

(AGs).[8] According to the Treaty[9] the number of AGs is eight, but at the request of the CoJ this number may be increased by unanimous decision of the Council. It has indeed been increased to eleven,[10] who according to an informal agreement between the member states are now divided as follows: six places to the six biggest member states[11] and five places that circulate among the smaller member states. The function of AG is borrowed from the member states that have been brought under French legal influence during the Napoleonic period, which happened to be a large majority of the original six. AGs are formally part of the Court, but have an independent function. In their conclusions, they set out the case fully and in neutral fashion, but also arrive at a well-reasoned proposal for a judgement.

The number of judges of the GC is determined in the same way as the number of AGs of the CoJ. A minimum number is mentioned in the Treaty, namely at least the number of the member states, and this number was also mentioned in the Statute and changed after every accession.[12] The Council and the Parliament then may use the power of Article 281 TFEU to increase this number. They have recently done so with a view to gradually doubling the number of the GC's judges to 56 in 2019.[13] The GC may also be assisted by AGs, but this possibility is hardly used at present.[14] The EUCST was created as a specialized court for personnel cases and was intended to lighten the burden of the GC; it was never meant to have at least one judge for each member state: it had seven.[15] That number was reintegrated into the GC with the transfer back of the jurisdiction over civil service cases on 1 September 2016.

The term of appointment for the judges of all courts and for the AGs of the CoJ is six years, and they may be reappointed.[16] In order to limit

[8] Article 19(2) TEU. [9] Article 252 TFEU.

[10] Council Decision 2013/336/EU increasing the number of Advocates-General of the Court of Justice of the EU, OJ 2013, L179/92.

[11] Germany, United Kingdom, France, Italy, Spain and Poland.

[12] Article 19(2) TEU and Article 48 Statute of the Court.

[13] Regulation (EU, Euratom) 2015/2422 of the European Parliament and of the Council of 16 December 2015, amending Protocol No 3 on the Statute of the Court of Justice, OJ 2015, L341/14.

[14] Article 49 of the Statute states that the members of the GC may be called upon to perform the task of Advocate General. In its initial years the GC availed itself of the possibility, but soon its docket became so full and the experience with the occasional AG's was not such that the GC continued the practice on a regular basis.

[15] Council Decision 2004/752/EC establishing the European Civil Service Court, OJ 2004 No. L333/7.

[16] Articles 253 and 254 TFEU and, formerly for the EUCST, Article 2 of Annex 1 (now abolished).

discontinuity in the Courts', composition renewal of half the courts' judges and AGs will take place every three years.[17] This possibility of renewal has often been considered, also for other international courts, as a weak point, where the independence of the judges was concerned. Their wish for renewal of their mandate might make them eager to take positions congenial to those of their member states or their interests. In a court like the CJEU, where there are no dissenting opinions, it is impossible to verify, as such personal tendencies at the time of the renewal of a judge's mandate are covered by the secret of the deliberation of the Court. The obvious remedy is to have one (longer) nonrenewable term, a solution that has also been advanced for, among others, the ICJ. It has been suggested that at least CoJ judges should be appointed for one term of twelve years, but this idea in the end found no traction in the European Convention.[18]

The qualifications and conditions that must be fulfilled by the judges and AGs who serve on the CoJ and the GC have not changed since the beginning of the European Union and the creation of the GC, respectively. The qualifications required are those for appointment to the highest judicial offices (or simply 'to high judicial office' in the case of the GC) or being a jurisconsult of recognized competence (in the case of the CoJ).[19] The sole other condition for all two courts is that they be persons whose independence is beyond doubt. What has changed, both in the Treaties and in the practice of many member states is the procedure by which the candidates for these functions are nominated by the member states and by which such candidates are subsequently selected at the level of the Union. And yet the procedure of

[17] Ibid.

[18] The Commission in the spring of 1999 stimulated the creation of an independent working party on 'the Future of the European Court of Justice' under former Court President Ole Due. This group issued its report in January 2000, in which it advanced, inter alia, the idea of a single twelve-year term. In 2003, in the framework of the European Convention, the so-called Discussion Circle on the Court of Justice, presided by Antonio Vittorino, was divided on the issue and did not fully support it, see *Final Report of the Discussion Circle on the Court of Justice*, doc. CONV 636/03 CERCLE I 13, para. 7.

[19] The category 'jurisconsult of recognized competence' opens the CoJ to practising lawyers, insofar as they would not qualify for the highest judicial offices, legal advisers of government departments (primarily Foreign Affairs), professors of law, etc. It remains a fact that, especially in its early years, (former) government ministers, other politicians, economists with a legal bent and others with minimal or even nonexistent legal expertise were appointed to the Court under the colour of this vague qualification.

appointment formally has not changed; it still requires the common accord of the governments of the member states.

In the past, the procedure of common accord led invariably to the result that the candidate nominated by a member state would be appointed. There were an equal number of candidates to the seats on the CoJ or the GC, and it is common knowledge that normally no member state ventured to put in doubt, or even seriously inquired after, the qualifications or independence of the candidates from the countries whose seats had to be filled at that particular moment, for fear of being confronted later to similar objections from other member states. Thus nomination by a member state equaled appointment. It is obvious that such a system carries the risk that persons are appointed to the CoJ and the GC who are not necessarily very well suited to their position. It could lead to the appointment of judges who were simply not good enough jurists, lacking in knowledge of EU law or of law in general. Or it might turn out that they were not good enough linguists, who could not adapt to working in French, the working language of the Court. Or it might be that they were not physically and mentally resistant enough to deal with the relentless stream of cases that as judge rapporteur were allocated to them.[20] Such 'wrong appointments' created a certain amount of deadweight in the courts. In the early days of the CJEU this was simply tolerated; it could be accommodated. How, then, did the dynamics of nomination change so as to change the outcome of the appointment by common accord?

There are three important factors that have influenced this change and the last one and most important of these is the creation of the panel established by Article 255 TFEU,[21] which in turn has been made possible by the two others.

The first one is the steady increase in the caseload and the certainty that it would continue to rise after the big accession of 2004. Moreover, the new member states would bring new judges from countries where the full independence of the judiciary had been vested only recently and the

[20] The author has been struck by how often judges from both the CoJ and the GC told him that the burden of continuously processing cases as judge rapporteur and preparing for discussions on other cases was high or that their period at the Court was surely the period they worked hardest in their lives.

[21] The best and most comprehensive treatment of this so-called Article 255 Committee is to be found in the various contributions to Michal Bobek (ed.), *Selecting Europe's Judges: A Critical Review of the Appointment Procedures to the European Courts* (Oxford University Press, 2015).

available expertise in European law was as yet limited and highly variable. Hence the growing realization[22] that the EU courts in the future could no longer accommodate a certain amount of deadweight in their midst. Thus, it became gradually accepted both inside the courts and in circles outside the courts, which were concerned by its functioning, such as the high national courts, the governments of the member states and the other EU institutions, and thus also of the European Convention of 2002–2003,[23] that the guarantees for selecting suitable candidates for the CoJ and the GC had to be higher than they were in the old system. This led to the inclusion in the text of the Constitution for Europe (2004)[24] of the provision that would later on become Article 255 TFEU.

It is here that the creation of the EUCST and the selection of its seven judges in 2005 helped. The Decision establishing the EUCST included a consultative Committee and gave it the task to give an opinion on each candidate selected by it for its shortlist of fourteen.[25] The way in which this Committee (the CST Committee) worked on the occasion of the first selection of the Civil Service Court has probably helped the advisory committee for the appointment of candidates for the CoJ and the GC (the 255 Committee) to find its footing and has accustomed the member states to receiving this kind of advice even before that committee started its work.[26]

[22] Other measures also needed to be taken, and were taken, to deal with the increasing caseload, also as a consequence of the creation of new and speeded up procedures, especially in the field of justice and home affairs. These consisted primarily in simplification of procedures and similar measures and will be discussed elsewhere in this contribution.

[23] The idea of an advisory committee 'consisting of highly qualified independent lawyers' to help the member states with judges' appointments without fundamentally changing the system of common accord was hatched in Ole Due's working party (see footnote 18 earlier), and the ideas of this group were then fed to the European Convention by the Discussion Circle on the functioning of the Court. On this episode, see Jean-Marc Sauvé, 'Le role du comité 255 dans la sélection du juge de l'Union' in A. Rosas, E. Levits, and Y. Bot (eds.), *The Court of Justice and the Construction of Europe: Analysis and Perspectives on Sixty Years of Case-Law* (The Hague: Asser & Springer, 2013), pp. 99–119, at p. 104.

[24] Article III-357 of the Draft Treaty establishing a Convention for Europe, as approved by the Intergovernmental Conference of 18 June 2004, OJ C 169, 18 July 2003, pp. 1–150.

[25] See Article 3(3) and (4) Annex 1 to Council Decision 2004/752/EC, fn. 14 above.

[26] Formally the task of the consultative committee for the EUCST was larger than that of the Committee for the CoJ and the GC. On these differences, see Georges Vandersanden, 'The real test – How to contribute to a better justice: The experience of the civil service court' in Michael Bobek (ed.), *Selecting Europe's Judges: A Critical Review of the Appointment Procedures to the European Courts* (Oxford University Press, 2015), pp. 86–94, at pp. 87–8.

Whereas in the CST Committee the former and present judges of the two courts were the dominant presence, which seems right given the intra-EU kind of work of the EUCST and its link with the GC, the seven-member 255 Committee consists primarily of former and actual presidents and members of Supreme Courts, Constitutional Courts or Councils of State of the member states. It also includes one member proposed by the European Parliament and one former member of one of the courts of the CJEU. Formally the number of former members of the EU courts could have been higher, and initially there were two, one from each court, but the members of the highest courts of the member states dominate the Committee

The 255 Committee has been very transparent about its activities. It has published three reports between 2010 and late 2013,[27] of which the last report is the most valuable, as it seeks to give an overview of the activities of the Committee during those four years.[28] Moreover, its members, and in particular its president, have also published on its activities.[29]

The workload of the panel is not negligible. In the four years between the entry into force of the Lisbon Treaty (December 2009) and December 2013, it met 24 times and issued 67 opinions, of which 32 were of new nominees. The procedure for renewals (35 cases) will be left to one side here.

The government proposing a new candidate for the CoJ or GC is required to present a comprehensive information package, including a detailed CV and a list of publications as well as information on the government's reasons to put this candidate forward and the candidate's personal motivations.[30] Moreover, the candidate will be interviewed for an hour by the 255 Committee. This will complement the information on the candidate's file and facilitate a judgement of the candidate's suitability for the job, based on a number of benchmarks that have been laid out by the 255 Committee in its Third Report.

The assessment criteria that the Committee uses fall into three groups. The first group consists of the qualities that a candidate needs to be able

[27] These reports are accessible through the website of the CJEU: http://curia.europa.eu/jcms/jcms/P_64268.

[28] The fourth report has been published in 2017, but could no longer be taken into account.

[29] See the publications by President Sauvé in fn. 24 and Lord Mance, 'The Composition of the European Court of Justice', talk given to the United Kingdom Association for European law, 19 October 2011, available at: www.supremecourt.uk/docs/speech_111019.pdf, accessed 16 March 2016.

[30] For all elements see Third Report, p. 9 and pp. 14–15.

to function as a high-level or very high level judge. The first of these qualities is high legal expertise, which in the view of the panel seems to consist of, on the one hand, a sufficient quantum of legal knowledge and expertise, in particular of European law, and on the other hand of a certain mind-set, a capacity for legal analysis of a problem of application of the law, in particular the application of EU law in the legal systems of the member states.[31] The panel has indeed encountered cases in which the required high legal expertise was absent and where candidates demonstrated a lack of knowledge with the basic structure of EU law and did not have the ability to analyse and reflect on the general issues in Union law.[32]

Linked to high legal expertise is the assessment of the professional experience of the candidates. The nature and the level of that experience have to be assessed within the context of their national legal, administrative and university systems. The Committee is very aware that it should not favour a specific candidate profile; national differences must be able to find their way into the EU courts.[33] The length of such high-level professional experience is set by the panel at twenty years for the CoJ and between twelve and fifteen years for the GC. Only in the face of demonstrated exceptional expertise of a candidate would the Committee be prepared to drop these requirements. There has been at least one case in which a youthful candidate could not convince the Committee that he possessed the qualities required to compensate for his limited professional experience.[34]

The third quality that falls into the first group of qualities needed to function as a (very) high-level judge, is the somewhat enigmatically formulated 'ability to perform the duties of a judge'. In more concrete terms the Committee puts it as follows: does the candidate have 'the ability to make a relevant and effective contribution, within a reasonable time, to the handling of disputes subject to the jurisdiction of the EU courts'? It is telling that the panel explicitly mentions the burden of work in this connection, thus intimating that 'passengers' can no longer be tolerated on the EU courts.

Here lies a link between the first group of qualities consisting of pure legal and judicial qualities and the second group distinguished by the

[31] Third Report, p.18. [32] Ibid., pp. 18 and 20.

[33] Ibid. Whether the Committee has succeeded in avoiding such a too uniform profile is questionable. More on that in fn 41below and accompanying text.

[34] Third Report, p. 20.

Committee, which includes the more practical qualities necessary to be effective on one of the EU courts. Does the candidate already have mastery of the working language or can the Committee be fairly sure that he/she will acquire sufficient proficiency in French 'within a reasonable time'?[35] Will the candidate have the aptitude for working in an international environment? The panel emphasizes that on these practical aspects as well as on 'the ability to perform the duties of a judge' candidates must be able 'to make an effective personal contribution ... to the judicial role for which they are being considered' after a period of adjustment that should 'be measured in months rather than years'.[36] It would seem that there has been at least one candidate that could not convince the panel that this was the case.

Finally, there is the third group of qualities that an EUCJ judge or AG must have: the requirements of impartiality and independence. The Committee clearly has confronted difficulties in operationalizing these qualities. They are not easy to assess on the basis of a CV or the professional experience of the candidates. Moreover, it is not easy to provoke candidates into being candid on these qualities, when asking them questions or to know what questions to ask of the nominating government on these issues. The third Committee report is rather vague and unsatisfactory on this point.[37] Doubts about independence could arise, if a candidate has been a high legal adviser serving a member state government or one of the institutions just before their nomination. Is it sufficient that such persons recuse themselves in cases on which they have advised their government or their institution in the past – which will presumably occur only during the early period of their service on the courts – or are they tainted by a suspicion of more permanent bias? In the past this last question has implicitly been answered in the negative by the Council, as there have been quite a few examples of high-ranking national legal advisers and Commission legal advisers being appointed to the Court, although it should be said that most of them also had a serious reputation as academics.[38] The CST Committee does not seem to have had any difficulty to go along with the nomination of EUCST judges who came from the legal services of the Commission and of the Parliament.

[35] Note the identical wording with the preceding requirement. Third Report, pp. 18–19.

[36] Ibid., p. 21. [37] Ibid., p. 19.

[38] Note that there is also a long tradition to elect legal advisors of the Ministries of Foreign Affairs to the International Court of Justice, without this having ever met serious criticism.

This brings up the question of the effectiveness of the advice of the 255 Committee. Have its negative opinions been followed? Of the thirty-two new candidates for a place on the CoJ and the GC, seven have been given a negative opinion, i.e. almost a quarter.[39] The reports of the Committee indicate that in all these cases the government concerned has proposed a new candidate, who has received a positive opinion from the Committee and has been duly appointed.[40]

There is no doubt, therefore, that the 255 Committee has been quite successful. Its activity and its reports have totally changed the dynamic of the appointment decisions by common accord between the governments of the member states. The dynamic of 'nomination equals appointment' has been broken. The decision to compose the Committee primarily of judges and even presidents of the highest civil, administrative or constitutional courts of the member states seems to have been vindicated; it is clearly extremely difficult for the member states to ignore the well-considered opinion of a Committee of this composition, even if the proportion of rejections of candidates was disconcertingly high. There can be little doubt that the work of the Committee and perhaps its mere existence has contributed to a higher quality of the judges on the EU courts and this is likely to have a positive effect on the legitimacy of the CJEU as a whole.

There have been two side effects of the work of the Committee, one of which is certainly positive, whereas the other is somewhat worrisome. Moreover, there is an omission by the Committee, which the Council has begun to remedy.

The positive effect has been that the member states' experience with the CST and 255 Committees has been instrumental in the decision of many member states to review their own internal selection procedures, often opening them up to a broader group of candidates, who can put themselves forward or who can be put forward by others.[41] Such open

[39] Negative opinions related to candidates from all categories of member states, from the original six and the early accession, from the accession of the nineties, and from the accession of the 2000s. See Henry de Waele, 'Not quite the bed that Procrustes built: Dissecting the system for selecting judges at the Court of Justice of the European Union' in Michael Bobek (ed.), *Selecting Europe's Judges: A Critical Review of the Appointment Procedures to the European Courts* (Oxford University Press, 2015), pp. 24–50, at pp. 45–6.

[40] Third Report, pp. 9–10. For a more extensive analysis, see De Waele, 'Not quite the bed that Procrustes built', pp. 45–7.

[41] On this development, see Dumbrovsky, Petkova, Van der Sluis, 'Judicial Appointments: The Article 255 TFEU Advisory Panel and Selection Procedures in the Member States', *Common Market Law Review*, 51 (2014), 455–82.

national procedures should enlarge the pool of judicial talent that can compete for a place on the EU courts and thus may enhance further the quality of the courts' work.

On the other hand it is an unmistakable fact that the criteria applied by the CST and 255 Committees seem to have a reinforcing effect on the preexisting trend of a large number of judges on the three courts previously having served as personal law clerks (so-called *référendaires*) to the judges of these courts.[42] Although the 255 Committee stresses the need for diversity in the composition of the Court and has certainly not designed the criteria for assessing the future judges with a view of selecting primarily *ex-référendaires*, these criteria seem nevertheless to have this effect. Who are likely to have good all-round knowledge of European Law; who are likely to be able to make a contribution, within a reasonable time, to the judicial work of the courts; who are likely to have the necessary language skills, including drafting skills, in the working language of the courts; who are likely to have the aptitude necessary to work in an international environment? The answer to all these questions is: people who have worked as law clerks at the EU courts. If in the meantime they have been able to acquire the necessary length of high-level legal experience, they will usually a have good chance to pass the test of the 255 Committee. Thus the search for diversity risks resulting in uniformity. The CST committee, which had a broader mandate than the 255-Committee, seems to have been somewhat aware of this risk,[43] and that may help the 255 Committee to avert this undesirable effect of the criteria they have developed.

Finally, the 255 Committee has not touched even with a barge pole another diversity question, namely gender. Although this is a serious question for all three courts, where women even today constitute a small minority,[44] the 255 Committee has obviously thought it wiser to concentrate exclusively on assessing ability and suitability. From its vantage point this is understandable, given that this question is not explicitly

[42] On these personal law clerks more in the next section on the internal functioning of the courts.

[43] Leif Sevon, 'The procedure for the selection of members of the Civil Service Tribunal: A pioneer experience', http://curia.europa.eu/jcms/upload/docs/application/2010-10/5anstfp_sevon_en.pdf, last visited 26/11/16.

[44] The Court of Justice in July 2016 had five women among the twenty-eight judges and two women among the eleven Advocate-Generals; the General Court at the same point in time had eight women out of thirty-five judges and the Civil Service Tribunal had seven male judges and two temporary judges, of whom one is a woman.

contained in its mandate, and raising it on its own initiative inevitably would have embroiled the Committee from the beginning of its existence in the well-known and politically charged discussion of gender versus merit, even if one considers that this is a false dichotomy. There is no denying, however, that it is a question of the utmost importance for the legitimacy of the EU courts, especially because (economic) discrimination against women has been a concern of the EEC from the very beginning and discrimination against women more generally is forbidden in Articles 8 and 19(1) TFEU and 21 of the Charter of Fundamental Rights.

Fortunately, here the Union legislator seems to be coming to the rescue. In their Regulation of 16 December 2015, doubling the number of GC judges, the Council and the European Parliament also decided that the member states, when making the necessary nominations for the three-yearly partial replacements with a view to arriving at 56 GC judges, should nominate two candidates for each seat. The objective of such double nominations is to choose more women, 'provided that the conditions and procedures laid down by the Treaties are respected'.[45] Given that the feminization of the law is visible in many member states, on the bench, in the law firms and on university staffs, it ought not to be difficult to reconcile these two requirements and appoint many well-qualified women lawyers to the EU courts.

2.2 *Internal Organization and Functioning of the EU Courts*

As explained earlier, the CJEU now consists of two courts. Thus, the first question that arises, once a case is brought, is which of the two courts it should be allocated to. With respect to the choice between the CoJ and the GC, the question is a bit more complicated. Broadly speaking, the CoJ presently is the constitutional court, the appeals court for the GC and the Court that guarantees the uniform interpretation of Union law, whereas the GC is rather the administrative court of the Union. That is the situation that flows from the present text of the Statute of the Court, but the Treaty leaves a greater leeway for the GC to be the Court of first instance for all annulment cases and for preliminary questions.[46]

[45] Recital 11 and Article 2 of Regulation (EU, Euratom) 2015/2422 of the European Parliament and of the Council of 16 December 2015 amending Protocol 3 on the Statute of the Court of Justice of the European Union, OJ 2015 No. L341/14, 24 December 2015.

[46] See Article 256(1) and (3) TFEU. Article 3(2) of Reg. 2015/2422 lays down that the CoJ will draw up a report for the EP, the Council and the Commission on possible changes in the distribution of competence for preliminary rulings.

For the moment the CoJ has the monopoly of all infringement cases and of all preliminary questions. It also deals exclusively with the requests for Opinions under Article 218(11) relating to the question of conformity or nonconformity with the Treaties of international agreements about to be concluded by the competent EU institutions. Furthermore, it also decides all claims for annulment and failure to act brought by a member state against the Council or the Parliament or against these institutions acting together as colegislators, except when the Council acts alone in the field of State aids or of protective trade measures against third countries under the common commercial policy, or if the Council takes implementing measures, where it has reserved these powers to itself, pursuant to Article 291 TFEU. The same logic of reserving the constitutional cases to the CoJ applies, when the institutions attack each other for annulment or failure to act, including when such a claim is brought by an institution against the European Central Bank.[47]

This leaves the GC with the normal annulment cases and actions for failure to act, which do not involve litigation between the member states and the major institutions of the Union (so-called privileged claimants)[48], with all damages cases, the civil service cases and the cases where the CJEU acts as an arbitral tribunal pursuant to a contractual clause.[49]

When a case is brought to the wrong forum, normally the Registry will make the claimant aware of this and redirect the case.[50]

Because the EUSCT has returned to the fold of the GC as from 1 September 2016, in the following we will concentrate the attention on how the CoJ and the GC process their cases and what are the features that stand out in this processing and how these features may influence the legitimacy of the courts. Both courts work in principle with a system of three- and five-person chambers and a Grand Chamber (consisting of 11, 13 or 15 members), depending on the importance of the case. Cases can always be upgraded to the next highest level, if the chamber asks for

[47] See Article 256 TFEU jo. Article 51 Statute of the Court. We do not deal here with the more arcane procedures, such as procedures against Commissioners, etc. See, e.g., Article 247 TFEU.

[48] Such privileged claimants, because of their position recognized by the Treaties, never need to demonstrate a legal interest, when appearing before the EU courts (the EP, the Commission, the Council and the member states). Others, the Court of Auditors, the European Central Bank and the Committee of the Regions have a guaranteed access to the courts, only if they act to protect their own prerogatives. They are the so-called semiprivileged claimants.

[49] See Article 272 TFEU. [50] Article 54 Statute EUCJ.

it or if a request for the Grand Chamber configuration is received from a party. Requests from member states and institutions have to be granted.[51] The CoJ meets in the Grand Chamber configuration more often than the GC.[52] In extremely important cases the CoJ may meet in plenary, although the number of judges needs to be made uneven for that occasion.

If a case comes in at either court, the president allocates it to a judge–rapporteur. The First AG of the CoJ then allocates the case to one of the AGs. If the Court, after having consulted the AG, is of the view that the case raises no new point of law, it can be decided without an opinion.[53]

It falls to the judge–rapporteur and his staff to prepare the so-called report for the hearing, after the parties and the intervening parties have lodged their written pleadings or written observations with the Court. That document is the basis on which the oral hearing will be held; it sets out the facts, the claims of both sides and the positions of the parties and the intervening parties in an objective manner. The parties and intervenors can ask for corrections of this report in writing or at the hearing. At the end of the hearing the AG announces when conclusions will be ready, and as soon as they are published the Chamber starts the real work of judging. In principle the Chamber begins with the question whether it will follow the AG. If the answer is broadly positive, the rest is simple: the judge–rapporteur starts writing a draft judgement in line with the conclusions of the AG, and that draft is honed during the deliberation. If the Chamber does not follow the AG's opinion, or only in part, the judge–rapporteur has more freedom to propose his or her own solutions for the case and prepare a draft, which is then adjusted and finally agreed in the deliberations of the Chamber.

There are a number of specific traits of the EU courts, which must be taken into account to complement this bare-bones outline of the process of producing a judgement. These are the typical civil law aspects in the character of the Court: it decides by majority vote (which is part of the secret of the deliberation), and there are no published dissents.[54] The consequence of this is that the judge–rapporteur can be appointed as the first step in the Court's process for making a judgement, whereas in

[51] Article 16 Statute EUCJ.

[52] The member states in particular are much more likely to ask for this in the kind of cases that go before the CoJ, as they are often about member state competences and infringements that are considered questions of principle.

[53] Article 20 (fifth alinea) Statute of the EUCJ. This alinea was added in 2012.

[54] Article 32 Rules of Procedure CoJ.

common law countries the task of writing a draft of the judgement is allotted only when the majority is well crystallized and is then given to a judge of that majority.

The specific role of the AG has been somewhat controversial because he or she sometimes came up with new viewpoints or solutions in his/her conclusions, without these having been sufficiently discussed at the hearing. This problem led to condemnations before the European Court of Human Rights of the way this function worked in some member states.[55] However, the creation of the possibility to reopen a case at any time, if inter alia the case must be decided on the basis of an argument that has not been discussed between the parties – a step that was taken in many member states that had AGs or comparable functions in their judicial system – protected the CoJ, when the issue came up indirectly in a case against the Netherlands.[56] So this potential threat to the legitimacy of the Court has been extinguished.

There also has been a lot of agonizing in the literature about the function of the AG. Does the AG produce some value added? Is the office absolutely necessary, or should it be reformed? What influence does the AG actually have on the Court? In discrete cases it is obvious that the AG can have influence on the Court and on other institutions. A clear example is AG Geelhoed, who was so shocked by the duplicity of the French authorities in an infringement case about overfishing and selling undersize fish[57] that *sua sponte* he advised the Court to go beyond the claim of the Commission and to impose, in addition to the usual penalty payments demanded by the Commission, a huge fine. When the Court followed him, this also had immediate repercussions on the Commission policy of exclusively demanding the imposition of penalty payments in nonimplementation cases.

[55] See ECtHR, *Vermeulen v. Belgium*, Judgement of 20 February 1996, Appl. No. 19075/91; *K.D.B. v. the Netherlands*, Judgement of 27 March 1998, No. 80/1997/864/1075.

[56] ECtHR, *Coöperatieve Producentenorganisatie van de Nederlandse Kokkelvisserij v. the Netherlands*, Order of 20 January 2009, Appl. No. 13645/05. The action was declared inadmissible. Presently the relevant provision is Article 83 of the Rules of Procedure of the CoJ.

[57] Case C-304/02, *Commission v. France*, EU:C:2005:444. For the Opinion of AG Geelhoed, see EU:2004:274. It appeared that France had not just tolerated continuing overfishing and selling of undersize fish but that French officials had insufficiently prosecuted these breaches of Union law and had attempted to hide this from the Commission and the Court, while France had already been condemned for the same facts in 1991 (Case C-64/88, *Commission v. France*, EU:C:1991:240).

It is more difficult to show that AGs have influence, not just in discrete cases but also over the long term and more globally on specific domains of Union law.[58] From those who have seriously researched different AGs and their influence on the Court, the answer is that they have had quite some influence, if they displayed a constant interest in certain problems over the years.[59] This would seem to apply to such AGs as J. P. Warner, Walter van Gerven and Francis Jacobs. Such studies rest on careful legal parsing of opinions and judgements, but necessarily remain somewhat impressionistic. However, there are now also quantitative studies that succeed in showing that over a long period of time the AGs active during this period do have a certain influence on the Court.[60]

Returning to the CoJ and the GC and how they handle a case, normally, the president of the Chamber and the judge–rapporteur will make an effort to be inclusive and thus to avoid a vote and aim for a consensus. The consequence is that many judgements are not as clearly and sharply formulated as might be desirable because there is quite some consensus language in the judgement. Sometimes the solution, in the interest of consensus, is to omit certain phrases and passages, and this can create the impression that the reasoning lacks a logical step or is otherwise enigmatic. In any case the CoJ has always had a somewhat enunciative/proclaiming style. Some have linked this to the drafting tradition of *cours de cassation* and *conseils d'état* from member states from the Napoleonic circle.[61] The GC has always had a more argumentative style than the CoJ,[62] while the CoJ itself from time to

58 See Takis Tridimas, 'The role of the advocate-general in the development of community law: Some reflections', *Common Market Law Review,* 34 (1997), 1349–87; and N. Burrows and R. M. Greaves, *The Advocate-General and EC Law* (Oxford University Press, 2007), pp. 7–9 and 12–14

59 See Burrows and Greaves, ibid., Chapters 5, 6 and 7.

60 Carlos Arrebola, Ana Julia Mauricio, and Hector Jiménez Portilla, 'An econometric analysis of the influence of the advocate general on the Court of Justice of the European Union', *Legal Studies Research Paper Series No. 3/2016, University of Cambridge Faculty of Law.* The study was restricted to annulment actions.

61 Mathilde Cohen speaks of the 'French judicial style', see 'On the linguistic design of multinational courts – The French capture', *International Journal of Constitutional Law,* 14 (2016), 498–517. Karen McAuliffe remarks that because so many nonnative speakers have influenced the French written at the Court, a special 'Court French' has been brought into being that is now also written by native French speakers, see 'Hybrid texts and uniform law? The multilingual case law of the Court of Justice of the European Union', *International Journal for the Semiotics of Law – Revue internationale de Sémiotique juridique,* 24 (2011), 97–115.

62 Examples of the (almost too) argumentative style of the GC are the so-called Kadi cases on the implementation of UN sanctions by the EU: Case T-315/01, *Yassin Abdullah Kadi*

time has made serious efforts to make its reasoning more elaborate and coherent.[63] Nevertheless, complaints about the quality of reasoning of the CoJ remain.[64]

Matters are further complicated by the language regime of the Court, which is, as we have already mentioned, a highly sensitive matter for the member states, witness the unanimity required for changing the relevant provision of the Statute,[65] as well as the relevant provisions of the Rules of Procedure.[66] The twenty-four languages of the Union are the languages of the Court, and each case is assigned one of these languages as 'language of the case' on the basis of the relevant rules.[67] On the other hand there is only one language of deliberation, namely French. The choice of one language is necessary so that the judges may deliberate without interpreters and the secrecy of the deliberation may be maintained. The choice of French in the early days of the Court of the European Coal and Steel Community was a natural one, and it has now become next to impossible to change it.[68]

There can be no doubt that the Court's language staff and interpreters are of exceptional quality, but it is obvious that the clarity of a judgement's

v. Council and Commission, EU:T:2005:332 and Case T-85/09, *Yassin Abdullah Kadi v. Commission*, EU:T:2010:418.

63 The CoJ, for instance, has been quite didactic in a long series of post-Lisbon external relations cases, probably because many member states intervened in them. A good example is Case C-73/14, *Council v. Commission*, EU:C:2015:663, on the Commission's powers and margin of manoeuver in international negotiations.

64 A good overview of the older literature criticizing the Court's quality of reasoning and the (resulting?) bias for further integration is Henri de Waele, 'The role of the European Court of Justice in the integration process: A contemporary and normative assessment', *Hanse Law Review*, 6 (2010), 3–26. A recent book-length and rather critical treatment is Gerard Conway, *The Limits of Legal Reasoning and the European Court of Justice* (Cambridge University Press, 2012).

65 Article 281 (2nd al.) TFEU.

66 Article 64 (2nd al.) Statute of the CJEU.

67 Articles 37 and 38 of the Rules of Procedure of the CoJ.

68 The great difficulty of changing the system toward another working language is a simple consequence of the fact that the whole system is geared to translate everything into and from French and to interpret the hearings primarily into French, as most of the judges try to listen to the French interpretation with a view to the coming deliberation. This means that, of the number of jurists-linguists and interpreters, those who are French language specialists are much more numerous than those who are specialists in other languages. Thus changing the working language would involve firing a large number of people at great cost and hiring a large number of specialists for the new working language within a very short time span, which in practice will be impossible and also highly costly for lack of immediately available offer. In any case, the chance of a change to English has become nil after the Brexit referendum.

text is not always enhanced by multiple translations and that the quality of the judgement in one or the other language may suffer from that. It is also obvious that using French as the single language for deliberation and drafting must have an influence on how the judgements are drafted and on their legal reasoning: there is indeed a certain 'French capture'.[69] However, it is submitted that it is at the same time so important for the legitimacy of the Court's judgements that the hearings are carried on in the language of the case (especially if individuals appear before the Courts) and that all cases are available in all languages, that the disadvantages (and the considerable costs) of the multilingual character of the procedures before the Court have to be accepted.

What other assistance, besides the linguistic support of the language staff and of course also the logistic assistance from the Registry of the CJEU, can the two courts still rely on, especially in respect of legal research and support? First there is the permanent staff of the library and research division of the Registry that stands ready to help the Court, when arcane issues of national law of a member state have to be researched for a particular case or when extensive comparative research has to be done with respect to how a certain legal question is dealt with in all member states. The most obvious example from the TFEU is Article 340, where reference is made to the general principles of noncontractual liability for government acts (government torts) common to the law of the member states with a view to awarding damages in cases, where the noncontractual liability of the Union is being invoked.[70]

Of greater interest to our topic of the legitimacy of the judgements of the EU courts is the personal assistance provided to the judges and AGs by their so-called cabinets. These consist, next to a personal secretarial staff, of so-called *référendaires*, that is to say law clerks, who help the judge or AG with case management, research and drafting. Their contracts are fixed term to discourage permanent employment.[71] Judges and AGs are encouraged to diversify their cabinets as to nationality, and most judges have an interest in any case to have a native French speaker in their cabinets, even if their own French is excellent, simply in order to be able to delegate to somebody the final legal polishing of all kinds of draft texts that leave or pass through the hands of the judge.

[69] See Cohen, 'On the linguistic design of multinational courts', footnote 61 above.

[70] See Case T-317/02, *FICF & Others v. Commission*, EU:T:2004:360.

[71] The times that a few réferendaires spent decades at the Court and they were more senior than the judges they counselled are clearly over.

The influence of the law clerks is nonnegligible. They write drafts for the judges and Advocates-General or polish drafts produced by the judges. They may be involved in discussions with the lawyer–linguists about the linguistic equivalence of the different language versions of a judgement. They may perform all kinds of different tasks, but as long as the ad hoc delegation by the judges to their cabinet members is circumscribed by a clear outcome and the judge–rapporteur continues to ensure supervision over the final result, this is a way of producing judgements that is rational and maintains sufficient control of the members of the Court over the process and the result.[72]

Finally, there is the question whether the CoJ and the GC need specialized chambers recognized as such. In the CoJ there has always been an understandable resistance to this. Its members needed to be generalists was the prevailing view, as the Court was constantly confronted with cases, especially those arriving by way of preliminary questions, that could cover all corners of Union and national law.

For the GC the situation is somewhat different. Its creation was, at least in part, due to the wish of CoJ to be rid of not only the staff cases,[73] but also of the large, facts-intensive competition and coal and steel cases that started to dominate its docket and began to demand more and more economic expertise in the early and mid-eighties. The CoJ itself was very aware that it lacked the time and the necessary professional expertise in these domains of the law.[74] This problem found an initial solution with the creation of the Court of First Instance, which has always counted a number of experts in staff matters and competition law among its judges, while also remaining what its present name says that it is, namely a general court. The spin-off of the EUCST from the GC, which took the staff cases off its docket, can also be seen as an attempt of the GC to remain a general court, while having sufficient expert judges who could deal well with competition and antidumping cases. For the tendency for

[72] See also Mathilde Cohen, 'Judges or hostages? The bureaucratization of the Court of Justice of the European Union and the European Court of Human Rights' in Fernanda Nicola and Bill Davies (eds.), *European Law Stories* (Cambridge University Press, 2017, Ch. 4).

[73] The wish to spin off staff cases to a separate court existed since the mid-seventies, when the Court for the first time launched this idea. See H. G. Schermers, 'The court of first instance', *Common Market Law Review*, 25 (1988), 541.

[74] For a contemporaneous view by a participant observer, see Gordon Slynn, 'Court of first instance of the European Communities', *Northwestern Journal of International Law & Business*, 9 (1988–1989), 542.

competition cases, and to a somewhat lesser extent antidumping cases, to become ever more massive and demand an ever-greater expertise in economics[75] has continued unabated.

The most recent reform of the GC, doubling its membership while at the same time 'repatriating' the EUCST into its fold, being the ugly political compromise that it also is,[76] can be seen as a new attempt at maintaining both the CoJ and the GC as general courts (the one administrative and the other rather constitutional), while giving the GC the possibility to dispose of sufficient economic expertise and expertise in personnel cases to deal with the growing caseload, where such expertise is needed. This may well lead to increased pressure on the GC, if not to formalize, at least de facto organize separate chambers for personnel, competition and antidumping cases. The evolution of the creation and expansion of the GC, spinning off and taking back a specialized court, warrants the conclusion that, once the evolution of the caseload and the nature of the available expertise on the Court leads to serious concerns that threaten the reputation of the CJEU as a whole and hence the legitimacy of its judgements, some kind of solution is found, together with the main institutions of the Union, to somehow remedy the situation.

3 Access to the Court: Bringing a Case and Intervening as Third Party

3.1 *Preliminary Issues*

First of all, it is important to recall briefly the ambition of the two courts to ensure a seamless web of judicial protection within the Union. This flows directly from the basic task of the CJEU to ensure 'that in the application and interpretation of the Treaties the law is observed'. In order to be able to carry out this mandate, the CoJ interpreted the Treaties as 'creating a complete and coherent system of judicial

[75] Parties in these cases present more and more expert studies in economics to the GC, which in turn has recourse to Court-appointed experts. A famous example is the Microsoft case (Case T-201/04, *Microsoft v. Commission*, EU:T:2007:289).

[76] As the Council of Ministers was incapable of finding the required unanimity for fixing a different number of judges than twenty-eight, as laid down in the Statute of the Court, since that would require some formula of rotation between member states for the number of judges above twenty-eight – which was not forthcoming, it was finally decided that the number would be doubled in stages to fifty-six. This was overkill (about ten more than necessary), which was compensated for by terminating the EUCST as an independent court and 'reintegrating' the members into the GC.

protection' in the European Union.[77] This implies that there are enough legal remedies and procedures available to be able to control the interpretation and application of Union law by the authorities of the Union and of the member states and to challenge it in the light of the basic norms laid down in, and derived from, the Treaties. In addition, these ways to interpret and challenge Union law should be coherent, that is to say that they should be available both at the level of the Union itself and at the level of the member states and be complementary of each other.[78]

However, it is important to point out that there is one sector of Union activity that is almost completely excluded from the jurisdiction of the EU courts, namely the Common Foreign and Security Policy (CFSP) by the terms of the TFEU itself.[79] This covers both judicial protection via the national route and, eventually, a preliminary question to the CoJ and direct judicial protection by the EU courts themselves. On the other hand the latter route remains open, where it concerns the rights of natural and legal persons who have been subjected to restrictive measures under the CFSP, primarily restrictions on entry into the Union member states.[80,81] Furthermore the Court is authorized by the TFEU to police the borders between the CFSP and the areas of Union law covered by the TFEU in cases between privileged claimants.[82] In this way the CoJ can have at least

[77] See Article 19(1) TEU, which now also lays down explicitly the obligation of the member states to provide remedies in the fields covered by Union law, and Case 294/83, *Les Verts v. European Parliament*, EU:C:1986:166.

[78] See inter alia Koen Lenaerts et al., *EU Procedural Law* (Oxford University Press, 2015), pp. 1–9. It is telling that *the* standard textbook on this subject, coauthored by the present president of the CoJ, starts with this presentation of the Court's doctrine on complete and coherent judicial protection in the European Union.

[79] Article 275, first sentence. Note that after the Area of Freedom, Security and Justice (AFSJ) had been shifted from the intergovernmental side of the European Union to the Community side through the Treaty of Amsterdam (1998), initially there remained important restrictions on the jurisdiction of the CJEU also in AFSJ, which were reduced by the Treaty of Nice and virtually eliminated after the entry into force of the Treaty of Lisbon (1 December 2014) with a remaining restriction of jurisdiction over police operations in the member states, Article 276 TFEU.

[80] Article 275 TFEU, second sentence, referring to measures adopted by the Council pursuant to Chapter 2 of Title V of the TEU.

[81] The most notorious example of such action for annulment was formed by the so-called Kadi cases (Case C-402/05 P, *Yassin Abdullah Kadi and Al Barakaat International Foundation v. Council of the European Union and Commission of the European Communities*, EU:C:2008:461, and Case C-584/10 P, *European Commission and Others v. Yassin Abdullah Kadi*, EU:C:2013:518).

[82] Article 275, second sentence.

some say over CFSP acts adopted by the Council[83], but this cannot replace the normal exercise of judicial review in the domain of CFSP, just as national courts have jurisdiction, at least in principle, over the area of foreign policy of their countries.

3.2 *Judicial Protection at the Union Level*

There is no controversy that the different actions available against the acts of the institutions, which have been borrowed from systems of national administrative law, i.e. the action for annulment, the action for failure to act, the objection of illegality and the action for damages, are sufficient, complementary the one to the other and effective. The aspects of the system of judicial protection, which have been contested and which could give rise to questions of legitimacy, are related to who, next to the privileged and semiprivileged complainants, can institute proceedings, and under which conditions, and whose acts can be complained of.

With respect to this last issue, the European Council has become an institution of the Union (Article 13(1) TEU) after Lisbon, and its acts intended to have effects on third parties outside the domain of CFSP (Article 263(1) TFEU) can now also be attacked before the CJEU. Furthermore, over the last two decades, during which many EU agencies and other bodies were created and bestowed with their own decision-making powers, there was growing concern that these new creations might not be covered by the wording of the relevant Treaty articles and that hence a gap in judicial protection was developing. This concern has been taken away by the broad formulation of the amended TFEU articles on the actions for annulment and for failure to act, which now refer also to acts of bodies, offices or agencies of the Union.[84]

Where the first issue is concerned, i.e. under which conditions non-privileged complainants can attack actions or inaction of the EU's institutions and bodies, it should be recalled that in most European countries it is not open to natural or moral persons to attack a law in the Courts for reasons of nullity unless that law is a disguised individual decision. This is also the basic design of the action for annulment at EU level. Only privileged complainants may attack legislative acts directly before the EU

[83] See Christoph Hillion, 'A powerless court? The European Court of Justice and the EU common foreign and security policy' (30 January 2014). Available at: http://papers.ssrn.com/sol3/papers.cfm?abstract_id=2388165, last visited 19 March 2016.

[84] See Articles 263 and 265 TFEU.

courts; and semiprivileged complainants may do so, only when they act in defence of their own prerogatives. Nonprivileged complainants should wait until the member states have implemented the legislative measures, attack the national measures before the national courts and at the same time turn against the EU legislative measure at the root of the national measure using the plea of illegality.[85] This should give the national court immediate cause to activate the preliminary question mechanism as only the Court of Justice can give a final decision on questions of nullity or invalidity of EU law.[86]

The problem with this conception of keeping the system of judicial review of legislative acts watertight was that in the past there was no discernible hierarchy of norms that had any basis in the Treaties. Regulations that were based on other regulations were still called regulations; the denomination implementing or regulatory regulations were totally informal. Hence all regulations (and directives for that matter) were very difficult for a moral or natural person to attack, as lastly Article 230 EC and its predecessors required that such a person should be directly and individually concerned. Moreover, these notions, of direct and individual concern have been interpreted restrictively by the CoJ since time immemorial.[87] Direct concern means basically that the legal act that an applicant complains of does not need any further implementation to affect his legal situation.[88] Individual concern means that an act that is not addressed to the applicants 'affects them by reason of certain attributes which are peculiar to them or by reasons or circumstances in which they are differentiated from all other persons and by feature of these factors distinguish them just as the person addressed' [by the act].[89] Although the CoJ developed and refined the two notions of direct and individual concern in many cases[90] to the point that one sometimes feels inclined to conclude that individual concern is excessively adapted to the peculiar circumstance of a case,[91] in the end the Court explicitly maintained its classic interpretation of these two concepts restricting direct access to the Courts by individuals.

85 See Article 277 TFEU. See in this vein Case C-321/95 P, *Greenpeace*, EU:C:1998: 153, paras. 32–4.
86 See Case C-314/85, *Foto Frost*, EU:C:1987:452.
87 Case 25/62, *Plaumann v. Commission*, EU:C:1963:17.
88 Case 294/83, *Les Verts v. European Parliament*, EU:C:1986:166, para. 31.
89 Case 25/62, *Plaumann v. Commission*, EU:C:1963:17, para. 107.
90 See the many cases discussed at length in Lenaerts, *EU Procedural Law*, pp. 318–54.
91 Case C-309/89, *Codorniu v. Council*, EU:C:1994:000.

The full hierarchy of norms foreseen in the draft Constitution was not maintained in the Lisbon Treaty, but at least in the context of an action for annulment brought by legal and moral persons Article 263 of the Lisbon Treaty created the distinction between a regulatory act and a legislative act. The European aversion from the idea that a single moral or natural person or even a group of such persons could have a truly legislative act annulled was maintained for the latter acts alone.[92] In the case of regulatory acts the requirement of individual concern disappeared, but the act could only be attacked if it did not need any implementation; direct concern therefore remained. The Court has interpreted the concept of a regulatory act as including all acts of a general nature that are not legislative acts, i.e. acts that have not followed the legislative procedure as laid down in Article 294 TFEU involving a proposal by the Commission followed by the two colegislators, Council and Parliament.[93] This includes also implementing regulations of a general nature adopted by the Commission pursuant to the implementing procedure of Article 291 TFEU.[94]

The changes included in Article 263 TFEU represent a certain amount of progress in the direct judicial protection of natural and moral persons against a certain category of acts of general application. Only the true legislative acts continue to require that individuals and companies overcome the hurdles of direct and individual concern, as narrowly interpreted by the Courts. This is in line with the constitutional tradition in most member states and is acceptable as long as the judicial protection via the national route and the preliminary question mechanism is operational and effective. However, serious doubt is warranted as far as the last-mentioned criterion is concerned, as there are quite a few member states where the putting of preliminary questions seems to be studiously avoided by the national judiciary. It is, therefore only a matter of time before the question of an important change in the *Plaumann* doctrine of the CoJ will raise its head again. The EU's infringement procedure remains a blunt instrument for changing long-standing habits of national judiciaries.[95]

92 On this aversion and how it was expressed in the preparatory texts of the Lisbon Treaty see the Conclusions of AG Kokott in Case C-583/11 P, *Inuit Tapiriit Kanatami et al. v. European Parliament and Council*, EU:C:2013:21, paras. 38–39 ff.

93 Case C-583/11 P, *Inuit Tapiriit Kanatami et al. v. European Parliament and Council*, EU: C:2013:625, para. 70.

94 Case T-262/10, *Microban International and Microban (Europe) v. Commission*, EU: T:2011:000, paras. 22–5.

95 The Commission has started infringement procedures against member states whose highest courts never referred a case to Luxemburg, notably Sweden. Insofar as the author has been able to verify, no case has as yet been brought against Sweden.

3.3 *Possibilities to Intervene in Cases before the Court*

The rules on intervention are near-identical for both Courts.[96] An intervener can only intervene in support of one of the parties and, more particularly, in support the form of order (i.e. the remedy) sought by that party. This means that amicus curiae interventions are in principle not allowed. Member states and institutions of the Union are privileged interveners and can intervene in any case without identifying any particular interest in the case. So may EEA member states and the EFTA Surveillance Authority in case provisions of the EEA Agreement and their application are at issue in a case before the CJEU. The other bodies, offices and agencies of the Union can intervene in a case, if they can establish that they have an interest in that case or if the intervention falls within the scope of the tasks conferred upon them.[97]

Nonprivileged intervenors, i.e. natural and legal persons, have no right to intervene in cases between members of the category of privileged intervenors. They will be admitted to intervene in other cases, if they can show an interest in the case. Both courts have taken this to mean that such a person, in all likelihood, will be directly affected in his legal position or in his economic interests by the operative part of the future judgement, more particularly by the form of order sought by the party in whose support he intervenes. This latter condition reinforces the tendency to exclude any form of intervention that might smack of 'mere' amicus intervention. It also has made the Court conclude that a person who is in a similar position as a party in the case should not ipso facto be admitted to intervene. For instance, a municipality that operates a subsidy scheme that is similar to a subsidy scheme used by a province that has seen that scheme prohibited by the Commission under Article 108 TFEU will not be easily admitted to intervene on the side of the province, if the Commission starts a case against that province for noncompliance with the Commission's decision. The municipality will have to show that truly its economic or legal position would be affected by a judgement by the GC (in this case) and is unlikely to succeed, unless it could show that its competitive position in relation to the province would be altered in the negative. In the case of other competition cases,

[96] See Article 40 of the Statute of the Court, Articles 129–132 of the Rules of Procedure of the CoJ and Articles 142–145 of the GC Rules of Procedure, available on the website of the CJEU: curia.europa.eu.

[97] Lenaerts, *EU Procedural Law*, p. 828.

however, it may be easier to show an interest: direct competitors of a dominant undertaking accused of abusing its dominance and attacking the Commission's decision, will almost certainly be accepted as interveners.[98]

The Court is fairly flexible insofar as it accepts associations of producers or consumers fairly easily as interveners in cases related to competition, state aids and antidumping. Such associations would have a hard time demonstrating that *their own* legal position would likely be affected by the possible decision of the Court, but given that filing of, and intervening in, court cases on behalf of its members is part of the association's task the Court accepts that its position should be appreciated as if it were the position of a member.[99] Although the acceptance of class actions after the US model is still controversial in European Law,[100] this attitude in respect of intervention by associations goes at least some way in that direction.

Everything taken together, the courts of the CJEU have been fairly flexible in the application of the rules on intervention by third parties. However, the rules themselves remain rather classic European and do not contain the possibility of amicus briefs and class actions. In the eyes of many it remains questionable whether one needs such rules in the European system of administrative law. Hence it is not clear whether the legitimacy of the Court would be better served by staying close to the European administrative law approach or by importation of certain aspects from the US legal system.

4 Fact-finding and Standards of Review

4.1 Ascertainment of the Facts

4.1.1 In Infringement Procedures

There is difference between the infringement procedure and the other procedures before the Court. In the infringement procedure the CJEU acts a bit more as an international court than in the other procedures, as the Court sits in judgement over (at least in principle) sovereign states. A separate place is reserved for the preliminary question procedure,

98 Ibid., pp. 828–9. 99 Ibid., pp. 831–2.

100 There are intensive discussions going on between academics, practitioners and representatives of the Commission about the introduction of class action suits in European law, especially in such fields as compensation of private parties that have suffered the consequences of anticompetitive practices, state aids law, consumer protection and environmental law.

where the national court posing the question has the duty to present the facts underlying the case as well as the questions to which these facts give rise. In these cases the CoJ has the habit of reformulating the questions from time to time, but never touches the facts as presented by the national court.

In infringement cases the burden of proof that an infringement has occurred rests entirely on the Commission. It has to show that a certain law, an implementing measure, an administrative practice or administrative and judicial decisions are contrary to the Treaties. The Commission has to do so entirely by itself; it cannot rely on an expert's report that the Court would have to ask for.[101] Neither can it rely on any presumption for discharging its burden of proof.[102] In the early years that was often easy enough; the Commission could simply show that certain laws or regulations were contrary to the Treaty or did not (sufficiently) implement the relevant directives. In later cases the Commission needed to prove more, such as administrative practices and a pattern of court cases being contrary to EU legislative and regulatory acts. The Court accepted that this was possible, but only if the Commission could advance 'sufficiently documented and detailed proof of the alleged practice of the national administration and/or the courts, for which the member state concerned is answerable'.[103] Moreover, such a practice must be of a consistent and general nature.[104] The Commission has even tried to demonstrate – and the Court has in principle admitted that this is possible – that a practice of the national authorities, which goes against a law that prima facie is in conformity with Union law, nevertheless constitutes an infringement. When the Commission came up with proof of fifty instances where the German national authorities had acted against such a law over a period of nine years, the Court was not satisfied that this constituted a consistent and general practice. This shows how

[101] See Case 141/87, *Commission v. Italy*, EU:C:1989:305, para. 17 on the refusal of the Court to ask for an expert report. The Commission otherwise failed comprehensively to show that Italy had applied the denomination (Lago di) Caldaro to wines that were not from this origin. Not that Italy's attempts at proving its point were very convincing, but the lack of factual proof on the part of the Commission was enough to reject the claim of an infringement, see paras. 22–4 and 27–36.

[102] Case C-287/03, *Commission v. Belgium* (Linked offers and freedom of movement of services), EU:C:2005:282, para. 27.

[103] Ibid., para. 28.

[104] Case C-387/99, *Commission v. Germany* (Vitamin supplements to foodstuffs), EU:C:2004:235.

stringent the Court is as far as the standard of proof for such infringements is.[105]

On the other hand, in order to amass such proof, the Commission can rely on the duty of loyal cooperation, as laid down in Article 4(3) TEU and further developed by the Court.[106] If the member state is not forthcoming with the documentation or information requested by the Commission, the Court normally draws negative inferences from such (illegal) lack of cooperation and this can lead to the member state being condemned.[107]

The duty of cooperation that applies inside the Union, in reality is an enhanced form of the good faith obligation from international law. The way it is applied by the EUCJ demonstrates that the infringement procedure does not take place in the ordinary international legal system, but in an at least partially constitutionalized environment. This is confirmed by the fact that the member states cannot invoke certain other defences that normally might be successful in international law, such as the *exceptio non-adimpleti contractus* recognized by the law of treaties[108] and the argument that the nonconforming measures were justified as countermeasures under the law of state responsibility.[109] This has been made unequivocally clear by the CoJ rather early in the existence of the EEC.[110]

105 Case C-441/02, *Commission v. Germany* (Administrative practice – Expulsion for criminal conviction), EU:C:2006:253. The Court accepted the German argument that the fifty instances were too widely spread out over nine years to constitute a consistent and general practice.

106 This duty has been developed by the Court over the years from a simple obligation of the EU institutions to help member states' judicial authorities by providing them with information from inspections carried out by Commission services (see Case-2/88, *Zwartveld*, EU:C:1990:440) into *i.a.* a far-reaching obligation of a member state to act in conformity with the Union interest in an international organization of which the Union was not a member, but the remit of which fell largely under Union competence (see Case-399/12, *Germany v. Commission (OIV)*, EU:C:2014:2258).

107 Case C-456/03, *Commission v. Italy* (Biotechnology inventions), EU:C:2005:388, para. 27. This case is also interesting for other aspects of the interplay between procedural rules, such as the duty of cooperation and the need to provide substantive proof on other aspects of the case.

108 Article 60 Vienna Convention on the Law of Treaties, Vienna, 23 May 1969, in force 27 January 1980, 1155 UNTS 331; (1969) 8 ILM 679; UKTS (1980) 58.

109 Articles 22 and 49 Draft Articles on the Responsibility of States for Internationally Wrongful Acts, Report of the ILC on the Work of its Fifty-third Session, UN GAOR. 56th Sess, Supp No 10, p. 43, UN DOC A/56/10 (2001).

110 Joined Cases 90–91/63, *Commission v. Belgium and Luxemburg* (Dairy Products), EU: C:1964:80, paras. 1–2.

4.1.2 In Other Procedures

If we turn to other procedures before the CJEU than the infringement and preliminary question cases, the 'normal' approach to the burden of proof, according to which each party is charged with proving the facts on which its claim or its defence is going to be based, is applied. The European Courts will base their judgement on the basis of the facts that have thus been advanced and that, in principle, should be fully known by both parties. This is the so-called adversarial principle.[111] In principle it cannot be abridged, except in very limited conditions. In competition and in state aid cases there can be legitimate reasons why confidential information on marketing strategies or on certain performance indicators of companies should not be shown to interveners in the case, which are often competitors. In such situations the Court can nevertheless demand that such information be produced. It can weigh up the importance of the adversarial principle against the interest of maintaining confidentiality. This can result in (1) the Court making the material available to the other party/ies under specific, restrictive conditions or (2) the Court not making the material available, but requiring that the party concerned produce a nonconfidential summary of the material.[112]

Another important and new exception to the adversarial principle is formed by information the communication of which would harm the security of the Union or one or more of its member states.[113] Such information can be requested by the Court by a measure of inquiry. If the request is rejected immediately, the Court will take formal note of that refusal. If the material is communicated to the Court, a weighing up of the interests involved will take place along the lines sketched earlier. If this leads the Court to the conclusion that the material should remain confidential *and* is relevant for its ruling in the case, a complicated procedure ensues, which may permit the Court to use the secret information without fully respecting the adversarial principle.[114]

This provision was the result of a dilemma that regularly recurred in sanctions cases, such as the Kadi cases,[115] namely that the member states

[111] Article 64 Rules of Procedure GC. [112] Article 103 Rules of Procedure GC.

[113] This is the new Article 105 of the Rules of Procedure of the GC, which constitutes a derogation from Article 103 of those Rules. A near-identical article will be included in the Rules of Procedure of the CoJ as well.

[114] The Court will also take a decision on the on the safekeeping of material for which confidential status is claimed in connection with the security of the Union or its member states.

[115] See the cases referred in footnote 81.

(and also non-member states) that disposed of secret information concerning terrorists and financiers of terrorism, who were blacklisted, were not inclined to put such information at the disposal of the Union institutions. It is to be hoped that the new Rule 105, and the accompanying security measures, will permit these states to modify their position. Otherwise the Courts will probably have to continue to accept claims for the removal of individuals from the EU sanctions list because of lack of information, and this may affect their legitimacy in the eyes the member states and third states.

Over the last ten to fifteen years the Courts have become much more assertive in taking so-called measures of organization of the procedure. Initially it was the GC (then still CFI) that, under pressure of big competition cases, began to take such measures. This consisted in making parties focus, in the period between the written procedure and the oral hearing or even in the second round of the written procedure, on specific legal issues or the proof of specific facts and to reply to questions in writing. Another technique was the organization meeting, held a few weeks before the oral hearing, during which the Court asked parties to adhere to a precise schedule for the hearing and to focus on specific problems. The CoJ very soon followed the example of the GC and even uses them nowadays in normal preliminary question cases, which usually take less than a day or just a morning. Such steps may be taken by the president in coordination with the judge–rapporteur and the AG or by the latter two under their own steam. These measures are informal and communicated by letter of the registrar; it is not unheard of that parties suggest to the Court to take such measures.

If the Court wants to be more formal and impose measures on the parties that have consequences if they are not followed or if truth is not observed in written documents or in oral declarations, it can take so-called measures of inquiry. These are decided upon by the Court, and that decision is officially communicated to the parties and interveners. Measures of inquiry, though relatively rare, nonetheless are applied fairly regularly. The production of documents is one of them, and we have already seen what happens if documents are refused for reasons of business confidentiality or the security of the Union and the member states. The official appointment of witnesses[116] in order to prove certain

[116] Article 66 Rules of Procedure CoJ. On request witnesses may be heard *in camera*.

facts is another, as is the appointment by the Court of an expert.[117] It is interesting to note that such Court-requested expert reports are most often requested in personnel cases in order to provide the Court with an authoritative view on medical and psychological questions. Another phenomenon that is mentioned neither in the Statute nor in the Rules of Procedure is the expert used by one of the parties in order to make a particular point. Again in competition cases companies now use expert reports in order to make fine points about the economics of dominance or of oligopoly, etc.[118] This is purely a tactic used by the parties; such experts are not neutral, as Court-appointed experts are supposed to be, and they are not placed under oath, unless they are heard as witnesses.

4.2 Standard of Review

The standard of review followed by the CJEU is basically uniform as between the two courts. For the purposes of this chapter the standard of review is of importance in two situations.

(1) Where the EU courts sit in judgement on the conformity of national law or practice with Union law, either directly in an infringement procedure, or indirectly in interpreting Union law or ruling on its validity in a preliminary question procedure. In the latter case confirming the validity of Union law or interpreting it in a certain way may spell the invalidity of national law as a consequence of the doctrine of supremacy of Union law.

(2) Where the EU courts sit in judgement on the legality or validity of the acts of the other institutions of the Union, in particular those acts that affect economic operators or groups of individuals in such areas as competition policy, state aids, antidumping, agricultural policy, etc.

Where the conformity of national law with Union law is concerned, the standard of review is normally strict. This is inherent in the Treaties, which declare respectively that the member states 'shall take any appropriate measure, general or particular, to ensure fulfillment of the obligations arising out of the Treaties or resulting from the acts of the institutions' (Article 4(3) TEU) and that 'Member States shall adopt all

[117] In Joined Cases C-89/85, 104/85, 114/85, 116/85, 117/85 and 125–129/85, *Ahlstrom et al. v. Commission*, EU:C:1993:120, paras. 31–2, the Court appointed two groups of experts, each with a distinctive task to accomplish.

[118] See Case T-201/04, *Microsoft v. Commission*, EU:T:2007:289, para. 100.

measures of national law necessary to implement legally binding Union acts' (Article 291 TFEU). The CoJ, if necessary, scrutinizes national laws or regulations in great detail for their conformity with Union law, but normally leaves the member states no margin of discretion, except insofar as directives inherently leave them a certain choice of means for implementation.[119]

The only exception is, when the member states may invoke an exception clause, such as Article 36 TFEU (which is largely based on Article XX GATT) or similar clauses, which recur from time to time in Union legislation. These exceptions that entitle member states to take certain unilateral measures to restrict the freedom of circulation in the internal market on the grounds of public morality, public policy or public security; the protection of the health and life of humans, animals and plants; and the protection of national treasures of artistic, historic or archaeological value have been reduced in importance inside the Union by harmonization and mutual recognition. And yet, if they are applicable, the Court is willing to grant the member states a certain margin of discretion, in particular in respect of public morality. However, this room for discretionary action remains subject to the presence of a genuine link between the measure's objective as advertised by the member state and the measure as it turns out in practice and to a test of proportionality between the measure and its objective.[120] In this way the Court nevertheless constrains the freedom that it has granted the member states in such cases.

Looking at the way the EU courts treat the acts of the EU legislature (since Lisbon the Council and Parliament acting in tandem) and of the EU Commission in such policy domains as agriculture, competition, state aids, antidumping, transport and the environment, one sees that the Court usually accepts that these are areas in which the legislature or the administration have to make assessments of complicated constellations of facts

[119] See, for example, Case C-456/03, *Commission v. Italy* (Biotechnology inventions), footnote 107 above. In practice other legal instruments, such as regulations or decisions, may also leave the member states certain discretion in specific instances.

[120] A good recent example of a classic Article 36 case is Case C-148/15, *Deutsche Parkinson Vereinigung e.V. v. Zentrale zur Bekaempfung unlauteren Wettbewerbs*, EU:C:2016:776. The CJEU declared the fixed price mechanism as operated by the German Pharmacists to be an obstacle to the free movement of goods because there was no sufficient link between the mechanism and its declared objective, whereas A. G. Szpunar had condemned the mechanism because it was not proportional, see *Opinion Szpunar* EU: C:2016:394.

involving complex 'political, economic and social choices'.[121] This is a mantra that regularly returns in the judgements of the Courts, whether it concerns (quasi-) legislative acts in the field of agriculture or antidumping or Commission decisions concerning cartels and mergers or state aids. It serves to justify leaving a considerable measure of discretion to the Union authorities, also because 'the Union Courts cannot substitute their own assessment of matters of fact for the Commission'. Hence in principle the Courts should limit themselves to determining 'whether the evidence put forward is factually accurate, reliable and consistent'. Sometimes the Courts stop there. In other instances, however, they go a step further and assert that 'they must also determine whether that evidence contains all the relevant data that must be taken into consideration in appraising a complex situation and whether it is capable of substantiating the conclusions drawn from it.'[122] That is to say that they can also review the internal logic of the decision.

It is obvious that insofar as the Courts become more and more familiar with certain types of cases and develop an increasing routine in handling them and the kind of arguments that are used in them, they are willing to conduct searching inquiries even into complicated decisions of the Commission, always remaining aware that they cannot sit in the chair of the executive and force it to redo its decision in a specific way. In this way the Union courts reflect a general tendency in the administrative courts of the member states.

5 Interpretative Approaches

5.1 Introduction and Interpretation of the Treaty

Because the Union Treaties are treaties between states, the Court has taken the logical view that it should follow the rules of treaty interpretation of the Vienna Convention on the Law of Treaties, although it often has recourse to those rules without explicitly mentioning the Convention, let alone its articles 31 and 32 on treaty interpretation.[123] However the

[121] Joined Cases C-154 and 155/04, *Alliance for Natural Health et al. v. Secretary of State for Health*, EU:C:2005:449, para. 52.

[122] All the quotes are from Case T-201/04, *Microsoft v. Commission*, EU:T:2007:289, paras. 88–9.

[123] A rare example, where the Court does refer explicitly to Articles 31 and 32, is when it wanted to distinguish the EU from a 'normal' international organization like the EEA in *Opinion 1/91*, EU:C:1991:490, para. 1.

use of the words *text*, *context*, *object* and *purpose* in the case law of the Court is telling. The Vienna Convention itself also states explicitly that it applies to founding treaties of international organizations.[124]

There is little doubt that the Court uses the elements of Article 31(1) of the Vienna Convention with a certain preference for the object and purpose of the Treaty and its system and structure.[125] A good example of such structural and systemic interpretation of an important treaty article by the CoJ is the way in which in the *Reyners* case it decided that the freedom of establishment as laid down in Article 52 EEC had direct effect after the expiry of the transitional period in 1970.[126]

The other elements of Article 31, outlining the broad meaning of context, i.e. agreements and other instruments between the parties agreed in connexion with the conclusion of the Treaties, and subsequent agreements and practice influencing the interpretation of the Treaties and finally the other relevant rules of international law in force between the parties, are treated by the Court with considerable eclecticism. The declarations attached to the Treaties are implicitly accepted by the Court as 'other instruments' to be taken into account in interpreting the Treaties. The chance that subsequent practice of the member states in the application of the treaty will be recognized as an agreement between the member states having modified the EU Treaties under Article 31(3)(b) Vienna Convention has been cut off by the consistent mantra of the Court that 'mere practice' cannot modify the Treaties.[127] Finally, it is obvious that the Court has never thought and would never think of interpreting the EU Treaty in the light of other trade and economic treaties that were in force at the time of the conclusion of the Rome Treaties and thereafter, such as the GATT, and the OECD Agreement.[128] The Court has always been of the view that in the field of market

[124] Article 5 of the Vienna Convention.

[125] G. Beck, *The Legal Reasoning of the Court of Justice of the EU* (Oxford: Hart Publishing, 2012), p. 322 ff.

[126] Case 2/74, *Reyners v. Belgium*, EU:C:1974:68, paras. 18–32, arguing in para. 22 and 23 that Article 52 should be interpreted in the light of the objective of the 'system' created by the chapter on the freedom of establishment and showing in para. 34 ff. that a restrictive interpretation of the 'public authority' exception of Article 55 can be reconciled with its object and purpose.

[127] One important example among others: *Opinion 1/94*, EU:C:1994:384, para. 52.

[128] Whereas the GATT had a number of provisions, such as Articles III, XI and XX that were models for key articles in the EEC Treaty at the time.

integration the European Union was a special case that went beyond anything that went before.[129]

In conclusion, it is perhaps better to say that the CoJ has made a very selective use of the elements of interpretation mentioned in Article 31 of the Vienna Convention.

It is also important to signal that the CoJ has initially never wanted to have recourse to the *travaux préparatoires* of the Treaty of Rome and its successors in order to solve problematic cases of interpretation, which did not yield a reasonable result after having applied the criteria of text, context and object and purpose. In such cases Article 32 Vienna Convention allows the recourse to the historical record. However, after the negotiations for the Treaty of Rome, the original six member states in Coreper decided to place the preparatory work and the negotiation record for the Treaty of Rome under lock and key.[130] The founding fathers were simply afraid that letting the public read the sometimes vivid discussions on controversial provisions of the Treaty would open old enmities once again.

In later negotiations about Treaty amendments the record was sometimes better kept and more accessible to the public. Nevertheless, the Court did not show any inclination to use the *travaux préparatoires* of the Single Act, Maastricht, or Amsterdam. This only changed with good records being kept of certain accession negotiations[131] and of the European Convention leading up to the Treaty on the Constitution for Europe. These records were trustworthy and widely available. Faced with these records being quoted in the written and oral pleadings, the Court in 2012, in the important *Pringle* case[132] on the legality of the creation outside the Union of the European Stability Mechanism (ESM) and in 2013 in the *Seal Products* case concerning the embargo on such products against Canada and Greenland, the CoJ finally embraced the possibility of historical interpretation. In *Seal Products* the CoJ, while referring to *Pringle*, explicitly states: 'The origins of a provision of European Union

[129] See *Opinion 1/91*, footnote 123 above.

[130] On this decision of Coreper and other aspects of early interpretation of the Treaties and Community acts, see R. Plender, 'The interpretation of community acts by reference to the intention of the authors', *Yearbook of European Law* (1982), 57–105, at 63.

[131] The Court resorted to historical interpretation in consulting the record of the Swedish accession in order to clear up the provisions about sugar, see Case T-187/99, *Agrana Zucker v. Commission*, EU:T:2001:149, paras. 64–70 and Case C-321/01 P, *Agrana Zucker v. Commission*, EU:C:2002:635, paras. 28–32.

[132] Case C-370/12, *Pringle v. Government of Ireland*, EU:C:2012:756, para. 135.

law may also provide information relevant to its interpretation.'[133] In the footsteps of many international courts and tribunals, the CoJ in these cases does not use historical sources only once it has exhausted all other methods of treaty interpretation, but rather as an instrument that can confirm and bolster an interpretation arrived at by using text, context, object and purpose, which is plausible, but perhaps not yet fully convincing.[134]

5.2 *Interpretation of Secondary Law*

It is likely that this acceptance of the historical method of interpretation will extend beyond the interpretation of primary law. The earlier quote from the *Seal Products* case not only points in this direction, speaking of 'a provision of European law' in general terms, but with the much-broadened legislative powers of the Parliament after Lisbon, the legislative process has become much more transparent. The Council as sole legislator was a black box, and it made no sense for the Court to go back to the history of a proposal, precisely when there was an enormous difference between the original Commission proposal and the final Council product. Now that the ordinary legislative procedure has become the 'new normal', it might be interesting for the Court to look into the legislative history, parse the legislative debates in the Parliament and critically review the back-and-forth between the Parliament and the Council in reconciliation committees, when the two institutions discuss how to reconcile two different versions of the legislative act in question, with the Commission in the middle.[135]

It is not necessary to go into detail once again about the approach to interpretation of the Court to EU secondary law; it does not differ dramatically from the approach to the EU Treaties themselves. All

[133] See C-583/11 P, *Inuit Tapiriit Kanitami et al. v. European Parliament and Council*, footnote 87 above, para. 50, where the recourse to the 'origins' is announced as relevant to it interpretation and para. 59, where the historical record is then used to complement the textual and contextual interpretation of the notion of 'regulatory act' in paras. 54–8.

[134] For a somewhat fuller treatment see PJK, 'From the board: International law in the case law of the Court of Justice: Recent trends', *Legal Issues of Economic Integration* 41 (2014), 1–8, at 3–5.

[135] The transparency of the reporting on the conciliation committees often leaves a lot to be desired, in particular, when for reasons of urgency Council and Parliament proceed to conciliation almost immediately after the first round of debate in Parliament, skipping the second round altogether. This may still prove a reason for the Courts not to look at the parliamentary history of legislative acts.

authors who have studied the subject in detail and from different angles come up broadly with the same elements: the relative emphasis on the object and purpose of the treaty and the context in which the provision requiring interpretation is to be found. The founding treaty of a purpose-oriented organization, such as the Union, contains inevitably a lot of vague language (that the founding states agreed upon as compromise) that is in need of interpretation. The difference between those who criticize this state of affairs and those who accept it is basically one of degree, as they agree on the underlying causes for the CJEU's course, but the degree easily grows to 180.[136]

If one wants the approach of the CoJ to the interpretation of secondary Union law encapsulated in a single paragraph from its case law, the following would be a good choice:

> Every provision of Community law must be placed in its context and interpreted in the light of the provisions of Community law as a whole, regard being had to the objectives thereof and to its state of evolution at the date on which the provision in question is to be applied.[137]

It neatly catches the feeling that the Court must have had during many years of its history that there were hardly any *'points de répère'* outside the Treaties and Union law itself to which the Court could turn in its work of interpretation and application. The only stable piece of soil, on which it could support itself with a view to lifting up the Community, was the Community and its founding treaty itself. Beyond that there was only unwritten Union law or principles of Union law.

5.3 Unwritten Union Law

Article 38 of the Statute of the International Court of Justice refers that Court to, among others, 'the general principles of law recognized by civilized nations'. The CJEU, when reflecting upon its task of ensuring 'that in the interpretation and application of the Treaties *the law* is observed', similarly found that in the process of doing so it is inevitable

[136] Cf. H. Rasmussen, *On Law and Policy in the European Court of Justice: A Comparative Study in Legal Policymaking* (Dordrecht: Kluwer Academic Publishers, 1986) and G. Beck, *The Legal Reasoning of the Court of Justice of the EU* (Oxford: Hart Publishing, 2013).

[137] Case 183/81, *CILFIT v Ministry of Health*, EU:C:1982:335, para. 20. Admittedly this was from a case about the interpretation and application of primary law, Article 177 EEC (now 267 TFEU), but it was intended as a general prescription.

to have recourse to certain principles, in this case common to the legal systems of the member states.[138]

It is in this way that the CoJ daringly constructed the liability of member states in situations in which the national authorities had stood in the way of timely implementing directives from which natural and moral persons could have derived rights or had obstructed the direct effect of provisions of regulations. In support the CoJ invoked also the fact that the notion of government tort was known generally in the member states.[139]

Similarly, the Court hit upon such principles as good faith and, closely related to that, estoppel. It introduced the principle of legitimate expectations into Union law[140] and subsequently limited it in the agricultural sector because the regulatory system had to change so often in response to market forces that legitimate expectations were unwarranted in many instances.[141] The principle of legal certainty is another notion common to nearly all legal systems of the member states that found its way into Union law.[142]

The principle of proportionality, known to most administrative law systems of the Union, became an important principle, initially applied by the Court for critically scrutinizing regulatory restrictions imposed by the member states within the internal market. It has now become a twin principle with subsidiarity that, together with the principle of conferral, is inscribed in Article 5 TEU with a view to limiting the legislative powers of the Union.

Another very important notion that came to play a big role primarily in the field of competition law is the rights of the defence. Originally it was controversial to what extent it was justified to apply such a principle (which actually was synonymous for a whole series principles of decent and proper procedure) originating in the national criminal law procedures to administrative and regulatory procedures, such as those of EU competition and

[138] In this vein: Joined Cases C-46/93 and C-48/93, *Brasserie du Pecheur and Factortame*, EU:C:1996:79, para. 27.

[139] Joined Cases C-6/90 and C-9/90, *Francovich et al.* EU:C:1991:428 and Joined Cases C-46/93 and C-48/93, footnote 138 above.

[140] An interesting example of the use of legitimate expectations (linked to principles of good faith in the law of treaties) is Case T-115/94, *Opel Austria v. Council*, EU:T:1997:3.

[141] For an older, but still very instructive article on the notion of legitimate expectations in Union law and its mitigation in agricultural law, see E. Sharpston, 'European community law and the doctrine of legitimate expectations: How legitimate, and for whom', *Northwestern Journal of International Law & Business*, 11 (1990–1991), at 90–6.

[142] The CoJ invokes the principle of legal certainty for instance with a view to limiting the temporal effects of its judgements in exceptional situations, see Case C-104/98, *Buchner and Others*, EU:C:2000:276.

antidumping law.[143] In the end, thanks to AGs like J.-P. Warner and CFI President Vesterdorf, the rights of the defence acquired their rightful place in various procedures.[144] In its wake came the recognition of protected privileged relations between an attorney and his/her client.[145]

In some instances, the Court developed a general principle of Community or Union law on the basis of an existing provision of the Treaty such as the duty of loyal cooperation.[146] Ostensibly building on the duty of cooperation, the Court subsequently developed the idea of the unity of representation of the Union on the international scene, and in particular within the framework of so-called mixed agreements.[147]

It is striking to note that most of the discoveries of general principles of Community/Union law have been wholly uncontroversial. These principles are so universal, or in any case so European, that they do not meet the slightest criticism, not even from those who are otherwise fiercely critical of the Court and its style of deciding cases. It is only when these principles lead to (new) obligations for the member states, as in the case of state liability and the unity of representation in international relations, that criticism has flared up.

5.4 *International Law*[148]

5.4.1 International Law as Law of the Union

The Treaty of Rome and its successors did not say a word about the way in which international law is, or becomes part of, the law of the Union. So it was up to the CJEU to find a solution for this problem. Relatively early

[143] It should be noted that in some national systems of economic criminal law, notably the German and Dutch systems, suspects could be obliged to give information to the prosecutor. This rested on the difference between true criminal offenses and what in German were called *Ordnungswidrigkeiten* or regulatory offenses. The right not to cooperate in one's own condemnation thus has not (yet) fully found a place among the general principles of Union law.

[144] Mostly as a right to be respected in respect of private parties during the preparatory procedure in competition and antidumping cases, but also in the procedure leading up to an infringement against a member state. See also Article 48(2) Charter of Fundamental Rights of the EU.

[145] Case T-30/89, *Hilti v. Commission*, EU:T:1991:70.

[146] Already discussed in footnote 106 and accompanying text.

[147] Launched for the first time in combination by the Court in *Opinion 1/94*, footnote 127 above, paras. 106–9.

[148] See for an ampler treatment of the role of the CJEU in dealing with international law, P. J. Kuijper, 'It shall contribute to...the strict observance and development of international law...' The role of the Court of Justice' in A. Rosas, E. Levits, and Y. Bot

in the EEC's existence a national court asked the question of whether the CJEU could interpret an international agreement concluded by the Community, *in casu* the old association agreement with Greece. The Court answered in the affirmative on the basis that the agreement had been concluded by an act of the Council and was thus an integral part of Community law.[149] The conclusion itself, therefore, made the agreement part of Community law and not some act of legislative transformation. In principle, therefore, the Community and the Union are and remain a monist system in this respect, but, as will be seen further on, this monism is more and more restricted to the sole aspect of the reception of international law in the Union legal order.

In many later preliminary question cases it became clear that, as one might expect, all kinds of treaties in all the expanding domains of Union law,[150] whether mixed agreements or not,[151] were ipso facto part of Union law and hence could be interpreted by the CJEU. This applies also to decisions of a binding character taken by a body established by an agreement concluded by the Union.

By assuming jurisdiction over the question of the validity and the interpretation of these agreements and the decisions taken by their organs, the CJEU sees itself as guaranteeing the uniform interpretation and application of this part of Union law throughout the Union and in relation to the treaty partners of the Union.[152]

Just as with international agreements, the Union courts have also accepted international customary law as part of Union law without much difficulty. It was simply seen as a determinant of the international environment that the Union had no choice but to accept as it found it, both by EU policy makers and the courts.

(eds.), *The Court of Justice and The Construction of Europe: Analyses and Perspectives on Sixty Years of Case Law* (The Hague: Asser Press & Springer, 2013), pp. 589–612.

149 Case 181/73, *Haegeman v. Belgium*, EU:C:1974:41, paras. 3–5.

150 For specific sectors see Case 87/75, *Bresciani*, EU:C:1976:18 (multilateral association agreement), Case C-104/81, *Kupferberg*, EU:C:1982:362 (free trade agreement),Case C-459/03, *Commission v. Ireland*, EU:2006:345 (UNCLOS Convention), Case C-344/04, *IATA and ELFAA*, EU:C:2006:10 (Montreal Convention), Case C-182/10, *Solvay and Others*, EU:C:2012:82 (environment, Aarhus Convention).

151 Only, when it is crystal clear that a particular part of a mixed agreement is clearly pure member state competence will the Court decline to answer a preliminary question about the interpretation or the validity of an international agreement, see Case C-431/05, *Merck v. Merck Genericos*, EU:C:2007:496.

152 Case C-192/89, *Sevince v. Staatssecretaris van Justitie*, EU:C:1990:322.

As to the rank order of international law, Article 218(11) TFEU implies that in principle international agreements concluded by the Union should respect the Union Treaties; in short, international agreements do not trump constitutional law. The CoJ has strongly upheld this principle, with a specific concern for its own role, including in the preliminary question procedure, as upholder of the law in the application and interpretation of Union law.[153]

Second, where the relation between international treaty law and secondary Union law is concerned, Article 216(2) TFEU declares that Union agreements are binding on the Union's institutions and on the member states. On this basis the courts have not shown any compunction to give precedence to international agreements concluded by the Union over secondary Union law and, mostly through answers to preliminary questions, also over national law. Moreover, the CoJ also construed this provision of Article 216(2) as an obligation of the member states to the Union. This put the Commission in a position to commence infringement procedures, if necessary, against member states for breaching Union agreements. It has used this capacity sparingly and not only to make member states toe the line with respect to their obligations under a Union agreement,[154] but also to respect Union law when allegedly applying a Union agreement.[155]

In the famous *Kadi* case the CoJ summarized its position with respect to the question fairly neatly, stating that, according to established case law, international agreements of the European Union had primacy over secondary Union law, but not over primary Union law, unless the primary law had been amended to allow the agreement to enter into force.[156]

5.4.2 Harmonious Interpretation and Direct Effect

Harmonious interpretation, that is to say, interpretation of the national laws or regulations in the light of international legal rules, is often the favoured treatment that national courts give to international agreements or international customary law. That stands to reason because in that way the court avoids placing its state in a position of international

[153] Opinion 1/2009 *European Patent Court*, EU:C:2011:123 and Opinion 2/13 *Accession to the ECHR*, EU:C:2014:2454.

[154] Case C-51/94, *Commission v. Germany* (Dairy Agreement), EU:C:1995:352.

[155] For example: Case C-459/03, *Commission v. Ireland* (MOX-plant), EU:C:2006:345.

[156] Joined Cases C-402/05 P and C-415/05 P, *Kadi and Al Barakaat v. Council and Commission*, EU:C:2008:461, paras. 306–9.

responsibility for breach of a treaty or a customary norm of international law, while at the same time leaving the national law or regulation intact. In doing so, moreover, the court respects the separation of powers, as it spares the executive the annoyance of having to deal with a complaint of treaty infringement and the parliament the effort of modifying a national law. The courts of the Union are no exception to this general rule. For the purposes of harmonious interpretation the CoJ uses the rules of treaty interpretation derived from the Vienna Convention.

In this way the Court has accepted inter alia that Union law on social security applies on the continental shelf of member states to the advantage of offshore workers, as the continental shelf automatically accrues to the member states according to the law of the sea.[157]

In the case concerning the application of the Union's energy trading scheme (ETS) to foreign aviation into and from the European Union, the Court clarified its position in respect to the question of the possible direct effect of customary rules of international law.[158] Direct effect of such basic principles as the complete sovereignty of states over their air space and the freedom to fly over the high seas was in principle possible. However, because principles of customary international law do not have the same degree of precision as provisions of international agreements, judicial review should be limited to the question of whether the EU institutions in adopting the act had made manifest errors of assessment of the conditions for applying those principles. The Union's ETS survived this reduced judicial review established by the CoJ for customary international law.[159]

The case law of the CoJ in respect of international agreements to which it otherwise refuses to accord direct effect shows that harmonious interpretation is important and that monism, as far as the reception of international law is concerned, is unaffected. Thus, the CoJ has often applied harmonious interpretation to parts of the WTO agreement, especially in the field of TRIPs. In some preliminary question cases on TRIPs the instructions to the national judges go so far that one may

[157] This was an approach initially based on customary international law and later, when the UN Law of the Convention had entered into force for the EC, on the Convention itself. See Case C-37/00, *Weber v. Universal Ogden Services*, EU:C:2002:122, para. 36; and Case C-347/10, *Salemink v. Raad van Bestuur van het UWV*, EU:C:2012:17, paras. 31–7.

[158] Case C-366/10, *Air Transport Association of America et al. v. Secretary of State for Energy and Climate Change*, EU:C:2011:864, paras. 107–11.

[159] Ibid., paras. 121–30.

wonder whether there is much of a difference with granting direct effect.[160] In the same way the CoJ has used Security Council resolutions in order to arrive at the proper interpretation of EU sanctions regulations based on such resolutions, even if such resolutions formally are not binding on the European Union, as it is merely an observer in the UN.[161]

As far as direct effect of international agreements is concerned, the CoJ's recourse to the Vienna Convention has led over the years to an increasing emphasis on the object and purpose of international agreements of the Union in order to decide whether these agreements as such are capable of having direct effect at all.[162] This began with the GATT and later the WTO, initially probably out of a fear of contamination.[163] Later reasons related to the balance between the institutions and deference to the Commission as negotiator and the Council (then still as sole legislator in the field of trade) became dominant, mixed with a hefty dose of reciprocity, as the other major trading powers in the world (United States, China and Japan) did not accord direct effect to the GATT and the WTO at all.[164] In the early 2000s the Court felt the need to develop its approach and place it on a more horizontal basis, arguing that there was a whole category of international agreements that, on the basis of their structure, object and purpose, should be analysed as being incapable of having direct effect *ab initio*. On this basis, the UN Convention on the Law of the Sea and the MarPol convention on pollution of the high seas were classified as such treaties.[165]

These restrictive tendencies in respect of direct effect of customary international law and of treaties have a negative effect on the access of natural and legal persons to the EUCJ with a view to obtaining remedies for breaches of their rights under such agreements. On the other hand, the CoJ continues to grant direct effect to treaty provisions and decisions

[160] Case C-89/99, *Schieving-Nijstad v. Groeneveld*, EU:C:2001:438.

[161] Case C-84/95, *Bosphorus Hava Yollari Turizm ve Ticaret v. Minister for Transport Energy and Communications*, EU:C:1996:312.

[162] The requirements for direct effect are those that one may expect and are found in other (national) jurisdictions: the provision contains a clear and precise obligation that is not subject, in its implementation or effects, to the adoption of any subsequent measure, see Case C-262/96, *Sema Sürül*, EU:C:1999:228, para. 60.

[163] See Joined Cases 21–24/72, *International Fruit*, EU:C:1972:115, paras. 20–7. Important provisions of GATT (Articles III, XI, XVII, XX and XXI) served as inspiration (even textually) for crucial articles of the EEC Treaty (30, 36, 95, etc.).

[164] Case C-377/02, *Van Parijs v. BIRB*, EU:C:2005:121, para. 54.

[165] See Case C-308/06, *Intertanko et al. v. Secretary of State for Transport*, EU:C:2008:312.

of treaty bodies, if these are clearly written with a view to granting rights to individuals and legal persons.[166]

6 Implementation by Member States and Interaction with Their Courts

6.1 *Member State Implementation and Infringement Procedures*

The Treaty of Lisbon has made it absolutely clear that ensuring the implementation of Union law is the foremost obligation of the member states. Article 4(3) TEU restates in no uncertain terms that member states have the positive duty to take all general and special measures necessary to this effect and that they have the negative duty to abstain from any measures that may endanger the realization of the objective of the European Union. The new Article 291 TFEU reaffirms that member states shall take all measures of internal law, which are necessary for the implementation of the legally binding acts of the Union. These provisions underline the importance of the infringement procedure.

At the time, it was created, the infringement procedure was a unique procedure, and it has remained so, finding an equivalent only in the similar procedure before the EFTA Court of the EEA. Although the classic state against state procedure, as it is used for example since 1995 in the WTO, remains an option (Article 259 TFEU), the reality is that it has seldom been used to the end – normally the Commission took responsibility for the member state's complaint – and, according to the Treaty, the procedure directed by the Commission sua sponte was the first option (Article 258 TFEU). The infringement procedure is the only procedure where all measures (whether legislative or not) taken by the member states[167] are directly reviewed by the CJEU for conformity with the EU Treaties.

Although some aspects of the infringement procedure have been discussed already, here the question is to what extent this procedure contributes to the proper implementation of Union law and to the enforcement of the Court's own judgements in infringement and other cases in the member states.

[166] Of particular importance are nondiscrimination provisions benefiting workers from the Maghreb countries and from Turkey, e.g. Case C-192/89, *Sevince*, footnote 152 above.

[167] There are a few other direct procedures, such as the special procedures for State aid (Articles 107 and 108 TFEU) and for abuse of the national security exceptions of Article 346 and 347 TFEU (Article 348 TFEU).

The sources of information that the Commission uses in starting infringement procedures are diverse: complaints by individuals, companies, trade organizations, etc. One important source of information for the Commission is the results of preliminary questions cases. It is a routine obligation for the Commission's services to report on averred or likely breaches of Union law by the authorities of member states that come to the fore during the procedure or in judgements of preliminary questions cases. They are inscribed in the Commission's register of suspected infringements and made subject to the usual procedure whether an infringement procedure should be brought. In this way, the preliminary question procedure and the infringement procedure form, as it were, are an integrated whole in order to suppress breaches of Union law by member states.

The infringement procedure is surrounded by many procedural guarantees that ensure that the litigation phase is only engaged, if the member state concerned has proved resistant to all nonlitigious means of solving the conflict.[168] First the Commission must send the member state that is accused of having infringed the Treaty a letter of formal notice. After the reply from the member state, the Commission reconsiders its case and may strengthen or abandon it. In the first hypothesis, the Commission sends a formal reasoned opinion to the member state, which concludes the administrative part of the procedure. If the reaction of the member state is considered inadequate by the Commission, the formal application for infringement of the Treaty by the member state may be submitted to the Court, and the judicial procedure begins. Throughout these three steps the contents of the Commission's submissions must be in the same line. There may not be sudden changes or breaks in the arguments of the Commission and the points on which the member state has allegedly breached the Treaty. Especially between the reasoned opinion and the application the breaches of the Treaty of which the state is accused must remain in principle the same. In that way, the rights of the defence are fully guaranteed, and member states cannot seriously claim unfairness in the procedure, if the Court

[168] Even the formal nonlitigious steps in the procedure are preceded in most cases by extensive informal contacts with the member state concerned in order to stimulate it to remove the alleged infringement voluntarily. The formal steps usually are only begun, when there is no hope left that the member state in question will so remove the offending national rules or practices.

condemns them after having rejected possible complaints about the preceding administrative procedure.[169]

As mentioned earlier, the burden of proof in infringement cases rests entirely on the Commission. However, once the Commission has discharged this burden of proof and the member state has been condemned, it is obliged to bring its measures or practices into conformity with Union law in line with the judgement of the Court.[170] If the state refuses to do so within a reasonable period of time to be determined by the Commission, the latter may start up a new procedure by simply putting it on notice. Here we come upon two improvements introduced by the Lisbon Treaty. First, according to Article 260(2) TFEU no new reasoned opinion is necessary, and the Court can then condemn the member state again to implementation of the earlier judgement and impose on the member state a fine and/or a penalty payment that will run until the day implementation is complete. Second, if the infringement is in the nature of a late transposition of a directive (one of the most frequent 'sins' of the member states), the Commission can immediately indicate what would be a reasonable fine or penalty payment to be imposed on the member state in question. If the Court proceeds indeed to the condemnation of the member state for late transposition, it can then impose a pecuniary sanction not higher than the one proposed by the Commission. In the past, late transposition cases required a second procedure for nonimplementation before a fine or a penalty payment could be imposed. These two improvements have certainly strengthened the infringement procedure.

One of the weak points of the infringement procedure is the discretion that the Court has allowed the Commission in choosing which infringement cases to prosecute and when to do so. It is not for the Court to assess whether it was appropriate to exercise that discretion. It has often been argued that this introduces an aspect of unequal treatment of countries and unfairness into the infringement procedure and hurts the

[169] Case C-350/02, *Commission v. Netherlands*, EU:C:2004:389, paras. 14–29. In these paragraphs the EUCJ sets out very clearly that the letter of formal notice and the reasoned opinion should be read together in order to give the member state concerned a clear picture of the case being advanced against it. This may lead to the Commission implicitly dropping one or more of the points of its case, as long as it is clear what the remaining points are and these are the same as some of the points contained in the letter of formal notice. Because the Commission had not formally dropped those points, the Court insisted that on these points the Commission's case was inadmissible.

[170] Article 260(1) TFEU.

reputation of both the Commission and the Court. The Court has taken the view, however, that a member state cannot invoke the possible infringement of the Treaty on the same issue by another member state in order to justify its own default.[171] The Court's legitimacy does not seem seriously affected by this position. Most observers realize that it is simply impossible, both from the viewpoint of manpower and finances, for the Commission to carry out a completely objective, nonselective and 'automatic' infringement policy.

In the end, however, it is the role of the Court that is decisive, and there are interesting indications in recent research that the member states may have considerable respect for this final judicial phase of the infringement procedure, even if the number of infringement cases has been going down over the last years.[172] This is likely to have something to do with the alternative procedures that have been created, such as the Internal Market Scoreboard (IMS), SOLVIT and EU Pilot, which have 'swallowed' many cases that otherwise would have become infringement cases. They have in common that they have no judicial phase built in to them and are pretty 'soft' in nature. They rely on such 'old techniques' as naming and shaming (the IMS), direct confrontation, in the presence of experts, between a private complainant and the government complained of (SOLVIT), and reporting and examination procedures as practiced inter alia in the OECD and the WTO Trade Policy Review Mechanism. These techniques proved to be more effective in the European Union than they had been in other international organizations. A reasonable explanation of this phenomenon is that in the European Union the Commission could always activate the infringement procedure, if the 'new procedures' were exhausted and that the member states knew this. Having been better informed of their real chances to survive an infringement procedure in the framework of the soft procedure, they were more inclined to give up than to risk the formal infringement procedure. The presence in the background of the infringement procedure made the soft procedures more effective in the European Union than in other international organizations where a judicial infringement procedure was lacking.[173] This shows that the reputation of the

171 These interconnected points are neatly summed up in para. 35 of Case C-266/03, *Commission v. Luxembourg*, EU:C:2005:341, with references to other cases.

172 See Pal Wenneras, 'Sanctions against member states under Article 260 TFEU: Alive but not kicking?' *Common Market Law Review*, 49 (2012), 145–76.

173 C. E. Koops, '*Contemplating Compliance: European Compliance Mechanisms in International Perspective*', unpublished PhD dissertation, University of Amsterdam (2014).

Court in the infringement procedure is and remains strong and that the decline of the number of infringement procedures that result in a condemnation by the Court is not necessarily the result of weak enforcement.

6.2 The Preliminary Question Procedure and Contacts with Courts of the Member States

6.2.1 The Acceptance and Interpretation of Questions Asked by National Courts

The CoJ, which is presently solely competent for preliminary questions, exceptionally rejects questions that are purely theoretical or too contrived. This is mostly based on the view that the question posed is not linked to any real underlying legal dispute. The Court has no problem with questions that arise from what are probably test cases, but a dispute that in reality is not a dispute goes too far.[174] Normally, however, the CoJ emphasizes the freedom of the national courts to decide on the need to pose preliminary questions, and because the Treaty and the Rules of Procedure set no requirements for the form in which they must be presented, it also leaves them free to draft them as they want.[175] The Court, as Lenaerts points out, has put the emphasis over the years more and more on the cooperation between the CoJ and the national courts.[176] From the early days of the EEC Treaty the Court has always helped the national judge or court that asked preliminary questions by reformulating these questions and to take care that they responded to the formal requirements, but in such a way that the replies were of real help for the national court in deciding the case before it,

[174] See Case 244/80, *Foglia/Novello II*, EU:C:1981:302. This was a case in which two Italian individuals had contrived to create a contractual conflict, which would provoke an Italian court in asking a question for a declaratory judgement from the CoJ that would declare the French taxation for liqueur wines contrary to Union law. The Court had already declared itself incompetent to answer the questions from the Italian judge, Case 104/79, *Foglia/Novello I*, EU:C:1980:73. In the second case the CoJ explains once again its refusal to answer the questions of the Italian judge.

[175] Case C-145/03, *Heirs of Annette Keller*, EU:C:2005:211, is a good example of a case where the CoJ (in Grand Chamber formation) relies on the freedom of the Spanish Court to ask the questions it deems necessary, but subsequently uses the maxim that the referring court must receive a reply that is helpful to it in order to first sort out the facts on the basis of elements present in the file received from the national court and then to reformulate the questions.

[176] Lenaerts, *EU Procedural Law*, p. 232.

including the question of whether national rules or practice were compatible with Union law.[177]

The CoJ is extremely pragmatic in managing the limited textual restraints inherent in Article 267 TFEU. If a matter has been sufficiently clarified by earlier answers to preliminary questions, there is no objection, according to the Court, that even the national courts that are obliged to ask questions do not do so and decide the case before them in their own corner on the basis of the old cases.[178] On the other hand, when a question arose on whether a provision of Union law should be annulled, the Court has taken the view that it should have the monopoly of such decisions of invalidity with a view to maintaining the uniform interpretation of Union law. This in turn entails the obligation of lower courts to ask a preliminary question about the validity of provisions of Union law.[179] Such obligation went beyond the wording of Article 267 TFEU, but was in line with its spirit.

This same mixture of pragmatism and principle characterizes the CoJ's recent case law about the duty of member states' highest courts to ask preliminary questions. It would go too far in the context of this contribution to discuss these cases in any detail. Let it suffice here to say that the CoJ accepts that it should give the highest courts some margin of manoeuver where their internal organization is concerned and in the application of CILFIT, but that in the end the duty to ask preliminary questions retains priority and that in the application of CILFIT the court concerned must assess whether there are conflicting lines of case law in the national courts or the provision of EU law gives rise to different interpretations in various member states. And if so, CILFIT should not be applied.[180]

Easy access to the CJEU for preliminary questions has also been threatened by the length of time necessary to process these cases. The

[177] See Case C-5/14, *Kernkraftwerke Lippe-Ems GmbH v. Hauptzollamt Osnabrück*, EU:C:2015:000, para. 34, in which the CoJ stressed that a national court must be able to exercise its right 'to refer to the Court of Justice questions concerning the interpretation or validity of EU Law in order to enable it to decide whether or not a provision of national law was compatible with that EU law'.

[178] Case 283/81, *CILFIT*, EU:C:1982:335, paras. 10–21. It should be noted that EUCJ also decided that national courts may also pose questions of interpretation and validity of Union law of their own initiative and not dependent on the wish of the party/ies, para. 9.

[179] Case 314/85, *Foto-Frost v. Hauptzollamt Lübeck-Ost*, EU:C:1987:452, paras. 12–20.

[180] Case C-5/14, *Kernkraftwerke*, see footnote 171, paras. 31–6. Case C-160/14, *Fereira da Silva e Brito et al. v. Estado Portugues*, EU:C:2015:565, paras. 40–4. Case C-689/13, *Puligienico Facility Esco SpA*, EU:C:2016:199.

perception among practitioners of European law, at the national bars as well as in Brussels and Luxemburg has always been that, if the length of time for answering a (set of) preliminary question(s) were to become too long, counsel and clients in national procedures and national judges would rather avoid asking preliminary questions. Hence the CoJ has always devoted great attention to keeping the processing time short, preferably at around a year in length. In the late nineties and early 2000s the duration of the average preliminary question case was over two years.

Internal reforms have brought this figure back to around fifteen months in 2014 and 2015,[181] which may no longer constitute a seriously discouraging factor. Moreover, the Court has created a special procedure, which makes it possible for the Court to send a reply to simple and evident questions by reasoned order, obviating the need for a full procedure.[182] In addition, the president can decide upon request to follow an expedited procedure where the nature of the case requires it to be dealt with within a short time.[183] Finally, in the field of Justice and Home Affairs, in preliminary question cases the national court may request a special urgent procedure or the president may at his own initiative propose such a procedure.[184] Such special urgent procedures, according to the text of Article 267 TFEU, were originally intended for persons in custody. In reality not only individuals in detention, but also persons at risk of deportation, or in need of having their personal status authoritatively determined (European arrest

[181] *CJEU Annual Report 2015*, 88. The modification of Article 20 Statute, allowing the Court to forego the conclusions of the Advocate-General in cases that posed no new legal question has also contributed to the shortening; see also footnote 53 and accompanying text.

[182] Rules of Procedure CoJ Article 99. This rule is applied with certain regularity. Precise data are as yet lacking.

[183] Rules of Procedure Article 105(1). From the judicial statistics of the CoJ it results that the vast majority of such requests in the last three years has been rejected by the Court; only three out of forty requests in preliminary questions cases have been accepted by the President over the last three years. *CJEU Annual Report 2015*, 91.

[184] Rules of Procedure Article 107(1). A report on the recourse to this urgent procedure during its first three years (2008–2011) has been published on the website of the Court under 'Procedures'. In that period twenty-two cases (out of 126 preliminary questions relating to the Area of Freedom, Security and Justice) were accompanied by a request for an urgent procedure, and the President proposed once to follow that procedure. In twelve cases the procedure was followed. The average duration of these procedures was sixty-six days. Since 2011 the number of requests has increased somewhat, but the number of granted requests has stayed proportionally the same: sixteen out of thirty-three, *CJEU Annual Report* 2015, 91.

warrant cases, expulsion of refused asylum seekers, parental authority or custody cases) profited from the special urgent procedure.[185]

6.2.2 Practical Measures for Stimulating Open Channels to National Courts

The Court of Justice and the General Court have developed over the years a number of instruments that clarify and simplify the procedures before the Court for the national courts of the member states and for the attorneys and counsel of the individuals and companies that appear before the CoJ and the GC. The 'Practice Directions to Parties concerning Cases brought before the Court'[186] form a reasoned commentary and explanation of the Rules of Procedure for those who practice before the Court. They are complemented by useful practical indications on how to plead under conditions of simultaneous translation, which can be found on the website of the CJEU. These contain both many rules and advice that are very useful and necessary to know for those who are involved in a CJEU preliminary question case.

Of particular importance for the national courts that wish to refer preliminary questions to the Court are the 'Recommendations to national courts and tribunals in relation to the initiation of preliminary ruling proceedings'.[187] They form in reality a short course on the preliminary question procedure and its important function in the EU system of legal protection of individuals and in maintaining uniformity of interpretation of Union law throughout the Union. They also contain practical guidelines for national courts on when and how to draft preliminary questions, taking into account that they will have to be translated into another language.

The importance of close contact between the CoJ and its Registry and the national court, so as to keep the latter abreast of the progress of the case in Luxemburg and the wish of the CoJ to be informed of the referring court's action upon receiving the reply to its questions and of being informed of its final judgement, are also highlighted.[188] The CoJ even goes so far as to request that referring courts asking for an urgent

185 Ibid.

186 See for the latest version: Practice Directions to Parties Concerning Cases Brought before the Court, OJ 2014 L31/1. The 'Practice Directions' belong formally to the new Rules of Procedure 2012.

187 See for the latest version: Recommendations to National Courts and Tribunals in Relation to the Initiation of Preliminary Ruling Proceedings, OJ 2012 C338/1. These 'Recommendations' are also based on the Rules of Procedure of 2012.

188 Ibid., paras. 1, 5, 8, 33 and 35.

procedure give a brief indication, if possible, of their views on the reply to be given to the questions referred. This will help the urgent procedure along.[189]

Beyond such written communications, the CoJ has also done its best over many years to have close relations on a personal level with first of all the highest courts in the member states that had an obligation to refer preliminary questions to the Court and, insofar as possible, with lower courts on a country-by-country basis as well. For the highest courts the CoJ could fall back on existing 'clubs' in Europe, such as the one for the Councils of State or for the Courts of Cassation (and equivalent civil courts) and for Constitutional Courts. It has regular meetings with these groups of highest courts, sometimes more scholarly in nature, at other times for discussing their mutual relations, in particular in relation with the preliminary question procedure.

There is no denying that with some of these highest courts relations are slightly more complicated than with others: the German *Bundesverfassungsgericht*, the French *Conseil d'Etat*, and the Italian *Corte Costituzionale* have always appeared in this list; it would seem that the Danish and the Czech Constitutional Court can be added. The possibility of a breach of human and fundamental rights by Community law originally played an important role in the problems between the CoJ and national highest courts,[190] but presently the shoe is on the other foot. Member states are much more likely to breach fundamental rights than the Union itself, also in the implementation of Union law, and it is they that run the risk of being sanctioned by the CoJ in the application of the new EU Charter of Fundamental Rights.[191] New tensions rather have to do with the remaining core of sovereignty that these courts see as essential for the survival of the member states as independent states on the international scene.[192]

[189] Ibid., para. 42. Although this request for the national court's opinion about its own question was placed in the context of the urgent procedure, it still throws a different light on the first request for a preliminary ruling of the German Constitutional Court in *Gauweiler*, which was accompanied by the *Bundesverfassungsgericht's* own suggestions for a reply, which in some circles in Europe was seen as horribly presumptuous.

[190] See the *Bundesverfassungsgericht* and its 'so lange' doctrine, BVerfGE 73, 339 2 BvR 197/83 *Solange II* decision.

[191] Some German scholars have suggested that the CoJ apply a 'so lange' doctrine in reverse: A. Von Bogdandy et al., 'Reverse solange – Protecting the essence of fundamental rights against EU member states', *Common Market Law Review*, 49 (2012), 489.

[192] See the largely *obiter dicta* of the *Bundesverfassungsgricht* on the German position in the WTO in its Lisbon judgement (BVerfGE 123, 267, 2BvE 2/08), which demonstrate a rather shocking lack of knowledge of the EU's common commercial policy and the practice of EU

Direct frontal collisions between a national highest court and the CJEU have not been entirely avoided in prejudicial cases, but fortunately remain rare.[193] These courts, even when there are frictions between them, seem still to have a shared sense of responsibility for maintaining what the president of the German Constitutional Court has characterised as the *Verbund* (Association) of European Courts.[194] Another expression of the existence of this *Verbund* is the fact that the former CoJ President Skouris invited the president of the *Bundesverfassungsgericht* and the vice-president of the French *Conseil d'Etat* into the so-called 255 Committee for the vetting of candidates for the Court of Justice, of which the latter became president.[195]

6.3 *Enforcement of Certain ECJ Judgements in the National Legal Order*

Judgements of the Courts of the European Union, which impose obligations, mostly of a pecuniary nature, on individuals or companies, are directly enforceable in the member states, according to Articles 280 and 299 TFEU. To this end such judgements are authenticated and appended to the order of enforcement according to a procedure determined by the state where the enforcement is carried out. This order will follow the national procedure for enforcement of judgements as if it were a judgement of a national court. Thus, it will not run the risk of encountering any of the obstacles that may be put in the way of an enforcement of a foreign judgement, even under the New York Convention. The national courts can only hear objections to the enforcement concerning the

representation inside the WTO and seem to put into question the exclusive character of the common commercial policy, as laid down in Article3(1)(e) TFEU.

193 There are two cases: (1) the Czech Constitutional Court's reaction to Case C-399/09, *Landtova*, EU:C:2011:415 (see Jan Komarek, 'Playing with matches: The Czech Constitutional Court's ultra vires revolution', available at: www.verfassungsblog.de and M. Bobek, 'Landtova, Holubec and the problem of an uncooperative court: Implications for the preliminary rulings procedure', *European Constitutional Law Review*, 10, 1 (2014), 54–89) and (2) the recent reaction of the Supreme Court of Denmark to Case C-440/14, *Ajos*, EU:C:2016:278 (see S. Klinge, 'Dialogue or disobedience between the European Court of Justice and the Danish Constitutional Court? The Danish Supreme Court challenges the Mangold-principle', *EU Law Analysis*, 13 December 2016).

194 See A. Vosskuhle, 'The cooperation between European Courts: The *Verbund* of European Courts and its legal toolbox', in A. Rosas, E. Levits, and Y. Bot (eds.), *The Court of Justice and the Construction of Europe: Analyses and Perspectives on Sixty Years of Case Law* (The Hague: T.M.C. Asser Press, 2012).

195 On this Committee, see Section 2.1 above.

irregular application of the national civil enforcement procedure. Suspension of the enforcement as such is reserved to the EU courts. Normally this procedure works smoothly and without any difficulty in the relatively few cases that a judgement of one of the EU courts has to be enforced, usually relating to fines in competition cases.

The execution of the CJEU's judgements concerning individuals and companies in the member states, as if they originated with a national court, is a simple and effective tool to ensure the authority of the EU courts in their dealing with private parties.[196] There are no known cases, where national courts have not loyally applied the provisions of Articles 280 and 299 TFEU for enforcement of the judgements of the CJEU, when asked to do so.[197]

7 Relationship to Other International Courts

7.1 Introduction

In the following sections the relations of the CJEU with international courts, three worldwide courts and two regional courts will be discussed in rather general terms, only buttressed by the occasional case, as in the framework of this contribution of necessity no justice can be done to the full richness of these relations.[198]

196 It is an instrument that cannot be used against the member states; their breaches of Union law can only be corrected through the infringement procedure, and any fines or penalty payments member states owe to the Commission after judgements under Article 260 TFEU are actually paid by the member states or withheld by the Commission from regional or agricultural subsidies granted to the member state concerned.

197 The author is personally acquainted with a case in the Netherlands, in which the Court of Appeal of Amsterdam approved the piercing of the corporate veil in order to enforce an antitrust fine after a judgement by the CoJ. It was a relatively small fine in a case concerning the anticompetitive use of intellectual property, in which the director of the company had turned it into a shell company without any assets in order to avoid paying the fine. The Commission took the precaution of seizing his personal immovable property as security, and the Court held him personally liable for the payment of the fine. As a matter of national law such piercing of the corporate veil was not at all commonplace at the time (the 1980s) and demonstrates the readiness of the Court of Appeal to make enforcement of Community antitrust fines fully effective.

198 For a more fulsome treatment, see T. Lock, *The European Court of Justice and International Courts* (Oxford University Press, 2015) and P. J. Kuijper, 'La jurisprudence *Usine Mox*, est-elle symptomatique d'un dialogue de sourds entre la CJCE et les autres juridictions internationales?' in Y. Kerbrat (ed.) *Forum shopping et concurrence des procédures dans le contentieux international* (Brussels: Larcier/Bruylant, 2011). Some parts of the following are based on that book contribution.

The two regional courts are the so-called EFTA Court and the European Court of Human Rights. These courts are so close to the CJEU that they are often grouped with the highest courts of the member states, as the group of courts that together with the CJEU are responsible for maintaining the rule of law in the European Union and the 'broader Europe', including the EEA and the Council of Europe Members.[199] Such a common responsibility, insofar as it is equally perceived to exist by all involved, breeds closer cooperation, but also a greater risk of collision from time to time. The three worldwide courts are the ICJ, the ITLOS and the WTO dispute settlement system.

7.2 *The International Court of Justice*

The EU, and the CJEU with it, have narrowly escaped a confrontation with the ICJ, and a concomitant internal confrontation with at least one member state, when Spain started a case before the ICJ in 1997–98 about the conflict with Canada on the North-West Atlantic cod fisheries around the Georges Bank. These fisheries and their conservation were regulated in an agreement between Canada and the EC, which had been implemented by a number of EC fisheries regulations.[200] Fortunately for the EC, the ICJ declared the case inadmissible for lack of a jurisdictional link between Spain and Canada, following the latter's reservation to its general acceptance of the jurisdiction of the ICJ linked to its new coastal fisheries regulation.[201] This spared the EC an internal conflict over the exclusive powers in the domain of fisheries conservation and hence Spain's right to represent itself or the Union before the ICJ on the merits.[202]

For the rest the CJEU has recourse to the case law of the ICJ and its predecessor the PCIJ to support its interpretation of international law, and in particular to confirm that a certain rule of international law is

[199] See A. Rosas, 'The status in EU law of international agreements concluded by the member states', *Fordham International Law Journal*, 34 (2011), 1304–45.

[200] The agreement was adopted by Council Decision 95/586/EC, OJ 1995, L327/35 and was provisionally applied since April 1995. The lawfulness of the agreement and of the regulations implementing it were put in question by a number of successive cases started by Area Cova and other Spanish fisheries companies against the Council and the Commission, which failed on grounds of inadmissibility, see *Area Cova SA and Others v. Council*, Cases T-194/95, EU:T:1999:141 and T-12/96, EU:T:1999:142 (first instance); C-300/99 P, EU:C:2001:71 and C-301/99 P, EU:C:2001:72 (appeals) and T-196/99, EU:T:2001:281 (damages).

[201] See R. Higgins, 'The ICJ, the ECJ, and the integrity of international law', *International & Comparative Law Quarterly*, 52 (2003), 151.

[202] Obviously, the European Union can act as a party in procedures before ITLOS in its quality of party to UNCLOS.

indeed a customary rule. Only some examples can be mentioned here. During the time when the EC had not yet ratified the Convention on the Law of the Sea, it was extremely useful and simple to rely on the ICJ's case law in order to be able to say with authority that the rules of the Convention on the nationality of ships, on the different sea zones and the powers that coastal states can exercise in these zones are customary rules of international law.[203]

More recent invocations of the case law of the ICJ in support of the interpretation of the CoJ of certain rules of international law are found inter alia in the law of treaties In a case concerning the interpretation of the Convention defining the Statute of the European Schools the Court ruled that this convention was obviously a treaty that should be interpreted according to the rules of Articles 31 and 32 of the Vienna Convention of 1969. Attention should be paid to the subsequent practice between the parties and on the basis of the ICJ's judgement in the *Temple of Preah Vihear*, the Court accepted that subsequent practice of the parties could modify the terms of the treaty, if that practice reflected the agreement between the parties. Such was the case with respect to the functioning of the Complaints Board of the European Schools as sole instance of a judicial character able to rule on disputes between the headmaster of a European School and a teacher.[204]

Most recently the GC, and on appeal the CoJ, in a case concerning the lawfulness of the conclusion of a free trade agreement with Morocco, especially in the light of the de facto incorporation of the former Spanish colony Western Sahara (Rio d'Oro) into Morocco, has paid ample attention to the ICJ's advisory opinion on the status of Western Sahara.[205]

7.3 *International Tribunal for the Law of the Sea (ITLOS)*

The Union has been the defendant in a case brought by Chile before ITLOS on the pacific swordfish fisheries,[206] but this case was soon

[203] Case C-286/90, *Anklagemyndigheden v. Poulsen & Diva Navigation Co.*, EU:C:1992:453, in which the CoJ relied on Case Concerning Delimitation of the Maritime Boundary in the Gulf of Marine Area (Canada *v.* US) ICJ Reports (1984) 217 and Case Concerning the Continental Shelf (Libya *v.* Malta) ICJ Reports (1985) 13.

[204] Joined Cases C-464 and C-465/13 *Europaeische Schule Muenchen v. Oberto and O'Leary*, EU:C:2015:163 paras. 60, 61 and 65.

[205] Case T-512/12, *Frente Polisario v. Council and Commission*, EU:C:2015:953. The case was decided on appeal in Case C-104/16 P, *Council v. Front Polisario*, EU:C:2016:973.

[206] Case No. 7 Conservation and sustainable management of Pacific sword fish stocks in the South-East Pacific (*Chile v. EC*).

suspended at the request of both parties and after several years finally withdrawn, after a compromise was reached between the parties.[207]

In theory, a direct conflict between ITLOS and courts of the European Union is not very likely. Article 282 of UNCLOS allows parties to the Convention, which are in a dispute on a matter falling under the Convention, to turn to other means of dispute settlement provided that it is binding. Therefore, if Union Member States have a dispute among themselves concerning the interpretation of UNCLOS, most likely, however, of the provisions of EU law implementing UNCLOS, such disputes should be brought to the Union courts without that being considered contrary to UNCLOS.[208] However, it is important to point out that ITLOS in its order relating to provisional measures in another dispute between the UK and Ireland on the nuclear installations at Sellafield has given a rather narrow interpretation of Article 282. ITLOS does not see an important risk of divergent interpretations between different jurisdictions on quasi-identical provisions, as such closely resembling provisions may be interpreted differently within the context of different treaties.[209] The germ of a conflict between ITLOS and the CJEU based on contradictory interpretations of Article 282 of UNCLOS has thus been sown, but thus far without any consequences.

7.4 *The Panels and the Appellate Body of the WTO*

The following analysis will deal with the question how the CoJ and the GC have dealt and are dealing with their obligation to regard the Panel and AB reports as binding on the European Union.

Neither of the EU courts has ever admitted that the Panel and AB reports are binding on the European Union or on the CJEU as one of the EU's main institutions. It is true that such recognition of these reports generally poses difficult problems to the judicial branch of the governments of the members of the WTO. In *Ritek*[210] the CFI argued that, if the

[207] The case was linked to a WTO case brought by the EU against Chile in reaction to the Chilean measures against transit and import of Pacific swordfish caught by Spanish fishing boats, Case DS 193, *Chile – Measures on Transit and Importation of Swordfish.*

[208] See Case C-459/03, *Commission v. Ireland*, EU:C:2006:345.

[209] This is a well-known argument of the EU courts in relation to the interpretation of clauses in free-trade agreements with third states that are quasi-identical to provisions of the EU treaties, but should be interpreted less broadly in a free-trade agreement than in a customs union context. The classic example is Case C-270/80, *Polydor v. Harlequin Records*, EU:C:1982:43.

[210] Case T-274/02, *Ritek et al. v. Council*, EU:T:2006:332.

situation in that case had been substantially the same as in the WTO Panel Report in the so-called *Bed-Linen case*,[211] it would have felt constrained to annul the antidumping decision at issue in that case. However, the CFI decided that such was not the case and hence it did not follow the *Bed-Linen report* that declared that the so-called zeroing technique was in breach of the general principle of a fair comparison between export price and normal value. Nevertheless, the implication of the CFI's reasoning was that, if the *Ritek* and *Bed-Linen* cases had been substantially the same, it would have had to follow the AB's report in the latter case. The CoJ was confronted with the *Bed-Linen* case in *Ikea Wholesale* and came to the same conclusions as the AB in that case, namely that the zeroing technique was discriminatory, purely on the basis of the nondiscrimination provisions of the European Union basic Anti-Dumping Regulation and without referring in any way to the *Bed-Linen* case itself.[212] When the CoJ in a later case was confronted with a request for the restitution of antidumping duties on textiles levied in a way contrary to the *Bed-Linen* principles, the Court finessed the consequences of its own ruling as follows.[213]

Acts of the EU institutions, bodies, offices and agencies are presumed to be lawful. They produce legal effects until such time as they are withdrawn by these institutions, or annulled or declared invalid by one of the EU courts. Only the CJEU has the power to declare an act such as an antidumping regulation null and void or invalid. Hence the fact that a panel or AB report has found that such an act is in breach of the WTO Anti-Dumping Agreement (ADA) does not affect this presumption of lawfulness. Therefore, as long as the Council (now: the Commission) had not yet used the power inherent in Regulation No. 1515/2001 to withdraw or modify an antidumping regulation that had been condemned by the AB, or the Court had not yet rendered its judgement in *Ikea Wholesale*, the old antidumping duties that were still lawful for the purposes of EU law and could be restituted only as from the moment that the Council or the CoJ would have acted.[214]

In a case handed down some seven months before the CoJ judgement, the GC had ventured to draw up a coherent position to take in WTO-related cases, which for the GC meant mainly antidumping and

[211] Panel Report, *EC – Bed Linen*, WT/DS141/R, adopted 12 March 2001.

[212] Case C-351/04, *Ikea Wholesale v. Council*, EU:C:2007:547.

[213] Case C-533/10, *CIVAD v. Receveur des douanes de Roubaix et al.*, EU:C:2012:347, paras. 37–44.

[214] It is important to note that the CoJ fails to say whether it would feel bound in such a situation to declare the act of an EU institution null or invalid.

countervailing duty cases.[215] The GC recalls that, when an act of the EU institutions is alleged to be in breach of provisions of the basic antidumping regulation, it is indicated to look into the wording, the object and purpose and the context of the basic regulation. As to the context, it follows from its preamble that most of the provisions of the EU antidumping regulation are a transposition of the provisions of the WTO ADA. Therefore, reference should be made to the relevant provisions of the ADA and their interpretation by the WTO Panels and the AB. On this latter aspect, the GC recalls that the reports of these (quasi-) judicial bodies cannot bind the Court in its assessment of whether the contested regulation is valid or not.[216] However, there is nothing to prevent the Court from referring to them, when a provision of the basic regulation has to be interpreted. This approach was implicitly approved by the CoJ on appeal, in which it applied itself the interpretation technique used by the GC, invoking an AB report in order to reject the appellant's arguments.[217]

On the basis of these two cases, one from the CoJ and the other of the GC,[218] the latter court constructs in the following years a growing line of judgements that do just that: they interpret the provisions of the European Union basic regulation in the light of the corresponding provisions of the WTO ADA, as interpreted by the WTO panels and AB reports. The General Court in doing so mostly calls on the reports of the panels and the AB in order to rebut the arguments of the claimants,[219] but also to reject arguments of the defendants, the Council and the Commission, and to rule in favour of the claimants.[220] This use of Panel and AB

[215] Case T-192/08, *Kazchrome and ENRC Marketing v. Council and Commission*, EU:T:2011:619, paras. 30–6.

[216] The GC bases this view on the CoJ's judgement in Case C-377/02, *Van Parys v. BIRB*, EU:C:2005:121, para. 54, but it must be doubtful if this is correct. However, in *CIVAD* the CoJ makes at the very least a distinction between validity under EU law to be decided by the Court and breach of the WTO ADA to be decided by the AB. Strictly speaking that is distinguishable from the bindingness of the AB's reports for the EU institutions, including the CoJ.

[217] Case C-10/12, *P Kazchrome and ENRC Marketing v. Council and Commission*, EU:C:2013:865, paras. 54–5.

[218] The GC later repeated and confirmed its judgement in *Kazchrome* in Case T-633/11, *Guangdong Kito Ceramics v. Council and Commission*, EU:T:2014:271, paras. 38–9.

[219] For example Case T-310/12, *Yuanping Changyuan Chemicals Co. Council and Commission*, EU:T:2015:295, paras. 140–6, which the GC invokes three different AB reports in order to reject claims from the complainant.

[220] For example Case T-425/13, *Giant China Co. v. Council and Commission*, EU:T:2015:896, paras. 56 and 84, in which the GC invokes two different panel reports in order to rebut arguments made by the Council and the Commission.

reports as part of the context for the interpretation of provisions of the European Union basic antidumping regulation is therefore in principle a neutral instrument.

Since the *Kazchrome* case in 2011 there have been roughly ten such cases until late 2015 in which the GC uses one or more AB reports as an aid in interpretation of the basic antidumping regulation and its application in specific cases. There is in these cases often a vivid back and forth between the applicants and the Union institutions that impose antidumping duties, the Council and/or the Commission, each advancing WTO cases that serve to bolster their arguments. The GC is an active participant in this process, rebutting or distinguishing the relevance of cases and sometimes invoking other cases in order to buttress parts of its judgements. In the process considerable authority is given from both sides to WTO case law. This should serve as a bit of a counterweight to the sometimes rather pessimistic view of the influence of WTO law and the authority of the WTO 'courts' in the EU's legal system. That pessimism is usually based on the lack of direct effect of WTO law in the EU legal order, but 'conforming' interpretation can have considerable effect and contributes to the authority of the panels and Appellate Body in the EU legal system as well.

7.5 *The EFTA Court*

The EEA includes, next to a free-trade agreement between the European Union and the remaining EFTA countries (Iceland, Norway and Liechtenstein), numerous aspects of the EU internal market in the field of establishment and trade in services. In these fields the three EFTA countries are obliged to follow the evolution of the *acquis communautaire*, and this *acquis* must be applied and interpreted by the EFTA authorities and the EFTA courts in the way it is interpreted and applied in the Union, in particular by the CJEU. However, the EFTA states, of which in particular the Nordic states had strong dualist systems of assimilating international law into their national legal order, were looking for a certain balance between the homogeneity of Union legislation, its interpretation and application on the one hand, and their dualist systems and their greater freedom in a free-trade area (compared to the EU customs union) on the other hand.

Thus it was the task of the EFTA court to follow the evolution of Union law and the case law of the Court of Justice in respect of the application and interpretation of Union law, but presumably not to imitate such typical EU notions as direct effect, supremacy and state liability in the case of nonimplementation of Union law. In the light of these expectations, it is remarkable to note that, though the EFTA Court dutifully followed the CJEU's case law and referred constantly to it,[221] it also managed to construe equivalents to direct effect and primacy. As the long-serving president of the EFTA Court, Carl Baudenbacher, has put it, the EFTA court's decisions in the *Restamark* and *Einarsson* cases[222] should be characterised as accepting a quasi-direct effect and a quasi-primacy through dualist means, notably by interpretation of the so-called Surveillance and Court Agreement and of Protocol 35 to the EEA Agreement.[223] Even without such support, but with recourse to very basic paragraphs in the preamble to the EEA Agreement on the role of individuals in the EEA, the EFTA Court managed to discover a principle of state responsibility vis-à-vis individuals for nonimplementation of EEA rules in line with the CJEU's *Francovich* case.[224] This was greeted with approval by the CJEU.[225]

The impression, however, that the EFTA Court is somehow constantly engaged in slavishly following the CJEU and that influence never flows the other way would be wrong. There are quite some instances in which the EFTA Court has inspired the CJEU and has been cited by the latter with approval. A well-documented example is the EFTA Court's views on foodstuffs fortified by vitamins and other allegedly beneficent substances.[226] In a number of cases the EFTA Court accepted that for precautionary reasons a state member of the EEA could refuse such fortified products, but at the same time emphasized that such precautionary measures should be based on scientific principles. Moreover, they

[221] Especially the early cases of the EFTA Court are shot through with footnotes referring to CJEU case law. The *Restamark* case referred to in the following footnote is a good example.

[222] Respectively Case E-01/94, *Restamark*, which interprets Article 11 EEA in line with Articles 30 and 36 EEC (free movement of goods) and the relevant case law of the CJEU, and Case E-01/01, *Einarsson v. Icelandic State* [2002] EFTA Court Report 1, which does the same for Article 15 EEA in line with Article 90 EEC (prohibition of tax discrimination).

[223] See C. Baudenbacher, 'The EFTA Court ten years on' in C. Baudenbacher, P. Tresselt, and T. Orlygsson (eds.), *The EFTA Court Ten Years On* (Oxford: Hart Publishing, 2005), pp. 13–51.

[224] Case E-09/97, *Sveinbjornsdottir* [1998] EFTA Court Report 95.

[225] Case C-140/97, *Rechberger*, EU:C:1999:306, para. 39.

[226] See M. Bronckers, 'Exceptions to liberal trade in foodstuffs: The precautionary approach and collective preferences' in C. Baudenbacher, P. Tresselt and T. Orlygsson (eds.) *The EFTA Court Ten Years On* (Oxford: Hart Publishing, 2005), pp. 104–19.

should be proportional, nondiscriminatory, transparent and consistent with earlier such measures.[227] In this way the EFTA Court was much more sophisticated and closer to the WTO SPS Agreement and the relevant case law of the Appellate Body in the *Hormones* case than the CJEU had hitherto been, but it was followed by GC and the CoJ fairly soon.[228] In the same way the GC has recently cited with approval the EFTA Court's view that a Statement of Objections in a competition case must respond to strict conditions, as there is a 'non-negligible stigma attached to a finding of involvement in an infringement of the competition rules for a natural or legal person'.[229] In the same way the CoJ followed the interpretation of the EFTA Court of a broad conception of the notion of 'personal injuries' in the directives on motor vehicle insurance as including physical and psychological suffering.[230]

There is probably only one case in which the EFTA Court and the CoJ have taken incompatible positions on the same question and that is the case of exhaustion of intellectual property rights, when goods covered by such rights move within a customs union, respectively a free-trade area. The CoJ had already foreseen this problem in the well-known *Polydor* case,[231] when it argued that in such situations different interpretations could be given of the same treaty text, as the purpose of an FTA and a customs union were different. In the *Maglite* case[232] the EFTA Court took the view that within the EEA worldwide exhaustion by individual countries could be accepted. In the *Silhouette* case,[233] the CoJ was fully informed on the *Maglite* judgement of the EFTA Court, but arrived at the conclusion that the Court should maintain its doctrine of Community exhaustion, also for the EEA (i.e. EEA exhaustion), as otherwise the distortions in the internal market would be too great. Ten years later,

227 A good example is Case E-03/00, *EFTA Surveillance Authority v. Norway*, [2000–2001] EFTA Court Report 73, commonly known as the Kellogg's case.

228 Case T-13/99, *Pfizer et al. v. Council*, EU:T:2002: 209.

229 Case T-442/08, *International Confederation of Societies of Authors and Composers v. Commission*, EU:T:2013:188, paras. 95–6, citing Case E-15/10, *Posten Norge v. ESA Surveillance Authority* [2012] EFTA Court Report 246, para. 90.

230 Case C-277/12, *Vitalijs Drozdovs v. Baltikums AAS*, EU:C:2013:685, para. 38, referring to Case E-08/07, *Celina Nguyen v. The Norwegian State*, [2008] EFTA Court Report 224, paras. 26–7.

231 Case 270/80, *Polydor v. Harlequin Records*, EU:C:1982:43.

232 Case E-2/97, *Maglite Advisory Opinion*, EFTA Court Report 127.

233 Case C-355/96, *Silhouette International Schmied v. Hartlauer Handelsgesellschaft*, EU:C:1998:374. The Opinion of AG Jacobs played an important role in the CoJ's judgement.

when the occasion presented itself to the EFTA Court to rule again on this matter, it followed the CoJ and opted for EEA exhaustion.[234]

On the whole, the relations between the CJEU and the EFTA Court are quite harmonious, and unexpectedly, the direction of influence does not always uniformly run from the CJEU to the EFTA Court, but also in the opposite direction. That influence has been limited, but is beneficial to the CJEU.[235]

7.6 *The European Court of Human Rights*

Real clashes between the courts of Luxemburg and Strasbourg have been avoided thus far. It has already been discussed earlier how the position of the Advocate-General in Luxemburg has been saved from the critical views expressed by the ECtHR on this function in several member states because the Strasbourg court seems to accept the possibility to reopen the hearing, in case the AG is about to bring up an argument in his conclusions that has not been treated at the hearing.[236] On the other hand, the Luxemburg courts have been willing to adapt their initially restrictive interpretation of the right to the inviolability of the home in connection with so-called dawn raids in competition cases to the evolution of the Strasbourg case law, which went from including lawyers' offices in 1992 to protecting all business premises in 2002. There is still an ongoing dialogue between the two Courts on the question of whether the obligation on individuals and companies to cooperate in competition and tax and customs law by giving certain information to the authorities on request, which was considered normal in the postwar economic order in West-European countries, should now be considered as contrary to the right against self-incrimination.[237]

It would seem logical to suppose that such references to case law of the Strasbourg court must have declined appreciably since the entry into force of the EU Charter of Fundamental Rights that can be applied directly by the EU courts, without reference to the Strasbourg jurisprudence. However, Article 52(3) of the Charter prescribes that in cases

[234] Joined Cases E-9/07 and 10/07, *L'Oréal v. Per Aarskog AS et al.*, [2008] EFTA Court Report 259.

[235] For a recent overview, see C. Baudenbacher, P. Speitler and B. Palmàrsdottir (eds.) *The EEA and the EFTA Court: Decentered Integration* (Oxford: Hart Publishing, 2015).

[236] See above footnote 55 *and* accompanying text.

[237] On all these points and with greater detail, see Lock, *The European Court of Justice and International Courts*, pp. 172–8.

where the provisions of the Charter correspond to rights guaranteed by the ECHR the meaning and scope of those rights shall be the same as those laid down by that Convention. This provision does not make the case law of the Strasbourg court binding on the CJEU because, as the CoJ has pointed out in some post-Charter cases, the European Union is not yet a party to the European Convention.[238]

The consequence of this provision has been in practice that the CoJ and the GC broadly continued their old practice of referring to the provisions of the old Convention and the relevant case law of the Strasbourg Court, after having referred to Article 52(3) and having pointed out that there is indeed a corresponding ECHR article to the article of the Charter that is being invoked.[239] Lock has pointed out that there were slight contradictions in the case law of the Luxemburg Courts and that not all the relevant Treaty and Charter provisions, including the Explanations to the Charter, were being done justice in these post-Charter cases. However, in an urgency procedure concerning the detention of an asylum seeker (who was also a petty criminal), awaiting his possible deportation from the Netherlands, the CoJ, in Grand Chamber formation, has laid down a new approach to the relation between the Charter, the European Convention and the weight to be accorded to the case law of the ECtHR, taking into account all the relevant factors, at least for as long as the European Union does not yet accede to the ECHR.[240]

The Court begins with recalling that Article 6(3) TEU qualifies the fundamental rights recognized by the ECHR as general principles of EU law and that Article 52(3) of the EU Charter lays down that the rights contained in the Charter and that correspond to the rights included in the ECHR are to have the same meaning and scope as the latter. However, such ECHR rights cannot yet be regarded as having been incorporated in EU law, as long as the European Union has not formally acceded to the ECHR. The validity of a provision of Union law allowing member state authorities to keep an asylum seeker in detention for reasons of public security or public order 'must be undertaken *solely* in the light of the fundamental rights guaranteed by the Charter'.[241]

[238] Among others, see Case C-617/10, *Aklagaren v. Akerberg Fransson*, EU:C:2013:280, para. 44 and Lock, *The European Court of Justice and International Courts*, pp. 180–4.

[239] See, for example, Case C-419/14, *WebMindLicenses Kft. v. Nemzeti Ado-es Vamhivatal Kiemelt Ado-es Vam Foigazgatosag*, EU:C: 2015:832, paras. 66 and 70.

[240] Case C-601/15, *PPU J.N. v. Staatssecretaris voor Veiligheid en Justitie*, EU:C:2016:84, paras. 45–8.

[241] Italics supplied.

However, the CoJ then continues with an analysis of the explanations attached to the Charter, in particular those relating to Article 6, the right to liberty and security of one's person, because according to Articles 6(1) TEU and 52(7) Charter these explanations have to be taken into account by the courts of the Union and of the member states, when interpreting the Charter provisions. The explanations with respect to Article 6 of the Charter make clear that this Article corresponds both in scope and meaning to Article 5 of the ECHR. This implies, according to the CoJ, in line with Article 52(3), that any limitations on Article 6 of the Charter may not go beyond those recognized by the ECHR, 'in the wording of Article 5 thereof'.[242] However, the Court also draws the attention to a phrase from the explanation of Article 52(3) to the effect that that article is intended to ensure the necessary consistency between the Charter and the ECHR, 'without thereby adversely affecting the autonomy of Union law and that of the Court of Justice of the European Union'. Finally the Court refers to 'a general principle of interpretation', namely that an EU measure must be interpreted, as far as possible, in such a way as to not affect its validity and in conformity with primary law as a whole and, in particular, with the provisions of the Charter.

It is perhaps too early to judge what will be the consequences of this judgement on the relations between the two Courts. There are good reasons to see it as an attempt to create some order in the relative chaos that reigned in the Court's case law concerning the relations between the Charter and the ECHR. In practice, one hopes, this precedent might be used by the Court's chambers in a more flexible way than one now expects. But the chances of this are limited. It is clear that the CJEU has drawn the tablecloth with a strong pull toward it, without taking account of the reality that the Charter could never have been conceived but in coexistence with the ECHR and the case law of the ECtHR. The existence of Article 6 of the Charter without a clause on limitations and a broader reading of the explanations to the Charter bear testimony to that.

The CoJ may well have done more damage to its relations with the ECtHR with its Judgement in Case C-601/15 than with its Opinion 2/13. One can have different views about the latter, and there are at least some

[242] Case C-601/15 PPU, para. 47 *in fine*. Note that there is no reference whatsoever to the case law of the ECtHR that has given shape to the permitted limitations on Article 5 ECHR. The role of ECtHR case law in interpreting and applying the ECHR was routinely referred to in all earlier post-Charter cases. Also in the later paragraphs of this judgement, where these basic principles are applied to the preliminary questions posed, no reference can be found to the case law of the ECtHR, whereas the Dutch *Raad van State* had specifically mentioned the ECtHR case *Nabil v. France* in the second question.

reputed academics who defended the Court's line,[243] but the Court overplayed its hand outside what is properly its domain, namely the negotiation of the accession agreement to the ECHR. The Court wanted to be able to feed the Commission and the member states, which participated in their own right in the negotiations as members of the Council of Europe, with its views and wanted to be at the table as part of the EU delegation. The most important demand of the Court was to be able to dispose of a Union variant of the exhaustion of local remedies rule that applied to all parties to the ECHR. In practice this so-called cor-espondent mechanism would mean that, if in practice the CJEU had not had the opportunity to rule on a case that was going to Strasbourg, because there had not been a prejudicial reference to Luxemburg, there would still be created an opportunity for the CoJ to express its views on it before the Strasbourg Court would take it on. In the end such a mechanism was obtained in the negotiations, but on further reflection the Court itself then rejected it in Opinion 2/13. This has done a lot of damage to the reputation of the European Union as a serious negotiator and a partner in the Council of Europe and will not be easily forgotten by the other EU institutions and member states involved.

8 Conclusions

If, on the basis of the preceding description and analysis, we take a look at the strong and the weak points of the EUCJ with respect to its legitimacy, the following overview results.

In respect of its selection, the work of the so-called 255 Committee has certainly strengthened the Court's legitimacy, where the quality of the judges is concerned. Remaining weaknesses in gender and colour diversity are addressed somewhat by a member state's obligation to propose two candidates per member state for the GC for the expansion of that court and in future for their replacement. The repeated reorganizations in which the EUCST was spun off from the GC and recently reintegrated again have not been good for the EUCJ's prestige. However, modernization of the Statute and the Rules of Procedure of the GC and the CoJ and other more informal measures of organization of the procedure have had a positive effect on the internal working of the Court.

[243] D. Halberstam, '"It's the autonomy, stupid!" A modest defense of Opinion 2/13 (Agreement on the EU Accession to the ECHR, and a way forward'. *German Law Journal*, 16, 1 (2015), 105–46 and C. Eckes, 'EU accession to the ECHR: Between autonomy and adaptation', *The Modern Law Review*, 76, 2 (2013), 254–85.

Where access to the EUCJ is concerned, on the downside there is the well-known restrictive interpretation that the CoJ has always given to the notion of 'direct and individual concern' that has limited direct access of individuals and legal persons to the courts. This has been partially remedied by changes in the Lisbon Treaty, but the CoJ has not fundamentally changed its interpretation of 'individual concern'. In the field of external relations access is limited by the exclusion of jurisdiction of the CJEU over the CFSP and the CoJ's tendency to become more and more restrictive in granting direct effect to provisions of international agreements. On the positive side one can mention the practical improvements in the time required to process preliminary question cases and the establishment of some specially speeded-up procedures for such cases, which are in favour of individual complainants.

With respect to fact-finding by the EUCJ and its application of standards of review, the situation was on the whole pretty good and largely noncontroversial.

The same cannot be said of the method of interpretation generally used by the Court over the years. This is where the Court has been most exposed to strong criticism, especially in its interpretation of primary law. There is no doubt that the EUCJ among the traditional elements of treaty and statutory interpretation has traditionally given pride of place to the object and purpose of the EU treaties and legislation. This was partly due to the decision of the member states not to make the historical record of the treaty negotiations public. There was nevertheless strong, sometimes strident criticism from academics, practitioners and public figures (such as Roman Herzog, Wolfgang Schuessel) that the EUCJ has been moving away much too far from the text of the treaties. Such criticism is shared nowadays by Eurosceptic parties in many member states. The CoJ has made more room for historical interpretation, especially because good records of the Constitutional Convention render recourse to the *travaux préparatoires* of the Lisbon Treaty much easier. It is also likely that the increased transparency of the legislative process will make the intention of the legislator more important in the CoJ's interpretation of secondary law. In any case, there is also quite prestigious support for the EUCJ's way of interpreting Union law, and the criticism is not so overwhelming as to create a true legitimacy problem for the EUCJ.

Where enforcement of Union law by the EUCJ against and inside the member states is concerned, it was already noted that the European Union has the strongest enforcement system of all international organizations. It is the combination of its role in the unique infringement system and in the equally unique preliminary question system, of which the latter puts the CoJ in the position to bring national judges to the disapplication of national law that is in conflict with Union law, that is at the root of this. The infringement procedure has been improved by the Lisbon Treaty so as to enable the CoJ to apply pecuniary sanctions even quicker, while the CoJ has also taken measures to make the preliminary question procedure faster and more effective. On enforcement, therefore, the legitimacy position of the EUCJ is quite good.

As to the relations with other international courts, the Court has the best relations with worldwide courts that have a mandate that is not too close to the substance of Union law, namely the ICJ and the ITLOS. Conflicts are unlikely, and the EUCJ can invoke case law of these courts to bolster its own reasoning on international law (of the sea), when necessary. The relations with the WTO panels and Appellate Body (AB) are more difficult, as the substance is close to that covered by the EUCJ and their reports are binding on the European Union. The EUCJ is still struggling to come to a better than ambivalent position in its relations with the WTO AB and panels: the CoJ is still standoffish, while the GC actively engages with the case law of the AB.

The relations with the ECtHR, after many years of broadly harmonious coexistence, have become fraught recently because of the treaty status given to the EU Charter of Human Rights and the projected accession of the European Union to the ECHR, which would make the ECtHR's judgements binding on the Union and the EUCJ. The accession has not yet come about, and the CoJ's Opinion 2/13 has not made this any easier. Moreover, the subsequent CoJ judgement in Case C-601/15 has overstated the independent position of the Charter as *the* source of fundamental rights for the Union and belittled the codependence between the Charter and the ECHR, as interpreted by the ECtHR. The CoJ may well have overplayed its hand in both cases and done its reputation no good.

On balance the EUCJ has a positive saldo of legitimacy in its selection and internal organization, in fact-finding and standards of review, and in enforcement. However, on access to the court, interpretation technique and relations with other courts, the balance seems to be on the negative side of the scale, but by a narrow margin only. One important element in favour of the EUCJ is without doubt that, like many national supreme courts, it is surrounded and critically accompanied in its case law by a large 'community' of academic and practising lawyers. This critical community of followers is now much more diverse than in the EUCJ's early days and helps to keep the Court aware of its weaknesses and may thus give a contribution to its legitimacy.

4

The EFTA Court

HALVARD HAUKELAND FREDRIKSEN

1 Introduction

The EFTA Court is a rather exceptional judicial body created by the equally exceptional Agreement on the European Economic Area (EEA).[1] Even the court's official name is a bit odd, as the EFTA Court is not an institution of the European Free Trade Association (EFTA), but rather an independent organisation under public international law[2] established by those EFTA states that are parties to the EEA Agreement (now only Iceland, Norway and Liechtenstein).[3] Consequently, the jurisdiction of the Court is limited to matters of EEA law – it has no jurisdiction to settle disputes between the EFTA states related to the EFTA Convention,[4] to the Lugano Convention[5] or to the many free trade agreements between

[1] The EFTA Court was formally established through the Agreement between the EFTA states on the establishment of a Surveillance Authority and a Court of Justice (Surveillance and Court Agreement - SCA). In reality, however, the Court was created by the EEA Agreement, whose Article 108 (2) states that '[t]he EFTA States shall establish a court of justice (EFTA Court).' Article 27 SCA is the fulfilment of this obligation.

[2] See Article 1 of Protocol 7 SCA: 'The EFTA Court shall possess legal personality.'

[3] The reason for the Court's official name was the expectation that all of the EFTA states would become parties to the EEA Agreement. However, the Swiss electorate rejected the agreement in a national referendum on 6 December 1992, leaving Switzerland as an EFTA state outside the EEA.

[4] Convention establishing the European Free Trade Association, signed in Stockholm on 4 January 1960, revised in Vaduz on 21 June 2001. The Convention has since been amended by the EFTA Council on a number of occasions. A consolidated version may be found at the EFTA homepage www.efta.int. In addition to institutional arrangements, the EFTA Convention regulates trade between the EFTA states. In practice, however, trade between the three EFTA states parties to the EEA Agreement is governed by the more far-reaching provisions of that agreement. The practical importance of the EFTA Convention is thus limited to trade between those states on the one hand and Switzerland on the other. According to Articles 47 and 48 of the Convention, disputes are to be settled by consultations or, as the last resort, arbitration.

[5] Convention on jurisdiction and the recognition and enforcement of judgements in civil and commercial matters, signed on 30 October 2007 by the European Community, Denmark, Iceland, Norway and Switzerland.

all of the (now only four) EFTA states on the one hand and various third countries on the other.[6] Even more important; the jurisdiction of the EFTA Court is limited to the EFTA pillar of the European Economic Area – jurisdiction to hear cases concerning the interpretation or application of EEA law in the European Union belongs exclusively to the Court of Justice of the European Union (ECJ).

The lack of a common 'EEA Court' is key to understanding the challenges faced by the EFTA Court. Indeed, the sole reason for the EFTA Court's existence is the fact that the ECJ in 1991 declared the proposition for a common EEA Court to be incompatible with the (then) EC Treaty.[7] The essence of the ECJ's objections was that it saw the creation of an EEA Court as a threat to its own position as the supreme authority on what was then Community law, in particular because the EEA Court, which was to be composed of judges from both the ECJ and the EFTA states, would be interpreting EEA provisions that are identical in substance to corresponding rules of EU law.[8] The solution was an independent court of justice for the EFTA pillar and the acknowledgement that any disputes between one or more of the EEA EFTA states on the one side and the European Union and the EU member states on the other would have to be settled by diplomatic means in the EEA Joint Committee.[9] When the ECJ the following year approved the renegotiated Agreement, it stressed that the EFTA Court would have no functional or personal connections to the ECJ and would exercise its jurisdiction only within the EFTA pillar.[10]

[6] Instead, free trade agreements negotiated between the EFTA States and third countries regularly foresee arbitration as the *ultima ratio* in order to settle disputes. These provisions apply also to possible (albeit improbable) 'internal' disputes between the EFTA states related to the agreement in question, leaving no role for the EFTA Court.

[7] Opinion 1/91, *EEA I*, [1991] ECR I-6079; [1992] 1 CMLR 245.

[8] See, e.g., T. Hartley, 'The European Court and the EEA', *International and Comparative Law Quarterly*, 41 (1992), 841–8 at 847, and, more recently, B. de Witte, 'A selfish court? The Court of Justice and the design of international dispute settlement beyond the European Union' in M. Cremona and A. Thies (eds.), *The European Court of Justice and External Relations Law* (Oxford: Hart Publishing, 2014), pp. 36–7.

[9] See Article 111 EEA. Note that in cases concerning the interpretation of EEA provisions taken over from EU law, the Contracting Parties to the dispute may agree to refer the matter to the ECJ. Twenty years on, it still remains to be seen if such judicial settlement of a dispute will be acceptable to the EFTA states if the occasion should arise. For the sake of completeness, it may be added that disputes concerning the scope or duration of safeguard measures, or the proportionality of any rebalancing measures taken may be referred to arbitration. However, it follows from Article 111 (4) that no questions of interpretation of EEA provisions taken over from EU law may be dealt with in such procedures.

[10] Opinion 1/92, *EEA II*, [1992] ECR I-2821; [1992] 2 CMLR 217.

The challenges facing the EFTA Court reflect the fact that the whole EEA project is an attempt to achieve the impossible: Full integration of the EEA EFTA states into the EU's internal market without any transfer of legislative, administrative or judicial powers to the European Union.[11] A sine qua non for the accomplishment of this attempt to 'square the circle' is the ability of the EFTA Court to gain (and keep) the trust of the European Union and the EU member states. If the EFTA Court was to be perceived by the ECJ as less committed to the judicial protection of the fundamental freedoms of the internal market and, conversely, more sympathetic toward the arguments of government lawyers than the ECJ itself, then the predictable response from the ECJ would be to invoke the principle of reciprocity and apply the feared *Polydor* doctrine to the EEA Agreement.[12] If the ECJ was to embark on an interpretation of EEA law differing from its own interpretation of corresponding provisions of EU law, the result would be the gradual undermining of the Agreement's overall goal to extend the internal market to include the EEA EFTA states. Thus, the lack of a common EEA Court essentially entails that the fate of the EEA Agreement depends on its continued acceptance by the ECJ.

To complicate matters even further, the position of the EFTA Court vis-à-vis the national courts of the EEA EFTA states is weaker than the ECJ's position within the European Union: for constitutional and political reasons concerning judicial sovereignty, the EEA EFTA states were (and still are) unwilling to submit their highest courts to the supremacy of the EFTA Court.

At the time of the EEA negotiations, few commentators thought that the compromises found would prove workable in the long term.[13] The fact that the EEA Agreement in 2014 celebrated its twentieth anniversary suffices to demonstrate that the EFTA Court has proven the sceptics wrong. Through dynamic interpretation of the Agreement, the EFTA

[11] In the literature, the EEA project is often referred to as an attempt to achieve the impossible. See, e.g., H. P. Graver, 'Mission impossible: supranationality and national legal autonomy in the EEA Agreement', *European Foreign Affairs Review* 73, 7 (2002), 90.

[12] Case 270/80, *Polydor*, [1982] ECR 329; [1982] 1 CMLR 677, where the ECJ interpreted provisions of the free-trade agreement between the EC and the then EFTA state Portugal differently from the virtually identically worded provisions in the EC Treaty, with justification in the different aims of the two treaties. This *Polydor* doctrine has since been applied to many free trade agreements between the European Union and third countries (including the bilateral agreements with Switzerland), but not to the EEA Agreement.

[13] See, e.g., M. Cremona, 'The "dynamic and homogeneous" EEA: Byzantine structures and various geometry', *European Law Review*, 19 (1994), 508–26 at 524: 'the compromises reached are unlikely to prove satisfactory'.

Court has managed – by and large – to achieve and maintain homogeneity between EEA and EU law.[14] In the process, it has gained a reputation as an independent guarantor of the EEA EFTA states' fulfilment of their obligations under EEA law and even established itself as a fairly regular dialogue partner of the ECJ.[15] The perhaps inevitable price to pay for this rather remarkable achievement is a somewhat troublesome relationship to the governments and highest courts of the EEA EFTA states. Right or wrong, they sometimes feel that the EFTA Court has become too immune to the arguments of government lawyers.

2 Nomination/Selection/Composition/Independence of Judges

The EFTA Court consists of one judge per EEA EFTA State. At the inauguration on 1 January 1994, the Court thus had five members. After the exit of Austria, Finland and Sweden and the entry of Liechtenstein, the Court has ever since 1995 consisted of only three judges (Article 28 SCA).[16] The judges are appointed by common accord of the governments of the EEA EFTA states (Article 30 (1) SCA). Both the principle of one judge per member state and the mode of their appointment are copied from EU law.[17] Even though the establishment of an independent court of justice for the EFTA pillar is required by the EEA Agreement itself (Article 108 (2) EEA), the Contracting Parties on the EU side have no say in the selection of its judges.

In addition to the regular judges, a system of ad hoc judges is established according to Article 30 (4) SCA for situations where a regular judge cannot act in a particular case. Just as the regular judges, the now six ad hoc judges – two for each EEA EFTA state – are appointed by common accord by the governments of the EEA EFTA states alone.

[14] See, e.g., H. H. Fredriksen, 'The EFTA Court 15 years on', *International and Comparative Law Quarterly*, 59 (2010), 731–60.

[15] Between them, the ECJ, its Advocates General and the General Court have over the last 20 years made over 150 references to EFTA Court case law in almost 100 judgements and opinions.

[16] The judges from Austria, Finland and Sweden left the EFTA Court on 30 June 1995, whereas the judge appointed in respect of Liechtenstein joined the Court on 6 September 1995. Thus, for a little more than three months, the Court had only two members. The solution found was for the Icelandic and Norwegian judge to agree on the designation of a third member of the Court on an ad hoc basis, but fortunately no cases had to be decided in this space of time.

[17] See now Article 19 (2) TEU.

Unlike the ECJ, the judges of the EFTA Court are not supported by any Advocates General. The original EEA EFTA states, of which none knew of any institution resembling that of the Advocate General from their domestic legal systems, were simply not prepared to bear the extra costs.[18]

In 2011, however, the EFTA Court proposed the creation of the post of an Advocate General as well the establishment of an 'Extended Court' for particularly important cases.[19] The Extended Court was to be composed of the three regular judges and two of the ad hoc judges.[20] The EFTA Court reasoned that an Advocate General and an Extended Court of five would reinforce its standing and credibility, whereby it presumably had both the ECJ and the national courts of the EEA EFTA states in mind. The proposals were withdrawn, however, after a rather chilling reception from the governments of the EEA EFTA states.[21]

The president of the EFTA Court is elected by the regular judges from among their number for a term of three years (Article 30 (3) SCA). Thus, the governments have no say in the Court's presidential elections.[22] Once again, this rule is taken over from EU law. Its consequences are mitigated by the fact that the president's powers are limited to administrative and certain procedural matters (interventions, interim measures, etc.) – all other decisions are to be made by the Court *en banc* (Article 29 SCA). The president may be reelected. Indeed, Carl Baudenbacher has been the

[18] L. Sevón, 'The EFTA Court – ten years on' in C. Baudenbacher, P. Tresselt, and Þ. Örlygsson (eds.), *The EFTA Court Ten Years On* (Oxford: Hart Publishing, 2005), pp. 185–6 at p. 186.

[19] See 'An Extended EFTA Court? The EFTA Court proposes amendments to the SCA', Press Release 11/11, 8 December 2011. For unknown reasons, the proposal is no longer available at the EFTA Court's homepage (www.eftacourt.int), but if may be obtained from the Court upon request to the Registrar.

[20] The decision to submit a case to the Extended Court was to be taken by the regular judges based on their assessment of the importance of each case. The two ad hoc judges were to be chosen randomly from a pool of nine (up from today's list of six). However, two ad hoc judges from the same EFTA state should not take part in the disposal of a case if ad hoc judges from other EFTA states were available.

[21] See in particular the response from the Norwegian government in Meld. St. 5 (2012–13) Report to Parliament (White Paper) 2012–13 'The EEA Agreement and Norway's other agreements with the EU' (English version), subchapter 2.3.5: 'Thus far, the Government has not seen a need to make amendments to the institutional setup of the EFTA Court.'

[22] According to the Court's president, however, some of the governments have nonetheless tried to influence the elections, cf. C. Baudenbacher, *The EFTA Court in Action* (Stuttgart: German Law Publishers, 2010), p. 8.

Court's president ever since 2003. In 2015, he was reelected for a fifth term as president.

Nomination of candidates for the Court is done individually by the governments; each government has the right to nominate one regular judge and two ad hoc judges. Even though appointment is made by common accord of the EEA EFTA states, a nominated candidate has never been rejected. In an exceptional move in 2007, the Norwegian government tried to block the reappointment of the judge nominated by Liechtenstein, putting the decision on hold for several months. However, as Liechtenstein refused to withdraw the nomination, the Norwegian government eventually gave in as the expiration of his term of office lay only a few weeks ahead.[23]

Just as in the ECJ, the judges of the EFTA Court are appointed for a term of six years, and they may – as demonstrated by the aforementioned example – be reappointed (Article 30 (1) SCA). There is no limit on the number of reappointments and no age limit. Carl Baudenbacher has been reappointed no less than three times and will be seventy-two years of age when his current term expires in 2019. The fact that he is a Swiss citizen also illustrates that the judges of the EFTA Court do not necessarily have to be citizens of the EEA EFTA states.[24]

Just like its EU law template (now Article 19 (2) TEU), Article 30 SCA as such does not give any priority to a sitting judge interested in a new term. However, refusal to reappoint a sitting judge, unless based on a preestablished and publically communicated policy that rules out reappointments in general or based on clear criteria (such as an upper age limit in line with what applies to national judges), will easily be politically controversial. This was aptly demonstrated by the controversy related to the reappointment of the Norwegian judge in 2016/2017. Despite the fact that the sitting Norwegian judge had signalled his interest in another term, the Norwegian government announced the vacancy in the press. This prompted the president of the EFTA Court to publish an open letter to the members of the government's evaluation panel, in which he set out some of the qualifications that he thought particularly important.[25] The letter was widely

[23] See, albeit without any naming of the involved governments, Baudenbacher, *The EFTA Court in Action*, p. 5.

[24] Still, the judges nominated by Iceland and Norway have always been Icelandic and Norwegian citizens.

[25] Letter of 27 July 2016, to the panel evaluating the candidates for the position of Norwegian judge on the Court, published on the EFTA Court's homepage (under 'Press and Publications').

read as support to the sitting Norwegian judge by highlighting the importance of parts of EEA law that he knows well (financial market law, etc.) and as an attempt to depreciate the importance of the field of expertise of one of his expected competitors (constitutional and institutional matters such as the questions of effect, primacy and state liability, the scope of application of the EEA Agreement, its 'sui generis' nature, etc.).[26] It prompted the Norwegian attorney general (civil affairs) to reply with an equally controversial letter, in which the attorney general not only contradicted the president's assessment of which parts of EEA law are of practical importance, but also added that he thought it to be important as a matter of principle to have regular replacements in the composition of the EFTA Court.[27] Both letters were picked up by the press, resulting in further escalation[28] and an unfortunate politicisation of the appointment. The Norwegian government's search for a compromise made things even worse – the Norwegian judge was reappointed by the governments of the EFTA states, but only 'for a nonrenewable term of three years, until he reaches the age of 70, which is the statutory retirement age for Norwegian Supreme Court Judges'.[29] This blatant violation of the wording of Article 30 (1) SCA caused a group of Norwegian academics to lodge a complaint with the EFTA Surveillance Authority; the Norwegian Judges' Association to write an open letter of concern to the Norwegian Government and a Liechtenstein court to ask the EFTA Court whether it considered itself to be lawfully composed in a manner that ensures its independence and impartiality.[30] When faced with the prospect of having to defend the decision before the EFTA Court, the Norwegian government retreated and allowed the Norwegian judge to be reappointed for a full period of

[26] It is true that the letter was published before the list of applicants was made public, but it was a well-known secret at the time that professor Finn Arnesen from the University of Oslo would be on that list.

[27] Letter of 19 August 2016, to the panel evaluating the candidates for the position of Norwegian judge on the EFTA Court, available (in Norwegian only) from the homepage of the Attorney General (www.regjeringsadvokaten.no).

[28] See, e.g., the article 'Advarer Norge' in the Norwegian newspaper *Verdens Gang*, 7 September 2016, in which the EFTA Court's president is quoted as saying that the nomination of someone who is not completely independent and impartial will damage the reputation of the nominating state.

[29] ESA/Court Committee Decision No 5 of 1 December 2016.

[30] For all the details, see Order of the President of 20.2.2017 in Case E-21/16, *Pascal Nobile*.

six years.[31] This again allowed the EFTA Court (sitting with two ad hoc judges) to conclude that the Court was indeed lawfully composed.[32]

As to the qualifications required, Article 30 (1) SCA states that the judges shall be chosen from persons whose independence is beyond doubt and who possess the qualifications required for appointment to the highest judicial offices in their respective countries or who are jurisconsults of recognized competence. Once again, the requirements are taken over from EU law.[33]

Unlike the current stand of EU law, however, the SCA does not provide for any external scrutiny of whether a candidate nominated for the EFTA Court actually fulfils the qualifications listed. The historic explanation is simply that neither did EU law at the time of the EEA negotiations. However, the Treaty of Lisbon introduced an independent panel entrusted with the task to give opinions on candidates' suitability before the governments of the member states make the appointments.[34] Interestingly, the EFTA Court in 2011 proposed a similar system.[35] According to the Court, this would reinforce its professional competence and, thus, its standing. In order to enhance its credibility vis-à-vis the ECJ in particular, one of the members of the evaluation panel was to be a former judge of the ECJ. The response from the EEA EFTA states was rather cold, however.[36] Unless the EU side should take an interest in the matter, the prospects for an independent evaluation panel for candidates to the EFTA Court therefore seem rather slim.[37]

As far as the internal selection procedures in each of the EEA EFTA states are concerned, the governments are firmly in control.[38] As a small sign of more openness, the two last Norwegian vacancies on the bench have been publicly announced in the press. A panel has been set up to

[31] ESA/Court Committee Decision 2017 No 1 of 13 January 2017 on the re-appointment of a Judge to the EFTA Court and repealing Decision 2016 No 5 of 1 December 2016.

[32] Decision of 14.2.2017 in Case E-21/16, *Pascal Nobile*.

[33] See now Article 253 TFEU on the qualifications required for the Judges and Advocates General of the ECJ.

[34] Cf. Article 255 TFEU. See further on this T. Dumbrovský, B. Petkova, and M. van der Sluis, 'Judicial appointments: The Article 255 TFEU Advisory Panel and selection procedures in the Member States', *Common Market Law Review*, 51 (2014), 455–82.

[35] See the Court's aforementioned Press Release 11/11.

[36] See in particular the aforementioned response from the Norwegian government in Meld. St. 5 (2012–13) Report to Parliament (White Paper) 2012–13 'The EEA Agreement and Norway's other agreements with the EU' (English version), subchapter 2.3.5.

[37] Unless the controversy related to the reappointment of the Norwegian judge in 2016/2017 should cause the Norwegian government to change its mind.

[38] See Baudenbacher, *The EFTA Court in Action*, p. 5.

evaluate the candidates for the current Norwegian vacancy, but two of its three members are (senior) officials from the Ministry of Foreign Affairs (the third being the president of the independent Judicial Appointments Board). Furthermore, the panel shall not rank the candidates – that is left to the government (in reality the Ministry of Foreign Affairs).

The fact that the EEA EFTA states appoint (and reappoint) their own judges could perhaps be expected to cause concern at the EU side,[39] but so far the case law of the EFTA Court seems to have put any such concern to rest. One may only hope that the aforementioned attempt by the Norwegian government in 2016/2017 to limit the new term of the Norwegian judge of the EFTA Court to only three years will not change this.

Just as with the ECJ, the possibility to reappoint the judges of the EFTA Court may only be reconciled with public confidence in their independence from their home states as long as the deliberations of the Court are kept secret (see Section 3 below). This is even more so for a court of only three judges who decides all cases *en banc*. Thus, a reform of the SCA introducing public voting would have to include the abolishment of the possibility to reappoint retiring judges.

The independence of the judges is further safeguarded by Article 4 of the Court's Statute, which states that they may not hold any political or administrative office. Furthermore, the judges may not engage in any occupation, whether gainful or not, unless exemption is granted by the Governments of the EEA EFTA states acting by common accord.[40]

The independence of the judges in each individual case is further secured by Article 15 of the Court's Statute, which states that no judge may take part in the disposal of a case 'in which he has previously taken part as agent or adviser or has acted for one of the parties, or in which he has been called upon to pronounce as a member of a court or tribunal, of a commission of inquiry or in any other capacity'.[41]

The EFTA Court interprets this provision rather strictly. As a result, there are quite a few cases from which one of the regular judges has withdrawn, including a couple where the reasons for doing so relate to legal opinions expressed in an extrajudicial capacity (academic writing).[42]

[39] See, e.g., J. Jonsdottir, *Europeanization and the European Economic Area* (London: Routledge, 2014), p. 71.

[40] A similar provision is found in Article 4 of the ECJ's Statute.

[41] A similar provision is found in Article 18 of the ECJ's Statute.

[42] Joined Cases E-9/07 and E-10/07, *L'Oréal* [2008] EFTA Court Report 258 (President Baudenbacher replaced by ad hoc Judge Ospelt) and Case E-16/11, *EFTA Surveillance*

Even if the independence of the EFTA Court is recognised and respected by all parties concerned, a row between the Court and the EFTA Board of Auditors that erupted in 2007 revealed fundamental disagreement concerning the external control of the judges' earning from extrajudicial occupational activities. The auditors refused to approve of the account of the EFTA Court for the previous year, citing the refusal of the judges to disclose their earnings from such activities.[43] In doing so, the EFTA Board of Auditors essentially advocated the view that the public confidence in the independence of the judiciary depends on external control of any possible conflicts of interest on the side of the judges. The EFTA Court, on the other hand, saw in such external control a threat to the very same judicial independence. The position of the EFTA Court appears to conform not only to that of the ECJ, but also to the civil law conception of judicial independence. Whereas Nordic lawyers are characterised by their far-reaching confidence in the administrative authorities, lawyers in the civil law tradition tend to be more concerned with the immanent possibility of abuse of any external control powers over the judiciary.[44] Unlike the EU Court of Auditors, the EFTA Board of Auditors is not a truly independent body – its three members are civil servants of the EEA EFTA states. The controversy ended only when the representatives of the EEA EFTA states in the Surveillance Authority and Court Committee found it to lie outside the competences of the Board of Auditors to look into the extrajudicial activities of the EFTA Court's judges.

3 Procedural Rules

3.1 Relationship to EU Procedural Rules

As the EFTA Court was established to fulfil a judicial function in the EFTA pillar more or less equalling that of the ECJ in the European

Authority v. Iceland ('Icesave') [2013] EFTA Court Report 4 (Judge Christiansen replaced by ad hoc Judge Mestad).

43 See, e.g., the article 'Efta-dommere tar hemmelige bijobber' ('EFTA judges with secret second jobs') in Norway's largest newspaper *Aftenposten*, 14 March 2007.

44 For a comprehensive analysis of the different perspectives of German and Norwegian lawyers when it comes to their confidence in the administrative authorities, see A. K. Sperr, *Verwaltungsrechtsschutz in Deutschland und Norwegen: Eine vergleichende Studie zur gerichtlichen Kontrolle von Verwaltungsentscheidungen* (Nomos: Baden-Baden, 2009). Of course, the very different historical experiences of the two countries are key to understanding these cultural differences.

Union, it is hardly surprising that it was modelled on the template of the latter. In the words of Leif Sevón, the head of the Preparatory Committee for (and later the first president of) the EFTA Court, the model of the ECJ was 'sufficiently strange and in part equally incomprehensible to all participants in the EFTA working group to convince them that none of them could smuggle in their own rules'.[45] It is, however, exactly this overall inspiration from EU law that makes the exceptions interesting.

Even though under no written obligation to do so, the EFTA Court has constantly taken the reasoning of the ECJ into account when interpreting procedural provisions of the SCA, the Statute and the Rules of Procedure, which are taken over from EU law. The EFTA Court has justified this 'principle of procedural homogeneity' with reference to the wish to ensure equal access to justice for individuals and economic operators throughout the EEA as well as reasons of expediency and enhanced legal certainty for all parties concerned.[46]

Furthermore, the EFTA Court has recognised the principle of effective judicial protection, including the right to a fair trial, as a general principle of EEA law.[47] It has done so by explicit reference to Article 6 of the European Convention on Human Rights and Fundamental Freedoms (ECHR), to which all of the EEA States are parties. As a result, the EFTA Court has acknowledged that the interpretation and application of its procedural rules must respect the obligations flowing from this provision.[48]

3.2 Categories of Cases

The by far two most important categories of cases before the EFTA Court are actions brought by the EFTA Surveillance Authority against an EEA EFTA state for infringement of the EEA Agreement (Article 31 SCA) and request for advisory opinions on the interpretation of the EEA Agreement from the national courts of the EEA EFTA states (Article 34 SCA). However, the Court is also competent to decide on actions concerning the settlement of EEA-related disputes between two or more EEA EFTA

[45] Sevón, 'The EFTA Court – ten years on', pp. 185–6.

[46] See, e.g., Case E-15/10, *Posten Norge v. EFTA Surveillance Authority* [2012] EFTA Court Report 246, paras. 109–10 and case law cited.

[47] See, e.g., Case E-2/03, *Ásgeirsson* [2003] EFTA Court Report 185, para. 23.

[48] See, e.g., Case E-15/10, *Posten Norge v. EFTA Surveillance Authority* [2012] EFTA Court Report 246, para. 110 *in fine*.

states (Article 32 SCA); actions for nullity brought by an EEA EFTA state or affected private parties against a decision of the EFTA Surveillance Authority (Article 36 SCA); actions for failure to act brought by an EEA EFTA state or private parties against the EFTA Surveillance Authority (Article 37 SCA) and damage claims against the EFTA Surveillance Authority (Article 39 SCA).[49]

Unfortunately, the EFTA Court lacks jurisdiction to rule on the validity of decisions from the institution that is vested with competence to incorporate novel EU legislation of EEA-relevance into the EEA Agreement – the EEA Joint Committee.[50] In direct actions, the Court can review the legality of decisions of the EFTA Surveillance Authority only (Article 36 SCA), whereas its jurisdiction under the preliminary reference procedure is limited to questions of interpretation of EEA law (Article 34 SCA).[51] It is uncertain to which extent the EFTA Court can remedy this deficiency in the judicial protection offered to individuals in the EFTA-pillar of the EEA by 'interpreting away' a decision from the EEA Joint Committee, which incorporates into the Agreement an EU legal act which the EU courts, in the setting of EU law, would declare null and void.[52]

Twenty-four years on, the Court has decided more than 240 cases.[53] Among these are more than 120 references from national courts and about 100 infringement proceedings brought by the EFTA Surveillance Authority. In addition, the Court has dealt with more than 40 actions for nullity against decisions of the EFTA Surveillance Authority, most of them brought by an affected EEA EFTA state but also some brought by private parties (primarily in the fields of state aid and competition law).

[49] Compare with Articles 258, 259, 263, 265, 267 and 268 TFEU.

[50] In order to ensure homogeneity between EEA law and the constantly evolving internal market acquis of the European Union, novel EU legislation of EEA relevance is continuously added to the Agreement through decisions of the EEA Joint Committee (Article 102 EEA). Since its entry into force in 1994, more than 7000 EU legal acts have been incorporated into the Agreement by amending its many annexes and protocols!

[51] See further on this N. Fenger, M. S. Rydelski, and T. van Stiphout, *The European Free Trade Association and the European Economic Area* (Alphen aan den Rijn: Wolters Kluwer, 2012), pp. 158–9 and 162–3.

[52] The EFTA Court's approach in Case E-6/01, *CIBA* [2002] EFTA Court Report 282 may suggest an affirmative answer, but it would certainly be preferable from the perspective of democratic legitimacy if the Contracting Parties were to amend the jurisdiction of the Court to solve the matter.

[53] See the overview of cases 1994–2016 provided for at the end of the EFTA Court's annual report for 2016.

Further, the EFTA Surveillance Authority has had to defend itself in a couple of cases concerning failure to act (all brought by private parties) and in one case concerning noncontractual liability.

3.3 *Access to the Court*

The issue of standing before the EFTA Court is rather straightforward when it comes to the EEA contracting parties: The EEA EFTA states have standing to bring actions against each other (Article 32 SCA) as well as against the EFTA Surveillance Authority (Articles 36 and 37 SCA), i.e. without the need to prove any particular interest in the subject matter of the case. On the other hand, neither the European Union nor any of the EU member states have standing to do likewise. As a consequence of the lack of a common EEA Court, the only option for the EU-side is to bring disputes with the EEA EFTA states and/or the EFTA Surveillance Authority before the EEA Joint Committee (Article 111 EEA).[54]

The consequences of these strict rules on standing are partly mitigated, however, by the fact that both the EU Commission and the EU member states are entitled to participate in cases pending before the EFTA Court. Article 20 of the Statute gives not only the EEA EFTA states and the EFTA Surveillance Authority, but also 'the Union and the European Commission' the right to submit statements of case or written observations in all cases before the EFTA Court. Furthermore, Article 36 of the Statute enables the said states and institutions to intervene in support of one of the parties to a pending case. Importantly, the reference to 'the Union' in both these provisions is understood by the Court to encompass all the EU member states. Consequently, not only the European Union as such but also all of the EU member states are routinely notified of all pending cases.[55] In practice, the Commission takes part in virtually all cases before the Court, whereas an EU member state does so only if it has a particular interest in the subject matter of the dispute.[56] In an order

[54] Note that only the EU as such, not the individual EU member state, has standing to bring such a dispute before the EEA Joint Committee. The explanation for this lies in the internal distribution of competences between the EU and its member states.

[55] Note that the EEA EFTA states and the EFTA Surveillance Authority enjoy similar rights to take part in at least certain categories of EEA-relevant cases before the ECJ. See further on this in Section 4 below.

[56] In high-profile cases, it seems that the involved EEA EFTA states sometimes ask like-minded EU member states to support their pleadings. An exceptional example is Case E-1/06, *EFTA Surveillance Authority v. Norway* [2007] EFTA Court Report 8 concerning

giving the Commission leave to intervene in the high-profile *Icesave* case, the president of the Court characterised the capability for any EEA state, the EFTA Surveillance Authority and the European Union and its institutions to intervene in cases before the Court as being 'of paramount significance for the good functioning of the EEA Agreement'.[57]

When it comes to individuals, the issue of standing is more complicated. According to Article 36 (2) SCA, any natural or legal person may institute proceedings before the EFTA Court against a decision of the EFTA Surveillance Authority, which is either (i) addressed to that person or (ii) of direct and individual concern to him. The former alternative is unproblematic, but as EEA law stands at present, it is only of practical interest in the field of competition law.[58] The latter alternative is anything but unproblematic, as is well demonstrated by several cases from the Court. In short, the EFTA Court follows the ECJ's narrow interpretation of the corresponding provision in Article 263 (4) TFEU.[59] Thus, persons other than those to whom a decision is addressed may only claim to be individually concerned within the meaning of Article 36 (2) SCA if the decision affects them by reason of certain attributes that are peculiar to them or if they are differentiated by circumstances from all other persons and those circumstances distinguish them individually just as the person addressed by the decision. In a case from 2003, the applicants – a Norwegian environmental foundation and a German consultancy firm within the field of renewable energy – invited the Court to adopt a more flexible interpretation of standing, thereby allowing them to challenge the EFTA Surveillance Authority's approval of Norwegian state aid to a

the Norwegian monopoly on gaming machines, where Belgium (and Iceland) intervened in support of Norway and no less than seven other EU member states submitted written observations and/or participated in the oral hearing.

[57] Order of 23 April 2012 in Case E-16/11, *EFTA Surveillance Authority v. Iceland ('Icesave')* [2013] EFTA Court Report 4, para. 33. The case is discussed further in section 6.

[58] Mirroring the competences of the Commission under EU competition law, the EFTA Surveillance Authority has competence to enforce the competition rules through decisions that are addressed to and binding upon private parties, see Articles 55 and 56 EEA. Note that the trend in the European Union toward more centralised control through the ever-increasing number of EU agencies has resulted in a number of new competences for the EFTA Surveillance Authority in recent years and that this development seems likely to continue. Thus, the action for nullity against addressed decisions of the EFTA Surveillance Authority may gradually become more important also outside the field of competition law.

[59] See, in particular, Case 25/62, *Plaumann v. Commission*, [1963] ECR 95; [1964] CMLR 29.

controversial liquefied natural gas project in the Barents Sea.[60] They failed to convince the Court, however, which chose to follow the established case law of the ECJ and which – by and large – has continued to do so thereafter.[61]

Consequently, access to the EFTA Court for private parties will in most cases be indirect through an action brought before a national court, who then decides to stay the proceedings and ask the EFTA Court for an advisory opinion on the interpretation of the relevant parts of the EEA Agreement (Article 34 SCA). The decision of whether to refer or not, however, lies exclusively in the hands of the national court. The parties before the national court – be they individuals or public authorities – can only ask and hope for such a referral to be made. As far as the lower courts are concerned, this is no different from the situation in the European Union. When it comes to national courts against whose decisions there is no judicial remedy under national law, however, there are important differences between EU and EEA law. Whereas Article 267 (3) TFEU obliges national courts of last instance to refer unresolved questions of EU law (and thus EEA law) to the ECJ, Article 34 SCA as such imposes no corresponding obligation on the national courts of the EEA EFTA states to turn to the EFTA Court.

Despite the clear wording of Article 34 SCA, the Court has recently embarked upon a highly controversial attempt to deduce an obligation to refer unresolved questions of EEA law to it from other sources of EEA law – first and foremost the general duty of loyal cooperation under Article 3 EEA; reasons of reciprocity with regard to judicial protection of rights in the European Union and in the EFTA-pillar of the EEA and the principle of access to justice enshrined in Article 6 § 1 of the European Convention on Human Rights (ECHR).[62] The campaign is understandable in light of

[60] Case E-2/02, *Technologien Bau- und Wirtschaftsberatung GmbH and Bellona Foundation v. EFTA Surveillance Authority* [2003] EFTA Court Report 52.

[61] In some cases decided after *Bellona*, the Court appeared a little more generous than the ECJ in the concrete application of the criteria for granting other persons than the addressees of a decision standing. However, this approach was left in Case E-5/07, *Private Barnehagers Landsforbund v. EFTA Surveillance Authority* [2008] EFTA Court Report 61. For a recent example in line with ECJ case law, see Case E-8/13, *Abelia v. EFTA Surveillance Authority* [2014] EFTA Court Report 638.

[62] See Case E-18/11, *Irish Bank* [2012] EFTA Court Report 592, paras. 58 ff.; Case E-3/12, *Jonsson* [2013] EFTA Court Report 136, para. 60; Case E-11/12, *Koch* [2013] EFTA Court Report 272, para. 117 and Case E-02/12 INT, *HOB-vín ehf.* [2013] EFTA Court Report 816, para. 11.

the disturbingly low number of references under Article 34 SCA,[63] but the legal reasoning behind may be questioned.[64] In a speech on the occasion of the EFTA Court's twentieth anniversary, the Chief Justice of Norway simply stated that he did not agree with those advocating the view that national courts of last instance have an obligation to refer unresolved questions on EEA law to the EFTA Court and that it would be very difficult – 'to put it mildly' – for Norwegian courts to disregard the political and constitutional considerations that lie behind the clear wording of Article 34 SCA.[65]

Turning to the statistics, it seems clear that the highest courts of the EEA EFTA states are reluctant to refer cases to the EFTA Court.[66] Twenty-three years on, the Supreme Court of Norway has only used Article 34 SCA on six occasions. What is more, before the much welcomed referral in 2015 the *Holship* case,[67] a period of more than twelve (!) years elapsed without any questions being sent to the EFTA Court. It is too early to tell whether the *Holship* referral sets a more cooperative tone from the Supreme Court of Norway, but an affirmative answer may be suggested by the fact that it was followed up by two referrals in 2016, first in the *Ski Taxi case*, then in the *Thue case*.[68] The Supreme Court of Iceland is only a little better at a total of eight referrals, but five of these have come in the last couple of years, suggesting a positive trend in the relationship between the justices in Reykjavik and the EFTA Court. Hopefully, a similar development is unfolding in Liechtenstein, as the principality's Constitutional Court referred its two first cases to the EFTA Court in 2013, and the Supreme Court followed up with its two first referrals in the autumn of 2015. The highest administrative court of the principality has long proven more cooperative with a total of seven referrals.

If the lower courts are included in the statistics, the total numbers of referrals under Article 34 SCA are fifty-seven from Norway, thirty-six from

63 See further below.

64 See, e.g., N. Fenger and M. Broberg, *Preliminary References to the European Court of Justice*, 2nd ed. (Oxford: Oxford University Press, 2014), p. 11, describing the case for an obligation on the highest courts of the EEA EFTA states to refer unresolved questions of EEA law to the EFTA Court as 'irreconcilable with the clear wording of Article 34 SCA and the deliberate intention of the EFTA States not to copy Article 267 TFEU in full'.

65 Speech delivered by (then) Chief Justice Schei in Luxembourg on 20 June 2014. The speech may be found at the homepage of the Supreme Court of Norway www.domstol.no/hoyesterett/ (last visited on 29 September 2017).

66 Source for the following numbers: The EFTA Court's homepage www.eftacourt.int.

67 Case E-14/15, *Holship Norge* [2016] EFTA Court Report 238.

68 Case E-03/16, *Ski Taxi and Follo Taxi*, [2016] EFTA Court Report 1000 and Case E-19/16, Thue [request received on 14 December 2016] (pending).

Iceland and twenty-five from Liechtenstein. In stark contrast, the courts of the former EEA EFTA state Austria (with a population of about 8 million) contributed with more than 500 cases to the ECJ in the same period of time.[69]

As suggested by these numbers and as confirmed by recent surveys from both Iceland and Norway, there are a substantial number of EEA-related disputes before the national courts that are never referred to the EFTA Court.[70] Possible reasons for this will be discussed in section 7. For the purpose of this section, the point is that Article 34 SCA neither in law nor in fact provides private parties with a right to access to the EFTA Court.

In cases that are referred to the EFTA Court, Article 97 (1) of the Court's Rules of Procedure makes sure that the parties to the dispute before the national court may take part in the proceedings before the EFTA Court. However, as Article 34 SCA establishes a special means of judicial cooperation between the EFTA Court and national courts, the parties to the proceedings before the national court are not considered as parties to the proceedings before the EFTA Court.

A final possibility for individuals to take part in proceedings before the EFTA Court lies in the right of 'any person establishing an interest in the result of any case submitted to the Court' to intervene in support of one of the parties (Article 20 of the Statute). However, there are important exemptions for cases between EFTA states as well as for cases between an EFTA state and the EFTA Surveillance Authority.

Apart from the possibilities set out earlier, the procedural framework for the EFTA Court does not give third parties any right to take part in the proceedings. On the other hand, the Court itself may at any time entrust any individual, body, authority, committee or other organization it chooses with the task of giving an expert opinion.[71]

3.4 Transparency

As to the transparency, Article 27 of the Statute states that hearing in court shall be public. The EFTA Court may, of its own motion or on application by the parties, decide otherwise for 'serious reasons', but in

69 Source: The ECJ's homepage www.curia.europa.eu.

70 Cf., e.g., P. Hreinsson, 'The Interaction between Icelandic Courts and the EFTA Court' and H. H. Fredriksen, 'The two EEA Courts – a Norwegian perspective', both in EFTA Court (ed.), *Judicial Protection in the European Economic Area* (Stuttgart: German Law Publishers, 2012).

71 Article 22 of the Court's Statute.

twenty-two years this exception has never been used. In cases involving individuals, the right to a public hearing may also be derived from Article 6 ECHR.

On the other hand, Article 30 of the Statute states that the deliberations of the Court 'shall be and shall remain secret'. Thus, as in the ECJ, no dissenting opinions can be made public. To Nordic lawyers in particular, this is very unfamiliar and a frequent source of criticism against the EFTA Court (as well as against the ECJ). The reason why the EFTA states nonetheless adopted the secrecy of the ECJ probably lies in the fact that it appears to be in accordance with the judicial traditions of three of the EFTA states at the time of the EEA negotiations (Austria, Liechtenstein and Switzerland). Interestingly, the secrecy has more recently been criticised by the Court's own president.[72] As mentioned in section 2 earlier, however, the introduction of dissenting opinions presupposes the abolishment of the current possibility to reappoint retiring judges. Further, the EEA EFTA states ought to consider the EFTA Court's proposal for an extended court of five judges as part of any such reform, thereby preventing potential damage to the Court's authority brought about by public display of narrow 2:1 decisions in politically sensitive cases.[73]

As to the transparency of the judicial reasoning of the EFTA Court, Article 32 of the Statute provides that the Court's judgements shall state the reasons on which they are based. Again, this provision is taken over from the ECJ's Statute, but through its practice the EFTA Court has adopted a judicial style that differs somewhat from that of the ECJ. Compared with the often quite brief and cryptic reasons offered by the ECJ, the decisions of the EFTA Court generally appear more argumentative and thus informative. A possible reason for this is the fact that none of the former or current judges of the EFTA Court hail from countries whose legal culture have been influenced by the postulating style of the French courts, even though it certainly also helps that there are only three judges and that the limited caseload leaves them with much more time to prepare their judgements. The EFTA Court's weaker

[72] Baudenbacher, *The EFTA Court in Action*, p. 7: 'In my view, the system is outdated and should be changed.'

[73] Prior to the judgement of the EFTA Court in the case of the Norwegian state-controlled monopoly on gaming machines (Case E-1/06, *EFTA Surveillance Authority v. Norway* [2007] EFTA Court Report 7) there were speculations in the Norwegian press as to the democratic legitimacy of a possible 2:1 decision against the vote of the Norwegian judge.

position vis-à-vis the national courts of the EEA EFTA states and its striving for recognition from the ECJ may also play a part – the authority of the EFTA Court is first and foremost of a persuasive character (see section 7). Regardless of the underlying reasons, the result is a more argumentative and open judicial style, with numerous references not only to the Court's own case law, but also to that of the ECJ, the General Court of the European Union and the European Court of Human Rights. Further, the EFTA Court has on a number of occasions cited Opinions of the ECJ's Advocates General[74] and, more recently, even some judgements from national courts as well as academic writing.[75]

A further element that distinguishes the EFTA Court from the ECJ is the fact that the *judge rapporteur* in charge of a case still prepares a comprehensive *Report for the Hearing*, in which the arguments of the parties and other participants to the proceedings are set out in detail. For reasons of workload of its judges and the time and costs related to translations, the ECJ limited and then gave up on this practice several years ago.[76] As the EFTA Court is not faced with similar problems, it continues to prepare and make public Reports for the Hearing in all substantial cases. To the parties and other participants to the proceedings, the report offers a possibility to assure themselves as they prepare for the oral hearing that their written arguments have been properly understood by the judge rapporteur. To outsiders, the report is a valuable source of information into the proceedings before the Court.

On the other hand, the lack of an Advocate General means that both the EFTA Court and its outside observers have to do without the analytical and often very thorough submissions that are offered by the Advocates General of the ECJ.

On balance, therefore, the transparency of the judicial reasoning of the EFTA Court is hardly much better than that of the ECJ.

[74] One recent example is to be found in Case E-15/10, *Posten Norge v. EFTA Surveillance Authority* [2012] EFTA Court Report 246, para. 88.

[75] References to national case law are to be found in Case E-11/12, *Koch* [2013] EFTA Court Report 272, para. 77 (a judgement from the German Bundesgerichtshof) and in Case E-7/13, *Creditinfo Lánstraust* [2013] EFTA Court Report 970, para. 48 (a judgement from the Supreme Court of Norway). References to academic writings are found in Case E-16/11, *EFTA Surveillance Authority v. Iceland ('Icesave')* [2013] EFTA Court Report 4, para. 167 and Case E-3/12, *Jonsson* [2013] EFTA Court Report 136, para. 56.

[76] See, e.g., A. Alemanno and O. Stefan, 'Openness at the Court of Justice of the European Union: Toppling a taboo', *Common Market Law Review*, 51 (2014), 97–139 at 130.

4 Fact-Finding

The rules on fact-finding in cases before the EFTA Court mirror those that apply to cases before the ECJ. As the process of fact-finding can be determinative for the outcome of a dispute, any other solution would threaten to undermine the objective of a homogeneous European Economic Area with equal conditions of competition and respect of the same rules (Article 1 EEA).

In cases referred to it by national courts under Article 34 SCA, the jurisdiction of the EFTA Court is limited to express itself upon the interpretation of the EEA rules in question.[77] Thus, the assessment of the facts in these cases is a matter for the national courts. For this reason, the EFTA Court will, as a point of departure, base itself upon the referring court's presentation of the facts of the case. Still, just as with the ECJ, the EFTA Court's Rules of Procedure allow it to admit evidence during a preliminary procedure. Hence, both the parties to the main proceedings and other participants to the proceedings before the EFTA Court may introduce facts not mentioned by the national court. Indeed, in its 'Notes for the Guidance of Counsel' the EFTA Court invites those participating in preliminary proceedings to bring to its attention 'the factual circumstances of the case before the national court'.[78] Just like the ECJ, the EFTA Court may supplement – and in very special circumstances even correct – the understanding of the facts expressed by the national court in order to provide an answer to the questions asked that it believes to be truly helpful for the resolution of the dispute before the national court. Still, the EFTA Court does not have the authority to decide the facts in the main proceedings with binding effect for the national court. Usually, the EFTA Court will note this explicitly, as it did in the *Philip Morris* case concerning the Norwegian prohibition on the visual display of tobacco products: 'it is for the national court to ascertain the facts which have given rise to the dispute and to establish the consequences that they have for the judgment which it is required to deliver.'[79]

In all other cases before it, the assessment of the facts is a matter for the EFTA Court. In short, the Court follows the general rule that a party

[77] For a thorough analysis of ECJ case law concerning the similar limitation of its jurisdiction under Article 267 TFEU, see Broberg and Fenger, *Preliminary References to the European Court of Justice*, pp. 362–72.

[78] Notes for the guidance of Counsel in written and oral proceedings before the EFTA Court, point B.10. The notes are available at the EFTA Court's homepage www.eftacourt.int.

[79] Case E-16/10, *Philip Morris* [2011] EFTA Court Report 330, para. 87.

who asserts a claim, be it the EFTA Surveillance Authority, an EEA EFTA State or an individual, must prove the matters that it asserts, whereas the defendant must establish the facts that disprove it in whole or in part. It is essentially for the parties to produce the evidence required to prove their case, but Article 21 (1) of the Court's Statute states that the Court may require the parties to produce all documents and to supply all information that it considers desirable.[80] Further, the Court may always require the EEA EFTA states (but not the EU-institutions or the EU member states) to supply all information that the Court considers necessary for the proceedings (Article 21 (2)).[81]

As to the standard of proof required, the EFTA Court has never elaborated upon this in general. However, the principle of homogeneity between EEA and EU law strongly suggests that the general requirement is the same as before the ECJ. Thus, much to the surprise of Norwegian lawyers, mere probability will not suffice – following the civil law tradition, the ECJ and the EFTA Court will have to be convinced by the evidence provided.[82] In practice, however, the standard of proof is often adjusted to fit the characteristics of a case. This is particularly evident in cases concerning national measures that restrict the free movement of goods, persons, services or capital within the EEA ('the four freedoms').[83] It is settled case law from both the ECJ and the EFTA Court that it is for the EEA states to show in each individual case that such a measure is appropriate for securing the attainment of a legitimate objective and does not go beyond what is necessary to attain it. In general, the EEA states are required to substantiate their arguments by 'specific evidence'.[84] However, in certain cases – in particular cases characterised by moral, religious or cultural factors or in cases where the precautionary principle applies – the standard of proof is lowered. An illustrative example of the former category from the EFTA Court is the high-profile case concerning the Norwegian monopoly on gaming machines, where the EFTA Court stated that moral concerns related to gambling served to justify a margin of discretion for the national authorities and where Norway was

[80] Cf. Article 24 (1) of the ECJ's Statute. [81] Cf. Article 24 (2) of the ECJ's Statute.

[82] Concerning the ECJ, see, e.g., K. Andová, 'Beweisrecht' in H.-W. Rengeling, A. Middeke, and M. Gellermann (eds.), *Handbuch des Rechtsschutzes in der Europäischen Union* 3rd ed. (Munich: Beck Verlag, 2014), § 24, para. 38.

[83] See, e.g., N. N. Shuibhne and M. Maci, 'Proving public interest: The growing impact of evidence in free movement case law', *Common Market Law Review*, 50 (2013), 965–1005.

[84] For a recent example from the ECJ, see Case C-379/11, *Caves Krier Fréres*, ECR not yet reported; [2013] 2 CMLR 14, para. 43.

acquitted because it was 'plausible to assume' that the state could more easily control and direct a wholly state-owned operator than private operators.[85] An example concerning the precautionary principle is the aforementioned *Philip Morris* case, where the EFTA Court stated that where there is uncertainty as to the existence or extent of risks to human health, 'an EEA State should be able to take protective measures without having to wait until the reality of those risks becomes fully apparent'.[86] Thus, it was sufficient for Norwegian authorities to demonstrate that it was 'reasonable to assume that the measure would be able to contribute to the protection of human health'.[87]

Another area of EU and EEA law where questions concerning proof are difficult and somewhat controversial is competition law. This is partly due to the fact that individual undertakings are involved, who regularly will invoke the guarantees enshrined in Article 6 ECHR, but also to the fact that competition law cases often involve highly complex economic assessments. The EFTA Court got an opportunity to elaborate upon this in the *Posten Norge* case from 2012.[88] Following a recent judgement from the European Court of Human Rights,[89] the EFTA Court essentially abandoned the 'manifest error' standard previously applied by the ECJ: Although the EFTA Court acknowledged that it may not replace the assessment of the EFTA Surveillance Authority by its own and, accordingly, that it does not affect the legality of latter's assessment if the Court merely disagrees with the weighing of individual factors in a complex assessment of economic evidence, the Court stated that it nonetheless had to be 'convinced that the conclusions drawn by ESA are supported by the facts'. The judgement has been hailed as a 'milestone judgment' by competition law experts who hope that it will encourage the ECJ to follow suit.[90]

[85] Case E-1/06, *EFTA Surveillance Authority v.* Norway [2007] EFTA Court Report 8, paras. 29 and 51.

[86] Case E-16/10, *Philip Morris* [2011] EFTA Court Report 330, para. 82.

[87] Ibid., para. 83.

[88] Case E-15/10, *Posten Norge v. EFTA Surveillance Authority* [2012] EFTA Court Report 246, paras. 84–102.

[89] European Court of Human Rights [Grand Chamber], judgement of 27 September 2011 in Case no 43509/08, *A. Menarini Diagnostics S.R.L. v. Italy*.

[90] See E. B. de la Serre, 'Standard of review in competition law case: *Posten Norge* and beyond' in EFTA Court (ed.), *The EEA and the EFTA Court – Decentred Integration* (Oxford: Hart Publishing, 2014), pp. 415–31.

5 Interpretative Approaches

5.1 *General*

In short, the interpretative methodology followed by the EFTA Court is that which the ECJ applies when it interprets EU law. Even though there is no denial that the EEA Agreement is an agreement under public international law, there is not a single reference to the 1969 Vienna Convention on the Law of Treaties to be found in the case law of the EFTA Court. This is certainly no coincidence. According to its president, the EFTA Court has not wished to be limited by what he sees as the Vienna Convention's 'conservative' components.[91] In an illustrative case from 2007 where the Liechtenstein government referred to the Vienna Convention and the general rules of public international law in an attempt to justify an interpretation of EEA law that differed from the ECJ's interpretation of the same rules in the EU law setting, the EFTA Court simply replied that it could not, in its interpretation of the EEA Agreement, be bound 'by mere expectations of the Contracting Parties as to the exact content of the obligations the Parties enter into'.[92]

As far as EEA rules taken over from EU law are concerned, the adoption of the ECJ's methodology is a direct consequence of the objective to integrate the EEA EFTA states into the EU internal market. During the EEA negotiations, the Contracting Parties were very much aware of the *Polydor* judgement, in which the ECJ interpreted the provisions of the free-trade agreement between the EC and the then EFTA state Portugal differently from the virtually identically worded provisions in the EC Treaty, with justification in the different aims of the two instruments.[93] In order to prevent this, Article 6 EEA states that the provisions of the Agreement, insofar as they are identical in substance to corresponding rules of EU law, shall be interpreted in conformity with the relevant rulings of the ECJ given prior to the date of signature of the Agreement (2 May 1992). Even if the EFTA states were not prepared to extend this obligation to encompass future case law from the ECJ, the Preamble of

[91] C. Baudenbacher, 'Der Beitrag des EFTA-Gerichtshofs zur Schaffung eines dynamischen und homogenen EWR' in T. Bruha et al. (eds.), *Liechtenstein – 10 Jahre im EWR* (Vaduz: Verlag der Liechtensteinischen Akademischen Gesellschaft 2005), pp. 32–5. It may be objected that the Vienna Convention hardly constrains dynamic interpretation of an international agreement as long as the agreement's object and purpose calls for such interpretation, but this is not the proper occasion on which to pursue this argument.

[92] Case E-5/06, *ESA v. Liechtenstein* [2007] EFTA Court Report 296, para. 63.

[93] Cases 270/80, *Polydor* [1982] ECR 329; [1982] 1 CMLR 677.

the EEA Agreement makes clear that the objective of the Contracting Parties is to arrive at, and maintain, a uniform interpretation and application of EEA law and the EEA-relevant parts of EU law. The EEA EFTA states followed up on this in Article 3(2) SCA, which obliges the EFTA Court (and the EFTA Surveillance Authority) to pay 'due account' to subsequent case law of the ECJ. Thus, the legitimacy of the EFTA Court's adoption of the ECJ's methodology seems beyond doubt in cases concerning the interpretation of the common EU/EEA rules of the internal market.[94]

5.2 *Dynamic Interpretation I: The Effect of EEA Law*

Far more controversial is the fact that the EFTA Court has extended its use of the ECJ's methodology to other parts of EEA law as well. This is particularly true for the Court's decisions on the legal effect of EEA law in the national legal orders of the dualist EFTA states (now only Iceland and Norway). It was only by applying the ECJ's distinctly teleological (or perhaps even 'constitutional') methodology that the EFTA Court was able, in the seminal *Sveinbjörnsdóttir* case from 1998, to deduce an unwritten principle of state liability for breach of EEA obligations from the object and purpose of the EEA Agreement, essentially mirroring the (in)famous *Francovich* ruling from the ECJ.[95] Unfettered by the lack of any express provision establishing a basis for state liability in the Agreement as well as the fierce opposition from the dualist EFTA states, the EFTA Court deduced an obligation to provide for compensation for loss and damage caused to individuals by breaches of the obligations under the EEA Agreement from the purposes and legal structure of the Agreement, in particular the Agreement's overarching objective of a homogeneous EEA with 'equal conditions of competition, and the respect of the same rules' (Article 1 EEA). In a striking parallel to the ECJ's characterisation of the EEC Treaty in the seminal judgement in *van Gend en Loos*, the EFTA Court declared the EEA Agreement to be an international treaty *sui generis*, which contains 'a distinct legal order of its own'.[96] Still, the EFTA Court cleverly avoided a claim of direct effect by acknowledging that the

[94] As a result, the EFTA Court's approach to the interface between trade and other areas of EEA law, such as the environment and human rights, mirrors the approach taken by the ECJ within the context of EU law. The same applies to the EFTA Court's approach with respect to domestic regulatory margin, included in sensitive policy fields.

[95] Case E-9/97, *Sveinbjörnsdóttir* [1998] EFTA Court Report 95.

[96] Para. 59.

principle of state liability might have to be made part of the national legal orders of the EEA EFTA states. Knowing that the main part of the Agreement had been implemented as such by the remaining dualist EEA EFTA states (Iceland and Norway), the Court noted that the principle of state liability was to be seen as an integral part of the EEA Agreement as such and that it was therefore 'natural to interpret national legislation implementing the main part of the Agreement as also comprising the principle of State liability'.[97]

To the dualist EEA EFTA states, *Sveinbjörnsdóttir* was a bitter pill. Practitioners and academics alike questioned both the conclusion reached and the underlying methodological approach.[98] When the question of EEA state liability resurfaced in the *Karlsson* case from 2002, the Norwegian government urged the EFTA Court to overrule *Sveinbjörnsdóttir.*[99] By then, however, *Sveinbjörnsdóttir* had been accepted by the Supreme Court of Iceland[100] and endorsed by the ECJ through an invaluable *dictum* in *Rechberger.*[101] It was thus hardly surprising that the EFTA Court stood its ground.[102] Later on, the Norwegian government gave in and accepted the existence of the principle when the question was raised before the national courts in the *Finanger II* case. In its final judgement in the case in 2005, the Norwegian Supreme Court followed suit and declared the EFTA Court's reasons for state liability to be 'convincing'.[103] The view that the EEA Agreement includes an unwritten principle of state liability has since also been accepted by the Liechtenstein courts,[104] leading to the conclusion that one may now speak of a well-established principle of EEA law.

From a methodological perspective, the essence of *Sveinbjörnsdóttir* is that the EFTA Court applied the fact that the EEA Agreement as such

[97] Para. 63. This interpretation of national law was subsequently accepted by both the Icelandic and the Norwegian Supreme Court.

[98] See, e.g., several of the contributions in *Forhandlingene ved Det 35 nordiske juristmøtet* [Proceedings of the 35th Nordic Law Conference] (Oslo, Det norske lokalstyret, 1999), pp. 977–1011.

[99] See the arguments of the Norwegian Government in Case E-4/01, *Karlsson* [2002] EFTA Court Report 240 (summarised at length in the Report for the Hearing).

[100] In its judgement of 16 December 1999 in Case 236/1999, *Iceland v. Sveinbjörnsdóttir.*

[101] Case C-140/97, *Rechberger,* [1999] ECR I-3499; [2000] 2 CMLR 1 para. 39.

[102] Case E-04/01, *Karlsson* [2002] EFTA Court Report 240, paras. 25–30.

[103] Judgement of 28 October 2005 in Case 2005/412 (Rt 2005 p 1365), *Finanger v. Norway,* para. 52.

[104] Judgement of the Supreme Court of Liechtenstein of 7 May 2010 in Case CO.2004.2, *Dr. Tschannet v. Liechtenstein.*

confers rights on individuals[105] and the fact that Article 3 EEA reproduces almost verbatim the loyalty clause of the EU Treaties (now found in Article 4(3) TEU) to support a *functional* (or *effect-related*) conception of the homogeneity objective: the objective of homogeneity does, *as a matter of a legal principle* (not only as a political goal), embrace the question of the effect of EEA law in the legal orders of the Contracting Parties. In doing so, the EFTA Court dismissed the understanding of the dualist EFTA states that the reach of the homogeneity principle was limited to the interpretation of the substantive content of the internal market *acquis*, leaving it to the Contracting Parties to secure the effect of the rules through national procedures. This functional conception of homogeneity has consequences far beyond the question of state liability, as it establishes *a general presumption for judicial protection of EEA-based rights, which, in effect, equals the protection offered in EU law.*[106] One such consequence is the EEA-based duty of national courts to do whatever lies within their competence to interpret and apply national law in conformity to obligations under the EEA Agreement;[107] another is the EEA-based duty of administrative authorities to do likewise;[108] a third is the EEA-based obligation to repay charges levied in breach of EEA law[109] and a fourth is what the EFTA Court more recently has described as the procedural branch of homogeneity.[110] At the same time, however, the EFTA Court acknowledged the limits of its dynamic approach to questions of the legal effect of EEA law when it held that the rather clear wording of Article 7 EEA and Protocol 35 EEA hinders the deduction of an unwritten EEA law principle of direct effect equalling that which exists under EU law.[111] It remains to be seen if the EFTA Court will

[105] See the fourth and eighth recitals of the Preamble.

[106] For a more comprehensive argument for this conception of the homogeneity objective, see H. H. Fredriksen, 'State liability in EU and EEA law: The same or different?' *European Law Review*, 38 (2013), 884–95, at 885–8.

[107] See Case E-1/07, *Criminal proceedings against A* [2007] EFTA Court Report 246, para. 39; Case E-15/12, *Wahl* [2013] EFTA Court Report 534, para. 54; Case E-6/13, *Metacom* [2013] EFTA Court Report 856, para. 69; Case E-7/13, *Creditinfo Lánstraust* [2013] EFTA Court Report 970, para. 47 and Case E-3/15, *Liechtensteinische Gesellschaft für Umweltschutz*, [2015] EFTA Court Report 512, para. 74.

[108] See Case E-1/04, *Fokus Bank* [2004] EFTA Court Report 11, para. 41.

[109] See Case E-7/13, *Creditinfo Lánstraust* [2013] EFTA Court Report 970, para. 43.

[110] See, e.g., Case E-14/11, *DB Schenker (No 1)* [2012] EFTA Court Report 1178, para. 77.

[111] See Case E-4/01, *Karlsson* [2002] EFTA Court Report 240, para. 28; Case E-1/07, *Criminal proceedings against A* [2007] EFTA Court Report 245, para. 40; Case E-2/10, *Kolbeinsson* [2009–2010] EFTA Court Report 234, para. 81; Case E-18/11, *Irish Bank*, [2012] EFTA Court Report 592, para. 121; Case E-15/14, *EFTA Surveillance Authority v.*

attempt to remedy this through the imposition of strict liability in cases where the lack of EU-style direct effect is a sine qua non for the loss suffered by an individual. The Court has not yet had the opportunity to express itself on the matter, but the by now well-established functional conception of homogeneity does suggest an answer in the affirmative.[112]

Looking back at the heated discussion in the wake of *Sveinbjörnsdóttir*, it can be argued that the opposition in the end proved beneficial to the EFTA Court as it only accentuated the court's achievement: it allowed the EFTA Court to demonstrate its independence of the EFTA states and its commitment to secure judicial protection of EEA-based rights, which equals the protection offered in EU law, if need be through a rather dynamic interpretation of the Agreement. From the perspective of the EU in general, and the ECJ in particular, the result has been increased trust in the credibility of the solution with an independent court of justice for the EFTA-pillar and thus in the viability of the EEA-project at the whole.[113] The assessment of the EFTA Court's president is telling: Without *Sveinbjörnsdóttir* and the deduction of an unwritten principle of state liability, 'the EEA Agreement and the EFTA Court would never have taken off'.[114]

5.3 *Dynamic Interpretation II: Bridging the Widening Gap between EU and EEA Law*

With the 'effect issue' largely settled, the most contentious issue concerning the interpretation of the EEA Agreement relates to the so-called widening gap between the main part of the EEA Agreement and the

Iceland, [2015] EFTA Court Report 40, para. 32 and Case E-3/15, *Liechtensteinische Gesellschaft für Umweltschutz* [2015] EFTA Court Report 512, para. 71. This is in line with the view of the ECJ in Opinion 1/91, *EEA I*, [1991] ECR I-6079; [1992] 1 CMLR 245, paras. 27–8 and of the Supreme Court of Norway in Rt. 2000 p. 1811 *Storebrand v. Finanger*.

112 See further on this, see H. H. Fredriksen, 'State liability in EU and EEA law: The same or different?' 884–95.

113 See, e.g., the very positive assessment of the EFTA Court delivered by the president of the ECJ on the occasion of the twentieth anniversary of the EEA Agreement: V. Skouris 'The role of the Court of Justice of the European Union in the development of the EEA single market' in: EFTA Court (ed.), *The EEA and the EFTA Court – Decentred Integration* (Oxford: Hart Publishing, 2014), pp. 3–12.

114 C. Baudenbacher, 'If not EEA state liability, then what? Reflections ten years after the EFTA Court's *Sveinbjörnsdóttir* ruling', *Chicago Journal of International Law*, 10 (2009), 333–58, at 358.

EU treaties. The root of the problem lies in the unfortunate fact that the EEA Agreement's main part has not been updated since the date of its signature (2 May 1992). Thus, the subsequent amendments to the EU treaties accomplished through the Treaties of Maastricht (1992), Amsterdam (1997), Nice (2001) and Lisbon (2007) are not reflected in the EEA Agreement. Unwilling to begin the strenuous work of updating the main part of the Agreement,[115] the Contracting Parties have long placed their trust in the ability of the EFTA Court to bridge the gap by interpreting EEA law in light of subsequent changes in the EU treaties. So far, the EFTA Court has, by and large, managed to maintain homogeneity between EU and EEA law, but sometimes only after engaging in rather creative interpretation of the EEA Agreement.

A telling example is the *LO* case, in which the ECJ's judgement in *Albany* was central.[116] In its assessment of whether collective agreements are exempt from the prohibition on cartels in Article 101 TFEU, the ECJ had included a number of provisions concerning the EU's social and labour market policy that were added by the Treaty of Maastricht, and therefore not mirrored in the main part of the EEA Agreement.[117] However, with reference to the goal of homogeneity and some rather vague statements in the preamble to the EEA Agreement and Part V Chapter 1 on social policy, the EFTA Court concluded that the social policy considerations that limited the application of Article 101 TFEU had a sufficient basis in the EEA Agreement to limit the application of Article 53 EEA in a corresponding manner.

More recent examples include *DB Schenker (No 1)* and *Deveci*, in both of which the EFTA Court managed to maintain homogeneity between EU and EEA law, despite the fact that the EU Charter of fundamental rights has not been made part of the EEA Agreement.[118] Particularly interesting from a methodological perspective is *DB Schenker (No 1)*, where the EFTA Court overcame the lack of an EEA parallel to Article 42

[115] Unlike the annexes and (most of) the protocols, the main part of the EEA Agreement can only be updated through the ordinary process of treaty amendment, involving all of the current thirty-two Contracting Parties (i.e., not only the three EFTA states and the EU, but also the 28 EU member states).

[116] Case E-8/00, *LO* [2002] EFTA Court Report 114.

[117] Case C-67/96, *Albany*, [1999] ECR I-5751; [2000] 4 CMLR 446, paras. 53–60.

[118] Case E-14/11, *Schenker (No 1)* [2012] EFTA Court Report 1179 and Case E-10/14, *Deveci* [2014] EFTA Court Report 1364. See further on this, see H. H. Fredriksen and C. N. K. Franklin, 'Of pragmatism and principles: The EEA Agreement 20 years on', *Common Market Law Review*, 52 (2015), 629–84 at 635 ff.

of the EU Charter of fundamental rights by holding that a right of access to documents of the EFTA Surveillance Authority had to be seen as 'an embodiment of the principles of transparency and good administration common to, and fostered by, the democratic traditions of the EEA/EFTA States'.[119] As EU law lawyers will recognise, there is a striking parallel here to the reasoning invoked by the ECJ when deducing general principles of EU law from the constitutional traditions common to the EU member states. A similar approach was taken in *Deveci* when the adoption of the ECJ's (controversial) interpretation of Article 16 of the EU Charter of fundamental rights on the freedom to conduct a business was justified with the argument that the freedom to conduct a business lies 'at the heart of the EEA Agreement and must be recognized in accordance with EEA law and national law and practices'.[120]

Unsurprisingly, the legitimacy of this judicial bridging of the widening gap between EU and EEA law has attracted attention from academic quarters. Whereas some commentators highlight the problematic aspects of letting treaty amendments in the European Union alone impact upon the interpretation of the EEA Agreement,[121] others point out that the Contracting Parties clearly wish for EEA Agreement to continue to deliver on its promise to integrate the EEA EFTA states into the EU internal market. In the opinion of the EFTA Court's president, the fact that the lack of an up-date of the main part of the Agreement is due to practical reasons alone, suggests that traditional perceptions of the division of competences between courts and legislatures are of little relevance ('weitgehend irrelevant') in the EEA context.[122] On this view, judicial bridging of the widening gap between the EU treaties and the unchanged main part of the EEA Agreement is justified by reference to the overarching object of the EEA Agreement and the presumed will of the Contracting Parties. However, according to the EFTA Court's

[119] Case E-14/11, *Schenker (No 1)* [2012] EFTA Court Report 1179, para. 118.

[120] Case E-10/14, *Deveci* [2014] EFTA Court Report 1364, para. 64.

[121] See N. Fenger 'Limits to a dynamic homogeneity between EC law and EEA law' in N. Fenger, K. Hagel-Sørensen, and B. Vesterdorf (eds.), *Festschrift Claus Gulmann* (Forlaget Thomson, 2006), 131–54; H. H. Fredriksen, 'Bridging the widening gap between the EU treaties and the Agreement on the European Economic Area', *European Law Journal*, 18 (2012), 868–86 and Graver, 'Mission impossible', 73–90.

[122] C. Baudenbacher, 'Der EFTA Gerichtshof, das EWR-Abkommen und die Fortentwicklungen des EG-Vertrages' in P. Monauni (ed.), *Liechtensteinisches Stiftungs- und Verfassungsrecht im Umbruch – Festschrift für Herbert Batliner* (Vaduz: ExJure Verlagsgesellschaft, 2004), p. 106.

president, the ultimate proof of the legitimacy of the EFTA Court's approach lies in the subsequent acceptance of its judgements by the Contracting Parties ('Konzept der Akzeptanz').[123]

To this, it has been objected that the objective of homogeneity has to be balanced against the EFTA states' equally clear intention that the EEA Agreement should not entail the transfer of legislative authority or other waiving of sovereignty and that the principle of legal certainty has to be added to the equation, at least in cases where dynamic interpretation of EEA law would impact negatively on the EEA-based rights of individuals.[124] Still, the EFTA Court is probably right in assuming that the Contracting Parties want it to do its outmost to preserve homogeneity between EU law and EEA law.

Unless the Contracting Parties take up their responsibility as masters of the EEA Agreement and bridge the widening gap between EU and EEA law, the EFTA Court will in the coming years be faced with an increasing number of cases that will test the limits to the dynamic homogeneity between EU law and EEA law.

5.4 *Dynamic Interpretation III: EU Citizenship*

In the last couple of years, the most controversial decisions from the EFTA Court concern the Citizenship Directive (Directive 2004/38/EC) and the EU law concept of Union Citizenship (Article 20 ff. TFEU). The explanation lies in the fact that at least two of the three EEA EFTA states (Iceland and Liechtenstein) originally rejected the EEA-relevance of the directive and only accepted its incorporation into the Agreement after considerable political pressure from the European Union.[125] By way of a compromise, the European Union accepted a Joint Declaration that makes clear that the concept of Union Citizenship as such has no equivalent in the EEA Agreement.[126] This declaration sets the interpretation of the Citizenship Directive apart from other cases concerning the widening gap between European Union and EEA law – in the context of Union Citizenship, certain divergences between European Union and EEA law are acknowledged and intended. It leaves the EFTA Court with

[123] Ibid. [124] See the literature referred to in footnote 112 above.

[125] See in detail J. Jonsdottir, *Europeanization and the European Economic Area* (London: Routledge, 2014), pp. 107–8.

[126] Joint Declaration by the Contracting Parties to Decision No. 158/2007 incorporating Directive 2004/38/EC into the EEA Agreement.

the very difficult task to interpret the Citizenship Directive in a legal context where the concept of Union citizenship is lacking.

The difficulty of the EFTA Court's job was firmly demonstrated through the *Gunnarsson* case from 2014 and the *Jabbi* case from 2016.[127] In both cases the EFTA Court was confronted with the question of whether Article 7 of the Citizenship Directive imposes obligations on the *home state* of an EEA EFTA state national. The wording of the provisions suggests an answer in the negative – it only expressly imposed obligations on *other EEA states* where the national in question is residing (i.e., the *host state*). The ECJ had nevertheless imposed obligations on home states not to hinder their own nationals from exercising their rights to free movement throughout the European Union, but it had done so on the basis of Article 21 TFEU – not on the basis of the Directive.[128] Before the EFTA Court, all of the three EEA EFTA states argued that there was no legal basis for a more expansive interpretation of the Directive in the context of EEA law.[129] In their view, the principle of homogeneity could not support different interpretation of common rules in an attempt to compensate for the existence of *other EU rules* without any counterparts in EEA law (i.e. Article 21 TFEU). The EFTA Court saw this differently, but without really explaining the broader understanding of the homogeneity principle upon which its dynamic EEA law interpretation of the Citizenship Directive is based. If limited to cases in which it can be reasonably argued that the ECJ would have interpreted the provision in question in a similar way, if this had been necessary to reach an outcome that in the context of EU law was secured by a different route, reasons of reciprocity may perhaps serve to justify the EFTA Court's approach. Still, the Court's critics are unlikely to be convinced. In light of compromise behind the Joint Committee's decision to incorporate the Directive into the EEA Agreement, and the wording of the accompanying Joint Declaration, it is understandable that the EEA EFTA States find it particularly hard to accept the EFTA Court's *analogous application* of the Directive's Article 7 in *Jabbi*.

127 Case E-26/13, *Gunnarsson* [2014] EFTA Court Report 254; and Case E-28/14, *Jabbi*, Advisory Opinion of 26 July 2016. See further on *Gunnarsson* Fredriksen and Franklin, 'Of pragmatism and principles', 638 ff. and C. Burke and Ó. Í. Hannesson, 'Citizenship by the back door? *Gunnarsson*', *Common Market Law Review*, 52 (2015), 1111–33.

128 See, in particular, Case C-456/12, *O. and B.*,[2014] ECR not yet reported.

129 Iceland and Norway in *Gunnarsson* and Norway and Liechtenstein in *Jabbi* (Liechtenstein did not make use of its right to take part in *Gunnarsson* and neither did Iceland in *Jabbi*).

6 Forum Shopping

The relationship between the dispute settlement mechanism under the EEA Agreement and overlapping trade agreements between some or all of the EEA Contracting Parties (the WTO Agreement, the EFTA Convention, the still existing bilateral free trade agreements between each of the EFTA States and the EU, etc.) is not particularly clear. There is no provision in the EEA Agreement or in the SCA equalling that of Article 344 TFEU, which obliges EU member states not to submit disputes concerning the interpretation or application of the Treaties to any method of settlement other than those provided for therein.[130] But neither are there any provision such as, e.g., Article 27 in the 2008 Free Trade Agreement between the EFTA States and Canada, which states that any dispute regarding any matter arising under both that Agreement and the WTO Agreement may be settled in either forum at the discretion of the complaining party.[131]

As far as the EEA EFTA states are concerned, Article 32 SCA states that the EFTA Court shall have jurisdiction in actions concerning the settlement of disputes between them regarding the interpretation or application of the EEA Agreement, the Agreement on a Standing Committee of the EFTA states or the SCA itself. Read together with the loyalty clause of Article 2 SCA, it could be argued that the EFTA states may not submit such disputes to any other method of settlement. It may perhaps even be argued that disputes between the EEA EFTA states regarding matters arising under both the EEA Agreement and other agreements (the EFTA Convention and/or the WTO Agreement) have to be settled in the EFTA Court. However, the fact that the provisions on the EFTA Court in the SCA so clearly are inspired by the provisions of EU law governing the ECJ

130 It follows from ECJ case law that this obligation encompasses disputes arising under other international agreements as long as the subject matter of the case is dealt with in parallel by EU law. See in particular Case C-459/03, *Commission v. Ireland*, [2006] ECR I-4635; [2006] 2 CMLR 59, concerning Ireland's decision to commence arbitral proceedings against the UK pursuant to the UN Convention on the Law of the Sea for environmental harm. The ECJ ruled that by bringing these arbitration proceedings Ireland had violated its obligations to accord the ECJ exclusive jurisdiction in disputes between EU member states in areas covered by the (then) EC Treaty.

131 Similar provisions are found in the other free trade agreements negotiated by the EFTA states in the last two decades ('second generation FTAs'). See, e.g., Article 37 (2) of the 2006 Free Trade Agreement between the EFTA states and the States of the Southern African Customs Union (SACU); Article 8.1 (2) of the 2009 Free Trade Agreement between the EFTA States and the Member States of the Co-operation Council for the Arab States of the Gulf and Article 12.1 (2) of the 2013 Free Trade Agreement between the EFTA States and the Central American States (Costa Rica and Panama).

strongly suggests that the absence of a provision mirroring that of Article 344 TFEU means that the jurisdiction of the EFTA Court is not exclusive. Still, it would be rather odd for the EEA EFTA states to submit EEA-related disputes to another forum. In practice, the EEA EFTA states leave the intra-EFTA enforcement of alleged breaches of EEA obligations to the EFTA Surveillance Authority – in twenty years Article 32 SCA has yet to be used.[132] Thus, the question of forum shopping in disputes between the EEA EFTA states is of a rather theoretical nature.

The same applies to EEA-related disputes handled by the national courts of the EEA EFTA states, even though Article 107 EEA gives the EFTA states the possibility to allow their courts to ask the ECJ to decide on the interpretation of EEA rules.[133] Use of this possibility would apparently allow the national courts of the EFTA state in question to choose whether to refer questions on the interpretation of EEA rules to the EFTA Court under Article 34 SCA or to the ECJ under Article 107 EEA.[134] In Norwegian literature, it has been argued that use of Article 107 EEA would give Norwegian courts access to the court, which actually determines the interpretation of the common rules of the EU/EEA internal market, and that it would enable the Supreme Court in particular to participate directly in the judicial dialogue that drives the evolution of EU/EEA law.[135] However, as a consequence of the ECJ's insistence on the binding effect of its preliminary rulings,[136] none of the EEA EFTA states have made use of this possibility. Even assuming that binding answers from the ECJ would be constitutionally acceptable,[137] the political expenses of giving

[132] This resembles the situation in the EU, where infringement proceedings brought by member states under Article 259 TFEU are few and far between.

[133] The details are found in Protocol 34 on the Possibility of Courts and Tribunals of the EFTA States to Request the Court of Justice of European Communities to decide on the Interpretation of EEA Rules corresponding to EC Rules.

[134] Provided that Article 34 SCA is not amended.

[135] H. H. Fredriksen, 'EØS-rett i norske domstoler [EEA law in Norwegian Courts]', *Europautredningen*, Report commissioned by the Norwegian EEA Review Committee (Oslo, 2011), p. 90.

[136] In the first draft of the EEA Agreement, the ECJ was only to 'express itself' on the interpretation of EEA law in cases referred to it from the courts of the EFTA states. This solution was rejected by the ECJ in Opinion 1/91 because it allegedly would change the nature of the function of the Court, namely that of a court whose judgements are binding. Thus, the wording of Article 107 EEA now ensures that the answers given by the ECJ will be binding.

[137] In Norwegian literature, it is disputed whether use of Article 107 EEA would be compatible with Article 88 of the Norwegian Constitution on the jurisdiction of the Supreme Court.

the 'foreign judges' of the ECJ jurisdiction in national cases are simply too high.[138] Furthermore, revival of Article 107 EEA after twenty years of sleep would represent a blow to the EFTA Court, which may have wider ramifications for the complex judicial architecture upon which the EEA rests.

Turning to disputes between one or more of the EEA EFTA states on the one hand and the European Union and its member states on the other, the question is whether the dispute settlement procedure under Article 111 EEA precludes the parties in dispute to refer the matter to another forum. This may be important because Article 111 (4) EEA states that no questions of interpretation of EEA provisions taken over from EU law may be referred to arbitration under the procedures laid down in Protocol 33 of the agreement. The matter was raised by the European Union when Norway in 2009 relied on the WTO dispute settlement mechanism in a case concerning the EU's ban on the importation and marketing of seal products.[139] According to the European Union, the WTO was not an appropriate forum to settle the dispute as it was of the view that the seal regulation fell within the scope of the EEA Agreement.[140] Referring to the 'special duty of loyal cooperation' under Article 3 EEA, the European Union argued that the Contracting Parties should not seek to evade the application of the specific rules governing the privileged relationship established by the EEA Agreement by resorting to dispute settlement under the WTO agreement. The case was complicated, however, by the fact that the regulation in question (Regulation No 1007/2009 on trade in seal products) had not been incorporated into the EEA Agreement due to Norwegian resistance.[141] The general provisions of EEA law concerning the free movement of goods may still apply, but the EEA rules on product coverage are complicated. As the European Union in the end declared that it 'stood ready to defend its measures

[138] Cf. the assessment of the Norwegian government on the occasion of parliament's ratification of the EEA Agreement; Royal Proposition No. 100 (1991–2), p. 340.

[139] WTO dispute DS401, European Communities – Measures Prohibiting the Importation and Marketing of Seal Products.

[140] WTO Dispute Settlement Body, Minutes of Meeting (21 April 2011), WT/DSB/M/295, para. 65.

[141] See the Commission's staff working document 'A review of the functioning of the European Economic Area', SWD (2012) 425 final, 7 December 2012, where the Commissions highlights this regulation as one of the rare instances where dialogue in the EEA institutional framework has not resulted in agreement concerning the EEA relevance of novel EU secondary legislation.

which it considered to be fully consistent with WTO law', the WTO Dispute Settlement Body established a panel to decide the dispute without going into the alleged EEA dimension of the case.[142]

At first sight, the choice of forum for the settlement of disputes between one or more of the EEA EFTA states on the one hand and the European Union and its member states on the other seems of little relevance to the EFTA Court. As stated in the introduction, the EFTA Court has no jurisdiction to decide such disputes, so that the choice appears to be only between the EEA Joint Committee[143] and – where applicable – the WTO regime.[144] However, the *Icesave* dispute between Iceland on the one hand and the Netherlands and the UK on the other shows that the EFTA Court may still be a forum to settle EEA-related disagreements. After prolonged consultations (including two referenda where Icelandic voters rejected suggested solutions), the parties in dispute decided to let the EFTA Court rule on whether Iceland had infringed its obligations under EEA law.[145] As neither the European Union nor its member states have legal standing to bring an infringement case against an EEA EFTA State (see section 3.3 earlier), the agreement was based on the assumption that the EFTA Surveillance Authority would pursue the matter before the EFTA Court. After the EFTA Surveillance Authority lived up to this expectation,[146] both the Commission and the governments of the UK and the Netherlands used their rights to take part in the proceedings before the EFTA Court.[147] In reality,

[142] The EU reserved the right, however, to pursue the matter under the EEA Agreement.

[143] With the possibility to refer questions concerning the interpretation of EEA provisions taken over from EU law to the ECJ and disputes concerning the scope or duration of safeguard measures (or the proportionality of any rebalancing measures taken) to arbitration, cf. Article 111 EEA.

[144] The bilateral free trade agreements between each of the EEA EFTA States and the European Union do not provide any judicial dispute settlement procedure.

[145] More precisely European Parliament and Council Directive 94/19/EC of 30 May 1994 on deposit-guarantee schemes and the general prohibition to discriminate on grounds of nationality enshrined in Article 4 EEA, OJ 1994 No. L135, 31 May 1994. For an introduction to the dispute, see the introductory parts of the EFTA Court's judgement in the case (Case E-16/11, *EFTA Surveillance Authority v. Iceland* [2013] EFTA Court Report 4).

[146] The real freedom of the EFTA Surveillance Authority to decide whether to bring the case before the EFTA Court may certainly be questioned, but legally the Authority was under no obligation to do so.

[147] In the *Icesave* case, the Commission intervened to support the EFTA Surveillance Authority, whereas the Netherlands and the UK submitted written observations (and participated in the oral hearing).

therefore, the EFTA Court was seized as a forum to decide an EEA-related dispute between an EEA EFTA state and two EU member states. This is not only an interesting bypass of the (insufficient) means provided for in Article 111 EEA, but it is also a clear salute to the EFTA Court from the European Union and the EU member states. This is even clearer when ones takes into account that the Netherlands and the UK accepted the fact that the EFTA Court in the end acquitted Iceland of all charges,[148] even though it follows from the two-pillar structure of the EEA that the judgement is not legally binding on them as EU member states.[149] Given the fact that Iceland originally was pressured into guaranteeing repayment of the minimum deposit guarantees in the amount of €4.0bn, the outcome of the saga certainly illustrates the worth to a small EFTA state of the fact that the EEA EFTA states have established an independent court of justice, which is recognised as such by the European Union and its member states.

At the same time, however, there is another form of tacit forum shopping in the EEA that is less flattering to the EFTA Court. In situations where similar questions of EEA law arise at the same time in the EFTA pillar and in the European Union (which they often do), there seems to be a quiet understanding between the EEA EFTA states and the EFTA Surveillance Authority to let the matter be decided by the ECJ.[150] Rather than parallel proceedings before the EFTA Court, both the EFTA Surveillance Authority and the EEA EFTA states concerned make use of their right to take part in EEA-related proceedings before the ECJ.[151] As long as the EEA EFTA states loyally adhere to the subsequent ruling of the ECJ, there is hardly any reason for the European Union to object to

148 Case E-16/11, *EFTA Surveillance Authority v. Iceland* [2013] EFTA Court Report 4.

149 It has to be added that the acceptance of the outcome was probably made a lot easier by the fact that the assets of the Landsbanki receivership turned out to be much bigger than feared, so that all priority claims (including minimum deposit guarantees) are to be repaid in full (but not secondary priority clams such as claims for interests).

150 Some examples are referred by Baudenbacher, *The EFTA Court in Action*, p. 14, but the list can easily be extended.

151 See the Statute of the ECJ Article 23 (3) (observations in preliminary reference cases) and Article 40 (3) (right to intervene in certain other types of cases). Note that the narrow interpretation of the latter provision favoured by the ECJ's president in C-542/09 *Commission v. Netherlands*, order of 1 October 2010, and C-493/09 *Commission v. Portugal*, order of 15 July 2010, has the regrettable consequence that the right of the EFTA Surveillance Authority and the EEA EFTA states to intervene before the ECJ is more limited than the right of the Commission and the EU member states to do likewise before the EFTA Court. In his order of 23 April 2012, in Case E-16/11, *EFTA Surveillance Authority v. Iceland*, the president of the EFTA Court rightly refused to let this impact negatively on the Commission's right to intervene in the *Icesave* case.

this indirect 'use' of the ECJ as a forum to decide such disputes. To the EFTA Court, however, this approach is problematic. First, it demonstrates that the EFTA Surveillance Authority and the EEA EFTA states acknowledge that the supreme authority on the interpretation of the common EU/EEA rules rests with the ECJ. Second, in particular the EEA EFTA states' support for this approach may arguably be interpreted as part of a strategy to prevent the EFTA Court from taking the lead in the judicial evolution of EU/EEA law. In Norway, the government's lawyers seem to fear that the EFTA Court will seize any such opportunity to make an impression on the ECJ and that it will do so through dynamic interpretation of EEA law against the interest of the state.[152] Third, this practice contributes significantly to the disturbingly low number of substantial cases before the EFTA Court. It is therefore unsurprising that the practice has been sharply criticised by the Court's president.[153]

Another, albeit related, type of tacit forum shopping in the EEA lies in the reluctance of the national courts of the EEA EFTA states to refer unresolved questions of EEA law to the EFTA Court under Article 34 SCA (section 3.3 earlier). In cases to which the governments are parties, they regularly oppose any suggestion for such referrals to be made.[154] As stated by the former EFTA Court Judge Henrik Bull, it is tempting to speculate that the government's lawyers hope that their arguments would be more persuasive in the ears of Norwegian judges than in the ears of the judges in the EFTA Court.[155]

7 Implementation and Interaction with National Courts

7.1 Implementation of Judgements

The EFTA Court's judgements are binding on the parties to the case. As far as private parties are concerned, Article 110 EEA states that any judgement by the EFTA Court that imposes a pecuniary obligation on them shall be enforceable throughout the entire EEA.[156] Enforcement may be suspended only by a decision of the EFTA Court itself (i.e., not by

[152] See further in section 7.

[153] See Baudenbacher, *The EFTA Court in Action*, pp. 17–19.

[154] Fredriksen, 'EØS-rett i norske domstoler [EEA law in Norwegian Courts]', p. 95.

[155] H. Bull, 'European law and Norwegian courts' in P.-C. Müller-Graff and E. Selvig (eds.), *The Approach to European Law in Germany and Norway* (Berlin: Berliner Wissenchafts-Verlag, 2004), pp. 95–114, at p. 113.

[156] Cf. Article 280 TFEU.

national courts). It follows from both Article 110 and the general duty of loyalty enshrined in Article 3 EEA that the EEA states are obliged to carry out enforcement in accordance with their general rules of civil procedure, thus securing the same enforcement of such judgements from the EFTA Court as they offer to domestic court decisions. It is noteworthy that this obligation applies to all of the EEA states (i.e., not only the EFTA states, but also the EU member states).[157] As EEA law stands at present, however, this is of practical interest in the field of competition law only. So far, private parties concerned have always complied with the judgement by the EFTA Court without any involvement from the EEA state in question.

As far as infringement cases against the EFTA states are concerned, Article 33 SCA states that the EFTA states 'shall take the necessary measures to comply with the judgments of the EFTA Court'. Once again, this provision is taken over from EU law. However, unlike Article 260(2) TFEU, there is no provision in the SCA providing for pecuniary penalties in case of nonimplementation of a judgement. The historical explanation is simply that neither did EU law at the time of the EEA negotiations – the possibility to fine an EU member state that has not taken the necessary measures to comply with the judgement of the ECJ was first introduced through the Treaty of Maastricht. The EFTA Court's president has suggested that the SCA ought to be amended accordingly.[158] It may be objected that the practical need for such a reform appears to be very limited: More than twenty years on, the EFTA Surveillance Authority has only twice brought an EEA EFTA state (Norway) before the EFTA Court for noncompliance with a judgement,[159] a figure that hardly compares to the significant problems of noncompliance with ECJ judgements that afflicted the European Union in the early 1990s and that prompted the introduction of what is now Article 260(2) TFEU. In addition to the EFTA Surveillance Authority's power to bring a noncompliant EEA EFTA state before the EFTA Court anew, the principle of state liability acts as an

[157] The corollary of this recognition within the European Union of EFTA Court judgements is the obligation on the EFTA states to enforce such judgements by the EU courts (as well as similar decisions by the Commission), see Article 110 EEA.

[158] C. Baudenbacher, 'Some Thoughts on the EFTA Court's Phases of Life' in EFTA Court (ed.), *Judicial Protection in the European Economic Area* (Stuttgart: German Law Publishers, 2012), pp. 2–28, at p. 23.

[159] Case E-18/10, *EFTA Surveillance Authority v. Norway* [2011] EFTA Court Report 202 and Case E-19/14, *EFTA Surveillance Authority v. Norway*, [2015] EFTA Court Report 300.

effective deterrent: As in EU law, noncompliance with a judgement will easily qualify as a sufficiently serious breach of EEA law and thereby expose the EFTA state in question for claims for economic compensation from affected individuals.[160]

Although Article 33 SCA does not specify the period within which measures necessary to comply with a judgement must be taken, the EFTA Court has followed the ECJ's lead and stated that the interest in the immediate and uniform application of EEA law 'requires that the process of compliance with a judgment must be commenced immediately and must be completed as soon as possible'.[161] The average time taken by the EFTA states to comply with judgements in infringement cases is 16,4 months, significantly shorter than the EU average of 21 months.[162] However, this figure conceals that most judgements are implemented much faster – the not very impressive average is primarily due to two unfortunate cases in which Norwegian authorities were excessively slow in their implementation of the judgements of the EFTA Court.[163]

For the sake of completeness, it may be added that the EFTA Surveillance Authority too is bound by the judgements of the EFTA Court in cases to which it is a party (Articles 38 and 46(2) SCA).

7.2 Implementation of Advisory Opinions

The assessment is more complicated when it comes to the implementation of the EFTA Court's Advisory Opinions under Article 34 SCA. For political and constitutional reasons, the EFTA states were unwilling to entrust the EFTA Court with jurisdiction to issue binding decisions on the interpretation of EEA law. It is noteworthy that the EFTA Court nonetheless renders its advisory opinions under the heading 'Judgments

[160] See, e.g., Case E-4/01, *Karlsson* [2002] EFTA Court Report 240, para. 40. The ECJ's introduction of the principle of State liability in Case C-6/90, *Francovich* [1991] ECR I-5357; [1993] 2 CMLR 66, was clearly a reaction to the tendency of certain EU member states at the time to simply ignore unpopular ECJ rulings. The wish to secure compliance with its judgements remains central to the ECJ's case law on State liability.

[161] Case E-18/10, *EFTA Surveillance Authority v. Norway* [2011] EFTA Court Report 202, para. 29; and Case E-19/14, *EFTA Surveillance Authority v. Norway*, [2015] EFTA Court Report 300, para. 42.

[162] Source: EFTA Surveillance Authority, *Internal Market Scoreboard No. 37*, July 2016, pp. 12–13.

[163] Case E-18/10, *EFTA Surveillance Authority v. Norway* [2011] EFTA Court Report 202, and Case E-19/14, *EFTA Surveillance Authority v. Norway*, [2015] EFTA Court Report 300.

of the Court', but the Supreme Court of Norway for its part has been careful to highlight the advisory character of the opinions and stress that it is thus for the Supreme Court itself to decide whether and to what extent they are to be followed.[164] At the same time, however, the Supreme Court has acknowledged that the fact that the EFTA states found it appropriate to establish a separate court of justice for the EFTA-pillar, the EFTA Court's expert knowledge of EEA law, the rules of procedure opening up for input from the Commission, the EFTA Surveillance Authority and the EEA member states and the clear intentions of the Norwegian parliament when approving the EEA Agreement, all suggest that an advisory opinion by the EFTA Court is to be accorded 'significant weight' by Norwegian courts when interpreting the EEA Agreement.[165] The situation appears to be more or less the same in Icelandic law.[166]

The question of the normative nature of the EFTA Court's Advisory Opinions under Article 34 SCA is complicated by the possibility of the EFTA Surveillance Authority to bring an infringement case against an EFTA state whose courts were to disregard the answers received from the EFTA Court. This would enable the EFTA Court to have the last word on the matter in the form of a binding judgement (Article 33 SCA), and it has been argued by the EFTA Court's president that the Advisory Opinions are thus 'indirectly binding'.[167] However, just like the European Commission in the European Union, the EFTA Surveillance Authority decides by itself whether to launch infringement proceedings.

Experience from the European Union suggests that the Commission only exceptionally regards infringement proceedings as an appropriate reaction to questionable rulings from the highest national courts, but it has happened on a few occasions.[168] For the EFTA Surveillance Authority, the pending investigation into the Norwegian Supreme Court's

[164] See Rt. 2000 p. 1811, *Finanger I*, at p. 1811 and Rt. 2013 p. 258, *STX*, para. 94.

[165] Cf. Rt. 2000 p. 1811, at p. 1827; Rt. 2004 p. 904, para. 67; Rt. 2005 p. 1365, para. 52; Rt. 2007 p. 1003, para. 79; Rt. 2009 p. 839, para. 7 and Rt. 2013 p. 258, para. 93.

[166] See Ó. Í. Hannesson, 'Giving effect to EEA law – The role of the Icelandic national courts and the EFTA Court in the European judicial dialogue' in M. E. Méndez-Pinedo and Ó. Í. Hannesson, *The Authority of European Law: Exploring primacy of EU Law and Effect of EEA Law from European and Icelandic Perspectives*, Series of the Law Institute of the University of Iceland No 11 (Reykjavik: Codex Publishing, 2012), pp. 156–279.

[167] Baudenbacher, Some thoughts on the EFTA Court's phases of life, p. 15.

[168] Two well-known examples are Case C-129/00, *Commission v. Italy* [2003] ECR I-14637, and Case C-154/08, *Commission v. Spain* [2009] ECR I-187*.

judgement in the 2013 *STX* case is a test case that is followed with considerable interest from both pillars of the EEA. In its judgement, the Supreme Court distanced itself in no uncertain way from the EFTA Court's interpretation of EEA law concerning the (politically very sensitive) matter of terms and conditions of employment for so-called posted workers in the maritime construction industry.[169] The EFTA Court responded through an equally harshly worded *obiter* in the subsequent *Jonsson* case.[170] Following a complaint from the Confederation of Norwegian Enterprise and, importantly, a subsequent judgement from the ECJ that arguably supports the view of the EFTA Court at least on one of the matters in dispute (the question of whether compensation for travel, board and lodging can be regarded as part of the minimum rates of pay to which posted workers are entitled), the EFTA Surveillance Authority sent the Norwegian government a letter in which it takes the view that the government's continued reliance on the Supreme Court judgement is incompatible with Norway's obligations under the Posted Workers Directive.[171] The Norwegian government has responded with a letter defending the judgement of the Supreme Court and questioning the EFTA Surveillance Authority's interpretation of the new judgement from the ECJ.[172] It remains to be seen whether the EFTA Surveillance Authority will proceed to initiate infringement proceedings against Norway. Even if this is to happen, however, the case will not be about the *STX* case as such, but rather about how the Posted Workers Directive is to be understood in light of the subsequent developments in ECJ case law. In a way, therefore, such a case will be more about the enforcement of ECJ case law than about the enforcement of the EFTA Court's advisory opinion as such.

In any event, it must be stressed that the (unfortunate) *STX* saga is very much the exception that proves the rule – in practice, the advisory opinions of the EFTA Court are implemented by the national courts of

169 Rt. 2013 p. 258, *STX*, deviating on several points from the EFTA Court's advisory opinion in the case (cf. Case E-2/11, *STX* [2012] EFTA Court Report 4). For an in-depth analysis of the row, see C. Barnard, 'Posting matters', *Arbeidsrett*, 1 (2014), 1–28.

170 Case E-3/12, *Jonsson* [2013] EFTA Court Report 136, paras. 56–60. The subject matter of this case had little to do with the *STX* case, but the EFTA Court's desire to defend itself at the very first possibility is easy to understand.

171 Letter of 10 July 2015, in Case No 74557 (Document No 762926) (available from the EFTA Surveillance Authority's Public Documents Database, see www.eftasurv.int).

172 Letter of 28 September 2015, in Case No. 74557.

the EEA EFTA states in much the same manner as the national courts of EU member states implement preliminary rulings from the ECJ under Article 267 TFEU.[173]

7.3 *Interaction with National Courts*

As suggested by the disturbingly low number for references (see section 3.3 earlier), the relationship between the EFTA Court and the national courts of the EFTA states is not as close as one may have hoped for. Once again, part of the explanation is likely to be the peculiarities of the judicial architecture of the EEA.

One of the most important reasons why the EEA Agreement has functioned well for over twenty years is the fact that the EFTA states, their courts included, have come to accept the hegemony of the ECJ. As most pleas for EEA-specific exceptions from the ECJ's interpretation of corresponding provisions of EU law have been rejected by the EFTA Court, their numbers have diminished.[174] This is no small achievement by the EFTA Court, but, unfortunately, one that has diminished the request for its services considerably. As the governments and courts of the EFTA states have grown accustomed to the idea that the internal market *aquis* is to be interpreted in line with ECJ case law, they may wonder how much there really is to gain from a referral to the EFTA Court and if the advantages outweigh the delay, work and cost entailed. The EFTA Court's expert knowledge of EEA law and the procedural rules that open up for valuable input from the Commission, the EFTA Surveillance Authority and interested EEA states suggest that there is a lot to gain, but it may well be that self-assured national courts still conclude

[173] As far as Norwegian courts are concerned, see H. H. Fredriksen, 'The Two EEA Courts – a Norwegian Perspective' in EFTA Court (ed.), *Judicial Protection in the European Economic Area* (Stuttgart: German Law Publishers, 2012). For an important recent example, see the final judgement of Eidsivating Court of Appeals in the Case of *Matja Kumba T. M'bye and Others v. Stiftelsen Fossumkollektivet* (LE-2014-56639), which loyally implements the Advisory Opinion obtained from the EFTA Court (Case E-5/15). Before the Court of Appeals, the employees argued that the EFTA Court's controversial interpretation of the Working Time Directive was at odds with ECJ case law, but the Court of Appeals could not be convinced. The judgement was appealed to the Supreme Court, but the Selection Appeals Committee denied leave to appeal (HR-2016-1553-U).

[174] See in detail Fredriksen, 'The EFTA Court 15 years on', 740 ff.

that they are capable to analyse ECJ case law with the same accuracy as the EFTA Court: Over the years, numerous pleas for referrals to the EFTA Court have been rejected by Norwegian courts citing the existence of what they deem to be sufficiently clear ECJ case law.

Fortunately to EU citizens and economic operators exercising their EEA-based rights in the EFTA states, the somewhat troubled relationship between the EFTA Court and the national courts of the EFTA states is of only limited practical interest. As long as the national courts of the EFTA States continue to adhere loyally to ECJ case law and protect EEA-based rights accordingly, it matters little to the parties concerned whether their case is dealt with by the national courts alone or in cooperation with the EFTA Court.

To the EFTA Court, however, the lack of references from the national courts is a very real problem. The current situation is also harmful more generally to the credibility of the judicial architecture of the EFTA pillar of the EEA. In the eyes of the ECJ, the position of the EFTA Court now appears to be of such a nature that even in a hypothetical case in which it should end up accepting national restrictions on the fundamental freedoms of the EEA Agreement that should have been disallowed pursuant to subsequent ECJ case law, no one will suspect it of wilful contribution to the feared 'cherry picking' of the EFTA states. By contrast, the 'margin of error' of the national courts is probably of a more limited nature – rightly or wrongly, there is something suspicious about national judges refusing to cooperate with the EEA judges in Luxembourg.

8 Tribunal-Specific Legitimacy Concerns

Any assessment of the legitimacy of the EFTA Court has to take into account the impossible task with which the Court is charged: The interpretation of an agreement under public international law that aims at full integration of the EFTA states into the internal market of the European Union. The goal of a homogeneous European Economic Area with 'equal conditions for competition' and 'respect of the same rules' (Article 1 EEA) can only be achieved if the EFTA Court follows the ECJ's lead. The reality of the EEA is that the EFTA states have to play by the rules of the internal market as they are interpreted by the 'foreign judges' of the ECJ. Criticism of this fact (or the obvious democratic shortcomings of the EEA Agreement more generally) is to be directed to the Contracting Parties (the EFTA states in particular) and not to the

EFTA Court. Unfortunately, critics of the EEA Agreement sometimes shoot the messenger and blame the EFTA Court as such, even though it essentially only transmits ECJ case law to the EEA EFTA states. A weakness frequently highlighted by its critics is the EFTA Court's small size. In the potentially turbulent times ahead as the UK seeks to secure continued access to the EU internal market from outside the European Union, the EEA EFTA states may be well advised to strengthen the credibility of the EFTA Court by blowing the dust off the Court's own proposal for an extended five-member bench.

5

The United States Court of International Trade

DONALD C. POGUE*

The United States Court of International Trade (CIT) is a domestic, federal trial-level court with nationwide geographic jurisdiction over certain trade-related cases. The court has a legislatively authorized complement of nine active judges,[1] including a Chief Judge,[2] and a courthouse in New York City.[3]

In considering whether the CIT may make a claim of legitimacy in resolving the trade disputes within its jurisdiction, this chapter will proceed as follows: After (1) a brief review of the CIT's historical background, the chapter will summarise (2) the framework for securing the court's judicial independence, (3) parties' access to the court, (4) the rule-based transparency of the court's legal process, (5) the court's fact-finding and interpretive role, (6) the court's relationship with other trade forums and tribunals, and (7) certain tribunal-specific considerations that may affect the court's legitimacy claim. This chapter concludes that the CIT may make a process-based legitimacy claim based on the independence, transparency and accountability of its decision making and a substantive legitimacy claim founded on the rules-based nature of its decisions.

* Judge Pogue has served on the United States Court of International Trade since 1995. The author is most grateful for the education, assistance and input provided by his colleagues at the court, including especially judges, court staff, and chambers clerks, staff and interns.

[1] An active judge is one who has not retired. Judges who are eligible to retire, may do so without relinquishing their office provided they continue to perform judicial duties. See 28 U.S.C. §371(c) (2012) (all subsequent citations to the U.S. Code are to the 2012 edition). Such judges are designated 'senior' judges. See 28 U.S.C. § 294(b).

[2] The Chief Judge is designated from among the nine by order of precedence, 28 U.S.C. § 258, and supervises the administration of the court, including its fiscal affairs and promulgation of its docket, 28 U.S.C. § 253.

[3] See 28 U.S.C. § 251(b) ('The offices of the [CIT] shall be located in New York, New York'.). The judges of the court are also authorized to preside, in the 'interests of economy, efficiency, and justice', in any port or 'place within the jurisdiction of the United States', or, under certain conditions, at evidentiary hearings in foreign countries. See 28 U.S.C. § 256; *Zoltek Corp. v. United States*, 13 CIT 1098, 1104, 728 F. Supp. 762, 766 (1989).

1 Background

The U.S. Constitution gives Congress the power to 'regulate Commerce with foreign Nations', requiring that 'all Duties, Imposts and Excises [be] uniform throughout the United States'.[4] This provision compels a single, national tariff schedule,[5] which both contributes to the creation of a nationwide market for imported goods and creates the need for an institution capable of achieving and administering uniformity. The CIT finds its primary roots here.

In addition, during the period prior to U.S. independence, colonial courts adopted British common law causes of action for the enforcement of bonds given to secure payment of duties for entry of goods and for assumpsit, an action to secure return of duties wrongfully charged. The litigation of these causes continued after Independence in the first federal courts.[6] But, during the nineteenth century, reforms – adopted both to achieve uniform administration and to stem the proliferation of lawsuits around the country – brought these causes of action into administrative (as opposed to judicial) forums.[7] The deficiencies of these reforms led to the return in the twentieth century to a judicial solution for the review of import disputes.[8]

[4] U.S. Const. ArticleI, § 8, cls. 1, 3.

[5] The uniformity requirement was originally adopted to ameliorate regional conflict by ensuring that 'Congress might not have the power of imposing unequal burdens [on different regions of the country]; that it might not be in their power to gratify one part of the Union by Oppressing another' *Annals of Congress* (3 Feb. 1792), vol. 2, p. 379 (statement of Hugh Williamson, Delegate from North Carolina).

[6] See D. Campbell, 'Customs Law Pre-1890', available at: https://prezi.com/h2fpm-cdbzvy/customs-law-pre-1890/ ('The first case tried before the first judge appointed to the first court organized in the United States was a Customs case [*United States v. Three Boxes of Ironmongery*]. On 3 November, 1789, as George Washington's first appointee, Judge Duane, convened the first session of the United States District Court for the District of New York in the Exchange Building near the foot of Broad Street, where Judge Duane ruled that $95 was the maximum amount of duty which could be claimed by the government.'); see also, H. P. Burak, *History of the United States District Court for the Southern District of New York* (New York: Federal Bar Association of New York, New Jersey, and Connecticut, 1962), pp. 1–2.

[7] See www.cit.uscourts.gov/BriefHistory.htm. The progress of reform faced obstacles in addition to regional and partisan conflicts. For example, the records of a special investigation commission created, at the direction of President Tyler, documented widespread bribery, fraud and conversion of public funds to private use in the N.Y. Customs House. H.R. Doc. No. 212, 27th Congress, 2nd Session, at 40–2, 56–7, 62–5 (1842) (Report by Commissioners Kelley and Steuart, submitted to Walter Forward, Secretary of the Treasury), *reproduced in Library of Congress, A Century of Lawmaking for a New Nation: U.S. congressional Documents and Debates, available at http://memory.loc.gov/ammem/amlaw/.*

[8] See www.cit.uscourts.gov/AboutTheCourt.html#history.

The search for a modern judicial solution initially led to the creation of the U.S. Customs Court[9] and its subsequent designation as an Article III court under the U.S. Constitution.[10] But the contemporary incarnation of a judicial home for the litigation of trade-related disputes was not created until the adoption of the Customs Court Act of 1980.[11] This act renamed the U.S. Customs Court, making it the Court of International Trade, and established the modern-day framework for Article III judicial review of U.S. administrative agency decision making in trade-related cases, as explained later.

2 The Framework for Judicial Independence

As with other Article III courts in the United States, such as the federal district courts and the regional courts of appeal (also called circuit courts), the CIT benefits from a Constitutional framework and decision-making process that secures judicial independence from the political branches while maintaining accountability.

Article III of the U.S. Constitution vests the judicial authority of the United States in the Supreme Court and 'such inferior Courts as the Congress may from time to time ordain and establish'.[12] Judges of these courts 'shall hold their Offices during good Behaviour, and shall, at stated Times, receive for their Services a Compensation which shall not be diminished during their Continuance in Office'.[13] In effect, this means that federal judges appointed pursuant to Article III have lifetime tenure (absent impeachment, discussed later), and a salary that is constitutionally protected from decrease during that tenure (e.g. by the political branches for political reasons).[14]

[9] See Act of May 28, 1926, ch. 411, 44 Stat. 669.

[10] See Act of July 14, 1956, ch. 589, 70 Stat. 532 (codified as amended at 28 U.S.C. § 251(a)). For further discussion of the implications of the court's Article III status, please see below.

[11] Pub. L. No. 96–417, 94 Stat. 1727 (1980).

[12] U.S. Const. ArticleIII, §1.

[13] Ibid.; see also 28 U.S.C. § 252 (providing the same for CIT judges specifically).

[14] See R. D. Rotunda and J. E. Nowak, *Treatise on Constitutional Law: Substance and Procedure* 5th ed., 6 vols., (St. Paul, MN: West Publishing Co., 2013), vol. I at § 2.9(a). The separation of powers doctrine – that is, the 'necessity of maintaining each of the three general departments of [U.S.] government, [Executive, Legislative, and Judicial,] entirely free from the control or coercive influence, direct or indirect, of either of the others', *Humphrey's Ex'r v. United States*, 295 U.S. 602, 629 (1935) –provides 'a basis for protecting the financial independence of the members of the judicial branch. Thus, Article III of the Constitution prohibits the diminution of a judge's compensation during his or her term in office. This clause is a specific means of ensuring the independence of the judiciary'. Rotunda and Nowak, *Treatise on Constitutional Law*, vol. 1 at § 2.9(a); see *United States v. Will*, 449 U.S. 200, 217–21 (1980) (discussing the origins of the Compensation Clause as means of ensuring separation of powers and, therefore, judicial

The appointment process for Article III judges is also specified in the U.S. Constitution. Article III judges must be nominated by the president and confirmed by vote of the U.S. Senate.[15] This process lends both democratic political accountability and legitimacy to the appointment.[16]

Except as explained later, Article III judges may be removed from office only after impeachment and conviction by the U.S. Congress.[17] Impeachment can only be for 'Treason, Bribery, or other high Crimes and Misdemeanors'.[18] If the person is impeached and convicted, the sanction does 'not extend further than to removal from Office, and disqualification to hold and enjoy any Office of honour, Trust or Profit under the United States'.[19] However, the person may still 'be liable and subject to Indictment, Trial, Judgment and Punishment, according to Law' in addition to impeachment.[20]

Judicial independence extends beyond appointment and tenure to the decision-making process at the CIT. Specifically, most cases are assigned for single-judge proceedings,[21] except where the Chief Judge designates a three-judge panel to hear constitutional issues or other issues of 'broad or significant implications'.[22] In addition, judges of the CIT are not bound by the other judges' decisions, even though they may strive for internal institutional consistency.[23]

independence); *Beer v. United States*, 696 F.3d 1174 (Fed. Cir. 2012) (legislation blocking five years of cost-of-living adjustments for judges constituted an unconstitutional deprivation of judicial compensation in violation of the Compensation Clause).

15 See U.S. Const. ArticleII, § 2, cl. 2 ('[The President] . . . shall nominate, and by and with the Advice and Consent of the Senate, shall appoint . . . Judges of the supreme Court, and all other Officers of the United States, whose Appointments are not herein otherwise provided for. . . .') See also 28 U.S.C. § 251 ('President shall appoint, by and with the advice and consent of the Senate' CIT judges). Such 'Advice and Consent' requires a two-thirds majority affirmative vote of the Senate. U.S. Const. Article II, § 2, cl. 2.

16 See *Edmond v. United States*, 520 U.S. 651, 659–60 (1997) (reviewing the history and purpose of the Appointments Clause of Article II).

17 The House of Representatives 'shall have the sole Power of Impeachment', U.S. Const. ArticleI, § 2, cl. 5, and the Senate 'shall have the sole Power to try all Impeachments. When sitting for that Purpose, they shall be on Oath or Affirmation . . . And no Person shall be convicted without the Concurrence of two-thirds of the Members present'. U.S. Const. ArticleI, § 3, cl. 6.

18 U.S. Const. Article II, § 4.

19 U.S. Const. Article I, § 3, cl. 7. Note, however, that the presidential pardon power does not extend to impeachment, so such relief is unavailable. U.S. Const. Article II, § 2, cl. 1 ('[The President] shall have Power to Grant Reprieves and Pardons for Offenses against the United States, except in Cases of Impeachment.').

20 U.S. Const. ArticleI, § 3, cl. 7.

21 See 28 U.S.C. § 254.

22 28 U.S.C. § 255.

23 The decision of a district court, like the CIT, is not binding authority on other district courts, or even itself, rather it is 'entitled only to comity in another district court'. *Mendenhall v. Cedarapids, Inc.*, 5 F.3d 1557, 1570 (Fed. Cir. 1993); see also *Camreta v. Greene*, 131 S. Ct. 2020, 2033 n.7 (2011).

As with other federal trial-level courts, accountability at the CIT is accomplished through appeal of final decisions to a higher court, in this instance to the Court of Appeals for the Federal Circuit (CAFC).[24] In each case, judges at the CIT must provide a statement of findings of fact and separate conclusions of law, or an opinion 'stating the reasons and facts upon which the decision is based'.[25] This ensures that the CAFC can provide meaningful review of CIT decisions.[26]

The CAFC's appellate review, however, is distinct in that the CAFC applies anew to each CIT decision the same statutory standard of review[27] used by the CIT to the agency decision under review.[28] Other (non-trade-related) agency decisions usually are appealed directly to a Court of Appeals (at the circuit level, without the intermediate step of a specialized trial court, like the CIT);[29] these decisions are then reviewed, upon grant of certiorari, by the Supreme Court, which uses a more deferential standard (upholding the appellate decision unless the Court of Appeals 'grossly misconstrued or misapplied' the lower courts' statutory standards), which usually avoids the repetitious application of the standard of review. It follows that this two-tier review is unique to trade-related administrative law.[30]

[24] See 28 U.S.C. § 1295(a)(5). Decisions of the CAFC, of course, are appealable by petition of certiorari to the Supreme Court. See U.S. Const. ArticleIII § 2, cl. 2 (vesting the Supreme Court with appellate jurisdiction); Sup. Ct. R. 10(a) (requiring petition for writ of certiorari).

[25] 28 U.S.C. § 2645(a).

[26] See *Camargo Correa Metais, S.A. v. United States*, 52 F.3d 1040, 1043 (Fed. Cir. 1995) ('[The CAFC] cannot provide effective and meaningful appellate review . . . in this case until we are supplied with the fruits of satisfaction of section 2645(a). Accordingly, the judgment of the Court of International Trade is vacated and the case is remanded to afford the court the opportunity to comply with the relevant statute.').

[27] See Section 3, for discussion of standards of review.

[28] See *Atlantic Sugar, Ltd. v. United States*, 744 F.2d 1556, 1559 n.10 (Fed. Cir. 1984) (repetitious application of statutory standard of review, as CAFC reviews CIT cases by same standard CIT used); see also *NSK Corp. v. U.S. Int'l Trade Comm'n*, 542 F. App'x. 950 (Fed. Cir. 2013).

[29] See Fed. R. App. P. 15 (providing how to obtain or intervene in an action to obtain review or enforcement of an administrative agency order).

[30] Only review of district court decisions under the Administrative Procedure Act – when there is no direct review provision for agency decisions – are similarly subject to two-tier review, with the appellate court reviewing the agency decision de novo and without deference to the district court decision. *See Aquarius Marine Co. v. Pena*, 64 F.3d 82, 87 (2d Cir. 1995) (citing *Ward v. Brown*, 22 F.3d 516, 521 (2d Cir. 1994); *Perales v. Sullivan*, 948 F.2d 1348, 1353 (2d Cir.1991)); City of New York *v.* Shalala, 34 F.3d 1161, 1166 (2d Cir. 1994); *Bellevue Hosp. Ctr. v. Leavitt*, 443 F.3d 163, 174 (2d Cir. 2006). But in these cases, of course, the district court is not acting with any special expertise.

Accountability is also provided by the mandatory availability of a procedure for filing complaints against judges,[31] when 'a judge has engaged in conduct prejudicial to the effective and expeditious administration of the business of the courts', or if a 'judge is unable to discharge all the duties of office by reason of mental or physical disability'.[32] In addition, federal judges are governed by a strict ethics code, subject to a process for sanctions or discipline.[33] Among other strictures, judges are not allowed to accept certain gifts, for example from a person 'whose interests may be substantially affected by the performance or non-performance of the [judge's] official duties',[34] and are not allowed to hold any financial interest in any company that is a party to a case (excluding stock held as part of a mutual fund).[35] To avoid political influence, judges are prohibited from any involvement in politics, including contributing to political campaigns.[36]

Finally on this issue, the CIT enjoys the support of an active bar composed of the approximately three hundred members of the Customs and International Trade Bar Association (CITBA).[37] The CITBA provides concrete and meaningful backing for securing both the court's expertise and its independence, by, for example, supporting, before Congress, the court's independent budget.

3 Access to the CIT

Although the CIT has exclusive subject matter jurisdiction to review certain trade-related decisions of a number of federal agencies,[38] most cases before the court are from Customs or Commerce, or are so-called residual jurisdiction cases involving the administration and enforcement of

[31] 28 U.S.C. § 363. [32] 28 U.S.C. § 351(a).

[33] See also *Code of Conduct for United States Judges*, Canon 4(D)(4) (2014), available at www.uscourts.gov/RulesAndPolicies/CodesOfConduct/CodeConductUnitedStatesJudges.aspx.

[34] 5 U.S.C. § 7353(a)(2); see ibid. at §§ 7351(a) and 7353(a)(1) for further restrictions on gifts; see also *Code of Conduct for United States Judges* at Canon 4(D)(4) (2014).

[35] *Code of Conduct for United States Judges* at Canon 3(C)(1)(c), 3(C)(1)(d), 3(C)(2), 3(C)(3)(c)(i)–(iv).

[36] Ibid. at Canon 5; see also ibid. at Canon 2(b). [37] See www.citba.org.

[38] These include the U.S. Department of Labor, the U.S. International Trade Commission (ITC), the U.S. Department of Commerce (Commerce), the U.S. Department of the Treasury, the U.S. Department of Homeland Security, and U.S. Customs and Border Protection (Customs). *See* 28 U.S.C. §§ 1581, 1582. Counterclaims, cross-claims and third-party actions may also proceed pursuant to 28 U.S.C. §1583.

U.S. trade laws.[39] This jurisdiction operates to limit access in the sense that the court will only make decisions about specified agency decisions and in accordance with a statutory schedule for review. In addition, the court's jurisdiction is also affected by the court's status as an Article III court.

First, as with other federal courts in the United States, the CIT's jurisdiction, and thus access to the court, is limited. The court will not make advisory opinions. Rather cases must be 'justiciable', meaning that they must not be moot, and must be 'ripe' for adjudication.[40] Second, parties must have 'standing' to bring a claim in federal court.[41] Such standing is broadly available in trade cases; in particular, it is available for all 'interested parties' who have participated in the administrative proceedings under review, including domestic producers or unions,

[39] Customs cases, brought under 28 U.S.C. § 1581(a) jurisdiction, include challenges, pursuant to 28 U.S.C. § 1515, of a Customs denial of a protest, *see* 19 U.S.C. § 1514, addressing issues of tariff classification, valuation, or exclusion orders. The CIT also reviews, pursuant to 28 U.S.C. § 1582, Customs enforcement actions and penalties assessed (including for misrepresentation of country of origin). Commerce and ITC cases, brought under 28 U.S.C. § 1581(c) jurisdiction, include review of affirmative or negative decisions regarding: the provision of a countervailable subsidy of merchandise imported into the U.S.; the sale in the U.S., at less than fair value, of foreign merchandise; whether a domestic industry in the U.S. is materially injured or threatened with material injury thereby. 'Residual' cases include jurisdiction under 28 U.S.C. § 1581(i) over actions arising out of U.S. law providing for revenue from imports, tariffs, duties fees or other taxes, embargoes, or the administration and enforcement thereof.

[40] The Constitution limits Federal court jurisdiction to 'cases' and 'controversies,' U.S. Const. ArticleIII, § 2, cl. 1., which excludes moot cases and advisory opinions, see *Aetna Life Ins. Co. of Hartford, Conn. v. Haworth*, 300 U.S. 227, 240–41 (1937) ('A justiciable controversy is thus distinguished from a difference or dispute of a hypothetical or abstract character; from one that is academic or moot. The controversy must be definite and concrete, touching the legal relations of parties having adverse legal interests. It must be a real and substantial controversy admitting of specific relief through a decree of a conclusive character, as distinguished from an opinion advising what the law would be upon a hypothetical state of facts.') (Internal citations omitted). Cases must also be ripe. *United Pub. Workers of Am. (C.I.O.) v. Mitchell*, 330 U.S. 75, 90 (1947) ('A hypothetical threat is not enough.').

[41] Standing in federal cases generally requires: (1) injury in fact, *Duke Power Co. v. Carolina Envtl. Study Grp., Inc.*, 438 U.S. 59, 72 (1978) ('The essence of the standing inquiry is whether the parties seeking to invoke the court's jurisdiction have "alleged such a personal stake in the outcome of the controversy as to assure that concrete adverseness which sharpens the presentation of issues upon which the court so largely depends for illumination of difficult constitutional questions".'), and (2) redressability, ibid. at 74 ('The more difficult step in the standing inquiry is establishing that these injuries fairly can be traced to the challenged action of the defendant, or put otherwise, that the exercise of the Court's remedial powers would redress the claimed injuries.') (Internal citations omitted).

importers, foreign producers or exporters, governments or associations.[42] Standing is available in Customs cases to anyone who has exercised a right to protest an administrative decision at the agency, including importers, agents, and persons seeking entry or delivery.[43] In 'residual' cases, the court has also recognized standing for foreign exporters and their governments' challenge to the unlawful administration and enforcement of provisions of the North American Free Trade Agreement (NAFTA) Implementation Act,[44] and the Uruguay Round Agreements Act (URAA).[45] Third, where appropriate, parties must have exhausted their administrative remedies in order to bring suit.[46] This requirement strengthens both the authority of the

[42] See 19 U.S.C. §§ 1516(a), 1677(9).

[43] See 19 U.S.C. § 1514(c)(2). Importantly this excludes domestic producers. See *Corning Gilbert v. U.S.*, CIT __, 837 F. Supp. 2d 1303 (2012) (no amicus standing for Patentee in Importer's challenge to Customs' exclusion). In addition, all duties must be paid before suit is brought, see 28 U.S.C. § 2637(a), such that the available remedy is reimbursement, with lawful interest.

[44] 19 U.S.C. §§ 3301–473.

[45] Pub. L. No. 103–465, 108 Stat 4809 (1994). Such standing was recognized, under 28 U.S.C. § 1581(i) and the Administrative Procedure Act, 5 U.S.C. § 702, for foreign exporters and their governments in *Canadian Lumber Trade Alliance v. United States*, 30 CIT 391, 425 F. Supp. 2d 1321 (2006) (invalidating application of the Continued Dumping and Subsidy Offset Act (the 'Byrd' Amendment), Pub.L. No. 106–387, § 1003, 114 Stat. 1549, 1623 (2000) (CDSOA), repealed by the Deficit Reduction Act of 2005, Pub.L. No. 109–171, § 7601(b), 120 Stat. 4, 154 (2006), to goods from Canada and Mexico), aff'd, 517 F.3d 1319 (Fed. Cir. 2008) and *Tembec Inc. v. United States*, 30 CIT 958, 441 F. Supp. 2d 1302 (2006) invalidating the application of Section 129 of the URAA, 19 U.S.C. § 3538, to negate effect of NAFTA decision).

[46] See 28 U.S.C. § 2637. Parties are, with some exceptions, required to not only have participated (if possible) in the administrative proceeding under review, but also to have unambiguously presented the specific arguments in question to the agency below. 28 U.S.C. §§ 2631, 2637. The CIT 'generally takes a "strict view" of the requirement that parties exhaust their administrative remedies before the Department of Commerce in trade cases'. *Corus Staal BV v. United States*, 502 F.3d 1370, 1379 (Fed. Cir. 2007) (internal citations omitted). This is because, while the: 'statutory injunction [in 28 U.S.C. § 2637(d)] is not absolute, it indicates a congressional intent that, absent a strong contrary reason, the court should insist that parties exhaust their remedies before the pertinent administrative agencies.' Ibid. Further, '[t]he exhaustion requirement [is] … not simply a creature of court decision, as is sometimes the case, but is a requirement explicitly imposed by the agency as a prerequisite to judicial review.' Ibid. Moreover, 'Commerce's regulations specifically address the exhaustion requirement, as applied to challenges to antidumping determinations, and require a challenger to submit a case brief to Commerce that contains all the arguments that the submitter deems relevant.' Ibid. (citing 19 C.F.R. § 351.309(c)(2)). There are, however, exceptions to the exhaustion requirement to accommodate situations where 'the benefits of exhaustion are inapplicable or outweighed by other concerns,' *Pakfood Public Co. Ltd. v. United States*, CIT, 724 F. Supp. 2d 1327, 1349–53 (2010), such as when further argument would be futile (that a

agency and the efficacy of judicial review by requiring parties to fully articulate their arguments to the agency and giving the court the opportunity consider the agency's response.

4 The Rule-Based Transparency of the CIT's Legal Process

The transparency of the CIT's legal process also has constitutional roots. Specifically, the First Amendment to the U.S. Constitution requires open court proceedings.[47] The only exception to this requirement is for the identification and transmission under seal of confidential information, usually proprietary information.[48]

In addition, the court's case management/electronic case filing system (CM/ECF)[49] makes all record documents and all filings, evidence and documents upon which the parties rely publicly available (with the limited exception for business proprietary information, which is redacted with great particularity from the otherwise publicly available filings). Ex parte communications are prohibited,[50] so that everything communicated to the judge with regard to the case will be similarly transparent. Consequently, anyone can see the documentary and evidentiary basis for both the agency's and the court's decisions. Further, because both the court and the agency must issue written decisions, stating the evidence considered, the standards used, and the conclusions reached,[51] the rationale of determinations and reviews is made public and transparent as well.[52]

The CIT's legal process is also governed by public rules of evidence and procedure. The Federal Rules of Evidence apply to all civil actions in

party would have to 'to go through obviously useless motions in order to preserve its rights'), *Mittal Steel Point Lisas Ltd. v. United States*, 548 F.3d 1375, 1384 (Fed. Cir. 2008) (internal citations, quotation and alteration marks omitted).

47 See *Richmond Newspapers, Inc. v. Virginia*, 448 U.S. 555, 575 (1980) ('The First Amendment, in conjunction with the Fourteenth, prohibits governments from 'abridging the freedom of speech, or of the press; or the right of the people peaceably to assemble, and to petition the Government for a redress of grievances.' These expressly guaranteed freedoms share a common core purpose of assuring freedom of communication on matters relating to the functioning of government.') (Quoting U.S. Const. amend. I).

48 See 28 U.S.C. §§ 2635(b)(2), 2635(c), and 2635 (d)(2).

49 Available at www.cit.uscourts.gov/CMECF/index.html.

50 See *Code of Conduct for United States Judges* at Canon 3(A)(4). The prohibition is with limited exception, including such communications as authorized by law. See Canon 3(A)(4)(a)–(d).

51 *See* 28 U.S.C. § 257.

52 The court's opinions are also available on the court's website, www.cit.uscourts.gov.

the CIT except as provided in 28 U.S.C. § 2639 or in § 2641(b) of that Title, or in the Rules of the Court.[53] While the CIT has rules of procedure distinct from the Federal Rules of Civil Procedure, the CIT's rules, as 'necessary to implement the Customs Court Acts of 1980, are styled, numbered and arranged to the maximum extent practicable in conformity with the Federal Rules of Civil Procedure'.[54] Thus, the procedural rules of the court are public, accessible, and familiar to any lawyer knowledgeable about federal court practice.

Further, an emphasis on timelines at the court makes its accessibility and transparency meaningful. The court makes every effort (through internal deadline-setting as well as expressly through USCIT Rule 1[55]) to issue decisions expeditiously, recognizing the importance of finality in matters involving commercial and economic transactions. As such, it serves as a realistic, accessible solution in trade disputes.

5 The Role of the CIT in the Process of Judicial Review

The CIT's function is shaped by the statutory standards Congress established for judicial review. These standards are best understood as word formulas communicating the court's function vis-à-vis administrative agencies.[56]

For customs cases, the statute provides for de novo review of both factual and legal issues.[57] This means that the court makes its own findings of the relevant facts based on the record presented and formulates its own interpretation of the statutory tariff provisions. Although the court also applies a statutory 'presumption of correctness' to the

[53] 28 U.S.C. § 2641.

[54] USCIT R. Preface, available at: www.cit.uscourts.gov/Rules/Rules_Forms%20Page/Rules_Forms_Guide_AO%20Page/Rules_Forms_Guide_AO%20PDF%27s/PREFACE.pdf.

[55] 'These rules govern the procedure in the United States Court of International Trade. They should be construed and administered to secure the just, speedy, and inexpensive determination of every action and proceeding. When a procedural question arises that is not covered by these rules, the court may prescribe the procedure to be followed in any manner not inconsistent with these rules. The court may refer for guidance to the rules of other courts. The rules are not to be construed to extend or limit the jurisdiction of the court.' USCIT Rule 1.

[56] See Charles H. Koch, Jr. and Richard Murphy, *Administrative Law and Practice*, 3rd ed., 5 vols. (St. Paul, MN: West Publishing Co., 2014), vol. III at §§ 9.24[1], 9.25[1].

[57] 28 U.S.C. § 2640(a); see also *United States v. Mead Corp.*, 533 U.S. 218, 230 (2001) (Customs statutory interpretations are not due special deference when they are not articulated in 'a relatively formal administrative procedure tending to foster the fairness and deliberation that should underlie a pronouncement' having the force of law).

agency's factual determinations,[58] this 'presumption' is more accurately described as a method of assigning the burden of production, going forward, of evidence of agency error.[59] The statutory presumption of correctness has no effect on legal determinations, which remain in the court's province.[60]

Trade cases are different. In trade cases, the court is generally charged to 'hold unlawful any determination, finding, or conclusion found . . . to be unsupported by substantial evidence on the record, or otherwise not in accordance with law',[61] a standard that is more deferential to the agency than the de novo review standard applied to customs cases. In either case, substantial evidence or in accordance with law, review is conducted on the grounds relied on by the agency.[62]

The substantial evidence standard applies to factual determinations. Under this standard, the court reviews the administrative record to

[58] See 28 U.S.C. § 2639(a)(1) ('[I]n any civil action commenced in the Court of International Trade under section 515, 516, or 516A of the Tariff Act of 1930, the decision of the Secretary of the Treasury, the administering authority, or the International Trade Commission is presumed to be correct. The burden of proving otherwise shall rest upon the party challenging such decision.'); see also *Chrysler Corp. v. United States*, 33 CIT 90, 97, 601 F. Supp. 2d 1347, 1354 (2009) (The presumption of correctness 'is a procedural device that codifies the presumption of regularity accorded government action').

[59] See *Universal Electronics Inc. v. United States*, 112 F.3d 488, 492 (Fed. Cir. 1997) ('The presumption of correctness is a procedural device that is designed to allocate, between the two litigants to a lawsuit, the burden of producing *evidence* in sufficient quantity. Specifically, the importer must produce evidence (the burden of production portion of the burden of proof) that demonstrates by preponderance (the burden of persuasion portion of the burden of proof) that Customs' classification decision is incorrect. The presumption of correctness certainly carries force on any factual components of a classification decision, such as whether the subject imports fall within the scope of the tariff provision, because facts must be proven via *evidence*.') (Footnote omitted, emphasis in original).

[60] See *Universal Electronics*, 112 F.3d at 492 ('The situation is quite different, however, with respect to pure questions of law, such as the proper interpretation of a particular tariff provision or term. Questions of law such as these lie within the domain of the courts, for "[i]t is emphatically the province and duty of the judicial department to say what the law is." In such a context, the importer has no duty to produce evidence as to what the law means because evidence is irrelevant to that legal inquiry. Therefore, we conclude that although the presumption of correctness applies to the ultimate classification decision . . . as a practical matter, the presumption carries no force as to questions of law.') (quoting *Marbury v. Madison*, 5 U.S. 137, 177 (1803)).

[61] 19 U.S.C. § 1516a(b)(1)(B).

[62] See *Sec. & Exch. Comm'n v. Chenery Corp.*, 318 U.S. 80, 95 (1943) ('[A]n administrative order cannot be upheld unless the grounds upon which the agency acted in exercising its powers were those upon which its action can be sustained.').

determine whether that record can reasonably be read to support the agency's determinations.[63]

'In accordance with law' applies to legal determinations. In applying this standard, the court follows the Supreme Court's two-step '*Chevron* doctrine': 'First, the court must determine whether Congress directly spoke to the precise question at issue and clearly expressed its purpose and intent in the governing statute.'[64] Second, 'if the statute does not clearly answer the relevant question, then the court must turn to the

[63] *Nippon Steel Corp. v. United States*, 458 F.3d 1345, 1351 (Fed. Cir. 2006) (holding that 'the substantial evidence standard requires review of the entire administrative record' and asks, in light of that evidence, whether Commerce's determination was reasonable); see also *Daewoo Elecs. Co. v. Int'l Union*, 6 F.3d 1511, 1520 (Fed. Cir. 1993) ('The specific determination we make is whether the evidence and reasonable inferences from the record support [Commerce's findings].') (internal citations and quotation marks omitted). Substantial evidence is 'such relevant evidence as a reasonable mind might accept as adequate to support a conclusion'. *Universal Camera Corp. v. N.L.R.B.*, 340 U.S. 474, 477 (1951). It 'is more than a mere scintilla'. *Consol. Edison Co. of New York v. N.L.R.B.*, 305 U.S. 197, 229 (1938). It 'must do more than create a suspicion of the existence of the fact to be established'. *N.L.R.B. v. Columbian Enameling & Stamping Co.*, 306 U.S. 292, 300 (1939). 'The substantiality of evidence must take into account whatever in the record fairly detracts from its weight.' *Universal Camera Corp.*, 340 U.S. at 488. See *Gallant Ocean (Thailand) Co. v. United States*, 602 F.3d 1319, 1323 (Fed. Cir. 2010) ('This court reviews the record as a whole, including any evidence that "fairly detracts from the substantiality of the evidence," in determining whether substantial evidence exists.') (quoting *Micron Tech., Inc. v. United States*, 117 F.3d 1386, 1393 (Fed. Cir. 1997)); but 'the possibility of drawing two inconsistent conclusions from the evidence does not prevent an administrative agency's finding from being supported by substantial evidence'. *Matsushita Elec. Indus. Co., Ltd. v. United States*, 750 F.2d 927, 933 (Fed. Cir. 1984) (quoting *Consolo v. Federal Maritime Comm'n*, 383 U.S. 607, 619–20 (1966)); '[w]e do not substitute our judgment for that of the board as to the weight of the evidence or the inferences to be drawn therefrom' *Cross v. Dep't of Transp.*, 127 F.3d 1443, 1448 (Fed. Cir. 1997) (citing *Consolo v. Federal Maritime Comm'n*, 383 U.S. 607, 620 (1966)).

[64] *Yangzhou Bestpak Gifts & Crafts Co. v. United States*, 716 F.3d 1370, 1377 (Fed. Cir. 2013) (citing *Chevron, U.S.A., Inc. v. Natural Res. Def. Council, Inc.*, 467 U.S. 837, 842–43 (1984)). In step one, '[t]he judiciary is the final authority on issues of statutory construction and must reject administrative constructions which are contrary to clear congressional intent. . . . If a court, employing traditional tools of statutory construction, ascertains that Congress had an intention on the precise question at issue, that intention is the law and must be given effect.' *Chevron*, 467 U.S. at 843 n.9; see *Robinson v. Shell Oil Co.*, 519 U.S. 337, 341 (1997) ('The plainness or ambiguity of statutory language is determined by reference to the language itself, the specific context in which that language is used, and the broader context of the statute as a whole.'); *Exxon Mobil Corp. v. Allapattah Servs., Inc.*, 545 U.S. 546, 568 (2005) ('[T]he authoritative statement is the statutory text, not the legislative history or any other extrinsic material.'); *Crawfish Processors Alliance v. United States*, 477 F.3d 1375, 1379 (Fed. Cir. 2007) ('In interpreting the statute, this court seeks first the unambiguous meaning of the language.'); *Fin. Planning Ass'n v. S.E.C.*, 482 F.3d 481, 487 (D.C. Cir. 2007) ('Applying the "traditional

second step and decide whether the agency's interpretation amounts to a reasonable construction of the statute.'[65] Under this framework, '[the court] defer[s] to an agency's reasonable interpretation of a statute it is charged with administering.'[66]

Last, in some instances of agency action, the court applies the even more deferential arbitrary, capricious or abuse of discretion standard.[67] This standard asks whether the agency has made a 'rational connection between the facts found and the choice made'.[68] Here too review is on the basis given by the agency.[69]

By performing its function in conformance with the statutory standard of review, the court is applying a standard that is reciprocal, that is, the court applies these standards to all issues, and to all parties, regardless of

tools of statutory construction," the court looks to the text, structure, and the overall statutory scheme, as well as the problem Congress sought to solve.') (citation omitted); *Jones v. Rath Packing Co.*, 430 U.S. 519, 525 (1977) (noting that Congress' intent may be 'explicitly stated in the statute's language or implicitly contained in its structure and purpose'); *Timex V.I., Inc. v. United States*, 157 F.3d 879, 882 (Fed. Cir. 1998) ('To ascertain whether Congress had an intention on the precise question at issue, we employ the "traditional tools of statutory construction." The first and foremost "tool" to be used is the statute's text, giving it its plain meaning.') (citations omitted).

65 *Yangzhou Bestpak*, 716 F.3d at 1377 (citing *Chevron*, 467 U.S. at 843); see *also Chevron*, 467 U.S. at 843 n.9 ('[I]f the statute is silent or ambiguous with respect to the specific issue, the question for the court is whether the agency's answer is based on a permissible construction of the statute.').

66 *Cuomo v. Clearing House Ass'n*, 557 U.S. 519, 524 (2010) (citation omitted); *Entergy Corp. v. Riverkeeper, Inc.*, 556 U.S. 208, 218 (2010) (footnotes & citations omitted) ('[An agency's] view governs if it is a reasonable interpretation of the statute – not necessarily the only possible interpretation, nor even the interpretation deemed most reasonable by the courts.').

67 19 U.S.C. 1516a(b)(1)(A). See *Citizens to Pres. Overton Park, Inc. v. Volpe*, 401 U.S. 402, 416 (1971) *abrogated on other grounds by Califano v. Sanders*, 430 U.S. 99 (1977) ('To make this [arbitrary or capricious] finding the court must consider whether the decision was based on a consideration of the relevant factors and whether there has been a clear error of judgment. . . . Although this inquiry into the facts is to be searching and careful, the ultimate standard of review is a narrow one. The court is not empowered to substitute its judgment for that of the agency.') (citations omitted); *Motor Vehicle Mfrs. Ass'n of U.S., Inc. v. State Farm Mut. Auto. Ins. Co.*, 463 U.S. 29, 43 (1983) ('Normally, an agency rule would be arbitrary and capricious if the agency has relied on factors which Congress has not intended it to consider, entirely failed to consider an important aspect of the problem, offered an explanation for its decision that runs counter to the evidence before the agency, or is so implausible that it could not be ascribed to a difference in view or the product of agency expertise.'); *State Farm*, 463 U.S. at 48 (The 'agency must cogently explain why it has exercised its discretion in a given manner'.).

68 *Burlington Truck Lines, Inc. v. United States*, 371 U.S. 156, 168 (1962).

69 See footnote 62 above.

which party to a case presents the issue for review. In this way, the court's consistent interpretative approach also models the even-handed, rule-based and transparent behaviour that it seeks from the agencies it reviews.

In applying these statutory standards of review, the court is essentially deciding questions of the reasonableness of agency action. In this context, the court may require consideration of societal interests broader than those articulated in trade remedy statues.[70]

The CIT's review function often results in the provision of meaningful relief to the parties to an action. First, the court grants relief in a majority of its cases. Of all cases that were fully briefed during the period 1 January 2007 through 1 January 2012, (the most recent five-year period for which data are available), the matter was remanded at least once in 53.33 per cent of the cases.[71] Second, the court has the remedial authority to provide meaningful relief. Specifically, the court is authorized to direct the return of excess duties, with interest, to the aggrieved party.[72]

[70] See, e.g., *Turtle Island Restoration Network v. Evans*, 284 F. 3d 1282 (Fed. Cir. 2002) (reversing CIT declaratory judgment invalidating regulations permitting importation of shrimp in individual shipments based on exporter representation regarding use of turtle protective commercial fishing technology rather than national certification of protective efforts); *Int'l Labor Rights Fund v. United States*, 29 CIT 1050, 391 F. Supp. 2d 1370 (2005) (holding plaintiffs lacked standing to challenge Commerce's decision not to investigate alleged forced child labor in Côte d'Ivoire cocoa industry); *Florsheim Shoe Co. v. United States*, 19 CIT 295, 880 F. Supp. 848 (1995) (affirming U.S. Fish and Wildlife Services denial of entry products based on embargo meant to discourage illegal trade in rhinoceros and tiger parts); *China Diesel Imports, Inc. v. United States*, 18 CIT 1086, 870 F. Supp. 347 (1994) (affirming Commerce's decision to exclude products produced with prison labour).

[71] Report of the United State Court of International Trade, Jan. 1, 2007 to Jan. 1, 2012 (Aug. 28, 2014) (on file with author).

[72] See 19 U.S.C. § 1516a(e) (2012) ('If the cause of action is sustained in whole or in part by a decision of the United States Court of International Trade or of the United States Court of Appeals for the Federal Circuit – (1) entries of merchandise of the character covered by the published determination of the Secretary, the administering authority, or the Commission, which is entered, or withdrawn from warehouse, for consumption after the date of publication in the Federal Register by the Secretary or the administering authority of a notice of the court decision and (2) entries, the liquidation of which was enjoined under subsection (c)(2) of this section, shall be liquidated in accordance with the final court decision in the action. Such notice of the court decision shall be published within ten days from the date of the issuance of the court decision.'); see also 28 U.S.C. § 1585 ('The Court of International Trade shall possess all the powers in law and equity of, or as conferred by statute upon, a district court of the United States.')

6 The CIT's Relationship with Other Trade Tribunals

6.1 *North American Free Trade Agreement (NAFTA)*

NAFTA 'binational panels' are an avenue of appeal, alternative to the CIT,[73] for parties seeking review of antidumping or countervailing duty determinations by the U.S. Department of Commerce or the International Trade Commission.[74]

NAFTA panels apply the same law as that applied by the CIT. The NAFTA itself instructs panels to apply the domestic law of the importing country.[75] Thus NAFTA is subordinate to U.S. law,[76] but NAFTA has also been fully implemented into U.S. law.[77] Accordingly, NAFTA panels apply the same standards applied by the CIT to the review of agency decisions. And, like the CIT, NAFTA panels may either affirm or remand the agencies' determinations,[78] and may invalidate agency action retroactively (in contrast with the World Trade Organization (WTO) Panel or Appellate Body (AB), which may only invalidate prospectively).[79]

[73] That is, if NAFTA panel review is not requested, parties may seek review before the CIT. If NAFTA panel review is requested, the action may not be brought to the CIT (with limited exceptions for certain issues under the U.S. Constitution). See *Ontario Forest Indus. Assoc. v. United States*, 30 CIT 1117, 1118–19, 444 F. Supp. 2d 1309, 1312–13 (2006).

[74] See 19 U.S.C. § 1516a(g)(8)(A)(i) ('An interested party who was a party to the proceeding in which a determination is made may request binational panel review of such determination by filing a request with the United States Secretary by no later than the date that is 30 days after the date described in subparagraph (A), (B), or (E) of subsection (a)(5) of this section that is applicable to such determination. Receipt of such request by the United States Secretary shall be deemed to be a request for binational panel review within the meaning of article 1904(4) of the NAFTA or of the Agreement. Such request shall contain such information and be in such form, manner, and style as the administering authority, in consultation with the Commission, shall prescribe by regulations.').

[75] NAFTA Article1904(2), 32 I.L.M. at 683; *Ontario Forest Indus. Assoc. v. United States*, 30 CIT 1117, 1120 (2006) ('The panel is empowered to sustain or remand the determination under review, NAFTA Article 1904(2), 32 I.L.M. at 683, and its findings are binding on the participating governments with respect to the matter at issue. NAFTA Article1904 (9), (11), (15), 32 I.L.M. at 683–4; 19 U.S.C. § 1516a(g)(2). See also S.Rep. No. 100–509, at 31 (1988), *reprinted in* 1988 U.S.C.C.A.N. 2395, 2426 ("Because binational panels act as a substitute for U.S. courts in deciding whether a determination is consistent with U.S. law, the Committee intends binational panel decisions to be implemented in the same manner that court decisions are implemented under the current law".)') (footnote omitted).

[76] See 19 U.S.C. § 3312(a)(1) ('No provision of the [NAFTA], nor the application of any such provision to any person or circumstance, which is inconsistent with any law of the United States shall have effect.').

[77] See 19 U.S.C. § 3311 and Exec. Order No. 12,889, 58 Fed. Reg. 69,681 (Dec. 27, 1993).

[78] NAFTA Article1904.8, 32 I.L.M. at 683.

[79] See Statement of Administrative Action to URAA, H.R.Rep. No. 103–316, at 1026 (1994), reprinted in 1994 U.S.C.C.A.N. 4040, 4313 ('Consistent with the principle that [General Agreement on Tariffs and Trade (GATT)] panel recommendations apply only

However, unlike CIT decisions, NAFTA panels may not be appealed to higher domestic courts;[80] instead for NAFTA panel decisions, either government may request that a binational extraordinary challenge committee review a panel decision.[81]

Despite the binding nature of NAFTA panel decisions, there have been cases in which the CIT has been a necessary forum for the implementation of the panel's action. For example, the final judgment in *Canadian Lumber*, discussed earlier, resulted in the return of duties upon the liquidation of the entries covered; a remedy the NAFTA panel was not empowered to order.[82]

6.2 *The WTO*

The CIT's relationship with the WTO agreements, and Panel and Appellate Body (AB) reports, is not as direct as its relationship with NAFTA and its panel decisions.

Like NAFTA, while the WTO agreements are subordinate to U.S. domestic law,[83] the agreements themselves have been implemented into U.S. law (through the URAA).[84] But the decisions resulting from the

prospectively, subsection 129(c)(1) provides that where determinations by the ITC or Commerce are implemented under subsections (a) or (b), such determinations have prospective effect only. That is, they apply to unliquidated entries of merchandise entered, or withdrawn from warehouse, for consumption on or after the date on which the Trade Representative directs implementation. Thus, relief available under subsection 129(c)(1) is distinguishable from relief available in an action brought before a court or a NAFTA binational panel, where, depending on the circumstances of the case, retroactive relief may be available. Under 129(c)(1), if implementation of a WTO report should result in the revocation of an antidumping or countervailing duty order, entries made prior to the date of Trade Representative's direction would remain subject to potential duty liability.'); see also *Andaman Seafood Co., Ltd. v. United States*, CIT, 675 F. Supp. 2d 1363, 1370 (2010).

80 See 19 U.S.C. § 1516a(g)(2) ('[N]o court of the United States has power or jurisdiction to review the determination on any question of law or fact by an action in the nature of mandamus or otherwise.')

81 See 19 U.S.C. § 1516a(a)(5)(C)(ii); NAFTA Article 1904.13, 32 I.L.M. at 683.

82 *Canadian Lumber Trade Alliance v. United States*, 32 CIT 936, 577 F. Supp. 2d 1313 (2008); see also *Tembec, Inc. v. United States*, 31 CIT 241, 243, 475 F. Supp. 2d 1393, 1396 (2007).

83 See 19 U.S.C. § 3512(a)(1) ('No provision of any of the Uruguay Round Agreements, nor the application of any such provision to any person or circumstance, that is inconsistent with any law of the United States shall have effect.').

84 Pub. L. No. 103–465, 108 Stat. 4809 (codified as amended at 19 U.S.C. §§ 3501–3624) (1994) and Exec. Order No. 13,042, 62 Fed. Reg. 18,017 (Apr. 9, 1997). According to its legislative history, the URAA 'is intended to bring U.S. law fully into compliance with U.S. obligations under [the Uruguay Round Agreements] ... by amending existing federal statutes that would otherwise be inconsistent with the agreements and, in certain

WTO dispute resolution process have a very different effect. Unlike NAFTA panel decisions, the compliance recommendations in WTO Panel and AB Reports do not command particular action by the United States (or WTO members generally).[85] This stems from the WTO agreements themselves, in that the Panel and AB Reports were not meant to compel a specific response from WTO member states.[86] Further, international trade law only has domestic effect in the United States insofar as it has been implemented by Congress.[87] In this context, WTO Panel and AB decisions are not viewed as binding precedent in U.S. courts.[88]

Instead, WTO Panel and AB determinations may be implemented into U.S. law through two different administrative proceedings: (1) a Section 123 proceeding (named for Section 123 of the URAA), which is 'the mechanism to amend, rescind, or modify an agency regulation or

instances, by creating entirely new provisions of law'. URAA Statement of Administrative Action, 1 H.R. Doc. 103–316, at 669 (1994).

[85] See 19 U.S.C. § 3538 (setting out the process (Section 123 and 129 proceedings) by which the U.S. Trade Representative may implement a WTO panel or AB decision).

[86] See Uruguay Round Agreement, Annex 2: Understanding on Rules and Procedures Governing the Settlement of Dispute, Article 19(1), Apr. 15, 1994 ('Where a panel or the Appellate Body concludes that a measure is inconsistent with a covered agreement, it shall recommend that the Member concerned bring the measure into conformity with that agreement. In addition to its recommendations, the panel or Appellate Body may suggest ways in which the Member concerned could implement the recommendations.'); see also *Tembec*, 30 CIT at 984–5, 441 F. Supp. 2d 1328.

[87] See H.R. Rep. 103–826(1), at 25 (1994) ('Since the Uruguay Round agreements as approved by the Congress, or any subsequent amendments to those agreements, are not self-executing, any dispute settlement findings that a U.S. statute is inconsistent with an agreement also cannot be implemented except by legislation approved by the Congress unless consistent implementation is permiss[i]ble under the terms of the statute.'); see also *Hyundai Electronics Co. v. United States*, 23 CIT 302, 311 (1999) ('[T]he response to a panel report is the prerogative of the executive branch, not the judiciary, because it implicates political decisions.') (citing *Footwear Distributors and Retailers of America v. United States*, 18 CIT 391, 852 F. Supp. 1078 (1994)).

[88] See *Corus Staal BV v. Dep't of Commerce*, 395 F.3d 1343, 1348 (Fed. Cir. 2005) ('WTO decisions are not binding on the United States, much less this court. Further, no provision of any of the Uruguay Round Agreements nor the application of any such provision to any person or circumstance, that is inconsistent with any law of the United States shall have effect. Neither the GATT nor any enabling international agreement outlining compliance therewith . . . trumps domestic legislation; if U.S. statutory provisions are inconsistent with the GATT or an enabling agreement, it is strictly a matter for Congress.') (internal quotation marks, citations, and original alterations omitted); see also *Koyo Seiko Co. v. United States*, 30 CIT 1111, 1113, 442 F. Supp. 2d 1360, 1363 (2006) ('It is a long standing principle that "while WTO adjudicatory decisions may be persuasive, they are not binding on Commerce or this court."') (quoting *NSK Ltd. v. United States*, 29 CIT 1, 13 n.13, 358 F. Supp. 2d 1276, 1288 n.13 (2005)).

practice in order to implement a decision by the WTO that such is inconsistent with U.S. treaty obligations',[89] and (2) a Section 129 proceeding (again, named for its provision in the URAA), which 'sets forth a procedure to implement a negative WTO decision with respect to a *specific* administrative determination that was the subject of a WTO dispute'.[90]

Despite this absence of direct effect, WTO agreements may still inform U.S. courts' interpretation of domestic law (i.e., courts interpret domestic law so that it does not directly conflict with applicable international law),[91] and Panel and AB Reports may be a persuasive guide, in some circumstances.[92] U.S. Courts have also considered WTO Reports, and the

[89] *Corus Staal BV v. United States*, 31 CIT 1442, 1447 n.8, 515 F. Supp. 2d 1337, 1341 n.8 (2007) (quoting *Corus Staal BV v. United States*, 31 CIT 826, 829 n.2, 493 F. Supp. 2d 1276, 1279 n.2 (2007)). Section 123 'requires the United States Trade Representative (USTR) to consult with appropriate congressional committees, private sector committees, and provide for public comment before determining whether and how to change an agency regulation or practice'. Ibid.

[90] Ibid. Section 129 determinations are 'prospective in nature,' as they are 'effective only for unliquidated entries of merchandise that are entered or withdrawn from warehouse for consumption on or after the date the USTR directs Commerce to implement that determination'. Ibid.; See *Andaman Seafood Co., Ltd. v. United States*, CIT, 675 F. Supp. 2d 1363, 1367 (2010); *U.S. Steel Corp. v. United States*, 33 CIT 984, 637 F. Supp. 2d 1199, 1205–6 (2009) *aff'd*, 621 F.3d 1351 (Fed. Cir. 2010); *Corus Staal BV v. United States*, 32 CIT 1480, 1484 n.11, 593 F. Supp. 2d 1373, 1377 n.11 (2008).

[91] See *Liugi Bormioli Corp, Inc., v. United States*, 304 F.3d 1362, 1368(Fed. Cir. 2002) ('the statute must be interpreted to be consistent with GATT obligations, absent contrary indications in the statutory language or its legislative history'); *Fed.-Mogul Corp. v. United States*, 63 F.3d 1572, 1581 (Fed. Cir. 1995) ('Yet GATT agreements are international obligations, and absent express Congressional language to the contrary, statutes should not be interpreted to conflict with international obligations.') (citing *Murray v. The Schooner States*, 304 F.3d 1362, 1368 (Fed. Cir. 2002) ('[W]e think that the statute must be interpreted to be consistent with GATT obligations, absent contrary indications in the statutory language or its legislative history.').

In this way, the agreements are a type of 'secondary legislative history,' used in *Chevron* step 2 analysis in conjunction with the *Charming Betsy* Doctrine. See *Hyundai Electronics Co. v. United States*, 23 CIT 302, 313, 53 F. Supp. 2d 1334, 1344 (1999) ('*Chevron* must be applied in concert with the *Charming Betsy* doctrine when the latter doctrine is implicated.'). (The *Charming Betsy* Doctrine provides that 'an act of Congress ought never to be construed to violate the law of nations if any other possible construction remains, and consequently can never be construed to violate neutral rights, or to affect neutral commerce, further than is warranted by the law of nations as understood in this country.' *Murray v. The Schooner Charming Betsy*, 6 U.S. 64, 118 (1804)).

[92] See *Allegheny Ludlum Corp. v. United States*, 367 F.3d 1339, 1348 (Fed. Cir. 2004) ('[T]he WTO's appellate report does not bind this court in construing domestic countervailing duty law. Nonetheless, this guideline supports the trial court's judgment.'); *Acciai Speciali Terni S.p.A. v. United States*, 28 CIT 2013, 2023 n.11, 350 F. Supp. 2d 1254, 1263 n.11

disputes which they reflect, to be relevant factual evidence to be taken take into account.[93]

7 The CIT's Tribunal-Specific Legitimacy Claims

In general, domestic law in the United States claims legitimacy as the result of how it is made: through a representative, democratic process with checks and balances to ensure an open system.

For administrative law at the CIT in particular, the legitimacy claim is based on a rule-based, transparent and meaningful process of judicial review. Because it is rule based and transparent, it corresponds to the expectations of those who use or rely upon it. This public transparency and accountability to objective, internally consistent, reciprocal and predictable standards lends legitimacy to the court's decisions in the eyes

(2004) ('Neither the WTO legal texts nor the AB and panel reports have direct applicability under U.S. law. The reasoning in those materials, however, can be useful for clarifying the subsidy provisions at issue in this case.'); *Usinor, Beautor, Haironville, Sollac Atlantique, Sollace Lorraine v. United States*, 28 CIT 1107, 1122, 342 F. Supp. 2d 1267, 1279 (2004) (considering a WTO AB decision as persuasive authority: 'The ITC's determination that U.S. law and the WTO Anti-Dumping Agreement are not in conflict is thus in accordance with the law.'); *Hyundai Electronics Co. v. United States*, 23 CIT. 302, 312 (1999) ('Congress provided that the response to an adverse WTO panel report is the province of the executive branch and, more particularly, the Office of the U.S. Trade Representative. *See* URAA § 129 (codified as 19 U.S.C. § 3538). Thus, the WTO panel report does not constitute binding precedential authority for the court. Of course, this is not to imply that a panel report serves no purpose in litigation before the court. To the contrary, a panel's reasoning, if sound, may be used to inform the court's decision.'). *Cf. Cummins Inc. v. United States*, 454 F.3d 1361, 1366 (Fed. Cir. 2006) (A '[World Customs Organization] opinion is not binding and is entitled, at most, to respectful consideration. It is not a proxy for independent analysis'.) (internal citation and quotation marks omitted).

93 See *Crosby v. Nat'l Foreign Trade Council*, 530 U.S. 363, 386 n.24 (2000) (finding that the existence of a WTO dispute was evidence toward establishing that a state law was interfering with federal diplomatic objectives and was ultimately invalid under the Supremacy Clause); *Allegheny Ludlum Corp. v. United States*, 29 CIT 157, 172 (2005) ('In this case, given that Commerce's methodology and its Section 129 determination are intended to implement WTO rulings, [that ruling, and Commerce's determination being a reaction thereto] is relevant. Accordingly, were the agency to construe an ambiguous statute so as to benefit domestic interests in violation of international agreements, retaliatory tariffs would result, a penalty which Congress presumably would wish to avoid. Consequently, courts should prefer adhering to international law standards unless otherwise indicated by Congress. Additionally, the WTO Appellate Body decisions have persuasive weight here because nonconformance of U.S. practice may result in retaliatory tariffs against U.S. exporters – a result that negates the U.S.'s benefit from the international agreement.') (internal citations omitted).

of both the parties to particular disputes (who seek an impartial, diligent and rational arbiter of disputes) and the general American public (who seek a just and reasonable application of the country's trade laws).

Substantively, despite the opportunity for two-tier review – through a second application of the same standard of review at the court of appeals for the federal circuit – most dispositive decisions by the CIT are not appealed, and most of those that are appealed are affirmed on appeal or the appeal is dismissed.

For the period 1 January 2007 through 1 January 2012 (the most recent five-year period for which data are available), more than 60 per cent of the CIT's dispositive opinions were not appealed, and more than two-thirds of those that were appealed were affirmed in all respects or the appeal was dismissed.[94]

This data must imply at least some level of acceptance of CIT decisions as meeting the expectations of the participants in the system.

[94] Report of the United State Court of International Trade, Jan. 1, 2007 to Jan. 1, 2012 (Aug. 28, 2014) (on file with author).

6

The Federal Courts of Canada

MAUREEN IRISH*

This chapter discusses aspects of Canadian international economic law and the Federal Courts of Canada. The chapter begins with a description of the mandate and operations of the Federal Courts and outlines the procedures involved in customs, antidumping and countervailing duty litigation. The next section addresses questions of deference to other decision-makers – in this case domestic administrative agencies – and the appropriate role for judicial review by courts, with an emphasis on customs and trade remedy matters. The following section on forum shopping discusses Canadian law on *forum non conveniens*, as well as NAFTA binational panels that can replace domestic judicial review on some trade files. The chapter then turns to the relationship between international law and domestic courts. Drawing on recent Canadian jurisprudence, the chapter comments on the task of domestic courts to apply international law in the internal legal system, while also having a role in the elaboration of that law as part of state practice and as a subsidiary source of law. The argument presented is that just as views on the proper role for judges have influenced the development of Canadian administrative law, so too have similar legitimacy concerns affected current doctrinal controversies over the treatment of public international law by Canadian courts, including in trade and economic disputes.

1 Court Mandate and Selection of Judges

The Federal Court of Canada was established in 1971, as the successor to the Exchequer Court of Canada.[1] The new court assumed the Exchequer

* Maureen Irish, Faculty of Law, University of Windsor, Windsor, Ontario, Canada. I am grateful for comments on earlier drafts from Judge Donald C Pogue and from Windsor Law Professors Laverne Jacobs, Christopher Waters and Sara Wharton. Excellent research support was provided by Vagmi Patel, Jessica Spina and Noah Haynes, with funding from the Faculty of Law.

[1] Federal Court Act, RSC 1970 (2nd Supp) c 10. For a history of the Court, see I. Bushnell, *The Federal Court of Canada: A History, 1875–1992* (University of Toronto Press, 1997).

Court's mandate for taxation and civil claims brought by the federal Crown. In succeeding years, the Federal Court acquired additional jurisdiction covering admiralty, intellectual property, immigration, actions against the Crown, specific statutory appeals and applications for judicial review of decisions of federal administrative agencies. In 1971, the Court consisted of a Trial Division and the Federal Court of Appeal. In 2002, the trial level was renamed the Federal Court. The Federal Court and the Federal Court of Appeal continue their functions, now as two separate courts.[2]

The Federal Court of Appeal consists of a chief justice and twelve other judges.[3] The Federal Court consists of a chief justice and thirty-six other judges.[4] At least five of the Federal Court of Appeal judges and at least ten of the Federal Court judges must be former judges of the Quebec Superior Court or Court of Appeal or former members of the Quebec bar.[5] Judges are appointed by the Federal Cabinet.[6] They hold office during good behaviour until age seventy-five, but may be removed by the Governor General on address of the Senate and House of Commons.[7] Judges of both Courts are to live in or near Ottawa, although a rota of judges of the Federal Court is established for the city of Vancouver, to ensure the continuous availability of judges for trials to be held there.[8]

The Federal Courts exercise authority that would otherwise be within the mandate of the provincial Superior Courts, the courts of general jurisdiction. Throughout their history, the mandate of the Federal Courts has been analysed and criticized within the context of federal–provincial relations.[9] Recently, a proposed nominee for the Supreme Court of Canada was found ineligible for one of the positions on that Court for judges from Quebec. The nominee was a judge of the Federal Court of Appeal and previously had been a member of the Quebec Bar for many years. The Supreme Court ruled that nominees for the Quebec seats had to be current judges of the Quebec Court of Appeal or Superior Court or current members of the Quebec Bar.[10]

[2] Courts Administration Service Act, SC 2002, c 8, s 16.

[3] Federal Courts Act, RSC 1985, c F-7, s 5(1). [4] Ibid., s 5.1(1). [5] Ibid., s 5.4.

[6] Ibid., s 5.2. [7] Ibid., s 8(1), s 8(2).

[8] Ibid., s 7(1), s 7(2), Federal Courts Rules, SOR/98-106, s 40.

[9] Bushnell, '*The Federal Court of Canada*, pp. 21–4, 157–67 and 195–202. Part of the impetus for the 1971 establishment of the Federal Court came from some conflicting views in the provincial courts over their jurisdiction to review federal agencies See *Canadian Transit Company v. Windsor (Corporation of the City)*, 2015 FCA 88, leave to appeal to the Supreme Court of Canada granted [2015] SCCA No 223.

[10] *Reference re Supreme Court Act, ss 5 and 6*, 2014 SCC 21, [2014] SCJ No 21 ('The purpose of s 6 is to ensure not only civil law training and experience on the Court, but also to ensure that Quebec's distinct legal traditions and social values are represented on the

The Federal Courts' trade-related work includes intellectual property, admiralty, customs law appeals from the Canadian International Trade Tribunal (CITT), judicial review of CITT decisions (antidumping duty, countervailing duty, government procurement), administrative law supervision of governmental action and cases brought by or against the Crown. An example of litigation brought by the Crown is the enforcement action against U.S. Steel relating to undertakings given as part of the process for foreign investment approval of a takeover of a Canadian business.[11] Actions to set aside investor–state dispute settlement awards may also be brought in the Federal Court.[12]

The Federal Courts supervise administrative agencies by way of appeals and judicial review. Much of the Courts' trade-related work comes from the CITT, an agency that has administrative and quasi-judicial functions.[13] The CITT hears appeals on customs and related duties, makes injury determinations in antidumping duty, countervailing duty and safeguard files and conducts inquiries[14] on matters referred by the federal Cabinet or the Minister of Finance. The CITT also hears bid challenges on government procurement.[15] The CITT consists of a

Court, thereby enhancing the confidence of the people of Quebec in the Supreme Court as the final arbiter of their rights' (para 49)).

11 *United States Steel Corporation and U.S Steel Canada Inc. v. Canada (Attorney General)*, 2011 FCA 176, [2011] FCJ No 726, leave to appeal dismissed [2011] SCCA No 364 (action originally brought in Federal Court).

12 *Canada (Attorney General) v. SD. Myers, Inc.*, 2004 FC 38, [2004] FCJ No 29. Provincial Superior Courts have concurrent jurisdiction for actions to set aside awards: *United Mexican States v. Metalclad Corp.*, 2001 BCSC 664, [2001] BCJ No 950; *United Mexican States v. Karpa*, [2005] OJ No 16, 74 OR (3d) 180 (CA); *United Mexican States v. Cargill, Inc.*, 2011 ONCA 622, [2011] OJ No 4320, leave to appeal dismissed [2011] SCCA No 528. The Ontario Superior Court of Justice heard an application for review of a jurisdictional decision made by an investor–state tribunal: *Bayview Irrigation District # 11 v. Mexico*, [2008] OJ No 1858. Actions for revision or annulment of investment awards may now be taken under the International Convention on the Settlement of Investment Disputes between States and Nationals of Other States (Washington, D.C, in force 14 October 1966), as Canada became a party in 2013 (signed by Canada 15 December 2006, in force 1 December 2013, Can TS 2013/24).

13 Canadian International Trade Tribunal Act, RSC 1985, c 47 (4th Supp).

14 See, for example, a report by a predecessor agency: Tariff Board, *Canada's Customs Tariff According to the Harmonized System*, Reference 163, 1985–8.

15 In addition, the Tribunal has jurisdiction over excise tax appeals, oil export charges and requests for tariff relief from textile imports. The Canadian International Trade Tribunal is the successor of several previous boards and tribunals: the Tariff Board, the Canadian Import Tribunal (previously the Anti-dumping Tribunal), the Textile and Clothing Board and the Procurement Review Board. The combination of administrative and quasi-judicial functions was also common in the predecessor institutions: Philip Slayton, *The*

chairperson and up to six other permanent members, appointed for terms of five years. Temporary members can be appointed for terms of three years. CITT members are appointed by the Federal Cabinet and can be removed at any time for cause.[16] In keeping with the functions of the CITT, members are not necessarily lawyers, but may have qualifications in other areas, such as commerce, economics, trade policy and public administration.

A person contesting a decision by customs authorities concerning origin, tariff classification, value for duty or marking can request two redeterminations within the Canada Border Services Agency (CBSA), the first by another officer, the second by the president of the Agency.[17] The decision of the president may be appealed to the CITT.[18] From the CITT, an appeal lies to the Federal Court of Appeal,[19] and thereafter to the Supreme Court of Canada, with leave.[20]

In antidumping and countervailing duty complaints, the CBSA investigates dumping and subsidization and is responsible for determining any margin of dumping or amount of subsidy. The CITT has responsibility for findings of injury. A complaint of dumping or subsidizing must be supported by producers having at least 25 per cent of total domestic production of like goods and by at least 50 per cent of domestic producers who express either support for or opposition to the complaint.[21] The president of the CBSA will initiate the investigation if there is evidence of dumping or subsidizing and of injury, retardation of the establishment of a domestic industry or threat of injury.[22] Within sixty days of the start of the investigation, the CITT decides whether to make a preliminary determination that there is a reasonable indication of injury, retardation or threat of injury.[23] Between sixty and ninety days after the start of the investigation, the president of the CBSA makes a preliminary determination of dumping

Anti-dumping Tribunal, Law Reform Commission of Canada (Minister of Supply and Services Canada, 1979); Philip Slayton and John J. Quinn, *The Tariff Board*, Law Reform Commission of Canada (Minister of Supply and Services Canada, 1981).

[16] Canadian International Trade Tribunal Act, RSC 1985, c 47 (4th Supp), s 3(4).

[17] Customs Act, RSC 1985, c 1 (2nd Supp), ss 59 and 60.

[18] Ibid., s 67.

[19] Ibid., s 68.

[20] Supreme Court Act, RSC 1985, c S-26, with leave of the Federal Court of Appeal (s 37.1) or with leave of the Supreme Court of Canada (s 40(1)).

[21] Special Import Measures Act, RS 1985, c S-15, s 31(2).

[22] Ibid., s 31(1).

[23] Ibid., s 37.1(1). This step was previously the responsibility of customs authorities, but was transferred to the CITT in 2000: P. M. Saroli and G. Tereposky, 'Changes to Canada's anti-dumping and countervailing duty laws for the new millennium', *Canadian Bar Review*, 79 (2009), 352.

or subsidizing, with estimates of the margin of dumping or amount of subsidy.[24] The final determination of dumping or subsidizing is made by the president along with the margins of dumping or amount of subsidy, within ninety days of the preliminary determination.[25] The CITT's inquiry into injury, retardation or threat of injury must be completed within 120 days of the CBSA's preliminary determination.[26] If the CITT finds that the dumping or subsidizing has caused injury, retardation or a threat of injury, duties are levied equal to the margin of dumping or the amount of subsidy.[27] The duties are retroactive to the date of the preliminary determination by CBSA if the CITT found that the dumping or subsidizing caused past injury.[28] Duties expire in five years, unless they are renewed.[29] The final determination of dumping or subsidizing and the CITT's injury finding are subject to review by the Federal Court of Appeal,[30] and that Court's decision may be appealed to the Supreme Court of Canada, with leave.[31]

2 Procedural Rules

Hearings of the Federal Courts are open and publicly accessible, unless an order is made for proceedings to be held *in camera*.[32] Material can be admitted on a confidential basis only if the court is satisfied that confidentiality is appropriate despite the public interest in open proceedings.[33] Hearings may take place by way of video conference or other form of electronic communication.[34] The Federal Court provides trials regularly in Ottawa, Toronto, Vancouver, Montreal and throughout the provinces.[35] The Federal Courts have discretion to grant intervener (i.e., amicus) status. An applicant must describe how the intervention will assist in determining a factual or legal issue before the court.[36]

CITT hearings are public, but may be held in camera to receive confidential information or if justified in the circumstances.[37] Hearings may take place in electronic form or by written submission.[38] In appeals on origin, marking, tariff classification, value for duty, dumping,

[24] Ibid., s 38(1). This time can be extended to 135 days after the initiation of the investigation: s 39(1).
[25] Ibid., s 41(1). [26] Ibid., ss 42(1) and 43(1). [27] Ibid., s 3(1). [28] Ibid., s 4(1).
[29] Ibid., s 76.03. [30] Ibid., s 96.1.
[31] Supreme Court Act, RSC 1985, c S-26, s 37.1, s 40(1).
[32] Federal Courts Rules, SOR/98-106, s 29. [33] Ibid., s 151. [34] Ibid., s 32.
[35] Ibid., s 34. [36] Ibid., s 109.
[37] Canadian International Trade Tribunal Rules, SOR/99-499, s 23. [38] Ibid., s 25.

subsidization, and the application of antidumping or countervailing duties to imported goods, any person who enters an appearance with the secretary of the CITT may be heard.[39] In contrast, investigations concerning injury in antidumping and countervailing duty matters are limited to evidence from complainants and directly interested persons.[40] If antidumping or countervailing duties are to be levied, the CITT has power to hold an inquiry to consider whether imposing duty in the full amount is in the public interest. If the Tribunal concludes that duties would not or might not be in the public interest, the Tribunal reports its opinion to the Minister of Finance, who decides what action to take in response.[41] Public interest inquiries have heard views from a wide range of participants, including community and labour representatives in the case of a factory threatened with closure, health and antipoverty groups concerned over pricing of essential products, the Competition Bureau and industry representatives.[42]

3 Fact-Finding

Trials in the Federal Court proceed by way of the examination and cross-examination of witnesses, who are subject to subpoena and can be ordered to produce documents and other material.[43] Expert witnesses may give testimony on specific questions, either orally or through affidavit.[44] The Federal Courts have discretion over the awarding of costs.[45]

The CITT has power to subpoena witnesses and documents or other material. Proceedings are by way of examination and cross-examination. Expert witnesses may give testimony and provide written reports.[46]

[39] Customs Act, RSC 1985, c 1 (2nd Supp), s 67(2); Special Import Measures Act, RSC 1985, c S-15, s 61(2). See *R.B. Packings & Seals Inc. v. Canada (Minister of National Revenue – M.N.R.)* [1995] CITT No 38. Competing domestic producers do not have standing to request advance rulings on tariff classification: *BalanceCo v. Canada (Border Services Agency)*, AP-2012-036, 3 May 2013, affd 2014 FCA 132.

[40] Special Import Measures Act, RSC 1985, c S-15, s 42; Canadian International Trade Tribunal Act, RSC 1985, c 47 (4th Supp), s 23; Canadian International Trade Tribunal Rules, SOR/99-499, s 41; L. L. Herman, *Canadian Trade Remedy Law and Practice* (Toronto: Emond Montgomery, 1997) p. 111.

[41] Special Import Measures Act, RSC 1985, c S-15, s 45. See Special Import Measures Regulations, SOR/84/927, s 40.1.

[42] Canadian International Trade Tribunal, Public Interest Investigation into Certain Prepared Baby Food Originating in or Exported from the United States of America, PB-98-001, 30 November 1998.

[43] Federal Courts Rules, SOR/98-106, s 41, s 91. [44] Ibid., ss 52.1 and 279.

[45] Ibid., s 400. [46] Canadian International Trade Tribunal Rules, SOR/99-499, ss 20–3.

4 Interpretative Approaches

The Federal Courts review decisions of federal administrators and hear appeals from federal statutory bodies such as the Canadian International Trade Tribunal. For this part of their mandate, the Courts follow Canadian judicial review law, which deals with the appropriate level of deference owing to administrative decision making. Canadian judicial review law follows the common law tradition and relies on stare decisis.[47] The Federal Court of Appeal and the Canadian Import Tribunal, a predecessor of the CITT, were involved in a significant dispute in judicial review law in the *National Corn Growers* case, a countervailing duty matter that was ultimately determined by the Supreme Court of Canada in 1990. The Canadian Import Tribunal found both injury and a threat of injury based on competition from potential – but not actual – imports, in a dispute over countervailing duties on grain corn from the United States.[48]

A central concern in judicial review law has been the appropriate role for judicial supervision of the institutions of the modern administrative state, reflecting the legislative decision to establish those institutions and endow them with certain powers. A wide role for courts is a means of controlling executive and administrative authority. The argument for a narrow role maintains that extensive review leads courts to substitute their decisions for those of expert agencies, at the risk of frustrating legislative policy. In the early 1970s, the Supreme Court of Canada adopted a very demanding standard that tended to treat any legal interpretation by an agency of its constitutive statute as a 'preliminary question' which the agency had to answer correctly in order to acquire and retain jurisdiction.[49] The preliminary question doctrine applied even

[47] This is so even when there is a statutory list of grounds for review, such as s 18.1(4) of the Federal Courts Act, which is read and understood against the background of evolving case law: *Canada (Citizenship and Immigration) v. Khosa* 2009 SCC 12, [2009] SCJ No 12 at para. 19. Canadian courts have tended to apply the same judicial review lens to applications to set aside decisions of investment tribunals See cases cited in footnote 12 above.

[48] *National Corn Growers Assn. v. Canada (Import Tribunal)* [1990] 2 SCR. 1324, [1990] SCJ No 110. The Supreme Court dismissed an appeal from the decision of the Federal Court of Appeal, [1989] 2 FC 517, [1988] FCJ No 1159, which upheld the finding of the Canadian Import Tribunal (1987) 14 CER 1.

[49] *Metropolitan Life Insurance v. International Union of Operating Engineers* [1970] SCR 425; *Bell v. Ontario* (Human Rights Commission) [1971] SCR 756. These cases were influenced by the reasoning of the House of Lords in *Anisminic v. Foreign Compensation Commission*, [1969] 2 AC 147, 2 WLR 163 (HL).

if the statute had a privative clause intended to bar or limit review by courts.[50] The privative clause would only protect while the agency was acting within its jurisdiction.

During the 1970s and 1980s, much academic commentary criticized this approach as overly intrusive. In *National Corn Growers*, the concurring minority decision by Wilson J. notes 'a growing recognition on the part of courts that they may simply not be as well-equipped as administrative tribunals or agencies to deal with issues which Parliament has chosen to regulate through bodies exercising delegated power, e.g., labour relations, telecommunications, financial markets and international economic relations'.[51] *National Corn Growers* was part of a line of more deferential decisions that would only reject an agency's interpretation of its constitutive statute if that interpretation were patently unreasonable.[52] In the case, the Canadian Import Tribunal's decision to consider potential imports as part of the injury determination was not a patently unreasonable interpretation of the legislation, and the Tribunal's determination was upheld by the Federal Court of Appeal and the Supreme Court of Canada. The 'pragmatic and functional' approach that developed in this line of decisions requires courts to analyse and choose the standard of review to apply in each case. As summarised in 1998 in *Pushpanathan*, one of three standards could apply: correctness, reasonableness simpliciter, or patent unreasonableness. The court's analysis is to consider four factors: (1) the presence or absence of a privative clause, (2) the expertise of the decision maker relative to the expertise of the reviewing court, (3) the purpose of the legislation as a whole and of the provision in particular and (4) the nature of the decision as relating to law or to fact.[53]

[50] See, for example, the privative clause in question in *Canadian Union of Public Employees Local 963 v. New Brunswick Liquor Corp.* [1979] 2 SCR 227: 'Section 101(1) Except as provided in this Act, every order, award, direction, decision, declaration, or ruling of the Board, the Arbitration Tribunal or an adjudicator is final and shall not be questioned or reviewed in any court. Section 101(2) No order shall be made or process entered, and no proceedings shall be taken in any court, whether by way of injunction, certiorari, prohibition, quo warranto, or otherwise, to question, review, prohibit or restrain the Board, the Arbitration Tribunal or an adjudicator in any of its or his proceedings.'

[51] *National Corn Growers*, above footnote 48, para. 9.

[52] Ibid., paras. 27–30. The judgement cites Canadian Union of Public Employees, *Local 963 v. New Brunswick Liquor Corp.* [1979] 2 SCR 227.

[53] *Pushpanathan v. Canada* (Minister of Citizenship and Immigration) [1998] 1 SCR 982, paras. 29–38.

In 2008, in *Dunsmuir*, the Supreme Court of Canada responded to criticism that this standard of review analysis was too complex and unpredictable. The Court collapsed the two reasonableness standards into one, so that the standard to be applied now is either correctness or reasonableness.[54] Correctness will apply to constitutional questions,[55] true questions of jurisdiction,[56] matters of general law 'of central importance to the legal system as a whole' and outside the decision makers' area of expertise,[57] and questions relating to the jurisdictional lines between two or more specialized tribunals.[58] Pursuant to the more deferential reasonableness standard, '[t]ribunals have a margin of appreciation within the range of acceptable and rational solutions.'[59] Reasonableness is usually the standard to be applied to decisions covered by a privative clause;[60] to questions of fact, discretion or policy; and to questions of mixed law and fact.[61] At the same time, the Court continued the basic factors of the earlier pragmatic and functional approach, while stating that a full analysis is not required in every case because existing jurisprudence could indicate that the analysis had already been completed earlier and did not need to be repeated.[62] Some initial fears over the revival of overly intrusive jurisdictional review have now subsided. At the moment, commentary is somewhat mixed on whether the *Dunsmuir* attempt to simplify has been successful.[63]

For review of decisions of the CITT, the Supreme Court of Canada has concluded that a reasonableness standard is appropriate in tariff classification matters, within the CITT's expertise, but that other areas such as customs valuation will be judged on a correctness standard if they depend on statutory interpretation and raise pure questions of law.[64]

54 *Dunsmuir v. New Brunswick*, 2008 SCC 9, [2008] 1 SCR 190, paras. 44–50.

55 Ibid., para. 58. 56 Ibid., para. 59. 57 Ibid., para. 60. 58 Ibid., para. 61.

59 Ibid., para. 47. Reasons given must be sufficient to allow a reviewing court to understand why the tribunal decided as it did, but there is no need for explicit findings on each element leading to the final conclusion: *Newfoundland and Labrador Nurses' Union v. Newfoundland and Labrador (Treasury Board)*, 2011 SCC 62, [2011] SCJ No 62.

60 *Dunsmuir*, above footnote 54, para. 52. 61 Ibid., para. 53. 62 Ibid., para. 57.

63 L. Jacobs, 'Developments in administrative law: The 2007–2008 term – The impact of *Dunsmuir*', *Supreme Court Law Review*, 43, 2, (2008), 1; G. P. Heckman, 'Substantive review in appellate courts since *Dunsmuir*', *Osgoode Hall Law Journal*, 47 (2010), 751; M. Lewans, 'Deference and reasonableness since *Dunsmuir*', *Queen's Law Journal*, 38 (2012), 59; P. Daly, 'The scope and meaning of reasonableness review', *Alberta Law Review*, 54, 4, (2015), 799.

64 *Canada (Deputy Minister of National Revenue) v. Mattel Canada Inc.*, 2001 SCC 36, [2001] 2 SCR 100.

The Federal Court of Appeal has reviewed valuation decisions on a correctness standard,[65] but used a reasonableness standard to dismiss an appeal from a CITT valuation decision regarding R & D payments, as the decision involved a factual assessment pursuant to a statute in which the Tribunal has expertise.[66] For review of CITT decisions on tariff classification, the Federal Court of Appeal applies the reasonableness standard.[67] In *Igloo Vikski*, the Court allowed an appeal and referred a classification decision on hockey gloves back to the CITT due to an interpretation of the Harmonized System General Rules for Interpretation that the Court found to be unreasonable. An appeal to the Supreme Court of Canada is pending at the time of writing.[68]

For review of CITT administrative determinations such as injury findings in antidumping duty matters, the Federal Court of Appeal applies a reasonableness standard.[69] In *Rio Tinto Alcan*, the Court reviewed a threat of injury finding for imports of silicon metal and considered an extract from a decision by a binational panel under the Canada–United States Free Trade Agreement as part of its reasons, in

[65] *AAi.Foster Grant of Canada Co. v. Canada* (Customs and Revenue Agency) 2004 FCA 259, 325 NR 122.

[66] *Skechers USA Canada Inc. v. Canada (Border Services Agency)*, 2015 FCA 58, [2015] FCJ No 276.

[67] *Costco Wholesale Canada Ltd. v. Canada (Border Services Agency)*, 2015 FCA 110, [2015] FCJ No 588; *Cycles Lambert Inc. v. Canada* (Border Services Agency), 2015 FCA 45, [2015] FCJ No 194; *Canada (Border Services Agency) v. Euro-Line Appliances Inc.*, 2014 FCA 208, [2014] FCJ No. 981; *Andritz Hydro Canada Inc. v. Canada (Border Services Agency)*, 2014 FCA 217, [2014] FCJ No 962; *Proctor-Silex Canada v. Canada (Border Services Agency)*, 2014 FCA 116, [2014] FCJ No 453; *Canada (Border Services Agency) v. SAF-HOLLAND Canada Ltd.*, 2014 FCA 3, [2014] FCJ No 13; *Canada (Border Services Agency) v. Masai Canada Ltd.* 2012 FCA 260, [2012] FCJ No 1350.

[68] *Igloo Vikski Inc. v. Canada (Border Services Agency)*, 2014 FCA 266, [2014] FCJ No 1134; leave to appeal granted: [2015] SCCA No 31. The Federal Court of Appeal recently allowed appeals of other CITT tariff classification decisions: *Eastern Division Henry Schein Ash Arcona Inc. v. Canada (Border Services Agency)*, 2015 FCA 220, [2015] FCJ No 1257; *Cross Country Parts Distribution Ltd. v. Canada (Border Services Agency)*, 2015 FCA 187, [2015] FCJ No 1067; *Marmen-Énergie Inc. v. Canada (Border Services Agency)*, 2014 FCA 118, [2014] FCJ No 454; *Wolsley Engineered Pipe Group v. Canada (Border Services Agency)* 2011 FCA 138, [2011] FCJ No 583.

[69] *Canadian Sugar Institute v. Canada (Attorney-General)*, 2012 FCA 163, [2012] FCJ No 668; *Owen & Company Limited v. Globe Spring & Cushion Co. Ltd.*, 2010 FCA 288, [2012] FCJ No 1338; *Zenix Engineering Ltd. v. Defence Construction* (1951) Ltd., 2008 FCA 109, [2008] FCJ No 1338. The reasonableness standard also applied to an expiry review of duties by the CITT: *Canadian Tire Corp. v. Koolatron Corp.*, 2016 FCA 2, [2016] FCJ No 18.

which it upheld the CITT's finding.[70] The Federal Court of Appeal also applies the reasonableness standard to review determinations of dumping by the president of the CBSA.[71]

The Federal Courts follow Canadian judicial review law and defer to the expertise of administrative agencies and authorities in trade and economic matters, reflecting the political choices of legislators.

5 Forum Shopping

Since 1990, Canadian law on court jurisdiction and recognition of foreign judgements is no longer based on a strict territorial analysis. Recognition and enforcement of foreign judgements previously depended on whether the defendant had been served with process in the foreign territory or had attorned to the jurisdiction of the foreign court. In *Morguard*, the Supreme Court of Canada added the further ground of real and substantial connection and enforced a judgement interprovincially against a defendant who had neither attorned nor been served in the originating province.[72] The real and substantial connection ground has been applied across international borders.[73] It is used both for the recognition and enforcement of foreign judgements and as the basis to determine whether a Canadian court will take jurisdiction over a dispute.[74]

Even once a real and substantial connection is established, Canadian courts have *forum non conveniens* discretion to decline to hear a matter if it is demonstrated that there is a clearly more appropriate forum elsewhere.[75] In the trade context, in *OT Africa Line*, the Federal Court of Appeal declined to take jurisdiction over a claim for cargo loss on a shipment of goods from New York to Liberia. The claimants relied on a provision of the Marine Liability Act that makes access to a Canadian

[70] *Rio Tinto Alcan Inc. v. Québec Silicon Limited Partnership*, 2015 FCA 72, 2015 Carswell-Nat 8211, citing Certain Hot-Rolled Carbon Steel Plate and High-Strength Low-Alloy Plate, Heat-Treated or Not, Originating in or Exported from the U.S.A., CDA-93-1904-06 (para. 50).

[71] *ABB Inc. v. Hyundai Heavy Industries Co.*, 2015 FCA 157, [2015] FCJ No 995. See *Canadian Tire Corp. v. Canada (Border Services Agency)*, 2016 FCA 20, [2016] FCJ No 94.

[72] *Morguard Investments Ltd. v. De Savoye*, [1990] 3 SCR 1107, [1990] SCJ No 135.

[73] *Beals v. Saldanha*, 2003 SCC 72, [2003] 3 SCR 416.

[74] *Club Resorts v. Van Breda*, 2012 SCC 17, [2012] 1 SCR 572.

[75] *Amchem Products Inc. v. British Columbia (Workers' Compensation Board)* (1993) 102 DLR (4th) 96 (SCC).

court available if the defendant has a branch or agency in Canada or if the contract was made in Canada. Although both of these factors were present in the case, the Federal Court of Appeal determined, on a purposive interpretation, that the legislation did not remove all judicial discretionary power. The claimants argued that the statutory provision ensured access to dispute settlement proceedings in Canada despite the terms of the forum selection clause in the contract. The Court reviewed submissions to Parliamentary committees when the provision was under consideration. The Court surveyed analogous legislation in Australia, New Zealand, South Africa, Denmark, Finland, Norway, Sweden and China and referred to the Hamburg Rules, an international treaty on the carriage of goods by sea that Canada has neither signed nor ratified.[76] In the result, the Court concluded that the provision was intended to benefit small and medium-sized Canadian enterprises that would be disadvantaged by having to pursue dispute settlement in distant locations. In this dispute, the head office of the carrier was in London, the head office of the seller was in New York, and the head office of the buyer was in Monrovia, Liberia. The Federal Court of Appeal allowed an appeal from the Federal Court and stayed the action, giving effect to the contractual forum selection clause, which chose dispute settlement at the High Court in London.[77]

For products from the NAFTA countries, private parties have a choice of forum for judicial review of antidumping and countervailing duty matters. A party that would be entitled to take a final determination to review before the Federal Courts of Canada can opt instead for review by a binational panel.[78] NAFTA panels apply the domestic trade law, administrative practice and judicial precedents of the importing country.[79]

The problem of overlap between the WTO and a regional agreement such as NAFTA is illustrated in the 2001–06 dispute over softwood lumber between Canada and the United States. In 2002, the U.S. Department of Commerce determined that imports of softwood lumber from Canada were subsidized and dumped,[80] and the U.S. International Trade Commission

[76] United Nations Convention on the Carriage of Goods by Sea, adopted at Hamburg, Germany, 31 March 1978, in force 1 November 1992, 1695 UNTS 3; 17 ILM 608 (1978). Canada is not a party to the Convention.

[77] *OT Africa Line Ltd. v. Magic Sportswear Corp.*, 2006 FCA 284. See Marine Liability Act, SC 2001, c6, s 46(1).

[78] North American Free Trade Agreement, 17 December 1992, in force 1 January 1994, 32 ILM 289, 605 (1993) Article 1904.5.

[79] NAFTA Article 1904.2.

[80] 66 Fed. Reg. 43,186, August 17, 2001; 66 Fed. Reg. 56,062, November 6, 2002.

(ITC) found that those imports threatened material injury.[81] The United States imposed countervailing duties and antidumping duties. Canada brought a number of reviews pursuant to chapter 19 of NAFTA, including a review of the 16 May 2002 finding by ITC of a threat of injury. The NAFTA panel dealing with injury remanded the matter twice on the basis, in part, that the finding of the Canadian industry's propensity to export was not supported by substantial evidence.[82] In the course of preparing its response to the second remand, ITC asked for permission to reopen the administrative record, which the panel denied. As the finding by ITC on the second remand did not change, the panel then directed ITC to make a finding that the evidence on the record did not support a finding of threat of material injury.[83] The United States brought the panel's decision before an Extraordinary Challenge Committee for review pursuant to NAFTA Article 1904.13. The Committee concluded that the panel had failed to apply the appropriate standard of review on the issue of export orientation of the Canadian industry. As this failure was not material, however, the Committee denied the challenge and affirmed the chapter 19 panel decision.[84]

In the meantime, Canada had also filed disputes before the WTO. The WTO panel dealing with the 16 May 2002 ITC finding of threat of injury decided that it was inconsistent with the WTO Anti-Dumping Agreement and the WTO Subsidies and Countervailing Measures Agreement, as the finding of a likely substantial increase in imports was not supported on the factors considered and the ITC's reasoning.[85] The ITC then reopened the record, gathered new evidence and found a threat of material injury. The WTO panel determined that the United States had implemented the decision of the panel and had now brought its measure

[81] U.S International Trade Commission, *Softwood Lumber from Canada*, Investigations Nos 701-TA-414 and 731-TA-928, USITC Pub. No 3509, May 16, 2002.

[82] *In the Matter of Certain Softwood Lumber Products from Canada*, USA-CDA-2002-1904-7, Decision of the Panel, September 5, 2003; *In the Matter of Certain Softwood Lumber Products from Canada*, USA-CDA-2002-1904-7, Remand Decision of the Panel, April 19, 2004.

[83] *In the Matter of Certain Softwood Lumber Products from Canada*, USA-CDA-2002-1904-7, Second Remand Decision of the Panel, August 31, 2004.

[84] *In the Matter of Certain Softwood Lumber Products from Canada*, ECC-2004-1904-01USA, Opinion and Order of the Extraordinary Challenge Committee, August 10, 2005.

[85] Panel Report, United States – Investigation of the International Trade Commission in Softwood Lumber from Canada, WT/DS277/R, adopted 26 April 2004, DSR 2004:VI, p. 2485

into conformity with its WTO obligations.[86] At this stage, the NAFTA process and the WTO process dealing with the same finding had gone in two different directions and reached two inconsistent results.

The contradiction did not remain. On appeal by Canada, the Appellate Body reversed the panel decision due to an insufficient level of scrutiny that failed to meet the standard under Article 11 of the Dispute Settlement Understanding.[87] Canada thus eventually won in both venues.[88] The hazards of parallel proceedings are illustrated in the unfolding of these decisions. Even though the original ITC ruling was found defective for just about the same reasons in both processes, the results were very different at one point. The ability of either system to resolve the dispute was undermined. The risks to parties involved in overlapping proceedings are apparent.[89]

Several suggestions have been made to deal with the problem of overlapping proceedings. Among them, relating to trade law, are the following: (i) forum selection clauses in regional agreements could be respected and used to determine admissibility of disputes;[90] (ii) international tribunals might exercise their inherent power to decline or suspend jurisdiction;[91]

[86] Panel Report, United States - Investigation of the International Trade Commission in Softwood Lumber from Canada - Recourse to Article 21.5 of the DSU by Canada, WT/DS277/RW, adopted 2 May 2006, as modified by Appellate Body Report WT/DS277/AB/RW, DSR 2006:XI, p. 4935

[87] Appellate Body Report, US - Softwood Lumber VI (Article 21.5 - Canada).

[88] For reviews and comments on the full proceedings in Softwood IV, see I. Sandford, 'Determining the existence of countervailable subsidies in the context of the Canada–United States Softwood Lumber Dispute: 1982–2005', *Canadian Yearbook of International Law*, 43 (2005), 297; C. Carmody, 'Softwood Lumber Dispute (2001–2006)', *The American Journal of International Law*, 100(3) (2006), 664; J. L. Dunoff, 'The many dimensions of *Softwood Lumber*', *Alberta Law Review*, 45 (2007), 319; L. C. Reif, 'Desperate softwood lumber companies?: The Canada–U.S Softwood Lumber Agreement and NAFTA chapter 11', *Alberta Law Review*, 45 (2007), 357.

[89] Parallel proceedings have been filed under the WTO and NAFTA chapter 19 over softwood lumber, high fructose corn syrup, oil country tubular goods, cement and wheat. As well, Canada filed parallel proceedings under GATT and chapter 19 of the Canada–US FTA (the predecessor of NAFTA chapter 19) over softwood lumber and pork. See Kevin C Kennedy, 'Parallel Proceedings at the WTO and under NAFTA chapter 19: Whither the Doctrine of Exhaustion of Local Remedies in DSU Reform?', *George Washington International Law Review*, 39 (2007), 47, esp. 82–7.

[90] J. Pauwelyn and L. E. Salles, 'Forum shopping before international tribunals: (Real) concerns, (im)possible solutions', *Cornell International Law Journal*, 42 (2009), 77.

[91] C. Henckels, 'Overcoming jurisdictional isolationism at the WTO-FTA Nexus: A potential approach for the WTO', *European Journal of International Law*, 19, 3, (2008), 571; C. Brown, *A Common Law of International Adjudication* (Oxford University Press, 2007).

and (iii) the WTO Dispute Settlement Understanding could be amended to provide an explicit power to stay proceedings under certain circumstances.[92] There is a forum selection clause in chapter 20 of NAFTA that binds parties to their initial choice of either NAFTA or WTO procedures once a dispute is initiated.[93] Chapter 20, however, does not apply to the system of binational panels under chapter 19.[94] As the chapter 19 panels depend, in fact, on private party initiation and apply the domestic law of the importing country, they differ from the state-to-state procedures of chapter 20. NAFTA's forum selection clause could have application in other contexts, but it was of no relevance in the softwood litigation.

Overlapping procedures could be addressed through the exercise of tribunal power to control admissibility or through enhanced discretion to decline jurisdiction. Without clear direction from national governments, tribunals may be reluctant to claim greater powers. As well, even if discretionary powers were well established, parallel proceedings could still arise. Canada and the United States are two common-law countries with very similar doctrines of *forum non conveniens* in their domestic legal systems. Nevertheless, in *Lloyd's v. Cominco*, courts in British Columbia recently refused to stay an insurance action against a smelter in the south of the province,[95] while a U.S. court also refused to stay a competing action brought by the smelter against the same insurer concerning the same alleged damage across the border in Washington State.[96] Complex multijurisdictional litigation is difficult for one court or one tribunal to control.

[92] B. E. Allen and T. Soave, 'Jurisdictional overlap in WTO dispute settlement and investment arbitration', *Arbitration International*, 30, 1, (2014), 1. I thank Miguel Villamizar for drawing this article to my attention.

[93] NAFTA Article 2005.6. The Article refers to dispute settlement under GATT or any successor agreement to GATT.

[94] NAFTA Article 2004.

[95] This smelter at Trail, B.C., was made famous in international legal circles in 'Trail Smelter Arbitration, United States *v.* Canada' (1941) 3 *Reports on International Arbitration Awards* 1905.

[96] *Lloyd's Underwriters v. Cominco Ltd.* 2007 BCCA 249, 279 DLR (4th) 257, affd *Teck Cominco Metals Ltd. v. Lloyd's Underwriters* 2009 SCC 11, 303 DLR (4th) 385. A *lis pendens* approach, more familiar in civil law jurisdictions, would also have been unsatisfactory. The parties had agreed to refrain from filing lawsuits for a certain period. The day after the truce ended, the Washington State action began at one second past midnight at a judge's residence. The B.C. plaintiffs filed their action later that morning when the courts opened in Vancouver.

6 Interaction between International and National Courts

Domestic courts serve a bridging function between public international law and national legal systems. In some respects, they provide the enforcement arm that public international law is said to lack. Courts can be called on to give effect to accepted international obligations where appropriate, ensuring that states comply with their commitments and the rule of law, and recognizing responsibilities through domestic constitutional, administrative or tort law.[97] National legal systems differ on whether international law applies directly or must be transformed to be considered in the domestic system. As well, the international obligation will be subject to varying interpretations by national courts.[98] It might be assumed that detailed international economic treaties provide little leeway for differing views and that the role of domestic courts would mainly involve enforcement and harmonization, but variations should be anticipated. In the *National Corn Growers* dispute, U.S. exporters argued that GATT subsidies obligations did not permit a finding of injury in the presence of only low volumes of imports. The Federal Court of Appeal and Supreme Court of Canada took the GATT provisions into account and still upheld the injury finding of the Canadian Import Tribunal, which was based on the economic influence of the U.S. market on Canadian prices.[99]

The involvement of domestic courts in international law is not simply unidirectional, as they also have a role in the elaboration of law. Court decisions can be evidence of state practice and of subsequent treaty interpretation by a state, and they are also a subsidiary source of public international pursuant to Article 38(1)(d) of the Statute of the International Court of Justice.[100] In this creative role, there might be a fear

[97] A. Nollkaemper, *National Courts and the International Rule of Law* (Oxford University Press, 2011) pp. 1, 40, and 194.

[98] R. Bahdi, 'Truth and method in the domestic application of international law', *Canadian Journal of Law and Jurisprudence*, 15, 2, (2002), 255.

[99] *National Corn Growers Assn. v. Canada* (Import Tribunal) [1990] 2 SCR. 1324, [1990] SCJ No 110. A dispute settlement panel of the GATT Committee on Subsidies and Countervailing Measures took a different view and ruled against Canada: GATT, *Panel on Canadian Countervailing Duties on Grain Corn from the United States*, SCM/140 and Corr.1, adopted by the Committee, 26 March 1992, BISD 39S/411.

[100] Statute of the International Court of Justice, Article 38(1): 'The Court, whose function is to decide in accordance with international law such disputes as are submitted to it, shall apply: (a) international conventions, whether general or particular, establishing rules expressly recognized by the contesting States; (b) international custom, as evidence of a general practice accepted as law; (c) the general principles of law recognized by civilized

that domestic decisions would reflect narrow parochial views, but careful analysis and discussion of international obligations can be helpful and persuasive for other interpreters.[101] The contribution of domestic courts in support of the international rule of law should not be overlooked.

Canada follows the British dualist tradition of separating treaty-making from treaty implementation.[102] The negotiation and ratification of treaties are executive functions, part of the Crown prerogative.[103] The implementation of any ensuing international obligations into domestic law is a separate process, as confirmed by the Privy Council in 1937:

> Within the British Empire there is a well-established rule that the making of a treaty is an executive act, while the performance of its obligations, if they entail alteration of the existing domestic law, requires legislative action.[104]

Implementation usually involves legislative approval.[105] It is possible that a treaty could become binding on Canada internationally without being implemented into domestic law. The federal executive negotiates treaties, but there is currently no explicit federal treaty-implementation power.[106] Any implementation involves federal and provincial legislatures, in

nations; (d) [. . .] judicial decisions and the teachings of the most highly-qualified publicists of the various nations, as subsidiary means for the determination of rules of law.'

101 Nollkaemper, *National Courts and the International Rule of Law*, pp. 217 and 235–42; A. Roberts, 'Comparative international law? The role of national courts in creating and enforcing international law', *International and Comparative Law Quarterly*, 60 (2011), 57.

102 For background, see J. H. Currie, *Public International Law*, 2nd ed. (Toronto: Irwin Law, 2008); J. H. Currie et al., *International Law: Doctrine, Practice, and Theory*, 2nd ed. (Toronto: Irwin Law, 2014).

103 In January 2008, the federal government announced that it will table treaties in the House of Commons for review and discussion twenty-one days before ratification. The government retains the authority to decide whether to ratify: 'Canada Announces Policy to Table International Treaties in House of Commons' Department of Foreign Affairs, Trade and Development Canada, News Release No 20, January 25, 2008.

104 *Attorney-General for Canada v. Attorney General for Ontario*, [1937] A.C 326 (P.C) at 347.

105 A treaty may require only executive action. See: *Rousseau Metal Inc. v. Canada*, [1987] FCJ No 40, 80 N.R. 74 (FCA); H. Kindred, 'The use and abuse of international legal sources by Canadian Courts: Searching for a principled approach' in O. E. Fitzgerald (ed.), *The Globalized Rule of Law: Relationships between International and Domestic Law* (Toronto: Irwin Law, 2006), p. 5.

106 Except for obligations of Canada as part of the British Empire, arising in treaties between the Empire and foreign countries, Constitution Act (1867), 30 & 31 Victoria, c 3 (U.K.), s 132.

accordance with subject-matter distribution of constitutional power.[107] For trade-related treaties, the federal mandate is quite wide, covering trade and commerce, navigation and shipping, patents and copyrights.[108] Provincial heads of jurisdiction are implicated if a treaty deals with the environment, labour, consumer rights, human rights, education, regulation of businesses and services, and any other matter relating to property and civil rights in the province.

In the case of an implemented treaty, it is the implementing domestic legislation that has legal force. In 1978, in *Capital Cities*, the Supreme Court of Canada (Laskin CJ) took a narrow view of whether an international treaty could be used to interpret domestic law, stating that the treaty could be consulted only in case of an ambiguity in the statute.[109] The *National Corn Growers* case, which was discussed earlier under standard of review, was also a landmark decision on the issue of the relationship between treaties and implementing legislation. The majority judgement in *National Corn Growers* rejected the strongly dualist approach of *Capital Cities*. In the judgement, Gonthier J. stated:

> In interpreting legislation which has been enacted with a view towards implementing international obligations, as is the case here, it is reasonable for a tribunal to examine the domestic law in the context of the relevant agreement to clarify any uncertainty. Indeed where the text of the domestic law lends itself to it, one should also strive to expound an interpretation which is consonant with the relevant international obligations.[110]

The majority held that it was not necessary to identify first an ambiguity in the text of the statute, but that consultation of the treaty was permitted at the outset in order to reveal any ambiguities.[111] The acknowledgement of the international source of legislation can be important to ensure

[107] *Attorney-General for Canada v. Attorney General for Ontario*, [1937] A.C 326 (P.C) at 354: 'While the ship of state now sails on larger ventures and into foreign waters she still retains the watertight compartments which are an essential part of her original structure.'

[108] Constitution Act (1867), s 91. Federal jurisdiction may also be based on the power in s 91 'to make Laws for the Peace, Order and good Government of Canada'.

[109] *Capital Cities Communications v. Canadian Radio-Television Commission*, [1978] 2 SCR141 at 173. Laskin CJ also noted that the legislation should state expressly the intent to implement the treaty.

[110] *National Corn Growers Assn v. Canada (Import Tribunal)* [1990] 2 SCR. 1324, [1990] SCJ No 110 at para. 74.

[111] Ibid., para. 75.

proper interpretation in accordance with treaty practice and within the context of the objectives of the treaty.[112]

The dualist approach on treaty law seems to involve courts in few possible challenges to the supremacy of the legislative branch of government – with the exception of unimplemented treaties to be discussed later. This contrasts markedly with the approach concerning customary international law.[113] Canada follows the common law tradition and considers custom to be automatically incorporated into the Canadian legal system, unless it is incompatible with domestic law.[114] A court that declares a rule to be customary international law and binding on Canada does so without legislative support, a situation that is quite different from the requirement for treaty implementation. This acceptance of monism reflects the treatment of custom as part of the common law. As with treaties, legislators remain supreme, and there could be a conflict between Canada's customary international legal obligations and its domestic law. Custom does not apply if domestic law is to the contrary.

For general statutory interpretation, the Supreme Court uses the presumption that legislatures do not intend to put Canada in breach of its international obligations.[115] The effect of this presumption of consistency is that a binding treaty can serve as an aid to interpretation, even if unimplemented, except where it would be in conflict with domestic law. It will be noted that this methodology is monist and similar to the treatment of international custom. In the presumption of consistency, the international treaty is merely an aid to interpretation, however, and does not have independent effect.

The exact impact of the interpretive presumption of consistency between international and domestic obligations is somewhat murky in Canadian law, as a result of the 1999 decision in *Baker*[116] and subsequent cases. In *Baker*, the Supreme Court took a weak monist view of what it considered an unimplemented treaty, the Convention on the Rights of

[112] O. K. Fauchald and A. Nollkaemper, 'Conclusions' in O. K. Fauchald and A. Nollkaemper (eds.), *The Practice of International and National Courts and the (De-) Fragmentation of International Law* (Oxford and Portland, Oregon: Hart Publishing, 2012), p. 343 at 356. The judgement of La Forest J. in *Thomson v. Thomson* [1994] 3 SCR 551 carefully explains the approach to treaty interpretation in public international law.

[113] And presumably also general principles of international law and jus cogens.

[114] *R. v. Hape*, 2007 SCC 26, [2007] 2 SCR 292 at para. 39; *Re Newfoundland Continental Shelf*, [1984] 1 SCR 86 at 95–97.

[115] *Merck Frosst Canada Ltd. v. Canada (Health)*, 2012 SCC 3, [2012] 1 SCR 23 at para. 117.

[116] *Baker v. Canada (Minister of Citizenship and Immigration)*, [1999] 2 SCR 817.

the Child.[117] L'Heureux-Dubé J. in the majority judgement stated that even though the treaty was unimplemented, 'the values reflected in international human rights law may help inform the contextual approach to statutory interpretation and judicial review'.[118] This 'values' approach is less forceful than the full presumption of consistency. If Canada has ratified a treaty and is bound internationally, as was the case in *Baker*, it can seem odd that only the 'values' reflected in the treaty are used in statutory interpretation, and not the provisions themselves.

Charter interpretation has used the looser 'values' approach. The Canadian Charter of Rights and Freedoms is presumed to provide at least as much protection as in international human rights treaties ratified by Canada.[119] In Charter litigation, nonbinding international sources such as declarations and soft law instruments might be cited to inform interpretation. This "values" approach is now moving out of Charter cases and seems to be added to the presumption of consistency, in a supplemental way. The Supreme Court has, on occasion, combined several approaches in the same judgement. In *Spraytech*, the Court recognizes the precautionary principle as a norm of customary international law, while at the same time noting that the values of international law inform the contextual approach to statutory interpretation.[120] In *Hape*, similarly, customary

[117] New York, 20 November 1989, in force 2 September 1990, Can TS 1992/3 (signed by Canada 28 May 1990, in force for Canada 12 January 1992). There is debate over whether the Convention was indeed unimplemented. Federal officials had consulted with provincial officials prior to ratification. It was likely that Canadian legislation already gave priority to the best interests of the child, and that there was no need for separate implementing legislation. See A. de Mestral and E. Fox-Decent, 'Implementation and reception: The congeniality of Canada's legal order to international law' in O. E. Fitzgerald (ed.), *The Globalized Rule of Law: Relationships between International and Domestic Law* (Toronto: Irwin Law, 2006), p. 31. As well, it has been suggested that federal officials could have used executive power to direct immigration officers to give the best interests of children primary consideration in deciding whether someone in the position of Ms Baker should be deported, despite negative effects on her Canadian-born children (R. Provost, 'Judging in splendid isolation', *American Journal of Comparative Law*, 56 (2008), 144).

[118] *Baker v. Canada (Minister of Citizenship and Immigration)*, [1999] 2 SCR 817 at 861.

[119] *Saskatchewan Federation of Labour v. Saskatchewan*, 2015 SCC 4, [2015] SCJ No 4 at para. 64; *Health Services and Support – Facilities Subsection Bargaining Assn. v. British Columbia*, 2007 SCC 27, [2007] SCJ No 27 at para. 79; *Slaight Communications Inc. v. Davidson*, [1989] 1 SCR 1038, [1989] SCJ No 45 at para. 23. See Canadian Charter of Rights and Freedoms, Part I of Constitution Act (1982), Canada Act, 1982, c11, Schedule B (U.K.).

[120] *114957 Canada Ltée (Spraytech, Société d'arrosage) v. Hudson (Town)*, 2001 SCC 40, [2001] 2 SCR 241. For discussion, see M. Valiante, 'Turf war: Municipal powers, the regulation of pesticides and the *Hudson* decision', *Journal of Environmental Law and Practice*, 11 (2001), 353–59.

international law is incorporated into domestic law,[121] courts try to avoid a construction in conflict with it,[122] and legislation is presumed to comply with its values and principles.[123] The general lack of precision has led some commentators to worry that the force of international law will be diminished by this tendency to 'treat all international law as inspirational but not obligatory'.[124]

There may now be some question about the treatment of international custom after the recent statement in the judgement of LeBel J. in *Kazemi* that 'the mere existence of a customary rule in international law does not automatically incorporate that rule into the domestic legal order'.[125] The judgement refers to situations where a customary rule permits states to exercise a certain jurisdiction or take a certain action but does not make such a step mandatory. If the customary rule allows a choice by the state, then normally any decision would be for the legislative or executive branches to make. It is difficult to see, however, why this would keep the customary rule with its full discretionary content outside the domestic order until the appropriate authority opts to bring it in. International custom covers such bedrock concepts as sovereignty,[126] territoriality and state recognition.[127] The idea that custom is not present domestically unless it is implemented in some way, as if it were a treaty, could be quite unsettling.[128]

121 *R. v. Hape*, 2007 SCC 26, [2007] 2 SCR 292 at para. 39. 122 Ibid., paras. 53 and 54

123 Ibid. For discussion, see J. H. Currie, '*Khadr* 's twist on *Hape*: Tortured determinations of the extraterritorial reach of the Canadian *Charter*', *Canadian Yearbook of International Law*, 46 (2008), 307. The 'values' approach is not mentioned in the most recent statement of the presumption of consistency, in *Merck Frosst*, but the Court cites to the analysis in *Baker*: *Merck Frosst Canada Ltd. v. Canada (Health)*, 2012 SCC 3, [2012] 1 SCR 23 at para. 117.

124 J. Brunée and S. J. Toope, 'A hesitant embrace: The application of international law by Canadian Courts', *Canadian Yearbook of International Law*, 40 (2002), 3 at 54.

125 *Kazemi Estate v. Islamic Republic of Iran*, 2014 SCC 62, [2014] SCJ No 62 at para. 61. LeBel J was discussing the possibility of a rule that allowed states to permit civil actions against foreign government officials in the case of torture – a rule that he finds is not part of customary international law. Even if such an exception to state immunity were to develop, he finds that it would likely allow legislatures to choose whether to permit such actions. For further elaboration on the idea of permissive custom, see G. van Ert, *Using International Law in Canadian Courts*, 2nd ed. (Toronto: Irwin Law, 2008), pp. 218–23.

126 *R. v. Hape*, 2007 SCC 26, [2007] 2 SCR 292.

127 *Reference re Secession of Quebec*, [1998] 2 SCR 217, [1998] SCJ No61.

128 Note the concern expressed by René Provost over statements in certain judgements that the Canadian government had supported rules the court found to be international custom, which he terms a 'radically consensual approach' not in accordance with established doctrine: R. Provost, 'Judging in splendid isolation', *American Journal of Comparative Law*, 56 (2008), 125 at 138, referring to *United States v. Rafay and Burns*,

In one particular area, Canadian law sets out a special link between domestic and international sources. For classification under the customs tariff, section 11 of the Customs Tariff Act states that 'regard shall be had' to the Explanatory Notes and Classification Opinions of the Harmonized Commodity Description and Coding System, published from time to time by the World Customs Organization.[129] In *Suzuki*, the Federal Court of Appeal held that, while the Notes and Opinions are not binding, the CITT below did not have the choice of rewriting an Explanatory Note and selecting its own meaning for a term defined in a Note.[130] This approach is similar to the presumption of consistency, but stronger. The reference in the section is a dynamic one, to versions of the Explanatory Notes and Classification Opinions as they are modified from time to time. Canada participates in WCO decision making, including revisions of the Explanatory Notes.[131] Section 11 may have been intended, in part, to counteract the extreme dualism of the Supreme Court's decision in *Capital Cities* in 1978, which prohibited reference to the source international treaty unless there was an ambiguity in the text of the domestic statute. The Harmonized System was adopted in Canada in 1988, prior to the liberalization of reference to international sources in the Supreme Court's 1990 decision in *National Corn Growers*. The Customs Tariff Act section responds to the challenge of trying to maintain harmonization among countries applying the same tariff nomenclature. When the goal is coordination at a detailed level, a specific section in the legislation was required.

In summary, Canadian domestic law is dualist on treaties and monist for the rest of public international law. Recent cases demonstrate some hesitation on the part of the Supreme Court of Canada to give legal effect to obligations that lack approval from a domestic legislative process. In one specific area, in the Customs Tariff Act, the statute establishes a link to international regulation with close to ongoing direct effect, to assist with interpretation of the Harmonized System of tariff classification.

[2001] 1 SCR 283, paras. 84–85 and *114957 Canada Ltée (Spraytech, Société d'arrosage) v. Hudson (Town)*, 2001 SCC 40, [2001] 2 SCR 241, para. 31.

[129] *Customs Tariff Act*, SC 1997, c 36, s 11.

[130] *Canada (Attorney General) v. Suzuki Canada Inc.*, 2004 FCA 131, [2004] FCJ No 615, leave to appeal dismissed [2004] SCCA No 243.

[131] Canada proposed the modification to clarify an Explanatory Note in *Canada (Border Services Agency) v. Decolin Inc.*, 2006 FCA 417, [2006] FCJ No 1963 covering 'articles for Christmas festivities' but then was prevented from applying the modification retroactively to goods already imported.

7 Legitimacy Concerns

René Provost identifies legitimacy concerns by Canadian judges over their two-way role in dealing with the increasingly frequent use of international law in argument before domestic courts. The dynamic involves the complicated constitutional balance of power among the judiciary, the executive and the legislative branches. The separate opinion of Iacobucci J. in *Baker* illustrates this tension:

> In my view, one should proceed with caution ... lest we adversely affect the balance maintained by our Parliamentary tradition, or inadvertently grant the executive the power to bind citizens without the necessity of involving the legislative branch.[132]

Iacobucci J, with the concurrence of Cory J., agreed with the majority in the disposition of the case, but disagreed with the idea of using an unimplemented treaty as part of the context for statutory interpretation. The separate opinion does not take account of the principle of consistency and does not reflect the views of the majority of the Court on this point. It demonstrates, however, the concern about the proper role for judges in the relationship between international and domestic law. Such questions of legitimacy are at the heart of recent doctrinal controversies in the area.

One response is that of the majority in *Baker*, opting for a largely comparative approach that treats international law as a source of ideas and solutions that the court may be persuaded to adopt. Karen Knop supports an emphasis on persuasiveness and the use of comparative law theory to enhance the study of domestic courts, as opposed to a limited focus on the binding nature of international law, which inappropriately views their role as merely enforcement.[133] As Patrick Glenn explained in 1987, Canadian courts generally have been receptive to the use of persuasive authority in domestic decision making, rather than adopting a strictly national, positivist approach.[134]

The Federal Court of Appeal decision in *OT Africa Line*[135] is an example of the use of persuasive authorities, including a treaty and

[132] *Baker v. Canada (Minister of Citizenship and Immigration)*, [1999] 2 SCR 817, para. 80.

[133] K. Knop, 'Here and there: International law in domestic courts', *New York University Journal of International Law and Politics*, 32 (2000), 501. See further S. Beaulac, 'International law and statutory presumption: Up with context, down with presumption' in O. E. Fitzgerald (ed.), *The Globalized Rule of Law: Relationships between International and Domestic Law* (Toronto: Irwin Law, 2006) p. 331.

[134] H. P. Glenn, 'Persuasive authority', *McGill Law Journal*, 32(2) (1987), 293–98.

[135] Above footnote 77.

developments in other jurisdictions, which helped the court to identify the policies surrounding the legislation at issue and reach an interpretation giving effect to the underlying purpose of the provision. Such attention to global context and legal sources elsewhere encourages coordination and balances the decentralized international legal structure.[136] The bridging role of domestic courts enhances communication and information, as judicial decisions can reflect a wide range of circumstances and policies,[137] while contributing to understanding and the development of international law.

Reliance on the use of persuasive authority, however, is an incomplete response to hesitation over applying international law. Karen Knop identifies the central question of the comparative approach as 'how and why we use the norms of other communities to judge our own'.[138] Although comparison can be helpful in many respects, international law does not belong to a separate community. Unless it conflicts with domestic law, international law is automatically part of the Canadian legal system, as custom or as an aid to interpretation. Even treaties, which are viewed through a dualist lens, are the product of elected political officials who decide to negotiate and ratify them on behalf of the Canadian public. Current doctrinal controversies may be tied partly to a perception of international law as external to the state, but mostly seem to reflect views of political legitimacy and the division of functions between judges and legislators.

8 Conclusions

This chapter has examined decisions of the Federal Courts of Canada on trade and international economic law. The discussion has outlined issues in Canadian legal doctrine relating to the role of courts in administrative law and to the treatment of public international law sources that are being presented by litigants with increasing frequency. International

[136] Fauchald and Nollkaemper, 'Conclusions', p. 343.

[137] See M. J. Tawfik, 'No longer living in splendid isolation: The globalization of national courts and the internationalization of intellectual property law', *Queen's Law Journal*, 32 (2007), 573, questioning a tendency toward hegemonic uniformity in the use of persuasive authority, and expressing concern over the choice of 'like-minded jurisdictions' for interpretation in *Théberge v. Galerie d'Art du Petit Champlain Inc.* 2002 SCC 34, [2002] 2 SCR 336 and *Harvard College v. Canada (Commissioner of Patents)* 2002 SCC 76, [2002] 4 SCR 45 (Binnie J, dissenting).

[138] Knop, 'International law in domestic courts', 507.

tribunals are not alone in being involved in debates over legitimacy and the relationship to political lawmakers. Domestic courts, as well, see their role in light of the presence of other decision makers and the authority of the legislative branch. This dynamic is an ordinary aspect of the judicial function. Both when looking inward to domestic constitutions and when looking internationally, courts operate within limits on their authority and responsibilities.

7

The Case of MERCOSUR[1]

PAULA WOJCIKIEWICZ ALMEIDA

1 Introduction

Since its inception, Mercosur has opted for a noncoercive and diplomatic dispute settlement system. The 1991 Treaty of Asunción that established Mercosur did not predict the creation of a permanent regional court. Disputes should have been solved, in the first place, by direct negotiations between interested states. If negotiations did not result in an agreement, the next step was a consensus-based recommendation of the Common Market Group (CMG), the Mercosur executive body. Should State Parties not reach a common solution, the procedure continued with the concurring opinion of the Common Market Council (CMC), the highest level body of Mercosur, also by consensus.

The Protocol of Brasília filled in the blanks of the procedure as initially foreseen in Asunción. It established a two-step process, with a political

[1] This chapter was first presented at the workshop organised by Pluricourts Oslo and the CIDS (Geneva Center for International Dispute Settlement at the University of Geneva; October 2014); then at the workshop organised by the Interest Group on International Courts and Tribunals held in the auspices of the LASIL/SLADI 2015 Annual Meeting in Rio de Janeiro (August 2015); and finally at the ESIL-ASIL Interest Groups on International Courts and Tribunals joint work-in-progress workshop held during the ESIL Annual Conference in Oslo (September 2015). I am grateful to the organisers and participants of those conferences for constructive suggestions for improvement. I would like to thank the following jurists interviewed during the development of this chapter for helpful comments and information: Alejandro Perotti, former legal advisor of the Mercosur Secretariat; Raphael Vasconcelos, current Secretary of the Permanent Review Court; Santiago Deluca, former Secretary of the Permanent Review Court; Magdalena Bas, professor from the Universidad de la Republica, Montevideo; as well as the following arbitrators from the Permanent Review Court: Welber Barral, Brazil; José Maria Gamio, Uruguay; and Roberto Ruiz Díaz Labrano, Paraguay. I express my gratitude to professors Geir Ulfstein (University of Oslo) and Hélène Ruiz-Fabri (Université Paris 1 Panthéon-Sorbonne) for reading and discussing earlier drafts of this chapter. And finally, I wish to thank the following Getulio Vargas Foundation Law School students for their commitment and interest in this project: Alessandra Spalenza Szpunar, Alice Régnier, Thaís Salvador and Marcos Patrick.

step that is binding before the arbitral phase can be activated. In 2002, the Protocol of Olivos (PO) was adopted and replaced the former Protocol of Brasília, entering into force on 1 January 2004. Among the most important innovations of the PO is the Permanent Review Court (PRC), established on 13 August 2004, and headquartered in Asunción. Responsible for controlling the interpretation and application of Mercosur law, the PRC has been lauded as the major innovation of the PO. The Court consists of an *ultima ratio* jurisdiction, capable of confirming, modifying or revoking the legal bases and decisions of the ad hoc Arbitral Tribunal. It can even pronounce itself, in the first instance, if the parties are willing. The PRC is also able to give advisory opinions on any legal question that involves the interpretation of Mercosur's primary and secondary law.[2]

Unfortunately, the Protocol has not led to a permanent jurisdictional body capable of ensuring legal security to Mercosur. The creation of a court with clear supranational characteristics implies considerable costs that State Parties have not been willing to bear. This lack of a jurisdictional body with all its related consequences implies serious challenges capable of compromising the legitimacy of the Mercosur dispute settlement system.[3]

There is no authoritative or generally accepted definition of 'legitimacy'. Indeed, 'legitimacy is used in a variety of ways regarding the international judiciary.'[4] Besides other analytical approaches of legitimacy,[5] this chapter will combine, in particular, both 'normative legitimacy'

[2] Like the European Union law, the sources of Mercosur law comprise both primary and secondary law. The main sources of primary law are the treaties establishing the Mercosur and other related treaties referring to the structure, distribution of competences between the Mercosur and its State Parties, and the main principles applied to the organisation. Secondary sources are legal instruments based on the treaties and include unilateral secondary law, such as decisions, resolutions and directives adopted by Mercosur decision-making bodies.

[3] The definition of *legitimacy* here accords with that adopted in the research conducted by Pluricourts Oslo, along with the Université Paris 1 Panthéon-Sorbonne and the University of New York.

[4] Andreas Follesdal, 'The legitimacy deficits of the human rights judiciary: Elements and implications of a normative theory', *Theoretical Inquiries in Law*, 14, 2, (2013), 345.

[5] This chapter does not deal with sociological legitimacy, which requires a more inductive or empirical approach, nor with political legitimacy, i.e., how international actors behave in order to legitimate themselves. For further details, see D. Behn, O. K. Fauchald, and M. Langford, 'How to approach "legitimacy"', for the book project *Empirical Perspectives on the Legitimacy of International Investment Tribunals*, (January 2015), available at: www.jus.uio.no/pluricourts/english/topics/investment/documents/1-2015-legitimacy-book-project.pdf.

and 'democratic legitimacy' in order to evaluate specific factors suggested by Pluricourts to assess the legitimacy of international trade tribunals.

The normative conception of legitimacy deals with 'the rightness of an institution's exertion of power within a society'; in other words, 'it is a set of moral standards by which an institution or regime is judged or justified.'[6] The concept is linked to 'legal legitimacy', which supposes the 'institution's observance of its legally constrained mandate'.[7] Normative legitimacy can be disaggregated into three elements: input, process and output. In terms of process, it includes 'the process by which rules, decisions, and actions are made, applied, or interpreted'.[8] If tribunals fulfil certain criteria such as transparency, accountability and due process, they may be viewed as legitimate.[9]

These criteria are also taken into consideration when assessing the 'democratic legitimacy' of global institutions. Indeed, transparency (the possibility of attributing accountability), the participation of those affected and deliberation are of particular significance for building up 'democratic legitimacy' of international courts.[10] These core elements may be applied to the election of judges, the procedure and reasoning.[11] Transparent procedure also implies the participation of affected or interested parties in proceedings, including a dialogue of the court with the parties, third parties and amicus curiae briefs.[12] Transparent reasoning concerns the decision-making process and tools according to which international courts and tribunals discuss and treat precedents.[13]

In order to assess the legitimacy of Mercosur tribunals, the first part of this research evaluates the legitimacy of Mercosur's procedures in dispute

[6] Ibid., p. 4. See also Buchanan and Keohane's definition of 'normative legitimacy' as 'the right to rule, understood to mean both that institutional agents are morally justified in making rules and attempting to secure compliance with them and that people subject to those rules have moral, content-independent reasons to follow them and/or to not interfere with others' compliances with them', A. Buchanen and R. Keohane, 'The legitimacy of global governance institutions' in R. Wolfrum and V. Röben (eds.), *Legitimacy in International Law* (Berlin: Springer, 2008), p. 25. According to A. Follesdal, 'normative legitimacy argues why should the decisions or recommendations of the international judiciary count as (defeasible) reasons for other actors when they decide what to do?', in 'The Legitimacy Deficits of the Human Rights Judiciary', 345; see also L. R. Helfer and K. J. Alter, 'Legitimacy and lawmaking: A tale of three international courts', *Theoretical Inquiries in Law*, 14, 2, (2013), 479–503.

[7] Behn, Fauchald, and Langford, 'How to approach "legitimacy"', p. 4. [8] Ibid., p. 6.

[9] Ibid.

[10] Armin von Bogdandy, 'The democratic legitimacy of international courts: A conceptual framework', *Theoretical Inquiries in Law*, 14, 2, (2013), 375.

[11] Ibid. [12] Ibid., 377. [13] Ibid., 376.

settlement (1). It identifies existing challenges that may compromise the desired legitimacy of the Mercosur dispute settlement system. The second part deals with the legitimacy of Mercosur arbitrators (2), while the third part addresses the legitimacy of Mercosur's judicial decision-making process (3).

Because data on intrinsic aspects of Mercosur remains obscure at times, this chapter relied on several interviews with officials and former officials of Mercosur, as well as with arbitrators from the PRC, who shared inside information on an intergovernmental organisation in which most dispute settlement procedures are kept confidential. These interviews were essential in revealing the 'real Mercosur', one based not only on treaties and norms, but also on subregional practice where politics play a fundamental role. The need to rely on interviews demonstrates that the Mercosur dispute settlement system lacks transparency, which is essential to ensure democratic legitimacy. This lack of transparency may compromise accountability.[14]

2 The Legitimacy of Mercosur Procedures in Dispute Settlement

Following an evaluation of Mercosur's primary and secondary law,[15] one can identify three challenges capable of compromising legitimacy: the possibility of State Parties seizing the WTO dispute settlement body and thereby authorising the choice of forum according to their interest and strategy (1.1); the lack of direct and indirect access of individuals and civil society to the Mercosur tribunals (1.2); and the absence of an institutionalised sanction mechanism in order to ensure implementation of the Mercosur awards by State Parties (1.3).

2.1 The Choice of Forum

Prior to the adoption of the PO, it was possible to simultaneously submit disputes to Mercosur tribunals and to other dispute settlement mechanisms. Indeed, Argentina and Brazil were involved in discussions related to the submission of already-decided cases under Mercosur ad hoc tribunals to WTO dispute settlement organs. This is particularly evident in the case *Application of Anti-dumping Measures on Exports of Whole*

[14] According to Armin von Bogdandy, 'The transparency of public action, that is its comprehensibility and the possibility of attributing accountability, is essential.' Ibid., 375.

[15] For further details on Mercosur's primary and secondary law, see footnote 2 above.

Chickens. Brazil lost this case before Mercosur tribunals in 2001[16] and then submitted the same dispute to the WTO DSB, which established a panel to entertain the case in 2002.[17] The WTO DSB considered that the Mercosur preclusion clause was not in force at that time (the PO was signed in February 2002) and did not apply to disputes already decided under the Protocol of Brasília.[18] The WTO panel found, therefore, that Argentina had acted inconsistently with its obligations under the provisions of the Anti-Dumping Agreement and its Annex II.

In 2004, the PO entered into force, thereby eliminating the duplicity of forum and the possibility of divergent decisions on the same matter. Article 1 determines that disputes falling within the scope of application of the Protocol may also be referred to the dispute settlement system of the WTO or other preferential trade systems that Mercosur State Parties have entered into (Article 1.1, PO). This fork-in-the-road clause demonstrates that the decision of one forum over another primarily depends on the discretion of the parties in dispute. The choice is to be made by the claimant state. In other words, being a Mercosur State Party does not prevent parties from submitting their disputes concerning subregional law to other tribunals.

There are few examples of the fork-in-the-road clause as applied by Mercosur State Parties, such as the *Anti-dumping Measures on Imports of Certain Resins from Argentina*, between Argentina and Brazil, submitted preferentially to the WTO DSB by Argentina in 2006, and not to the

[16] Brazil submitted an application to the Mercosur dispute settlement mechanism on antidumping measures applied by the Argentinean Ministry of Economy (Res. 574/2000) against its exports of whole chicken. Brazil considers that the referred resolution and its antidumping investigation procedures are incompatible with Mercosur norms on the matter. The ad hoc Arbitral Tribunal formed in March 2001 decided that the Argentine measures were reasonably acceptable and did not breach Mercosur law. Brazil then requested the establishment of a panel before the WTO DSB. See Ad hoc Tribunal, *Application of Anti-dumping measures on exports of whole chickens from Brazil*, Brazil *v.* Argentina, Arbitral Award of 21 May 2001.

[17] The case concerns definitive antidumping measures, in the form of specific antidumping duties, imposed by Argentina on imports of poultry from Brazil for a period of three years. In 2001, Brazil requested consultations with Argentina on the grounds that the definitive antidumping duties imposed, as well as the investigation conducted by the Argentine authorities, might have been flawed and based on erroneous or deficient procedures. This would be inconsistent with Argentina's obligations under several provisions of Annex II of the Anti-Dumping Agreement, Article VI of the GATT 1994, and Articles 1 and 7 of the Customs Valuation Agreement.

[18] Panel Report, *Argentina – Definitive Anti-Dumping Duties on Poultry from Brazil*, WT/DS241/R, adopted 19 May 2003, DSR 2003:V, p. 98.

Mercosur dispute settlement system.[19] It is worth noting that Mercosur State Parties did not apply the mechanism of choice of forum in the cases concerning the *Blockage of roads in Argentina giving access to the bridges linking it to the Uruguayan territory* brought before the Mercosur Tribunal,[20] as well as the *Pulp mills case* filed before the International Court of Justice (ICJ).[21] Indeed, despite the close connection between these cases, the distinction regarding their object did not allow for the activation of the fork-in-the-road rule.

These cases demonstrate that disputing states can elect to resolve their disputes under the Mercosur dispute settlement system, or under other systems to which Mercosur States are individual parties. Should the credibility of the Mercosur dispute settlement mechanism become compromised,[22] arbitrators have pointed out that the choice of one forum over another is essentially a matter of strategy.[23] However, this choice may endanger 'social legitimacy'. Indeed, decisions by a judiciary that actors do not believe is normatively legitimate are less likely to have impact or produce social legitimacy.[24] This may in turn decrease the 'normative legitimacy' and the effectiveness of Mercosur tribunals because actors do not believe that the judiciary body would respect, protect and further the best interests of individuals globally.[25]

Moreover, the fork-in-the-road clause may result in the politicisation of the dispute settlement mechanism and contribute to only a few cases being brought before Mercosur tribunals. Since 1991, Mercosur tribunals have rendered only eighteen decisions, including advisory opinions.

[19] This case was mentioned during the interview with Magdalena Bas, professor from the Universidad de la República, Montevideo (interview dated 15 August 2014). Panel Report, *Argentina – Poultry Anti-Dumping Duties*.

[20] Ad hoc Tribunal, *Blockage of roads in Argentina giving access to the bridges linking it to the Uruguayan territory*, Uruguay *v.* Argentina, Arbitral Award of 6 September 2006. For more details concerning the influence of politics in the Mercosur dispute settlement mechanism, see P. Wojcikiewicz Almeida, 'O caso das papeleras', *Casoteca Latino-Americana de Direito e Política Pública* (São Paulo: FGV Direito SP, 2007), p. 49; see also D. Ventura, 'O caso das papeleras e o papelão do MERCOSUL', *Revista Pontes*, 2, 2, (2006), 17.

[21] Case Concerning the Pulp Mills on the River Uruguay (*Argentina v. Uruguay*), Judgement, ICJ Reports (2010) 14.

[22] Interview with Magdalena Bas dated 15 August 2014.

[23] Interview with Welber Barral, Brazilian arbitrator of the PRC, dated 10 July 2014. It appears that the choice of the ICJ was influenced by its previous judgements regarding environmental law issues and by the feeling that Mercosur tribunals would have a tendency to confer primacy to free trade issues over environmental protection.

[24] Follesdal, 'Human rights judiciary', 346. [25] Ibid., 349.

Brazil, for instance, was very active under the Brasília Protocol, but has not appeared before subregional tribunals in any other situation since 2004, when the Olivos Protocol entered into force.

2.2 The Lack of Direct and Indirect Access of Individuals and Civil Society

The Mercosur dispute settlement mechanism does not permit private parties, natural persons or legal persons to submit their claims against State Parties for arbitration. There is a specific procedure to accommodate private parties' claims, but this mechanism can only be activated through the intervention of the CMG.[26] These claims can be related to the adoption or application by a State Party of legal or administrative measures of a restrictive or discriminatory nature or those leading to unfair competition in violation of Mercosur treaties and secondary norms (Article 39).

Because individuals do not possess an active legitimacy before Mercosur tribunals, the case becomes an interstate dispute to be submitted to arbitral proceedings in case the State Party in question does not comply with the requirements established by the Group of Experts (Article 42). This procedure established by the PO to entertain private parties' claims has only been applied once, in the case concerning *Discriminatory and restrictive measures on trade of tobacco and tobacco products* against Brazil.[27] The complaint was judged admissible by the Mercosur Group of Experts. Considering that Brazil failed to comply with it within the prescribed period of time, Uruguay resorted directly to arbitral proceedings and requested the installation of an ad hoc Tribunal.

Clearly, the overall system to entertain private-party claims depends upon the political decisions of those State Parties directly concerned. The decision of the CMG not to reject the claim requires the unanimous consensus of State Parties, including that of the state allegedly responsible for the violation. According to ex-arbitrator Vinuesa (R. E.), '[A]t the very end of the entire process, interested Member States will have the

[26] See Articles 40 and 41 of the Olivos Protocol.

[27] Ad hoc Tribunal, *Discriminatory and restrictive measures on trade of tobacco and tobacco products*, Uruguay *v.* Brazil, Arbitral Award of 5 August 2005. The dispute originated from an application filed by a domiciled Uruguayan company, *Compañía Industrial de Tabacos Monte Paz SA*, before the National Chapter of the CMG in Uruguay.

same remedy that they already have if they had decided to submit the claim as a dispute among State Parties.'[28]

If individuals do not have direct access to Mercosur tribunals, their claims can be pursued through proceedings before national courts. National courts may apply Mercosur law and recur to the PRC in case of doubt via the mechanism of advisory opinions, which is similar to EU preliminary rulings.[29] As a consequence, civil society organisations can only obtain access to Mercosur tribunals via advisory opinions. The PO does not provide for amicus curiae briefs.

As mentioned in the introduction, the participation of affected individuals and interested parties in proceedings is of utmost importance in order to ensure normative and democratic legitimacy.[30] The possibility to apply for amicus curiae briefs in the judicial proceedings could also help Mercosur tribunals to strengthen their democratic legitimacy.[31]

2.3 *The Absence of an Institutionalised Sanction Mechanism*

The noncompliance with arbitral awards pronounced by Mercosur's tribunals authorises the complainant state to unilaterally apply 'compensatory measures' against the recalcitrant state.[32] This authorisation to use coercion to impose justice unilaterally differs from the logic of the European integration, in which the European Commission may propose the application of a lump sum and/or a penalty payment by the Court.

The possibility of introducing unilateral measures does not exclude the obligation to formally inform the recalcitrant state, at least fifteen days before its implementation.[33] This is similar to the World Trade Organization's Dispute Settlement Mechanism, which served as an inspiration

[28] R. E. Vinuesa, 'Enforcement of Mercosur arbitration awards within the domestic legal orders of member states', *Texas International Law Journal*, 40 (2005), 429.

[29] For further details regarding the mechanism of advisory opinions, see Section 2, Subsection 2.2, Title 2.2.2.

[30] Bogdandy, 'Legitimacy of international courts', 377. [31] Ibid.

[32] The application of a 'compensatory measures' mechanism is authorised under Chapter IX of the *Protocol of Olivos* (see notably Article 31).

[33] Parties in Mercosur have to previously inform the Mercosur Secretariat on the retaliatory measures to be imposed. The obligation to inform, however, does not mean that the complaining state should request an authorisation from the Mercosur tribunal to suspend the application of concessions or other obligations under the covered agreements. In other words, suspending Mercosur obligations in relation to another State Party does not require a previous authorisation of the Mercosur dispute settlement body.

for Mercosur.[34] There is no control over the possibility to impose 'compensatory measures' such as in the WTO DSB. This lack of a 'collective' or institutional system in order to ensure compliance in Mercosur may have an impact on its legitimacy.

The 'compensatory measures' mechanism was implemented for the first time in the case *Retreaded Tyres*, referring to the Argentine customs authorities' prohibition of importing retreaded tyres from Uruguay. The *Retreaded Tyres* dispute concerns the first time a State Party was held responsible by the Permanent Review Court for not complying with Mercosur law, being unilaterally forced to pay 'compensatory measures' by the complainant State Party. On this occasion, the referred Tribunal delivered its first award.[35]

Despite the legal basis of Mercosur law and the pronounced objective to rebalance mutual trade benefits, the 'compensatory measures' constitute a new commercial barrier and compromise the common market. This seems contrary to Mercosur objectives, which are not limited to commercial relations between State Parties. Indeed, the damage inflicted on Uruguay cannot be limited to just the economic sphere, in contrast with the GATT/WTO mechanism, which inspired the dispute settlement system of Mercosur. Also, it is difficult to settle a correspondent value on the damage suffered in order to apply compensatory measures in an effective way. This difficulty is reinforced due to economic asymmetry among Mercosur States, resulting in inefficacy of the referred measures.

Moreover, these measures are not sufficient in order to motivate Mercosur State Parties to comply with the awards. In the *Retreated Tyres* case, Argentina failed to comply with the arbitral award, despite the imposition of compensatory measures by Uruguay. Litigation involving the legality of these measures may serve to extend the proceeding of dispute settlement before the PRC, due to the plurality of recourses available.

[34] The mechanism of 'compensatory measures' in Mercosur is similar to that of retaliatory measures in the auspices of the WTO. Its objective is to ensure compliance by the recalcitrant state. Technically, the possibility for the complainant to ask the WTO DSB for permission to impose trade sanctions against the recalcitrant state is called 'suspending concessions or other obligations under the covered agreements' (Article 22.2 of the DSU). Although the term used in Mercosur may appear confusing, Mercosur's 'compensatory measures' are different from the WTO's 'compensation', which is negotiated between the parties involved in the dispute (see Article 22.1 and 22.2 of the DSU).

[35] PRC, Appeal for review presented by the Oriental Republic of Uruguay on the case concerning the prohibition of importing retreaded tyres from Uruguay, *Uruguay v. Argentina*, Award No 01/2005.

The referred case also demonstrates that decisions of international courts are not complied with simply because of the threat of any kind of sanctions.[36] The legitimacy of international tribunals is more linked to the authoritative character of the decision and less to the possibility to exercise coercion to ensure compliance. If Mercosur tribunals are considered legitimate, it means their judgements, views and recommendations are taken into consideration without the threat of formal sanctions.[37] A state that decides to defer to the authority of an international tribunal must thus be convinced to comply because of the perceived 'normative legitimacy' of the authority.[38] As a consequence, if Mercosur tribunals fail to reach the intended objective, their 'normative legitimacy may suffer, and social legitimacy may unravel partly as an effect'.[39]

3 The Legitimacy of Mercosur Arbitrators

This section will assess the nomination and composition of Mercosur tribunals (2.1), and the independence of arbitrators (2.2) by evaluating: the profile of each arbitrator both from the ad hoc Tribunal and the PRC according to the information available on their website; and interviews, particularly with arbitrators from the PRC, that focus on their personal perspectives on being designated to the tribunal, their function and their independence. The transparency of the nomination process and the independence of arbitrators are both essential in order to build up the democratic legitimacy of Mercosur tribunals.[40]

3.1 The Nomination and Composition

The nomination and composition of Mercosur ad hoc Tribunals (2.1.1) and the PRC (2.1.2) follow the rules established in the Olivos Protocol dealing with the appointment of arbitrators, as well as those indicated in the Regulation of the Olivos Protocol (Regulation of the PO) and

[36] Follesdal, 'Human rights judiciary', 342. [37] Ibid., 343. [38] Ibid., 346. [39] Ibid.

[40] According to Armin von Bogdandy, 'the election of judges, the procedure and the reasoning are to be construed and developed in their light. Transparency, participation and deliberation, the core elements of Article 11 of the TEU, are of crucial importance for international courts as they indicate strategies through which they can build up proper democratic legitimacy', Bogdandy, 'Legitimacy of international courts', 376.

secondary norms adopted by Mercosur decision-making bodies. It is important to highlight that there is no election of Mercosur arbitrators.

3.1.1 Mercosur Ad Hoc Tribunals

In terms of ad hoc Arbitral Tribunals, twelve arbitrators are nominated by State Parties to be included in a list filed with the Mercosur Secretariat (Article 11.1). There is also a list of third arbitrators, which is composed of four candidates proposed by each State Party (Article 11.2). State Parties maintain total control over this process because they have discretion in nominating the most appropriate candidate. This flexibility also applies to the possibility of modifying the list of arbitrators as duly proposed (Article 11, PO and Article 24, ROP).

The lack of any domestic rule concerning the nomination of arbitrators to Mercosur tribunals suggests that the nomination departs from the Ministry of Foreign Affairs of each State Party, but can also originate from the Ministry of Justice (this is the case of the last nomination of Argentine arbitrators for the Permanent Review Court).[41] This decision is frequently criticised as being nontransparent, which does not allow for accountability; it is not even published in the official bulletin of State Parties, with the exception of Uruguay.[42] There is no doubt that political actors are frequently involved in the process of nomination and selection of Mercosur arbitrators. However, when interviewed, some arbitrators insisted that there is no direct influence on their respective government: being an arbitrator in Mercosur is not perceived as a popular or important function.[43]

If the establishment of the list including the arbitrators nominated by State Parties officially occurs via the adoption of a Common Market Council decision (which, as a general rule, depends on the common agreement of all State Parties), this possibility implies that the

[41] Interview with Santiago Deluca, former Secretary of the Permanent Review Court and professor from the Universidad Buenos Aires, dated 14 April 2015 and 11 May 2015; interview with Welber Barral, Brazilian arbitrator of the PRC, dated 10 July 2014; and interview with Alejandro Perotti, former legal advisor of the Mercosur Secretariat and professor from the Universidad Austral, Buenos Aires, dated 12 July 2014 and 10 May 2015.

[42] According to Alejandro Perotti, Uruguay publishes in its official diary the executive decree that nominates its arbitrators. Argentina only did that once. The process would be completely unheard of in Brazil and Paraguay (Interview with Alejandro Perotti dated 12 July 2014 and 10 May 2015).

[43] Interview with Welber Barral dated 10 July 2014.

nomination of an arbitrator can be obstructed by another State Party.[44] Indeed, in order to ensure neutrality, other State Parties can request additional information on proposed individuals or raise objections on the designated candidates (Articles 11.1 and 11.2, PO and Articles 22 and 23, ROP). To date, no state has activated this procedure.[45] This may suggest that the Mercosur dispute settlement mechanism very much relies on diplomacy among State Parties and does not ensure transparency or neutrality in the nomination process, thereby compromising the 'democratic legitimacy'.

Once the full list has been established, the arbitration procedure is held before an ad hoc Tribunal comprised of three arbitrators: one appointed by each state in dispute and one Presiding Arbitrator chosen by the states or appointed by the Administrative Secretariat in case the disputing states are not able to reach an agreement. A total of three alternate arbitrators are also appointed to replace each of the arbitrators in the event of the inability to act or of excusing oneself during any stage of the arbitration procedure. The Olivos Protocol is clear in the sense that nationals of those states involved in the dispute are not permitted to act in the role as presidents during the arbitration procedure.

3.1.2 Permanent Review Court (PRC)

As far as the arbitrators of the PRC are concerned, these are also nominated via adoption of a decision by the Common Market Council. Four arbitrators, one per State Party, and their alternates are appointed for a two-year term,[46] renewable for two consecutive periods. The fifth arbitrator is to be appointed for a three-year nonrenewable period and must be chosen unanimously by State Parties from their nationals. With the exception of Brazil's replacement of an alternate arbitrator in 2008 and the renouncement of the Paraguayan arbitrator in 2007 (Dr. Wilfrido Fernández),[47] State Parties tend to renew the mandate of their

[44] Interview with Raphael Vasconcelos, current Secretary of the Permanent Review Court and professor from the Universidade do Estado do Rio de Janeiro (UERJ), dated 4 August 2014 and 10 May 2015.

[45] This information was obtained with the assistance of Mercosur officials and former officials interviewed by the author.

[46] The last nomination of arbitrators of the Mercosur PRC was held in December 2014, by MERCOSUR/CMC/DEC. nº 29/14.

[47] The former arbitrator claimed that the Mercosur dispute settlement mechanism was dependent totally upon State Parties' discretion: 'Denuncian dictadura del Mercosur',

arbitrators to the fullest extent.[48] This may suggest the influence of politics on the renewing process.

Those five arbitrators decide on a majority basis, and there is no advocate general. Despite the theoretical permanent character of the PRC, the arbitrators meet only when necessary during the actual proceedings. According to the Olivos Protocol, 'the members of the Permanent Review Court shall be permanently available to act whenever they are called upon to do so' (Article 19, PO). This means that the PRC's sole permanent body is its Secretary.[49] When required, the arbitrators will be paid according to the specific proceeding in question.[50]

The norm establishing these fees was adopted approximately eleven years ago and has yet to be revised by State Parties. The last example of its application concerns the award of the PRC rendered in 2012, Case No. 01/2012, on *Exceptional and Urgent Procedure requested by the Republic of Paraguay regarding the suspension of its participation in the Mercosur bodies and the incorporation of Venezuela as a full member.*[51] Because this proceeding was legally qualified as being a matter of an 'exceptional and urgent' case, the three participating arbitrators earned US$ 2,000 each per arbitral award.[52]

Following the creation of a mechanism on advisory opinions (similar to the preliminary rulings in the EU), arbitrators of the PRC may be required to render such 'opinions'. Similar to the EU context, the advisory opinion also plays a fundamental role in ensuring that Mercosur law produces the same effect in all circumstances for all State Parties. In such a case, the fees incumbent upon the arbitrators will be assumed in equal proportions by all Mercosur State Parties,[53] this being only US$ 2,000 per

ABC Color, 18 October 2007, available at: www.abc.com.py/edicion-impresa/politica/denuncian-dictadura-del-mercosur-1017388.html.

[48] S. Deluca, 'Metodología para la selección de árbitros del sistema de controversias del Mercosur (*Ad hoc* y TPR)' in M. H. Ramos and S. Deluca (eds.), *Tribunales en organizaciones internacionales: Mercosur, Comunidad Andina y Union Europea* (Madrid: Editorial Aranzadi, 2012), pp. 27–50, Nº 7.

[49] The tribunal is supported at its seat by one legal secretary and four administrative staff members (see MERCOSUL/GMC/RES Nº 64/14). The current secretary of the PRC is Dr. Raphael Carvalho de Vasconcelos.

[50] See MERCOSUL/GMC/RES Nº 40/04.

[51] PRC, Exceptional and urgent procedure requested by Paraguay with respect to its participation in Mercosur bodies and to the incorporation of Venezuela as a Full Member, Paraguay *v.* Argentina, Brazil and Uruguay, Arbitral Award No 01/2012.

[52] A total of US$ 786,839 was allocated to the Secretary of the PRC in 2015. For further details on the current budget of the Secretary of the PRC, see GMC Resolution Nº 59/14.

[53] MERCOSUL/GMC/RES Nº 40/04 and MERCOSUL/GMC/RES Nº 41/04.

rapporteur and US$ 1,000 for the other arbitrators for the most relevant proceeding before the Mercosur dispute settlement system![54]

One may wonder whether these very low fees could impede attraction of good members to compose the tribunals. However, it seems that being part of Mercosur tribunals is mostly regarded as a strategic international function, capable of conferring a relevant status to academics specialised in international law. One may also wonder whether these low fees could somehow compromise the impartiality of the arbitrators because they end up assuming a great variety of domestic functions as discussed later.

The expenses referred to may be paid through the Special Fund for Disputes ('Fondo Especial para Controversias'), duly established in 2004 and designed to ensure that fees, travel expenses and general costs are paid to Mercosur dispute settlement employees.[55] The Special Fund consists of contributions of US$ 50,000 forwarded by each member state.[56]

3.2 Common Provisions Regarding the Qualification and Independence of Arbitrators

The Olivos Protocol and its Regulation and other secondary norms also contain rules on the qualification of the arbitrators, stating that they 'shall be lawyers possessing the recognised expertise in the fields that may be subject matter of disputes, and shall be acquainted with the body of Mercosur regulations. Besides being capable of applying the Mercosur *acquis*, these arbitrators shall be necessarily impartial and functionally independent with regards to the central public administration of their respective State Party. They shall not pertain interests at stake in the dispute, being appointed due to their "objectivity, reliability and good judgment"' (Article 35, PO).

In order to maintain independence, the Regulation of the PO (Article 19, ROP on the impediments to be appointed arbitrator) mentions a list

[54] According to informal discussions with Jose Manuel Zarate, professor of International Law (Externado University of Colombia) and lawyer pleading before the Court of Justice of the Andean Community, the judges earn between US$ 20,000 and 25,000 per month.

[55] MERCOSUR/CMC/DEC. Nº 17/04, Article1.

[56] The existence of this Fund is considered positive by many Mercosur specialists because it confers transparency to process and guarantees payment to judges and arbitrators. There are other dispute settlement mechanisms that do not operate on the basis of special funds, such as the Andean Community (according to informal discussions with Jose Manuel Zarate, lawyer before the Court of Justice of the Andean Community).

of situations in which an arbitrator shall not be appointed. The impediment also occurs should a State Party object to the appointment of an arbitrator, according to the provisions of Article 19.3, ROP.[57] The arbitrator's appointment depends upon a decision adopted *huis clos* within the CMC, this being without any participation of civil society.[58] In any case, such an impediment has not yet occurred since the entry into force of the Olivos Protocol in 2004.[59] Once appointed to act in a particular case, both arbitrators from ad hoc Tribunals and from the PRC must sign a declaration stating their independence and impartiality (Articles 10 and 19, PO and Articles 21 and 32, ROP).

In addition to these rules, the CMC has recently adopted a Code of Conduct for the Mercosur arbitrators, experts and employees working within the subregional dispute settlement mechanism.[60] The referred document is said to have been manufactured out of the blue, without any previous notice to Mercosur arbitrators.[61] It reinforces the duties and obligations incumbent upon arbitrators and experts with a view to ensure their independence and impartiality, to avoid conflicts of interest, to maintain confidentiality of the proceedings and to restrain any kind of additional remuneration related to the arbitral proceedings (apart from those already due in accordance to Mercosur norms and regulations) (Article 2).

In the case of an alleged violation of the duties and obligations as mentioned earlier, a State Party involved in a dispute may request the CMG, Mercosur's executive body, to initiate an investigation proceeding, bringing to light the arguments supporting its allegations (Article 4). As a

[57] The only case where a State Party objected to the appointment of an arbitrator relates to the current renewal of the fifth Brazilian arbitrator, Dr. Jorge Luiz Fontoura Nogueira, as Mercosur rules do not explicitly allow for a second renewal period (see CMC decision 29/11). Argentina objected to the reappointment of the referred arbitrator, but failed to nominate another candidate. During the last GMC meeting in April 2015, State Parties decided the CMC would again renew the mandate of the Brazilian arbitrator. Interview with Raphael Vasconcelos dated 4 August 2014 and 10 May 2015; and interview with Alejandro Perotti dated 12 July 2014 and 10 May 2015.

[58] Interview with Santiago Deluca dated 14 April 2015 and 11 May 2015.

[59] The Argentine *manoeuvre* in order to object the Spanish presiding Arbitrator of the ad hoc Tribunal, Dr. Luis Martí Mingarro, in the case *Blockage of roads in Argentina giving access to the bridges linking it to the Uruguayan territory*, was unfruitful (Interview with Alejandro Perotti dated 12 July 2014 and 10 May 2015).

[60] MERCOSUR/CMC/DEC. N° 31/11.

[61] Interview with Alejandro Perotti dated 12 July 2014 and 10 May 2015. In his view, the Code of Conduct appears to be an attempt by national diplomacies to control and restrict the activities of Mercosur Tribunals.

consequence, the CMG, among others, may suspend the dispute settlement procedure or replace the arbitrator with his/her alternate. This type of violation and its consequences have yet to occur in Mercosur.[62] As noted later, politics play a fundamental role in the Mercosur dispute settlement mechanism, thereby compromising transparency and accountability.

In practice, the current arbitrators of the ad hoc Tribunal and the PRC tend to be high-level academics and recognised lawyers in the State Party concerned. This has been the rule, particularly under the auspices of the PRC[63]: according to their profile, they are all PhDs, with links to several universities as academics and have exercised private and public professional activities. They are all specialised in international law and Mercosur law. According to Alejandro Perotti, a former official of the Mercosur Secretariat and renowned jurist, arbitrators from small countries such as Paraguay and Uruguay who were elected during the last ten years possessed a sound knowledge of Mercosur law.[64]

4 The Legitimacy of the Mercosur Judicial Decision-Making Process

In terms of the legitimacy of the Mercosur judicial decision-making process, the objective is, first, to evaluate the use of precedents and reference to other international, regional and subregional tribunals (3.1). Transparent reasoning, which implies discussing and treating precedents, is certainly an important factor to strengthen the 'democratic legitimacy' of the Mercosur decision-making process.[65] Second, their deliberation process and interaction with national courts through the cooperation mechanism established through advisory opinions (which is similar to preliminary rulings under the auspices of the EU) (3.2) are also

62 This information was obtained with the assistance of Mercosur officials and former officials interviewed by the author.

63 A Common Market Council decision adopted in 2013 (MERCOSUR/CMC/DEC. nº 18/03) renewed the mandate of the current arbitrators of the Permanent Review Court for the period 14 August 2013 to 14 August 2015. From the arbitrators contacted by the author, only Drs. Welber Barral (Brazil), José Maria Gamio (Uruguay) and Roberto Díaz Labrano (Paraguay) accepted the invitation to be interviewed.

64 Interview with Alejandro Perotti dated 12 July 2014 and 10 May 2015. The author was not able to conclude that the size of a country is decisive for finding enough specialists on international and Mercosur law.

65 Bogdandy, 'Legitimacy of International Courts', 376.

important criteria in order to assess their 'normative and democratic legitimacy'.

4.1 *The Use of Precedents and Reference to Other Tribunals*

Mercosur ad hoc Tribunals have consistently referred to previous Mercosur awards as precedents as well as to judgements of the European Court of Justice (ECJ), the ICJ and the Permanent Court of International Justice (PCIJ), and to the decisions of the WTO DSB. This seems to 'reinforce the idea of recognizing common patterns in the application and interpretation of Mercosur law'.[66]

Indeed, it is important to evaluate to what extent Mercosur tribunals refer to judgements of other international courts and whether this referral influences the decision-making process. This referral to other courts or, in other words, the 'unilateral jurisprudential dialogue', may serve to confirm the Court's reasoning, help filling the gap or contribute to the definition of applicable legal standards and concepts.[67]

Several examples are to be found in different arbitral awards issued under the Brasília and Olivos Protocols. This is particularly evident with regards to advisory opinions issued by the Permanent Review Court, which constantly refer to ECJ judgements on preliminary rulings. The first advisory opinion made extensive use of precedents: the arbitrators mentioned previous ad hoc Tribunals' awards, as well as jurisprudence of the ECJ, particularly the cases *Costa v. Enel* and *Van Gend Loos*, and judgements of the Andean Community Court of Justice. Reference was made to several European and Latin American jurists, as well as to international conventions applicable to the matter, particularly those rules of the Vienna Convention on the Law of Treaties regarding *pacta sunt servanda* and internal law and observance of treaties (Articles 26 and 27, VCLT).[68] By incorporating these precedents, the arbitrator's intent (notably the rapporteur of the advisory opinion, Dr. Wilfrido Fernández, Paraguayan arbitrator), was to clearly apply the principles of EU law, i.e., primacy and direct effect, to the Mercosur legal system.[69]

[66] Vinuesa, 'Enforcement of Mercosur Arbitration Awards', 443.

[67] P. Wojcikiewicz Almeida, 'The challenges of the judicial dialogue in Mercosur', *The Law and Practice of International Courts and Tribunals*, 14 (2015), 1–15.

[68] Vienna Convention on the Law of Treaties, Vienna, 23 May 1969, in force 27 January 1980, 1155 UNTS 331; (1969) 8 ILM 679; UKTS (1980) 58.

[69] The arbitrators of the first advisory opinion transposed the principles of primacy and direct effect to the Mercosur legal system. However, the mechanism of advisory opinions

Conversely, the second and third advisory opinions were far less ambitious and mentioned only Mercosur precedents and the VCLT.

The contentious cases submitted to Mercosur tribunals also tend to make extensive use of precedents and reference to other tribunals and international treaties. The first arbitral award issued under the Brasília Protocol made reference to the EU doctrine, in order to apply the teleological interpretation to Mercosur treaties.[70] It also made extensive use of international law doctrine[71] so as to apply the rules concerning *pacta sunt servanda* and good faith, also recognised by the VCLT. A number of subsequent arbitral awards also mentioned the VCLT, particularly provisions on the observance and interpretation of treaties, by emphasising the relevance of a teleological interpretation.[72] Consequently, not only has the VCLT been used consistently as a source of interpretation of Mercosur treaties, but Mercosur tribunals also acknowledged the need to observe and apply the rules and principles of international law when deciding a case based on Mercosur law.[73]

in Mercosur is not binding to the national court that requested it. As a consequence, the recognition of primacy and direct effect remains in the hands of the national courts. For further details on the mechanism of advisory opinions, see section 3.2 of this chapter.

[70] The referred award explicitly cited the works of Dr. Robert Lecourt, Antonio Remiro Brotons and Fausto Quadros.

[71] Particularly Anzilotti, Kelsen, Verdross, Sinclair and others.

[72] See the ad hoc Tribunal, *Clarification of the Arbitral Award on the application of antidumping measures on exports of whole chickens from Brazil, Brazil v. Argentina*, Arbitral Award of 18 June 2001; ad hoc Tribunal, *Prohibition of importing retreaded tyres from Uruguay, Brazil v. Uruguay*, Arbitral Award of 01 September 2002; PRC, Excess in the application of compensatory measures on the case concerning the prohibition of importing retreaded tyres from Uruguay, Award issued on 8 July 2007 (No 1/07); PRC, Divergence as to the enforcement of the Award No 1/05, *Uruguay v. Argentina*, Arbitral Award No 01/2008; PRC, Exceptional and urgent measures requested by Paraguay with respect to its participation in Mercosur bodies and to the incorporation of Venezuela as a Full Member, *Paraguay v. Argentina, Brazil and Uruguay*, Arbitral Award No 01/2012; PRC, Appeal for review presented by the Oriental Republic of Uruguay on the case concerning the prohibition of importing retreaded tyres from Uruguay, *Uruguay v. Argentina*, Award No 01/2005; PRC, Blockage of roads in Argentina giving access to the bridges linking it to the Uruguayan territory, *Uruguay v. Argentina*, 2006.

[73] According to the ad hoc Tribunal, 'regardless of the application of the specific rules of Mercosur, the Court is bound to observe, to the extent possible, the rules and principles of international law' (translation by the author), ad hoc Tribunal, *Discriminatory and restrictive measures on trade of tobacco and tobacco products, Uruguay v. Brazil*, Arbitral Award of 5 August 2005, p. 6 (citing other cases, such as ad hoc Tribunal, *Prohibition of importing retreaded tyres from Uruguay, Brazil v. Uruguay*, Arbitral Award of 01 September 2002; and ad hoc Tribunal, *Restriction to the access of Uruguayan bicycles in the Argentinean market, Uruguay v. Argentina*, Arbitral Award of 29 September 2001).

Four Mercosur arbitral awards have notably referred to judgements (mostly contentious cases) of the International Court of Justice (ICJ) and the Permanent Court of International Justice (PCIJ)[74]: (i) *Application of protective measures on textile products*; (ii) *Application of antidumping measures on exports of whole chickens from Brazil*; (iii) *Discriminatory and restrictive measures on trade of tobacco and tobacco products*; and (iv) *Blockage of roads in Argentina giving access to the bridges linking it to the Uruguayan territory*. Arbitrators repeatedly mentioned PCIJ and ICJ jurisprudence in order to define the concept of dispute within Mercosur, this being 'a disagreement on a point of law or fact, a conflict of legal views or interests between parties'.[75]

If international law is to be taken into account in order to interpret and apply Mercosur law, WTO law is also a relevant source of interpretation. Under the Brasília Protocol, eight arbitral awards referred to WTO DSB case law, while under the Olivos Protocol, four arbitral awards mentioned WTO DSB case law. The Mercosur ad hoc Tribunal in the *Bicycles Case* made it clear that WTO principles and rules are part of

[74] For the PCIJ cases cited, see: Case Concerning the Mavrommatis Jerusalem Concessions, Judgement, PCIJ Reports (1925), Series A-Nº 5; Case Concerning Certain German Interests in Polish Upper Silesia, Judgement, PCIJ Reports (1926), Series A-Nº 7; Case Concerning the S.S. "Wimbledon", Judgement, PCIJ Reports (1923), Series A-Nº 1; Advisory Opinion Concerning the Treatment of Polish Nationals and Other Persons of Polish Origin or Speech in the Danzig Territory, PCIJ Reports (1932), Series A/B-Nº44; Case Concerning the Free Zones of Upper Savoy and the District of Gex, Second Phase, PCIJ Reports (1930), Series A-Nº 24; Advisory Opinion Concerning the Greco-Bulgarian Communities, PCIJ Reports (1930), Series B-Nº 77. As for the ICJ, the arbitrators pointed out the following cases: Case Concerning South West Africa (Liberia/Ethiopia *v.* South Africa), Second Phase, Judgement, ICJ Reports (1966) 6; Case Concerning the Northern Cameroons (*Cameroon v. United Kingdom*), Preliminary Objections, Judgement of 2 December 1963, ICJ Reports (1963) 15; Case Concerning East Timor (*Portugal v. Australia*), Judgement, ICJ Reports (1995) 90; Case Concerning Nottebohm (*Liechtenstein v. Guatemala*) (second phase), Judgement, ICJ Reports (1955) 4. Only one advisory proceeding issued by the ICJ was cited: Advisory Opinion Concerning the Interpretation of Peace Treaties (second phase), Advisory Opinion, ICJ Reports (1950) 221.

[75] Ad hoc Tribunal, *Application of antidumping measures on exports of whole chickens from Brazil, Brazil v. Argentina*, Arbitral Award of 21 May 2001, pp. 9 and 8; and ad hoc Tribunal, *Discriminatory and restrictive measures on trade of tobacco and tobacco products, Uruguay v. Brazil*, Arbitral Award of 5 August 2005, p. 7, footnote 7, both citing the Case Concerning the Mavrommatis Jerusalem Concessions, Judgement, PCIJ Reports (1925), Series A-Nº 5, p. 11. This interpretation has been reiterated by the ICJ in the following cases also cited by both arbitral awards: Case Concerning the Northern Cameroons (*Cameroon v. United Kingdom*), Preliminary Objections, Judgement of 2 December 1963, ICJ Reports (1963) 15, p. 27 and Case Concerning East Timor (*Portugal v. Australia*), Judgement, ICJ Reports (1995) 90, p. 99.

international law and constitute an integral source of Mercosur law (Article 19, Protocol of Brasília).[76] In the *Pork Meat Case*, arbitrators considered that the WTO definition of the term 'subsidies' should apply within the Mercosur legal system.[77] Being focused on trade since its inception, most Mercosur arbitral awards made extensive reference to the WTO agreements. However, in the case concerning the *Application of anti-dumping measures on exports of whole chickens from Brazil*, arbitrators limited the application of WTO law by indicating that recourse to WTO norms and principles was exceptional and dependent upon an expressed authorisation to apply WTO principles according to Mercosur norms.[78] The effect of this limitation is yet to be found in future cases involving the matter.

With regard to other subregional organisations, the ECJ and Andean Community Court of Justice's case laws are consistently cited as 'external' precedents. The first reference to ECJ precedents by Mercosur Arbitral Awards in contentious proceedings has proven to be very cautious.[79] Insofar as the Arbitral Award recognised the importance of these precedents in the context of regional integration, they also underlined the peculiarity of the Mercosur integration process. This would require a particular solution not necessarily transposed from the EU legal framework.

The second allusion to ECJ precedents was clear enough in the case concerning the *Industrialization of wool*.[80] The respondent argued for the applicability of the international rule, *exceptio non adimpleti contractus*, in Mercosur. The ad hoc Tribunal firmly opposed this argument by

[76] Ad hoc Tribunal, *Restriction to the access of Uruguayan bicycles in the Argentinean market, Uruguay v. Argentina*, Arbitral Award of 29 September 2001, p. 8.

[77] Ad hoc Tribunal, *Subsidies to the production and exportation of pork meat, Argentina v. Brazil*, Arbitral Award issued on 27 September 1999, p. 19–22.

[78] Ad hoc Tribunal, *Application of anti-dumping measures on exports of whole chickens from Brazil, Argentina v. Brazil*, Arbitral Award issued on 21 May 2001, p. 32. This arbitral award made explicit reference to renowned jurists, such as Dr. Gabrielle Marceau, *Anti-dumping and Anti-trust Issues in Free Trade Areas* (Oxford: Clarendon Press, 1994), p. 141.

[79] The Arbitral Award cited the following ECJ judgements: Case 06/60, *Humblet v. Belgium* [1960] ECR 1125; Case 48/71, *Commission v. Italy* [1972] ECR 529; Case 167/73, *Commission v. France* [1974] ECR 359, [1974] 2 CMLR 216; Joined Cases 24 and 97/80, *Commission v. France* [1980] ECR 1319, [1981] 3 CMLR 25 (see *Clarification of the Arbitral Award on the restriction to the access of Uruguayan bicycles in the Argentinean market, Uruguay v. Argentina*, Arbitral Award issued on 29 September 2001).

[80] Arbitral Award, Incompatibility of the Uruguayan regime that stimulates the industrialization of wool, *Argentina v. Uruguay*, Arbitral Award of 4 April 2003.

asserting that the mechanism of self-defence is incompatible with sub-regional integration organisations, such as Mercosur. Thus State Parties shall not take the law into their own hands. Mercosur treaties (*dans le cas d'espèce*, Brasília Protocol) expressly provide means and special procedures for remedying the difficulties encountered by State Parties as a consequence of a breach of Mercosur law.[81] The ad hoc Tribunal followed the reasoning of the ECJ[82] and the Andean Community Court of Justice[83] in order to render its award.

The Arbitral Award on the *Appeal for review presented by the Oriental Republic of Uruguay on the case concerning the prohibition of importing retreaded tyres from Uruguay* was based almost entirely on ECJ precedents.[84] In order for the PRC to establish criteria for evaluating restrictions to free trade in Mercosur, it made extensive reference to settled case law of the ECJ. According to Mercosur arbitrators, ECJ reasoning on the case *Commission v. Austria* is perfectly transposable to Mercosur.[85] Any obstruction to the free movement of goods and services must 'be regarded as constituting a measure having equivalent effect to quantitative restrictions' (Para. 69). This was judged incompatible with EU law, unless the measure in question could be objectively justified. Arbitrators applied the same reasoning, explicitly mentioning the opinion of advocate general Geelhoed (14 July 2005) to stress that the measure applied within Mercosur was not justified by overriding requirements related to the protection of the environment, nor was it proportionate to the aim pursued.[86] Like in the European Union, the evaluation of the proportionality of a measure taken by a Mercosur State Party also required determination of whether it was necessary and appropriate in order to secure the legitimate objective.[87]

[81] Arbitral Award, *Incompatibility of the Uruguayan regime that stimulates the industrialization of wool, Argentina v. Uruguay*, Arbitral Award of 4 April 2003, p. 19–20, paras. 65–6.

[82] Joined Cases 90/63 and 91/63, *Commission v. Luxembourg and Belgium* [1964] ECR 625, [1965] CMLR 58.

[83] Andean Community Court of Justice, Case No I-A1-97, 20 October 1999 (Gaceta Oficial del Acuerdo de Cartagena, No 500, 25 October 1999).

[84] PRC, *Appeal for review presented by the Oriental Republic of Uruguay on the case concerning the prohibition of importing retreaded tyres from Uruguay, Uruguay v. Argentina*, Award No 01/2005.

[85] Case C-320/03, *Commission of the European Communities v. Republic of Austria* [2005] ECR I-09871, paras. 69–71 and para. 85, cited by the PRC, Award No 01/2005, pp. 6 and 7.

[86] The PRC also mentioned the following ECJ precedents: Case C-463/01, *Commission v. Germany* [2004] ECR I-11705, para. 75 and Case C-309/02, *Radlberger Getränkegesellschaft and S. Spitz* [2004] ECR I-11763, [2005] 1 CMLR 35 para. 75.

[87] Case 104/75, *De Peijper* [1976] ECR 613, [1976] 2 CMLR 271, paras. 16 and 22, cited by the PRC, Award No 01/2005, p. 9.

A further referral to ECJ case law concerns Argentina's noncompliance with the Arbitral Award of the case concerning the *Prohibition of importing retreaded tyres from Uruguay*, which justified the possibility of Uruguay adopting compensatory measures. The legality and proportionality of these measures were argued by Argentina before the Mercosur PRC. In its award, the Court comprehensively referred to ECJ judgements and those of the Andean Community Court of Justice delivered in 'proceedings for failure to fulfil obligations under EU law' in order to criticise the unilateral mechanism applied by Mercosur State Parties. The PRC emphasised their reproachable character as well as their intrinsic contradiction as far as the free movement of goods and services are concerned.[88]

Finally, the case concerning *Blockage of roads in Argentina giving access to the bridges linking it to the Uruguayan territory* represents the latest time a Mercosur contentious case mentioned ECJ case law. However, reference to the ECJ was only marginal, as the arbitral award proved to be much more comprehensive of international law practice in the field. On the one hand, as a claimant, Uruguay invoked the ECJ case *Commission v. France* to endorse the responsibility of States for failing to take all necessary measures in order to prevent the free movement of goods from being obstructed by private individual action.[89] Argentina, on the other hand, tried to justify its supposed omissions by alluding to the ECJ *Schmidberger* case, which recognised the legitimate aim of a demonstration organised by an environmental group on a Member State motorway, any such action not giving rise to liability on the part of the Member State concerned.[90] Despite their connection to the facts in dispute, Mercosur arbitrators expressly disregarded these precedents.[91]

[88] Case C-387/97, *Commission v. Hellenic Republic* [2000] ECR I-5047, paras. 89–90; Case C-278/01, *Commission v. Kingdom of Spain* [2003] ECR I-14141, paras. 41–62; Case C-304/02, *Commission v. French Republic* [2005] ECR I-6263, [2005] 3 CMLR 13, paras. 80 and following; Case C-177/04, *Commission v. French Republic* [2006] ECR I-2461, paras. 59 and following. All cases city by: PRC, *Excess in the application of compensatory measures on the case concerning the prohibition of importing retreaded tyres from Uruguay*, Award issued on 8 July 2007 (No 1/07), pp. 8–9, paras. 10.2–10.4.

[89] Case C-265/95, *Commission v. French Republic* [1997] ECR I-06959, cited by ad hoc Tribunal, *Blockage of roads in Argentina giving access to the bridges linking it to the Uruguayan territory, Uruguay v. Argentina*, Arbitral Award of 6 September 2006, para. 31.

[90] Case C-112/00, *Schmidberger* [2003] ECR I-5659, [2003] 2 CMLR 34 cited by ad hoc Tribunal, *Blockage of roads*, p. 9.

[91] The arbitrators disregarded the EU case law on the basis of distinctions between the power devoted to EU and Mercosur structures and the singularity of the cases compared to the situation in dispute in Mercosur. See ad hoc Tribunal, *Blockage of roads*, paras. 150–2.

It seems that in especially controversial or politically sensitive cases, arbitrators tend to look consistently to other prestigious and influential courts, such as the ECJ, in order to search for guidance, inspiration and to confer legitimacy to their decisions.[92] Even if precedents of international courts are not entirely transposed to the disputed case in Mercosur, this practice of looking *ailleurs* may be considered a positive assessment for strengthening the 'normative and democratic legitimacy' of the judicial decision-making process.

4.2 The Interaction with National Courts

The interaction with national courts occurs predominantly via the mechanism of advisory opinions, which is exercised before the Mercosur PRC. This procedure enables national courts to question the PRC exclusively with regard to the interpretation of Mercosur law. Contrary to the EU reference for preliminary ruling whereby the mechanism occurs 'from one judge to another', Mercosur expands the number of those capable of requesting advisory opinions: State Parties acting together along with decision-making bodies and the Parliament are all empowered to request an advisory opinion on *any legal question arising from Mercosur law* to the PRC.[93] However, advisory opinions requested by national judges via their Supreme Courts may only concern the *interpretation of a Mercosur norm* (not the validity of Mercosur law).[94] Moreover, first instance national judges other than Supreme Courts are not permitted to directly access the PRC.

The importance of this mechanism is well known, as is the preliminary ruling in the European Union. Its objective is to guarantee uniform application of Mercosur law throughout the organisation by promoting active cooperation between national courts and the PRC. This objective can be hardly achievable because the PRC's reply does not bind the national court to which it is provided.[95] Likewise, the Court's opinion does not legally bind any other national courts before which the same problem is raised. This double nonbinding character implies that national courts, even those acting as a final resort, are not obliged to exercise the advisory opinion mechanism, nor are they bound to apply

[92] See Wojcikiewicz, 'Judicial dialogue in Mercosur', 10. See also D. S. Law and W.-C. Chang, 'The limits of global judicial dialogue', *Washington Law Review*, 86 (2011), 571.

[93] Article 2 and 3 of the Regulation of the PO.

[94] Article 4 of the Regulation of the PO.

[95] See Article 11 of the Regulation of the PO.

the interpretation rendered by the Court. The national court therefore remains competent for the original case and may decide whether or not to apply the PRC's advisory opinion.[96] It seems that Mercosur State Parties opted for this nonbinding character in order to avoid the risk of judicial law-making by its courts, taking into account the experience of the ECJ in the 1960s.

According to the Regulation of the PO adopted in 2003, the procedure to request advisory opinions to the PRC must be regulated by the High Courts of Justice of Mercosur State Parties (Article 4). Four years later, the Common Market Council adopted decision N° 02/07 regulating the referred mechanism. From that moment on, it was up to national Supreme Courts to specify the formal requirement to be complied with by first instance national judges intending to submit advisory opinions. It took a while until all national courts were finally able to apply this mechanism. Uruguay was the very first State Party to adopt rules authorising the national request of advisory opinions (2007), followed by Argentina and Paraguay one year later (2008). Brazil was by far the last State Party allowing its nationals to indirectly clarify a question on the interpretation of Mercosur law (2012).[97]

Concretely, the PRC has issued a total of three advisory opinions exclusively related to the interpretation of Mercosur law: one submitted by the Supreme Court of Paraguay and two by the Supreme Court of Uruguay.[98] Similar to the European Union, several important principles of Mercosur law have been laid down by advisory opinions. The first advisory opinion transposed EU principles of primacy and direct effect to the Mercosur legal order, whereas the second and third advisory opinions were far less ambitious.[99]

[96] This may indicate that a power relationship is at stake because it will depend on whether national courts follow the PRC's interpretation according to their own interest.

[97] See also Uruguay, Circular 86/2007 of the Supreme Court of Justice; Argentina, Acordada N° 13/08 of the Supreme Court of Justice of the Nation; Paraguay, Acordada N° 549/2008 of the Supreme Court of Justice; and Brazil, Emenda Regimental N° 48/2012 of the Federal Supreme Court.

[98] Demand No. 01/2007, submitted by the Supreme Court of Paraguay; Demand No. 01/2008, submitted by the Supreme Court of Uruguay; Demand No. 01/2009, submitted by the Supreme Court of Uruguay.

[99] See Section 2, Subsection 2.2, Title 2.2.2 for a summary of the reasoning of the arbitrators applied by the first advisory opinion. For more details, see C. Esposito and L. Donadio, 'Inter-jurisdictional co-operation in the MERCOSUR: The first request for an advisory opinion of the MERCOSUR's Permanent Review Tribunal by Argentina's Supreme Court of Justice', *The Law and Practice of International Courts and Tribunals*, 10 (2010), 261–84.

The national tribunals that made the request of advisory opinions, however, did not accurately follow the interpretation issued by the PRC. In the Paraguayan situation (the first advisory opinion), the national requesting judge ended up reaching a similar solution for the case, even when applying distinct reasoning from that of the PRC.[100] In the second and third advisory opinions, originating from Uruguay, the national requesting judges followed the exact opposite path and, thus, did not comply with the PRC's opinion.[101] The national judges' choice of an alternative path can indicate that national actors do not respect the analytical approach, the interpretation and/or the conclusion of Mercosur tribunals as authoritative.[102]

This low number of advisory opinions may result from four main challenges within Mercosur.[103] First, the 'double' nonbinding character of advisory opinions; second, the delay in regulating the submission mechanism by national courts, as previously indicated;[104] third, the lack

[100] Interview with Alejandro Perotti dated 12 July 2014 and 10 May 2015.

[101] Interview with Alejandro Perotti dated 12 July 2014 and 10 May 2015. The Uruguayan Supreme Court considered that domestic law had the same hierarchy as international treaties and prevailed over the Asunción Treaty. Interview with Magdalena Bas, professor from the Universidad de la República, Montevideo, dated 15 August 2014. For more details on the referred cases, see M. B. Vilizzio, *Solución de Controversias en el MERCOSUR: Análisis de resultados 2004–2011 desde la perspectiva jurídico-política* (Montevideo: ed. CSIC: UdelaR: Universidad de la República, 2013), pp. 34–6.

[102] Behn, Fauchald, and Langford, 'How to approach "legitimacy"', p. 3.

[103] These are not the sole advisory opinions ever submitted to the PRC. Indeed, the tribunal has recently terminated two official requests submitted by Argentine tribunals via resolutions N° 01/2014 (PRC Presidency, Resolution N° 01/2014, adopted under the auspices of advisory opinion N° 01/2014 requested by the Argentine Supreme Court of Justice on the case concerning 'Dow Química Argentina S.A. c/ E.N. -DGA.- (SANLO) Resol. 583/10 y otros s/ Dirección General de Aduanas'.) and 02/2014 (PRC Presidency, Resolution N° 02/2014, adopted under the auspices of advisory opinion N° 02/2014 requested by the Argentine Supreme Court of Justice in the case concerning 'S.A. LA HISPANO ARGENTINA CURTIEMBRE Y CHAROLERIA C/ E.N. -DGA.- (SANLO) s/ Dirección General de Aduanas'.). In several other cases originating from the Argentine Supreme Courts, parties withdrew the request of advisory opinions or abandoned the original case before the national tribunals. Most of them dealt with intrazone export duties. See A. Perotti, *La judicatura argentina y las opiniones consultivas: el 'largo' camino a Asunción* (Buenos Aires: CARI, 11 November 2014). For further details concerning the Argentine cases, see M. P. Pinon, 'Una Mirada al Mercosur desde la Corte Suprema de Justicia de la Nación. Comentario al fallo Bio Sidus', *Revista de Doctrina Judicial*, 35 (2013), 17–21 and 21–7, available at: http://grupodeintegracion.blogspot.com.br/2013/09/una-mirada-al-mercosur-desde-la-corte.html.

[104] The nonadoption of internal regulations authorising the submission of advisory opinions does not preclude a tribunal from requesting it from the PRC. Indeed, the

of incorporation of Mercosur law in State Parties, which would allow individuals and legal persons to invoke a subjective right based on Mercosur; and finally, the lack of knowledge of Mercosur law and its mechanisms among lawyers and national judges.

The interaction with national courts also occurs via 'judicial dialogue' with representatives of the Mercosur tribunals.[105] National Supreme Courts of Mercosur State Parties have established a forum known as 'Supreme Court Meetings', which consist of annual meetings designed to discuss legal aspects related to the regional integration system. These official meetings were held consecutively in 2006, 2007, 2008, 2009 and 2010. Other subsequent meetings did not specifically concern Mercosur-related topics. A great supporter of the project of the Mercosur Court of Justice was the Brazilian Minister Gilmar Mendes from the Federal Supreme Court, during his presidency between 2008 and 2010.[106]

5 Conclusion

This chapter highlighted numerous challenges within the Mercosur dispute settlement mechanism, which are capable of compromising the desired legitimacy of its tribunals. These challenges are linked to the concepts of 'normative and democratic legitimacy' discussed in the introduction of this chapter and encompass three main factors: procedures in dispute settlement; nomination and composition of tribunals; and decision-making process. Such factors seem closely interrelated and interdependent in terms of their effects on legitimacy.[107]

In terms of procedures in dispute settlement, it is currently not possible to evaluate the legality of Mercosur normative acts because Mercosur decision-making bodies are the masters of their own procedures. Also, the Mercosur Secretariat does not have the power to initiate infringement procedures. The limitations of the current mechanism

Paraguayan Supreme Court submitted a request even before the adoption of the respective domestic regulation. See Pinon, 'Una Mirada al Mercosur', 23.

105 On the importance of formal meetings or information gatherings for the formation of the judges' understandings and opinions, see A. Tzanakopoulos, 'Judicial dialogue as a means of interpretation' in H. P. Aust and G. Nolte (eds.), *Interpretation of International Law by Domestic Courts* (Oxford University Press, 2016), available at: Oxford Legal Studies Research Paper 71 (2014), pp. 6 and 7.

106 Interview with Alejandro Perotti, former legal advisor of the Mercosur Secretariat and professor at the Universidad Austral, Buenos Aires, dated 12 July 2014 and 10 May 2015.

107 Behn, Fauchald, and Langford, 'How to approach "legitimacy"', p. 3.

result from its transitory aspect; the absence of obligatory submission to Mercosur courts because Article 1 from the *Protocol of Ouro Preto* allows the activation of Dispute Settlement Body (DSB) of the WTO; the *inter partes* effect of the arbitral award, endangering the uniform application of Mercosur law; the limited access of individuals who are only able to present their demands via the National Section of the Common Market Group of the Member State in question; and the absence of an autonomous coercive power capable of enforcing arbitral awards.

As far as the nomination and composition of Mercosur tribunals are concerned, the current rule contained in the Olivos Protocol does not allow for the election of arbitrators. The system depends entirely on the political will of the State Parties; it is not designed in a way as to guarantee the independence of the arbitrators. This does not ensure the necessary transparency, thereby compromising proper accountability. Although the decision-making process may appear closely interrelated to the nomination and composition of Mercosur tribunals, arbitrators tend to confer greater 'normative and democratic legitimacy' to their reasoning because there is an extensive use of precedents and reference to other tribunals by Mercosur awards. This reference may serve multiple purposes: to define applicable legal standards and concepts and, more generally, to help filling the gap; to confirm the tribunal's decision; and finally, to search for guidance or inspiration.[108] It is undeniable that the education and professional background of Mercosur arbitrators often shape their decision-making process because there is a relationship between judicial background and foreign or international law usage.[109]

Finally, the interaction with national courts as part of the decision-making process, which occurs via direct and indirect judicial dialogue, is also an important criterion in order to assess the 'normative and democratic legitimacy' of Mercosur tribunals. If this interaction exists in a flexible way, the 'double' nonbinding character of the advisory opinion may endanger the uniform application of Mercosur in State Parties, putting at risk the 'normative legitimacy' of its dispute settlement mechanism. The possibility to engage in a constructive dialogue with Mercosur tribunals is thus dependent upon the discretion of national courts.

Taking all these challenges into consideration, some initiatives have been adopted recently in order to enhance 'normative and democratic legitimacy', paving the way to the creation of a permanent court for

[108] Wojcikiewicz, 'Judicial dialogue in Mercosur', 14. [109] Ibid.

Mercosur. Numerous reform initiatives were adopted by member state Supreme Courts (Mercosur Supreme Court meetings), as well as Mercosur institutional organs, including the Mercosur Parliament. They both consist of adopting a binding mechanism based on the creation of a permanent court for Mercosur.[110] Because there is no institutional mechanism authorising the Mercosur Parliament to participate in the decision-making process, any proposal originating from the Parliament has to be necessarily submitted to Mercosur's intergovernmental decision-making bodies (CMC, GMC or CCM). To date, there is no consensus among State Parties with regard to the creation of a permanent Court for Mercosur; all proposals in this sense are thus constantly and unilaterally barred.

In any case, it is undeniable that the absence of a jurisdictional solution cannot ensure the necessary legal security of the Mercosur dispute settlement system.[111] A permanent and independent Court for Mercosur would be the result of a coherent approach in which the legal instrument should result from objectives followed by international organisations. If the objective of State Parties limited itself to the creation of a simple common market in Mercosur, it would be sufficient to obtain reciprocal compromises through a mere treaty of commerce.[112]

[110] The project was submitted to Mercosur's Parliament on 30 April 2009 and presented by Mercosur's parliamentarian Rodriguez Sáa, from Argentina, and Salum Pires, from Paraguay.

[111] P. W. Almeida, *La difficile incorporation et mise en œuvre des normes du Mercosur. Aspects Généraux et exemple du Brésil* (Paris: LGDJ, 2013), pp. 168–9.

[112] Ibid.

8

The Andean Court of Justice

MIGUEL ANTONIO VILLAMIZAR*

1 Introduction

The Andean Court of Justice was created on 28 May 1979 and began operating in January 1984.[1] At that time it became the jurisdictional organ of the 'Cartagena Agreement' (the CA),[2] a scheme created to achieve regional integration between countries from the Andean region of South America.[3]

Over thirty years after its creation, the Court has been recognised as one of the most active international tribunals. According to the statistics published on the Court's webpage, as of 31 December 2014 it had received a total of 2961 cases.[4] Up to the end of 2007, approximately 97 per cent of the cases had dealt with aspects related to intellectual

* The views expressed herein are the personal views of the author, and do not represent a position, official or unofficial, of the WTO Secretariat or WTO Members. I would like to thank Jorge Castro, Valerie Hughes, and Dean Merriman for their useful comments, as well as the doctoral students who provided an editorial review of the footnotes to this chapter. All remaining errors are mine. I would also like to thank Alan Yanovich for his invitation to participate in the preparation of this chapter.

1 J. A. Quindimil López, *Instituciones y Derecho de la Comunidad Andina* (Valencia: Tirant Lo Blanch, 2006), p. 323. See also Treaty Creating the Court of Justice of the Cartagena Agreement, Cartagena, 28 May 1979, in force 19 May 1983, I.L.M. *American Society of International Law*, 18(5) (1979), 1203; and 'Andean Group: Commission Decision on the Statute of the Court of Justice of the Cartagena Agreement', I.L.M. *American Society of International Law*, 23, 1, (1984), 425–41.

2 Agreement on Andean Subregional Integration, Bogotá, 26 May 1969, in force 16 October 1969, I.L.M. *American Society of International Law*, 8(5), 910.

3 The Cartagena Agreement was signed on 26 May 1969. 'Agreement on Andean Subregional Integration', 910.

4 Of these, 2769 corresponded to prejudgement interpretations, 55 to annulment actions, 113 to noncompliance actions, 6 to the resource of omission, and 18 to labour claims. Court's Statistics Report: 1984–2014, p. 2. Available at: www.tribunalandino.org.ec/sitetjca/index.php?option=com_wrapper&view=wrapper&Itemid=80.

property.[5] This trend has led authors like Helfer and Alter to sustain that the Court has become a tool for litigants to protect their rights and interests, especially with respect to intellectual property.[6] Although this predominance remains,[7] the Court's mandate encompasses areas beyond intellectual property, such that the Court has played a nonnegligible role in solving disputes related to other subject matters (e.g. regarding compliance with market access commitments through noncompliance actions).

The objective of this chapter is to provide a brief description of the Court's origins and current operation.[8] In addition, it will delve into certain aspects of the Court's legitimacy. In line with the main legitimacy-related topics suggested by the editors, the Court's legitimacy will be assessed as it relates to the independence of its judges, its procedural rules, its fact-finding powers, the interpretative approaches that it has followed in its case law, its relationship with other international dispute settlement fora, its interaction with domestic courts, and to particular features of its performance. This chapter is divided into sections that address each of these aspects.

1.1 Background: Emulating the European Model

1.1.1 Cartagena Agreement (1969–1979)

On 26 May 1969, representatives of Bolivia, Chile, Colombia, Ecuador and Peru gathered in Quito and signed the CA. Through this subregional

[5] L. R. Helfer, K. J. Alter, and F. Guerzovich, 'Islands of effective international adjudication: Constructing an intellectual property rule of law in the Andean community', *American Society of International Law*, 103, 1, (2009), 14.

[6] Ibid., 1–47; and L. Helfer and K. J. Alter, 'The Andean Tribunal of Justice and its interlocutors: Understanding preliminary reference patterns in the Andean community', *New York University*, 41, 4, (2009), 872–930.

[7] Of the 265 prejudgement interpretations requests that the Court received in 2013, 242 were related to intellectual property (including trademarks, patents, copyrights and other forms of protection). This means that approximately 91 per cent of the prejudgement interpretations in that year were related to intellectual property. See Court's Annual Report: 2013, p. 12. Available at: www.tribunalandino.org.ec/sitetjca/index.php?option=com_filecabinet&view=files&id=3&Itemid=35.

[8] The introductory section delves into certain detail on the Court's history and operation, in order to provide a proper context for the reader. However, it does not aim to be a comprehensive or extensive narrative of all the political, economic and legal intricacies of how the Cartagena Agreement came into existence and how it has been modified throughout time.

agreement, the Andean countries attempted to create an economic bloc that would be able to compete with its more industrialised neighbours in South America.[9] Although Venezuela was not initially part of the Agreement, it joined in 1973.[10]

The CA's initial institutional arrangement did not envisage a 'rules-oriented' dispute settlement mechanism. At its outset, the CA foreshadowed negotiations, good offices, mediation and conciliation coordinated by its main administrative organ (the Cartagena Agreement Board) and referred to a nonoperative dispute settlement mechanism of the Latin America Free Trade Association. Therefore, the main avenue to address potential disputes between the member states was diplomatic in nature.[11]

Chile's withdrawal from the CA in October 1976 raised certain questions about the stability of the CA.[12] Moreover, during the 1970s, member states were reluctant to accept the direct application of Andean law developed domestically. In particular, the Colombian Supreme Court rendered a judgement through which it denied the binding nature of secondary law in the regional institutional setting. The Supreme Court ruled in 1972 that the Andean Investment Code, a cornerstone of the regional integration process, had no direct effect in the Colombian legal system; therefore, it required the approval of national parliaments in order to be legally binding within the domestic legal system.[13] This undermined the support for a permanent court in the CA.

Despite the obstacles, there were attempts within the institution of the CA to add a permanent court to the existing institutional setting.[14] These attempts led to the commissioning of a report by the Institute for the Integration of Latin America and the Caribbean – INTAL (associated with the Inter American-Development Bank) on the need to create a

[9] E. B. Keener, 'The Andean Common Market Court of Justice: Its purpose, structure, and future', *Emory University School of Law*, 2, 1, (1987), 39–41.

[10] N. de Pierola, 'The Andean Court of Justice', *Emory University School of Law*, 2, 1, (1987), 11.

[11] Keener, 'The Andean Common Market Court of Justice', 43. See also Article 23 of the CA.

[12] Ibid., 40–1.

[13] 'Colombia: Supreme Court Decision Concerning Andean Foreign Investment Code', *American Society of International Law*, 11, 3, (1972), 574–83. See K. J. Alter, L. R. Helfer and O. Saldías, 'Transplanting the European Court of Justice: The experience of the Andean Tribunal of Justice', *American Society of Comparative Law*, 60, 3, (2012), 642–3.

[14] O. Saldías, *The Judicial Politics of Economic Integration: The Andean Court as an Engine of Development* (Abingdon: Routledge/Glass House, 2014), pp. 61–2; Alter, Helfer, and Saldías, 'Transplanting the European Court of Justice', 644–7; and Keener, 'The Andean Common Market Court of Justice', 43–9.

court for the CA.[15] It seems as if this report triggered the network that Osvaldo Saldías has studied, which led to the adoption in the integration project of the Andean countries of a system modelled on the institutions of the European Community. Among the most notable individuals involved at the time of the preparation of the report were Felix Peña and a young lawyer recently graduated from a European University, Francisco Orrego-Vicuña.[16] The outcome of that report was a recommendation to create a regional court. However, it was not until 1977 that the Andean presidents committed to achieving the creation of the new court. At this stage, the influence of the advocates for the European Model grew strong and led to the participation in the creation of the court of notable European figures such as Professor Gerard Olivier and Justice Pierre Pescatore.[17]

1.1.2 Creation of the Court (1977–1984)

Member states of the CA supported the creation of the Court with a view to establishing an institutional framework that would secure a uniform interpretation of Andean law that in turn would contribute to the application of a common economic policy.[18] In addition, member states of the CA considered that the Court could safeguard compliance with the supranational policies.[19] This was also an opportunity to clarify the issue of the relationship between the regional legal framework and each party's domestic legal system.

On 28 May 1979, in the city of Cartagena, the representatives of the governments of Bolivia, Colombia, Ecuador, Peru and Venezuela signed the Treaty Creating the Court of Justice of the Cartagena Agreement (Court's Treaty).[20] As reported by some authors, the Venezuelan Congress was opposed to recognising a binding character to supranational regulations, which led to delaying Venezuela's deposit of its instrument of ratification of the Treaty creating the Court of Justice of the CA until 1983.[21]

15 Alter, Helfer, and Saldías, 'Transplanting the European Court of Justice', 644–52.

16 Saldías, *The Judicial Politics of Economic Integration*. pp. 66–78.

17 Ibid., pp. 69–70; and Keener, 'The Andean Common Market Court of Justice', 49–50.

18 Keener, 'The Andean Common Market Court of Justice', 49–50; and De Pierola, 'The Andean Court of Justice', 15–18.

19 Ibid., 58–61.

20 'Andean Group: Treaty Creating the Court of Justice of the Cartagena Agreement', 1203.

21 Keener, 'The Andean Common Market Court of Justice', 61; and 'Andean Group: Commission Decision on the Statute of the Court of Justice of the Cartagena Agreement', 421 and 424.

This treaty entered into force on 19 May 1983. In August of that year, the CA's Commission approved Decision 184, through which it adopted the Court's Statute.[22] On 5 January 1984 the Court was formally inaugurated at its seat in Quito, Ecuador, with an initial annual budget of US$ 1.4 million.[23]

Among the most notable features of the new Court's Treaty was that it expressly provided for the direct effect of secondary law in the member states' legal systems (Articles 2 and 3 of the Court's Treaty). In addition, the Court was mandated with the task of providing a single and coherent interpretation of the Andean legal instruments. This way, the Court would guide the way in which domestic judges would apply the Andean legal framework. The key course of action for the Court to do this was the 'prejudgement interpretation', which largely mimicked the European equivalent (i.e., preliminary ruling). The Court would also have authority to hear actions of nullification and actions of noncompliance, and to issue advisory opinions. In brief, the Court's original mandate included deciding on the following matters: the legality of the decisions of other institutions of the CA (internal rule of law), noncompliance by member states of the CA (infringement), and interpretation of the Andean legal framework. With this new institutional setting, the member states of the CA attempted to provide stability in the development of what could be called an Andean legal system, which would provide certainty and stability to the operation of the system of subregional integration.

1.1.3 The Revamp of the Andean Integration System (Late 1990s): The Trujillo Protocol and the Cochabamba Protocol

Toward the end of the 1980s, the main common policy pursued by the member states of the CA underwent an overarching review. The outcome of the review was to strengthen the protection to foreign investment, including stricter norms for the recognition and enforcement of intellectual property.[24] In addition, members attempted to create a common market, through a free trade area and a common external tariff. These changes highlighted the need of reassessing the institutional arrangement

[22] 'Andean Group: Commission Decision on the Statute of the Court of Justice of the Cartagena Agreement', 425–41.

[23] Ibid., 422.

[24] Text in Spanish available at: http://intranet.comunidadandina.org/Documentos/Decisiones/DEC220.doc.

of the CA. The result of this process was a revamp of the CA called the Andean Integration System, which led to the creation of the Andean Community. These changes were put in place through the Trujillo Protocol,[25] which modified the CA and updated the Andean institutional arrangement,[26] and the Cochabamba Protocol (CP),[27] which modified the Court's Treaty.

Regarding dispute settlement, the main changes that came about in 1996 in light of the CP were directed to address the past ineffectiveness of noncompliance actions (against member states) and the participation of private litigants in the Andean dispute settlement system. Those modifications included (a) broadening of standing regarding noncompliance actions (i.e., a legal claim brought against a member state because it has acted in a manner inconsistent with the Andean legal framework – Articles 23–31 of the CP); (b) introducing a new omissions procedure to address those situations in which the Andean Council of Foreign Affairs Ministers, the Commission or the General Secretariat refrain from carrying out any activity for which they are expressly responsible under the Andean legal framework (Article 37 of the CP); (c) broadening the grounds for national judges to request prejudgement interpretations (Articles 32–36 of the CP); (d) introducing two new causes of action under the Court's jurisdiction: arbitration (Articles 38 and 39 of the CP) and labour disputes (Article 40 of the CP); (e) a shift in the requirements for standing of private parties when exercising the annulment action with respect to acts from certain Andean institutions (Article 19 of CP); and (f) an increase in the statute of limitations for the exercise of annulment actions (Article 20 of the CP).

In brief, the CP attempted to increase the access of private parties to the actions subject to the Court's jurisdiction and adjust certain aspects of the types of procedures already under the Court's jurisdiction. These aspects seemed to have enhanced the Court's legitimacy among citizens, companies and the public at large in the member states of the Andean Community.

[25] Text in English available at: www.un.org/documents/ga/docs/51/plenary/a51-87.htm.

[26] The revamp of the system included institutional adjustments such as moving from the Board to the General Secretariat, creating the Council of Foreign Affairs Ministers, as well as adding other institutions to the Andean System of Integration. See Alter, Helfer, and Saldías, 'Transplanting the European Court of Justice', 650–2.

[27] Text in English available at: www.wipo.int/wipolex/en/other_treaties/text.jsp?file_id=224429.

1.1.4 The 'Andean Legal System'

A crucial aspect of the creation and development of the Court was to clarify the status of the regulations derived from the institutions that were constituted as part of the regional integration project. The Court's Treaty, as well as its Statute,[28] clarified this and established the so-called Andean legal system. According to Article 1 of the CP, the Andean legal system is comprised of: the CA, its Protocols and additional instruments; the Court's Treaty and its amending Protocols; the Decisions of the Council of Foreign Affairs Ministers and of the Commission; the Resolutions of the General Secretariat; and the Industrial Complementation Agreements.[29] Article 2 of the Court's Statute clarifies the two types of rules that comprise the Andean legal system: primary rules, which refer to the treaties signed by the member states, along with their amending and additional protocols, and secondary (or derived) rules, which refer to the Decisions of the Council of Foreign Affairs Ministers and of the Commission, the Resolutions of the General Secretariat and the Industrial Complementation Agreements.

Drawing largely from the European model, the provisions of the Court's Treaty as well as those from the Court's Statute have been interpreted by the Court as enshrining the principles of autonomy, preeminence and direct effect of community law.[30] The Court also developed in its case law the principle of *complemento indispensable* (indispensable complement), which refers to the possibility that domestic regulators from the member states have of enacting complementary regulation to the one approved in the regional level by the Andean institutions.

[28] The Court's Statute currently in force has been codified in Decision 500 of the Andean Council of Foreign Affairs Ministers, available at: www.tribunalandino.org.ec/sitetjca/T_Estatuto%20del%20Tribunal%20de%20Justicia%20de%20la%20Comunidad%20Andina.pdf.

[29] Articles 2 and 3 of the original Court Treaty (1984) provided for the binding character and the direct effect of Decisions from the Commission. The 1996 amendment extended the application of these features to Decisions from the Council of Foreign Affairs Ministers and clarified that in addition to Decisions of those two institutions, Resolutions from the General Secretariat shall be directly applicable in the member states (Articles 2 and 3 of the CP).

[30] The Court ruled on the application of these principles as features of the Andean legal system in Case 1-IP-87 (a request for prejudgement interpretation from the Colombian *Consejo de Estado*, regarding the registration of the trademark VOLVO). These principles have been confirmed in a number of decisions that followed the Court's ruling in 1-IP-87, particularly Case 2-IP-88 (regarding the precedence of Decision 85 of the Commission over a Colombian law on intellectual property that predated Decision 85) where the Court referred to the case law of the European Court of Justice in Costa/Ennel (1964) and Simmenthal (1978).

The Court has ruled that it is not possible to issue domestic regulations regarding the same subject matter covered by regional regulations, unless the domestic regulations are necessary for the correct application of the ones at the regional level.[31]

Despite the efforts to create a robust legal system, the withdrawal of Venezuela from the Andean Community in 2006 has had adverse consequences for the system. It has been said that Venezuela's withdrawal calls into question the pertinence of the Andean Community as a means for regional integration.[32]

In summary, the Court is the jurisdictional organ of the Andean Community, which has a supranational and community character, established in order to declare Andean law and ensure its uniform application and interpretation in all the member states (Article 4 of the Court's Statute). We now turn to assess the independence of the Court's judges.

2 Judges' Independence

The independence of the Court's judges is examined in this section with respect to: the Court's composition, the nomination and selection process of judges, the judges' duties and responsibilities and the rules for the removal of judges.

2.1 Composition

Initially, the Court was comprised of five judges who must be nationals of the member states (Article 6 of the CP). However, in light of Venezuela's withdrawal from the Andean Community and the number of member states falling from five to four, the Andean Council of Foreign Affairs Ministers decided that the number of judges that comprise the Court would be equal to the number of member states of the Andean Community.[33]

[31] The Court has applied this doctrine in a number of cases. The following cases are among the first ones where the Court addressed this matter: 2-IP-88 (where the Court assessed the prevalence of Decision 85 over a Colombian law regarding intellectual property); 2-IP-90 (where the Court reviewed the consistency of a Colombian law with the regional regulations on technology transfer); and 1-IP-96 (regarding the compatibility of the *Paris Convention for the Protection of Industrial Property* with Andean intellectual property regulations).

[32] C. Malamud 'Venezuela's Withdrawal from the Andean Community of Nations and the Consequences for Regional Integration', Working Paper, 28/2006, Real Instituto Elcano, 15 November 2006.

[33] See Decision 633 of 12 June 2006 of the Council of Foreign Affairs Ministers, available at: http://intranet.comunidadandina.org/Documentos/decisiones/DEC633.doc.

For someone to be appointed as a judge, that person must enjoy a good moral reputation and fulfil the necessary conditions for exercising the highest judicial functions in their respective country of origin or be a highly competent jurist.[34]

As of December 2015, the Court had four main judges,[35] each of whom had two substitute judges.[36] Luis José Diez Canseco Núñez, a Peruvian national, was appointed as the Court's president for 2015. His background covers practice in the Peruvian competition and intellectual property agency and consulting with different international organisations such as WIPO, UNCTAD and the Andean Community.[37]

The other three judges in 2015 were Leonor Perdomo, a Colombian national, who developed her career in the Colombian judiciary, focusing in labour, civil and commercial litigation, as well as in management positions within the Colombian judiciary;[38] Cecilia Luisa Ayllón Quinteros, a Bolivian national, who developed her career in the Bolivian judiciary and actively participated in politics advocating for reforms in the judicial sector and was the Bolivian Minister of Justice between 2012 and 2014;[39] and José Vicente Troya Jaramillo, an Ecuadorian national, who developed his career in Ecuador's judiciary, acting as justice of high courts in his country.[40]

The background of the current and past judges indicates that the individuals appointed as judges to the Court have usually been experienced adjudicators who have had a prominent career in their domestic jurisdiction. Interestingly, most of the judges also have broad academic experience and have been involved in teaching different subjects in

[34] Article 6 of the CP. For instance, in Colombia, for someone to exercise the highest judicial functions, they have to: (a) be a lawyer, (b) not have been sentenced to imprisonment, except in cases of political or culpable (*culposos*) crimes, and (c) have been on duty for at least ten years in a position in the Judicial Branch or the Public Ministry, or have exercised, with good performance, during the same time, the legal profession, or university lecturing in legal disciplines at officially recognised establishments (Article 232 of the Colombian Constitution).

[35] According to Article 9 of the Court's Statute, each principal judge has two substitute judges who will replace the principal judge in case of temporary or definitive absence.

[36] See Article 7 of the Court's Statute.

[37] See www.tribunalandino.org.ec/sitetjca/index.php?option=com_content&view=article&id=22&Itemid=69.

[38] See www.tribunalandino.org.ec/sitetjca/index.php?option=com_content&view=article&id=23&Itemid=71.

[39] See www.tribunalandino.org.ec/sitetjca/index.php?option=com_content&view=article&id=24&Itemid=70.

[40] See www.tribunalandino.org.ec/sitetjca/index.php?option=com_content&view=article&id=25&Itemid=72.

several universities in the region. However, it is not a general rule for them to have broad expertise in Andean Community law.[41]

The current four-judge composition of the Court raises practical problems reaching the three-judge majority vote required in situations of a split bench (Article 32 of the Court's Statute). To cope with this challenge, the Court has followed a practice that it recently codified in Resolution 01/2014 establishing a procedure by which one of the substitute judges would be called upon to participate in the proceedings in order to achieve the quorum required for the Court to decide the matter before it.[42]

2.2 *Nomination, Selection and Oath of Office*

Responsibility for nomination of prospective judges of the Court lies with each member state. According to the applicable rules (Article 7 of the CP and Article 7 of the Court's Statute), each member state has the right to submit to the host country of the Court (Ecuador) the names of the principal and substitute judges. Once the host country has received the nominees, its authorities will then convene a meeting amongst the member states' plenipotentiaries for them to select the preferred candidate.

Each member state has autonomy concerning who they nominate to the Court. As mentioned earlier, it is generally the case that the Court's judges are legal professionals with a broad background in adjudication in their respective countries of origin. Certain past and present judges have a background both in judicial activities and in the practise of intellectual property law.

The Court does not openly provide any information regarding the applicable procedures that are followed by each member state in the nomination process of potential judges. In addition, there is no accessible information publicly furnished by the member states in this respect. Those following the Court's work will probably welcome having more readily available information regarding this selection process.

The Court's judges are appointed for a six-year period; appointments can be renewed once, for an additional six-year period (Article 8 of the

[41] For an account of the profiles of the Court's judges up to 2008, see: *Testimonio Comunitario*, available at: www.tribunalandino.org.ec/sitetjca/index.php?option=com_filecabinet&view=files&id=7&Itemid=35.

[42] Resolution N° 01/2014 of 13 May 2014, issued by the Andean Court. Available at: www.tribunalandino.org.ec/sitetjca/RESOLUCION%2001-2014.pdf.

CP). The appointment and reappointment of judges is staggered, such that half of the seats are open for appointment or reappointment every three years, on a rotating basis.

After appointment, the judges must take an oath of office where they swear before the Court's president or whoever is exercising his functions and the Court's registrar, to perform their task with awareness and absolute impartiality, safeguard the confidentiality of those actions that require it and fulfil the duties inherent to their functions (Article 9 of the Court's Statute).

Interestingly, the Court's Treaty provides that judges shall not undertake any other professional activities, remunerated or not, except for teaching (Article 6 of the CP). This was intended to avoid potential conflicts of interest and reflects the full-time employment commitment that the judges undertake when accepting their office.

2.3 *Immunities and Removal*

In order to safeguard the Court's independence, member states (including the host country) shall provide the Court, its judges and its registrar everything necessary to ensure compliance with their duties, including privileges and immunities as recognised by international law. Those privileges and immunities encompass, in particular, those contemplated in the Vienna Convention on Diplomatic Relations regarding the inviolability of persons, archives and official correspondence, as well as in respect of immunities from civil and criminal jurisdiction (Article 12 of the CP and Article 6 of the Court's Statute).

Another legal aspect aimed at safeguarding the judges' independence and good behaviour is the removal procedure. The removal procedure can only be initiated upon the request of a member state and is limited to situations that amount to a serious misconduct (Article 10 of the CP). The situations deemed to be serious misconduct are (a) notoriously bad conduct; (b) any comportment incompatible with the nature of the judge's office; (c) repeated failure to fulfil the duties inherent to the judge's responsibilities; (d) the undertaking of professional activities, whether or not remunerated, except for those of lecturing or academic nature; and (e) the breach of the oath of office (Article 11 of the Court's Statute).

Based on the information publicly available, there is no reported case of removal. However, this procedure provides a mechanism to discipline judges who might eventually undertake actions contrary to the high responsibilities with which they were entrusted. This provides an overall degree of legitimacy to the judges' fulfilment of their duties, as it ensures an accountability mechanism.

2.4 *Conflicts of Interest*

Another tool included in the Court's Statute to avoid situations where a judge might have conflicts of interest is the procedure for self-declared conflict (*impedimento*) or a challenge of disqualification (*recusación*). These options seem to contribute to the Court's legitimacy, as they warrant the possibility of a conflicted judge to step down from the bench and be replaced by a nonconflicted judge.

The Court's Statute foreshadows four situations where a judge should declare an existing conflict or could be subject to a challenge for disqualification. These situations are (i) family ties with the parties or their representatives; (ii) direct or indirect personal or spouse's interest in a matter submitted to the Court or on another that deals with a similar object; (iii) having issued extrajudicial opinions on matters submitted to the Court or having participated as a party, attorney or counsellor in such a matter; and (iv) close and manifest personal or spouse's friendship or enmity with the parties or their representatives (Article 67 Court's Statute).

The self-declaration or challenge of disqualification can be made or raised at any point of the proceedings. Upon the declaration of the first or the request of the latter, the Court will stay the proceedings until it decides on the matter (Articles 68 and 69 of the Court's Statute). If there is merit to either, the corresponding judge shall be replaced by its replacement judge on the specific dispute (Article 70 of the Court's Statute).

2.5 *Budget*

An interesting aspect related to the Court's operation, which is somewhat related to the judges' independence, is the Court's budget. In 1984, when the Court began operating, it had an approved budget of US$ 1.4 million for its first year. According to the most recently published Court's Annual Report, corresponding to the year 2013, it operated under a budget of US$ 1.17 million.[43]

[43] This situation is due in part to the fact that in 2009, the Commission decided that if it did not adopt a new budget for the Court the one from the preceding year would apply (Decision 714 of 8 September 2009). The most recent approved budget for the Court corresponds to the year 2008, which was set at US$ 1,170,667.00 (Decision 680 of 30 January 2008).

As reported by Quindimil,[44] in its initial days, the Court saw a drastic cutback in its budget, which in his view was due to a lack of political commitment on the part of the member states in order to provide the Court with sufficient resources to fully undertake its task.

The Court has received an increasing number of cases, most of which have been prejudgement interpretations (approximately 94 per cent of the Court's total caseload).[45] In its first six years of operation, the Court only received eighteen prejudgement interpretation requests. This number has systematically grown since. The Court has received the following numbers of requests: between 1991 and 1995 it received 57; between 1996 and 2000 it received a yearly average of 46; between 2001 and 2005 it received a yearly average of 142; between 2006 and 2010 it received a yearly average of 161; and between 2011 and 2014 it received a yearly average of 236.75 (with the highest peak in 2014, with a total of 325).[46]

The Court has pursued a number of agreements with universities in order to further its activities related to the dissemination of the Andean Community law. This seems to be contributing to the increased number of cases witnessed in the past four years.

If we compare this rather stagnant budget with the increasing number of cases, it is clear that the Court is doing an amazing job in addressing the large number of prejudgement interpretation requests from different domestic courts. This can also be interpreted as evidence of the Court's ability to overcome a setting of limited resources and pursue its adjudicative tasks with integrity and dedication. In this sense, the Court's legitimacy seems to be growing. If looked at in detail, the latest statistics report of the Court shows how new courts within the member states are becoming more frequent users of the prejudgement interpretation.[47]

2.6 *Final Remarks on the Judges' Independence*

The rules regarding how the Court operates provide a high degree of confidence that the judges are independent in the performance of their duties. If a judge does not act independently, the rules provide for a

[44] Quindimil, *Instituciones y Derecho de la Comunidad Andina*, pp. 366–8.

[45] Court's Statistics Report: 1984–2014, p. 2. Available at: http://tribunalandino.org.ec/sitetjca/index.php?option=com_wrapper&view=wrapper&Itemid=80.

[46] Court's 1984–2014 Statistics Report, pp. 31–3.

[47] Court's 1984–2014 Statistics Report, pp. 34–6. See also Helfer and Alter, 'The Andean Tribunal of Justice and its interlocutors', 889–93.

removal procedure. This procedure can only be initiated by a member state and can lead to the replacement of the judge who committed serious misconduct. As stated earlier, there is no formal indication that this has happened. These rules seem to contribute to the Court's reputation, and consequently to its legitimacy.

Although the Court has a public website and is a known institution among those involved in the substantive areas within the Court's jurisdiction (and, in particular, intellectual property), it remains a generally unknown institution in the region.

As Quindimil points out,[48] among the most significant cutbacks in the Court's budget are the expenses related to dissemination of community law.[49] Despite this, the Court has undertaken efforts to inform the public of its activities through its webpage and through the related webpage of the Andean Community (handled by the Andean Community's Secretariat). However, there is limited information publicly available on the Court's activities. In the future, the Court could make readily available updated information of its activities and work. The Court could also benefit from enhancing the research tools available for external people interested in accessing the Court's case law.

3 Procedural Rules

This section delves into the legitimacy concerns related to the Court's procedural rules. Before referring to specific legitimacy concerns, this section begins with an overview of the Court's jurisdiction.

3.1 Overview of the Court's Jurisdiction

The Court has general jurisdiction over legal issues related to the legal framework of the Andean Community, described earlier as the Andean legal system (Article 5 of the Court's Statute). There are a limited number of causes of action through which the Court can exercise that general jurisdiction. They include the annulment action (*acción de nulidad*), the noncompliance action against member states' measures (*acción de incumplimiento*), prejudgement interpretation (*interpretación prejudicial*),

[48] Quindimil, *Instituciones y Derecho de la Comunidad Andina*, p. 368.

[49] In 2013, the sum spent in dissemination of community law was US$ 3910. See the Court's Annual Report: 2013, p. 146.

actions of omission (*acción de omisión*), arbitration (*arbitraje*) and labour disputes (*controversias laborales*).

3.1.1 Annulment Procedure

The annulment procedure can be used to seek the Court's declaration of the nullity of: (a) Decisions of the Andean Council of Foreign Affairs Ministers, (b) Decisions of the Andean Commission, (c) Resolutions of the General Secretariat or (d) Specific agreements between members (relating to issues such as industrial complementarity).[50] The Court shall annul those decisions that oppose the Andean legal system, including those adopted *ultra vires* (Article 17 of the CP and Article 101 of the Court's Statute).

Member states, the Andean Council of Foreign Affairs Ministers, the Commission, the General Secretariat, interested individuals and legal entities all have standing to bring an annulment request to the Court. However, a member state who voted in favour of a decision is barred from challenging it through an annulment procedure (Article 18 of the CP and Article 102 of the Court's Statute). Individuals and legal entities may request an annulment procedure if their rights or legitimate interests are affected by the challenged decision (Article 19 of the CP and Article 102 of the Court's Statute). In the context of an annulment procedure, the requesting party may ask the Court to grant the provisional suspension of the challenged decision (Article 21 of the CP and Article 105 of the Court's Statute).

The statute of limitations for the presentation of an annulment procedure is two years following the entry into force of the challenged decision, resolution or agreement (Article 20 of the CP and Article 103 of the Court's Statute).

The CP provides that a party to a dispute in a domestic proceeding can seek an injunction to prevent that domestic court from applying a particular instrument of secondary law made by an Andean institution. Whenever this request is presented, the domestic court shall consult the Court on the legality of the allegedly illegal instrument of secondary law and shall stay the proceedings until it receives the Court's views. Such views will be binding on the ruling of the domestic court (Article 20 of the CP and Article 104 of the Court's Statute).

[50] Decisions of the Andean Council of Foreign Affairs and of the Andean Commission are regulatory, whereas the Resolutions of the General Secretariat may be regulatory or individual. Specific Agreements are normally agreed by two or more member states.

As of 31 December 2014, the Court had received a total of fifty-five annulment requests.[51] The Court has already ruled on fifty-four of those requests, finding in sixteen that the challenged decisions were contrary to the Andean legal system.[52]

3.1.2 Noncompliance Request against Member's Measures

The assessment of noncompliance by a member state is a shared function between the General Secretariat and the Court. At an initial stage, it is the General Secretariat who examines whether a member state is not complying with its obligations under the Andean legal system. After the General Secretariat has done an initial assessment of the matter and only if a member state persists in acting in a manner contrary to its obligations, will the Court be able to address the matter (Article 23 of the CP). Thus, the purpose of the noncompliance request is to ask the Court to order an infringing member state to bring its measures into conformity with its obligations (Article 107 of the Court's Statute).[53]

The General Secretariat, a member state or individuals or legal entities whose rights are affected by the allegedly noncomplying measure may present a noncompliance request to the Court (Articles 23–25 of the CP and Article 108 of the Court's Statute). In the course of such a request, the complaining party may seek the provisional suspension of the application of the challenged measure (Article 28 of the CP and Article 109 of the Court's Statute).

Whenever the Court has found a member state's measures to be in breach of its obligations, and such a member state is reluctant to bring its noncomplying measures into conformity with its obligations, other member states, institutions of the Andean Community or private actors may seek a summary process to request the Court to impose sanctions (retaliatory measures) on the noncomplying member state (Article 119 of the Court's Statute). Through this procedure the Court will determine the limits within which the member state may restrict or suspend the benefits owed to the noncomplying member state (Article 27 of the CP).

[51] Court's Statistics Report: 1984–2014, p. 2.

[52] Court's Statistics Report: 1984–2014, pp. 4–9.

[53] Those measures include the issuance of domestic regulations contrary to the Andean legal system, the nonissuance of regulations that fulfil such legal system or any act or omission contrary to the Andean legal system or which in some way limits or bars its application (Article 107 of the Court's Statute).

As of 31 December 2014, the Court had received 113 noncompliance actions. In 69 of those cases, the Court ruled that the challenged measure was contrary to the member's obligations under the Andean legal system.[54]

3.1.3 Prejudgement Interpretation (Preliminary References)

The prejudgement interpretation is the avenue most frequently used to activate the Court's jurisdiction. It was crafted following its European model; however, it has its own features that have affected the development of the Court's activities.

The purpose of the prejudgement interpretation is to allow the Court to interpret the norms that make up the Andean legal system, with the objective of ensuring its uniform application in the territory of the member states (Article 121 of the Court's Statute). Therefore, only a domestic court (*juez nacional*) has standing to request a prejudgement interpretation from the Court (Article 33 of the CP).

Domestic courts issuing a judgement not subject to appeal have the obligation to request a prejudgement interpretation from the Court in cases where Andean Community law will be applied or is challenged as part of the matter being litigated. In this scenario, the judge requesting such an interpretation must stay the proceedings until she receives the Court's prejudgement interpretation (Article 123 of the Court's Statute).

Other domestic courts or judges, whose judgements are subject to appeal and who are involved in a case where Andean Community law will be applied or is part of the matter being litigated, may request a prejudgement interpretation from the Court. In this scenario, the requesting judge is under no obligation to stay the proceedings and must issue its judgement within the relevant deadlines under domestic law, even if she has not yet received the Court's prejudgement interpretation (Article 122 of the Court's Statute).

Domestic Courts may request a prejudgement interpretation on their own initiative or upon request from a disputing party in the domestic litigation (Articles 122 and 123 of the Court's Statute). The reference to domestic courts in Article 33 of the CP had systematically been interpreted as meaning that only domestic courts, i.e. judges, have standing to request prejudgement interpretations from the Court.[55] However, the Court has broadened its interpretation of the term *domestic courts* to

[54] Court's Statistics Report: 1984–2014, p. 10.

[55] Quindimil, *Instituciones y Derecho de la Comunidad Andina*, pp. 406–7.

mean that administrative entities or regulatory agencies with jurisdictional powers, as defined in the domestic legal system, also have standing to request prejudgement interpretations from the Court.[56] The Court has gone even a step further and developed a legal test to assess when a particular entity in a member state's legal system can be deemed to be a domestic court for the purposes of the CP and the Court's Statute.[57] In a judgement of 20 November 2014, the Court concluded that the Peruvian competition and intellectual property agency was entitled to request prejudgement interpretations from the Court.[58]

The shift in the Court's case law is a notable example of how the Court has extended its jurisdiction by opening up its most frequently used proceeding. This could be read as a way to open additional channels to communicate with its interlocutors, in the sense discussed by Helfer and Alter.[59] This allows for more open interpretations of standing requirements, which may further open the possibility for domestic actors to request the Court's views on the application of Andean Community law.

However, prejudgement interpretations were designed with a limited scope in order to avoid further resistance from domestic adjudicators. The main limitation that the Court has when issuing its prejudgement interpretations is that in its decision the Court cannot make findings on the merit of domestic laws nor can it make factual findings regarding the dispute in which the Andean Community law would be applied (Article 34 of the CP). This means that the Court is only expected to refer to the Andean Community legal provisions with respect to which the domestic court seeks guidance, and to the facts of the case in as much as necessary to render its interpretation of the relevant Community legal provisions (Articles 34 of the CP and 126 of the Court's Statute).

As of 31 December 2014, the Court had received 2769 prejudgement interpretation requests. Domestic courts that had issued judgements not subject to appeal requested 2695 of those, while domestic courts whose judgements could be appealed requested the other 74.[60] This seems to indicate that to a large extent the nonmandatory use of prejudgement interpretation by domestic courts in the member states remains scarce.

[56] Andean Court, Case 14-IP-2007, pp. 7–8.
[57] Andean Court, Case 121-IP-2014, para. 29.
[58] Andean Court, Case 121-IP-2014, paras. 30–50.
[59] Helfer and Alter, 'The Andean Tribunal of Justice and its interlocutors'.
[60] Court's Statistics Report: 1984–2014, p. 31.

3.1.4 Omission Procedure

The omission procedure is designed to address situations where the Andean Council of Foreign Affairs Ministers, the Andean Commission and the General Secretariat have not fulfilled an obligation that they have pursuant to the Andean legal system (Articles 37 of the CP and 129 of the Court's Statute). The mentioned Andean institutions, the member states and individuals or legal entities have standing to present an omission procedure (Articles 37 of the CP and 130 of the Court's Statute).

A requirement for the admissibility of a request for an omission procedure is that the claimant previously requests, in writing, that the noncomplying institution undertake the omitted action. Only once thirty days have elapsed after the presentation of this written request will the complainant be able to trigger the omission procedure before the Court (Article 131 of the Court's Statute).

As in the case of the annulment action, individuals and private entities will only have standing if they are able to demonstrate that their subjective rights or their legitimate interests are affected by the alleged omission (Articles 37 of the CP and Article 132 of the Court's Statute).

As of 31 December 2014, the Court had received six omission procedure requests. All those requests concerned alleged inactions by the Secretariat General. In three of those cases the Court found that the Secretariat had failed to fulfill its obligations.[61]

3.1.5 Labour Disputes

The Court also has jurisdiction over labour disputes arising between the organs and institutions of the Andean Integration System and their staff (Articles 40 of the CP and 136 of the Court's Statute). Labour disputes subject to the Court's jurisdiction are governed by the applicable law provided for in the Headquarter Agreement, and by the general principles of labour rights (a) recognised by the International Labour Organization and (b) those principles of labour law common to the member states (Articles 135 and 136 of the Court's Statute).

Staff from any organ or institution of the Andean Integration System has standing to bring labour claims to the Court (Article 137 of the Court's Statute).

[61] Court's Statistics Report: 1984–2014, p. 30.

As of 31 December 2014, the Court had received nineteen labour disputes.[62]

3.1.6 Arbitration

The final type of proceeding contemplated in the CP is arbitration (Articles 38 and 39 of the CP). It was originally envisaged that the Court would be able to act as an arbitral tribunal in cases between private parties, or between private parties and institutions of the Andean Integration System where parties agreed to such arrangement. The disputes that could be submitted to the Court's arbitral function are those related to contractual matters subject to the 'Andean legal system' (Article 38 of the CP).

Pursuant to the provisional provisions of the Court's Statute, the Council of Foreign Affairs Ministers would adopt a Decision relative to the Court's arbitral function. As of mid-2015, this Decision had not been issued. Therefore, the Court has not had the opportunity to exercise its arbitral function and has not provided any particular guidance as to the precise scope of this function.

3.2 Confidentiality

Article 30 of the Court's Statute provides that the Court's deliberations shall be confidential until the final solution in the corresponding proceeding is reached. This rule is aimed to secure the Court's independence throughout its decision-making process, thus contributing to the Court's legitimacy.

3.3 Concerns Regarding the Court's Legitimacy under Its Procedural Rules

The Court's legitimacy, as derived from the normative structure of its founding legal texts (the CP and the Court's Statute), can be seen as robust in terms of the wide access that the basic rules provide to the Court's jurisdiction. Table 8.1 summarises this situation with respect to each type of proceeding.

[62] Court's Statistics Report: 1984–2014, p. 29.

Table 8.1 *Standing under the Court's main proceedings*

Type of proceeding	Standing
Annulment procedure of: (a) Decisions of the Andean Council Foreign Affairs Ministers, (b) Decisions of the Andean Commission, (c) Resolutions of the General Secretariat, or (d) Specific agreements between members (relating to issues such as industrial complementarity)	Member states, the Andean Council of Foreign Affairs Ministers, the Commission, the General Secretariat, individuals and legal entities. The latter two's standing is conditional on a demonstration that their rights or legitimate interests have been affected by the challenged decision.
Noncompliance request against member's measures	The General Secretariat, a member state or individuals or legal entities whose rights are affected by the allegedly noncomplying measure.
Prejudgement interpretation (preliminary references)	Domestic courts (which have been understood to include any entity, within a member state's legal system, that exercises a judicial function).
Omission procedure	Andean Council of Foreign Affairs Ministers, the Andean Commission and the General Secretariat, the member states and individuals or legal entities.

As shown in Table 8.1, with the exception of prejudgement interpretations,[63] the Court's jurisdiction is widely available to a number of international and domestic entities, both public and private.

3.4 *An Assessment of the Participation of Private Parties, Nongovernmental Organizations (NGOs) and the Court's Caseload*

Helfer and Alter's research has provided some valuable insights regarding what they describe as the Court's 'interlocutors' (i.e., the Court's most frequent users). Their key finding in this regard is that

[63] However, the Court's Statute clarifies that a party in a proceeding upon a domestic court can request that Court to request a prejudgement interpretation from the Court (Article 123 of the Court's Statute).

there was a boom in the cases brought to the Court that began in the mid-1990s, which is largely explained by two factors: (a) a higher demand by private actors in Colombia and Ecuador for domestic courts to request the Court's prejudgement interpretations with respect to domestic disputes (largely in IP-related matters); and (b) the effect of undertaking outreach activities by Andean judges with former colleagues in the national courts (this was particularly the case of Ecuador).[64] The authors also note that Peru has incrementally increased the use of the system.[65]

The participation of private actors and NGOs seems to have changed recently due to some changes in the Court's jurisdiction. First, the Court has broadened the scope for the standing of domestic courts to request prejudgement interpretations. Second, the Court has increased its outreach activities. Third, private law firms seem to have increased the marketing of their services in connection to litigation under the Court's jurisdiction. Each of these is addressed in turn.

As mentioned earlier, in a judgement of 20 November 2014, the Court clarified the necessary requirements for a domestic authority to be considered to act as a domestic court.[66] This particular decision broadened the scope for the standing of domestic authorities to request prejudgement interpretations. Before this judgement it was not clear under which circumstances an administrative authority could be said to exercise judicial functions in order to have standing to request a prejudgement interpretation from the Court.

Although it remains to be confirmed, this decision seems to pave the way for new pressure from private entities to request administrative authorities at the domestic level to have recourse to the Court's prejudgement interpretations. It would not be surprising if private entities counselled by attorneys seize the opportunity to request additional judicial input to administrative decisions from a Court sensitive to the protection of intellectual property. It might also be the case that if and when the Court diversifies its reputation on the subject matters it deals with, prejudgement interpretations may relate to topics beyond intellectual property.

The second element that has changed is the way the Court has increased its outreach activities, including interaction with private entities and NGOs in the region. As can be identified from the Court's

[64] Helfer and Alter, 'The Andean Tribunal of Justice and its interlocutors', 901–5.
[65] Ibid., 905–10. [66] See footnotes 57 and 58 above.

webpage, its outreach activities have increased in 2011, 2012 and 2013, as compared with the figures in 2010.[67] If this trend continues, one can expect the Court to have a broader outreach, beyond current or former colleagues in the domestic judiciary, who might be increasingly interested in using its services. This could eventually be confirmed through the increase in the number of cases that are presented to the Court.

The third element points to the perceived increased interest in law firms and legal practitioners that seem to be addressing their clients' interests through disputes brought to the Court. Although this hypothesis is difficult to test empirically, due to the lack of clear information from the past, there seems to be such a growing number of law firms and practitioners who litigate cases in the Court, such an increase especially where this use goes beyond local and transnational players in the IP area, may draw more attention from the legal community in the region and abroad regarding the Court's role. Recent cases adjudicated by the Court in areas like telecommunications[68] demonstrate that there is scope for expansion of the Court's work to other novel areas, such as trade in services.

4 Fact-Finding

Generally speaking, with the exception of prejudgement interpretations, the Court has broad fact-finding powers. Articles 73–81 contain the general rules that the Court must follow with respect to evidentiary matters. They largely reflect the common evidentiary practice of courts under the civil law tradition in Latin America. Those rules cover basic areas such as: procedural opportunity regarding evidentiary matters (Articles 74 and 75 of the Court's Statute), type of evidence (Article 76

[67] In the 2011, 2012 and 2013 annual reports, the Court participated in at least twenty-three academic events and celebrated cooperation and technical agreements with administrative and judicial entities in different member states. In contrast, in the 2010 report the Court only participated in five academic events and did not undertake any cooperation activities with the judicial or administrative entities of the member states. The text of those four annual reports is available at: www.tribunalandino.org.ec/sitetjca/index.php?option=com_filecabinet&view=files&id=3&Itemid=35.

[68] Andean Court, cases: 16-IP-2014 (Telefónica Móviles de Colombia S.A. *v.* Empresa de Telecomunicaciones de Bogotá S.A. E.S.P. – ETB); 14-IP-2014 (COMUNICACIÓN CELULAR S.A. COMCEL S.A. (COMCEL) *v.* ETB); 261-IP-2013; 255-IP-2013; 181-IP-2013; and 89-IP-2013. All of these cases involved the preliminary interpretation of Decision 462 that governs the process of integration and liberalisation of trade in telecommunication services.

of the Court's Statute), the Court's authority to request evidence (Article 77 of the Court's Statute), standard of proof (Articles 78 and 79 of the Court's Statute), cooperation with domestic judges in the collection of evidence (Article 80 of the Court's Statute) and distribution of costs and expenses regarding evidentiary matters (Article 81 of the Court's Statute).

The Court has ample powers to order the production and collection of evidence. It can do so within a limited time frame, because all evidence should be collected within thirty days from the date in which the Court's issues the procedural ruling regarding the collection of the relevant evidence (Article 77 of the Court's Statute).

As explained in Section 3.1.3, when requested to render a prejudgement interpretation, the Court is barred from weighing or assessing disputed facts in a case pending before a domestic court (Article 34 of the CP).

Recent fact-intensive cases, such as the ones relating to the telecommunications sector in Bogotá (Colombia), involving Comcel and ETB, are examples of the way in which the Court deals with evidence in the context of prejudgement interpretations, where it has the obligation to refrain from making factual findings when interpreting Andean regulations.[69]

5 Interpretative Approaches

Neither the CP nor the Court's Statute contain specific rules on the manner in which the Court shall interpret the provisions of the norms that comprise the Andean legal system. However, in its initial judgements, the Court provided clear guidance on what later came to be core principles for the interpretation of the Andean legal framework. These principles include teleological and systemic interpretation.

The Court explained that in deciding to pursue interpretations based on the principles of teleological and systemic interpretation it was following the guidelines developed by its European counterpart, in what the Court called 'integration law'.[70] The Court observed that teleological interpretation was of particular importance in the context of Andean law

[69] See previous footnote.

[70] Andean Court, Case 1-IP-87, section 3.5. Despite the direct reference to the European Court of Justice, the Andean Court did not refer to particular instances where the European Court had applied the principles of systemic or teleological interpretation.

because it allowed the interpretation of specific provisions on the basis of the object and purpose of the CA, and more generally of the Andean integration project. Such an interpretation would secure the integrationist objectives set out by the architects of the regional integration project.[71]

Saldías argues that the Court initially followed these interpretive principles to advocate for integration as initially envisaged in the Cartagena Agreement. That is, where foreign intellectual property was viewed as a vehicle for technology transfer into the region, this in turn would contribute to an increase the region's development. In that context, Article 5 (c) of Decision 85 (on intellectual property) excluded pharmaceutical products from patentability. Based on the teleological interpretation of this provision the Court held in a number of cases that herbicides would fall under that clause, thus being excluded from patentability.[72]

However, due to a normative change in the regulation applicable to the protection of intellectual property, pharmaceutical products were no longer excluded from patents. Decision 85 (on intellectual property) was replaced by Decision 344 (later replaced by Decision 486) toward the beginning of the 1990s, broadening the scope of what could be subject to a patent. The Court had to reconcile its interpretative approach with these new norms that favoured a broader protection of intellectual property.[73]

This normative change could explain the shift in the Court's interpretative approach. However, based on the teleological interpretation, the Court could have reiterated its previous rulings. If the Court had not followed this approach, it might have been accused of engaging in judicial activism that would oppose those changes, by providing a teleological interpretation that would run against the amendments of secondary law. However, when faced with an institutional limitation, which barred it from pursuing a teleological interpretation as just described, the Court opted to change its approach on the basis of an amendment to preexisting regulations. Acceptance of the patentability of certain herbicides that had been found not to be patentable before could thus be seen to reflect a preference for a textual interpretation. With this attitude, the

[71] Andean Court, Case 1-IP-87, section 3.5. The Court observed that the use of teleological interpretation was particularly relevant when ruling on a prejudgement request.

[72] According to Saldías in *The Judicial Politics of Economic Integration*, pp. 101–4, the Court followed this approach in a number of subsequent cases related to requests for patents over herbicides. Andean Court, cases: 1-IP-88; 3-IP-88; and 7-IP-89.

[73] Saldías, *The Judicial Politics of Economic Integration*, pp. 105–12.

Court seems to have supported the integration project and the adjustment in the policy goals pursued by the Andean Community. Such an outcome could be said to derive its legitimacy from the common policy objectives sought by the Andean Community member states.

6 Forum Shopping

Among the issues that may raise legitimacy concerns in international adjudication is so-called forum shopping. In other settings, states that have acknowledged the jurisdiction of one of the international courts studied could have also accepted the jurisdiction of another court or tribunal. This might lead to a situation where a state shops for the most convenient forum, depending on the particular nature of its dispute.

In the context of the Andean Community, member states have strictly complied with Article 42 of the CP, which provides that they should only pursue the settlement of disputes related to the Andean legal system through the Court. To date, there is no record of Andean Community member states having referred a dispute between them to a court or tribunal other than the Court. Although all four members of the Andean Community are also members of the WTO, none of them has filed a dispute against another within the WTO dispute settlement mechanism.[74]

This attitude has been reinforced by the legal commitment undertaken by Colombia and Peru, the two most active member states in extraregional trade negotiations, in the framework of their negotiations under the Pacific Alliance. In that context, these member states agreed to include a footnote to Article 17.3 of the Additional Protocol to the Framework Agreement of the Pacific Alliance,[75] which clarifies that 'the present Chapter [17 on Dispute Settlement] shall not apply to the disputes between the Republic of Colombia and the Republic of Peru in respect of the norms that make up the Andean Community legal system.'

The member states' behaviour toward the Court's jurisdiction seems to indicate a high degree of confidence in the Court's ability to address

[74] As provided in the WTO website (www.wto.org/english/tratop_e/dispu_e/dispu_by_country_e.htm#complainant), Bolivia has only been involved in a dispute as a third party; Colombia has only filed disputes against Chile, the European Communities (currently the European Union), Nicaragua and the United States; Ecuador has only filed disputes against the European Union, Turkey and the United States; and Peru has only filed disputes against Argentina and the European Union.

[75] Done in Cartagena, on 10 February 2014. Available in Spanish at: www.sice.oas.org/Trade/PAC_ALL/Index_PDF_s.asp; or at: http://alianzapacifico.net/documentos/.

disputes among the member states. This behaviour also seems to reflect a commitment on the part of the member states to sustain Andean regional integration.

7 Implementation and Interaction with National Courts

As a normative matter national courts are bound to follow the Court's judgements in the context of prejudgement interpretations. Article 35 of the CP provides that the domestic court hearing the case subject to a prejudgement interpretation must adopt the Court's interpretation in its ruling.

This was not always the case. During the 1980s the member states struggled to overcome the resistance that domestic judges had against the Court having mandatory jurisdiction over matters handled by domestic courts and related to Andean rules. Venezuela was the strongest advocate against this approach, which was reflected in the difficulties surrounding Venezuela's acceptance of the Court's Treaty.[76]

In addition, the situation of the applicability of the Court's jurisdiction and the implementation of the obligations enshrined in the Court's Treaty with respect to domestic courts varies from one member state to another. In the case of Bolivia, it was not until 2009 that the new Constitution created a legal basis for the binding nature of supranational law developed in the context of Andean regional integration. This in turn may have had an impact on the lack of use of the prejudgement interpretation by Bolivian courts.[77] The situation in Colombia has been quite different. Since the end of the 1980s, Colombian Courts have acknowledged the mandatory nature of the prejudgement interpretations and have been frequent users of this cause of action in the Court.[78]

[76] Keener, 'The Andean Common Market Court of Justice', 61; and 'Andean Group: Commission Decision on the Statute of the Court of Justice of the Cartagena Agreement', 421 and 424.

[77] S. Manrique, 'Bases Jurídicas Institucionales y Doctrinales para la Proyección Internacional de la Comunidad Andina' (General Secretariat, Lima, 2000, SG/di 283), pp. 11–12, available at: www.comunidadandina.org/Documentos.aspx?GruDoc=02. See also Articles 257, 265 and 266 of the Constitution of the Plurinational State of Bolivia, available in Spanish at: www.oas.org/dil/esp/Constitucion_Bolivia.pdf.

[78] See Ibid., pp. 12–14 and J. D. Barbosa, M. Salcedo, and M. Villamizar, 'Los tratados de libre comercio y su aplicación en el derecho colombiano' in G. Pardo Carrero (ed.), *Acuerdos Comerciales y Aspectos Relacionados con el Comercio Exterior* (Bogotá: Editorial Universidad del Rosario, 2014), pp. 94–102.

In Ecuador, the acceptance of the Court's jurisdiction and the use of the mandatory prejudgement interpretation began in 1994. Originally, there were uncertainties as to the domestic legal basis for these international commitments; such uncertainties have now been addressed, thus paving the way for domestic courts in Ecuador to use the Court's jurisdiction.[79] Last, in Peru the Court's jurisdiction has been gradually accepted and incrementally used by domestic courts.[80]

More recently, some domestic courts have become frequent users of the Court's prejudgement interpretation. As Helfer and Alter have identified, the most common users of mandatory prejudgement interpretation are the Colombian *Consejo de Estado*, Ecuador's *Tribunal de lo Contencioso* and Peru's *Corte Suprema de Justicia*.[81] Moreover, new actors such as certain civil courts in Colombia and Peru's competition and intellectual property agency, have been requesting the Court's prejudgement interpretation.[82]

Although there is no systematic study of the degree of domestic courts' compliance with the Court's judgements, there is no report of widespread disregard of the Court's interpretation in the context of prejudgement interpretations. On the contrary, the Court seems to have played an important role in the consolidation of the rule of law in areas such as intellectual property.[83] Helfer and Alter's findings in this sense highlight the Court's legitimacy in the view of domestic IP agencies and administrative judges entrusted with handling IP matters.

There is still a need to study further the extent of the Court's interaction with domestic courts in the context of disputes concerning other subject matter. Issues that could be further researched include a comparative analysis of how domestic courts in the four member states have followed the Court's prejudgement interpretations.

8 Legitimacy Concerns Specific to the Court

Alter and Helfer have explored, through a largely statistical analysis of the Court's case law and an interview process with relevant stakeholders

79 Salazar, 'Bases Jurídicas Institucionales y Doctrinales para la Proyección Internacional de la Comunidad Andina', pp. 14–15.

80 Ibid., pp. 15–16.

81 Helfer and Alter, 'The Andean Tribunal of Justice and its interlocutors', 889–93.

82 Court's Statistics Report: 1984–2014, pp. 34–6.

83 Helfer, Alter, and Guerzovich, 'Islands of effective international adjudication', 21–5.

in the region, how the Court has become an intellectual property tribunal. It is beyond the purpose of this chapter to delve into the reasons for this trend; however, Alter and Helfer's research provides useful insights regarding the close link between law firms, specific lawyers and judges in promoting the rule of law through the Court, especially with respect to the protection of intellectual property.[84] What is relevant for this chapter is whether the Court's focus toward intellectual property cases has had any impact on the Court's legitimacy.

The Court's focus on intellectual property is striking at first, if compared with the wide array of areas where there is secondary Andean law in place. These areas include customs, trade in goods, energy, price band system for agricultural products, investments, rules of origin, intellectual property, macroeconomic policy, environment, immigration, small and medium enterprises, standards, SPS (sanitary) measures, telecommunications, transportation, external relations, human health, safety, trade in services, international cooperation, cultural policies, trade remedies and consumer protection.[85]

From the perspective of the Court's goal of setting out a uniform and harmonious interpretation of the Andean legal framework, the Court seems to have provided extensive guidance concerning the Andean regulations on intellectual property, whilst remaining silent on other areas. Alter and Helfer's research highlights the role of specific private-sector interests in driving the consolidation of the rule of law with respect to intellectual property. This view would seem to support a conclusion that the Court enjoys wide legitimacy among intellectual property practitioners in particular.

It goes beyond the objective of this chapter to explain why the Court has not produced the same amount of decisions in other subject areas. However, the Court has been willing and able to handle disputes related to other normative areas of law in the Andean Community. Those areas include member states' compliance with market access commitments, telecommunication and the extent to which member states may broker

[84] Helfer, Alter, and Guerzovich, 'Islands of effective international adjudication', 13–21. See also Helfer and Alter, 'The Andean Tribunal of Justice and its interlocutors'.

[85] It is noteworthy that as a result of the Andean Community's most recent process of reengineering, a number of the organisation's activities were curtailed in order to focus in a smaller group of policy areas. The results of this process have been enshrined in Comission's Decisions 792 (19 September 2013) and 797 (14 October 2014). Available at: www.comunidadandina.org/Documentos.aspx?GruDoc=07.

trade deals with other states on a bilateral basis. The Court's contributions in these areas are yet to be studied in more detail.

Despite the Court's limited role by virtue of the predominance of intellectual property issues in its work, it will be interesting to see how the Court keeps on engaging with judges, academics, governmental agencies and other relevant stakeholders in order to continue contributing to securing the rule of law in the region, including areas beyond intellectual property.

9 Conclusion: A View Toward the Future

In the almost five decades of its existence, the Court has faced great challenges in order to consolidate its judicial function. The reform process pursued through the CP attempted to broaden the access of private entities to the Court's jurisdiction and improve its position in the region as a reputable dispute settlement body.

Notwithstanding the limited outcome of the so-called reengineering process of the Andean Community thus far, it seems that the Court has still an important role to play in the process of regional integration. The construction of common policies might be further subject to the Court's scrutiny as some of its members further engage in other economic integration projects (i.e. Colombia and Peru's participation in the Pacific Alliance).

In addition, the Court has recently moved forward in providing clear guidance on the circumstances under which domestic agencies would be allowed to request prejudgement interpretations to the Court. Currently these efforts seem to be aimed at consolidating the Court's exchange with intellectual property agencies. In the future, it might be the case that the Court's clarity on this matter might lead agencies handling other issues subject to the Andean legal framework to reach for the Court's guidance, particularly when those agencies are exercising judicial functions. Such areas might include the telecommunications sector, competition law and policy and consumer protection.

Moreover, as new substantive developments in the Andean Community's regulatory framework are slow to materialise, the Court might find some room to further consolidate its interpretative approaches and build a strong body of case law in areas beyond intellectual property, which might be of interest to the member states or to other stakeholders in the region.

We have yet to see what the future will bring for the Andean Community. Venezuela's withdrawal from the Andean Community and the separate efforts of member states to negotiate free trade agreements with third parties cast doubts about the extent to which deeper integration could be sought. It is also yet to be seen whether, regardless of institutional changes in the CA, the Court could play an important role in holding together the integration attempts, or even driving such endeavours.

9

The Case of the Economic Court of the CIS

RILKA DRAGNEVA

The Economic Court of the Commonwealth of Independent States (ECCIS) is the oldest regional court in the post-Soviet space, having come into being more than twenty years ago. Until recently the Court has been a functioning institution, albeit being active more in an advisory than in an adjudicatory role. This chapter analyses the setup and the work of the Court in assessing its importance and legitimacy as an international trade tribunal.

The existence and role of the Court, it can be argued, has been closely affected by the nature and fate of the regional organisation within which it was originally embedded, namely the Commonwealth of Independent States (CIS), particularly the degree to which this organisation was used as a functioning framework for economic integration. The first part of this chapter introduces the design, development and activity of the Economic Court of the CIS by placing it within the broad context of regional integration in the post-Soviet space. It explores the extent to which the legitimacy of the Court is influenced by the member states' overall commitment to the CIS as well as their integration behaviour and trade relations more generally. Against this context, the second part analyses the specific legitimacy characteristics examined in this book as they apply to ECCIS. The discussion reveals the case of the Court as highly instructive in understanding the legitimacy of regional trade tribunals in circumstances where interstate cooperation is driven by strong legacies and sensitivities, but also asymmetric relations, where regional hegemons, such as Russia, have determined the agenda of economic integration and the development of institutions in its service.

1 Institutional Setting and Regional Integration Context

The origin of the ECCIS is inseparable from the emergence and development of the CIS. In December 1991 the CIS replaced the dissolved Soviet Union and as such it was a vehicle for holding together countries in the process of consolidating their newly acquired independence. Sovereignty sensitivity and mistrust in Russia's regional ambitions were paramount in defining the commitment to the new grouping. The member states were keen to assert the need to engage with each other on the basis of international relations in contrast with the previous federal unity. Accordingly, there was an emphasis on structuring relations via international agreements and political coordination at the level of heads of state and government, and a strong reluctance to commit to a binding framework or a system of common bodies that might entail loss of sovereignty. Of particular importance, as will be seen in Section 1.1, was the so-called interested party principle, whereby no member could be obliged to participate in a certain agreement or decision adopted within the organisation if they had no interest in it.[1]

Following these initial terms of engagement, the organisational structure of the CIS developed incrementally, reflecting the realisation of the enormity of economic interdependence. Gradually, common bodies were agreed upon, including the creation of a permanent dispute resolution body. Yet, this process revealed the difficulty in searching for a common vision for a new style of CIS cooperation beyond the need to deal with the past.[2]

1.1 Legal Basis and Jurisdiction

The idea of a court was first mentioned in an international agreement of May 1992, which envisaged its creation for the purpose of 'resolving inter-state economic disputes which could not be submitted to the high economic (arbitration) courts of the member states'.[3] This impulse was very much in the context of the inherited system of planned interstate

[1] Article 3 of the Temporary Agreement on the Council of Heads of State and the Council of Heads of Government of the CIS, Minsk, 30 December 1991, in force 30 December 1991; Article 23 of the Charter of the Commonwealth of Independent States, Minsk, 22 January 1993, in force 22 January 1994.

[2] In the early 1990s, many CIS countries were preoccupied with their own domestic developments, political consolidation and trade collapse as a result of the breakup of the USSR. Russia's commitment, in particular, was limited as it viewed the other CIS members as economic burdens and focused on improving relations with the West.

[3] Article 5 of the Agreement on the Measures for Ensuring the Improved Settlement between Economic Organizations, Tashkent, 15 May 1992, in force 15 May 1992. This was a very general agreement, leaving any detail to a future Statute of the Court to be prepared by the High Economic or Commercial Courts of the member states and submitted for approval to the Council of Heads of State.

deliveries (or barter), which was only gradually supplemented and then replaced by market-based trade relations.[4] Thus, initially the Court was tasked with a role residual to that of the existing judicial institutions of the member states competent to settle disputes subject to the principles of conflict of laws. In July 1992, another agreement was signed whereby the Statute of the Court was adopted.[5] This agreement was clearly influenced by the process of seeking to strengthen the foundations of the CIS as an international organisation, providing a somewhat wider definition of the role of the Court in terms of ensuring the 'uniform application of the agreements of the CIS and the economic obligations and contracts based on them'.[6] Finally, when the Charter of the CIS was adopted in January 1993, the Court was proclaimed to be one of the 'organs of the CIS' with the task of 'ensuring the implementation of economic obligations within the Commonwealth'.[7]

This incremental genesis of the Court, however, led to lasting problems and tensions with important legitimacy implications. First, the resulting legal framework was incoherent, with contradictions between the founding agreements.[8] At the same time, important design issues were not dealt with in any detail in the founding agreements. Some of them were dealt with by the Court itself in its Rules of Procedure.[9] This, however, remains an internal document without a necessarily clear external legitimacy. Second, given the interested party principle characterising relations within the CIS, the founding agreements of the Court do not necessarily have the same signatories (Table 9.1). This put in

[4] Initially only a small percentage of total trade (mainly consumer goods) was outside the deliveries system, R. Dragneva and J. De Kort, 'The legal regime for free trade in the Commonwealth of Independent States', *International and Comparative Law Quarterly*, 56 (2007), 233–266.

[5] Agreement on the Statute of the Economic Court of the CIS, Moscow, 6 July 1992, in force 6 July 1992. This is a short Agreement consisting of four articles, to which the Statute is attached.

[6] Article 1 of the 1992 Statute. [7] Article 32 of the Charter of the CIS.

[8] The resulting legal confusion has also been noted in academic commentary, M. Kleandrov, 'Ekonomicheskii sud SNG: Chto Takoe?' *Khoziaistvo i pravo*, 198 (7) (1993), 60–9, E. Dovgan', 'Ekonomicheskii sud SNG – organ dlia razresheniia mezhdunarodnykh sporov publichnogo kharaktera na prostranstve SNG', *Zhurnal Mezhdunarodnogo prava i mezhdunarodnykh otnoshenii*, 1 (2008), 3–9, Shinkaretskaia, 'Sud Evraziiskogo Ekonomicheskogo soobshchestva i tamozhennogo soiuza', *Mezhdunarodnoe pravosudie*, 1 (2012), 98–106.

[9] Its Procedural Rules (*Reglament*) were adopted in July 1994 with a Decree of the Plenum of the Economic Court. New Procedural Rules were adopted 10 July 1997, and amended numerous times thereafter.

Table 9.1 *Legal basis of the Economic Court of the CIS: founding agreements and their signatories*

CIS member state	May 1992 agreement	July 1992 statute	January 1993 charter
Armenia	S, R	S, R, Den 2006	S, R
Azerbaijan	S (Res), Not R	- -	S, R
Belarus	S, R	S, R	S, R
Georgia (withdrew 2009)	- -	- -	S, R
Moldova	S (Res), Not R	S (Res), R, Den 2009	S, R
Kyrgyzstan	S, R	S, R	S, R
Kazakhstan	S, R	S, R	S, R
Russia	S, R	S, R	S, R
Turkmenistan	S, R	- -	- -
Tajikistan	S, R	S, R	S, R
Ukraine	S (Res), R	- -	- -
Uzbekistan	S, R	S, R	S, R

S – signed, R – ratified, Res – reservation, Den – denounced.

question the legitimacy of the Court as an 'organ of the CIS', but also created important practical complications for its work.[10]

The founding agreements limited the obligatory jurisdiction of the Court to *interstate economic disputes*. Two kinds of such disputes were specifically mentioned: disputes arising from the states' implementation of the economic obligations envisaged in international agreements or acts of the CIS organs; and disputes related to the conformity of member states' economic legislation to the agreements and other acts of the CIS.[11] Thus, the subject-matter jurisdiction of the Court depends on what constitutes 'economic obligations'. In its own interpretations, the ECCIS

[10] E.g. G. Danilenko, 'The Economic Court of the Commonwealth of Independent States', *NYU Journal of International Law and Politics*, 31 (4) (1999), 893–918; G. Simonian, 'K voprosu o priznaniia iurisdiktsii Ekonomicheskogo suda SNG', *Moskovskii zhurnal mezhdunarodnogo prava*, 4 (2000), 104–11, G. Shinkaretskaia, 'Sud Evraziiskogo Ekonomicheskogo soobshchestva i tamozhennogo soiuza', *Mezhdunarodnoe pravosudie*, 1 (2012), 98–106.

[11] Article 3 of the 1992 Statute, Article 32 of the Charter.

has narrowly defined such 'economic obligations' as actions directly connected with property-related performance, such as handing over objects, payment of money, performance of work, or services, i.e., obligations concerned with 'tangible benefits with monetary value'.[12] At the same time, the Court took the view that such obligations can arise in the areas of trade, transport or finance, but also humanitarian, cultural or other forms of cooperation. In terms of personal jurisdiction, the Court deals only with disputes between states. Thus, disputes involving private parties or territorial or other public units within states are excluded. As far as states are concerned, the Court's obligatory jurisdiction has been interpreted as limited to the state signatories of the 1992 Statute.[13]

This jurisdiction can be expanded to *other interstate disputes* when envisaged by an agreement.[14] Thus, the existence of a compromissory clause allows noneconomic disputes to be brought before the Court, but also for extending its jurisdiction to non-1992 Statute signatories. Indeed, subsequent developments show that compromissory clauses have been included in many CIS agreements.[15] Upon review, the majority of these agreements relate to economic cooperation, thus asserting the perception of the primary purpose of the Court.

The Court was also granted important interpretative powers. This area, however, is one of the prime examples of the conflicts between the founding agreements of the Court. According to the 1993 Charter, the Court can interpret the agreements and other acts of the CIS 'on economic matters'.[16] The 1992 Statute, however, refers to interpreting (a) agreements and other acts of the Commonwealth in general, and (b) the legislation of the USSR for the duration of its application.[17] The approach of the Court itself has shown its support for a broad advisory jurisdiction in line with the 1992 Statute. As will be shown later, a range of important advisory opinions on noneconomic matters have been issued. The Court can engage in interpretation either in the process of deciding specific cases or at the request of the highest state organs, the CIS institutions, and the highest economic or commercial courts of the member states.

[12] Advisory Opinion Nr.C-1/1-97, 11 November 1997.

[13] Advisory Opinion Nr. C-1/1-97, 11 November 1997. Moldova signed with a reservation that the submission of specific disputes can be only with the consent of the government.

[14] Article 3 of the 1992 Statute, Article 32 of the Charter.

[15] At the time of writing the full list of such agreements stands at 37, see http://sudsng.org/competence/sng.

[16] Article 32, paragraph 3 of the Charter.

[17] Article 5 of the 1992 Statute.

1.2 The Pursuit of Economic Integration and Its Effect on the ECCIS

The design of the Court as developed in 1992 and early 1993 reflected the limited commitment of its member states to the CIS. In the following two decades, as the economic agenda for the CIS evolved, there were various attempts or opportunities to enhance the role of the Court and revise its legal basis, yet hardly any of them proved to be effective.

In 1993 Russia, asserting its role as a regional leader, took the initiative to set up an Economic Union, modelled on a progressive, EU-style integration process, starting with a free-trade area. An ambitious, but brief and general Treaty on the Economic Union (TEU) was signed,[18] accompanied by a plan for the adoption of a range of implementing agreements, including a multilateral free trade agreement. The TEU attempted to boost the role of the Court in relation to the Economic Union agenda. The TEU contained a compromissory clause expanding the Court's jurisdiction to 'disputes related to the interpretation and implementation of the Treaty'.[19] In the Court's view, this provision conferred a wide jurisdiction not just in terms of what is envisaged in the Treaty, but also the other agreements adopted in implementing its economic agenda.[20] Yet, this conclusion is difficult to support given the lack of formal priority of the TEU over such other 'implementing' agreements. Furthermore, while other agreements were signed, they often had a varying number of signatories and envisaged their own compromissory clauses differing significantly from that of the 1993 Treaty.

Even more important, the formula for integration proposed with the 1993 TEU proved to be short-lived, reflecting the member states' diverging positions. Given Russia's highly asymmetric importance as a trade partner and energy supplier, its motivation was critical. Moscow was keen on integration rhetoric, but in practice it was reluctant to undertake the costs of trade liberalisation. Russia signed the 1994 Free Trade Agreement (FTA), yet it never ratified it.[21] Instead, it proceeded to

[18] Treaty on the Creation of an Economic Union, Moscow, 24 September 1993, in force 14 January 1994. The Treaty was signed by (or acceded to) by all CIS countries, except Ukraine, which declared interest in associated membership.

[19] Article 31, first paragraph of the TEU.

[20] Advisory Opinion Nr. C-1/19-96, 15 May 1997.

[21] Agreement on the Creation of a Free Trade Area, Moscow, 15 April 1994, in force 30 December 1994. The agreement was ratified by all its signatories apart from Russia and Turkmenistan.

manage relations on a bilateral basis,[22] with only certain special issue agreements (e.g. on rules of origin) adopted within the CIS multilateral framework. It also turned its attention to small integration formats, initially loosely related to the CIS but increasingly acquiring a life of their own, with a view of becoming a nucleus for attracting other member states. Thus, in 1995, Russia, Belarus and Kazakhstan signed a Customs Union agreement, later joined by Kyrgyzstan and Tajikistan. Like processes within the CIS-wide framework, however, this remained a weak, ineffective regime that did not produce practical results. In 1999, another attempt to set up a CIS free trade area was made, which also largely remained on paper.[23]

Thus, while intra-CIS trade and economic cooperation remained important, the CIS as a multilateral organisational platform failed to become an effective vehicle for its facilitation. There were various attempts to reform the institutions of the CIS in making it more suitable for the developing integration agenda,[24] including the design of the Court.[25] Drafts amending the 1992 Statute were prepared, which sought to strengthen the effect of its decisions and expand its jurisdiction to deal with a wider range of disputes. The 2002 draft, in particular, envisaged the creation of an Arbitration Chamber (*Treteiskaia palata*), where disputes between private parties in the context of the free trade agenda could be heard. Yet, despite the activism of the Court itself in promoting these drafts, no such changes were made.[26] The only measure to 'promote the effectiveness' of the Court member states agreed on, was to reduce the

[22] Thus, a web of bilateral FTAs sprang into being, most of them of a very weak, basic nature, envisaging diplomatic mechanisms for resolution of disputes, Dragneva and De Kort, 'The Legal Regime', 25.

[23] Protocol for amending the Agreement on the Creation of a Free Trade Area, Moscow, 2 April 1999, in force 24 November 1999.

[24] R. Dragneva, 'Is "Soft" Beautiful? Another Perspective on Law, Institutions, and Integration in the CIS', *Review of Central and East European Law*, 29(3) (2004), 279–324.

[25] The critique of the Court's design was there virtually from the start. In a sequence of articles, for example, the Russian representative to the Court, Justice Kleandrov, made the case for the extension of the Court's jurisdiction over what he terms 'non-standard' disputes (including human rights or territorial disputes) in M. Kleandrov, 'Ekonomicheskii sud SNG: Problemy i perspektivy', *Khoziaistvo i Pravo*, 7 (1995), 115–20. M. Kleandrov, '"Nestandartnye" spory *v.* SNG—Komu ikh razreshat'? *Gosudarstvo i pravo*, 10 (1995), 146–56.

[26] In 2007–2008 there was another failed attempt for reform, F. Abdulloev and I. Mishal'chenko, 'O sovershenstvovanii deiatel'nosti Ekonomicheskogo Suda Sodruzhestva Nezavisimykh Gosudarstv', *Evraziiskii Iuridicheskii Zhurnal*, 16(9) (2009), 22–26.

member states' quota for appointing judges from two to one. Ironically, this had a lasting opposite effect, as will be discussed in Section 2.1.

Critically, Russia increasingly lost interest in the CIS as a platform for fostering economic integration in the post-Soviet space. In 2000 the Eurasian Economic Community (EEC) between Russia, Belarus, Kazakhstan, Kyrgyzstan and Tajikistan was set up, as a new international organisation with a broad set of objectives, including 'deep' economic cooperation. The EEC founding treaty envisaged the setting up of a dedicated Court of the EEC (CEEC).[27] Nonetheless, little progress was achieved in the EEC format until 2010 when the Customs Union between Russia, Belarus and Kazakhstan was launched as a treaty regime partially embedded in the organisational structure of the EEC.[28] This latest initiative was a key priority for the Kremlin, driven by strong geopolitical motives.[29] The ambition of the project was notable, with a swift launch of a Single Economic Space in 2012.

The refocus of integration interest to the Eurasian structures, nonetheless, gave a certain lease of new life to the ECCIS insofar as no Court of the EEC was set up until 1 January 2012. Instead, in the autumn of 2003, the decision was taken for the ECCIS to perform the role of a Court of the EEC.[30] This decision was not necessarily driven by a view of the effectiveness of the ECCIS. As noted, it overlapped with plans to reform it, which failed to materialise. Paradoxically, despite the resulting potential increase of the caseload of the Court, the decision was taken to transform it from functioning on a permanent to a sessional (twice a year) basis. Thus, the reliance on the ECCIS is best explained by the use of institutional economy and the limited interest in binding dispute

[27] Treaty on the Creation of a Eurasian Economic Community, Astana, 10 October 2000, in force 30 May 2001.

[28] R. Dragneva. 'The Legal and Institutional Dimensions of the Eurasian Customs Union' in R. Dragneva and K. Wolczuk (eds.), *Eurasian Economic Integration: Law, Policy and Politics* (Cheltenham: Edward Elgar, 2013), pp. 34–60. The Customs Union remained a treaty regime embedded in the EEC until 1 January 2015, when the Eurasian Economic Union came into effect as a new international organisation and the EEC was dissolved.

[29] R. Dragneva and K. Wolczuk, 'Commitment, asymmetry and flexibility: making sense of Eurasian economic integration' in R. Dragneva and K. Wolczuk (eds.), *Eurasian Economic Integration: Law, Policy and Politics* (Cheltenham: Edward Elgar, 2013), pp. 204–21.

[30] Council of Heads of Government, Decision on Assigning the ECCIS the Functions of the CEEC, Yalta, 19 September 2003; Agreement between EEC and the CIS on the functioning of the Economic Court of the CIS as a Court of the EEC, Minsk, 3 March 2004, in force 3 March 2004.

resolution, evident from the early design of the Court of the EEC as largely modelled on the ECCIS. This did not change until the launch of the Customs Union in 2010, when stronger differences were introduced both in relation to the jurisdiction of the Court and the effect of its rulings. At the same time, the manner of the transfer of functions did not serve to maximise the potential role of ECCIS. The provision was for ECCIS to use its own Rules of Procedure except where specific departures from them were envisaged in the founding documents of the Court of EEC, in particular its Statute.[31] This framework was rudimentary despite the important differences between the two regimes. Thus, again, the Economic Court was left to deal with these matters, which it did on an ad hoc basis.[32]

Russia's relations with countries outside the Customs Union, given the described state of the CIS regime, largely remained based on weak, bilateral agreements. In those settings, Russia's strong bargaining position had important implications for how disputes were settled, as will be discussed in Section 2.7. In seeking to deal with their vulnerability, some CIS countries, such as Moldova, Georgia, Armenia and Ukraine, increasingly sought to reorient trade toward the European Union and engage in agreements to facilitate this. Furthermore, these countries also sought to join the multilateral trade structures, WTO in particular, in facilitating this trade reorientation (Table 9.3). Notably, in 2006 Armenia denounced the 1992 Agreement and ceased its participation in the ECCIS, followed by Moldova at the end of 2009. In justifying this step, both countries emphasised the Court's irrelevance to how economic disputes are resolved in reality, and its weak legal basis.[33]

In the late 2010s, Russia's integration interest toward the 'outer ring' of countries increased, largely in response to the changes in the geopolitical environment and these countries' growing Euro-Atlantic affiliation. Russia's motivation with regard to setting up a CIS free trade area changed, and an agreement to this effect was concluded in

[31] Article 4 of the EEC-CIS Agreement.

[32] A partial attempt to ensure a better institutional fit followed the launch of the Customs Union and a new Statute of the CEEC in 2010, yet it remained fairly basic, see Protocol amending the EEC-CIS Agreement, 17 January 2011.

[33] 'Parlament Armenii prinial reshenie o vyhode respubliki iz Ekonomicheskogo suda stran SNG', Novosti Armenia, 22 December 2006, at www.newsarmenia.ru/arm1/20061222/41621684.html; 'Moldova denonsirovala soglashenie o statuse Ekonomicheskogo suda SNG', Interlic, 23 December 2009, at http://ru.interlic.md/2009-12-23/moldova-denonsirovala-soglashenie-o-statuse-ekonomicheskogo-suda-sng-13785.html.

October 2011.[34] Relative to its predecessors, the 2011 FTA represented a major step in providing compatibility with the WTO rules.[35] Importantly, the agreement contained a compromissory clause, referring to the Court as one of the possible forums for dispute resolution. Article 19 provides that disputes under the agreement can be brought before the Court, if both parties to it are signatories to the 1992 Statute, thus expanding its subject matter, but not its personal jurisdiction to other states. This, again, has the potential to enhance its role, yet its effects are yet to materialise.

Importantly, the Eurasian integration project grew in ambition with plans for the setting up of a Eurasian Economic Union (EEU) being made as of 2011. A new treaty was negotiated setting up the Union as a fully fledged international organisation with a developed system of bodies, including a new Court of the Eurasian Economic Union (CEEU). The result was the dissolution of the EEC, the closure of its court and the de facto transition of its work to the CEEU.

The developments described show that the interest in the CIS as a format for economic cooperation – other than in dealing with the legacies of the past – was lost. Thus, a certain paradox occurred. On the one hand, the CIS was hollowed out of economic contents in favour of cooperation at bilateral or Eurasian level. The CIS became more and more a vehicle for broad political and cultural cooperation. On the other hand, the Court's relevance was limited as its functions were restricted to the area of economic relations, with reform plans to expand and strengthen those functions failing repeatedly.

1.3 ECCIS and the International Centre for Dispute Resolution

Since its inception, the Court has endeavoured to promote itself as an important, functioning institution. Repeatedly, yet unsuccessfully, it lobbied the CIS member states to agree to amend its 1992 Statute. In these

34 Treaty on the Free Trade Area, St. Petersburg, 18 October 2011, in force 20 September 2012. Despite the launch of the Customs Union, the Treaty was signed by its members individually; yet, the rules took account of its existence. The Treaty was also signed by Kyrgyzstan and Tajikistan, members of the EEC at the time, as well as Armenia, Moldova and Ukraine.

35 At the time of signing, Russia's accession to the WTO was nearing completion, and the questionable relationship with Russia's membership in the Customs Union was satisfactorily resolved by asserting the primacy of WTO rules and Russia's undertakings before it in a Customs Union agreement of May 2011.

circumstances, the Court sought the support of the Inter-Parliamentary Assembly of the CIS and the International Union of Lawyers to develop its role. Most important, in October 2008, an International Centre for Dispute Resolution attached to the ECCIS was set up. The Court was instrumental in preparing the procedural rules of the Centre, which was registered as a noncommercial organisation under Russian law with a seat in St. Petersburg. The Centre consists of an Arbitration Tribunal, able to settle disputes initiated by business entities as well as states on the basis of an arbitration agreement, and a Chamber of Representatives, with its main focus on conciliation. Thus, in the absence of commitment to strengthening the Court as an international judicial institution, the Court allied with professional lobbies to set up an international arbitration tribunal affiliated to it.[36]

1.4 *Operational Status*

Despite the complications described earlier, the two decades of existence of the Court show it as a functioning institution. Nonetheless, only a small number of interstate disputes (eight) have been brought before it. A closer look shows that in fact very few of them relate to market-based trade relations. Half of the disputes were brought in the early years of the existence of the Court and relate to the failure to implement specific obligations, envisaged in bilateral interstate agreements for delivery of goods.[37] As such they deal with aspects of relations inherited from the USSR planned system of deliveries. Another dispute relates to the contested ownership rights over assets, also resulting from the nature of relations between former Soviet republics.[38] Only two of the disputes brought before the Court relate to trade policy. The first claim was brought by Tajikistan against Uzbekistan on account of its unilateral import and transit ban on ethanol in 1998. This remains the only case where the conformity of domestic acts with CIS agreements was under

[36] It is still early to draw a conclusion on the viability of this tribunal and the Court's involvement in it. In January 2014 the first request for conciliation between subjects of Belarus and Russia was reported, resulting in a settlement of the dispute via an agreement in March 2015.

[37] *Belarus v. Kazakhstan* (1994), *Belarus v. Kazakhstan* (1995), *Russia v. Kazakhstan* (1996), *Moldova v. Kazakhstan* (1997). Another dispute, *Belarus v. Moldova* (2000), related to the failure to pay for military training pursuant to a bilateral agreement. The latter two disputes were rejected as falling outside the Court's jurisdiction.

[38] *Kazakhstan v. Russia* (2008). This was the only case to be appealed before the Plenum.

Table 9.2 *Overview of the acts of the ECCIS issued in relation to interpretations and interstate disputes (March 1994–December 2014): type of appellant/claimant*

Appellant/claimant	Interpretations[i]	Disputes[ii]	Total
CIS integration or cooperation bodies	82		82
Own initiative	3		3
Armenia	1	0	1
Belarus	6	4	10
Moldova	2	1	3
Kazakhstan	7	2	9
Kyrgyzstan	2	0	2
Russia	5	2	7
Tajikistan	5	1	6
Uzbekistan	0	0	0
EEC bodies	1	0	1
Total	114	10	124

[i] Including 'advisory opinions', 'decisions' or 'rulings' (*opredeleniia*).
[ii] Including 'decisions', 'rulings' or Plenum 'resolutions' (*postanovleniia Plenuma*).

examination.[39] The second case was the only dispute brought before the ECCIS in its capacity of a Court of the EEC, whereby Belarus challenged Russia's application of export duties on oil and oil-related products.[40] Notably, no country other than a 1992 Statute signatory has brought a dispute before the Court on the basis of a compromissory clause.

By far the main focus of the Court's activity has been related to interpretations of the provisions of various CIS agreements through advisory opinions (114 out of 124 judicial acts, see Table 9.2). In understanding the role of the Court, it is worth providing an overview of the subject matters to which those opinions were dedicated. There are three main groups of issues that have come under discussion:

First, opinions related to the socioeconomic rights of citizens. The largest group of advisory opinions focus on the interpretation of agreements guaranteeing the socioeconomic rights and privileges of certain categories of citizens, particularly ex-military personnel and their

[39] *Tajikistan v. Uzbekistan* (2004). [40] *Belarus v. Russia* (2011).

families, Second World War veterans or refugees/migrants. These agreements typically sought to ensure the uniform realisation of rights that have arisen prior to the breakup of the USSR with the motivation to ensure that the resulting divergence in member states' legislation and economic policy, or lack of capacity to protect them, does not result in the violation of such rights. Similar issues were raised in relation to pension rights, rights of compensation for serious illness, and recognition of work experience for those purposes. Thus, while individuals cannot bring cases before the Court, its interpretative opinions have informed the practice of domestic institutions, ultimately helping citizens to benefit from the rights conferred in CIS agreements.

Second, opinions related to the legal and institutional basis of the CIS. This group of opinions includes interpretations of the founding acts of the CIS as well as agreements dealing with the status and powers of CIS bodies and various transborder entities. Similarly, the Court has issued interpretations of various international agreements and their conformity to the principles of international law. Given the highly complex and incrementally developed legal framework of the CIS, the opinions have made an important contribution to clarifying fundamental issues, such as the membership in the organisation, its international legal personality or the legality of the numerous reservations to agreements used regularly by member states. Finally, the Court has sought to develop its own institutional regime, seeking to enhance its own significance in dispute resolution in the region. Notably, it is within that category that the only interpretation by the ECCIS in its capacity of a Court of the EEC was sought. The advisory opinion issued dealt with the fundamental matter of the legal status of the acts of the bodies of the EEC.

Third, opinions related to the functioning of the free trade area. As previously noted in Section 1.1, the Court can interpret agreements and other acts on the CIS 'on economic matters'. On this basis, the Court has issued a number of interpretations of the 1994 Free Trade Agreement, subsequent specific issue agreements, related, for example, to rules of origin, the common customs nomenclature, or rules on transport, as well as some bilateral free trade agreements. In quantitative terms, such opinions do not represent a large amount (about 10 per cent of all opinions issued), yet they deal with some fundamental concepts and principles. For example, the Court took the opportunity to clarify concepts, such as 'customs tariffs, taxes and fees with equivalent effect' or 'quantitative restrictions'.

2 Specific Legitimacy Issues

2.1 Nomination, Composition and Independence of Judges

The ECCIS was structured to operate as Full Court (*polnoi sostav*), chamber (*kollegiia*), and Plenum (*plenum*). The main judicial task of the Full Court, formed of all judges, is to issue interpretative advisory opinions.[41] The Full Court also appoints judges to the chamber, which then operates as a court of first instance composed of three or five judges.[42] The chamber decisions can be challenged in the Plenum, which consists of the regular judges of the Economic Court as well as additional, ex officio judges, namely the chairs of the high economic or commercial courts of the member states that are signatories to the 1992 Statute.[43] Further to its operating as an appellate body, the Plenum is the highest collegiate body of the Court with an important organisational role, including the approval of its Rules of Procedure.[44]

The process of appointment of judges and the guarantees for their independence has been one of the main areas of concern for the legitimacy of the Court. First, the selection and nomination of judges is a process entirely determined by the respective member states, with no input from the CIS institutions. Regular judges are elected or appointed for a term of ten years in accordance with the domestic procedure applied for the election or appointment of judges to the highest economic or commercial courts.[45] Although there are some variations between the constitutional provisions in this respect, a common feature is the prominence of the executive branch in the process.[46] This prominence is even greater given the political nature of domestic regimes, exhibiting strong authoritarian features, including dominance of the legislature by strong [residential parties. The 1992 Statute formulates only the general requirement that the selection should be made at the state's discretion 'on a strictly professional basis' from the body of existing commercial or arbitration court judges or other persons with a law degree who are also highly qualified specialists in the area of economic relations.[47] In effect, the domestic criteria for electing judges to the highest courts can be stricter in that, for example, a certain minimum prior judicial

[41] Articles 24 and 123 of the 1997 Rules of Procedure.

[42] Article 9 of the 1997 Rules of Procedure.

[43] Article 13 of the 1997 Rules of Procedure.

[44] Article 2 of the 1992 Statute.

[45] Article 7, first paragraph of the 1992 Statute.

[46] In the RF, for example, they are nominated by the President and approved by the Parliament.

[47] Article 7, first paragraph of the 1992 Statute.

experience is required. A symbolic role for the CIS institutions is reserved only in the shape of the requirement for the CIS Council of Heads of Government to approve the Chair of the Court and its deputies, following their election by the majority of regular judges.[48]

These provisions become even more problematic in view of their implications for the independence of the Court, underlying its declarative rather than substantive nature. On the one hand, the 1992 Statute provides that individual judges are independent and cannot represent any states, state organs or organisations, commercial structures, political parties or movements, or any nations, peoples, social or religious groups or persons. On the other hand, clearly the judges owe their position entirely to the state and state organs that have appointed them with no transparency of selection criteria. More important, judges can be removed from office before the end of their term by being recalled by the state organs that have appointed them.[49] Although the Statute provides that this can be done only in cases of abuse of office, crime or illness, there are no guarantees against the possible arbitrary use of these provisions. Furthermore, judges are deemed to be immune from prosecution; they cannot face criminal or administrative trials or be arrested without the consent of the Court.[50] Yet, the wording of the provision suggests that this applies only to the immunity from the jurisdiction of the country of residence of the Court, Belarus, which has been interpreted as an important deficiency of the regime.[51] Ultimately, the independence of judges is only as strong as the quality of domestic rule of law, which has been a cause for consistent concern in the region.

Second, independence concerns are also raised at the institutional level in relation to the composition of the Plenum. The argument for the participation of the chairs of the high judicial or arbitration institutions of the member states was, according to Genadii Danilenko, stemmed from 'the desire of the CIS states to build more confidence in the Court' and the need to apply and interpret not only CIS agreements, but also former USSR law as well as principles of domestic law.[52] Yet, this also raises the issue of the Court's cohesion and efficiency, given the busy schedules of such officials. Indeed, despite the move to a sessional mode of work,

[48] Article 7, paragraph 2 of the 1992 Statute.
[49] Article 7, third paragraph of the 1992 Statute.
[50] Article 8, first paragraph of the 1992 Statute.
[51] Shinkaretskaia, 'Sud Evraziiskogo Ekonomicheskogo soobshchestva', 101.
[52] Danilenko, 'The Economic Court of the CIS', 897.

attendance has remained a practical concern, resulting in absences and delegated representation.[53] Even more important, the participation based on official position makes even more questionable the passing of impartial judgement as an appeals body if the interests of their own country are at stake. Notably, in 2009, the addition to the Procedural Rules of the Court was made whereby these judges participate in the work of the Plenum in a 'personal capacity'. Yet, given the internal nature of this document, as noted earlier, and the lack of a corresponding amendment to the 1992 Statute, the effectiveness of this provision remains questionable.

Third, the 1992 Agreement established a quota of two judges per country,[54] which was reduced to one in 2002.[55] The analysis of the appointments to the Court since its launch is highly instructive of the member states' limited commitment to it. The ECCIS has never operated with the full possible set of appointments (two regular judges from eight countries) or even, initially, with an equal number of judges per country. Thus, the premise of the ECCIS being formed on the basis of equal representation of member states failed to materialise.[56] Uzbekistan never sent any regular judges to the Court, limiting its participation only to the Plenum. Some countries appointed two judges, others just one. Russia, for example, had no appointed judges in the period 2001–2002. Tajikistan has not appointed regular judges since 2009, and Kyrgyzstan since 2013. These countries are only represented in the Plenum of the Economic Court. This pattern, in combination with the reduction of the number of judges to one per country, has had an important effect on the ability of the Court to operate. There have been renewed calls to reverse the 2002 move, yet, given the evidence of member states' waning commitment to the Court, it is doubtful that this step would solve the problem. Ultimately, since January 2015 the Court has faced a crisis: it has not been able to legitimately operate either as a chamber (for which a minimum of three judges is needed) or as a full court (requiring a quorum of two-thirds).[57]

[53] Accordingly, in 2009 amendments to the Rules of Procedure were introduced, requiring absence to be notified in advance, and due authorisation presented if representatives are sent, Article 15, paragraph 3.

[54] Article 2 of the 1992 Agreement.

[55] Decision of the Council of Heads of State, 7 October 2002.

[56] Article 6 of the 1992 Statute.

[57] Kazakhstan transferred its judge to the Court of the Eurasian Economic Union, launched on 1 January 2015, and has not yet nominated a new judge at the ECCIS. At the time of writing, the ECCIS has regular judges from only Russia and Belarus.

2.2 Procedural Rules and Issues

As mentioned, the ECCIS jurisdiction is limited to interstate disputes. Such disputes can be brought before it by two categories of public actors: the interested states acting through their competent organs and by the institutions of the Commonwealth.[58] In practice, petitions have been filed only by member states represented by their governments or government committees. In the latter case, the Court has been particularly attentive to the issue of the proper claimant, verifying the existence of due authorisation[59] and rejecting claims in its absence.[60]

Apart from the direct access to the Court resulting in the standing as a party to the proceedings, it is also possible for a third party (again, only a member state or a CIS body) to acquire such status when its 'legal interests are at stake'.[61] No other state or nonstate interests can be represented in the proceedings, other than views of the expert community when acting in the capacity of general counsel, specialist or an expert. In such circumstances, it is within the power of the chamber to select and appoint such persons and determine the scope of their contribution.[62]

A specific issue of particular relevance for the legitimacy of the Court's rulings relates to the nonparticipation of a party in the proceedings. This was an issue in many of the disputes actually dealt with by the Court.[63] According to the Rules of Procedure, a party not attending a hearing or refusing to participate in the process altogether does not present a barrier to the proceedings.[64] Yet, this has clear consequences for the implementation of the Court's decision and its general relevance.[65]

[58] Article 3, third paragraph of the 1992 Statute. The latter situation has been deemed unrealistic to arise, I. Fisenko, 'Mekhanizmy razresheniia sporov mezhdu gosudarstvami-uchastnikami SNG', *Moscow Journal of International Law*, 26, 2, (1997), 122–33.

[59] In *Kazakhstan v. Russia*, Decision Nr. 01-1/3-06, 18 April 2008, the Court verified that the claimant, the Committee of State Property and Privatisation was duly authorised by the Prime Minister.

[60] For example, a claim by a district public authority in *Russia v. Kazakhstan*, Nr C-1/8-96. The Court also rejected claims filed by companies as falling beyond its jurisdiction.

[61] Article 39, paragraph 1 of the 1997 Rules of Procedure.

[62] Articles 33, 40, 42 and 42 of the 1997 Rules of Procedure.

[63] For examples, see I. Fisenko, 'Practika Ekonomicheskogo Suda Sodruzhestva Nezavisimykh Gosudarstv', *Moscow Journal of International Law*, 27, 3, (1997), 26–32.

[64] Article 64.

[65] For example, in the case of *Tajikistan v. Uzbekistan*, which had potential importance for promoting the compliance of domestic acts with the country's trade undertakings, Uzbekistan did not submit formal positions or appointed representatives at the proceedings, nor did it implement the ruling.

The right to request advisory opinions is granted to the CIS institutions as well as the highest state organs and the highest economic or commercial courts of the member states. Over the last two decades the majority of such requests (82 out of 114) have been submitted by CIS bodies (Table 9.2), such as the CIS Executive Committee or the CIS Inter-Parliamentary Assembly. Yet, the Court has adopted a very wide, pragmatic interpretation of 'CIS institutions', including not just bodies envisaged in the CIS charter, but also various bodies for sector-specific cooperation (e.g. the Interstate Bank). Similarly, in line with the broad view of its advisory jurisdiction, it has dealt with requests from non-governmental organizations (e.g. Confederation of Trade Unions) and transnational public monopolies (e.g. Interstate Telecom Company).

Another important procedural issue relates to the transparency of the Court's work. The Rules of Procedure provide that the oral proceedings before it are open, unless otherwise decided.[66] The deliberations of the Court, however, are strictly confidential and cannot be disclosed.[67] Dissenting opinions are allowed; however, they cannot be published.[68] Thus, they can contribute to debates and the evolution of practice within chambers, but do not become available to the public at large. It is the decision of the majority that becomes the decision of the Court and is then disclosed to the parties and the public. According to the 1992 Statute, the acts of the Court are officially published in a CIS journal and the member states' mass media.[69] Currently, they are also available on the Court's website in full and in annotated versions. In addition, the Court has regularly undertaken reviews of its practice in particular areas. This has had a positive effect on the legal and academic community's familiarity with the work of the Court.

2.3 *Fact-Finding*

During the initial stage of the proceedings, the parties submit documentary and other evidence in support of their claims and counterclaims. Every party bears the burden of proof for the facts on which it relies.[70] In deciding on the admissibility and relevance of the evidence, the chamber

[66] Article 63 of the 1997 Rules of Procedure.
[67] Article 45 of the 1997 Rules of Procedure.
[68] Article 86 of the 1997 Rules of Procedure.
[69] Article 16 of the 1992 Statute.
[70] Article 31 of the 1997 Rules of Procedure.

is guided by the work of the General Counsel, which submits a conclusion and formulates the Court's position.[71] The chamber is also able to investigate facts on its own initiative, request additional evidence from the parties, as well as commission expert opinions or request specialist advice. The chamber also has wide powers to call witnesses from amongst the civil servants and other officials of the bodies of the CIS, domestic bodies, commercial and noncommercial organizations, as well as individuals.[72] Thus, in terms of fact-finding, the Court's setup allows it to operate as a legitimate institution.

2.4 *Interpretative Approaches*

According to its Rules of Procedure, in deciding disputes the Court applies: the international agreements between the parties to the disputes, the acts of the CIS bodies, the applicable norms of the former USSR, the domestic law of the member states that are parties to the dispute, the general and specific international conventions recognised by the parties, the generally accepted principles of international law, international custom as evidence of general practice accepted as law, the general principles of law recognised by the parties, the resolutions of the Plenum and other decisions of the Court having the nature of a precedent and the Plenum resolutions and other decisions of the Court with preliminary force regarding the present case.[73] A number of issues need to be noted with regard to this list as well as the Court's practical activity in this respect.

First, as noted by Danilenko, the reference to the explicit role of the Court's decisions as precedents is fairly uncommon in a civil law context.[74] Yet, it is conducive to the building up of a body of consistent case law and the predictability of judicial outcomes. Certainly, the approach to deciding similar disputes (the only example being the three decided cases relating to obligations in the context of the deliveries system), show that the Court was guided by its previous decisions.

Second, in terms of reliance on international law, the ECCIS has regularly applied the 1969 Vienna Convention on the Law of Treaties. The 2011 FTA is particularly important as it requires the Court to apply the various WTO rules referred to in the agreement. Similarly, recent

[71] Article 40^1 of the 1997 Rules of Procedure.
[72] Article 41 of the 1997 Rules of Procedure.
[73] Article 29 of the 1997 Rules of Procedure.
[74] Danilenko, 'The Economic Court of the CIS', 909.

changes to the 1997 Rules of Procedure require the Court to take into account the case law related to applying the relevant WTO agreements.[75] It must be noted, however, that the Court had already referred to a number of fundamental GATT provisions in interpreting the various trade-related agreements concluded within the CIS. It remains to be seen how well the ECCIS will apply the WTO rules as and when the occasion arises. Its regional counterpart, the CEEC, in the two years of its separate existence, certainly applied those rules, yet sometimes reached surprising conclusions about their relationship to the legal order of the Customs Union.[76]

Third, there are various examples of the Court's willingness to refer to and apply domestic legislation both in its decisions and advisory opinions.[77]

In general, the Court has applied extensively literal and systematic methods of interpretation, but has also provided examples of considering the objectives behind the adoption of certain CIS agreements, such as the 1993 TEU. This has been very helpful in providing clarity to what, as described, has been a very confusing and overlapping system of hundreds of international agreements. Yet, the formal legality applied by the Court has often proved to be at odds with the reality of the member states' commitment and economic relations. Certainly, the focus on the 1994 FTA in many advisory opinions has been in sharp contrast with the failure of that agreement to deliver practical results.

2.5 *Forum Shopping*

For most of the last two decades, forum shopping has not been a key issue in the post-Soviet world. In principle, a number of CIS agreements have explicitly referred to a choice between various international fora. To start with, the 1993 Treaty on the Economic Union provided that countries can resolve their disputes by negotiations or by turning to the Economic Court; yet, in case of a failure to settle their disputes through the aforementioned ways, they can submit them to 'other international judicial organs' in accordance with their rules and procedures.[78] In its

[75] Article 113 of the 1997 Rules of Procedure.

[76] A. Smbatian, 'Kontzeptziia 'osobosti' pravoporiadka Tamozhennogo soiuza *v.* reshenii suda Evrazes po prokatnym valkam', *Evraziiskii Juridicheskii Zhurnal*, 8 (2013), 31–36.

[77] For example, in its recent high-profile Advisory Opinion 01-1/1-14 of 23 September 2014 on interpreting Article 11 of the CIS Convention on Protecting Investor Rights of 28 March 1997, the Court confidently examined and applied the domestic laws on investment of the signatories of that Convention as well as the related practice of these countries' supreme judicial institutions.

interpretations, the ECCIS was keen to assert its importance, underlining that this can occur only when there are no grounds for the consideration of the case according to its own Procedural Rules.[79] In fact, it argued that with regard to disputes falling within what the Court deems the mandatory jurisdiction under the Treaty, the member states of the Economic Union have no right to turn to other international judicial organs.

Particularly as of the late 1990s onward, however, many CIS agreements have referred either to abstract 'procedures envisaged by international law' without mentioning the Court at all or have allowed parties to choose between the ECCIS and other international judicial bodies as equally possible options. These references have been general and unspecific. In its advisory opinions the ECCIS took the view that, as such, these clauses do not provide a clear alternative of another tribunal, but leave that to be specified between the parties at a later stage. Therefore, the possibility to turn to such bodies, it held, would be ultimately determined by their own subject matter, personal or territorial jurisdiction as well as the parties' clear and unambiguous consent to refer their dispute to particular bodies.[80]

Through most of the 1990s its alternatives, according to the ECCIS, were restricted to bodies such as the International Court of Justice or the Permanent Court of Arbitration.[81] Following the setting up of the EEC, there was the possibility for the Court of the EEC to also become such an alternative. As Table 9.3 shows, the members of the EEC were also signatories of the 1992 Statute of ECCIS; both organisations included trade and economic cooperation amongst their objectives. In fact, some agreements, which were part of the multilevel CIS economic integration formula, such as the 1995 Customs Union agreement, were also deemed to be part of the legal basis of the EEC and the 2010 Customs Union, opening the possibility for overlap in subject-matter jurisdictions.

Yet, this was more of a hypothetical issue, not least while the ECCIS performed the task of a Court of the EEC. In that period there was only one dispute brought before the Court in 2011, which concerned Russia's alleged breach of its undertakings under its bilateral FTA with Belarus and other agreements, concluded under the CIS period, but also the latest agreements

[78] Article 31, paragraphs 1 and 4. [79] Advisory Opinion C-1/19-96 of 15 May 1997.

[80] This issue came under discussion in a widely discussed Advisory Opinion of September 2014, Case 01-1/1-14, where Kyrgyzstan requested the interpretation of the jurisdictional clause, Article 11, of the Convention on the protection of investor rights of 28 March 1997, Moscow, in the context of a large number of investor claims being filed against it at the Arbitration Court at the Moscow Chamber of Commerce.

[81] Advisory Opinion C-1/19-96 of 15 May 1997.

Table 9.3 *Possible fora for trade disputes in the post-Soviet region*

	ECCIS (1992)	Court of EEC (2004–2014)	Court of EEU	WTO DSM	2011 FTA regime
Belarus	Yes	Yes*	Yes	–	Yes
Kazakhstan	Yes	Yes*	Yes	December 2015	Yes
Kyrgyzstan	Yes	Yes	–	20/12/1998	Yes
Russia	Yes	Yes*	Yes	22/08/2012	Yes
Tajikistan	Yes	Yes	–	2/03/2013	Yes
Uzbekistan	Yes	2006–2008	–	–	–
Armenia	Denounced 2006	–	Yes	5/02/2003	Yes
Moldova	Denounced 2009	–	–	26/07/2001	Yes
Azerbaijan	–	–	–	–	–
Georgia	–	–	–	14/06/2000	–
Turkmenistan	–	–	–	–	–
Ukraine	–	–	–	16/05/2008	Yes

* Includes Customs Union matters.

between them, part of the legal framework of the Customs Union.[82] The dispute also arose in the context of the political negotiations surrounding the launch of the Customs Union in June 2010 and was clearly treated falling within the subject matter of the CEEC. Notably, no interstate dispute has been filed since. In practice, since its start in 2012 the CEEC has been an active court, but almost exclusively in relation to claims of commercial actors against the acts of the permanent regulator of the grouping, the Eurasian Economic Commission, where no competition with the ECCIS is possible.

This seems to be also the tendency with the Court of the Eurasian Economic Union (EEU), which started work in January 2015, and which provides similar direct access to proceedings for commercial actors. Nonetheless, given that the Statute of the Court of the EEU allows that not only disputes related to the legal basis of the Union can be brought before it, but also related to 'other international agreements between the member states',[83] it is possible that states will make a choice to litigate on

[82] *Belarus v. Russia* (2011). The agreements represented the legal basis of the Customs Union were clearly determined, Dragneva, 'The Legal and Institutional Dimensions', pp. 43–44.
[83] Article 40 of the Statute of the CEEU, Annex 2 of the Treaty on the EEU.

CIS agreements before the Court of the EEU as opposed to the ECCIS. As far as disputes with non-EEU members are concerned, the Statute of the EEU refers only to a jurisdiction over disputes related to agreements between 'the Union and third parties'. Thus, the literal interpretation of this provision will entail that the Court of the EEU will not be an alternative with regard to agreements between individual members and third parties, which can be brought under the jurisdiction of the ECCIS, either by virtue of the 1992 Statute or a compromissory clause.

As noted, the 2011 FTA also gave parties a choice in dispute resolution fora. Article 19 (2) provided that if the attempts to settle a dispute consensually fail, the claimant can choose between bringing the case before the ECCIS, if both parties are signatories of the 1992 Statute, or a commission of experts. This commission will then act on the basis of a procedure approved as Appendix 4 to the Treaty. Nonetheless, this provision is currently of limited importance for 1992 Statute signatories who also are predominantly members of the Eurasian structures (Table 9.3). For the 1992 signatories who are not in the EEU, the choice of the ECCIS is a highly symbolic possibility given their de facto limited participation in it.[84] Choosing the commission of experts might have certain advantages, such as greater confidentiality, speed and control over the members of the panel. However, its use is yet to be established.

The other possible forum for settling disputes is offered by the WTO system. As shown in Table 9.3, eight post-Soviet countries have become members of the WTO, Kazakhstan being the most recent accession. Furthermore, Article 19 (3) of the 2011 FTA provides that disputes over issues dealt with by reference to WTO rules can chose the WTO settlement system. In principle, there has been a limited number of requests made before the WTO. Most of them precede the conclusion of the 2011 FTA and involve disputes between Armenia, Moldova and Ukraine.[85] Thus, the extent to which the WTO will be a preferred route is still to be established.[86]

[84] These are Kyrgyzstan, which is currently negotiating accession to the EEU, Tajikistan, which is discussing possible accession, and Uzbekistan. As noted earlier, despite the formal participation in the 1992 Statute, Uzbekistan has not given any credence to the Court. Kyrgyzstan and Tajikistan have also stopped appointing regular judges.

[85] *Ukraine v. Armenia*, July 2010 (import and internal sale of cigarettes and alcoholic beverages), *Moldova v. Ukraine*, March 2011 (tax discrimination against imported distilled spirits), and *Ukraine v. Moldova*, February 2011 (environmental charge on imports).

[86] Most recently Ukraine, and Moldova in one instance, have joined the requests of the European Union against Russia as third parties.

2.6 Implementation and Interaction with National Courts

The lack of bindingness of the decisions of the Court and its implications for their implementation is an issue widely noted in the commentaries on the ECCIS.[87] In fact, it could be argued that this feature deprives the ECCIS of its essential adjudicating legitimacy, despite it being called a 'Court'.[88] Article 4 of the 1992 Statute provides that the Court's decisions establish the fact of the violation and recommends suitable measures for adoption by the country found in violation; 'the state with respect to which a decision was adopted, ensures its implementation.' The Court has viewed this provision as unclear in terms of its binding force or recommended nature. In this sense, it has opted for a literal interpretation, arguing that its decisions establish the facts that might amount to a violation, but the measures to eliminate this violation can only be treated as a recommendation.[89]

The issue of bindingness was raised in the context of the 1993 Treaty on the Economic Union, which is one of the 'other' agreements containing a reference clause to the ECCIS. In particular, Article 31 of the Treaty provides that 'if the Economic Court recognizes that . . . a member state has not fulfilled an obligation ensuing from the Treaty, this state is obliged to take measures connected with the implementation of the decision of the Economic Court.' According to the Court, the signatories of the Treaty have specifically undertaken to be bound by its rulings.[90] Yet, this view did not meet a wider acceptance. The granting of a binding force to the Court's decisions has also been a part of the failed reform rounds, described in Section 1.2 earlier. As argued, it was unrealistic to expect that given the nature of the integration processes in the CIS and the lack of bindingness granted to the acts of the other bodies of the CIS, this would be a step to which member states would agree.[91]

Ultimately, the implementation of decisions remains within the state's discretion. There is no common enforcement or disciplinary mechanism to ensure this. In the event of noncompliance, the aggrieved state can turn to the Council of Heads of State, the highest decision-making body

87 E.g. L. Anufrieva, 'Mezhdunarodnoe pravosudie: regional'nye sudebnye uchrezhdeniia *v.* evraziiskoi integratzii', *Evraziiskii Iuridicheskii Zhurnal*, (2013), 14–22, F. Abdulloev and I. Mishal'chenko, 'O sovershenstvovanii deiatel'nosti Ekonomicheskogo Suda Sodruzhestva Nezavisimykh Gosudarstv', *Evraziiskii Iuridicheskii Zhurnal*, 16 (9) (2009), 22–26.

88 Thanks to the reviewers for drawing attention to the contradiction.

89 Interview with Justice L. Kamenkova, 21 December 2009, news.tut.by/economics/155728.html.

90 Advisory Opinion C-1/19-96 of 15 May 1997.

91 Fisenko, 'Mekhanizmy razresheniia sporov', 129.

of the CIS, which is a 'soft' and politically uncertain route. The Council decides by consensus, so any decision can be blocked, and it can do no more than 'recommend to the parties an appropriate procedure or method of settling' the dispute.[92]

It has to be noted that often decisions have given rise not to implementation but to a process of negotiating a solution through political means, as in the 1995 *Belarus v. Kazakhstan* dispute, where a resolution was eventually found after extensive bilateral negotiations. At the same time, several requests for advisory opinions have actually been related to disputes that were dealt with through other means. Some scholars have argued, however, that the ECCIS's willingness to use advisory proceedings to resolve actual disputes is problematic insofar as the conclusions are reached without the participation of all parties concerned and that such nonparticipating states are likely to reject opinions as lacking legitimacy.[93]

The Court's advisory opinions have had a generally positive effect in domestic settings, certainly according to the Court's own assertions: its interpretations, particularly in relation to the rights of military personnel, have been taken into account and referred to by domestic high courts as well as by executive agencies.[94] Similarly, it has been argued that customs agencies have followed opinions on CIS transit rules or rules of origin.[95] Generally, there has been a framework for strong interaction between the ECCIS and national courts. In addition to the structural links via the composition of the Plenum, the ECCIS has participated in various fora for regional judicial dialogue and cooperation.

2.7 Disputes in the CIS: Adjudication, Consensus or Coercion

As discussed, the legitimacy of the Court has been dependent on multiple factors, ranging from the members' integration behaviour and trade relations, their commitment to the CIS, and various aspects of the design of the Court. The decision of whether to resort to it has also been affected by a general unwillingness to commit to adjudicative methods as well as, especially in the case of Russia, the ability to reach the desired outcomes by exploiting regional asymmetries.

[92] Article 18 of the CIS Charter. [93] Danilenko, 'The Economic Court of the CIS', 905.

[94] Interview with the Chair of the Court, L. Kamenkova, 16 March 2012, at www.gazeta-yurist.ru/prn_article.php?i=1840.

[95] Information at http:sudsng.org/analytics/sudobzor/practik.

In principle, it has been argued that the region has inherited the Soviet legacy of mistrust of international judicial institutions.[96] In combination with the sovereignty sensitivities of the newly independent republics, this has resulted in prominence of consensual mechanisms in the various CIS agreements. Most bilateral free trade agreements envisaged settlement of disputes purely by negotiation. The multilateral agreements similarly have made the submission of a claim to an international judicial body either alternative to negotiations or subsequent to it, i.e. in the event of the failure of negotiations. Over time, there has been the tendency to put stronger emphasis on pretrial procedures – negotiations, structured consultations, conciliation – particularly evident in comparing the 1994 and 1999 Free Trade Agreements.[97] Similarly, the 2011 FTA provides for resort to the ECCIS or the experts' commission only as a last resort.

This overall trend is also clearly seen in the approach of the ECCIS. In relation to several disputes, the Court has taken the initiative to recommend further negotiations between the states concerned and the settlement of relations via international agreements.[98] Importantly, the Court's latest amendments of its Rules of Procedure envisage its own right to initiate conciliation as well as an important role for it in determining the list of recommended conciliators.[99] As with other examples of the Court's activism, however, the legitimacy effect of such a measure remains uncertain.

In general, looking at trade relations in the post-Soviet space, it can be established that there has been an abundance of disputes. For example, there has been a long history of concerns over the discriminatory use of trade protection measures, including tariff changes, antidumping or taxation.[100] In those situations, Russia has shown a consistent preference for diplomatic solutions, but has also resorted to extensive issue-linkages. Given its partners' high dependence on energy supply, migrant labour

[96] Danilenko, 'The Economic Court of the CIS', 914.

[97] Dragneva and De Kort, 'The Legal Regime', 259.

[98] This most notably the case in the controversial 2011 Belarus–Russia dispute on export duties on oil. It is not easy to establish to what extent the Court was driven by legal consideration, political pragmatism or, indeed, member states' pressure.

[99] Article 115 as amended on 9 October 2014. Previously, the provision entailed only the right of either party to request conciliation.

[100] For discussion of this pattern in, for example, Russia–Ukraine relations, see R. Dragneva and K. Wolczuk, *Ukraine between the EU and Russia: The Integration Challenge* (Basingstoke: Palgrave, 2015).

remittances or security guarantees, Russia has often tied the resolution of trade concerns to such issues, thus maximising its bargaining power. Certainly, it has become clear that the formal provision of the various dispute settlement mechanisms of the 2011 FTA has had little effect on Russia's preference for coercive measures against Ukraine, Moldova or Georgia in seeking to dissuade them from entering into an Association Agreement with the European Union.[101] In this context, relations have been additionally complicated by the use of trade policy to achieve geopolitical priorities, particularly in relation to Russia's challenge of the perceived expansion of the Euro-Atlantic structures.

Notably, the preference for political resolution of disputes and 'gas' diplomacy is also evident in relations between the members of the Eurasian Customs Union, followed by the Eurasian Economic Union, despite the highly legalised nature of that regime. Recent disputes between Russia, Belarus and Kazakhstan, for example, have revealed continued preference for retaliatory measures and highest-level dialogue.[102]

3 Conclusions

The ECCIS, it can be argued, started its life in circumstances that had important implications for its design and expected role. Its functioning has shown its limited use for resolving trade disputes outside the framework of the inherited USSR framework for economic relations. The member states' use of the Court has been circumscribed by their regional integration behaviour, in general, and attitudes to the CIS, in particular. Ultimately, the ECCIS has been marginal in a context where trade relations have been embedded in strong asymmetric arrangements and preference for consensual modes of settling disputes. As shown, however, the Court has built a body of interpretative opinions. In the conditions of limited member states' commitment – both in terms of ex ante design and ex post willingness to support its reform – the Court has taken a proactive stand, seeking to maximise its own role.

101 E.g. see D. Cenusa et al., 'Russia's Punitive Trade Policy Measures towards Ukraine, Moldova and Georgia', CEPS Working Document Nr. 400, September 2014, at: www.ceps.be/system/files/WD%20300%20Punitive%20Trade%20Measures%20by%20Russia_0.pdf.

102 Russia's introduction of bans on Belorussian meat on grounds of SPS violations, for example, resulted in the reintroduction of customs controls by Belarus in the late 2014, thus unravelling the achievements of the Customs Union altogether.

What is also clear is the importance of the ECCIS as a 'testing ground' for the development of later regional courts, particularly the Court of the Eurasian Economic Community and, now, the Court of the Eurasian Economic Union. The design of those institutions around problematic issues, such as the selection and appointment of judges or the legal force of its decisions, show significant learning from the ECCIS and the critique thereof.

The present role of the Court, however, is critically constrained by the waning member states' participation in its organisational setting, endangering its ability to act. It is uncertain whether, given the changes in the regional context in terms of the shift to Eurasian integration, but also Russia's pronounced use of coercive measures in the region, the Court can maintain its importance. It increasingly looks unlikely that the ECCIS will survive as something more than the ceremonial role of an emeritus institution.

10

The COMESA Court of Justice

JAMES THUO GATHII*

1 Introduction

There is almost no scholarship focusing on the Common Market for Eastern and Southern Africa (COMESA) Court of Justice.[1] This is the first attempt to provide a comprehensive discussion of the cases decided by the COMESA Court of Justice from its founding.[2] In addition, this chapter relied on an interview with the President of the Court in the summer of 2013 and from perusing the records of the minutes of various COMESA organs and press reports.

The COMESA Court of Justice has a major similarity with other African subregional ICs. Although it is established as a regional trade court, it has barely handled any trade cases. However, while the other subregional ICs like the East African Court of Justice (EACJ) and the Economic Community of West Africa (ECOWAS) Court of Justice (ECCJ) have mostly decided human rights cases, the COMESA Court of Justice has primarily decided disputes between various COMESA institutions and their employees. This chapter compares and contrasts the reasons underlying the COMESA Court of Justice's trajectory in

* Wing-Tat Lee Chair in International Law, Loyola University Chicago School of Law.
I thank Laurence Helfer for very helpful comments on an earlier draft of this paper.

[1] Notable but now dated exceptions are, P. K. Kiplagat, 'Dispute recognition and dispute settlement in integration processes: The COMESA experience', *Northwestern Journal of International Law and Business*, 15 (1994–1995), 437; K. K. Mwenda, 'The common market for Eastern and Southern Africa (COMESA) and the COMESA Court: Immunity of international organization from legal action', *Miskolc Journal of International Law*, 6 (2009), 60; and H. K. Mutai, *Compliance with international trade obligations* (Alphen aan den Rijn: Kluwer Law International, 2007).

A more recent brief analysis is G. Erasmus, 'The COMESA Court of Justice: Regional Trade Agreements Do Protect Private Parties', TRALAC Trade Brief No. S13TB09/2013 (2013)

[2] That is not surprising in part because its case law has to date not been publicly available. In addition, unlike other African International Courts (ICs), it has been largely invisible.

becoming an administrative tribunal for COMESA employees, with how the EACJ and the ECCJ became human rights courts.

Although African subregional courts are established to ensure trade integration is rule based,[3] they have overwhelmingly decided human rights rather than trade cases. The COMESA Court of Justice is unique; rather than deciding human rights cases, it has overwhelmingly decided employment disputes between COMESA and its employees. This chapter therefore seeks to fill the lacunae in our current understanding of the COMESA Court of Justice, first by showing that like other subregional African courts, it has not decided trade cases with the exception of a recent and remarkable exception, and second, by showing that while other subregional courts have primarily decided human rights cases, the COMESA Court of Justice has mostly decided employment disputes.[4]

This chapter argues that assessing the legitimacy of newer courts such as the COMESA Court of Justice has to go beyond merely asking the following questions: First, whether the court is composed of competent and appropriate judges. Second, whether the court fulfils certain procedural requirements, such as providing due process for all affected parties. Third, whether the court properly applies the applicable law as consented through ratification by member states. Last, whether the court produces judgements and rulings that are actually adhered to.

Instead, to understand the trajectory of the COMESA Court of Justice, which is only about a decade and a half old, other concerns have to enter into the picture. The reasons why the COMESA Court of Justice's docket is dominated by cases filed by COMESA employees are: First, unlike other subregional courts in Africa, the Court has lacked mobilized constituencies such as a regional bar association or nongovernmental organisations, (NGOs), to bring cases before the Court, to lobby for court reform to make

[3] For the COMESA Court of Justice, this was clearly the goal as illustrated by this quote early in its life: In his opening statement at the Sixth Meeting of the COMESA Ministers of Justice and Attorneys General held on 12th April, 2002, His Excellency, the Rt. Hon. Prime Minister of Swaziland, Dr. B. S. S. Dlamini, made the following remark about the role of the COMESA Court of Justice: 'We are all aware that the growth of the European Community was largely facilitated by the existence of a Court of Justice that had been established in 1952, providing a forum for the uniform interpretation of (what are now) EU rules and regulations, particularly with regard to issues affecting competition. It is, therefore, important that, as Ministers of Justice and Attorneys General, you will continue to strengthen the COMESA Court to ensure that the integration process of COMESA is rule based.'

[4] On the East African Court of Justice, see James Gathii, 'Mission creep or a search for relevance: The human rights strategy of the East African Court of Justice', *Duke Journal of Comparative and International Law*, 24 (2013), 249.

it more accessible or to defend it when it gets into trouble with member governments. Second, the Court started its work in the 2000–2001 period when it was difficult for a new international court to begin exercising its authority in a context in which governments were particularly hostile to any form of judicial review. Third, the location of the Court, first in Lusaka, Zambia, and currently in Khartoum, Sudan, has not provided a base with interlocutors in the same way Arusha, Tanzania, has for the East African Court of Justice and Abuja, Nigeria, has for the ECOWAS Community Court of Justice. Sanctions against the government of Sudan hampered fund-raising for the Court's new premises and have severely limited the ability of NGOs involved in human rights and the rule of law to be based in Khartoum, further inhibiting the growth of the Court along the lines of other African subregional courts. Fourth, the Court has adopted a very restrictive interpretive approach that further compounds its other limitations and that makes it an unattractive litigation forum both for human rights groups and business actors.

What implications does this experience of African subregional courts have for legitimacy? The fact that governments do not litigate against each other and that private-sector groups do not sue governments in these courts with a view to promote trade integration strongly suggests that these courts do not enjoy the legitimacy of governments and the private sector. By contrast, courts like the East African Court of Justice that repeatedly entertain human rights cases enjoy legitimacy among human rights groups. In West Africa, the ECOWAS Community Court of Justice has built its legitimacy and had its jurisdiction to decide human rights cases accepted by ECOWAS member states through the publicity and extrajudicial advocacy of human rights NGOs working together with the judges of that court. On its part, the COMESA Court of Justice primarily enjoys the legitimacy of COMESA employees in large part because its restrictive interpretive approach has not appealed to traders or even human rights groups.

This chapter proceeds as follows. Part One provides a comprehensive introduction to the Court. Part Two discusses the decisions of the Court. Part Three reflects on the decisions of the Court in light of the experience of other subregional African courts with particular reference to the East African Court of Justice.

2 Introducing the COMESA Court of Justice

The Court of Justice for the Common Market for Eastern and Southern Africa (COMESA) is an 'organ of the Common Market' whose purpose is '[ensuring] the adherence to law in the interpretation and application of [the] Treaty'.[5] COMESA, established in 1994, is a nineteen-member free trade area with plans to become a customs union and eventually a monetary union.[6] The Court was established in 1998 at the Third Summit of the COMESA Authority in Kinshasa, Democratic Republic of Congo.[7] The Court has jurisdiction to 'adjudicate upon all matters which may be referred to it pursuant to [the] Treaty'.[8]

At the Seventh Summit of the COMESA Authority held 23–24 May 2002 in Addis Ababa, Ethiopia, the decision was made by the Authority, the highest decision-making organ in COMESA, to create an Appellate Division, thereby bifurcating the Court into a First Instance and an Appellate Division.[9] The First Instance Division functions as a trial court. Seven judges sit on the First Instance Division. The Appellate Division, on which five judges sit, serves as an appellate court over decisions of the First Instance Division.

The Court's initial location was within the COMESA Secretariat in Lusaka, Zambia.[10] In March of 2003, the COMESA Authority decided to relocate the seat of the Court to Khartoum, Sudan.[11] Sudan signed the agreement to host the Court in January 2004 but Sudan did not complete the courthouse until the summer of 2014.[12] The Court heard its first cases in Khartoum in the autumn of 2014.[13]

[5] Treaty Establishing the Common Market of Eastern and Southern Africa, Kampala, 8 December 1993, in force 8 December 1994, 2314 UNTS 265, Article7 [hereinafter Treaty Establishing COMESA].

[6] See James Gathii, *African Regional Trade Agreements as Legal Regimes*, (Oxford University Press, 2011).

[7] Reports and Decisions: Seventeenth Meeting of the COMESA Council of Ministers Report, 4–5 June 2004, Nile International Conference Centre, Kampala, Uganda.

[8] Treaty Establishing COMESA, Article23.

[9] Report and Decisions: Fifteenth Meeting of the COMESA Council of Ministers, 13–15 March 2003, Friendship Hall, Khartoum, Sudan.

[10] Ibid.

[11] *COMESA Court of Justice*, About COMESA (31 August 2014, 2:00 PM), available at http://about.comesa.int/index.php?option=com_content&view=article&id=83&Itemid=133.

[12] 'Sudan Hands Over $4.2m COMESA Court.' 25 August 2014, 8:00 PM), available at www.comesa.int/index.php?option=com_content&view=article&id=1230:comesa-court-handing-over-&catid=5:latest-news&Itemid=41.

[13] COMESA, 'COMESA Court Holds First Sitting in Sudan', September 2014 available at http://comesa.int/index.php?option=com_content&view=article&id=1326:comesa-court-holds-first-sitting-in-sudan&catid=5:latest-news&Itemid=41. (The building consists of two separate Court Chambers, one each to house the Court's First Instance Division and the Appellate Division. Of the $4.2 million dollars used to renovate the facility,

No more than two citizens of the same member state may sit on the Court.[14] The judges and the president of the Court are appointed by the Authority of the Common Market, which comprises the heads of state or government of the member states.[15] The Court may request the Authority to appoint additional members as need may arise.[16] The judges are immune from 'legal action for any act or omission committed in the discharge of their functions under [the] Treaty'.[17] The judges hold office for a period of five years and are eligible to be reappointed for another term of five years.[18] The president and judges are expected to hold their offices for their entire terms of appointment unless they pass away, resign or are removed from office for cause.[19]

Judges of the Court can only be removed from office by the Authority for 'misbehavior or for inability to perform the functions of his office due to infirmity of mind or body or due to any other specified cause'.[20]

The Court can entertain cases from COMESA member states, where a member state believes that another member state or the Council has failed to fulfil its duties under the Treaty or has 'infringed a provision of [the] Treaty'.[21] A member state may also bring to the Court's attention 'the legality of any act, regulation, directive or decision of the Council on the grounds that such act, regulation, directive or decision is ultra vires or unlawful or an infringement of the provisions of [the] Treaty or any rule of law relating to its application or amounts to a misuse or abuse of power'.[22]

The Secretary-General of COMESA is also permitted to bring certain issues before the Court.[23] Where the Secretary-General believes that a member state is not fulfiling its duties under the Treaty or has violated a provision of the Treaty, the Secretary-General must submit his findings to that particular member state so that that member state may in turn submit its own observations regarding those findings.[24] The member state has a period of two months during which to submit its observations.[25] If that time period expires or the member state's observations are not satisfactory, the Secretary-General is required to then refer the matter to the Bureau of the COMESA Council of Ministers, which will make a

$695,000 went toward furnishings and communications equipment, such that each Court Chamber contains information technology and interpretation equipment to enable the court to 'cater for up to 12 languages'.)

[14] Treaty Establishing COMESA Article20(1–2). [15] Ibid. Article20(1).
[16] Ibid. Article20(3). [17] Ibid. Article39. [18] Ibid. Article21(1).
[19] Ibid. Article21(2). [20] Ibid. Article22(1). [21] Ibid. Article24(1).
[22] Ibid. Article24(2). [23] Ibid. Article25(1). [24] Ibid. [25] Ibid. Article25(2).

determination as to whether the Secretary-General must then refer that matter to the Court or whether the matter must be referred to the Council.[26] In the event that the matter is referred to the Council and the Council is unable to resolve the issue, the Council will then instruct the Secretary-General to refer the matter to the Court.[27]

Residents of member states are also permitted to refer issues to the Court, where there are disputes as to 'the legality of any act, regulation, directive, or decision of the Council or of a Member State on the grounds that such act, directive, decision or regulation is unlawful or an infringement of the provisions of this Treaty'.[28] However, individuals must first have exhausted all other remedies in the national courts before referring the matter to the Court.[29]

The Court also has jurisdiction to adjudicate disputes between COMESA and its employees that pertain to the Staff Rules and Regulations of the Secretariat or the terms and conditions of employment with COMESA.[30] Additionally, the Court has jurisdiction to adjudicate claims made by individuals against COMESA as a result of the actions of COMESA's employees done in their capacity as employees of COMESA.[31] The Court may also hear and determine matters arising as a result of arbitration clauses contained within a contract that gives the Court jurisdiction to hear the matter, where COMESA or its institutions is a party, or with regard to issues that arise as a result of disputes between the member states as to the Treaty, and where the dispute is submitted to the Court 'under a special agreement between the member states concerned'.[32]

National courts may still have jurisdiction over matters where COMESA is a party, unless the COMESA Court of Justice is explicitly given jurisdiction under the Treaty for that particular issue.[33] Regarding the provisions of the Treaty, decisions of the Court will take precedence over decisions made in national courts regarding the provisions of the Treaty.[34]

The Court is allowed to make preliminary rulings on questions of the application or interpretation of the Treaty if the court or tribunal of the member state that is raising the question believes such a ruling will be necessary for it to come to a decision.[35] In such issues, if there is no judicial remedy available under the national law of that member state, then that

[26] Ibid. The Bureau of the Council of Ministers constitutes of its Chairperson, Vice-Chairperson and Rapporteur, *Ibid.* Article2.
[27] Ibid. Article25(3). [28] Ibid. Article26. [29] Ibid. [30] Ibid. Article27(1).
[31] Ibid. Article27(2). [32] Ibid. Article28. [33] Ibid. Article29(1).
[34] Ibid. Article29(2). [35] Ibid. Article30(1).

court or tribunal must refer the issue to the Court.[36] If a party discovers some new fact that might have had a significant effect on the judgement following the delivery of the judgement, and both the party and the Court were unaware of the fact and it could not have been discovered even with due diligence by the party, it can make an application for revision of the judgement to the Court.[37]

The Court also has the power to give advisory opinions about questions of law regarding the provisions of the Treaty that affect COMESA upon request from the Authority, the Council or a member state.[38] This request must be made in writing and specify clearly the question being asked.[39] The Court is still governed by the provisions of the treaty in exercising its advisory function.[40] In addition, judgements of the Court, if applicable, can govern the actions of the COMESA Customs Union.[41]

If necessary, the Court may issue interim orders, which have the same effect as final decisions of the Court.[42] Disputes that arise out of interpretation or application of the Treaty can only be settled by methods set out within the Treaty.[43] Once a judgement has been rendered, the member states must take whatever steps are necessary to implement the judgement of the Court.[44] In the event that a party defaults in implementing the Court's judgement, the Court is permitted to impose those sanctions it deems appropriate against that party.[45] In the event that the Court's judgement imposes a financial obligation on a person, the execution of that judgement will be governed by the rules of civil procedure as they exist in the member state where the execution of that judgement will take place.[46]

With the Court's permission, member states, the Secretary-General or a resident of a member state who are not parties to a particular case may intervene in that case.[47] However, they are limited to only providing evidence that supports or opposes the arguments of one of the parties to the case.[48] A recent addition to the jurisdiction of the Court arises from COMESA Competition Regulations under which an appeal may lie from decisions of the Board of Commissioners responsible for enforcing the regulations.[49]

36 Ibid. Article30(2). 37 Ibid. Article31(3). 38 Ibid. Article32(1).
39 Ibid. Article32(2). 40 Ibid. Article32(4).
41 Official Gazette of the Common Market for Eastern and Southern Africa, Volume 15, number One, 9 June 2009.
42 Treaty Establishing COMESAArticle35. 43 Ibid. Article34(1).
44 Ibid. Article34(3). 45 Ibid. Article34(4). 46 Ibid. Article40.
47 Ibid. Article36. 48 Ibid.
49 COMESA Competition Commission, FAQs – General, available at www.comesa.int/competition/?page_id=267.

3 Analysis of the Decisions of the COMESA Court of Justice

3.1 *Jurisdiction over Employment Disputes*

To recap briefly, Article 27(1) of the Treaty for the Establishment of COMESA provides that the COMESA Court of Justice shall have jurisdiction 'to hear disputes that arise out of the application and interpretation of the Staff Rules and Regulations of the Secretariat or the terms and conditions of employment of the employees of the Common Market'. The mere fact of a COMESA employee bringing a reference to the Court is therefore sufficient to trigger its jurisdiction.[50] Further, Article 28(a) of the Treaty for the Establishment of COMESA can confer jurisdiction on the Court by virtue of an arbitration clause in a contract to which COMESA or any of its institutions is a party. Where a contract in which COMESA or any of its institutions is a party specifies that the Court shall have jurisdiction but specifies an alternative dispute settlement system such as conciliation, parties must first exhaust those other alternatives before approaching the COMESA Court of Justice.[51] Even though internal dispute resolution mechanisms within COMESA must first be exhausted, the Court has asserted it has Article 27 jurisdiction to review the proceedings of such internal mechanisms.[52] In effect, the

[50] The Court has affirmed this jurisdiction in *Eastern and Southern African Trade and Development Bank v. Yvonne Nyagamukenga* (Ref. No. 3, Judgement of 18 September 2009) at p. 5 where the court held it has jurisdiction under Article 27 'to hear industrial disputes involving COMESA and its employees, arising out of the application and interpretation of the Staff Rules and Regulations of such institutions or the terms and conditions of employment of its staff members'.

[51] In *Eastern and Southern African Trade and Development Bank v. Yvonne Nyagamukenga* (Ref. No. 3, Judgement of 18 September 2009) at p. 5 the Court held: 'Article 27 of the Treaty does not specify the nature of jurisdiction regarding employment disputes. It seems clear to this Court that primary or first instance jurisdiction must be assumed where there are no internal dispute resolution mechanisms provided for in the terms and conditions of the contract. . .The Court ought not to assume primary jurisdiction in such cases where the parties have agreed in their contract as to the procedure for dispute resolution and such procedure has been complied with.' Notably, in *Eastern and Southern African Trade and Development Bank v. Yvonne Nyagamukenga* (Application of a Suspension Order Under Rule 75 of the Rules of the Court and Article 35 of the COMESA Treaty, Order of the Lord President dated 17 April 2007), the Court ordered COMESA not to proceed with enforcing an arbitral award against the applicant until the COMESA Court of Justice had had an opportunity to hear and determine the Applicant's case.

[52] *Eastern and Southern African Trade and Development Bank v. Yvonne Nyagamukenga* (Reference No. 3, Judgement 18 September 2009) at p. 5 where the Court held: 'However, where such internal dispute resolution mechanisms exists, there is nothing to preclude the Court from assuming its Article 27 jurisdiction in the form of review proceedings over decisions of internal mechanisms.' See also *COMESA v. Samuel Anderson Mwambazi*, Preliminary Application No. 2 of 2011 at p. 6 (Judgement of 23 November 2011).

Court has determined it has exclusive jurisdiction over COMESA employment law, which means that COMESA employees invariably choose to go to the Court even when they have the option of going to a national court that might be a more attractive forum.[53]

The Court has justified this power of reviewing its own judgements or rulings or decisions of an Arbitration Tribunal set up with the acquiescence of a national court as arising from the common law.[54] The East African Court of Justice's Appellate Division has cited with approval the COMESA Court of Justice's power of review of its own judgements (even though they are final) to justify a similar power of review.[55] Another source of the Court's review authority has been traced to Article 31(3) of the COMESA Treaty.[56] In *COMESA v. Kabeta Muleya*,[57] the COMESA Court of Justice held that this power of revision was contingent on discovery of

[53] Notably, the suspension of the Southern African Development Tribunal (SADC) in 2010 by the Heads of States of SADC, member states left SADC employees without a forum to bring their employment disputes. The High Court of Botswana (A SADC member state national court) in October 2011 successfully brought a case against SADC for failure to renew the employment contract of a Botswana citizen working for SADC. Thus even though the case involved interpretation of SADC rather than Botswana law, the Court nevertheless exercised jurisdiction noting that in the absence of the SADC Tribunal being able to decide the case, the SADC employee would be denied access to justice and that the Botswana High Court had jurisdiction to review the case on the basis of 'illegality, unlawfulness, irrationality or procedural irregularity,' see Gerhard Erasmus, 'High Court of Botswana Steps into Void Left by SADC Tribunal', TRALAC Trade Brief No. S14TBO3/2014 at p. 4.

[54] *Kabeta Muleya (Dr.) v. COMESA and others*, Reference No. 1 of 2003 (Judgement of 18 September 2009) at Paragraph 12 where the COMESA Court decided that it has 'jurisdiction under Article 27 to review the proceedings of the Arbitral Tribunal but only where such intervention is justified. The Court ought not to assume primary jurisdiction in such case where the parties have agreed in their contract as to the procedure for dispute resolution and such procedure has been complied with'. Notably, what was in issue in this case was whether the COMESA Court could review the decision of an Arbitration Tribunal in a dispute between COMESA and one of its employees. The Court decided that although it had jurisdiction to review those proceedings, there were no grounds for reviewing the Tribunal.

[55] *Independent Medical Legal Unit v. AG of Kenya*, here In the Matter of Application No. 2 of 2012 Arising from Appeal No.1 of 2012 available at http://eacj.huriweb.org/wp-content/uploads/2013/09/AG_MedLegalUnit_v_Kenya.pdf.

[56] Article 31(3) provides: 'An application for revision of a judgment may be made to the Court only if it is based upon the discovery of some fact which by its nature might have had a decisive influence on the judgment it had been known to the Court at the time the judgment was given, but which fact, at the time, was unknown both to the Court and the party making the application, and which could not, with reasonable diligence, have been discovered by that party before the judgment was made, or on account of some mistake or error on the face of the record.'

[57] Revision Application No. 1 of 2002.

some new fact(s) or on account of some mistake or error on the face of the record. Mistake or error cannot, however, be used to affect the substantive issues or the validity of the Court's judgement – it involves formalities such as 'misnaming of parties, errors in calculation, clerical mistakes or obvious slips that appear on the fact of the record which can be corrected without changing the validity or effect of the judgment'.[58] In essence, prior to the Court being split into a First and Appellate Division, it held that its revision jurisdiction did not amount to appellate jurisdiction.[59] Let us first look at the breakdown of the types of cases the COMESA Court of Justice has decided before proceeding to examine them more closely:

Nature of *cases[60]	Number of Cases	Status
Staff matters between COMESA and Institutions	26	Determined
Between governments	3	Determined
Between private sector and government	5	Determined
Between private sector and private sector	4	Determined[61]
COMESA institutions and COMESA	4	Determined
COMESA institutions and government	4	Determined
Revisions in reference	2	Determined
Advisory opinions	1	Pending
Appeals filed	2	One determined and one appeal pending

[58] *Eastern and Southern African Development Bank (PTA Bank) and Dr. Michael Gondwe v. Martin Ogang*, Reference Revision No. 1 of 2001.

[59] *COMESA v. Kabeta Muleya* Revision Application No. 1 of 2002 (ruling of 16 October 2002 at p. 5).

[60] This table comes from the Report of the Thirty Second Meeting of the COMESA Council of Ministers, Kinshasa, Democratic Republic of Congo, 22–24 February, 2014 Doc. CS/CM/XXXII/2(February, 2012) at paragraph 373 on p. 91.

[61] The COMESA Establishment Treaty does not provide for proceedings between private parties. Although the treaty (Article 28) does provide for jurisdiction in disputes arising from an arbitration clause, such jurisdiction only arises when the Common Market or any of its institutions or a COMESA member state is a party to such an arbitration clause. These four cases between the private sector must therefore have been wrongly categorized by COMESA.

What can one make of the fact that the largest portion of the docket of the COMESA Court of Justice consists of employment disputes? The disputes are primarily routine employment disputes.[62] These employment disputes do, however, reflect larger institutional questions that seem to have pervaded the newly formed COMESA institutions: Employees of COMESA's bank (the Preferential Trade Area (PTA) Bank), which faced allegations of corruption, repeatedly resorted to the Court. More cases arose from the decision to relocate the Bank's headquarters from Burundi to Kenya, resulting in laid-off employees filing suit. Further, the fact that the PTA Bank generated the bulk of employment disputes may itself not be surprising given that the Bank was one of COMESA's first institutions to be set up.

The most dramatic series of cases are those initiated by the president of the PTA Bank, Martin Ogang, against the PTA Bank. The case centered whether he had irregularly been removed from his position by the Bank's Board of Directors. This dispute spawned at least six concurrent applications after the original case contesting his removal. To illustrate how this particular case crowded the calendar of the newly formed COMESA Court of Justice, I will briefly go through the filings Mr Ogang made in the Court. The main case he brought was named Reference 1B of 2000 – it contested his removal as president of the PTA Bank as null and void and sought damages; Application 1A of 2000, which was filed concurrently with 1B, sought orders suspending the decision to remove him from office; on orders by the President of the Court to serve Application 1A on COMESA for an interparties hearing, Mr Ogang filed Application 1C ex parte, seeking to suspend orders to preempt a meeting of the Bank's Board of Governors that would have discussed his replacement. The Bank ignored the Court's orders and brought Reference 1D, in which it raised preliminary objections to the Court's jurisdiction in entertaining Reference 1B and applications 1A and 1C.

So bitter were the series of cases filed that in Application 1E, in which Mr. Ogang sought orders for contempt of court and sequestration of the Bank's property, the lawyers representing COMESA walked out of the court and declined to participate in the proceedings.[63] These contempt

[62] See, for example, *In the Matter of Nkurunziza and others v. Eastern and Southern African Trade and Development Bank*, Reference No. 1 of 2004, decision of 26 July 2006 (where the employees unsuccessfully challenged their termination as being inconsistent with COMESA Staff Manual rules requiring prior notification).

[63] *In the Matter of the Eastern and Southern African Trade and Development Bank* and *In the Matter of Sequestration Orders Against Eastern and Southern African Trade and*

proceedings arose from the fact that the president of the Court, pursuant to the Rules of the Court, had issued orders suspending and refraining the Bank and its agents from removing Mr Ogang from office until the case was heard and determined, and compelling them and the Bank's Board to reverse the decision terminating him as president. These decisions were issued ex parte and therefore without giving the Bank and its officers a chance to be heard before the decision. Subsequently, the COMESA Court of Justice reversed the decision as being inconsistent with the Rules of the Court requiring that such matters involve a hearing of both sides before a decision is rendered and further declined to issue orders to commit the Bank's officers to jail for contempt of court or sequestration of their property.[64] After the Court ordered Mr Ogang to be reinstated, a later decision overturned the reinstatement because one of the judges who had sat on that decision, Justice Ogoola, had not declared a meeting he had had with one of the respondents that created a conflict of interest.[65]

In a different stage of the prolonged proceedings, the Bank argued that the COMESA Treaty made it inviolable to suit by virtue of its privileges and immunities. The COMESA Court rejected this argument and held that the Bank is not exempt from its jurisdiction and that the Bank's

Development Bank and Committal to Civil Jail of Dr. Michael Gondwe, Kifle Hamza and Sylvia Kitonga, Reference No. 1B/2000 Ruling of 27 March 2000. See also *Martin Ogang v. Eastern and Southern African Development Bank and Others*, Preliminary Plea of Protest 1F/2000, decision of 28 March 2001 where the court held in its brief decision: 'The preliminary plea of protest filed by the First and Second Respondents, namely the PTA Bank and Michael Gondwe, was set down for hearing today. Although the Agents representing the Respondents were well aware of this hearing date of the preliminary plea of protest, they have not bothered to come to Court today to prosecute the same. We have no alternative, but as requested by Ochieng Oduol Esq appearing for the Applicant herein, Martin Ogang, to dismiss the preliminary plea of protest which we hereby do with costs for the Applicant.' In *Eastern and Southern African Trade and Development Bank v. Martin Ogang*, Reference 1B/200 judgement of 29 March 2001 at p. 13 the court said of the nonappearance of the respondent's lead counsel on a prior hearing date and the refusal of the assisting counsels to proceed with the case: 'This Court has a very tight schedule arising from the fact that it is composed of Judges from different countries, and we consider the omission of leading counsel to appear on the scheduled date to argue the application, and the refusal of his juniors to move the Court in terms of the application, a slight on this court. It is for Counsel to wait on the Court and not the Court to wait on Counsel. Such a situation is unacceptable and one for which the party asking deferment must be mulcated (sic) in costs.'

64 Ibid., at pp. 5 and 6.

65 *Eastern and Southern African Trade and Development Bank v. Martin Ogang*, Reference No. 2 of 2002 judgement of 21 October 2002.

charter 'is subservient to the Treaty which endowed the Court with jurisdiction over all organs and institutions of the Common Market inclusive of their employees'.[66] In yet another part of this series of litigation, Mr Ogang failed to convince the Court that the appointment of a new president of the Court and the appointment of an accounting firm to investigate allegations levelled against him for corruption had been done in violation of the rules governing the Bank or of COMESA law.[67] Repeat litigants like Ogang are not unique to the COMESA Court of Justice. Other African regional trade courts have had similar experiences. For example, in the ECOWAS Court of Justice, there is another series of employment cases brought by an especially litigious ECOWAS employee.[68] Indeed, employee cases dominate the caseload of many African trade courts.

One takeaway from these employment cases is the manner in which the new COMESA Court was overwhelmed with multiple employment cases and how it used its review authority to reverse decisions that were quickly being challenged within a short period. We also see COMESA institutions defending their employment decisions, particularly through their innovative use of the Court's review jurisdiction to reverse decisions they did not like. The backtracking by the COMESA Court in a number of its early employment decisions using this review jurisdiction very early in its existence says at least two things. First, the new Court was feeling the pressure of COMESA members in cases where it had ruled in favour

[66] *Eastern and Southern African Trade and Development Bank v. Martin Ogang*, Reference 1B/2000 judgement of 29 March 2001 at pp. 8–9 (holding that the Bank's immunity provisions are limited to national courts of member states). Notably, the Kenyan Court of Appeal rejected this argument regarding the immunity of the Bank in the national courts of member states by invoking the commercial activity exception, *Tononoka Steels Limited v. The Eastern and Southern Africa Trade and Development Bank*, Civil Appeal No. 255 of 1998. See also *In the Matter of Article 32 of the Treaty for the Establishment of the Common Market for Eastern and Southern Africa* and *In the Matter of the Rule 107 of the Rules of the Court of Justice of the Common Market for Eastern and Southern Africa 2006*, Reference No. 1 of 2013 (Advisory Opinion of the Court) at pp. 33–34 (where the COMESA Court of Justice followed the decision of the Kenyan Court of Appeal finding that COMESA and its institutions do not enjoy immunity for commercial transactions).

[67] *Martin Ogang v. Eastern and Southern African Trade and Development Bank*, Reference 1A/2000 and 1C/2000 judgement of 30 March 2001.

[68] Thanks to Laurence Helfer for pointing this out to me. These cases are *Mrs. Tokunbo Lijadu Oyemade v. Council of Ministers* and 4 Others, ECW/CCJ/APP/04/07 (2008); *Executive Secretary ECOWAS v. Mrs. Tokunbo Lijadu Oyemade*, ECW/CCJ/APP/04/06 and *Executive Secretary ECOWAS v. Mrs. Tokunbo Lijadu Oyemade*, ECW/CCJ/APP/05/06.

of employees. This trend would not augur well for a new court seeking to establish its credibility among COMESA member states. Second, the backtracking of the Court evidenced in the reversals of its pro-employee decisions is the only explanation available for the decision by COMESA member states to split the new Court into a First Instance and an Appellate Division. By splitting the Court, the members provided for a safety valve that guaranteed a right of appeal where they were unhappy with a decision of the First Instance Division. Fast forward to 2007, when Kenya was unhappy with a decision of another regional trade court, the East African Court of Justice, it quickly proposed amendments that split the court into a First Instance and an Appellate Division as an insurance mechanism to ensure the right of appeal for East African Community member states unhappy with that court's decisions.[69]

3.2 *Jurisdiction over Cases Involving the Conduct of COMESA Employees*

Article 27(2) provides that the Court 'shall have jurisdiction to determine claims by any person against the Common Market or its institutions for acts of their servants or employees in the performance of their duties'. Dr. Kabeta Muleya invoked the Court's jurisdiction alleging that the Secretary-General of COMESA had defamed him by publishing untrue words about him that damaged his professional reputation and had made it difficult for him to obtain employment.[70] He sought damages for libel and an injunction restraining COMESA from further publishing the defamatory words. The case had arisen from a suit to reinstate Dr Kabeta Muleya as a COMESA employee in the COMESA Court of Justice. Having won the case, COMESA issued a press release stating in part that the Court had decided not to reinstate Dr Muleya 'on the basis of poor performance'.[71] The Court awarded Dr Kabeta Muleya USD 2,000 for the libelous press release.[72] It is notable that this decision has been repeatedly cited in Kenyan courts for the proposition that damages, rather than

[69] For more on this and other backlashes against Africa's international courts, see K. Alter, J. Gathii, and L. Helfer, 'Backlash against international courts in West, East and Southern Africa: Causes and consequences', *European Journal of International Law*, 27 (2016), 293–328.

[70] *Kabeta Muleya (Dr.) v. COMESA and Erastus J.O. Mwencha*, Reference No. 1 of 2003

[71] *Kabete Muleya (Dr) v. COMESA*, Reference No. 1 of 2003, decision of the First Instance Decision delivered at Khartoum, Sudan 1st of July 2003 at p. 2.

[72] Ibid., at p. 8.

compelling an employer to reemploy a dismissed employee through an order of specific performance, is the appropriate common law remedy for a breach of a contract of service.[73]

Insofar as I can tell, no other African subregional trade court has jurisdiction to entertain tort claims. The COMESA Treaty also permits the Court to give monetary relief to a party.[74] The ECOWAS Court of Justice has similar powers of issuing monetary relief, but neither the East African Court of Justice nor the Southern Africa Development Community Court (SADC) Tribunal have such power.

3.3 *Exhaustion of Domestic Remedies*

Unlike the treaties establishing the EACJ, the ECCJ or the SADC Tribunal, the treaty that establishes the COMESA Court of Justice requires an exhaustion of domestic remedies.[75] This rule of customary international law seeks to balance two competing interests. First, it gives the country where a claim arises the opportunity to have its courts decide the availability of a local remedy before an international remedy is sought. Second, it gives a claimant an opportunity to seek an international remedy where the local remedy was not available, effective or adequate. As I show later, this rule has been a major reason accounting for the dearth of cases brought to the Court.[76]

In the 2001 case of *Republic of Kenya and the Commissioner of Lands v. Coastal Aquaculture*,[77] the issue was whether the applicant in the case had exhausted domestic remedies. The applicant filed the case to stop the

[73] See, for example, *Zadock Liyosi Mmberia v. St. Mark's Church Westlands*, Industrial Court of Kenya Cause No. 1216 of 2012 available at http://kenyalaw.org/caselaw/cases/view/87655.

[74] This power arises by virtue of Article 40 of the COMESA Establishment Treaty, which provides in the relevant part that 'the execution of a judgment of the Court which imposes a pecuniary obligation on a person shall be government by the rules of civil procedure in force in the Member State in which execution is to take place.'

[75] Article 26 of the Treaty for the Establishment of COMESA which provides in the relevant part 'Provided that where the matter for determination relates to any act, regulation or decision by a Member State, such person shall not refer the matter for determination under this Article unless he has first exhausted local remedies in the national courts or tribunals of the Member State.'

[76] The immediate former President of the Court has made this point as well. See Philip Muyanga, 'COMESA Court Underutilized, Senior Counsel Nzamba Kitonga Says,' Daily Nation, 1 August 2015 available at http://nation.co.ke/news/Comesa-court-underutilised-Nzamba-Kitonga-/-/1056/2816492/-/xo384z/-/index.html.

[77] Reference No. 3 of 2001.

Government of Kenya from compulsorily acquiring its two pieces of land and jeopardizing its investment worth over US$ 24 million. The applicant had already prevailed in the High Court and the Court of Appeal in Kenya (the highest court at the time) in stopping the acquisitions as being inconsistent with Kenyan law. The case before the COMESA Court of Justice arose when the government engaged in a third attempt to compulsorily acquire the applicant's property. Rather than go back to Kenyan courts, the applicant argued before the COMESA Court of Justice that the continued attempts by the Kenyan government to compulsorily acquire its property disabled it to continue with its investment projects worth US$ 24 million in preoperational expenses. The COMESA Court of Justice was preferred over Kenyan courts because of the uncertainty arising from the repeated acquisition attempts and the lack of a satisfactory settlement. The applicant contended that it was experiencing an 'unbearable situation for which the national courts are powerless to provide relief'.[78] Although the COMESA Court of Justice expressed 'sympathy' with the applicant arising from the 'frustration' of its projects, it held that there was no exhaustion of domestic remedies because the applicant had withdrawn a case before the Kenyan High Court just before filing the case in the COMESA Court of Justice.[79] In this sense, the COMESA Court of Justice was dodging having to decide a politically sensitive case from one of the more powerful COMESA members by hiding behind the technicality that there was no exhaustion of remedies. This was notwithstanding the fact that the applicant had prevailed in previous cases in Kenya, and that the government had nevertheless continued in its efforts to compulsorily acquire its property.

More than a decade later in *The Republic of Mauritius v. Polytol Paints and Adhesives Manufacturers Co. Ltd.*, the First Instance Division of the Court re-interpreted the circumstances under which the rule of exhaustion of domestic remedies applies. The First Instance Division did so by not strictly applying this rule as it had in the *Aquaculture* case. Hence in *Polytol*, the Court held that domestic remedies ought to be considered to have been exhausted where the applicant could not be expected to get an effective and sufficient remedy even though the *Polytol* applicant had not exhausted administrative remedies available to it after the highest Mauritian rejected Polytol's case a second time.

It is quite clear that in the 2001–2 period when the *Aquaculture* case was argued and decided, the Kenyan government had an extremely

[78] Ibid., at p. 10. [79] Ibid., at p. 10.

authoritarian president. The Court may have been unwilling at that early stage in its life to antagonise Kenya and risk a backlash against it. In fact, in the 2001–2 period, no other subregional court in Africa was in operation. The COMESA Court of Justice had started its operations in 2000.[80] It was not until 2005 that the East African Court of Justice decided its first case. The SADC Tribunal decided its first case in 2007. The ECOWAS Court of Justice decided its important human rights cases only after its jurisdiction was extended in 2005. Clearly, the COMESA Court of Justice was established at a moment when the forces of democratisation and human rights – particularly human rights groups – had not coalesced as much as they had a few years later. For example, when the Mike Campbell case was filed in 2007 against Zimbabwe challenging land acquisitions in the SADC Tribunal, the case was framed as a violation of the right not to be discriminated against on the basis of race, deprivation of property without due process and denial of access to Zimbabwe's courts.[81] What is remarkable is that to date, although the COMESA Treaty has similar aspirational language on human rights as the East African and SADC Establishment Treaties, no cases have been decided arising from these human rights clauses. I will return to this point in the conclusion.

In *Itelsolmac v. Rwanda Civil Aviation Authority*,[82] the First Instance Division of the COMESA Court of Justice held that a party seeking to show impossibility of exhausting domestic remedies occasioned by the conduct of a COMESA member state 'must produce clear evidence of the steps he took in the pursuit of the local remedies and describe the nature of the acts used by the State party or its agents to prevent him from accessing the local remedies... Bald and unsubstantiated allegations of obstruction by the State party would not meet the standard of proof required'.[83] In this case involving a claim of contractual breach, a Ugandan company alleged that it had unsuccessfully tried to hire eight law firms and that all of them were reluctant to 'prosecute its claim against the government of Rwanda'.[84] The First Instance Division held that there

[80] Address by Hon. Yatin Varma, AG of Mauritius, at the COMESA Court of Justice Retreat, Intercontinental Hotel, Balaclava, Mauritius, 12–16 July 2010, available at http://attorneygeneral.gov.mu/English/Documents/Speeches/speech-12%20july%202010.pdf.

[81] See S. T. Ebobrah, 'Human rights developments in African sub-regional economic communities during 2010', *African Human Rights Law Journal*, 11 (2011), 216.

[82] Reference No. 1 of 2009 (Ruling of 7 May 2010). [83] Ibid., at p. 11.

[84] Ibid., at p. 11.

was no evidence that met its clear evidence threshold that the applicant had vigorously pursued local remedies for resolution of the case.

In a case instituted against the government of Burundi for preventing the PTA Bank from leasing its building in Bujumbura, Burundi, to the United Nations Development Programme, the issue arose whether the exhaustion of domestic remedies was a prerequisite in a case arising from an international agreement between the PTA Bank and the government of Burundi.[85] In the proceedings, the PTA Bank sought orders to compel the government of Burundi to enter into arbitration proceedings as required by their agreement. Burundi failed to appear in the proceedings and the Bank prevailed. According to the Court, it was effectively being invited to rule on the legality of the decision of the government of Burundi to prohibit the leasing of the building, even though the Bank had not shown the government was about to commit such conduct. More significantly, the Court found that the Bank had not exhausted domestic remedies. This reasoning was not convincing because the agreement between it and the government of Burundi provided for determination through arbitration.[86] The decision reflected the reluctance of the COMESA Court of Justice to rule against governments, even when those governments do not appear before it.

The upshot of these decisions of the COMESA Court of Justice on the exhaustion of domestic remedies is that they have served to effectively foreclose substantive determinations against COMESA member states. One may regard this approach as legal diplomacy – a strategy of avoiding decisions that would in essence constitute a review of sovereign decisions and prerogatives. This self-constraining strategy adopted by the COMESA Court of Justice may very well reflect its reluctance to adopt expansionist interpretations that may put it on a collision course with member states. In fact, expansionist decision making among Africa's subregional courts has been met with backlash and in one instance the suspension of a court.[87] This careful attitude in declining to reverse member states is reflected in the COMESA Court of Justice case in *Itelsolmac*. Here, the Court gave no weight to evidence that strongly suggested that the government of Rwanda had rendered obtaining a domestic remedy impossible. In the PTA Bank case, discussed earlier, Burundi prevailed even after failing to appear before the Court. The

[85] *Eastern and Southern African Trade and Development (PTA Bank) v. The Republic of Burundi represented by the Minister of Justice*, Reference No. 1 of 2006 and Applications No. 1 and 2 of 2006 (Decision of the First Instance Division of 16th August 2006).

[86] Ibid., at p. 9.

[87] See Alter, Gathii, and Helfer, 'Backlash against international courts'.

COMESA Court of Justice has shown little creativity in its interpretations of the exhaustion of domestic remedies. It has narrowly construed impossibility of getting domestic remedies in a way that has discouraged cases from coming to its docket. This strict interpretation of the exhaustion of domestic remedies has provided COMESA member states lots of wiggle room not to have to defend themselves in the Court. This deference to COMESA member states is demonstrated by how the Court ignored and justified the nonappearance of states in cases filed in the Court. It did so by invoking the exhaustion of domestic remedies rule to dismiss cases on its own motion. This is very much unlike the East African Court of Justice, which declined the invitation to find the exhaustion of domestic remedies was a customary international law rule in a way that would have achieved the same pro-member state results as the series of decisions of the COMESA Court of Justice have done. Unsurprisingly, by excluding the applicability of the exhaustion of domestic remedies rule, the East African Court of Justice has had a much broader array of cases coming before it.

3.4 *The Republic of Mauritius v. Polytol Paints and Adhesives Manufacturers Co. Ltd.*

The COMESA Court of Justice is the only African Trade IC that has received what is purely a trade dispute. *The Republic of Mauritius v. Polytol Paints and Adhesives Manufacturers Co. Ltd.* was filed in 2012 after the applicants had exhausted domestic remedies.[88] The applicant was a Mauritian manufacturer and seller of auto parts among other things. They imported paints from Egypt, another COMESA member with no customs duty; as of 1 November 2000, Mauritius removed customs duties from COMESA member states. Thereafter, Mauritius re-imposed a 40 per cent duty on the paint products, and the applicant paid customs duties. The Mauritian Supreme Court dismissed the applicant's claim that the payments constituted a violation of COMESA Treaty law on the basis that the Treaty was not enforceable by domestic courts. The COMESA Court dismissed Mauritius's application challenging its jurisdiction and the locus standi of the applicant to bring the case.[89]

[88] Reference No. 1 of 2012.

[89] *The Republic of Mauritius (Applicant) v. Polytol Paints and Adhesives Manufacturers Co. Ltd.*, Preliminary Application No. 1 of 2012 (Arising from Reference No. 1 of 2012) Decision of the COMESA Court of Justice, First Instance Division, Ruling of 6 December 2012.

What is also really important about this case is that it gave the First Instance Division an opportunity to talk about the nature of COMESA Treaty obligations for member states. Noted the Court, 'Any Member State that acts contrary to the Treaty cannot, therefore, plead the nature of its legal system as a defence when citizens or residents of that State are prejudiced by its acts. This is clearly stipulated in Article 27 of the Vienna Convention on the Law of Treaties, 1969 which provides that "[a] party may not invoke the provisions of its internal law as justification for its failure to perform a treaty".'[90] Recently, the COMESA Council of Ministers invoked this observation by the Court in its review of COMESA Treaties and Protocols that had not been domesticated by member states and urged member states to domesticate all outstanding obligations by the end of 2014.[91]

3.5 *Legitimacy Implications Arising from These Cases*

While international courts have engaged in an ever-increasing number of functions, the COMESA Court of Justice has confined itself to primarily resolving employment disputes. Unlike the East African Court of Justice, which has gone out of its way to develop jurisdiction to decide human rights cases even while it has no explicit treaty basis for doing so, the COMESA Court of Justice has been content not to use its interpretive authority expansively. Courts like the East African Court of Justice contribute to the legitimisation of human rights even though it was established as a trade court.[92] Why has the COMESA Court of Justice avoided going beyond resolving employment disputes to promoting the rule of law and human rights like the East African Court of Justice?[93] As Geir Ulfstein argues, the different functions of the international courts carry implications that require different methods of assessing their legitimacy.[94] For example, the impression that international courts are only legitimised by state consent may inadequately capture the importance of international

[90] Ibid.

[91] Report of the Thirty Second Meeting of the COMESA Council of Ministers, Kinshasa, Democratic Republic of Congo, 22–24 February, 2014 Doc. CS/CM/XXXII/2 (February, 2012) at paragraph 46.

[92] Geir Ulfstein, 'International courts and judges: Independence, interaction, and legitimacy', *NYU. Journal of International Law and Politics*, 46 (2014), 849 (discussing the increased judicialization of the international legal order and the legitimacy of international courts).

[93] Ibid., 861. [94] Ibid., 861.

courts to various constituencies. Thus, although the COMESA Court of Justice lacks legitimacy among human rights NGOs who do not take cases there, it is quite clear that employees of COMESA accept its normative and descriptive legitimacy. I adopt Ulfstein's definition of normative legitimacy as being centered on an 'analysis of whether an institution is worthy of support and whether its decisions merit deference', and descriptive legitimacy as resting 'on whether the actors accept the institution's authority and that the actors are therefore willing to implement even unpopular decisions'.[95]

To the extent that COMESA States so far appear indifferent to the Court because they do not provide strong support for it or file cases there demonstrates that from their perspective it has no normative or descriptive legitimacy. In addition, they have not had any reason to want to curb any of its decisions so far. COMESA employees and institutions appear to accept the COMESA Court of Justice's descriptive and normative legitimacy. By contrast, actors external to COMESA such as human rights NGOs or business actors do not.

Considering whether the COMESA Court of Justice has normative legitimacy goes beyond asking whether the following minimal criteria for assessing legitimacy have been met. First, whether the court is composed of competent and appropriate judges. Second, the court fulfils certain procedural requirements, such as providing due process for all affected parties. Third, whether the court properly applies the applicable law as consented through ratification by member states. Last, whether the court produces judgements and rulings that are actually adhered to.[96] Going by these minimalist criteria, COMESA employees perceive the COMESA Court of Justice as having the legitimacy and right to decide their employment disputes – particularly because, as I noted earlier, the Court has construed its jurisdiction over COMESA employment cases as exclusive.[97]

[95] Ibid., 862. For other ways of thinking about legitimacy, see also Armin von Bogdandy, 'The democratic legitimacy of international courts: A conceptual framework', *Theoretical Inquiries in Law*, 14 (2013), 361 (arguing international courts are legitimate when they are worthy of public support); Nienke Grossman, 'The normative legitimacy of international courts', *Temple Law Review*, 86 (2013), 61 and 64, (arguing that one has to look beyond state consent to factor such as moral, political and legal theory to determine the legitimacy of a court) and J. Pauwelyn, R. A. Wessel, and Jan Wouters, 'When structures become shackles: Stagnation and dynamics in international lawmaking', *European Journal of International Law*, 25, 3 (2014), 733 (arguing that we must look beyond 'the framework of traditional actors, processes, and outputs' to establish the legitimacy of courts).

[96] Ulfstein, 'International courts and judges', 864.

[97] Ibid., 864.

In summary, therefore, even though the COMESA Court of Justice does have the legitimacy to decide employment disputes, this legitimacy does not expand beyond that to include other groups such as human rights or business actors. In addition, it does not extend to COMESA states who have all hardly brought any cases against each other in the Court. To the extent that the COMESA Court of Justice's docket is so limited means we have to expand our inquiry of its legitimacy beyond formal inquiries as to whether the Court is composed of competent and appropriate judges, fulfils certain procedural requirements or whether it applies the applicable law as consented through ratification by member states.[98] The next part of this chapter explores the factors that have limited the expansion of the Court's docket beyond these criteria. These additional important criteria include whether there are well-organized constituencies who regularly bring cases to the Court and who are willing and ready to defend the Court when it is under assault and the location of the Court as well as the kind of message the interpretive approach (e.g. restrictive or expansionist) sends to constituencies who might then consider using the Court.

4 Factors That Have Limited the Development of the COMESA Court

4.1 Cases and Constituencies

The fact that the overwhelming number of cases that have come before the COMESA Court of Justice are employment disputes has effectively turned the Court into an industrial court for resolving disputes between COMESA and its institutions, on the one hand, and its employees, on the other. The Court has not created a cause of action in human rights like the East African Court of Justice has done. This has not served the COMESA Court of Justice well in building organised constituencies like human rights or environmental groups to bring cases to the Court. Because states in Africa rarely bring cases in African subregional courts against each other, and since it is lacking in other mobilized constituencies to bring cases that it

[98] See also R. F. Oppong, 'Legitimacy of regional economic courts in Africa', *African Journal of Legal Studies*, 7 (2014), 84–5 (examining legitimacy of Africa's international courts to include concerns such as their actual day-to-day operations, their liberal interpretations on standing, 'willingness to take on difficult and controversial subjects, desire to enhance their physical accessibility, and the fairness of their procedures').

could use to build its reputation, the Court has remained relatively obscure unlike other subregional courts such as the East African Court of Justice.

The COMESA Court of Justice inherited its jurisdiction over employment disputes from an industrial court that preceded the formation of COMESA, the Preferential Trade Area Administrative Appeals Tribunal. The accessibility of the Court for employees became evident in the initial series of cases that the COMESA Court of Justice decided, such as those involving PTA Bank President Martin Ogang. Those cases lay the foundation for future cases.

In my view, there are a number of reasons why employment cases do not augur well for enhancing broad legitimacy of a new court such as the COMESA Court of Justice. First, employment cases are often very nasty, with mudslinging accompanied by embarrassing disclosures. That kind of dirty laundry cannot enhance the visibility, profile and stature of a court. Second, given that employment cases are by far the largest number of cases on the COMESA Court of Justice docket, this means these cases cannot be marginalised in the Court's efforts to publicise the potential utility or effectiveness of the Court. Thus it may not be surprising that litigants and bar associations have largely stayed away from the Court.

As noted earlier, a primary reason for the COMESA Court of Justice not becoming like the East African Court of Justice, the SADC Tribunal or the ECOWAS Court of Justice has to do with its having started operations in 2001 – a few years before organised interest groups, particularly bar associations that have been critical in bringing cases before these subregional courts, were organised and mobilised around these new international courts. The East African Court of Justice established the human rights cause of action in 2005, the same year that in West Africa, the treaty was amended to give the ECOWAS Court of Justice jurisdiction over human rights. The Campbell case that brought prominence to the SADC Tribunal was first handed down in 2007. In short, timing was of the essence.

To date, there is no regional bar association around COMESA as there is with regard to the East African Community, ECOWAS and SADC. With nineteen very diverse member states, COMESA may be too large for such a bar association. There are countries using Roman-Dutch law (e.g. South Africa, Zimbabwe, Namibia and Swaziland), civil law (e.g. Angola and Mozambique) and common law (e.g. Kenya and Uganda), and a mix of common and civil law countries (such as Mauritius) within COMESA. The countries vary widely in other ways – from countries with extremely repressive governments like Sudan to others with democratically elected governments and very active civil society groups like

Kenya; from countries like Egypt that are relatively wealthy, to small, least-developed economies like Swaziland. This makes it hard to have collaboration among the various members of the bar in the COMESA region in the same way that lawyers in the relatively homogenous East African Community have formed an extremely active regional bar association, the East African Law Society, which litigates repeatedly before the East African Court of Justice.[99]

The judges of the East African Court of Justice capitalised on opportunities to decide controversial cases, such as the *Katabazi* decision of 2007, which created a cause of action for human rights. These cases legitimised the East African Court of Justice as an independent actor not subject to the political control of the executive organs of the EAC nor beholden to the conservative and positivist judicial tendencies that characterise national judiciaries. Further, every subsequent set of EACJ judges has demonstrated forcefulness in some decisions balanced with well-measured decisions.

In addition, unlike the COMESA Court of Justice, the EACJ was established at a moment when a new ideational context involving respect for human rights and constitutional governance was taking shape.[100] This new context arose in part as a result of dramatic social and political changes in East Africa during which one-party states gave way to varying degrees of multiparty democracy and competitive politics. For the first time since independence from colonial rule, civil society groups, especially in the human rights, pro-democracy and rule of law arenas, emerged and became established players in initiatives to hold their governments accountable for excesses that had often gone unchallenged under authoritarian rule.[101] The judges of the court worked closely with

[99] Other scholars studying international courts in the developing country context have also observed the importance of having NGOs and civil society groups interacting with the judges, bringing cases and defending an international court as critical to its trajectory in engaging in expansionist judicial decision-making, see L. Helfer and K. Alter, 'Nature or nurture? Judicial law making in the European Court of Justice and the Andean Tribunal of Justice', *International Organization*, 64 (2010), 563.

[100] East African Court of Justice Strategic Plan (2010–2015) at 10 (noting that the court operates in a context where there 'has been an upsurge in advocacy for good governance, human rights and democracy' and the fact that East African citizens 'are more enlightened and more knowledgeable about their rights', as well as 'more assertive and demanding').

[101] The spread and effectiveness of the civil society movement in the five East African countries is very uneven. Kenya certainly has the best organized civil society movement, particularly in the rule of law, democracy and human rights sectors, followed by Uganda, Tanzania, Burundi, and Rwanda. Interview with Leading Civil Society Member, in East Africa (Oct. 2012).

these civil society groups, in particular the East African Law Society, in defining the court's place among the EAC organs.[102] The judges of the COMESA Court of Justice were not favoured with a similar ideational context or interest groups like the East African Court of Justice. In this context, it becomes clear why the efforts to popularise the COMESA Court of Justice have not worked as well as those in East Africa.[103]

4.2 Location Matters

Another major limitation that has faced the COMESA Court of Justice is its location. Lusaka, Zambia, is an inconvenient location for litigants and their lawyers. To fully appreciate the importance of location for a court, let us look at the East African Court of Justice, which is based in Arusha, Tanzania.

A cadre of regional human rights lawyers, activists, academics, organisers, and civil society groups, led by the East African Law Society, Kituo Cha Katiba and the East African Civil Society Organizations' Forum, have coalesced in Arusha and have played a catalytic role in the establishment of the human rights practice before the Court[104] and bringing together a unique skill set and a vibrant community. The growth in the EACJ's caseload is the result of this cadre's success in convincing the judges that the Court should take human rights cases. Informal contacts, media campaigns, appeals to donors, meetings in EAC countries, conferences, symposia and workshops all played an important role in building the space within which the Court operates.

This coalescence has been facilitated by the location in Arusha of the headquarters of the EAC and other human rights and international law-oriented groups, including the African Court of Human and Peoples' Rights, the African Union Advisory Board on Corruption, the International

[102] Ibid. E-mail correspondence with an official at the Raoul Wallenberg Institute between November and December 2012 confirmed that the cooperation between the Court and the Institute started in 2003, was funded by the Swedish government, and was initiated by the Swedish Embassy in Nairobi. That cooperation continues to date. See 'Training for the East African Court of Justice', *Raoul Wallenberg Institute of Human Rights and Humanitarian Law* (9 October 2013), http://rwi.lu.se/training-east-african-court-justice/ (last visited 26 January 2014). ('The Institute is currently conducting a two-week training in Nairobi for the judges of the East African Court of Justice, as part of its cooperation programme with the Court under the Regional Africa Programme.')

[103] For an extensive analysis, see Gathii, 'Mission creep or a search for relevance'.

[104] See Interview with Human Rights Advocate L, in Arusha, Tanzania (30 July 2013).

Criminal Court for Rwanda, which has now wound up its operations and been replaced by the Mixed International Criminal Tribunal, and the African Institute of International Law.[105] Arusha has been flush with donor funding as a destination of choice for regional human rights and trade meetings.[106] Unsurprisingly, the EACJ has now expanded its docket of possibilities to include environmental cases following the important decision that barred the government of Tanzania from building a highway across the Serengeti National Park – the series of decisions from the EACJ over a two-year period helped catapult domestic and international support both for the Court and against environmental damage of a United Nations Educational, Scientific and Cultural Organization (UNESCO) World Heritage site.[107]

Contrast this with Lusaka, Zambia, where there is nearly nothing like the international institutions and NGOs present in Arusha. Further, now the COMESA Court has been relocated to Khartoum, Sudan. Khartoum is difficult for human rights groups to get to because of President Bashir's dictatorial rule and his repression of human rights groups who have supported his indictment at the International Criminal Court. In fact, it is quite paradoxical that the COMESA Court of Justice is now located in a country that has shown little regard for international courts.

4.3 *Restrictive Interpretive Approach*

The East African Court of Justice and the SADC Tribunal established their profiles because of their broad constructions of their Establishment Treaties. Although neither were explicitly conferred with a human rights jurisdiction, they nevertheless decided they had jurisdiction to decide human rights cases. Both these ICs (EACJ and SADC Tribunal) read preambular human rights commitments as proper sources of law upon which litigants could sue and decisions made to establish if state conduct was consistent with these commitments.

Like the Treaty for the Establishment of the East African Community, the COMESA Treaty includes as part of the Fundamental Principles

[105] African Union [AU], Decision on the Establishment of an African Institute of International Law in Arusha, the United Republic of Tanzania, 18th Ordinary Sess., Doc. Assembly/AU/14 (XVIII) Add.5 (29–30 Jan. 2012).

[106] Interview with EACJ Appellate Judge A and President, in Arusha, Tanzania (30 July 2013); Interview with EACJ Judge B of the First Instance Division (Principle Judge), in Arusha, Tanzania (30 July 2013).

[107] See J. Gathii, 'Saving the Serengeti: The new judicial environmentalism of Africa's international courts', *Chicago Journal of International Law*, 16, 2 (2016), 386–438.

of COMESA, the 'recognition and observance of the rule of law' (Article 6(g)); the 'recognition, promotion and protection of human and peoples' rights in accordance with the provisions of the African Charter on Human and Peoples Rights' (Article 6(e)); and 'the promotion and sustenance of a democratic system of governance in each Member State' (Article 6(h)). Why have litigants not asked the COMESA Court of Justice to interpret these provisions? Quite clearly, a major reason is that the Court sent a signal to potential litigants in the 2002 *Aquaculture* case against Kenya that it would read the exhaustion of domestic remedies rule restrictively. The 2002 *Aquaculture* case against the government of Kenya challenging the acquisition of an investor's property was the first time an African government had been challenged in a subregional court. This perhaps explains the COMESA Court of Justice's strict application of the exhaustion of domestic remedies rule. Ten years after the *Aquaculture* case, the COMESA Court of Justice in *The Republic of Mauritius v. Polytol Paints and Adhesives Manufacturers Co. Ltd.* abandoned its strict application of the exhaustion rule by holding it did not apply where the applicant could not be expected to get an effective and sufficient remedy from the highest national court even though not all other administrative remedies available had been exhausted. A major difference between this 2012 decision and the 2002 decision in *Aquaculture* is that unlike *Aquaculture*, which was a direct challenge to the exercise of a sovereign prerogative in acquiring land, *Polytol* was a classic trade case involving a tariff. So it is not entirely clear how the COMESA Court of Justice would respond to a case raising primarily human rights rather than trade issues.

In fact, if one considers that human rights cases often receive unfavourable reception in many COMESA member states, it follows that having a restrictive interpretation of the exhaustion of domestic remedies acts as a difficult barrier. This is because even national courts are often wary of deciding human rights cases and so they languish long in national courts. Bringing a human rights case in the COMESA Court of Justice therefore makes it hard for an applicant to prove that all remedies have been exhausted. The extent to which the exhaustion of domestic remedies rule has been narrowly construed means that unlike the East African Court of Justice, the COMESA Court of Justice has not become a platform for opposition activists to antagonise member states – something perhaps the judges of the COMESA Court of Justice prefer not to do.[108]

[108] The East African Court of Justice angered the Kenyan government following a decision challenging its slate of representatives for the East African Legislative Assembly. Kenya

The East African Court of Justice's decision in *Katabazi v. Uganda* is illustrative of the kind of jurisdictional expansion that the COMESA Court has avoided. In that case, involving the arrest by state agents within the precincts of the High Court of Uganda of citizens who had just been released on bail, the East African Court of Justice determined that while it did not have jurisdiction over human rights, 'it will not abdicate from exercising its jurisdiction of interpretation under Article 27(1) [of the EAC Establishment Treaty] merely because the [case] includes allegation[s] of human rights violation[s]'.[109] In other words, the EACJ held that it could not abdicate its responsibility to interpret the provisions of the EAC Treaty, including those relating to the rule of law, human rights and democracy even though the Establishment Treaty explicitly provided that it would be granted jurisdiction over human rights at a future date. Moreover, it held that Article 23, which provides that the EACJ 'shall ensure the adherence to law', conferred jurisdiction on it to decide cases involving human rights because the Establishment Treaty included references to human rights.[110] The Court referred to Articles 5(1), 6, 7(2), and 8 (1)(c), which refer to human rights, the rule of law, good governance and democracy, and held that partner states were obliged to comply with these provisions.[111] Citing cases from the African Commission on Human and Peoples' Rights and from the United Kingdom, the East African Court of Justice held that it had an obligation to 'provide a check on the exercise of the responsibility ... to protect the rule of law'.[112] The EACJ held that to accept Uganda's defence that the rearrest and detention of the complainants had been necessary for security reasons 'would lead to an unacceptable and dangerous precedent, which would undermine the rule of law'.[113] This case created a cause of action based on the preambular provisions relating to human rights, the rule of law, good governance and democracy that has opened the doors of the East African Court of Justice to many human rights cases.

The restrictive interpretive approach of the COMESA Court of Justice is a major reason that explains why it has not engaged in such expansive judicial decision making as the East African Court of Justice has done.

then quickly and successfully lobbied the other East African Community member states to restrict the jurisdiction of the court. The COMESA Court has avoided such a backlash or even the possibility of a suspension as happened to the SADC Tribunal following unpopular decisions against Zimbabwe's land reform program.

109 *Katabazi v. Uganda*, Ref. No. 1 of 2007 at p. 16. 110 Ibid., at p. 23.

111 Ibid., at pp. 15–23. 112 Ibid. 113 Ibid., at p. 22.

Further, its geographical inaccessibility to human rights NGOs because of its location, first in Lusaka, Zambia, and currently in Khartoum, Sudan, makes it an unlikely venue to repeatedly nudge it in the same direction as the East African Court of Justice. The fact that there is no regional bar association that is specific to the COMESA region is a further explanation accounting for the fact that only those with access to it, primarily COMESA employees, are the ones most likely to use it.

5 Conclusion

The COMESA Court of Justice shares one commonality with other subregional African trade judiciaries – its docket hardly includes cases relating to the trade commitments that the COMESA member states have entered into. While other subregional courts in Africa have predominantly decided human rights cases, the COMESA Court of Justice has primarily decided employment disputes between COMESA and its employees.

This chapter advances four key arguments that account for the COMESA Court of Justice becoming an employment dispute tribunal more than an international trade court over the last several years: First, the significance of timing with regard to when the Court started its work, second the lack of mobilised constituencies, third, the Court's location and fourth, the interpretive approach pursued by the Court. I summarise the claims on each of these points next.

First, unlike the other subregional trade courts, the COMESA Court of Justice started its operations in a political context in which African governments were particularly hostile to judicial oversight of any nature. According to Freedom House, the year 2001 was characterised by 'little evidence of forward momentum towards greater openness' in Africa.[114] While Freedom House's 2005 report does not report an appreciably higher number of free countries in 2005 as opposed to 2001,[115] by 2005, litigants were successful in advancing cases against governments before subregional courts such as the East African Court of Justice than had been the case a few short years before in the COMESA Court of Justice. In West Africa, the 'mid-2000s created an opportunity for an

114 Freedom House, Freedom in the World 2001, available at http://freedomhouse.org/report/freedom-world/freedom-world-2001#.VCWc_Wd0zcs.

115 Freedom House, Freedom in the World 2005, available at http://freedomhouse.org/report/freedom-world/freedom-world-2005#.VCWiTxaiHwk.

alliance of civil society groups and supranational actors to mobilize in favor of court reform' that resulted in the ECOWAS Court of Justice getting jurisdiction over human rights from private litigants.[116] Thus mobilisation by the judges of the ECOWAS Court of Justice joined by the West African Bar Association and human rights groups successfully resulted in enabling that court to be conferred with jurisdiction over human rights.

Therefore, the second major finding of this chapter that is closely related to the timing of the establishment of African subregional courts, the importance of mobilisation of litigants as a critical factor that accounts for how the East African Court of Justice came to entertain an increasing number of human rights cases. In East Africa, the East African Law Society played a catalytic role. There has been no similar regional mobilisation of civil society groups around the COMESA Court of Justice.[117] In fact, unlike in East Africa, Southern Africa and West Africa, there is no regional bar association in the COMESA region. Perhaps an explanation for this is because COMESA overlaps substantially with the East and Southern African countries. This means that COMESA member states are also members of regional groupings to which they have closer geographical and historical proximity. Namibia and Tanzania have withdrawn from SADC as a result of these overlaps. COMESA also has a heterogeneous mix of legal regimes and the vastness of its geographical reach, from Egypt and Libya to the north to Zimbabwe and Swaziland to the south, makes it difficult for civil society groups to operate effectively.

Third, and closely related to the lack of organised constituencies who can bring cases or organise reform of COMESA rules to make the

[116] K. Alter, L. Helfer, and J. R. McAllister, 'A new international human rights court for West Africa: The ECOWAS Community Court of Justice', *American Journal of International Law*, 107 (2013), 739.

[117] In a rather curious effort to suggest that the COMESA Court of Justice has decided human rights cases, Lord Justice Kalaile of the Court in an undated speech in my view unconvincingly states without much discussion that the PTA Bank, Muleya and Republic of Kenya (Aquaculture) cases related to human rights (access to justice and legal remedies, access to administrative justice and right to property, respectively). Even if one was to agree with Justice Kalaile that these cases touched on aspects of human rights, the restrictive and formalistic approaches of the court denied it the opportunity for more favourable remedies to the litigants in the ways other subregional courts like the East African Court of Justice have done, see Lord Justice Kalaile, 'Building Effective Regional Strategies: The Role of Regional and Sub-Regional Organizations in Strengthening Judicial Systems', undated paper available at: http://unictr.org/Portals/0/English%5CNews%5Cevents%5CMay2002%5CKalaileEN.pdf.

COMESA Court of Justice a forum where litigants would want to litigate is its location. Until recently, it has been located in Lusaka, Zambia. Lusaka, unlike the locations of other subregional African courts, is far from ideal. Lusaka has not attracted civil society groups or NGOs with foreign funding to support human rights, the rule of law and democracy the same way similar groups have done in Arusha, Tanzania, in the case of the East African Court of Justice or in Abuja, Nigeria, for the ECOWAS Court of Justice. Since it commenced its operations in 2000, uncertainty about its permanent location enveloped the Court. Until the summer of 2014, the Court did not have its own fixed premises. It shared office space within the COMESA Secretariat, a factor the Court president argued 'negatively impacted' on its operations.[118] To compound this problem, the Court faced financial constraints that resulted in its annual work programme not being approved. In September 2009, these constraints resulted in 'about 40 preliminary applications still pending trial'.[119] Even though the Court has now moved to a permanent location in Khartoum, several COMESA members 'continued to lag behind making their financial contributions to the court of Justice'.[120] Khartoum is the capital of the Sudanese government that has clamped down on the activities of human rights groups and nongovernmental groups who have supported the indictment of Sudanese President Bashir in the International Criminal Court. Khartoum is not going to be a destination of choice for human rights and other groups who would provide the COMESA Court of Justice with the kind of constituencies that have supported the work of other African subregional courts. The practice of law in Sudan is primarily in Arabic while the language of the COMESA Court of Justice is in English. This language barrier may create additional barriers that may be exacerbated by the Sudanese government's security apparatus set up to purge human rights promoters.[121]

118 Lusaka Times, 'COMESA Court of Justice Meeting Opens in Lusaka', 9 September 2009 available at http://lusakatimes.com/2009/09/09/comesa-court-of-justice-meeting-opens-in-lusaka/.

119 Ibid.

120 COMESA, Court of Justice Meets, Report of the 15th Administrative Meeting of the COMESA Court of Justice, Lusaka, Zambia, April 28–29, 2014 available at: http://comesa.int/index.php?option=com_content&view=article&id=1142:court-of-justice-meets&catid=5:latest-news&Itemid=41.

121 M. F. Massoud, *Law's Fragile State: Colonial, Authoritarian and Humanitarian Legacies in Sudan* (Cambridge University Press, 2013), p. 209.

The fourth and last challenge that has hampered the effectiveness of the COMESA Court of Justice is its very restrictive or formalistic interpretive approach. According to leading commentator Frans Viljoen, the COMESA Court of Justice's jurisprudence 'teems with procedural matters and intricate legal arguments'.[122] This restrictive interpretive approach sharply differs from the approach taken by the East African Court of Justice and the suspended SADC Tribunal. It is not inevitable that the COMESA Court would adopt a restrictive interpretive approach, given that Article 23 of the COMESA Establishment Treaty gives it rather broad jurisdiction 'to adjudicate upon all matters which may be referred to it' pursuant to the Treaty. It would seem that for an African subregional court to attract constituencies to bring cases before it and defend it when it gets into trouble, having a more expansive interpretive approach, particularly around human rights issues, has been the way to go. Even though the COMESA Court of Justice has the longest history of the African subregional courts discussed in this chapter, it has by far remained the weakest of them particularly by virtue of having attracted no external constituency to bring cases to it or to lobby for additional resources or changes to its rules to make it a more attractive court for litigants. Instead, the COMESA Court of Justice has remained an insider affair within COMESA. COMESA employees have been the primary litigants before the court. Amendments to the COMESA Treaty to bifurcate the Court into a First Instance and an Appellate Division involved no NGO or external input. Further evidence of how the Court has remained an inside affair include the fact that no outside groups have mobilised or been mobilised to raise funds to build the premises of the Court in Khartoum. This is because many rule of law and human rights donors who have funded similar initiatives in East, West and Southern Africa are restricted by economic sanctions imposed against Sudan by the United States, the European Union and the United Nations, among others, to fund the Court's new premises in Sudan.[123]

[122] Frans Viljoen, *International Human Rights Law in Africa*, 2nd ed. (Oxford University Press, 2012) p. 494.

[123] For an overview of the sanctions, see US Office of Foreign Assets Control, Sudan Sanctions Program, updated 5 November 2013, available at: http://treasury.gov/resource-center/sanctions/Programs/Documents/sudan.pdf. See also Interview with the President of the COMESA Court of Justice, 2 August 2013, Nairobi, Kenya, confirming the difficulty of raising funding because economic sanctions against Sudan limits the ability of financial assistance from western governments and NGOs.

The COMESA Court of Justice has very commendable goals on paper: providing security and predictability to the COMESA trading system; preserving the rights and obligations of COMESA members; clarifying the rights and obligations of COMESA member states through treaty interpretation; promoting amicable and timely settlement of disputes, among other roles. Yet, the COMESA Court of Justice has hardly played any of these roles. Notwithstanding the challenges facing the Court, there are two signs of a potential change of direction. First, the COMESA Court of Justice is the only African subregional court to have entertained a case between African states. That case, filed by the government of Ethiopia against the government of Eritrea, was subsequently withdrawn.[124] The rarity of African governments suing each other in international courts makes the Ethiopia/Eritrea filing unique and perhaps serves as an indicator that the diverse and heterogeneous nature of COMESA makes it more likely than other regions to have cases filed between governments.[125] Second, the 2012 decision of the COMESA Court of Justice case, *Republic of Mauritius v. Polytol Paints and Adhesives Manufacturers Co. Ltd.*, is the first real trade case to have come before any African subregional court and to have been affirmatively decided. In February of 2015, the COMESA Court of Justice delivered an important and lengthy advisory opinion that confirmed that the immunities and privileges of COMESA and its institutions do not extend to commercial transactions.[126] This advisory opinion adopting the commercial activity exception for COMESA and its institutions also eschewed the highly legalistic and restrictive interpretations that characterised a majority of the Court's previous decisions. Perhaps these decisions will signal a new direction as private actors begin looking to the COMESA Court of Justice as a viable alternative when they have

[124] *Ethiopia v. Eritriea*, COMESA Court of Justice, Reference No. 1 of 1999.

[125] One limitation of this argument was made by the president of the COMESA Court of Justice, who in an interview noted that the decisions of the SADC Tribunal in the Campbell cases against Zimbabwe had made COMESA member states very skeptical of amending the COMESA Treaty to remove the provision relating to exhaustion of domestic remedies. See Interview with the President of the COMESA Court of Justice, 2 August 2013, Nairobi, Kenya.

[126] *In the Matter of Article 32 of the Treaty for the Establishment of the Common Market for Eastern and Southern Africa* and *In the Matter of the Rule 107 of the Rules of the Court of Justice of the Common Market for Eastern and Southern Africa 2006*, Reference No. 1 of 2013 (Advisory Opinion of the Court) at pp. 33–34.

exhausted domestic remedies.[127] In conclusion, the COMESA Court of Justice, like other African subregional courts, does not enjoy legitimacy as an adjudicator of trade disputes in the eyes of African traders and states. Only where there have been mobilised constituencies around issues of human rights, the rule of law and democracy, such as in East and West Africa, have these courts been able to build their legitimacy to address these issues. Yet once these courts succeed in building their legitimacy with such external constituencies and when they use expansive interpretive strategies, they face the risk of having their powers whittled down by the member states when they decide in ways objectionable to the states.[128]

Ultimately, this chapter demonstrates that the legitimacy of an international court is very context dependent. Contextual factors such as where the court is located, whether there are constituencies engaging the court and the judges by bringing cases or defending the court when it falls into trouble with member states, are all relevant factors in assessing the legitimacy of a new court. In other words, it is not simply the design features of a court such as individual access, the independence of judges, pursuit of procedural fairness and proper application of the law that matter for the legitimacy of a court. Having independent judges does not matter if the court is inaccessible to litigants who can form the constituencies that design strategic litigation around issues such as human rights and the rule of law. In addition, in the absence of opportunities for formal and informal contacts between judges, civil society groups and donor agencies, such as has been the case for the COMESA Court of Justice, means the court has much less space for creative decision making. Without the opportunity to develop its reputation as a court that defends rights or the rule of law, the COMESA Court of Justice has been relegated to a forum for resolving disputes between COMESA and its employees. Without a caseload and a legacy for defending values such as human rights and the rule of law, the COMESA Court of Justice is invisible as an alternative to discredited national political institutions such as courts that lack independence from their executive branches.

[127] On the reluctance of private actors to use subregional courts in Africa, see James Gathii, 'The variation in the use of sub-regional integration courts between business and human rights actors: The case of the East African Court of Justice', *Law and Contemporary Problems*, 79 (2016), 37.

[128] For a different view, see Laurence R. Helfer and Karen J. Alter, 'Legitimacy and lawmaking: A tale of three international courts', *Theoretical Inquiries in Law*, 14 (2013), 479; see also Alter, Gathii, and Helfer, 'Backlash against international courts'.

This in turn means that it is primarily the judges of the COMESA Court of Justice who have largely determined its restrictive jurisprudential approach thus far. Because these judges are appointed from national judiciaries that do not have a legacy of defending individual rights against government encroachment, they have not been anxious to do so when sent to COMESA Court of Justice. In fact, not breaking with the tradition of conservative judicial decision making in which restrictive or formalistic approaches are a hallmark is a great way to guarantee the perk of being appointed or reappointed to a subregional court. The opposite is true of the East African Court of Justice, which has both engaged in defending important values such as individual rights and the rule of law, but has also done so because of the close-knit connections geographically, professionally and in terms of shared values with an engaged network of regional NGOs, particularly the East African Law Society but also with donor agencies and other support networks outside East Africa.

11

The WAEMU Court of Justice

OUSSENI ILLY

1 Introduction

The West African Economic and Monetary Union (hereinafter WAEMU, also known by its French acronym, UEMOA[1]) is one of the myriad Regional Economic Communities (RECs) that the African continent is cluttered with.[2] It was created by the Treaty of Dakar (Senegal), signed on 10 January 1994 between Benin, Burkina Faso, Côte d'Ivoire, Mali, Niger, Senegal and Togo.[3] Founded primarily for the purpose of promoting economic integration between its members, WAEMU is actually an attempt by the seven West African francophone countries to go beyond the monetary union that they inherited from their former colonial power, i.e. France, and to establish a fully-fledged economic (and political) union. On 2 May 1997, Guinea-Bissau, a former Portuguese colony, became the eighth member of the Union.

WAEMU has entrusted itself with an essential mission: the building, in the West African region, of a fully integrated economic area, characterised by free movement of goods, persons, services and capital (Article 4 of the revised treaty). Since its inception, the Union has gathered some successes, ranging from the realisation of a complete free trade area (at least on paper) and a customs union, to the establishment of common sectorial policies on industry, mining, environment, agriculture, etc. Although WAEMU still faces notable challenges, mainly in terms of implementation of the community law and policies by the member states,

[1] Union Economique et Monétaire Ouest-Africaine

[2] Africa is indeed the home of some fourteen RECs, with overlapping mandates and memberships, and which an overarching African Union project attempts to organise and rationalise in the ultimate goal of creating an African Economic Community (AEC). See O. Illy, *L'OMC et le régionalisme: le régionalisme africain* (Bruxelles: Larcier, 2012), p. 131.

[3] The Dakar Treaty was revised on 29 January 2003. See www.uemoa.int/Documents/TraitReviseUEMOA.pdf.

the Union is often cited among the (quite) well-functioning RECs in Africa. Indeed, it has one of the highest intracommunity trade rates on the African continent (15%)[4] and has been experiencing a certain degree of free movement of people.[5]

Among the pillars put in place to sustain the integration process of WAEMU is the WAEMU Court of Justice.[6] Enshrined in Article 39 of the Treaty, the Court is one of the centrepieces of the Union. Its mission, pursuant to Additional Protocol N°1 of 1996 relating to the judicial bodies of WAEMU, is to ensure the observance of the Union law by member states, both in terms of implementation and interpretation.[7] In other words, the main role of the Court is to ensure the prevalence of rule of law within the Union. Such a mission is crucial, given that no regional integration process can succeed without the rule of law. The member states seem to have realised that, and every effort was made from the beginning to make the Court operational as quickly as possible. The Court was officially set up on 27 January 1995, and by the end of 1996, it was ready to render its first decisions.

However, despite this good intention, the WAEMU Court of Justice has not been very active so far. Indeed, in almost twenty years of functioning, only some thirty-seven decisions have been rendered by it, which makes less than three decisions per year.

This situation, which is not unique in Africa,[8] may be explained by several factors.[9] First of all, one needs to take into account the nascent

[4] The average of intracommunity and intra-African trade is about 11 per cent. See UNCTAD, *Intra-African Trade: Unlocking Private Sector Dynamism* (2013), p. 13.

[5] For example, there is no visa requirement for the citizens of the Union travelling from one member state to another member state (contrary to many other African RECs).

[6] The other bodies of the Union are: the Authority of Heads of State and Government, the Council of Ministers, the Commission, the Parliament and the Court of Auditors (see Article 16 of Treaty).

[7] See Article 2 of the Protocol. In addition to the Treaty and the Additional Protocol N°1, the WAEMU Court of Justice is governed by two other important legal instruments: the Additional Act N°10/96 of 10 May 1996 relating to the Statute of the Court, and Regulation N°1/96/CM of 5 July 1996, relating to the Rules of Procedure before the Court. See www.uemoa.int/Pages/ACTES/ConseildesMinistres.aspx.

[8] One can indeed observe an extreme restraint across Africa for the use of regional courts in general and trade courts in particular. See D. Sanou, 'La juridictionnalisation des organisations d'intégration économiques régionales en Afrique', unpublished PhD thesis, University Paris 1 (2012), p. 524.

[9] But it does not mean in any way that there are no infringements of the Union law. The Commission and independent organisations document each year many cases of violations of the Union law, mainly by member states.

nature of these courts on the continent. Indeed, although regional integration is not new in Africa, the first RECs did not put in place trade courts.[10] Second, most of these courts are not open to individuals (except in rare situations, see later discussion), a situation that impacts their potential caseload. Last, political factors intervene in the decisions by the Commissions not to bring cases against member states and member states not to bring cases against each other.

Another thing that deserves to be mentioned in WAEMU is the nature of the Court's decisions. Indeed, among the aforementioned thirty-seven decisions, more than three-quarters are related to disputes between the Union and its staff, and advisory opinions. Although the Court has jurisdiction on such matters, its primary role was intended to be to support the integration process by ensuring the observance of Union law. Meant to be the watchdog of the integration process, the WAEMU Court of Justice has turned out to be a sort of 'administrative tribunal' and 'legal counsel' for the Commission and other Union bodies and institutions.

Furthermore, the WAEMU Court of Justice is not the unique regional trade court within the West African region. As mentioned earlier, the African continent is cluttered with regional integration projects, and the West African region is not immune to this situation. In addition to WAEMU, one can mention the Economic Community of West African States (ECOWAS) and the Organization for Harmonization of Business Law in Africa (OHADA), among others. These two organisations, which have overlapping mandates and memberships with WAEMU,[11] have their own courts: the Community Court of Justice for ECOWAS and the Common Court of Justice and Arbitration for OHADA. The existence of these three courts raises some issues of conflicts of jurisdiction and forum shopping.

[10] Sanou, 'La juridictionnalisation des organisations d'intégration économiques régionales en Afrique', p. 20.

[11] ECOWAS was founded on 28 May 1975 and is composed of fifteen West African countries – the eight WAEMU countries, plus Cape Verde, Gambia, Ghana, Guinea, Liberia, Nigeria and Sierra Leone. As for OHADA, it was created by the Treaty of Port-Louis signed on 17 October 1993; it is composed of seventeen Central and Western African States: Benin, Burkina Faso, Cameroon, Central African Republic, Chad, Comoros, Congo, Côte d'Ivoire, Democratic Republic of Congo, Equatorial Guinea, Gabon, Guinea, Guinea-Bissau, Mali, Niger, Senegal and Togo.

In addition to these potential conflicts with other regional courts, one should mention the WTO. Indeed, as a REC with trade liberalisation objectives, WAEMU has some similar provisions as the WTO; this leads to potential conflicts between the WAEMU Court of Justice and the WTO Dispute Settlement Body.

This chapter aims to shed some light on the WAEMU Court of Justice, its legitimacy and its future within a region marked by an ongoing transformation of regional economic communities. Indeed, from January 2015, ECOWAS became a customs union, which questions the relevance of WAEMU as a trade bloc. As mentioned earlier, all eight members of WAEMU are also members of ECOWAS.

The remainder of the chapter is structured as follows: Section 2 casts light on the members of the Court (judges) and their statute; Section 3 discusses the procedural rules before the Court; Section 4 discusses the fact-finding process; Section 5 raises the issue of forum shopping; Section 6 discusses the issue of implementation and interaction with national courts, and finally Section 7 concludes.

2 Members of the Court

2.1 Composition and Selection Process

The Court of Justice of WAEMU is composed of eight judges, one from each member state. They are chosen among nationals of member states who present 'all guaranties of independence and qualification required for appointment to the highest judicial officers' in their home country (Article 2 of Additional Protocol N°1). The Protocol does not indicate who chooses these persons and how they are chosen. It simply mentions that the judges 'are appointed by the Authority of Heads of State and Government' (Article 4 of Additional Protocol N°1). The Authority has therefore full discretion in the choice and nomination of the judges. In comparison, in ECOWAS, even though the nomination power is vested in the Authority of Heads of State, there is a national selection process, where any qualified person can take part.[12]

The judges are appointed for a term of office of six years. This term is renewable.[13]

[12] See Article 6 of the Rules of the Court of Justice of ECOWAS.
[13] Article 4 of Additional Protocol N°1.

2.2 *Independence of Judges*

As stated earlier, judges in WAEMU are chosen and nominated in full discretion by the Authority of Heads of State. This may impact in some way their independence, as the Heads of State have the tendency to choose judges they can 'control'. As is well known, political leaders in Africa (and elsewhere) dislike to be 'admonished', even on a legal ground.

Nonetheless, the Additional Act N°10/96 relating to the Statute of the Court attempts to find a way out of this flaw linked to the nomination process. According to Article 12 of this Act, once appointed, a judge can no longer be dismissed or get his salary or rights to pension suspended, unless the Court, meeting in plenary session, takes cognisance that he (or she) no longer fulfils the conditions and the obligations required to be a member of the Court. Moreover, the members of the Court enjoy privileges and immunities. In particular, they are not liable to prosecution or arrest for acts carried out or statements made in the exercise of their functions (Article 8 of Additional Act N°10/96). This immunity can only be waived by the Court itself and continues, for the acts carried out and the statements made in the exercise of their functions, even after the cessation of their activities. Finally, before assuming office, members of the Court take an oath of office, by publicly and solemnly swearing to perform their duties 'in full independence, impartially, honourably and faithfully, and to keep secret of deliberations' (Article 6 of Additional Act N°10/96).

All these arrangements could somewhat balance the flaw linked to the nomination process and should guaranty a certain independence for the Members of the WAEMU Court. However, the Additional Act N°02/2016/CCEG/UEMOA taken by the Authority of Heads of State and Government casts some doubts on this assertion. On 8 January 2016, the Heads of State dismissed all the judges except one,[14] on the ground that they impede the functioning of the Court. Due to some misunderstanding between the president of the Court and his colleagues, no session had been convened since February 2014. This brought the Court into a stalemate. The move of the Heads of State, although understandable, has no legal foundation in the community law. As stressed before, only the Court itself can dismiss one of its members.

In addition to the judges, the Court has a Registry, headed by a Registrar, appointed by the Court for a term office of six years, renewable

[14] The judge who was not dismissed was a newly sworn-in judge from Côte d'Ivoire.

once (Article 19 of Additional Act N°10/96). The Registrar is in charge of the administrative matters of the Court.

3 Procedural Rules

3.1 Jurisdiction of the Court

The Court of Justice of WAEMU is given a broad jurisdiction in order to fulfil its mission of ensuring the observance of the Union law by all the stakeholders of the integration process. In total, eight types of proceedings could be identified pursuant to the Regulation N°1/96/CM of 5 July 1996 relating to the Rules of Procedure before the Court (Article 15). These procedures, however, can be regrouped in two categories: those related to the contentious jurisdiction of the Court, on the one hand, and those related to the advisory jurisdiction of the Court, on the other hand.

3.1.1 Contentious Jurisdiction

It is the most important part of the jurisdiction of the Court and seven proceedings related to this jurisdiction are listed by Regulation 1/96:

3.1.1.1 Actions for Infringements Provided for in Article 15(1) of the Regulation N°1/96, this proceeding allows the Court to determine whether a member state has honoured its obligations under WAEMU law; more specifically, it allows the Court to determine whether a member state has broken the Union law. Such actions belong in priority to the Commission. They may also be brought by a member state. In that case, however, the member has to submit the case first to the Commission.

Before the Commission brings a case to the Court, it must allow the state concerned the opportunity to present its arguments, after having sent it a written notice. It should be noted that there is no specified deadline for the state's response after having been summoned by the Commission. Regulation 1/96 leaves the Commission free to set that deadline (Article 15(1)). If the member state does not react or terminate the infringement within the deadline set out by the Commission, this latter could refer the case to the Court.

If the Court finds that an obligation has not been fulfilled, the state must end the infringement. If the state fails or refrains from implementing the Court's decision, the Commission could refer the case to the Authority of Heads of State and Government.

It should be mentioned that there is no explicit sanction in Regulation 1/96 for failure to implement the WAEMU Court's decision. In particular, the Court has no power to impose sanctions on states. However, the Regulation seems to suggest that the sanctions provided for within the framework of the Multilateral Surveillance Mechanism[15] of the Union may be applied in infringement procedures. These sanctions,[16] administered by a political body (the Council of Ministers), seem not fit for a court decision. In comparison, in the case of the Court of Justice of the European Union, if the Court finds that a country has not followed its ruling, it can issue a fine to that country. No similar procedure exists in WAEMU, which leaves room for potential high rates of unimplemented decisions.

Since the inception of the Court of Justice of WAEMU, no infringement case has ever been brought before it. This does not mean in any way that the law of the Union is fully observed by member states. The Commission and independent nongovernmental organisations (NGOs) document each year numerous cases of law infringements by the member states.[17] However, the Commission prefers to use political or diplomatic means in attempt to solve them, rather than bringing them before the Court; political and diplomatic means have proven though not to be very successful when one looks at the number of cases that remain unresolved.[18]

3.1.1.2 Actions for Annulment of the Union Acts The actions for annulment of the Union acts are provided for in Article 15(2) of Regulation 1/96. By such action, the applicant seeks to repeal a measure (in particular a regulation, directive or decision) adopted by an institution or body of the Union. These actions may be brought to the Court by anyone. The member states, the Council and the Commission can initiate an action against any regulation, directive or decision. However, for natural and legal persons, the Union acts that they seek the annulment

[15] The Multilateral Surveillance Mechanism, organised by Articles 63 to 75 of WAEMU Treaty, aims to coordinate the macroeconomic policies of the member states in order to ensure convergence and macroeconomic stability within the Union. See Articles 63 to 75, WAEMU Treaty, Dakar, 10 January 1994, in force 1 August 1994. See www.uemoa.int/Documents/TraitReviseUEMOA.pdf.

[16] The sanctions, which are essentially financial, include recommendations to the West African Development Bank (BOAD) to reconsider its financial assistance to the concerned state, suspensions of the Union assistance to the state, etc.

[17] See, for example, the quarterly reports of the *Observatoire des pratiques anormales* (OPA), an independent body of WAEMU and ECOWAS Commissions (www.uemoa.int/Pages/PUBLICATIONS/rapports_OPA.aspx).

[18] Ibid.

of must have been addressed to them or have direct effect on them. As regard to the nature of the act, the Court has decided that they are not limited to legal instruments, as the provisions of Regulation 1/96 may seem to provide. Any decision that is binding could be brought to the Court.[19]

An action for annulment shall be brought to the Court within a time period of two months from the publication of the act or its notification to the concerned or from the day he or she took cognisance of the act (in case of absence of notification). Nonetheless, the annulment could still be sought on the occasion of any dispute involving the act.[20]

3.1.1.3 Actions Relating to Competition Matters These actions, provided for in Article 15(3) of Regulation 1/96, are not much different from the foregoing (actions for annulment of the Union acts). However, the Court's power here goes beyond a mere annulment power. Indeed, pursuant to Article 15(3), in reviewing the sanctions imposed by the Commission on companies for breaches of the Union competition law, the Court may 'modify or repeal these decisions, reduce or increase the amount of the fines and the penalties, make findings, impose obligations on the companies'. This state of fact, which can result in practice in the Court substituting its own decision to that of the Commission, gives a kind of competing decision power to the Court on competition issues.

3.1.1.4 Disputes between the Union and Its Staff Pursuant to Article 15(4) of Regulation 1/96, the WAEMU Court of Justice has jurisdiction to hear disputes between the Union and its staff. As Article 15(4) explicitly refers to the 'Union bodies' as far as this proceeding is concerned, some related but independent institutions of WAEMU, such as the West African Central Bank (BCEAO), argued therefore that they are excluded from the Court's jurisdiction. The Court rejected that argument and stated its competence over all related institutions and agencies of WAEMU in a landmark decision rendered on 19 December 2012.[21]

[19] See WAEMU Court of Justice, Case 01/2001, *Société des Ciments du Togo, SA, v. Commission de l'UEMOA*, in Recueil des textes fondamentaux et de la jurisprudence de la Cour de Justice de l'UEMOA, November 2008, p. 272.

[20] Additional Protocol N°1 relating to the judicial bodies of WAEMU, Article 11.

[21] See WAEMU Court of Justice, Case 02/2012, *Dame M. S. SODABI et M. L. KOUGBENOU v. BCEAO*, 19 December 2012.

Table 11.1 *Cases before the WAEMU Courts of Justice (1996–2013)*

Proceeding	Number
Actions for infringements	0
Actions for annulment of the Union acts	3
Actions relating to competition matters	2
Disputes between the Union and its staff	17
Actions relating to noncontractual liability and compensation	0
References for preliminary ruling	1
Arbitration	0
Advisory opinions	12
Others	2
Total	37

Source: Compilation by the author from various sources of WAEMU case law.

Disputes between WAEMU and its staff turned out to represent so far the vast majority of the contentious cases brought before the Court (almost half: see Table 11.1). This is unfortunate as the Court was built primarily to support the integration process by ensuring the observance of the Union law, particularly by member states.

3.1.1.5 Actions Relating to Noncontractual Liability and Compensation

The WAEMU Court of Justice has exclusive jurisdiction to determine the noncontractual liability of the Union and to order the payment of compensation for damages caused by it or its staff in the exercise of their functions or while on official duties (Article 15(5) of Regulation 1/96). This procedure is open to any natural or legal person, including the Union's staff. On the other side, the Union can also seek the liability and compensation from its staff for damages caused to it due to personal misconduct in the exercise of their functions.

Actions for compensation (against the Union or by it) expire after three years from the day of occurrence of the damaging fact.

As regard to contractual liability of the Union, the jurisdiction of the Court is not automatic. The parties remain free to choose any tribunal or court when concluding the contract.[22]

22 Article 9 of the WAEMU Treaty.

3.1.1.6 Reference for Preliminary Ruling National courts of the member states are the primary and ordinary courts of WAEMU law. However, in order to ensure uniform interpretation and application of the Union law, the Court of Justice has been given a special mandate, consisting of receiving, for preliminary rulings, all the cases before national courts and involving the interpretation and application of the Union law. The reference for preliminary ruling also concerns any issue of legality of a Union act raised before a national court (on the occasion of a dispute, for example). The reference is mandatory for national courts whose decisions are final under national law (no judicial remedy) and optional for the others.[23]

One case of preliminary ruling has been so far referred to the Court of Justice.[24]

3.1.1.7 Arbitration The Court may act as an arbitration tribunal for any dispute regarding the interpretation and application of the WAEMU Treaty between member states.[25] This special jurisdiction is, however, neither automatic nor compulsory. The member states involved must so agree through a submission agreement notified to the Court.[26] Although the disputing parties are free to choose the procedural rules applicable to their dispute, the applicable law remains WAEMU law.[27] Moreover, there is no freedom of choice of arbitrators.[28] The use of the term *arbitration* by the treaty could therefore be misleading as regards normal international arbitration.[29]

No arbitration case has ever been brought so far before the Court. One could wonder, however, what difference does exist between this arbitration procedure and the actions for infringements discussed earlier. As we remember, these actions are open both to the Commission and member states for infringement of WAEMU law by a member state (see earlier, Section *3.1.1.1*). Should a member state go for a dispute with another member, it would certainly choose the infringement procedure, as there is no need for a submission agreement there. The arbitration procedure might therefore remain unused.

[23] Article 15(6) of Regulation 1/96.

[24] Case 02/2005, *Compagnie Air France v. Syndicat des agents de voyage et de tourisme du Sénégal*, 21 January 2005 (reference made by the Conseil d'Etat of Senegal).

[25] See Article 15(8) of Regulation 1/96. [26] Ibid. [27] Ibid. [28] Ibid.

[29] The usual components of international arbitration are freedom of choice of arbitrators, procedural rules and applicable law.

3.1.2 Advisory Jurisdiction

Pursuant to Article 27 of Additional Act 10/96 and Article 15(7) of Regulation N°1/96/CM, the WAEMU Court of Justice may give advisory opinions and recommendations. The right to seek advisory opinions from the Court was initially reserved to the Commission, the Council of Ministers, the Authority of Heads of State and Government and the member states (see Article 15(7) of Regulation N°1/96/CM). However, the Court has extended this right to all the Union bodies and institutions.[30]

The advisory jurisdiction of the Court is separated into three categories:

- *Opinions on the Union texts*: the Commission may ask the opinion of the Court on any legal text in preparation. The opinion is not binding.
- *Opinions on international agreements*: the Council of Ministers, the Commission or a member state may seek the opinion of the Court on the compatibility of any existing international agreement (or an agreement under negotiation) with the WAEMU Treaty. There is no specification about the nature of this opinion; in particular, whether the member state should withdraw from the agreement if the Court found it incompatible with the provisions of the Union Treaty.
- *Opinions on any difficulty regarding the application or the interpretation of the Union law*: this opinion may be sought by the Council of Ministers, the Commission, the Authority of Heads of State or a member state.

The WAEMU Court has been quite active in giving advisory opinions. Indeed, one out of five of its decisions (20 per cent) have been so far advisory opinions (see Table 11.1). These opinions are mainly on the Union texts in preparation and the interpretation of the Union law. No advisory opinion has been given on international agreements.

This active role of the Court in advisory opinions has brought many to question whether it has not turned into 'legal counsel' for the WAEMU Commission, deviating from its core and intended mission, which is to ensure the observance of the Union law by member states.

[30] See WAEMU Court of Justice, Case 003/96, Demande d'avis de la Banque centrale des Etats de l'Afrique de l'Ouest (BCEAO) sur le projet d'agrément unique pour les banques et les établissements financiers, 10 December 1996; in Recueil des textes fondamentaux et de la jurisprudence de la Cour de Justice de l'UEMOA, p. 110; also WAEMU Court of Justice, Case 01/2011, Demande d'avis de la Banque Ouest-Africaine de Développement (BOAD) relative à son éligibilité au système judiciaire de la Cour de Justice de l'UEMOA, 30 October 2011.

3.2 *Access to the Court and Procedure*

As shown through the different proceedings listed, the WAEMU Court of Justice is open to a variety of actors: the Union bodies, institutions and agencies, member states, national courts, natural and legal persons, etc.

As far as procedural rules are concerned, however, a distinction must be drawn between the ordinary jurisdiction of the Court on the one hand, and the arbitration jurisdiction on the other.

Cases related to the ordinary jurisdiction of the Court are filed through written applications addressed to the registry. Such applications must indicate the name of the applicant, the party against whom the proceedings are being instituted, a brief statement of the facts of the case and the orders being sought by the plaintiff.[31]

As regards arbitration cases, they are initiated through notification of a submission agreement to the Court. This notification can be made jointly by the concerned states or by either of them.[32] The agreement must indicate the subject of the dispute and the parties involved.

Whatever the type of case, however, there is always a written stage and, if appropriate, an oral stage, which is normally public (Article 36 of Additional Act 10/96, Article 18 of Regulation N°1/96/CM). Third-party interventions are allowed up to the end of the written procedure.[33] During the written stage, the Court may also receive amicus curiae submissions.[34] However, amicus curiae must prove their interests to the solution of the case. Moreover, amicus curiae submissions are not allowed in disputes between member states, between the Union bodies, and disputes between the Union bodies and member states.[35]

According to Article 45 of Additional Act 10/96, third-party interventions, including amicus curiae, have to support the conclusions of one party to the dispute. These restrictions may impact negatively on any interest for amicus curiae interventions before the WAEMU Court.

During the oral stage, the Court may hear anyone, including witnesses, experts, etc.[36]

Decisions of the Court are binding to all parties to the dispute. They are final and not subject to appeal, except in cases of applications for revision or interpretation by the Court itself.[37] Furthermore, decisions of

[31] See Article 26 of Regulation 1/96. [32] Article 27 of Regulation 1/96.
[33] Article 45 of Additional Act 10/96. [34] Ibid. [35] Ibid.
[36] Article 41–3 of Regulation 1/96.
[37] Article 48 of Additional Act 10/96, and Article 82–5 of Regulation 1/96.

the Court may also come under objection from parties to the dispute that failed to take part in the proceeding and from third parties.[38]

In sum, access to the WAEMU Court of Justice depends on the proceeding, as shown earlier. However, overall, the access to the Court is limited for natural and legal persons. Indeed, apart from the proceedings for annulment of the Union acts, competition matters, staff disputes, and contractual and noncontractual liability, individuals and legal persons do not have access to the Court. In particular, they cannot bring cases for infringement of the Union law, even though infringements are commonplace in WAEMU and the Commission is not doing anything to counter them. Moreover, there is not, like in the European Union, a procedure for failure to act,[39] anything that would have widened the access to the Court by individuals and enhance its legitimacy.

4 Fact-Finding

In all cases before the WAEMU Court, the president of the Court shall appoint a judge rapporteur (Article 7 of Regulation N°1/96/CM). The mission of the judge rapporteur is to examine the case on preliminary ground and propose a draft report for ruling to the members of the Court. As stated earlier (Section 3.2), the Court may order any investigations and hear anyone, including witnesses, experts, amicus curiae, etc.

In addition to the judge rapporteurs, the Court comprises advocates general, whose mission is to assist the Court to render its judgments. The advocates general are appointed among the members of the Court, but they act independently.[40]

5 Forum Shopping

The West African zone is home to two major Regional Economic Communities: the Economic Community of West African States (ECOWAS) and the West African Economic and Monetary Union (WAEMU). Both RECs pursue the same objective in the trade domain, i.e. the

38 Article 80–1 of Regulation 1/96.

39 Actions for failure to act are provided for in Article 265 of the Treaty on the Functioning of the European Union and allow any natural or legal person to bring a case against any institution, body, office or agency of the European Union that has failed to address to that person any act other than a recommendation or an opinion.

40 Article 9 of Regulation 1/96.

creation of common markets, with free trade areas and customs unions as main features.[41] Moreover, all members of one REC are also members of the other: all eight members of WAEMU are also parties to the ECOWAS Treaty. Finally, as stated before, both WAEMU and ECOWAS have set up regional courts, which have jurisdiction over their respective member states and on the matters covered by their respective treaties.

This situation leads to potential forum shopping and conflict of jurisdictions. Conflict of jurisdictions may be positive or negative. The conflict is positive if several tribunals seized at the same time declare themselves competent and negative if no tribunal declares itself competent. In the first situation, the risk is contradictory decisions, complicating the implementation for the concerned party. In the second situation, the risk is simply denial of justice for the complaining party. This is what occurred in 2011 in the case *El Hadji Aboubacar v. Banque centrale des Etats de l'Afrique de l'Ouest (BCEAO) et Etat du Niger*. Mr. Aboubacar, who is a businessman from Niger, brought BCEAO and the Government of Niger before ECOWAS Community Court of Justice for violation of his property right after the Council of Ministers of WAEMU decided to demonetise previous currency in circulation in the area. The ECOWAS Court, without denying its competence, preferred, in a judicial comity, to leave the case to the WAEMU Court of Justice. However, when the WAEMU Court was later seized, it also declared itself incompetent (although on other grounds: individuals cannot bring cases against states before the WAEMU Court).[42]

6 Implementation and Interaction with National Courts

As stated before, the Court of Justice of WAEMU has been more active on staff disputes and advisory opinions (Table 11.1). Therefore, implementation has not been so far such an issue. However, some high-profile staff disputes showed that it could be in the future, especially when the intended party is a political body. Indeed, in 2004, Mr. Eugène Yayi, a commissioner, was dismissed without reason by the Authority of Heads of State and replaced by another commissioner. Mr. Yayi brought the

[41] See Article 3 of the ECOWAS Treaty, and Article 4 of the WAEMU Treaty.

[42] See Community Court of Justice, ECOWAS, Case ECW/CCJ/APP/13/08, *El Hadji Aboubacar v. La Banque centrale des Etats de l'Afrique de l'Ouest (BCEAO) et l'Etat du Niger*, 8 February 2011; and Court of Justice of WAEMU, Case 01/2013, *El Hadji Aboubacar v. Etat du Niger*, 16 January 2013.

case to the Court of Justice, claiming the illegality of his dismissal. He was followed by the Court, who annulled the dismissing act. Nonetheless, the Authority went ahead and took another act (Additional Act 01/2005) confirming the dismissal. This second act was annulled in its turn by the Court, but the Authority persisted. On 11 May 2006, another act was taken to dismiss again Mr. Yayi. This act coincided with the end of his mandate, and therefore the Court found it unnecessary to annul it.[43]

This situation shows how hard it can be for courts in general in Africa and regional courts in particular to have political leaders abide by their decisions. Nonetheless, the Yayi case also showed the 'audacity' of the WAEMU Court of Justice and the independence of its judges.

7 Conclusion

The Court of Justice of the WAEMU has been set up to support the integration process taking place in the area. According to its mandate, it shall be the 'watchdog' of the good implementation of the Union law, in the ultimate goal of insuring the achievement of its objective, i.e. the creation of a common market where free movement of people and goods is guaranteed.

Considering the work of the Court so far, one could wonder if it is accomplishing its mission. As shown earlier, more than two-thirds of its activity is based on staff disputes and advisory opinions. A trade court turned out to be an 'administrative tribunal' and a 'legal counsel', as stated earlier. This could raise questions about the legitimacy of the Court. Not only has it had very few cases (thirty-seven cases over seventeen years, in other words, less than three cases per year!) but it seems also to have deviated from its core mission.

Nonetheless, one should bear in mind that if the Court has been idle so far (and on trade matters in particular), this is far from its fault. As shown earlier, it has no power to seize itself, and individuals cannot bring cases before it against member states. Only the Commission or other member states can do that. This strongly restricts the ability of the Court to adjudicate on the numerous Union law violations that are commonplace

[43] See Court of Justice of WAEMU, Case 03/2005, YAÏ Eugène *v.* La Conférence des Chefs d'Etat et de Gouvernement de l'UEMOA, 27 April 2005; Case 01/2006, YAÏ Eugène *v.* La Conférence des Chefs d'Etat et de Gouvernement de l'UEMOA, 5 April 2006; and Case 01/2008, YAÏ Eugène *v.* La Conférence des Chefs d'Etat et de Gouvernement de l'UEMOA, 30 April 2008.

in WAEMU. Because of the political climate within the region, the Commission refrains from bringing cases against member states and member states also refrain from doing so against each other.

If reforms were to take place, they should be oriented toward opening the Court to natural and legal persons on infringement actions, rather than, as one can hear from time to time, extending the jurisdiction of the Court on human rights issues (short of copying ECOWAS). Regional courts created within the framework of regional integration mechanisms have the primary role to support the integration process, not to become human rights courts. The ECOWAS Community Court of Justice is a bad example in that regard, and WAEMU should not follow that example.

Finally, regional judges on the continent should find other ways to get out of idleness and not tend to push for 'mission creep' of regional trade courts.

12

The ASEAN Trade Dispute Settlement Mechanism

MICHAEL EWING-CHOW AND RANYTA YUSRAN

1 Introduction

The Association of Southeast Asian Nations (ASEAN) was established in 1967 amid regional security tensions among its founding members, Indonesia, Malaysia, Singapore, Philippines and Thailand.[1] ASEAN initially was not conceptualised as an economic grouping but rather more as a confidence-building and political-security forum. Therefore, the early ASEAN agreement on dispute settlement, the Treaty of Amity and Cooperation in Southeast Asia (TAC), reflects this focus.[2] It was only in 1977 that ASEAN started to focus on regional economic integration[3] and finally adopted the 1996 Protocol on Dispute Settlement Mechanism, which later would be succeeded by the 2004 Protocol on Enhanced Dispute Settlement Mechanism (EDSM) to address intra-ASEAN disputes arising from the interpretation or application of certain ASEAN economic agreements, including trade disputes. However, the legalisation of ASEAN only started in late 2008 after the entry into force of the ASEAN Charter.[4] The ASEAN Charter then prescribes a number of dispute settlement mechanisms to cover disputes that may arise from all fields of ASEAN cooperation.[5] It affirms the continuance of the application of the EDSM and expands its coverage to disputes arising from *all* ASEAN economic agreements, including

[1] ASEAN Declaration, Bangkok, 8 August 1967, 6 ILM 1233 (1967). Today ASEAN comprises of ten member states namely Brunei, Cambodia, Indonesia, Laos, Malaysia, Myanmar, the Philippines, Singapore, Thailand and Vietnam.

[2] Treaty of Amity and Cooperation in Southeast Asia (TAC), Bali, 24 February 1976, in force 21 June 1976, 1025 UNTS 297.

[3] On 24 February 1977, ASEAN adopted the Agreement on ASEAN Preferential Trading Arrangements. It is the first ASEAN economic agreement since its inception in 1967. It is the root agreement for the establishment of ASEAN Free Trade Area.

[4] Charter of the Association of Southeast Asian Nations (ASEAN Charter), Singapore, 20 November 2007, in force 15 December 2008, 2624 UNTS 223.

[5] Ibid., Articles 24–25.

agreements on free trade area and the liberalisation of goods and services.[6]

If one takes the entry into force of the ASEAN Charter as the effective beginning of the legalisation of ASEAN, it is not surprising that none of ASEAN dispute settlement mechanisms have ever been invoked, as there has not been a lot of time for legal disputes to develop. However, we think that beyond the limited time for disputes to have been brought there exists some pathologies in ASEAN that mitigate against disputes being resolved by any of the ASEAN dispute settlement mechanisms. Bearing in mind the limited number of intra-ASEAN trade disputes (out of seven intra-ASEAN disputes that were brought before third-party dispute settlement mechanisms, only two related to trade), it is our opinion that it is therefore worthwhile to also consider the ASEAN culture relating to dispute settlement and management in general, including nontrade disputes.

2 ASEAN Dispute Settlement Mechanisms and Their Lack of Usage

As a general rule under the ASEAN Charter, all disputes pertaining to the interpretation or application of a specific ASEAN instrument shall be settled through the dispute settlement mechanism specifically provided under such instrument.[7] The Charter prescribes the use of the High Council of the TAC,[8] the EDSM[9] and the Protocol to the ASEAN Charter on Dispute Settlement Mechanisms (DSMP)[10] to address disputes falling outside the general rule. The EDSM is the only ASEAN dispute settlement mechanism that addresses intra-ASEAN disputes pertaining to economic cooperation, including trade. To date, none of these mechanisms has been invoked.

2.1 1976 Treaty of Amity and Cooperation in Southeast Asia

The TAC was signed on 24 February 1976 at the first ASEAN Summit. It is ASEAN's first dispute settlement and principal political-security treaty.[11] The TAC codifies for the first time the Association's guiding

[6] Ibid., Article 54(2). [7] Ibid., Article 24(1). [8] Ibid., Article 24(2).
[9] Ibid., Article 24(3). [10] Ibid., Article 25.
[11] The TAC also allows ratifications by non-ASEAN states making it the only regional dispute settlement that can be used for disputes arising between an ASEAN state and a non-ASEAN state.

principles on international relations, which includes ASEAN's revered principle of noninterference in the internal affairs of one another.[12] Initially the TAC might apply to any kind of disputes 'likely to disturb regional peace and security'[13] however, the 2006 Eminent Person Group Report suggested limiting the application of the TAC to political-security disputes.[14] The ASEAN Charter later specified that the TAC should be used to address intra-ASEAN disputes unrelated with the interpretation and application of the Charter and ASEAN economic agreements.[15]

Under the TAC, states are obliged to settle their disputes through friendly negotiations.[16] If the disputes remain unresolved, such disputes may be brought before the High Council – a political body consisting of Foreign Ministers of all ASEAN member states.[17] The decision to submit a dispute to the High Council must be agreed by all parties to the dispute. The High Council then recommends to the disputing parties appropriate means to settle the dispute, including the High Council's good offices. The High Council may also with the agreement of the parties, constitute itself into a mediation committee, inquiry or conciliation.[18] It should be noted that the TAC does not provide a time frame within which the High Council shall render its decisions. The High Council shall make its decisions by consensus,[19] but nothing in the TAC obliges state parties to comply with the decisions of the Council.

Despite nearly forty years of existence, the TAC has never been utilised. In the event of disputes among state parties, they show a high preference to utilise other third-party international dispute settlement mechanisms rather than the TAC. The state parties' reluctance to utilise the TAC dispute settlement is most likely due to the political nature of the High Council and the lack of confidence in the TAC procedures. The fact that disputing parties are also part of the High Council and that any decision must be taken by consensus makes it less likely that any satisfactory outcome can emerge as such procedures would only further politicise such sensitive disputes instead of resolving them.

[12] TAC, Article 2. [13] Ibid., Article 13.

[14] 2006 Report of the Eminent Persons Group, at 46. The Eminent Persons Group was established to prepare the drafting of the ASEAN Charter.

[15] ASEAN Charter, Article 24(1). [16] TAC, Article 13.

[17] Rules of Procedure of the High Council of the Treaty of Amity and Cooperation in Southeast Asia (Rules of Procedure of the TAC High Council), Hanoi, 23 July 2001, Rule 3. In the event of a dispute involving a non-ASEAN state, then a representative of that state will also sit in the High Council.

[18] TAC, Article 15. [19] Rules of Procedure of the TAC High Council, Rule 19.

2.2 *2004 Protocol on Enhanced Dispute Settlement Mechanism*

The EDSM was signed on 29 November 2004 and supersedes the 1996 Protocol on Dispute Settlement Mechanism.[20] It is the main mechanism for trade dispute resolution in ASEAN. Article 1 stipulates that the EDSM applies to disputes arising from the interpretation and application of forty-six ASEAN economic agreements listed under Appendix I of the EDSM. The EDSM also applies automatically to disputes arising from ASEAN economic agreements adopted after 2004.[21] In 2008, the ASEAN Charter expanded the applicability of the EDSM to include disputes arising from *all* ASEAN economic agreements.[22] The Charter provides that all disputes arising from all ASEAN economic agreements shall be resolved through the EDSM.[23] The EDSM is the only dispute settlement regime to address state-to-state disputes arising from 1992 Agreement on the Common Effective Preferential Tariff Scheme for the ASEAN Free Trade Area (CEPT). The system adopted under the EDSM is modelled on that of the World Trade Organization's (WTO) Dispute Settlement Understanding (DSU), albeit with shorter timelines. However, recourse to the EDSM is without prejudice to the rights of ASEAN member states to bring their disputes before other dispute settlement mechanisms.[24]

2.2.1 Adjudication

The ASEAN Senior Economic Officials Meeting (SEOM), roughly analogous to the WTO Dispute Settlement Body (DSB) if not modelled on it, is responsible in administering the EDSM. It has the authority to establish panels, adopt panel and Appellate Body reports, monitor the implementation of findings and recommendations of panel and Appellate Body and authorise suspension of concessions and other obligations under ASEAN economic agreements.[25] Similar to the WTO DSB, SEOM

20 Protocol on Enhanced Dispute Settlement Mechanism (EDSM), Vientiane, 29 November 2004, in force on 24 November 2004.

21 Ibid., Article 1(1).

22 ASEAN Charter, Article 24(2).

23 Ibid. Prior to the Charter, the EDSM allowed member states to have their economic disputes, including those arising from ASEAN economic agreements, resolved in other forum outside of ASEAN (see Article 1(3) of the EDSM).

24 EDSM, Article 1(3).

25 Ibid., Article 2(2). This is provision is parallel to/ to be applied in conjunction with Article 24(2) of the ASEAN Charter.

operates by 'Negative Consensus'.[26] This means, unless SEOM decides by consensus *not* to establish a panel and to adopt a report of the panel and/or the Appellate Body, SEOM will establish and adopt the reports within the time frame prescribed in the EDSM. The application of negative consensus limits the possibility of blockage by any party to the dispute. It is interesting to note that the EDSM specifically provides that nonreply by any member of SEOM is taken as an agreement to the establishment of a panel. The inclusion of this WTO DSU practice may represent ASEAN's intention to address the organisation's well-known culture of dispute avoidance by invoking the consensus rule.

Central to the mechanism under the EDSM is the automatic process involving a panel established by SEOM to consider disputes that cannot be resolved through consultation.[27] Unlike other ASEAN dispute settlement mechanisms, SEOM has the power to establish a panel based only on the request of a party to the dispute within forty-five days upon the receipt of the request. Appendix II of the EDSM provides that after the establishment of the panel, the parties are given ten days to decide on the individuals who will sit on the panel.[28] The panel is composed of three or five panellists, subject to the agreement of the parties. If the parties fail to reach an agreement on appointment of panellists, within twenty days after the establishment of the panel a party may request the Secretary-General of ASEAN to determine the composition of the panel.[29] The Secretary-General is then given ten days to determine the composition of the panel by appointing panellists whom the Secretary-General considers most appropriate after consulting with SEOM and the parties in the dispute.

The function of the panel is to make an objective assessment of the dispute brought before it and to make its findings and recommendations in relation to the case.[30] The working procedures of the panel are similar to those provided under the WTO DSU.[31] After assessing such disputes,

[26] Ibid., Article 5(2), 9(1), and 12(13).

[27] Ibid., Article 5(1). See also, Agreement Establishing the World Trade Organization, Annex 2: Dispute Settlement Rules: Understanding on Rules and Procedures Governing the Settlement of Disputes (WTO-DSU), Marrakesh, 15 April 1994, in force 1 January 1995, 1869 UNTS 401, 33 ILM 1226. Similar to the WTO DSU, the panel mechanism of the EDSM will only be triggered if consultation fails to solve the dispute within sixty days after the receipt of request for consultation or the responding party fails to response to such request within ten days or fails to enter into consultation within thirty days.

[28] EDSM, Appendix II: Working Procedures of the Panel, I. Composition of Panels (Appendix II.1), pt. 5.

[29] Ibid., Appendix II.1, pt. 7. [30] Ibid., Article 7.

[31] Ibid., Appendix II.2. The procedures are similar to Appendix III of the WTO DSU.

the panel is required to deliver its findings and recommendations to SEOM within sixty days of its establishment.[32] The panel may seek an additional ten days to submit its report to SEOM. The panel shall give adequate time to the parties to review the report prior to submitting it to SEOM.[33] Unless SEOM, by consensus, refuses to adopt the panel's report or a party decides to file an appeal, SEOM has to adopt the panel's report within thirty days of its submission.[34]

The EDSM prescribes for the establishment of a standing Appellate Body by the ASEAN Economic Minister Meeting (AEM).[35] The Appellate Body is to be composed of seven persons, three of whom shall serve on any appeal case on a rotation basis. All members of the Appellate Body will be appointed by the AEM for a four-year term.[36] The working procedures of the Appellate Body will be drafted by SEOM and any subsequent changes and additions shall be decided by the Appellate Body in consultation with SEOM and the Secretary-General of ASEAN.[37] Only parties to a dispute may appeal a panel report.[38] The Appellate Body will decide on the issues of law and legal interpretation in the panel's report within sixty days after the appeal request was filed.[39] The Appellate Body will also inform SEOM if it believes it cannot deliver its report within sixty days but in no case may the proceedings exceed ninety days. The Appellate Body's report shall be adopted by SEOM and unconditionally accepted by parties to the dispute, unless SEOM decides by consensus not to adopt the report.[40] ASEAN has yet to establish the Appellate Body; however, a list comprising qualified individuals from all ASEAN member states has been procured.[41]

2.2.2 Compliance

The implementation procedure of the EDSM also includes a compliance phase and compensation or suspension of concessions. Article 15 of the EDSM stipulates that parties to the dispute are required to comply with the findings and recommendations of panel or Appellate Body within

[32] Ibid., Article 8(2). In exceptional cases, the panel may take an additional ten days to submit the report to SEOM.

[33] Ibid., Article 8(3).

[34] Ibid., Article 9.

[35] Ibid., Article 12(1).

[36] Ibid., Article 12(2).

[37] Ibid., Article 12(8).

[38] Ibid., Article 12(4).

[39] Ibid., Article 12(5) and (6).

[40] Ibid., Article 12(13).

[41] This information was collected during the Workshop on ASEAN Enhanced Dispute Settlement Mechanism at the ASEAN Secretariat, Jakarta, Indonesia, on 30 October 2012. This information is still valid based on our interview with an ASEAN Secretariat official on 27 September 2014.

sixty days after their adoption by SEOM. Parties to the dispute may decide on a longer time period for compliance, and this decision for extended time lines must be made within fourteen days after SEOM's adoption of the reports.

The EDSM applies specific rules, which differ from the WTO DSU, with regard to a request for a longer time period for compliance. The EDSM stipulates that when a party to a dispute requests a longer period of time for compliance, the other party will take into account the circumstances of the case and consider the complexity of actions required to comply with the findings and recommendations of panel and Appellate Body adopted by SEOM. The request shall not be unreasonably denied.[42] Furthermore, when compliance requires the passing of a national legislation, a longer period appropriate for that purpose shall be accorded.

Similar to Article 21(5) of the WTO DSU, the EDSM also provides a compliance adjudication process, which shall not exceed ninety days.[43] Issues with regard to compliance may be raised at SEOM meeting and, unless SEOM refuses to consider them, the issues shall remain in SEOM agenda until they are resolved. In this case, parties are required to provide SEOM with regular status reports of their progress in implementing the findings and recommendations of the panel and Appellate Body. The meetings of SEOM itself are governed by Article 20(1) of the ASEAN Charter, which stipulates that every decision of an ASEAN organ shall be made based on consultation and consensus. However, Article 16(1) of the EDSM provides that if SEOM fails to resolve these issues within sixty days or within the longer time period agreed by the parties in accordance with Article 15, then the concerned party of the dispute may trigger the process of compensation and the suspension of concessions.

The EDSM provides compensation and suspension of concessions or other obligations as temporary measures that may be taken in the event of nonimplementation of the findings and recommendations of the panel and Appellate Body reports.[44] The procedures for resorting to and the criteria for the granting of these temporary measures under the EDSM are very similar to those of the WTO DSU. Arbitration is provided under Article 16 of the EDSM to resolve disputes arising from suspension of concessions.

The Arbitration process under Article 16 is similar to that of the WTO DSU. The arbitration will be carried out by the original panel or by an

[42] EDSM, Article 15(2). [43] Ibid., Article 15(5). [44] Ibid., Article 16.

arbitrator appointed by the ASEAN Secretary-General. The arbitration needs to be completed within sixty days after the date of expiry of the time period to comply with the panel and Appellate Body reports adopted by SEOM under Article 15. The parties shall accept the arbitration decision as final and promptly notify SEOM. Upon a request, SEOM will grant authorisation to suspend concessions or other obligations in accordance with the decision of the arbitration, unless it decides to reject the request by consensus.

2.2.3 Selection of Panellists and Members of the Appellate Body

Appendix II of the EDSM stipulates that preference is to be given to nationals of ASEAN states to be appointed as panellists. They are required to be well-qualified and experienced legal professionals or academics in the field of international trade law and policy. Nationals of any of the disputing parties cannot serve on a panel concerned with that dispute. The ASEAN Secretariat is responsible for maintaining the indicative list of qualified individuals from which members of a panel may be drawn. Member states may periodically suggest names of governmental and nongovernmental individuals to be included in the indicative list, providing relevant information on their knowledge and experience of international trade and of the ASEAN economic agreements. The list shall indicate specific experience or expertise of each individual in the ASEAN economic agreements. Member states shall undertake to permit their officials to serve as panellists.

Article 12 sets out the requirements of Appellate Body's members. They shall consist of individuals of recognised authority and shall demonstrate expertise in law, international trade and subject matter of ASEAN economic agreements. These individuals shall not be affiliated with any government. A member will be appointed by AEM for a four-year term and may be reappointed once.

2.2.4 Administrative Body, Funding and Cost

The ASEAN Secretariat is tasked with the secretarial duties for the purposes of the EDSM. Under Articles 17 and 19 of the EDSM, the ASEAN Secretariat is responsible for (1) administering the ASEAN DSM Fund for the purpose of the EDSM; (2) assisting the panels and Appellate Body, especially on the legal and procedural aspects, and providing secretariat and technical support; (3) assisting SEOM to monitor and maintain surveillance of the findings and recommendations of the panel and Appellate Body reports; and (4) receiving all documentations pertaining to disputes. Apart from these, the ASEAN Secretariat is responsible in maintaining an indicative list of qualified individuals for the purpose of creation of a panel. It also has a duty to propose nominations of the panel to the parties to the dispute and inform all member states of the composition of a panel thus formed.[45]

As of 2009, ASEAN has already established the ASEAN DSM Fund as required under Article 17 of the EDSM.[46] The EDSM applies a rather innovative approach to the financing of its application; the EDSM stipulates that the ASEAN DSM Fund shall be a revolving fund and the initial sum of the Fund shall be contributed equally by all the member states. Any drawdown from the Fund shall be replenished by the parties to the dispute. The Fund will be used to meet the expenses of the panels, Appellate Body and any related administration costs of the ASEAN Secretariat. In relation to the replenishing of the Fund by the parties to a dispute, the panel and the Appellate Body will also make recommendations about the expenses to be borne by the parties as part of their findings and recommendations.[47] They may apportion the expenses in a manner appropriate to a particular dispute. The AEM shall approve a set of criteria on which subsistence allowance and other expenses of the panel and the Appellate Body shall be based.

2.2.5 Issues

Similar to other ASEAN dispute settlement mechanisms, the EDSM has never been invoked by any ASEAN member state. This is not because ASEAN states are particularly averse to bringing their dispute before third-party adjudication or because there is no economic disputes among ASEAN states. The first trade dispute brought before the WTO was in fact a dispute between two ASEAN member states, Malaysia and Singapore, in 1995 regarding Malaysia's prohibition on the importation of polyethylene and polypropylene.[48] Another trade dispute brought before the WTO DSU in 2008 concerned Thai fiscal and custom measures

[45] EDSM, Appendix II.A, pts. 6–7.

[46] ASEAN Secretariat, 'ASEAN Dispute Settlement System – Fact Sheet', 24 February 2009.

[47] EDSM, Article 14(3).

[48] WTO dispute DS1, *Malaysia – Prohibition of Imports of Polyethylene and Polypropylene*, Request for Consultation, 10 January 1995. The parties finally resolved their dispute through consultation and withdrew the request on 19 July 1995. Because Singapore already requested the establishment of a panel, Singapore announced that it withdrew its complaint completely.

affecting cigarettes from the Philippines.[49] The former could not be brought before the EDSM because it was not in existence in 1995, the later, however, could have been brought before the EDSM.

Setting this issue temporarily aside, although the EDSM procedures closely resembles the procedures of the WTO DSU, there are several features in the EDSM that may raise concerns when the EDSM is finally invoked.

2.2.5.1 Limited Time Frame for the Adjudication Process As mentioned before, the EDSM adjudication process is supposed to run on a very strict and limited time frame. The whole process of dispute settlement under the EDSM, from the moment when a party files a request for consultation until the adoption of the report of the Appellate Body by SEOM (in the event of an appeal), should only take up to 325 days, or about eleven months.[50] By contrast, the WTO DSU provides a time frame of almost sixteen months from the time a party files a request for consultation until the adoption of the Appellate Body report by the WTO DSB.[51]

The most striking difference in relation to the issue of time frame is the time period allocated for the panel process. A panel under the EDSM has seventy days at the most[52] since its establishment to deliver its report to SEOM. Effectively, the panel only has sixty days for deliberations and submission of report. The first ten days is carved from the panel time frame for the appointment of panellists' process.[53] However, if the parties cannot agree on the appointment of the parties then after twenty days of the establishment of the panel, a party may ask the Secretary-General of ASEAN to appoint the panellists within the next ten days.[54] In this case, the panel will only have forty days at maximum for deliberations and submission of report. Within this time

49 WTO dispute DS371, *Thailand – Customs and Fiscal Measures on Cigarettes from the Philippines*, Appellate Body Report, 17 June 2011.

50 EDSM, Articles 3, 5, 8 and 12.

51 WTO DSU, Article 4(7), 7, 12(9) and 17(14). According to these provisions, the WTO process takes exactly 12 months and 115 days. See also WTO, 'Flowchart of the Dispute Settlement Process', retrieved on 10 October 2016 from the official website of the WTO: www.wto.org.

52 EDSM, Article 8(2). Compare this to the time frame granted to a panel of WTO DSU, up to nine months *after* the selection of panellists. See WTO, 'Flowchart of the Dispute Settlement Process'.

53 Ibid., Appendix II.1, pt. 5.

54 Ibid., pt. 7.

frame somehow the panel is required to fit in, among others, two rounds of submissions by the parties,[55] two rounds of meetings,[56] an interim review of the report[57] and, when necessary, expert advice.[58] Again by contrast, in the WTO DSU process the time frame accorded to the panel is an ample nine months, which only kick-starts after panellists are selected.

The Appellate Body, on the other hand, is given a longer period of time to deliver its report to the SEOM, up to ninety days. Although this is the standard given to the WTO DSU Appellate Body, it is normally the case that a panel process is afforded more time than the appeal process considering the bulk of work that the panel has to do. Additionally, the EDSM does not provide for a grace period after the submission of the panel report for the parties to decide whether any of them wants to appeal the panel report.[59] As a comparison, the WTO DSU procedures provide for a twenty-day period for the parties to consider the panel report, and during this period, the report will not be considered for adoption by the DSB.[60] If the parties decide not to appeal the report, the DSU provides another sixty days for the DSB to consider the adoption of the report.[61]

Thus, the time frame accorded under EDSM appears to be unachievable, especially if we consider that in the WTO even a time frame of nearly sixteen months, on occasions, is not sufficient. For example, the *Boeing v. Airbus* disputes took more than five years before the WTO Appellate Body's Report was circulated.[62] This overly ambitious time frame and the inflexibility of the EDSM may cause a major obstacle to the application of the EDSM when member states decide to invoke it, or these considerations may even dissuade member states from bringing their disputes to the EDSM at all.

2.2.5.2 The ASEAN DSM Fund Article 17 of the EDSM established the ASEAN DSM Fund. The purpose of the Fund is to cover all expenses arising from the functions of the panellists and members of the Appellate

[55] Ibid., Appendix II.2, pts. 4 and 7. [56] Ibid., pt. 5 and 7. [57] Ibid., Article 8(3).
[58] Ibid., Article 8(4).
[59] Ibid., Article 9(1). The EDSM only provides thirty days time frame for the consideration of the report by SEOM.
[60] WTO DSU, Article 16(2). [61] Ibid., Article 16(4).
[62] WTO dispute DS316, *European Communities and Certain Member States – Measures Affecting Trade in large Civil Aircraft* and WTO dispute DS353 *United States – Measures Affecting Trade in Large Civil Aircraft – Second Complaint*.

Body and administrative costs of the ASEAN Secretariat. All member states are required to contribute equally to the initial sum of the Fund. The Fund is a revolving one, and the disputing parties shall replenish any drawdown from it. At first glance, Article 17 appears to be an innovative approach to the financing of dispute settlement mechanism, especially if we consider the ASEAN culture of dispute management. However, this provision comes with a number of problems. The first problem is the absence of a provision that stipulates the amount that each member state has to contribute to the Fund or a method through which the amount of contribution will be decided. In the WTO, on the other hand, there is a detailed method to calculate the amount of contribution that each member state should give.[63]

Second, considering the level of economic development of every ASEAN State, equal contribution to the ASEAN DSM Fund means that the Fund will be determined by the lowest offer by a member state. As a comparison, in the WTO the amount of a member state's contribution to the WTO budget is determined according to that member's share of international trade for the last five years.[64] This leads to an important question on the ASEAN DSM Fund: will the equal contributions of all member states to the ASEAN DSM Fund be sufficient to cover the costs associated with panellists, Appellate Body and administrative cost of the ASEAN Secretariat? The answer is, unfortunately, unclear. According to the ASEAN Secretariat, ASEAN has established the ASEAN DSM Fund as of 2009.[65] However, the amount of the initial Fund is not public. A number of sources has informed us that the ASEAN DSM Fund has reached US$ 345,000. It is unlikely that this amount will be sufficient to cover all expenses of the panel, Appellate Body and the ASEAN Secretariat in the course of a dispute. At a minimum the administrative cost to ASEAN for a dispute would be in the region of US$ 55,000 per case.[66] This is based on an estimate of the time cost of a technical officer in ASEAN to manage the case and an estimate of the administrative cost for the period of fifteen months (from the time a party files a request for consultation to the time of implementation of the reports). If the estimate

[63] Joint WTO/GATT Committee on Budget, Finance and Administration, 'Method of Calculation of Contributions Assessed on Members of the WTO', WTO Secretariat, retrieved on 10 October 2016 from the official website of the WTO: www.wto.org.

[64] Ibid. [65] ASEAN Secretariat, 'ASEAN Dispute Settlement System – Fact Sheet'.

[66] This estimate is based on the average salary of a midlevel technical officer at the ASEAN Secretariat, which is US$ 3,000 per month and the minimum administrative expenses for fifteen months.

of the administrative cost incurred by a dispute already consumes about 20 per cent of the total ASEAN DSM Fund, it is most likely that the ASEAN DSM Fund will not be sufficient to cover all expenses occurring from panels and Appellate Body proceedings.

The third problem is related to the obligation of the parties to a dispute to replenish the Fund in accordance with the panels and Appellate Body's apportioning of the expenses. The obligation to replenish the ASEAN DSM Fund might prove to be a deterrent factor for member states to utilise EDSM procedures, especially for the economically less-developed member states. This problem, combined with the potential insufficiency of the ASEAN DSM Fund to cover the cost of the Panel, Appellate Body and the Secretariat, might also contribute to member states' preference to bring their disputes before the WTO DSU, as the costs of dispute settlement are covered by the budget of the WTO.[67]

With regard to the role of the panel and Appellate Body in apportioning the expenses of the dispute, the EDSM does not provide any guidelines on how panels and the Appellate Body should apportion the expenses of the dispute appropriately. Last, indeed the EDSM expressly stipulates that parties to the dispute shall replenish the Fund. However, it is silent on the proportion of the sum that each party should bear.

Finally, there is nothing in Article 17 and the EDSM in general that suggests any other source of funding to maintain the Appellate Body, which is a standing body under Article 12 of the EDSM. It seems that there is a significant gap in the setup with regard to this, and it needs to be addressed before ASEAN establishes the EDSM Appellate Body.

2.3 *2010 Protocol to the ASEAN Charter on Dispute Settlement Mechanisms*

The DSMP applies to disputes arising from the interpretation or application of the ASEAN Charter and other ASEAN instruments that do not have any specific means of resolving disputes and do not fall within the ambit of the TAC and the EDSM.[68] It is unlikely, but not impossible, that a trade dispute may be characterised in a manner that would necessitate recourse to the DSMP. The DSMP also applies to other ASEAN

[67] WTO DSU, Article 8(11). [68] ASEAN Charter, Article 25 and DSMP, Article 2.

instruments that expressly provide for its application. Taking the EDSM as a template, the DSMP operates on strict time periods, which cannot be modified by parties to a dispute.[69] The means of resolving disputes under the DSMP consist of consultation, good offices, mediation and conciliation, and arbitration.[70] The DSMP is also equipped with rules of good offices, mediation, conciliation and arbitration in its Annexes 1–4. Unlike the EDSM, the DSMP does not establish a standing body for dispute settlement. Any means of dispute settlement, including arbitration, which a member state may invoke, will operate on an ad hoc basis. Therefore, there are no specific Fund and secretariat dedicated on a permanent basis to support the functions of the DSMP.

It is notable that the DSMP enables a member state to lodge a claim against another member state without needing to seek the consent of the latter first.[71] However, this does not mean that the DSMP is a compulsory mechanism. Unlike the EDSM, any means to resolve dispute under DSMP is only triggered when all parties to the dispute agree to use it.[72] Although the ASEAN Coordinating Council (ACC) has the power to direct disputing parties to resolve their dispute through arbitration, the ACC is less likely to do so because it has to base its decision on consensus.[73] A consensus to direct disputing parties is very unlikely to be achieved because the representative of the party that refuses to be brought to arbitration, in all likelihood, will not agree to such decision. The DSMP entered into force in July 2017, seven years after its adoption.[74]

Despite the DSMP entry into force, it would still be doubtful that ASEAN states would invoke any dispute settlement mechanism under the DSMP. This problem of the DSMP automaticity was demonstrated in 2010 when Cambodia attempted to activate the good offices of the ASEAN Chair (at that time, Vietnam) to mediate between Cambodia and Thailand in the dispute concerning the temple Preah Vihear.[75] The attempt failed because consensus of all disputing parties was needed to

[69] DSMP, Article 4. [70] Ibid., Articles 5–8. [71] Ibid., Article 5.

[72] For instance, Articles 8(3) and 10 of the DSMP stipulates that arbitration can only be established based on the mutual consent of the disputing parties.

[73] DSMP, Article 9.

[74] ASEAN Secretariat, 'ASEAN Legal Instruments', retrieved on 11 September 2017 from the official website of the ASEAN Secretariat http://agreement.asean.org.

[75] ASEAN Charter, Article 23.

activate the good offices of the ASEAN Chair, and Thailand refused. Even though the ASEAN Chair's good office to mediate was finally activated in 2011 when Indonesia held the ASEAN Chair, it was most likely due to the perceived referent authority of Indonesia as the largest of the ASEAN states rather than the authority vested in an organ of ASEAN (the ASEAN Chair).[76]

2.4 *The ASEAN Summit – Unresolved Disputes and Noncompliance with ASEAN Dispute Settlement Mechanism Findings and Recommendations*

Under Article 26 of the ASEAN Charter, in the event a dispute 'remains unresolved', after the parties have utilised the mechanisms available within the Charter, they can refer the unresolved dispute to the ASEAN Summit for its decision. Article 27 further stipulates that the ASEAN Summit also decides on the case of noncompliance with findings and recommendations resulting from an ASEAN dispute settlement mechanism. In this sense, ASEAN framework positions the ASEAN Summit as the final de facto arbitrator and enforcer of a decision that has been reached in any ASEAN dispute settlement mechanism. Additionally, the ASEAN Summit is to decide in the case of serious breaches of the Charter or noncompliance.

ASEAN member states may be reassured that a political body like the ASEAN Summit is the final arbitrator and enforcer for noneconomic disputes. However, it creates structural uncertainties about how the ASEAN Summit should apply its power to address the aforementioned matters. First, nothing in the Charter prescribes any mechanism enabling the ASEAN Summit to make its decision on the matters explained earlier. Second, even if the Summit is to make its decision based on consensus in accordance with Article 20 of the ASEAN Charter, the Charter is still silent on how the Summit should make its decision where consensus cannot be reached. Finally, nothing in the Charter explicitly obliges member states to comply with the Summit's decisions and the consequences of noncompliance to a Summit decision. So far no member state has brought any unresolved dispute to the attention of the ASEAN Summit.

[76] W. Woon, 'Dispute Settlement in ASEAN,' Conference Paper, 17 October 2011.

3 They Have Never Been Used: Addressing Legitimacy

Despite the limitations of the dispute settlement processes in ASEAN, no stakeholder that we know of, e.g. state, general public and academic, has raised legitimacy concerns about the processes. It could be because no disputes have been brought to the EDSM or that the public and other stakeholders have not become aware or unduly concerned about the EDSM. However, adopting the 'international pedigree view', the EDSM may find its legitimacy based on the fact that it was established by the consensus of all ASEAN member states.[77] Nevertheless, the lack of concern about the legitimacy of the EDSM and the fact that it was established through international consensus does not mean that consensus is the only touchstone of legitimacy. Having pointed out that ASEAN is in theory equipped to address intra-ASEAN trade disputes, why is it then that the EDSM is still not used? Does this affect the legitimacy of the EDSM within the framework of ASEAN? To answer this question, then, it may be beneficial to address the issue of legitimacy of the EDSM.[78]

The epistemic conditions of legitimacy as proposed by Buchanan and Keohane of minimal moral acceptability, comparative benefit and institutional integrity may serve as a practical approach to evaluate the EDSM.[79] Buchanan and Keohane proposed these aspects to evaluate global governance institutions, and thus they may be used to evaluate the EDSM as an institution for governing intra-ASEAN economic disputes. While Buchanan and Keohane point out that these conditions are 'best thought of as what Rawls calls "counting principles": the more of them an institution satisfies, and the higher degree to which it satisfies them, the stronger its claim to legitimacy',[80] the legitimacy of the EDSM may well be examined by applying these conditions on the EDSM's and ASEAN's own terms.

ASEAN arguably has satisfied the first condition of legitimacy, the 'minimal moral acceptability', i.e. this requires an institution to commit to 'minimal moral acceptability' and also accommodate and encourage 'the possibility of developing more demanding requirements of justice'.[81]

[77] A. Buchanan and R. O. Keohane, 'The legitimacy of global governance institutions' in R. Wolfrum and V. Roben (eds.), *Legitimacy in International Law* (Heidelberg: Springer, 2008), p. 35. *See also* R. Wolfrum, 'Legitimacy in international law' in R. Wolfrum, *The Max Planck Encyclopaedia of International Law Vol. IV* (Oxford University Press, 2012), p. 809.

[78] Buchanan and Keohane, 'The legitimacy of global governance institutions', p. 25.

[79] Ibid., p. 49. [80] Ibid., p. 50. [81] Ibid., p. 46.

ASEAN has formally fulfilled this condition through the pronouncement of a number of moral standards in its Charter, namely: (1) respect for and protection of human rights and fundamental freedoms; (2) adherence to the rule of law, good governance and the principles of democracy; (3) reliance on peaceful settlement of dispute; and, specifically on trade matter; and (4) adherence to multilateral trade rules and ASEAN's rules-based regime toward elimination of all barriers of regional economic integration in a market-driven economy.[82] These are a number of fundamental principles of ASEAN, and nothing in the EDSM or any of ASEAN economic agreements undermines these principles.

The second condition of legitimacy, which is 'comparative benefit', refers to the ability of an institution to provide benefits to states that otherwise cannot be obtained.[83] Unfortunately, the nonutilisation of the EDSM may emphasise the *lack* of comparative benefit. Despite the stipulation in the ASEAN Charter that the EDSM has exclusive jurisdiction to resolve disputes arising from the interpretation and application of *all* ASEAN economic agreements (which on the surface gives a semblance of comparative benefit), most trade-related obligations in ASEAN economic agreements are also covered in the GATT, which may explain ASEAN states' preference to bring their trade disputes before the WTO DSB (see later). The absence of disputes before the EDSM has resulted in the absence of information on the economic cost of resolving a dispute before the EDSM, which forms a significant element in supporting a claim of comparative benefit. Even with the absence of such data on cost, an educated calculation that we presented in the previous section shows that the economic cost of bringing a dispute before the EDSM may be higher compared to the cost that states have to spend to bring their disputes before the WTO. However, the EDSM may have a claim to comparative benefit for ASEAN trade disputes, which involve WTO plus obligations. For ASEAN obligations beyond their WTO obligations, ASEAN states will have no other option to resolve their disputes than the EDSM.

'Institutional integrity' as the last condition of legitimacy suggests that in order for an institution to be legitimate, there should not be 'egregious disparity' between its performance and its procedures or goals or its practice or procedures should not frustrate its goals, which justify its existence.[84] Again, the lack of disputes brought before the EDSM

[82] The ASEAN Charter, Article 2

[83] Buchanan and Keohane, 'The legitimacy of global governance institutions', p. 47.

[84] Ibid., pp. 47–8.

provides us with no data beyond the textual procedures for us to evaluate the EDSM. Nonetheless, assuming that there were disputes brought before the EDSM, would the EDSM procedures (at the very least) serve its main goal set out in the ASEAN Charter? Is there any possibility that the EDSM procedures may thwart its goal?

As has been established previously, the EDSM procedures are modelled on those of the WTO DSB, albeit with shorter timelines. Most important, the EDSM procedures include the negative consensus rule when it comes to its decision making, thereby depoliticising disputes and emphasising the rule of law. However, in the EDSM procedures all roads lead to SEOM; every stage of dispute resolution under the EDSM is concluded by SEOM. The crux of the problem here is that there are limited rules or information available about the procedures and workings of SEOM, especially on the internal procedures of its meetings. Considering that the ASEAN Way may be considered as the golden rule of ASEAN and it continues to hold a prominent position in the ASEAN Charter, it may be the case that SEOM would probably, at this stage in time, operate based on the ASEAN Way rather than sticking to the procedures of the EDSM. SEOM's transparency and procedures may become clearer and more accountable in the future as ASEAN economic disputes are brought to the EDSM. Until such a time, it can only be said that at least the text of the EDSM evidences institutional integrity.

Thus, as the EDSM has not yet been tested, the best that we can say at the moment is that the EDSM displays some functional legitimacy in that its procedures could work in theory and correspond to some extent with Buchanan and Keohane's counting principles. However, Buchanan and Keohane also warn that the availability of 'factual knowledge' of an institution, e.g. procedures and practices, is pivotal in producing 'reasonable judgments' about whether an institution satisfies any of these conditions.[85] And 'factual knowledge' vis-à-vis the EDSM is, sadly, absent.[86]

Nonetheless, we would argue that the EDSM is legitimate also because of a lack of alternatives for ASEAN WTO plus obligations. Despite its

[85] Ibid., p. 50.

[86] For instance, a discussion on the lack of factual knowledge on ASEAN economic integration, which is highly relevant in the context of the EDSM, i.e. procedures, accountability, enforcement etc., *see* M. Ewing-Chow, 'Culture club or chameleon: Should ASEAN adopt legalisation for economic integration?', *Singapore Yearbook of International Law and Contributors*, 12 (2008), pp. 225–37.

forty-eight years of existence, ASEAN only started its legalisation process in 2007 when it adopted the ASEAN Charter. ASEAN states are still in the process of developing their own domestic legal procedures, and although ASEAN states recognise the principle of democracy enshrined in the ASEAN Charter, they practice political systems that vary from liberal democracy to absolute monarchy.[87] In many of the ASEAN states the option for a legal solution to disputes is further hampered by a limited rule of law and high corruption perception.[88] The EDSM therefore represents a real viable alternative to domestic courts in lieu of anything else. Thus, we believe that a functional approach to legitimacy at this stage of ASEAN will be a better benchmark to evaluate the EDSM and, hopefully, strengthen its claim of 'institutional integrity'. Through this approach we will attempt to evaluate the legitimacy of the EDSM through its function in contributing toward the achievement of ASEAN's goals vis-à-vis the AEC.

Under the Blueprint of the AEC, the establishment of the AEC aims at the transformation of ASEAN into a region with 'free movement of goods, services, investment, skilled labours and freer flow of capital' by 2015.[89] The Blueprint specifically stipulates the EDSM as a tool to enhance the implementation and realisation of the AEC with a specific function 'to promote a rules-based community'.[90] This implies a range of functions of the EDSM, as opposed to merely resolving ASEAN economic dispute. Taking into consideration ASEAN states' subtlety in managing disputes and penchant for the ASEAN Way, the absence of disputes before the EDSM does not pose as a legitimacy problem for

[87] The ASEAN Charter does not require ASEAN members to be democratic because the principle of democracy is subordinate to the principle of sovereignty and noninterference. *See* D. E. Weatherbee, *Indonesia in ASEAN: Vision and Reality* (Singapore: Institute of Southeast Asian Studies, 2013), p. 34. Although Buchanan and Keohane argue that apart from the three epistemic conditions of legitimacy, ongoing consent of democratic states is generally necessary for legitimacy. *See* Buchanan and Keohane, 'The legitimacy of global governance institutions', pp. 37–8.

[88] According to the 2014 Corruption Perception Index generated by Transparency International only Singapore is listed as one of the least corrupt countries (rank 7 out of 175 countries). In an ascending order, the rank of ASEAN countries in TI's Corruption Perception Index is as follows: (1) Malaysia (52/175); (2) Thailand (85/175); (3) the Philippines (85/175); (4) Indonesia (107/175); (5) Vietnam (119/175); (6) Laos (145/175); (7) Cambodia (156/175); and (8) Myanmar (156/175). See Transparency International, 'Corruption Perception Index 2014: Results', retrieved on 10 October 2016 from the official website of Transparency International www.transparency.org.

[89] ASEAN Economic Community Blueprint, Singapore, 20 November 2007, para. 4.

[90] Ibid., para. 72.iv.

ASEAN. The EDSM serves as an additional option to solve complaints; it potentially equalises the power asymmetry between member states. It also adds pressure on member states to comply with measures leading up to the achievement of AEC goals because under the shadow of possible litigation parties are more reasonable with their commitments and lead up to the promotion of compliance. There are only very few things in the world that focuses the mind and encourages reasonable behaviour for compliance than the threat of litigation and liability.

4 Why Are ASEAN Dispute Settlement Mechanisms Still Not Used?

The fact that the ASEAN dispute settlement mechanisms have never been used does not mean that intra-ASEAN disputes do not exist. However, ASEAN member states seem to prefer bringing their disputes to third-party dispute settlement mechanisms outside of ASEAN. We believe that there are a number of pathologies in ASEAN that mitigate against disputes being resolved by any of ASEAN dispute settlement mechanisms, including the EDSM. Because these pathologies are also pervasive in other ASEAN dispute settlement mechanisms and considering the very small number of intra-ASEAN trade disputes that have been brought in any fora, it is in our opinion that it will be worthwhile to consider the ASEAN culture relating to dispute settlement in general, including nontrade disputes. Although we recognise that the dynamics of nontrade disputes are different from trade disputes, we believe that they provide extra evidence of a regional culture of dispute management within ASEAN and hence are worth exploring. Table 12.1 below shows known disputes between ASEAN states that were brought before third–party dispute settlement fora.

Based on our analysis of the case precedents described in Table 12.1 and ASEAN's practice in handling intra-ASEAN dispute, we list three possible explanations that may contribute to the nonutilisation of ASEAN dispute mechanisms. The first possible explanation is ASEAN states' persistent practice of dispute management through the exercise of the 'ASEAN Way' of diplomacy and the numerous regular meetings of ASEAN organs, which substantially reduce the need for a legalised mechanism. Second, when diplomacy does not result in satisfactory resolution and when member states indeed agree to bring their disputes before a formal and binding dispute settlement mechanism, they show a high degree of confidence in, and preference for, extra-ASEAN dispute settlement mechanisms. Third, it appears that member states realise the

Table 12.1 *List of disputes between ASEAN states before third-party dispute settlement*

No	Dispute	Parties	Year	Third-party dispute settlement	Base of jurisdiction
1.	The Railway Land Arbitration[1]	Malaysia/ Singapore	2012–2014	Permanent Court of Arbitration (PCA)	Art. 1 of the Submission Agreement between Singapore and Malaysia of 9 January 2012
2.	Request for Interpretation of the Judgement of 15 June 1962 in the Case concerning the Temple Preah Vihear (Cambodia *v.* Thailand)[2]	Cambodia *v.* Thailand	2010–2013	International Court of Justice (ICJ)	Art. 60 of the ICJ Statute – interpretation of a judgement upon the request of a party
3.	Thailand – Cigarettes (Philippines)[3]	Philippines *v.* Thailand	2008–2011	WTO DSB	WTO DSU
4.	Land Reclamation by Singapore in and around the Straits of Johor[4]	Malaysia *v.* Singapore	2003	Ad Hoc Tribunal	Annex VII of the United Nations Convention on the Law of the Sea (UNCLOS)
5.	Sovereignty over Pedra Branca/Pulau Batu Puteh, Middle Rocks and South Ledge[5]	Malaysia/ Singapore	2003–2008	ICJ	Special Agreement made under Art. 36(1) of the ICJ Statute
6.	Sovereignty over Pulau Sipadan and Pulau Ligitan[6]	Indonesia/ Malaysia	1998–2002	ICJ	Special Agreement made under Art. 36(1) of the ICJ Statute

Table 12.1 (*cont.*)

No	Dispute	Parties	Year	Third-party dispute settlement	Base of jurisdiction
7.	Malaysia – Prohibition of Imports of Polyethylene and Polypropylene[7]	Singapore *v.* Malaysia	1995	WTO DSB	WTO DSU
8.	The Case concerning the Temple Preah Vihear[8]	Cambodia *v.* Thailand	1959–1962	ICJ	Optional Clause Declarations made under Art. 36(2) of the ICJ Statute

1 *Railway Land Arbitration (Malaysia v. Singapore)* PCA Case (2014) no. 2012–01.

2 Request for Interpretation of the Judgement of 15 June 1962 in the case concerning Temple of Preah Vihear (*Cambodia v. Thailand*) (*Cambodia v. Thailand*) ICJ Reports (2013) 151.

3 WTO dispute DS371, *Thailand – Cigarettes (Philippines)*. This is the second dispute brought by an ASEAN state against another ASEAN state before the WTO DSB.

4 *Land Reclamation by Singapore in and around the Straits of Johor (Malaysia v. Singapore)*, Provisional Measures, 2003 ITLOS Rep. 10. Malaysia and Singapore signed a settlement agreement in 2005 and thereafter jointly submitted a letter to ITLOS requesting ITLOS to deliver a final binding award in the terms set out in the settlement agreement.

5 Sovereignty over Pedra Branca/Pulau Batu Puteh, Middle Rocks and South Ledge (*Malaysia v. Singapore*) ICJ Reports (2008) 12.

6 Sovereignty over Pulau Sipadan and Pulau Ligitan (*Indonesia v. Malaysia*) ICJ Reports (2002) 625.

7 Request for Consultation, *Malaysia –Polyethylene and Polypropylene*. It is the first dispute brought before the WTO DSU. The two parties managed to resolve their dispute through consultation and Singapore withdrew its complaint completely on 19 July 1995.

8 *The Case concerning the Temple of Preah Vihear (Cambodia v. Thailand)*, ICJ Reports (1962) 24. Cambodia managed to bring Thailand before the ICJ based on optional clause declarations that both parties had made under Article 36(2) of the ICJ Statute, accepting the compulsory jurisdiction of the Court. After the Court rendered its judgement giving the sovereignty over the temple Preah Vihear to Cambodia, Thailand stopped renewing its declaration.

institutional and resource limitations of ASEAN organs, especially the ASEAN Secretariat, vis-à-vis the exercise of the functions of ASEAN dispute settlement mechanisms. With that said, data from other Free Trade Area dispute settlement mechanisms, which show a similar limited utilisation rate, suggest that ASEAN is not alone in these pathologies.[91]

4.1 *Dispute Management: ASEAN Way of Diplomacy and ASEAN Meetings*

Although ASEAN states are not averse to submitting their dispute before third-party dispute settlements outside ASEAN dispute settlement mechanisms, dispute management still takes precedent in ASEAN. In the ASEAN context, dispute management is usually aimed at deescalating the dispute.[92] The most common practice of dispute management in ASEAN is through the ASEAN Way of diplomacy; it is commonly used to address territorial sovereignty disputes, which may affect the region's peace and security.[93]Another possible method of dispute management in ASEAN is, theoretically, through the utilisation of numerous regular meetings of ASEAN organs as strategic forums of dispute management through continued discussion. This method may be utilised to manage disputes arising from interpretation and implementation of ASEAN instruments. As the following discussions will explain, ASEAN's prioritisation of dispute management might be another reason why (possible) ASEAN disputes do not go before any ASEAN dispute settlement mechanism.

4.1.1 'ASEAN Way' of Diplomacy to Manage Intra-ASEAN Disputes

ASEAN is well known for its 'ASEAN Way' of diplomacy to manage disputes, which mainly consisted of three revered principles of ASEAN:

[91] C. Chase, A. Yanovich, J.-A. Crawford and P. Ugaz, 'Mapping of Dispute Settlement Mechanisms in Regional trade Agreements – Innovative or Variations on a Theme?', *WTO Economic Research and Statistic Division*, Staff Working Paper, ERSD-2013-07.

[92] H. D. Phan, 'Procedures for peace: Building mechanisms for dispute settlement and conflict management within ASEAN', *UC Davis Journal of International Law and Policy*, 20 (2013), p. 49; D. E. Weatherbee, *International Relations in Southeast Asia: The Struggle for Autonomy*, 2nd ed. (Singapore: Institute for Southeast Asian Studies, 2010), pp. 131–2; and M. Caballero-Anthony, 'Mechanisms for dispute settlement: The ASEAN experience', *Contemporary Southeast Asia*, 20 (1998), pp. 39 and 51–3.

[93] Ibid.

reliance on consultation and consensus in decision making, nonconfrontation and noninterference in the internal affairs of one another.[94] Based on these principles, disputes among ASEAN states, especially territorial sovereignty, are settled through diplomacy (read: bilateral consultations).[95] Diplomacy as means to deescalate disputes has been observed strictly by ASEAN member states since the beginning of ASEAN. Informality and closed-door policy are the key signatures of ASEAN Way of diplomacy, and third-party involvement is strictly prohibited unless the disputing parties agreed otherwise.[96] The methods usually involve informal summits, instead of formal ASEAN meetings/forums, at the level of head of government/state or ministers of foreign affairs, and discussions are usually conducted over cocktails or lunch.[97]

This practice keeps ongoing intra-ASEAN disputes from public attention, and as a result, the general public only know of an intra-ASEAN dispute when the disputing parties have agreed to bring their dispute before a third-party dispute settlement forum or from bits and pieces of the dispute mentioned in newspaper coverage or books written by former diplomats. In the Thai cigarette case, for instance, the three-year negotiation between Thailand and Philippines flew below the ASEAN public's radar until Philippines filed a request for consultation before the WTO in 2008. Similarly, in the Polyethylene and Polypropylene case between Singapore and Malaysia, the negotiation process was never revealed to the public until Singapore brought the dispute before the WTO. This is not to say that this practice is an exclusive trait of ASEAN states, but it is the persistence of ASEAN states to pursue negotiations and consensus-building before finally bringing their disputes before a third-party dispute

94 ASEAN Charter, Articles 2(2)(e) and 20. These principles have a long-standing history in Southeast Asia dating back to Maphilindo in 1963. For further discussion on the ASEAN Way, see N. Sopiee, 'ASEAN and regional security' in K. S. Sandhu et al. (eds.), *The ASEAN Reader* (Singapore: Institute of Southeast Asian Studies, 1992), pp. 391–2; Weatherbee, *International Relations in Southeast Asia*, p. 128; and S. Narine, *Explaining ASEAN Regionalism in Southeast Asia* (London: Lynne Riener Publishers, 2002), pp. 31–3.

95 R. C. Severino, *Southeast Asia in Search of an ASEAN Community: Insights from the Former ASEAN Secretary-General* (Singapore: Institute of Southeast Asian Studies, 2006), pp. 164–6.

96 Narine, *Explaining ASEAN Regionalism*, p. 31; and Weatherbee, *International Relations in Southeast Asia*, p. 131. Since 1967, parties to intra-ASEAN disputes never requested the involvement of a third party in the negotiation of their disputes. The only exception is the Preah Vihear dispute in 2010.

97 Ibid.

settlement forum that marks the particularity of ASEAN culture in managing dispute.

There are also other intra-ASEAN trade disputes that were resolved through negotiations and not made public. Two cases that we are aware of are the Singapore–Philippines trade dispute concerning measures affecting petrochemical products and the dispute between Thailand and Malaysia on the delay in automotive tariff reductions.[98] In the dispute concerning petrochemical products between the Philippines and Singapore, Singapore sought compensation from the Philippines due to measures affecting the importation of petrochemical resins and certain plastic products. The Philippines' government issued an Executive Order in January 2003 that temporarily suspended the tariff set out under the CEPT in order to protect domestic production facilities. Although the CEPT requires that tariff rates between ASEAN member states on a broad range of products be reduced from 0 per cent to 5 per cent, the 2003 Executive Order raised rates on a number of products from 5 per cent to 20 per cent.[99] The dispute was settled through negotiations, which resulted in a US$ 8 million compensation arrangement.[100] In the trade dispute between Thailand and Malaysia on measures affecting the importation of cars and automotive parts, Malaysia constantly refused to lower its automotive tariff in accordance with the CEPT's 2002 schedule.[101] As the biggest cars and automotive parts producer in the region, Thailand sought compensation from Malaysia as Malaysia's delay in reducing its automotive tariff was an impediment to the successful implementation of AFTA 2002.[102] This dispute was never brought before any third-party dispute settlement forum, and it seems that this dispute was settled by negotiations. This is indicated by Malaysia's gradual

98 D. F. binte Abdul Aziz, G. G. Meishan and E. Lim Wee Kuan, 'Southeast Asia and international law: July – December 2001', *Singapore Journal of International and Comparative Law*, 5 (2001), pp. 833–5; and L. Toohey, 'When 'failure' indicates success: Understanding trade disputes between ASEAN members' in R. P. Buckley, R. W. Hu, and D. W. Arner (eds.), *East Asian Economic Integration: Law, Trade and Finance* (Northampton: Edward Elgar Publishing Limited, 2011), p. 165.

99 Executive Office of the President of the United States of America, '2004 National Trade Estimate Report on Foreign Trade Barriers', Office of the United States Trade Representative, 31 March 2004, p. 378.

100 'Singapore Agrees to Compensation Package in Petrochem Dispute with Philippines', retrieved on 10 October 2016 from Plastemart website: www.plastemart.com.

101 1992 ASEAN Agreement on the Common Effective Preferential Tariff Scheme for the ASEAN Free Trade Area, Singapore, 28 January 1992, Article 4.

102 'ASEAN must Get Serious about AFTA', Straits Times, 17 July 2001, p. 6.

automotive tariff reduction.[103] However, it is not clear whether Thailand received any compensation from Malaysia.

These disputes were settled far away from the eyes of the public, and negotiations were conducted behind closed doors in numerous ASEAN meetings.[104] It is interesting to note that unlike intra-ASEAN political disputes, handling or settlement of economic disputes arising from interpretation or application of ASEAN economic agreements is more amenable to pressure by other ASEAN states not parties to the dispute. Kenevan and Winden even argue that peer pressure is likely to be a particularly effective element in the ASEAN Free Trade Area due to the widespread consensus among ASEAN member states to maintain rapid economic growth.[105] Though the CEPT lacked a concrete dispute settlement provision, it was designed to encourage peer pressure to advance economic integration.[106] The CEPT has been replaced by the ASEAN Trade in Goods Agreement in 2009.

ASEAN experience shows that when bilateral consultations failed to contain or resolve a dispute to the satisfaction of the parties, the disputing parties will only bring their dispute before a third-party dispute settlement if they can reach a mutual agreement to do so. This was the case with both the Sipadan–Ligitan and Pedra Branca disputes. All disputing parties to those disputes spent decades in bilateral negotiations and consultations before they finally gave their consent to bring their disputes before the ICJ.[107] Another instance is the Thai cigarette dispute.

103 Executive Office of the President of the United States of America, '2004 National Trade Estimate Report on Foreign Trade Barriers', Office of the United States Trade Representative, 31 March 2004, p. 320.

104 Please see the discussion in the next section on 'ASEAN Meetings to Manage Disputes Arising from Interpretation or Application of ASEAN Instruments'.

105 P. Kenevan and A. Winden, 'Flexible free trade: the ASEAN free trade area', *Harvard International Law Journal*, 34 (1993), pp. 228–9.

106 Ibid., p. 229.

107 Indonesia and Malaysia had conducted negotiations to resolve the Sipadan-Ligitan dispute since 1969 before they finally brought the dispute before the ICJ in 1997. Similarly, the Singapore and Malaysia negotiation process to resolve the Pedra Branca dispute had taken decades since the emergence of the dispute in 1979 until a decision was taken by both parties to bring the dispute to the ICJ. Even after a decision was made to take the Pedra Branca dispute before the ICJ in 1995, it took another nine years before the parties finally ratified the Special Agreement. See S. Jayakumar and Tommy Koh, *Pedra Branca: the Road to the World Court* (Singapore: National University of Singapore Press, 2009), pp. 35 and 41; R. R. Bundy, 'Asian Perspective on Inter-State Litigation' in Natalie Klein (ed.), *Litigating International Law Disputes: Weighing the Options* (Cambridge University Press, 2014), pp. 157–9.

Although it was Philippines that initiated the consultation, and finally panel process, under the WTO DSU against Thailand, this was done after years of bilateral consultation between the two states consistent with the 'ASEAN Way' of diplomacy.[108] In the dispute between Singapore and Malaysia before the WTO DSU in 1995, Singapore even withdrew its request because the dispute had been settled through bilateral consultation.[109] This shows that even when an intra-ASEAN dispute has been brought before a dispute settlement mechanism, the ASEAN way of diplomacy may still continue to run its course.

If the disputing parties cannot reach a mutual agreement to bring the dispute before a third-party dispute settlement system and the dispute is so politically charged that it stirs up the domestic populations within both states, often ASEAN states will implicitly avoid the dispute altogether. By avoiding the dispute, the disputing states implicitly agree not to escalate the dispute and not to initiate any discussion with regard to the dispute in any forum, including an ASEAN forum, for an indeterminate period of time. An example of this practice is the Sabah dispute between the Philippines and Malaysia from 1968 to the early 1970s.[110] After two 'cooling-off' periods and years of suspension of all ASEAN meetings during this period, Malaysia and the Philippines still could not agree on a solution or whether to bring their dispute before a dispute settlement body. In 1976, the Philippines finally agreed not to raise its claim over Sabah in any ASEAN forum. This gesture was welcomed by Malaysia, and Malaysia indicated this by attending the First ASEAN Summit, the first meeting that it attended together with the Philippines. Since then, the Sabah dispute has never been raised in any ASEAN meeting and Malaysia and the Philippines have long since normalised their diplomatic relations.[111] It appears that they tacitly agreed to put this dispute on the back burner indefinitely.

Since the adoption of the ASEAN Charter, however, ASEAN has evolved from informality to a more formal form of diplomacy within the framework of the Charter. As explained earlier, in 2010 Cambodia

[108] International Centre for Trade and Sustainable Development, 'Appellate Body Upholds Ruling against Thailand in Philippines Cigarette Dispute' (2011) 15 *Bridges*, retrieved on 10 October 2016 from the official website of ICTSD: www.ictsd.org.

[109] Request for Consultation, *Malaysia – Polyethylene and Polypropylene*.

[110] Details of the dispute can be found in Severino, *Southeast Asia in Search of an ASEAN Community*, pp. 164–6; Weatherbee, *International Relations in Southeast Asia*, pp. 131–2; and Caballero-Anthony, 'Mechanisms for dispute settlement', pp. 53–5.

[111] Ibid.

requested the good office of Indonesia as the ASEAN Chair of that year to mediate its dispute with Thailand over the temple of Preah Vihear. The request was made based on Article 23 of the ASEAN Charter and Thailand agreed with the request.[112] The acceptance set an unprecedented move of invoking the good offices of an ASEAN organ to mediate an intra-ASEAN dispute.

4.1.2 ASEAN Meetings to Manage Disputes Arising from Interpretation or Application of ASEAN Instruments

The ASEAN Secretariat organises more than 600 regular meetings of ASEAN organs every year.[113] These include meetings at the ministerial level down to sectoral bodies' meetings. Regular meetings of ASEAN organs may constitute yet another method of ASEAN dispute management, especially the meeting of organs that are responsible for the implementation, coordination, monitoring, review and/or evaluation of ASEAN instruments. From 1967 to date, the ASEAN Secretariat has recorded eighty-nine ASEAN umbrella and independent agreements and more than one hundred derivative and amendment protocols.[114] Almost all of these agreements have specific ASEAN organs that are responsible for their implementation, coordination, monitoring and/or review.[115] Pursuant to these agreements, these bodies are required to hold regular meetings vis-à-vis their functions and responsibilities.[116]

In practice, these meetings take place within the time frame of the ASEAN Summit.[117] The agenda of these meetings usually consists of regular items and irregular items.[118] The agenda is first distributed to all

[112] H. D. Phan, 'Institutional design and its constraints: Explaining ASEAN's role in the Temple of Preah Vihear Dispute', *Asian Journal of International Law*, 5 (2014), p. 4.

[113] S. Pitsuwan, 'ASEAN's Challenge: Some Reflections and Recommendations on Strengthening the ASEAN Secretariat', Report submitted to H.E. M. Natalegawa, Chair of ASEAN Coordinating Council, 2011, p. 26.

[114] ASEAN Secretariat, 'ASEAN Legal Instruments'.

[115] Robert C. Beckman et al., *Promoting Compliance: The Role of Dispute Settlement and Monitoring Mechanisms in ASEAN Instruments* (Cambridge University Press, 2015), Appendix 2.

[116] Ibid. [117] ASEAN Charter, Article 7(3).

[118] Regular items include deliberation on the implementation of ASEAN instruments or any other functions that a particular ASEAN organ is required to perform under an ASEAN agreement. Irregular items may include questions that arise from the implementation of an ASEAN agreement. To the knowledge of the authors, ASEAN has not adopted any Rules of Procedures or Standard Operating Procedures pertaining to regular meetings of ASEAN organs. All information in this Article in relation to the practice of ASEAN meetings are based on information provided by former government officers of ASEAN

member states' delegations for approval, and such approval has to be reached by consensus. During this process, a member state may raise an issue/dispute to be included as an irregular item in a particular meeting. If they cannot reach a consensus on the inclusion of such item, then the item will not be included in the agenda or, depending on the gravity of the issue/dispute raised, the heads of delegation may hold a private informal meeting among them to discuss the issue/dispute.[119]

Considering that these meetings are closed to the public and, in the case of informal meetings, the meetings' reports are not always made public, it is hard to determine the number of issues/disputes arising from the interpretation or application of any ASEAN agreement that have been included as irregular items in any of these meetings. However, the inclusion of irregular items in the agenda of a regular meeting of an ASEAN organ may serve as a viable option for member states to bring a dispute over the interpretation and implementation of an ASEAN agreement. We have been told by various officials involved in these processes that many disputes are resolved in this way. As mentioned before, the dispute between Singapore and Philippines over measures affecting petrochemical resins and certain plastic products and the dispute between Thailand and Malaysia over automotive tariff serve as notable examples of disputes resolved through this mechanism.

4.2 *Preference to Utilise International Third-Party Dispute Settlement Mechanisms*

Although no dispute has ever been filed under any ASEAN dispute settlement mechanisms, ASEAN states are not averse in resorting to international third-party dispute settlement. ASEAN states' culture in managing disputes requires the disputing parties to undergo rigorous bilateral consultation to resolve their dispute and only when they consider that the dispute cannot be resolved through consultation will they begin *another* consultation to reach a consensus to submit their dispute to a dispute settlement body. The Singapore–Malaysia's Polyethylene and Polypropylene trade dispute demonstrated that consultation was actively pursued as a preferred solution.

states who attended regular meetings of ASEAN organs. The interviews were conducted between 22 and 24 July 2014.

[119] Ibid.

Case precedents show that when it comes to disputes over territorial sovereignty and trade, ASEAN states have become more open to dispute resolution before international judicial bodies. Cambodia and the Philippines even still maintain their optional clause declaration accepting the compulsory jurisdiction of the ICJ indicating their readiness to resort to ICJ to solve their dispute.[120] ASEAN states are also not averse from bringing non-ASEAN states to third-party dispute settlement or to participate as a third party for both territorial sovereignty and trade disputes as shown in the South China Sea dispute under Annex VII of UNCLOS between the Philippines and China[121] and ASEAN states' involvement in WTO disputes before the WTO DSB.[122]

So why do ASEAN states prefer to bring their disputes to international third-party dispute settlement notwithstanding the possibility that it is also possible to bring their disputes before an ASEAN dispute settlement mechanism? For instance, in the Thai cigarette dispute, Philippines filed for consultation and eventually for panel establishment due to Thai fiscal and custom measures affecting cigarettes from the Philippines. The Philippines claimed that Thailand administered these measures in violation of the GATT. Though ASEAN trade agreements at this time were not comprehensive, the Philippines still could have brought its complaint for possible breach of the 1997 ASEAN Agreement on Customs before the EDSM. Similarly, territorial sovereignty disputes such as the Sipadan–Ligitan and Pedra Branca disputes could also be brought before the TAC High Council, and yet ASEAN states chose not to.

There are certain reasons why ASEAN states prefer to utilise extra-ASEAN dispute settlement mechanisms. First, prior to the entry into force of the ASEAN Charter, there was nothing in any ASEAN's instrument on dispute settlement mechanism, that gives exclusive jurisdiction to the

[120] International Court of Justice, 'Declarations Recognizing the Jurisdiction of the Court as Compulsory', retrieved on 10 October 2016 from the ICJ official website: www.icj-cij.org.

[121] In the Matter of the South China Sea Arbitration before an Arbitral Tribunal Constituted under Annex VII to the 1982 United Nations Convention on the Law of the Sea (the *Republic of the Philippines v. the People's Republic of China*), Arbitral Award, PCA Case No. 2013–19, 12 July 2016, paras. 28 and 36. On 22 January 2013, the Philippines initiated an arbitral proceeding against China pursuant to Articles 286 – 287 and Annex VII of UNCLOS on disputes over maritime features in the South China Sea. On 5 December 2014, Vietnam submitted a statement to the arbitral tribunal in which, among others, it reserved 'the right to seek to intervene' in the proceedings in accordance with international law.

[122] WTO Dispute Settlement, 'Dispute by Country/Territory', retrieved on 10 October 2016 from the official website of the WTO www.wto.org.

respective mechanism to address disputes arising from ASEAN agreements or intra-ASEAN disputes. On the contrary, there is a standard clause in the TAC and the EDSM, which gives free reign to ASEAN states to decide on the mode and forum to settle their disputes.[123] Therefore, nothing obliges ASEAN states to bring their trade disputes or territorial sovereignty disputes before ASEAN dispute settlement bodies. Although this was the case prior to the entry into force of the Charter, the Charter strengthens the jurisdiction of these mechanisms by making them applicable to all disputes arising from the interpretation and application of all ASEAN agreements. The Charter even goes so far as to oblige member states to bring *all* intra-ASEAN disputes, including those that do not arise from the interpretation and application of ASEAN agreements, to the TAC for settlement.[124] It will be interesting to know how this seemingly exclusive provision affects the dynamics of post-Charter intra-ASEAN disputes.

The second reason is related to the reputation, proven track record and/or higher enforceability of particular extra-ASEAN dispute settlement mechanisms. Compared to the untried ASEAN dispute settlement mechanisms, the option of bringing intra-ASEAN disputes to external forum seems to offer more assurance for the disputing parties. To start with, these mechanisms have a proven track record in resolving disputes on the basis of international law, and they have built a body of case law, which might provide disputing parties with more assurance about the predictability of the outcomes.[125] Another aspect that may also be of crucial consideration of the states in this regard is the issue of costs. Especially for trade disputes, bringing trade disputes to the WTO will possibly cost compared to than bringing disputes to the EDSM. For instance, while the WTO DSU provides that the costs of a panel and secretariat will be covered by the budget of the WTO Secretariat, under the EDSM the disputing parties are basically required to pay for the costs of the panel, Appellate Body and Secretariat.

The third reason relates particularly to ASEAN trade agreements. It appears that in the period prior to the adoption of the ASEAN Trade in Goods Agreement,[126] ASEAN trade provisions were not as comprehensive

[123] TAC, Article 17 and EDSM, Article 1(3). [124] ASEAN Charter, Article 24(2).

[125] M. Lewis and P. van den Bossche, 'What to do when disagreement strikes? The complexity of dispute settlement under trade agreements' in S. Frankel and M. Lewis (eds.), *Trade Agreements at the Crossroads* (New York: Routledge, 2014), p. 15; and Bundy, 'Asian perspective on inter-state litigation', pp. 159–60.

[126] 2009 ASEAN Trade in Goods Agreement, Cha-am, 26 February 2009, in force 30 April 2010.

as the provisions of the WTO. For instance, to our knowledge until the adoption of the ASEAN trade in Goods Agreement, ASEAN did not have any provision on National Treatment. Therefore, it does not come as a surprise that ASEAN states preferred to bring their trade disputes to the WTO, and this is what happened in the Thai cigarettes dispute. Although various Southeast Asian scholars have suggested that the Philippines could have resorted to the EDSM procedures,[127] it is pertinent to note that at this time the only relevant ASEAN instrument on goods was the CEPT, which dealt with the reduction of tariff rates on certain products, but the CEPT did not include a national treatment clause, unlike the GATT. Arguably a claim could have been brought under the ASEAN economic agreements for breaches of the 1997 ASEAN Agreement on Customs which Article 5 incorporates the GATT Article VII on custom valuation. Of course, while this would have dealt with the Philippines' concern with regard to custom valuation and tariff rates, it would not have resolved the problem behind the border measures by Thailand, namely the excise tax and other nontariff measures affecting Philippines cigarettes.[128] Thus, beyond the institutional advantages, reputational gains and high compliance likelihood provided by bringing a dispute to the WTO there were clear legal advantages to do so as well.

The fourth consideration is with regard to the presence of the political content in some aspects of ASEAN dispute settlement mechanisms. The starkest example of this is the TAC's High Council, which is practically a political body[129] instead of an adjudicative one. An example of member states' reluctance to utilise the TAC due to this consideration can be illustrated through the experience of the Sipadan–Ligitan dispute. Prior to bringing the Sipadan–Ligitan dispute to the ICJ, Indonesia suggested to Malaysia to bring the dispute to the TAC. However, the suggestion was met with a refusal. The main reason of Malaysia's refusal was because Malaysia feared that a number of ASEAN states would be partial to Indonesia's claim.[130] Malaysia's fear was reasonable since at that time Malaysia had territorial disputes with all of its immediate neighbours.[131] It might be perceived that due to these reasons the proceeding would be biased and highly charged with various political interests. By jointly submitting their disputes to the ICJ, ASEAN states had most likely agreed

127 See for instance, Woon, 'Dispute Settlement in ASEAN'.

128 Appellate Body Report, *Thailand – Cigarettes (Philippines).*

129 See discussion on the membership of TAC above.

130 Severino, *Southeast Asia in Search of an ASEAN Community*, p. 12.

131 Ibid., p. 13.

to separate the legal and political aspects of the disputes,[132] hence depoliticising the disputes and conceivably making the ICJ's judgement more acceptable to both parties. It is also worth mentioning that depoliticisation also formed a part of ASEAN consideration to establish the EDSM.[133] However, practice suggests that they still prefer the even more depoliticised processes of the WTO.

4.3 *The Lack of Capacity of ASEAN Organs vis-à-vis The Exercise of the Functions of ASEAN Dispute Settlement Mechanisms*

Notwithstanding the similarities of the EDSM procedures with the WTO DSU, there are significant capacity issues concerning the organs of the EDSM. Limited capacity and lack of resources, especially on the part of the ASEAN Secretariat, constitute some of ASEAN's infamous constraints. Although it is hard to determine how far these issues might affect member states' decisions on dispute settlement mechanisms, these problems impose great constraints in the execution of ASEAN organs' functions in general, and dispute settlement in particular.

4.3.1 The ASEAN Secretariat – Obligations and Implementation

The ASEAN Secretariat plays significant roles and functions under the ASEAN Charter and hundreds of ASEAN agreements. The Secretariat's functions under the EDSM only constitute a small part of the Secretariat's responsibilities, a fact that most observers tend to overlook when they compare the ASEAN Secretariat with the WTO Secretariat. Under the Charter alone, the Secretary-General of ASEAN and the Secretariat are responsible for, among other roles, facilitating and monitoring progress in the implementation of all ASEAN agreements, maintaining treaty records and depository of ratifications, monitoring member states' compliance with decisions of ASEAN dispute settlement bodies, preparing for ASEAN meetings, administrative matters of the Association and providing an interpretation of the Charter upon the request of any

[132] For a discussion on the depoliticisation of international disputes through an international court see J. G. Merrills, *International Dispute Settlement*, 5th ed. (New York: Cambridge University Press, 2001), pp. 152–6.

[133] High-level Task Force on ASEAN Economic Integration, 'Recommendations of the High-Level Task Force on ASEAN Economic Integration', retrieved on 10 October 2016 from the official website of the ASEAN Secretariat www.asean.org.

member states.[134] The ASEAN Secretariat is also charged with responsibilities specific to certain ASEAN agreements from all fields of cooperation namely political-security, economic and sociocultural.[135] A number of the Secretariat's functions demand a certain degree of legal expertise. For instance, the secretariat role as the Association's depository requires sound knowledge of the law of treaties and treaty management, and its role to support the EDSM panel in conducting legal research requires in-depth knowledge on international and regional trade law and policy. However, despite these responsibilities the Secretariat has not been provided with the financial resources to match. Furthermore, the Secretariat's capacity is currently more limited particularly with regard to legal expertise.

The Secretariat has been facing constant problems of the lack of resources and a severe shortage of funds.[136] As the issue of the ASEAN DSM Fund has been discussed earlier, this part will focus solely on the ASEAN Secretariat's lack of resources to perform its administrative duties under the EDSM and lack of legal professionals to provide legal support for the EDSM panels and Appellate Body. As of May 2011, the ASEAN Secretariat employs about 260 staff including 79 openly recruited from all member states.[137] They are responsible for the execution of the Secretariat's administrative functions as well as other functions in all fields of ASEAN cooperation. To illustrate the overly burdened workload of the Secretariat, we take the Secretariat's responsibility to administer all ASEAN meetings as an example.[138] Every year, the Secretariat organises more than 600 meetings of ASEAN organs, most of which are regular meetings. This means on average there are two ASEAN formal meetings every day all year round.[139] Considering the amount of work that these staff have to do to prepare for every meeting and the limited number of

[134] ASEAN Charter, Articles 11, 27 and 51.

[135] For instance, under the 2009 ASEAN Political-Security Community Blueprint, the ASEAN Secretary-General, supported by the Secretariat, is responsible to conduct monitoring on the implementation of the Blueprint and to report back to the ASEAN Summit. Another example is the 2009 ASEAN Trade in Goods Agreement that tasks the Secretariat to monitor and report on the implementation of the Agreement.

[136] Pitsuwan, 'ASEAN's Challenge', pp. 26 and 34.

[137] K. Shongkittavorn, 'ASEAN Secretariat must be empowered', *The Nation*, 21 May 2012, retrieved on 10 October 2016 from the official website of National Multimedia: www.nationmultimedia.com.

[138] ASEAN Charter, Article 11(3).

[139] Pitsuwan, 'ASEAN's Challenge', p. 26.

staff, it is hard to imagine how the ASEAN Secretariat could manage to perform even the basic administrative functions under the EDSM properly in the event of a dispute. By contrast, the WTO Secretariat employs more than 600 staff to handle *only* trade cooperation and disputes, albeit for a larger pool of members.[140]

Turning to the issue of lack of legal professionals, the Legal Services and Agreements Directorate (LSAD) was initially established to provide legal advice on trade disputes and, consequently, assist the ASEAN Secretariat in executing its functions under the EDSM.[141] However, in reality the LSAD, being the only legal division in the ASEAN Secretariat, ends up taking on more responsibilities than those initially assigned to it. According to our latest interviews with the ASEAN Secretariat, the LSAD is at present also tasked with assisting the Secretariat in interpreting the Charter, giving legal opinions on matters outside of economic cooperation and issues pertaining to technical commercial agreements (e.g. consultancy, procurement and vendor agreements).[142]

In relation to the functions of the Secretariat under the EDSM, the LSAD basically mirrors the Legal Affairs Division (LAD) of the WTO but with an extra responsibility to assist the Appellate Body.[143] However, unlike its counterpart, the LSAD only consists of a very small team. While the LAD has seventeen lawyers specifically dedicated to provide legal advice to the WTO dispute settlement panels, other WTO bodies and WTO members,[144] the LSAD only employs in total five staff (two senior officers and three technical assistants) to provide legal advice to the EDSM panels and Appellate Body and to various other ASEAN bodies, and at times, ASEAN member states on various legal issues arising from ASEAN commitments.[145] When a dispute actually appears before the EDSM it is hard to imagine how the five staff of the LSAD might cope.

140 WTO, 'Overview of the WTO Secretariat', retrieved on 10 October 2016 from the official website of the WTO www.wto.org.

141 High-level Task Force on ASEAN Economic Integration, 'Recommendations'.

142 Interview with an ASEAN Secretariat official on 27 September 2014.

143 This is because, unlike the WTO DSU that provides for a separate secretariat for the WTO Appellate Body, the EDSM does not provide for a specific secretariat to assist its Appellate Body; hence it falls to the ASEAN Secretariat to assist both the EDSM panel and the Appellate Body.

144 WTO, 'Overview of the WTO Secretariat'; and WTO, 'Divisions', retrieved on 10 October 2016 from the official website of the WTO www.wto.org.

145 High-level Task Force on ASEAN Economic Integration, 'Recommendations'; and an Interview with an ASEAN Secretariat official on 27 September 2014.

4.3.2 The Senior Economic Officials Meeting

Under the Agreement Establishing the WTO, the DSB is a session of the General Council of the WTO on dispute settlement.[146] The DSB consists of representatives, usually ambassadors or equivalent, of all WTO member states who are specifically appointed to deal with WTO issues. In contrast, not much is known about SEOM on paper. The composition and qualification of SEOM is unclear. However, secondary sources suggest that ASEAN states' representatives sitting in SEOM are at the level of deputy-directors of international relations within the trade and investment ministries.[147] Members of SEOM are not exclusively assigned to SEOM; they hold other formal positions in other ASEAN organs and in their home countries. There is nothing in ASEAN instruments that describes the procedures of SEOM's meetings.

The fundamental difference between SEOM and the WTO DSB is that members of SEOM are not residents (exclusively assigned to SEOM); they resemble the Ministerial Meeting of the WTO but with more frequent meetings. Because they are not residents, SEOM's meetings do not by themselves evidence an internally developed culture similar to that of the WTO DSB. Members of SEOM do not spend any time in residence in Jakarta and only met each other briefly twice a year. Although this is obviously more than the Ministerial Meeting of the WTO, it is significantly less than the General Council and the DSB in Geneva.

All roads lead to the SEOM, complaints are initiated by submissions to SEOM, panels are composed by SEOM, appeals to the Appellate Body are made to SEOM, arbitration requests for noncompliance are made to SEOM and reports from the arbitration are also authorised by SEOM. This is not dissimilar to the WTO DSB; indeed, the adoption of negative consensus rule for the empanelment of a case, the adoption of reports and the authorisation of retaliations make the process even more like that of the WTO DSB. It remains to be seen whether the practice will be more similar to that of the WTO DSB or because of the cultural preferences and more limited legal capacity in ASEAN that SEOM will rely more on the ASEAN Way to resolve disputes. We predict that so long as capacity within ASEAN states and within the ASEAN Secretariat is limited, despite the clear legalised process found in the EDSM, SEOM would

146 Agreement Establishing the World Trade Organisation, Marrakesh, 15 April 1994, in force 1 January 1995, 1867 UNTS 154; 33 ILM 1144 (1994), Article IV(3).

147 Toohey, 'When 'failure' indicates success', p. 175.

probably operate more by way of consultation and negotiation than by strictly relying on the letter of the law.

5 The Future of ASEAN Dispute Settlement Mechanisms

The fact that the EDSM has never been used in the past does not mean that it will not be used in the future. Although we have suggested that ASEAN member states do not have significant confidence in an untried dispute settlement mechanism, this does not mean that they may not be forced in the future to rely on the EDSM. We have suggested that ASEAN states prefer to manage dispute rather than litigate them. We have also provided examples of situations where ASEAN states have been able to avail themselves of extra-ASEAN dispute settlement mechanisms such as those provided by the WTO. However, as ASEAN economies integrate more, it is not hard to imagine a situation where the dispute is about a WTO plus commitment found in an ASEAN agreement such as a WTO plus tariff reduction or a WTO plus services market access concession where ASEAN states would not be able to rely on the WTO system for a resolution of dispute. As suggested by some scholars, 'the WTO dispute settlement mechanism may not be available to enforce deeper RTA commitments (WTO+) or commitments in areas not currently covered by the WTO (WTO-X).'[148] In such a situation, while ASEAN states may well acknowledge and recognise the imperfection and limitations of the EDSM, they may have no choice than to refer the dispute for settlement to the EDSM. It will only be then that the EDSM will be tested.

We also believe that not all disputes, even on WTO+ and WTO-X issues need to be resolved at the state-to-state level. The ASEAN economic community also has the ASEAN Comprehensive Investment Agreement (ACIA) that allows investors to bring claims directly against states for breaches of ACIA's obligations.[149] Thus, investors affected by measures that are in violation of ACIA's National Treatment clause may prefer to bring their claims directly against the state for this rather than seeking their home state's espousal of their claims. Indeed, the one intra-ASEAN case that finally resulted in a third-party adjudicated award was the well-known case of *Yaung Chi Oo Trading Pte. Ltd. v. Myanmar*, which involved a

[148] Chase, Yanovich, Crawford, and Ugaz, 'Mapping of Dispute Settlement Mechanisms in Regional trade Agreements', p. 8.

[149] 2009 ASEAN Comprehensive Investment Agreement (ACIA), Cha-am, 26 February 2009, in force 24 February 2012, Article 29.

Singapore incorporated investor bringing claims against the Myanmar government for, among others, an expropriation of the investor's properties and assets in Myanmar.[150]

Finally, some domestic jurisdictions in ASEAN have become more receptive toward submissions that suggest that international treaties are directly applicable in those jurisdictions. The acceptance of claims on violations of international human rights by courts in Indonesia, Malaysia and Philippines are notable examples of this.[151] We predict that the trend in these jurisdictions will lead to arguments and maybe even greater acceptance of arguments that ASEAN agreements are directly applicable in these jurisdictions. If so, it is likely that aggrieved individuals would choose the most efficient mechanism to resolve their disputes with ASEAN governments, which in this case could include recourse to the domestic courts of some ASEAN jurisdictions.

With that said, we believe that the creation of these state-to-state dispute settlement mechanisms in ASEAN is not in vain. These mechanisms provide a tool kit or options for individuals and states to enforce bargains made by ASEAN states. The fact that they may not be directly used belies their value in putting pressure on ASEAN states during dispute management negotiations to resolve a dispute. The more effective a mechanism is, the more likely that a party aware of being in breach of an obligation will be receptive to a reasonable solution or compromise. Under the shadow of litigation and third-party adjudication, parties are often more conciliatory. What is important is for all parties to be aware and knowledgeable of their obligations, the options for the enforcement of those obligations and the need to promote the rule of law within ASEAN. As one of the authors of this chapter once said in a previous publication: 'Education and the rule of law are great equalizers.'[152]

[150] *Yaung Cho Oo Trading Pte. Ltd. v. Government of the Union of Myanmar*, ARB/01/1, 42 ILM 540 (2003).

[151] Human Rights Law (Undang Hak Asasi Manusia), Law No. 37, dated 23 September 1999, Article 7 (for Indonesia); High Court of Malaysia, *Noorfadilla binti Ahmad Saikin v. Chayed bin Basirun and Ors (2012)*, 1 CLJ 769; and Rules of Civil Procedure, Resolution of the Supreme Court No. 803, dated 8 April 1997, Rule 65 (for the Philippines).

[152] M. Ewing-Chow, A. Goh and A. K. Patil, 'Are Asian WTO members using the WTO DSU "effectively"?', *Journal of International Economic Law*, 16 (2013), 705.

PART II

Cross-Cutting Studies

13

A Comparative Analysis of Formal Independence

THERESA SQUATRITO

1 Introduction

When asked to identify the central features to a legitimate court, most people would likely cite criteria concerning independence. The typical court would be expected to be unbiased and insulated from political pressure. This is no less true for international trade courts than any other type of court. In other words, the legitimacy of international trade courts and tribunals (ITCs) is likely to be, in part, related to their independence. Although scholars agree that judicial independence has general importance for international courts, they debate whether international courts are independent. This debate has, in fact, not been based upon broad comparative analysis of the extent to which independence is formally safeguarded by the design of international courts. What formal institutional safeguards do ITCs have to ensure independence? How do ITCs compare in their formal independence? And, what might their formal independence mean for their legitimacy? These are only a few of the questions that remain unanswered. This chapter aims to address this gap in the literature by exploring these questions.

The chapter argues that judicial independence is a crucial aspect of the legitimacy of an international trade court or tribunal. I develop an understanding of the formal judicial independence that emphasizes the formal rules that safeguard the independence of an ITC. Based on this understanding, I operationalize and measure formal independence on the basis of formal rules governing the selection and tenure of judges, the eligibility criteria for judges, court resources, court rules of procedure, recusal and limits on activities incompatible with judicial office, the confidentiality of deliberations, a judicial oath to independence, and privileges and immunities granted to judges. The chapter compares the formal independence of sixteen permanent international trade courts or tribunals. These sixteen constitute the universe of permanent international trade courts operational prior to 2015. This includes the WTO Appellate Body (AB) and all courts that are embedded within regional integration systems.[1] The analysis reveals that ITCs vary in their level of formal independence, with varying consequences for their legitimacy.

The chapter develops in four parts. In the first part, the chapter discusses how judicial independence is linked to the legitimacy of an international court. Second, the chapter reviews how current literature debates whether international courts are independent. The review of this debate illustrates how current perspectives on judicial independence tend to focus on only a few courts, and thus a broad comparative analysis of international courts is merited. The third section of the chapter develops a methodology for studying formal independence based upon institutional rules that can safeguard independence. In other words, this section provides an operationalization of formal independence and specifies how it might be measured. The fourth section then uses this methodological approach to comparatively analyze the formal independence of international trade courts, revealing important patterns of similarities and differences. The chapter then concludes with a discussion of how these patterns in formal independence are useful for understanding the legitimacy of ITCs.

2 Judicial Independence's Significance to Legitimacy

Judicial independence relates to the ability of courts to deliberate and reach judgments in light of the law and without any undue pressure or influence from external sources, governmental or otherwise. Thus, judicial independence is understood here as an institutional feature, although it is closely linked to independence of the individual judges siting on a court. Specifically, independence, as an institutional feature, is shaped by the autonomy and the impartiality of judges. To be autonomous, judges must be willing and able to act free from the control of political actors. Impartiality, on the other hand, requires that judges be able to act as neutral arbiters without interests or ideological preferences that would bias them in favor of a disputing party. Thus, independence of an international court

[1] Many of the ITCs included in this analysis are addressed in this volume. Six ITCs included here are not otherwise included this volume; they are the Benelux Court of Justice (BCJ), the Caribbean Court of Justice (CCJ), the Central American Court of Justice (CACJ), the Court of Justice of Economic Community of West African States (ECOWAS CJ), the Organization for the Harmonization of Business Law in Africa Common Court of Justice and Arbitration (OHADA CCJA), and the Tribunal of the Southern African Development Community (SADC). Also, the ASEAN dispute settlement mechanism is not included because it does not have a permanent body in operation. Domestic trade courts are also excluded from this analysis. For a complete list of the sixteen ITCs, see Appendix.

connotes the ability of judges to act autonomously, especially free from the pressures and influences of states, and without bias.[2]

Moreover, independence of a court can be conceived along two dimensions. First, *formal independence* concerns how judicial independence is embedded in the formal institutional design of a court through institutional safeguards, such as how it is codified in the rules governing the functioning of the court. This is what elsewhere has been labeled de jure independence.[3] Second, informal independence is independence in practice. Others call this de facto independence.[4] This chapter focuses on the former dimension of judicial independence.

Independence for international courts, in general, and ITCs, in particular, is desirable for several reasons. First, independence can enable an international court to have greater authority and influence and thus enhance its effectiveness. Some scholarship associates the effectiveness of an international court, in part, to the degree of independence that it enjoys.[5] Guillaume argues, "[t]he international judiciary, like national judiciaries, cannot effectively perform its functions unless it enjoys the requisite independence and hence the trust of those subject to its jurisdiction."[6] Second, the independence of a court can help to garner the rule of law in society.[7] Third, yet related to effectiveness and the rule of law, judicial independence can be instrumental in shaping the legitimacy of international courts.

[2] Y. Haftel and A. Thompson, "The independence of international organizations: Concept and applications," *Journal of Conflict Resolution*, 50, 2, (2006), 255–6.

[3] J. Melton and T. Ginsburg, "Does de jure judicial independence really matter?: A reevaluation of explanations for judicial independence," *Journal of Law and Courts*, 2, 2, (2014), 187–217.

[4] Ibid.

[5] R. Keohane, A. Moravcsik, and A.-M. Slaughter, "Legalized dispute resolution: Interstate and transnational" (2000) 54 *International Organization*, 3, 457–88; L. Helfer and A.-M. Slaughter, "Towards a theory of effective supranational adjudication," *Yale Law Journal*, 107, 2, (1997), 273–391; L. R. Helfer and A.-M. Slaughter,"Why states create international tribunals: A response to professors Posner and Yoo," *California Law Review*, 93, 3, (2005), 899–956; Y. Shany, *Assessing the Effectiveness of International Courts* (Oxford University Press, 2014). The reverse argument has been made as well, associating effectiveness of international adjudication to dependence; see E. Posner and J. Yoo, "Judicial independence in international tribunals," *California Law Review*, 93, 1, (2005), 1–74.

[6] G. Guillaume, "Some thoughts on independence of international judges," *The Law & Practice of International Courts and Tribunals*, 2, 1, (2003), 163–8 at 163.

[7] T. Meron, "Judicial independence and impartiality in international criminal tribunals," *The American Journal of International Law*, 99, 2, (2005), 359–69.

The independence of international courts is crucial to understanding their legitimacy. I conceive of legitimacy as the right to govern or rule.[8] Legitimacy can be a normative concept, understood as whether an actor has the right to govern because it fulfills desired normative criteria for rightful authority (known as normative legitimacy), or it can be a sociological concept referring to whether an actor is believed or perceived by others to have the right to rule (known as sociological legitimacy). I would argue that existing research relates judicial independence to some conceptions of normative legitimacy and shows independence enhances sociological legitimacy.

First, some conceptions of normative legitimacy of international courts and tribunals include independence among the values that must be had to be legitimate. For example, Von Bogdandy and Venzke argue that an important element of democratic legitimacy for international courts is their independence.[9] Similarly, Esty suggests independence can advance legitimacy.[10] Although independence is not often referenced in normative conceptions of legitimate international courts, it is often implicit. That is, the ideal international court is generally assumed to be comprised of judges who are impartial to the interest of states and other political actors as well as insulated from their political control. This assumption is closely linked to what is associated with legitimate governance – a separation of political powers.[11]

Second, previous research has demonstrated that independence, among other things, confers sociological legitimacy on an international court, improving how a court is perceived by other actors. As Benvenisti and Downs argue, "[T]he perceived independence of a given international tribunal from the handful of powerful states that have tended to dominate the institutional design process continues to be the most significant factor in shaping the extent to which judge made law is regarded as legitimate in the eyes of less powerful states. Such political independence on the part of

[8] D. Bodansky, "Legitimacy in international law and international relations" in J. Dunoff and M. Pollack (eds.), *Interdisciplinary Perspectives on International Law and International Relations: The State of the Art* (Cambridge University Press, 2013), p. 324.

[9] A. von Bogdandy and I. Venzke, "In whose name? An investigation of international courts' public authority and its democratic justification," *European Journal of International Law*, 23, 1, (2012), 7–41; A. von Bogdandy and I. Venzke, "On the democratic legitimation of international judicial lawmaking," *German Law Journal*, 12, 5, (2011), 1341–70.

[10] D. Esty, "Good governance at the supranational scale: Globalizing administrative law," *Yale Law Journal*, 115, 7, (2006), 490–562.

[11] D. Zimmermann, *The Independence of International Courts: The Adherence of the International Judiciary to a Fundamental Value of the Administration of Justice* (Baden-Baden: Nomos, 2014).

the international tribunals continues to be a necessary, if not sufficient, condition for the perceived legitimacy of their lawmaking."[12] By one argument, independence confers legitimacy on international courts because judicial independence contributes to perceptions that they are fair and unbiased.[13] Cali et al. find through an extensive interview study that the independence of the ECtHR shapes interviewees' perceptions of the Court.[14] Likewise, Brems, and Lavrysen suggest that independence plays a role in the legitimacy of a court because it advances procedural justice.[15]

In all, judicial independence is linked to normative conceptions of legitimacy and evidence shows it is also related to sociological legitimacy. Independence, thus, should be conceived as a normatively valuable feature of international courts, as well as a crucial element to how they are perceived and supported by various audiences. Given the importance that independence has for the legitimacy of ITCs, a closer examination of how independent ITCs are merits further exploration. Are ITCs independent? The next section turns to this question.

3 The Debate: Are International Courts Independent?

While courts are traditionally assumed to be a neutral third party that intervenes to solve a dispute between two parties, as depicted by the concept of triadic dispute resolution, recent scholarship has questioned this assumption as it applies to international courts.[16] Two general perspectives are etched in this debate. The first perspective claims that international courts are constrained politically and lack independence.[17]

12 E. Benvenisti and G. Downs, "Prospects for the increased independence of international tribunals," *German Law Journal*, 12, 5, (2011), 1057–82 at 1058.

13 N. Grossman, "Legitimacy and international adjudicative bodies," *George Washington International Law Review*, 41, 1, (2009), 107–80.

14 B. Cali, A. Koch, and N. Bruch, "The legitimacy of human rights courts: A grounded interpretivist analysis of the European Court of Human Rights," *Human Rights Quarterly*, 35, 4, (2013), 955–84.

15 E. Brems and L. Lavrysen, "Procedural justice in human rights adjudication: The European Court of Human Rights," *Human Rights Quarterly*, 35, 1, (2013), 177–200.

16 For a typical characterization of courts in terms of triadic dispute resolution, see A. S. Sweet, "Judicialization and the construction of governance," *Comparative Political Studies*, 32, 2, (1999), 147–84.

17 M. Elsig and M. Pollack, "Agents, trustees, and international courts: The politics of judicial appointment at the World Trade Organization," *European Journal of International Relations*, 20, 2, (2014), 391–415; G. Garrett, R. D. Kelemen, and H. Schulz, "The European Court of Justice, national governments, and legal integration in the European Union," *International Organization*, 52, 1, (1998), 149–76; C. J. Carrubba, M.

One strand of this literature draws heavily on principal-agent theory from political science. The central premise of this strand of literature is that international courts are agents of states, who are the principals responsible for delegating authority to courts. Courts, actors in their own right, have interests that can diverge from those of states. States seeking to minimize "agency slack," where a court will follow its own preferences rather than those of states, will use various mechanisms to curb or rein in the autonomy of a court. These court curbing mechanisms can be ex ante controls on a court, such as nomination and selection procedures that may aim to identify judges whose ideological preferences will be closely aligned with those of states. Court curbing mechanisms can also be ex post reactions to specific decisions or actions of a court, such as actions to undermine the reappointment of a judge or to change the jurisdiction or powers of the court following a controversial decision.[18] As a result of these court curbing mechanisms, it is argued that international courts are not truly independent. A second strand of this literature draws less from principal-agent theory, but nonetheless still arrives at the conclusion that international courts have "bounded discretion," "constrained independence," and operate within a "strategic space."[19] Both strands, however, recognize that the judicial independence of courts is limited because they operate in the context of state power and political limitations to judicial authority.

A second main perspective on the independence of international courts maintains that international courts are generally independent of states and exercise their authority without deference to the preferences of states.[20] This perspective largely holds that states have very limited

Gabel, and C. Hankla, "Judicial behavior under political constraints: Evidence from the European Court of Justice," *American Political Science Review*, 102, 4, (2008), 435–2.

[18] T. Ginsburg, "Political constraints on international courts" in C. Romano, K. Alter, and Y. Shany (eds.), *The Oxford Handbook of International Adjudication* (Oxford University Press, 2013); Elsig and Pollack, "Agents, trustees, and international courts"; R. D. Kelemen, "The political foundations of judicial independence in the European Union," *Journal of European Public Policy*, 19, 1, (2012), 43–58.

[19] For "bounded discretion," see T. Ginsburg, "Bounded discretion in international judicial lawmaking," *Virginia Journal of International Law*, 45, 3, (2005), 631–73. For "constrained independence," see Helfer and Slaughter, "Why states create international tribunals." For "strategic space," see R. Steinberg, "Judicial lawmaking at the WTO: Discursive, constitutional, and political constraints," *American Journal of International Law*, 98, 2, (2004), 247–75.

[20] K. Alter, "Agents or trustees? International courts in their political context," *European Journal of International Relations*, 14, 1, (2008), 33–63; R. Cichowski, *The European Court and Civil Society: Litigation, Mobilization and Governance* (Cambridge University

control over international courts, or that an international court "operates in an unusually permissive zone of discretion."[21] A prominent strand found within this perspective is work that views international courts as "trustees." Unlike delegation to an agent, delegation to a trustee has the foremost objective of making state commitments credible, and thus independence is of extreme importance.[22] According to this logic, an international court's independence from states is supported by their authority as guardians of the law. That is, a court draws legitimacy from its professional and moral authority. Judges and courts have moral authority, as they serve higher ideals, or "the law," and expert authority based on respect for their expertise.[23] This perspective also argues that international courts are generally independent because court curbing mechanisms are typically ineffective and that courts can lead states to revise their preferences.[24]

The question of whether international courts, and ITCs in particular, are independent remains an empirical question. In fact, much of the debate so far has been largely focused on only the Court of Justice of the European Union (CJEU) and WTO dispute settlement mechanism. Little examination of independence of other international trade courts has arisen in this debate. The purpose of this chapter is to offer a broad comparative analysis that looks beyond the CJEU and WTO to assess whether ITCs are independent. To do so, I look at formal judicial independence.

Although formal measures of judicial independence may not give a complete picture of the actual practice of independence, it can broaden our understanding of the extent to which ITCs are designed with institutional safeguards intended to ensure judicial independence. The extent to which there are informal means of restricting judicial behavior and the extent to which political constraints are in practice faced by courts is a

Press, 2007); A. S. Sweet and T. Brunell, "The European Court of Justice, state noncompliance, and the politics of override," *American Political Science Review*, 106, 1, (2012), 204–13.

21 A. S. Sweet and T. Brunell, "Trustee courts and the judicialization of international regimes. The politics of majoritarian activism in the European Convention on Human Rights, the European Union, and the World Trade Organization," *Journal of Law and Courts*, 1, 1, (2013), 61–88 at 65.

22 G. Majone, "Two logics of delegation: Agency and fiduciary relations in EU governance," *European Union Politics*, 2, 1, (2001), 103–21.

23 Alter, "Agents or trustees? International courts in their political context."

24 Ibid. K. Alter, *The New Terrain of International Law: Courts, Politics, Rights* (Princeton University Press, 2014).

more complex matter. The aim here is thus to offer an initial comparative approach that speaks to judicial independence.

4 Measuring the Judicial Independence of ITCs

To examine the extent to which ITCs have formal institutional safeguards that foster independence, we must first specify what types of formal rules can shape judicial independence. Existing literature puts forward a variety of rules that are likely to foster or impede independence. Mackenzie and Sands suggest that the dimensions of judicial independence include "the procedures for the nomination, selection, and re-election of international judges; the relationship between the international judges and the parties or issues before the court the outside activities of international judges; and finally, the relationship between judicial and political organs."[25] Keohane, Moravscik, and Slaughter claim independence is reflected in "selection and tenure, legal discretion, and control over material and human resources."[26] Shany argues that "court's freedom to determine its own internal administration, the confidentiality of court deliberations, the elaboration of judicial service conditions in legally binding instruments, the conferment of diplomatic privileges and immunities upon international judges, and adequate budgeting of the court" also determine a court's independence.[27] Meron also includes rules on when judges should recuse themselves as an important element of judicial independence.[28]

Although all ITC treaties assert that judges are to be independent and impartial, these provisions do not necessarily safeguard independence. Rather, a variety of rules are likely to foster independence in practice. As Shany argues, "[t]he combination of rules and conditions relating to judicial independence and impartiality enable us to assess whether or not the court in question has an institutional design that enshrines freedom from external interference and improper bias."[29] Building from existing literature that considers judicial independence of international courts, I include eight types of rules that safeguard of judicial independence: (1) selection and tenure, (2) eligibility criteria, (3) resources, (4) rules of

25 R. Mackenzie and P. Sands, "International courts and tribunals and the independence of the international judge," *Harvard International Law Journal*, 44, 1, (2003), 271–85 at 276.

26 Keohane, Moravcsik, and Slaughter, "Legalized dispute resolution," 460.

27 Shany, *Assessing the Effectiveness of International Courts* p. 100.

28 Meron, "Judicial independence and impartiality in international criminal tribunals," 359–69.

29 Shany, *Assessing the Effectiveness of International Courts*, p. 102.

procedure, (5) recusal and activities incompatible with judicial office, (6) confidentiality, (7) oath to independence, and (8) privileges and immunities. All permanent ITCs ($N = 16$) are analyzed along the eight rule types, based on their founding treaties, regulations and rules of procedure (or similar). These sixteen ITCs are permanent international trade courts that were created and have been operational within regional economic integration systems, such as the European Union, or the World Trade Organization. These ITCs are listed in the chapter appendix.[30] The following section discusses how each type of rule provides an institutional safeguard to independence and specifies how independence is measured for the purpose of comparative analysis.

4.1 Selection and Tenure

Selection, including the nomination and election of judges, and tenure processes vary among ITCs, and some appointment procedures better safeguard judicial independence than others. Five aspects of selection and tenure in particular shape judicial independence. First is the nomination process. Nomination procedures are often not codified in the rules of an ITC; rather, states have discretion to determine how they will identify for nomination particular candidates. Second are the decision rules governing the election of judges, which range from direct appointments by individual states, election by a unanimous decision of states or a majority vote of states, to election by an independent commission.[31] In practice, judicial appointments can be highly politicized, and political concerns affect judicial appointments to international courts.[32] Elsig and Pollack argue that states "can and will utilize their individual right to nominate and their collective right to appoint in order to influence

[30] The Court of the Eurasian Economic Community is not included in the analysis because it was just becoming operational when the coding began. ITCs that were never operational or quickly died are also not include; see, C. Romano, "Trial and error in international judicialization" in C. Romano, K. Alter, and Y. Shany (eds.), *The Oxford Handbook of International Adjudication* (Oxford University Press, 2014).

[31] The CCJ is the only ITC where judges are appointed by an independent commission, which is composed of persons nominated by nongovernmental entities as well as some persons from member state governments. See Article 5(1) of the Agreement Establishing the Caribbean Court of Justice, St. Michael, Barbados, 14 February 2001.

[32] Mackenzie and Sands, "International courts and tribunals and the independence of the international judge," 271–85; E. Voeten, "The politics of international judicial appointments: Evidence from the European Court of Human Rights," *International Organization*, 61, 4, (2007), 669–701.

ex ante the endogenous preferences of international judges."[33] Nevertheless, Keohane, Moravscik, and Slaughter suggest that when judges are appointed either directly by individual states or by consensus (thereby providing any one state with a veto), the level of independence is likely to be low because nominees will need to gain the favor of all states to be elected.[34] Majority voting rules enable more independence because nominees need to gain the favor of fewer states, and thus judges will be beholden to fewer states. Another aspect of selection concerns reappointment. If judges can be reappointed, they have more incentives to maintain the goodwill of states, and for this reason, rules that enable the reappointment of judges effectively reduces independence.

Tenure also shapes independence, such that longer term lengths bolster independence. When a judge's appointment to a bench is for only a few years, they may have insecurities about their career once their judicial office expires. So, judges, especially if they are younger, may seek to protect their long-term career by remaining in the high esteem of states. Voeten finds that there is some indication that career insecurities make judges more likely to favor their national governments in disputes.[35] All else equal, longer terms can help to isolate judges somewhat from such political retribution of judges for unpopular decisions. Another aspect of tenure to affect judicial independence is rules governing the dismissal or removal of judges from office.[36] When states control the removal of judges from the bench, judges have greater incentive to remain in the good esteem of states, negatively impacting independence.

To measure selection and tenure rules for each ITC, I identify the provisions that specify: (1) what decision rules apply to judicial appointments, (2) whether judges can be reappointed, (3) the length of judicial tenure, and (4) the procedure for the removal of judges.[37] Each rule is then coded along a 0 to 1 scale, where 0 represents low independence and 1 is high independence. If judicial appointments are by a unanimous decision of states or a direct appointment by a single state, the rule is coded as 0. If appointments are made on the basis of a majority voting rule it receives a

33 Elsig and Pollack, "Agents, trustees, and international courts," 409–10.

34 Keohane, Moravcsik, and Slaughter, "Legalized dispute resolution," 457–88.

35 E. Voeten, "The impartiality of international judges: Evidence from the European Court of Human Rights," *American Political Science Review*, 102, 4, (2008), 417–33.

36 Zimmermann, *The Independence of International Courts.*

37 This measure does not include the rules on nomination of candidate for appointment because most ITCs do not have formal rules on the process of nomination. Rather, nomination procedures are at the discretion of the state in most cases.

score of 0.5, or 1 if appointments are made by an independent body.[38] If judges can be reappointed, it is scored as a 0, and if they cannot be reappointed it is coded as a 1. Tenure is measured against the average tenure length. The average for all ITCs is six years. International trade courts that have six-year term lengths for judges are scored as .5, while those with a shorter term receive a score of 0 and those with more than six years receive a score of 1. Lifetime tenure (or tenure until the age of retirement) is coded as a 1, signifying greater independence.[39]

4.2 *Eligibility Criteria*

"High standards of qualifications are important both for giving credibility to the judgments of international courts, as well as for ensuring judicial independence and fair and unbiased tribunals."[40] The most relevant eligibility requirement that may affect independence is the type of professional experience or expertise a judge must have to be appointed to the bench. In most instances, there are requirements that appointees be of high "moral character," but in addition there may be provisions that speak to whether appointees must have legal or judicial experience or expertise. This is important because career diplomats or politicians may be more likely to show allegiance to governments than career judges. For example, European Court of Human Rights judges who are former diplomats were more likely than judges with other professional backgrounds to vote in favor of their national governments.[41] Thus, it is likely that eligibility criteria that appointees have related legal expertise or experience may act as an institutional safeguard for greater independence.[42]

To measure eligibility criteria, for each court I identify the rule that specifies whether appointees must have legal or judicial experience or expertise. The rule is coded on a binary scale of 0 (low independence) to 1 (high independence). In many instances, the rule states that an appointee must fulfill the criteria for national high or the highest judicial office. I assume that national criteria for high judicial office require at

[38] The CJEU, with its new procedure where an independence panel is consulted, is unique. For this reason, it is coded as .5.

[39] Judges appointed to the CCJ hold their tenure until the age of 72. See Article 9(2) of the Agreement Establishing the Caribbean Court of Justice.

[40] Grossman, "Legitimacy and international adjudicative bodies," 133.

[41] Voeten, "The impartiality of international judges," 428.

[42] Former diplomats or government officials may nevertheless meet the formal requirements for legal or judicial office in some instances.

least some degree of legal expertise or experience. Thus, when the eligibility rule states that an appointee must have legal or judicial experience or expertise, or fulfill the criteria for a national high judicial office, the rule is coded as 1. Conversely, if there is no requirement of legal or judicial expertise or experience, the rule is coded as a 0.

4.3 Resources

The extent to which a court has control over its resources is likely to be an important factor shaping judicial independence. Resources will affect their ability to process their caseloads, and to do so independent of states. For example, resources "may permit a court or tribunal to develop a factual record independent of the state litigants before them."[43] The relevant resources for a court include both material and human resources.[44] A court's ability to determine its budget provides it with discretion to determine how its resources are allocated. On the other hand, if states control the budget, states can affect the amount of funding (e.g. states could opt to funnel money away from the court to another organ of an international organization), as well as how resources are allocated, including funding for fact-finding, expert testimony, support staff, and the remuneration of judges. Human resources, such as the support staff for the court, are also an important aspect of a court's overall resources. Thus, the ability to control human resources is critical for a court, including decisions on who comprises the registry or secretariat of an international court. As much of the staffing and managerial decisions may be made by a registrar or secretary, the appointment of the highest officials of the court's secretariat or registry may overall affect the ability to exercise control over its resources. Overall, we can assume that the more influence a court has over their budget and the appointment of its registrar or secretary, the greater its independence.

To measure an ITC's control of its resources, I look at two provisions for each ITC. First is the rule on who approves the budgets of the court, and whether states have sole responsibility to approve the court's budget (scored as a 0), whether states approve the court's budget based on recommendations of the court (score = .5), or whether the court approves its own budget (score = 1), where the latter is assumed to be the highest form of independence when it comes to budgetary control.[45] Second is the

[43] Keohane, Moravcsik, and Slaughter, "Legalized dispute resolution," 462. [44] Ibid.

[45] While the size of the budget is significant for the independence of a court, I assume the most relevant aspect of budgeting for independence is who controls the allocation of resources.

rule concerning the appointment of the court's registrar or secretary. Where states appoint the registrar, independence is assumed to be lower and is coded as a 0. Where appointments are jointly made on the recommendations of the court and then approved by states, the provision is coded as a .5. If the court is solely responsible for the appointment, the provision is coded as 1, signifying a higher level of independence.

4.4 *Rules of Procedure*

The control over a court's rules of procedure can also affect a court's level of independence. No court has the ability to override their founding treaty. However, rules not specified by treaties can sometimes be determined and modified by the courts themselves. When courts are able to determine these rules of procedure on their own, they have some autonomy over the internal administration of the court, the functioning of its registry, as well as aspects of judicial proceedings. Thus, courts that are able to determine their rules of procedure, so long as they do not conflict with the treaty, are likely to have more discretion over their internal operation, and thus functionally have greater independence.

I measure whether independence is safeguarded through the control over rules of procedure according to provisions that specify who has the authority to determine and approve a court's rules of procedure, using a scale of 0 (low independence) to 1 (high independence). A rule that provides that a state organ determines and approves the rules of procedure is coded as a 0. If the rule specifies that a state organ approves the rules based on the court's recommendation, it is coded as a .5. If the rule states the court has the sole authority to determine and approve its own rules of procedures, independence is higher, and the provision is coded as a 1.

4.5 *Recusal and Limits of Activities*

Another form of institutional safeguard to independence is rules addressing activities that are incompatible with the office or when a judge is disqualified from adjudicating a dispute. Grossman suggests that "[r]equirements for disclosure of potential conflicts, disqualification provisions, and limitations on activities during tenure" can reduce bias in international adjudication.[46] Others also suggest rules concerning incompatibilities with judicial office

[46] Grossman, "Legitimacy and international adjudicative bodies," 137.

enhance independence.[47] Rules that govern recusal or activities incompatible with judicial office are twofold. First, there are those that specify what external activities judges may not participate in while in office. Usually these speak to restrictions on paid professional services and political functions for judges while serving on the bench. Additionally, there are also rules that address when a judge is disqualified to adjudicate a dispute and must recuse him or herself. These rules usually assert that a judge is disqualified to hear a case if he or she has previously rendered judgment on the case, served as an advisor on the case, or has personal interests in the dispute.

I measure recusal and limits on activities incompatible with judicial office on a scale of 0 to 1. If there are no rules requiring judges to recuse themselves or limit their activities, the court receives a score of 0 (low independence). If there are rules on recusal but not on incompatible activities, or vice versa, the score is .5. When there are rules requiring a judge to recuse themselves and there are rules limiting incompatible activities, the court receives a score of 1 (high independence).

4.6 *Confidentiality*

Rules governing the secrecy or confidentiality of judicial deliberation may foster independence. When courts have confidential deliberations, we can assume that the secrecy enables judges to more freely deliberate without concern for how their statements may be perceived, interpreted, or used against them by external actors. Thus, secret deliberation may go a long way toward enhancing judicial independence. Guillaume argues "the secrecy of deliberations is a crucial guarantee of a judge's independence."[48] To measure confidentiality of deliberations, I look for provisions that specify whether deliberation must occur in "closed" session, are "secret" and shall remain so, or that they are confidential. If a court's treaty, regulations, or rules of procedure have such a rule, it is coded as a 1, representing higher independence, and if not it is coded as a 0.

4.7 *Oath*

Another means of safeguarding independence may be an oath. Grossman argues, a "mechanism states appear to value in promoting adjudicator

[47] Guillaume, "Some thoughts on independence of international judges"; Zimmermann, *The Independence of International Courts*; Shany, *Assessing the Effectiveness of International Courts*.

[48] Guillaume, "Some thoughts on independence of international judges," 165.

independence and impartiality is an oath or solemn declaration made upon taking office."[49] Guillaume similarly suggests that an oath of office helps to ensure independence.[50] Taking an oath, or signing disclosure statements of independence is an institutional safeguard because it binds a judge to remain independent. Also, it is a public assertion of independence. To measure independence, I identify whether each court has a rule requiring newly appointed judges take an oath affirming their independence. If there is such a provision, it is coded as 1. I treat disclosure statements to independence as equivalent to an oath. If there is no such provision, it is coded as a 0 to represent low independence.

4.8 *Privileges and Immunities*

Provisions that grant diplomatic privileges and immunities to judges can also safeguard judicial independence. Protections for judges from politically motivated prosecutions may be essential to their ability to act free from pressure of states. "If the individual judges cannot feel safe from sanctions for the decisions he makes on the bench, if he has to fear negative consequences that affect other aspects of his life, then the most competent individual will either decline to serve as a judge or be disposed to surrender to the pressure."[51] The necessary privileges and immunities for a judge to have independence include protections from prosecution both during and after their tenure that arise as a consequence of their judicial service. To measure privileges and immunity provisions, I determine whether the court's treaty or rules of procedure state that judges shall be granted privileges and immunities of their office. If there are such rules it is coded as a 1, and 0 if not.

The measurement of rules is summarized in Table 13.1. In total, each court is coded along twelve different rules governing formal independence.

It should be recalled that this method to measure independence only captures formal safeguards for independence. It does not capture actual behavior or informal safeguards. That said, the institutional safeguards are likely to influence whether or not judges actually behave independently or not because the institutional safeguards, among other things, shape the incentive structure affecting judicial behavior. For example, a judge knows that the formal rules permit a state to affect his or her removal from the bench, may ultimately factor that state's preferences into how he or she decides a dispute. Or, knowing that a court's budget can become a tool through which states can

49 Grossman, "Legitimacy and international adjudicative bodies," 107–80.
50 Guillaume, "Some thoughts on independence of international judges," 164.
51 Zimmermann, *The Independence of International Courts*.

Table 13.1 *Measurement of formal independence*

		Low independence = 0	Moderate independence = .5	High independence 1
Selection and tenure	• Appointment of Judges	Direct appointment or unanimity decision rule	Majority voting rule on appointments	Appointment by an independent body
	• Reappointment	Judges can be reappointed	n/a	Judges cannot be reappointed
	• Tenure	Less than average tenure (<6 years)	Average tenure (6 years)	Greater than average (>6 years) or life tenure/retirement
	• Removal	States decide on removal of judges	States decide, but court is consulted	Court decides on removal of judges
Eligibility criteria		No required legal qualifications		Legal qualifications are required
Resources	• Budget	States control the budget of the court	States control the budget of the court, but the court is required to be consulted	Court governs its own budget
	• Appointment of Registrar/ Secretary	States decide on appointment	States and Court jointly appoint	Court decides on appointment
Rules of procedure		States adopt	Court adopts its rules of procedure with approval by states	Court adopts
Recusal and limit on activities		No rules on either	A rule in place requiring *or* limitation on other activities	Both rules on recusal and limit on activities
Secret deliberations		No rules	n/a	Yes
Oath to independence		No oath	n/a	Yes
Diplomatic privileges & immunities		No rules granting	n/a	Yes

punish a court could affect how a court exercises its authority. In other words, the institutional safeguards condition how judges anticipate court curbing.

5 Evaluating the Judicial Independence of ITCs

Having described the operationalization and measurement of formal independence, this section analyzes the formal independence of international trade courts and tribunals. The analysis reveals several points of comparison. This section first illustrates which rules safeguarding independence are more and less commonly featured by ITCs. Second, I present findings based on a composite index that incorporates all of the rules determining the institutional safeguards to independence and highlight some important differences among the various ITCs. I also explore regional differences in ITC independence. Third, this section looks more closely at differences in selection and tenure rules as well as rules governing resources.

The data collected on the sixteen international trade courts' formal independence address several questions. What institutional safeguards for independence are most frequently featured by ITCs? What safeguards are the least common? Also, what international trade courts have the greatest degree of formal independence, and conversely which have the least? Are there any significant regional patterns in formal independence of international trade courts?

Figure 13.1 illustrates what portion of ITCs feature the various rules safeguarding independence. Several key findings can be identified from this figure. First, the most common institutional safeguard is the requirement that judicial nominees have legal or judicial expertise or experience. All sixteen ITC are formally designed so that judges must meet this eligibility criterion. Rules requiring judges to take an oath affirming independence, diplomatic privileges and immunities, as well as secret deliberations are the second most common types of institutional safeguard; roughly 94 percent of ITCs have these three types of rules in place. On the other hand, selection and tenure rules that correspond to high judicial independence are among the least commonly found institutional safeguards (see following discussion). Specifically, judicial independence through majority voting is featured by only one ITC (the OHADA CCJA) and only one ITC has selection by an independent body (the CCJ), tenure appointments for more than six years occur in 38 percent of ICT, and in only 44 percent of ITCs are decisions on the removal of judges left solely to the court. ITCs generally also lack independence to determine their resources. Only 13 percent of ITCs, or two courts,

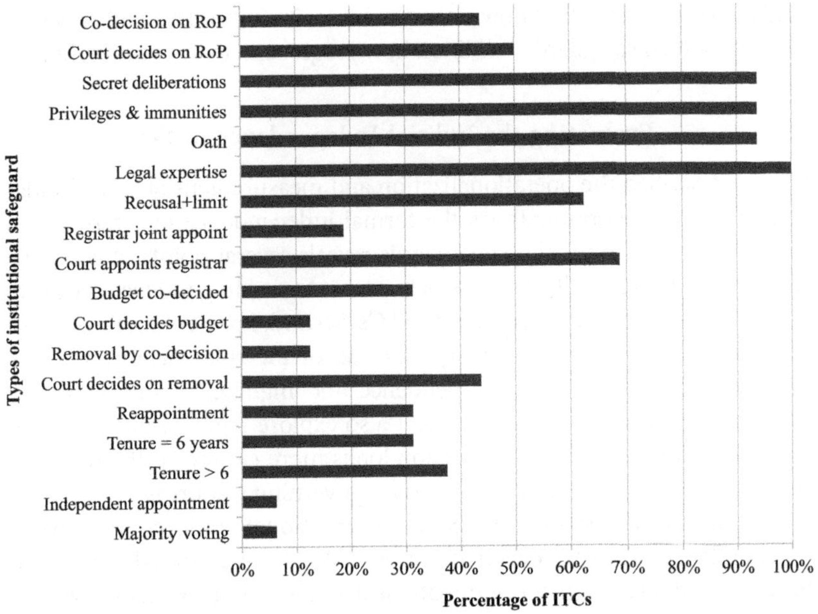

Figure 13.1 Percentage of Courts with Institutional Safeguards to Independence

independently decide on the allocation of their budget resources. In another 13 percent, courts recommend their budgets. This suggests that the vast majority of courts (74 percent, not shown) have limited discretion over their material resources. ITCs, however, tend to be more independent regarding the appointment of their registrar or secretary. In fact, roughly 69 percent of ITCs have sole discretion to appoint their registrar or secretary. An additional 19 percent of ITCs are consulted on the appointment.

We might be interested in how ITCs compare among one another on formal independence. To do so, I develop a cumulative index, which equally weights all twelve rules on independence and then normalizes the value to range from 0 (low independence) to 1 (high independence).[52]

[52] An alternative is to weight rules differently. I use equal weighting for three reasons. First, proportional weighting requires additional empirical insights into what rules determine independence the most. This is an empirical question and not a theoretical one. Second, the rules that are arguably less significant for independence, such as expertise, are the same across most if not all the courts. Third, I am most interested in the relative independence ITCs. In other words, the cumulative index does not reveal much about the independence of any one court per se.

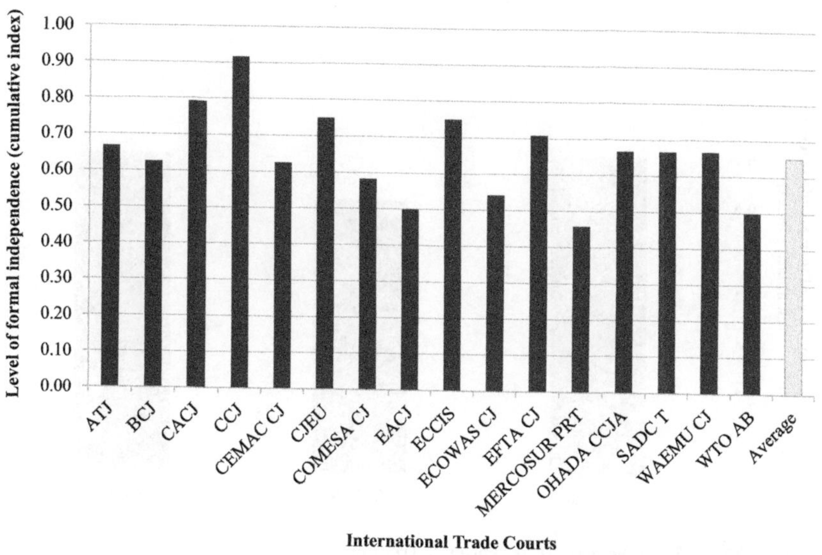

Figure 13.2 Degree of Formal Independence of ITCs (cumulative index, $N = 16$)[53]

The comparison of the sixteen ITCs on the basis of this cumulative index is depicted in Figure 13.2.

This figure reveals that the least formally independent ITC is the Mercosur Permanent Review Tribunal (PRT). The Mercosur PRT scores low in independence for several reasons. First, arbitrators are appointed for only two years, which is renewable.[54] Also, arbitrators maintain other professional activities while appointed, the Common Market Group (a state body) controls their removal, and the Olivos Protocol establishing the PRT (or its corresponding regulations) does not guarantee arbitrators immunities and privileges. Conversely, the international trade court with the highest level of formal independence is the CCJ, scoring 0.92. The CCJ scores high because it has most institutional safeguards, and it has a unique structure that ensures independence in judicial appointments. Judges, as well as the registrar, are elected by an independent

[53] For the individual court scores and abbreviations of ITCs, see Appendix.

[54] See Article 18 of the Olivos Protocol for the Settlement of Disputes in MERCOSUR, Olivos, Argentina, 18 February 2002, in force 10 February 2004, 42 ILM 2 (2003). The fifth arbitrator is appointed for a nonrenewable three-year term.

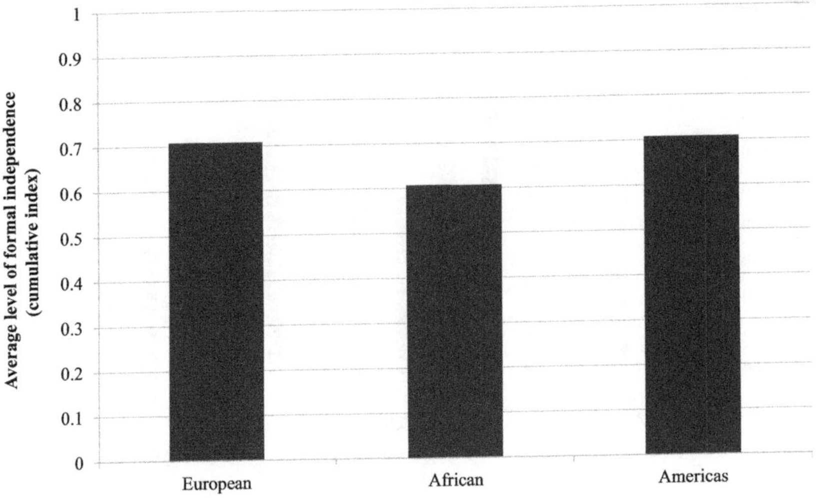

Figure 13.3 ICTs Formal Independence (regional average)

commission whose members represent not only governments but nongovernmental entities (such as bar associations). Also, its budget is governed by an independent trust fund. The CACJ also scores high, in part, because its judges are appointed for a ten-year, nonrenewable term, it has most institutional safeguards in place and it has input on its budget and autonomy on the appointment of its registrar.

Another interesting question pertains to whether there are any notable patterns across world regions. Figure 13.2 suggests that some European and American regional trade courts have a higher level of independence than several of the African trade courts. Figure 13.3 illustrates the average degree of independence for the regional trade courts (by region).

As can be seen, the average level of independence for European regional trade courts is the same as those in the Americas.[55] However, African regional trade courts score lower than those from Europe and the Americas. What contributes to the average lower level of independence among African regional trade courts? First, all regional trade courts in

[55] The European trade courts include the BCJ, CJEU, EFTA CJ, and the ECCIS. The regional trade courts in the Americas include the ATJ, CACJ, CCJ, and the Mercosur PRT.

Africa score low on control of their budgets, with the exception of the COMESA Court of Justice. Second, with the exception of the OHADA CCJA, all regional trade courts in Africa use unanimous voting for judicial appointments. Third, some of the African regional trade courts do not have formal rules governing recusal and limits on activities incompatible with judicial office. Also, several of the African regional trade courts score low on independence of rules of procedure. The regional differences are important to highlight because existing research suggests that most regional trade courts are emulations of European courts, especially the CJEU.[56] Yet, Figure 13.3 suggests that there are important dissimilarities between the European (score = 0.71) and African (score = 0.61) regional courts in terms of formal independence, suggesting that this feature of institutional design cannot be easily attributed to diffusion from the European model international court. Moreover, if we compare the African courts to the CJEU alone, the difference is even more striking. The CJEU scores 0.75 (see Appendix), while the average for the African regional courts is lower.

Another possible way to perhaps comparatively assess independence among ITCs is to look at the types of rules that ensure independence. For example, we might be interested in variation across ITCs in terms of their selection and tenure rules. To do so, I create a *selection and tenure index* that includes the four rules addressing selection and tenure (appointment, reappointment, length of tenure, and removal of judges). The index is then a cumulative score of these four rules, equally weighted and normalized on a scale of 0 (low independence) to 1 (high independence). The comparison of all sixteen ITCs on the basis of the selection and tenure index is presented in Figure 13.4.

Figure 13.4 shows that selection and tenure rules for the CCJ and the OHADA CCJA are the most amenable to higher independence. As mentioned before, the CCJ stands out because the election of judges as well as their removal is determined by an independent commission and is not decided upon by states, even though two representatives of states sit on the commission of eleven members. In addition, judges have appointments that run until the age of retirement, and thus reappointment does not apply. The judges of the OHADA CCJA are elected by an absolute majority by the Council of Ministers, a state organ, for a seven-year,

[56] K. Alter, "The global spread of European style international courts," *West European Politics*, 35, 1, (2012), 135–54.

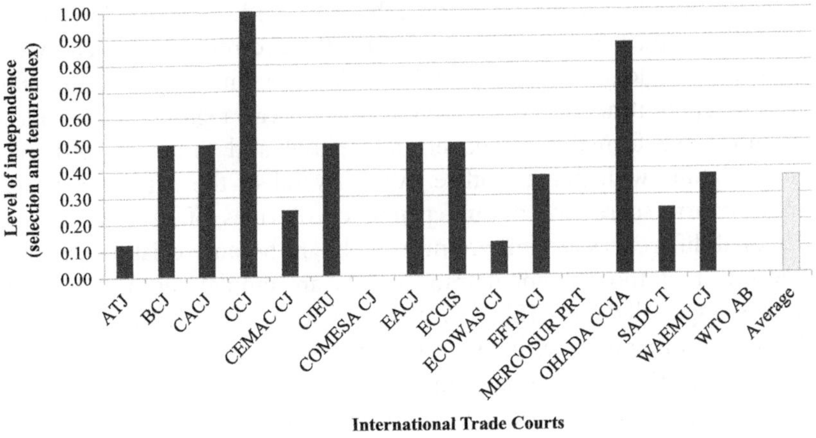

Figure 13.4 ITCs' Formal Independence on Basis of Rules on Selection and Tenure ($N = 16$)[57]

nonrenewable term.[58] On the other end of the spectrum, the COMESA Court of Justice and the Mercosur PRT scores 0 on the selection and tenure index. Figure 13.4 also illustrates that European regional courts score similar to one another (except the EFTA CJ, which has a slightly lower score) on the selection and tenure index, and African regional trade courts all score .5 or less (except for OHADA CCJA). This helps to explain the regional variation depicted in Figure 13.3. Last, Figure 13.3 also suggests that selection and tenure tends to reduce the degree of independence of ITCs, as reflected by the average among all ITCs. The average on the selection and tenure index is lower than in the cumulative index (see Figure 13.2).

Finally, another comparative assessment of the independence among international trade courts can be made on the basis of this data. We can look at the variation in ITCs concerning the independence in the governance of court resources. How do ITCs compare in the ability to control their material and human resources? To address this question, I create a resource index that includes the scores for the rules on the control of a court's budget and the appointment of the registrar/secretary of the court. The index is then a cumulative score of these two rules,

[57] See Appendix for more detail.

[58] See Article 31 of the Revised Treaty on the Harmonization of Business Law in Africa, Quebec, 17 October 2008.

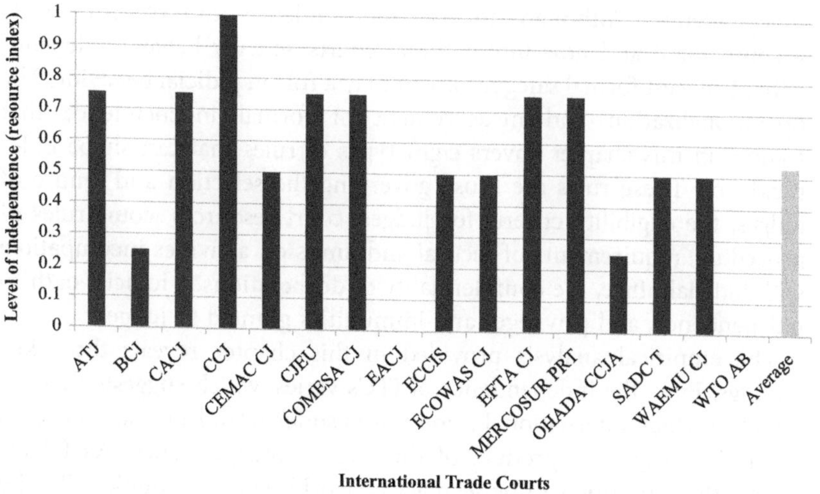

Figure 13.5 ITCs' Formal Independence on Basis of Rules Governing Resources ($N = 16$)

equally weighted and normalized on a scale of 0 (low independence) to 1 (high independence). The comparison of all sixteen ITCs on the basis of the resource index is presented in Figure 13.5.

Figure 13.5 reveals again that the CCJ stands out. It scores 1.0 on the resource index, suggesting that it has high independence when it comes to the governing of its resource. As explained earlier, the CCJ's resources are decided upon by an independent commission. The East African Court of Justice (EACJ) and the WTO AB stand out for having low independence over resources, both scoring 0 on the resource index. The Benelux Court of Justice and the OHADA CCJA also score on the lower side of the resource index.

6 Conclusion

In this chapter, I have argued that judicial independence is an important aspect of understanding the legitimacy of an international trade courts. Yet, existing literature has given little comparative analysis the level to which ITCs are formally independent. I have set out to provide such a comparative analysis looking at all sixteen permanent international trade courts. I have argued that formal independence can be understood as comprising the formal rules that are in place to safeguard judicial independence. Although formal independence cannot completely account for if and how international courts actually behave independently, I suggest formal safeguards can play a role in judicial behavior. The operationalization and measurement of formal independence that I adopt in this chapter covers eight types of rules that can shape independence. These rules are those governing the selection and tenure of judges, the eligibility criteria for judges, court resources, court rules of procedure, requirements of recusal and limits on activities incompatible with judicial office, the confidentiality of deliberations, a judicial oath to independence, and privileges and immunities granted to judges.

The empirical analysis provided in this chapter reveals three key findings. First, the independence of ITCs varies, which suggests that the extent to which international trade courts suffer from legitimacy crises is to varying degrees a product of the judicial independence. As I have shown, this variation can be seen across world regions. Additionally, the CCJ stands out in many ways as an ITC that has a high level of independence because of formal institutional safeguards. The CCJ's legitimacy is thus likely to be supported by its higher level of independence. On the other hand, the overall independence of the EACJ, the WTO AB, and the Mercosur PRT tend to be lower than other ITCs. The latter two of these are appeals bodies, which may contribute to why states have opted to design them with less independence. This suggests that an important source of a legitimacy deficit for these three courts may indeed be the weakness of their institutional safeguards for judicial independence. African regional courts may also suffer from weaker forms of independence, with consequences for their legitimacy.

Second, selection and tenure rules tend to be the way in which courts lack independence. In general, ITCs score low in terms of their independence based on the rules governing the selection and tenure of judges. In many ITCs, judges are selected on the basis of unanimity rules, they are eligible for reappointment, and the removal or dismissal of judges is controlled by states. In all, these features hinder judicial independence. This suggests that the extent to which international courts may suffer from legitimacy deficits, the process of selecting judges and the terms of their tenure could be an important source of such deficits. The question remains whether those courts with more independent selection and tenure rules are likely to in practice demonstrate independence in their behavior. Nomination procedures, which are predominantly determined at the national level, may play an equally if not more important role in shaping independence along this dimension.

Third, several institutional safeguards are found in most if not all ITCs. Oaths to independence, guarantees to privileges and immunities for judges, the confidentiality of deliberations, and eligibility based on legal or judicial experience or expertise are most commonly featured by ITCs. These frequently used means of safeguarding judicial independence thus can be understood as important supports to the legitimacy of international trade courts. In other words, the legitimacy deficits of ITCs are not likely to come from a lack of these forms of institutional safeguards.

This chapter has offered one approach to understanding the independence of international trade courts. Yet, it does not capture all aspects of independence. For example, some who study independence suggest that independence is also shaped by factors such as the feasibility of changing a court's jurisdiction as well as overriding the decisions of a court. Additional research is necessary to examine the extent to which such feasibility varies across international trade courts. As I have also mentioned, this chapter only captures *formal* independence. Formal independence is limited in how much it can tell us about the autonomy and impartiality that judges can exercise in practice, and thus further research is needed to tackle this aspect of judicial independence. Despite shortcomings, this chapter suggests that the extent to which ITCs vary in their formal independence can inform our discussions of their legitimacy.

Appendix

Court	Year in Operation	Cumulative Index Score	Selection and Tenure Index Score	Resource Index Score
Andean Tribunal of Justice (ATJ)	1984	0.67	0.13	0.75
Benelux Court of Justice (BCJ)	1974	0.63	0.50	0.25
Central American Court of Justice (CACJ)	1992	0.79	0.50	0.75
Caribbean Court of Justice (CCJ)	2005	0.92	1.00	1.00
Central African Economic and Monetary Community Court of Justice (CEMAC CJ)	2000	0.63	0.25	0.50
Court of Justice of the European Union (CJEU)	1952	0.75	0.50	0.75
Common Market for Eastern and Southern Africa Court of Justice (COMESA CJ)	1998	0.58	0.00	0.75
East African Court of Justice (EACJ)	2001	0.50	0.50	0.00
Economic Court of the Commonwealth of Independent States (ECCIS)	1993	0.75	0.50	0.50

(*cont.*)

Court	Year in Operation	Cumulative Index Score	Selection and Tenure Index Score	Resource Index Score
Economic Community of West African States Court of Justice (ECOWAS CJ)	2002	0.54	0.13	0.50
European Free Trade Agreement Court of Justice (EFTA CJ)	1994	0.71	0.38	0.75
Mercosur Permanent Review Tribunal (Mercosur PRT)	2002	0.46	0.00	0.75
Organization for the Harmonization of Business Law in Africa Common Court of Justice and Arbitration (OHADA CCJA)	1996	0.67	.88	0.25
Tribunal of the Southern African Development Community (SADC Tribunal)	2005–2010	0.67	0.25	0.50
Western African Economic and Monetary Union Court of Justice (WAEMU CJ)	1995	0.67	0.38	0.50
World Trade Organization Appellate Body (WTO AB)	1994	0.50	0.00	0.00
Average		0.65	0.37	0.53

14

Judicial Interaction of International Trade Courts and Tribunals

MICHELLE Q. ZANG

1 Introduction

Recent decades have witnessed the significant rise of regional trade agreements (RTAs). This is not only reflected in terms of quantity of regimes in force; more important, the content of the new generation RTAs has also evolved over time. In particular, they have become quite expansive in their regulatory coverage, moving from the reduction of tariffs to behind-the-border issues such as the harmonisation of standards, and further, to the so-called WTO-extra issues such as competition and investment.

The fact that almost all the RTAs have established their own dispute settlement mechanisms leads to the coexistence of a high number of international fora, either judicial or quasi-judicial in nature, where trade disputes are adjudicated.[1] The relationship among them has incurred intensive debates among academics and practitioners.[2] This contribution

[1] International trade adjudication is a combined system because it covers both judicial and arbitral mechanisms, e.g. EUCJ vs. NAFTA panel; it is combined also in the sense that both types of mechanisms exist within one single regime setting, e.g. the WTO panel and the Appellate Body. Trade disputes can be adjudicated between the member governments of the WTO with private individuals or companies having no direct access except filing their amicus curiae submissions. Indeed, the WTO dispute settlement is the only forum with exclusive jurisdiction of interstate disputes. In numerical terms, regional courts established on the basis of economic integration agreement comprise the majority of the international trade adjudicators. Different from exclusively specialised dispute settlement bodies, e.g. the WTO panel and Appellate Body, regional courts are normally bestowed with jurisdiction over a wide range of subject matters, and trade disputes might be just the tip of the iceberg. In sum, international trade adjudication is a landscape of perplexity with a high number of diversified mechanisms, at bilateral, regional, plurilateral and multilateral levels, of judicial, arbitral or combined nature.

[2] J. Hillman, 'Conflicts between dispute settlement mechanisms in regional trade agreements and the WTO – What should WTO do', *Cornell International Law Journal*, 42 (2009), 194–208; G. Marceau, A. Izaguerri, and V. Lanovoy, 'The WTO's influence on

thus joins the discourse with a specific research focus upon an emerging phenomenon, namely, judicial interaction between the adjudicators.

Courts are talking to one another all over the world; and there are many types of interjurisdictional communication among courts across borders.[3] Among different types of interjurisdictional communication, the subject of this chapter is the interaction among different trade courts and tribunals. The term 'judicial interaction' refers to the action initiated by the adjudicator referring, discussing and assessing the norms and judicial decisions from another jurisdiction. Judicial interaction distinguishes from the concept of 'judicial dialogue' in that, strictly speaking, the latter refers to a communicative exchange in a responsive manner. The classic example of dialoguing activity is the preliminary reference mechanism setting up the exchange protocol between the Court of Justice of the European Union (CJEU) and the domestic courts of the EU member states. By contrast, judicial interaction usually takes the form of monologue, as opposite to dialogue, referencing, deliberating and comparing the relevant decisions of another judiciary that is not necessarily aware of the ongoing adjudication. While dialogue inherently aims to reach certain conclusion or agreement, interaction focuses on the course of deliberation and comparison with regard to the persuasiveness and applicability of the judicial decision and practice being invoked. In some cases, it is a posture that occupies a large middle ground on the continuum between resistance and convergence, highlighting the motion of the participating adjudicator to consider external sources in appropriate cases, denoting commitments to judicial deliberation but open to the outcome of either harmony or dissonance. Furthermore, it includes but is not limited to the use and/or disuse of precedents from other international courts and tribunals. Judicial interaction might also stem from issues such as overlapped jurisdiction and conflict of obligations between different trade and economic regimes. As discussed later, this function is

other dispute settlement mechanisms: A lighthouse in the storm of fragmentation', *Journal of World Trade*, 47 (2013), 481–574; C. Chase et al., 'Mapping of dispute settlement mechanisms in regional trade agreements – innovative or variations on a theme?', WTO Staff Working Paper, ERSD-2013-07, 10 June 2013; J. Pauwelyn and L. E. Salles, 'Forum shopping before international tribunals: (real) concerns, (im)possible solutions', *Cornell International Law Journal*, 42 (2009), 77–117.

[3] A.-M. Slaughter, 'A typology of transjudicial communication', *University of Richmond Law Review*, 29 (1994), 99–137.

clearly demonstrated in a number of WTO disputes, e.g. *Mexico – Taxes on Soft Drinks* and *Brazil – Retreaded Tyres*.

Judicial interaction is by no means a natural corollary of the proliferation of international judiciaries during the postwar era; rather, its emergence is based on a number of preconditions.[4] Among others, the departure point must be normative: in most cases, the interacting judiciaries share in common a certain normative framework, not necessarily identical normative rules and principles, to allow them to be able to transpose each other's decisions or practice to their own circumstances. From this perspective, it is not surprising that one of the most active areas of judicial communication is among courts charged with the interpretation and application of international instruments concerning human rights.[5] However, what has been often forgotten is the substantial normative convergence in the field of international trade regulations. In particular, there are apparent trends of normative convergence and policy repetition, despite the complicated network consisting of numerous treaty-based regimes. Most treaty regimes of economic integration revolve around the themes of trade liberalisation and market access, which consequentially guarantee essential policy resemblance in areas such as tariff reduction, nondiscrimination and prohibition on quantitative restrictions.

Another cause of interaction among trade courts and tribunals is the overlapped jurisdictions thereof over the same, or inextricably linked, subject matter under dispute. It emanates from the simple fact that there are myriad adjudicatory fora, and the same dispute might well be subject to more than one dispute settlement mechanism. In practice, the RTA parties that are also members of the WTO often have different views regarding the proper, or the best, forum for dispute resolution.[6] As shown later, jurisdiction-related claims have been deeply debated in

[4] Ibid., 122. [5] Ibid., 128.

[6] In the saga of the soft lumber case between the US and Canada, the same set of US measures was litigated at both NAFTA and the WTO, and parallel proceedings have lasted for decades. In *Mexico – Taxes on Soft Drinks* concerning certain tax measures imposed by Mexico on beverages with sweetener, Mexico contested the admissibility of the dispute on the grounds that the US's claims are inextricably linked to a broader dispute between the two countries related to trade in sweeteners under NAFTA. In Mexico's opinion, under those circumstances, it would not be appropriate for the WTO panel to issue findings on the merits of the US's claims. Panel Report, *Mexico– Tax Measures on Soft Drinks and Other Beverages*, WT/DS308/R, adopted 24 March 2006, as modified by Appellate Body Report WT/DS308/AB/R, DSR 2006:I, p. 43, para. 7.11.

several WTO disputes, where the panels and the Appellate Body faced challenges arising from the coexisting jurisdiction of another forum.

What are the legitimacy indications of such interjurisdiction interaction between trade adjudicators? Adjudicatory activity as such responds to several legitimacy questions discussed in the first part of this volume. For example, instances of forum shopping have continuously emerged in trade litigations and have resulted in numerous debates as regards its impact on the effectiveness of the adjudicators involved. Judicial interaction speaks directly to such phenomenon, verifying and measuring the empirical consequence of this conflict that revolves around theory. Also, discussion and valuation of decisions from another adjudicator often take place during the process of fact-finding and legal interpretation, which are considered significant elements in gauging the overall legitimacy of the adjudicator concerned.

Furthermore, interaction activities among adjudicators also highlight legitimacy issues such as inconsistent decisions issued by different tribunals and regulatory fragmentation that stems from institutional pluralism. Legitimacy deficiency as such is inextricably linked to the approach and strategy of the adjudicator when dealing with judicial externality from another jurisdiction, e.g. practice and decisions of the adjudicator therein.

This contribution is therefore arranged as following. The first section starts with an overview of two different types, as well as the status quo, of interaction activities currently engaged by international trade adjudicators. The second section explores in details the interaction of the WTO adjudicators with RTAs and the tribunals established therein. The third section investigates several legitimacy-related aspects of the current practice. The last section concludes.

2 The Typology of Judicial Interaction

To date, the overall picture generally involves two types of interactions among international trade adjudicators, which are, respectively, proactive and passive in nature. Proactive interaction takes place when the adjudicator, in its judgement and more important, on its own initiative, looks into and makes reference to relevant decisions and practice of another adjudicator. It has been widely addressed as cross-judging[7] or a cross-fertilising

[7] R. Teitel and R. Howse, 'Cross-judging: Tribunalization in a fragmented but interconnected global order', *NYU Journal of International Law & Politics*, 41 (2008), 959.

exercise. The premise for interaction of this type is that the adjudicators involved are facing similar substantive or procedural questions, and the referencing adjudicator is convinced by the authority and persuasiveness of the decisions and practice of the other.

In contrast, passive interaction happens when the decisions and practice of another adjudicator are brought to the adjudicator's attention by parties to the dispute. Such interaction is passive in nature as the acting adjudicator is asked, rather than willing, to look into the judicial externalities being invoked. Under this circumstance, the adjudicator is, to a certain extent, 'obligated' to examine the value and viability of the decisions and practice from another jurisdiction. In most cases, they are invoked as evidence in support of various legal claims, ranging from jurisdictional questions and procedural matters to legal interpretation and applicable rule of law.

A couple of observations can be drawn as regards the two types of interacting activities among adjudicators. First, the aim of interaction and the role of the judicial externality differ from each other. In the case of proactive interaction, the adjudicator is mainly motivated by concerns over functionality or/and coherence.[8] It is primarily based on the recognition that, although they have different functions, arbitrators, judges, WTO panellists, and members of the Appellate Body 'use a common discourse of justification, which permits and often requires decision-makers in different regimes to situate their decisions in relation to other regimes'.[9] Ultimately, it is self-consciously using the judicial externality, as source of authority or inspiration, to buttress its own legal reasoning and conclusions. By contrast, in the case of passive interaction, judicial externality is submitted by the disputing parties as evidence in support of their legal claims, and the interaction on the part of the adjudicator simply demonstrates the process of evidence verification.[10]

[8] For functionality, it happens most frequently when the judiciary is searching for an appropriate answer to issues raised by the dispute under scrutiny, to which the case law or practice of another adjudicator offers a functional solution. The consideration of coherence reflects the desire to maintain a certain degree of coherence between the regime under adjudication and other legal regimes. Marceau, Izaguerri, and Lanovoy, 'The WTO's influence on other dispute settlement mechanisms', 489–91.

[9] D. Pulkowski, 'Universal International Law's Grammar' in U. Fastenrath et al. (eds.), *From Bilateralism to Community Interest: Essays in Honour of Bruno Simma* (Oxford University Press, 2011), p. 139.

[10] For example, in *Argentina – Poultry Anti-dumping Duties*, Argentina was of the view that Brazil was 'estopped' by the principle of good faith from initiating the case at the WTO as it had already challenged the same measure at Southern Common Market (MERCOSUR)

Second, distinct outcomes arise from each type of interaction. On the one hand, borrowing and referencing of rulings and practice between different legal regimes has been widely considered as a process of cross-fertilisation. With the ultimate purpose of consolidating its legal analysis, the adjudicator, when carrying out proactive interaction, stands mainly in agreement with the judicial externality being invoked. On the other hand, by looking into judicial externality as part of the evidence, the result would be either endorsing or dismissing its applicability as regards the argumentation being claimed. In addition to such dichotomous outcomes, passive interactions by WTO adjudicators have on a number of occasions also incurred debates over questions of systemic importance. For example, in *Mexico – Taxes on Soft Drinks*, Mexico was of the view that a panel at the North American Free Trade Agreement (NAFTA) was better positioned to 'address the dispute as a whole',[11] and it would not be appropriate for the WTO Panel to issue findings until a parallel NAFTA proceeding had been completed.[12] Consequently, the WTO Panel in that case and the Appellate Body have addressed, although to a limited extent, the issue of jurisdiction overlap between the WTO and other regional regimes.

Third, the type of judicial interaction leads to different involvement of the parties to the dispute. In the case of passive interaction and when judicial externality constitutes part of evidence, the disputing party bears the 'burden of proof' in proving the relevant legal pleas. In other words, the relevance of judicial externality is part of the reasoning to establish the prima facie case. However, it will not be the case for proactive interaction: when the decision or practice from another jurisdiction is quoted, the adjudicator has already shown the perceived relevance and acceptance of the judicial externality.

The preceding typology of judicial interaction has been plainly demonstrated among international trade courts and tribunals. On the one hand, a high number of bilateral and regional trade adjudicators have heavily referenced WTO jurisprudence for the purpose of functionality and coherence, achieving a high level of cross-fertilisation evolving around WTO *acquis*.[13] There are plenty of proactive interactions and

and lost the case; and in *Brazil – Retreaded Tyres*, Brazil invoked an early MERCOSUR ruling to justify under Article XX GATT on the exception clauses the alleged WTO breach of its import ban over retreaded tyres.

[11] Panel Report, *Mexico – Taxes on Soft Drinks*, para. 7.11. [12] Ibid.

[13] Marceau, Izaguerri, and Lanovoy, 'The WTO's influence on other dispute settlement mechanisms'.

engagements on the part of RTA adjudicators toward the WTO dispute settlement. On the other hand, as the only multilateral tribunal, the WTO adjudicators have been highly prudent in making reference to other RTA courts and tribunals, the decisions and practice of which have been dealt with mainly as evidence submitted by the disputing parties. As shown in the following discussion, by conducting such a passive interaction, the WTO adjudicators have, to a varying extent, dealt with several systemically important matters.

3 Interacting Activities of WTO Adjudicators

The approach of WTO panels and the Appellate Body toward regional trade courts and tribunals is embedded in, and cannot be detached from, the broader issue of the role of RTAs in the WTO dispute settlement and their status in WTO law in general. To date, the WTO-RTA debates have revolved mainly around three core questions. The first one concerns the jurisdiction of the WTO DSM and the exercise of it. Typical enquiry includes under what circumstances and to what extent WTO adjudicators should compromise their jurisdiction and defer to the overlapped, or conflicting, jurisdiction of the RTA. In practical terms, it relates to the question of whether WTO adjudicators should dismiss a dispute for the reason that the same or related dispute has already been decided by another RTA adjudicator, or the WTO DSM might not be the most appropriate forum for the pending dispute as compared to other regional fora. The second question refers to the role of RTAs in the interpretative exercise of the WTO laws. As the state concerned is committed to obligations under both the WTO and the RTA, the question thus arises of whether the latter would be of any value when interpreting certain WTO obligations of the same state, particularly in the light of systemic interpretation principle[14] as reflected in Article 31(3) of the Vienna Convention on the Law of Treaties (VCLT). Last but not least, in the case of conflict of obligations, would the WTO rules prevail or should the RTA commitments be prioritised? Alternatively, it can be questioned whether states can modify, among themselves, the WTO obligations

[14] M. Koskenniemi, 'Fragmentation of international law: Difficulties arising from the diversification and expansion of international law', Report of the study group of the international law commission (2007); C. McLachlan, 'The Principle of Systemic Integration and Article 31(3)(c) of the Vienna Convention', *International and Comparative Law Quarterly*, 54 (2005), 279–319.

through concluding, or on the basis of, RTAs. The Appellate Body offered its position in the early *Turkey – Textiles* case, but the recent *Peru – Agricultural Products* case brought in certain new dimensions of this classic issue. The following part will offer a brief overview of the existing WTO case law where the WTO-RTA debate was raised, as well as the approach adopted by the panels and the Appellate Body therein.

3.1 *WTO vs. RTA: Jurisdiction and Admissibility*

The conflict of jurisdiction between the WTO and RTAs was presented in two disputes, namely, *Argentina – Poultry Anti-dumping Duties* and *Mexico – Taxes on Soft Drinks*. In *Argentina – Poultry Anti-dumping Duties* and before initiating this WTO dispute, Brazil challenged the Argentine antidumping measure at a MERCOSUR ad hoc tribunal but lost the case. Afterward, Brazil then brought the same case to the WTO against Argentina, which claimed that Brazil was 'estopped' by the principle of good faith from initiating the case at the WTO.

According to the Panel, there are several essential elements of estoppel that must be fulfilled. However, the Panel found that it was not the case in *Argentina – Poultry Anti-dumping Duties*. In particular, the Panel did not 'consider that Brazil has made a clear and unambiguous statement to the effect that, having brought a case under the MERCOSUR dispute settlement framework, it would not subsequently resort to WTO dispute settlement proceedings'.[15] Also, at the time of the previous MERCOSUR case, the relevant MERCOSUR agreement, namely the *Protocol of Brasilia*, imposed no restrictions on Brazil's right to bring subsequent WTO proceedings in respect of the same measure. It is only its successor, the *Protocol of Olivos*, that provides once a party decides to bring a case under either the MERCOSUR or WTO dispute settlement forums, that party may not bring a subsequent case regarding the same subject-matter in the other forum. The Panel was therefore of the view that this 'fork-in-the-road' clause in the *Protocol of Olivos* is not of relevance because it was not yet in force and thus cannot apply in respect of disputes already decided in accordance with its predecessor.[16]

Another jurisdiction-related conflict arose between the WTO and NAFTA. In *Mexico – Taxes on Soft Drinks*, Mexico took issue with the

[15] Panel Report, *Argentina – Definitive Anti-Dumping Duties on Poultry from Brazil*, WT/DS241/R, adopted 19 May 2003, DSR 2003:V, p. 1727, para. 7.38.
[16] Ibid., para. 7.38.

jurisdiction of the WTO adjudicator on the basis that 'the United States' claims are linked to a broader dispute between the two countries related to trade in sweeteners under a regional treaty, the NAFTA'.[17] In Mexico's opinion, under those circumstances, it would not be appropriate for the Panel to issue findings on the merits of the United States' claims until a parallel NAFTA proceeding had been completed,[18] and only such a panel under the NAFTA would be in a position to 'address the dispute as a whole'.[19]

The Panel declined Mexico's requests. On the appeal, the Appellate Body, while agreeing with Mexico that 'panels have the right to determine whether they have jurisdiction in a given case, as well as to determine the scope of their jurisdiction', nevertheless dismissed the argument that 'once jurisdiction has been validly established, WTO panels would have the authority to decline to rule on the entirety of the claims that are before them in a dispute.'[20] According to the Appellate Body, a decision by a panel to decline validly established jurisdiction would seem to 'diminish the right of a complaining Member to seek the redress of a violation of obligations' within the meaning of Article 23 of the *Dispute Settlement Understanding* (DSU), and the right to bring a dispute pursuant to Article 3.3 of the DSU.[21] The Appellate Body nevertheless acknowledged that there may be a legal impediment to the exercise of a panel's jurisdiction. However, due to the precise scope of Mexico's appeal, the Appellate Body did not consider it necessary to elaborate on the types of situations that could give rise to an impediment as such.[22] In any event, the Appellate Body saw no legal impediments applicable in this case.[23]

Therefore, the essential question raised in *Argentina – Poultry Anti-dumping Duties* and *Mexico – Taxes on Soft Drinks* is whether the WTO jurisdiction, or the exercise of it, could be affected by the parallel jurisdiction of a RTA, and if so, to what extent and in what manner. Following the reasoning of the Appellate Body, jurisdiction of the panel and admissibility of the pending dispute are two distinct issues from each other. As part of its inherent power in relation to its adjudicative functions, the panel is entitled to determine its jurisdiction and to deal

[17] Panel Report, *Mexico – Taxes on Soft Drinks*, para. 7.11. [18] Ibid., para. 7.11.
[19] Ibid., para. 7.11.
[20] Appellate Body Report, *Mexico – Tax Measures on Soft Drinks and Other Beverages*, WT/DS308/AB/R, adopted 24 March 2006, DSR 2006:I, p. 3, paras. 45–6.
[21] Ibid., para. 53. [22] Ibid., para. 54. [23] Ibid., para. 54.

with specific situations that may arise in a particular case.[24] The issue of admissibility comes in the form of 'legal impediment to the exercise of a panel's jurisdiction'.[25] At this juncture, the Appellate Body did nothing more than confirm the possibility of such a scenario without defining any concrete circumstance where legal impediment as such might arise. As shown in these two disputes, it remains unsolved whether the 'fork-in-the-road' clause in a RTA or an existing decision from a RTA adjudicator would fall into this category.

3.2 WTO vs. RTA: Legal Interpretation

The possible involvement of RTAs in interpreting the meaning of WTO rules stems from Article 31(3) VCLT, according to which any 'subsequent agreement between the parties' and 'relevant rules of international law' should be taken into account during the interpretative exercise. Thus, the central question focuses upon whether the RTA concerned can be considered as either of the two terms within the meaning of Article 31(3) VCLT.

In *Argentina – Poultry Anti-dumping Duties*, Argentina argued that the earlier MERCOSUR ruling is part of the normative framework to be applied by the Panel as a result of Article 31(3)(c) of the VCLT; in particular, it constitutes the 'relevant rules of international law applicable in the relations between the parties'.[26] The Panel observed that Argentina's claim, rather than focusing on *interpreting* specific WTO provisions in a particular way, actually was equal to requesting the Panel to *apply* the relevant WTO provisions in a particular way. This argument of Argentina was rejected as the Panel considered it to have no basis in the DSU. The Panel was of the view that 'we are not even bound to follow rulings contained in adopted WTO panel reports, so we see no reason at all why we should be bound by the rulings of non-WTO dispute settlement bodies.'[27] In this case, although without specific conclusions on the role of RTAs in WTO interpretation, the Panel made an interesting distinction: it is one thing to *interpret* a WTO agreement taking into account the

[24] It is also clear that the panel cannot decline to exercise the jurisdiction because, by doing so, it would deprive the member of its right under the WTO. Appellate Body Report, *Mexico – Taxes on Soft Drinks*, para. 45.

[25] Ibid., para. 54.

[26] Panel Report, *Argentina – Poultry Anti-dumping Duties*, para. 7.40.

[27] Ibid., para. 7.41.

provisions of a RTA, it is quite another to *apply* the WTO agreement in the light of the same RTA provisions.

Similar issues once again emerged in the recent *Peru – Agricultural Products* dispute, where the measure under dispute was the tariff regime of Peru imposing additional duties on imports of a number of agricultural products. In the free trade agreement (FTA) concluded but not yet in force between Peru and Guatemala, the regime under dispute is specifically and explicitly mentioned and recognised as an option available for Peru. However, Guatemala, for various reasons, decided to bring this regime to the WTO and challenge its consistency with Peru's WTO obligations. Among a number of defences, Peru contended that its WTO obligations, particularly those under Article 4.2 of the *Agreement on Agriculture* and Article II:1(b) GATT, should be interpreted in the light of the provisions of the FTA as meaning permitting the tariff regime at dispute exclusively in the relations between Peru and Guatemala, who are the parties to the FTA.[28] According to Peru, the FTA should be considered as 'subsequent agreement between the parties' and 'relevant rules of international law' within the meaning of Article 31(3) VCLT.

To date and insofar as legal interpretation is concerned, the Appellate Body has applied a strict approach revolving around Articles 31 and 32 VCLT in that any element being involved in the interpretation of WTO rules must qualify the requirement and criteria stipulated in these two articles. The relevant terms and tests have already been debated and established in a number of WTO disputes. In brief, for 'subsequent agreement between the parties', the Appellate Body holds that agreements 'regarding the interpretation of the treaty or the application of its provisions' have to be those 'bearing specifically upon the interpretation of a treaty'.[29] For 'relevant rules of international law', it is established

[28] Appellate Body Report, *Peru – Additional Duty on Imports of Certain Agricultural Products*, WT/DS457/AB/R and Add.1, adopted 31 July 2015, paras. 5.93 and 5.95.

[29] Appellate Body Reports, *European Communities – Regime for the Importation, Sale and Distribution of Bananas – Second Recourse to Article 21.5 of the DSU by Ecuador*, WT/DS27/AB/RW2/ECU, adopted 11 December 2008, and Corr.1 / *European Communities – Regime for the Importation, Sale and Distribution of Bananas – Recourse to Article 21.5 of the DSU by the United States*, WT/DS27/AB/RW/USA and Corr.1, adopted 22 December 2008, DSR 2008:XVIII, p. 7165, para. 390. In *US – Clove Cigarettes*, the Appellate Body found that it was not possible to discern a function of paragraph 5.2 of the 2001 Doha Ministerial Decision 'other than to interpret the term "reasonable interval"' in the Agreement on Technical Barriers to Trade (TBT Agreement), and it was therefore considered to 'bear specifically upon the interpretation' of that term (Appellate Body Report, *United States – Measures Affecting the Production and Sale of Clove Cigarettes*,

WTO jurisprudence that in order to be 'relevant' for purposes of interpretation, rules of international law must concern the same subject matter as the treaty terms being interpreted.[30] The disputing parties in *Argentina – Poultry Anti-dumping Duties* and *Peru – Agricultural Products* raised claims under Article 31 VCLT; however, both the MERCOSUR tribunal ruling and the Peru-Guatemala FTA were not accepted.[31]

3.3 *WTO vs. RTA: Obligation Conflicts*

In several disputes, obligations arising from a RTA or customs union have been invoked to justify certain domestic measures that would otherwise violate a member's WTO obligations. In *Turkey – Textiles*, India brought a case against certain import restrictions imposed by Turkey. Turkey argued that the Panel should dismiss India's claims because measures at issue were taken pursuant to an RTA between Turkey and the European Communities. It claimed that its import restrictions on textiles and clothing, which were inconsistent with Article XI GATT on the elimination of quantitative restrictions, could be justified under Article XXIV:5 GATT. In particular, the chapeau of Article XXIV:5 provides that 'the provisions of this Agreement shall not prevent,

WT/DS406/AB/R, adopted 24 April 2012, DSR 2012: XI, p. 5751, para. 266 (emphasis in original)). In *US – Tuna II (Mexico)*, the Appellate Body found that a TBT Committee Decision could be considered as a 'subsequent agreement' within the meaning of Article 31(3)(a) of the Vienna Convention. The Appellate Body considered that the extent to which the Decision would inform the interpretation and application of a term or provision of the TBT Agreement would depend on the degree to which it 'bears specifically' on the interpretation and application of a term or provision 'in a specific case' (Appellate Body Report, *United States – Measures Concerning the Importation, Marketing and Sale of Tuna and Tuna Products*, WT/DS381/AB/R, adopted 13 June 2012, DSR 2012:IV, p. 1837, para. 372).

30 See Appellate Body Reports, Peru – Agricultural Products, para. 5.101; *United States – Definitive Anti-Dumping and Countervailing Duties on Certain Products from China*, WT/DS379/AB/R, adopted 25 March 2011, DSR 2011:V, p. 2869, para. 308; and *European Communities and Certain Member States – Measures Affecting Trade in Large Civil Aircraft*, WT/DS316/AB/R, adopted 1 June 2011, DSR 2011:I, p. 7, para. 846.

31 In both cases, the Panel and the Appellate Body declined the application of Article 31 VCLT to the MERCOSUR tribunal ruling and the Peru–Guatemala FTA on the basis that the involvement and function of these two documents do not concern the issue of interpretation but the issue of application. Furthermore, the Appellate Body disagreed with the claim that the Peru–Guatemala FTA constitutes 'rules concerning the same subject matter as the WTO provisions under dispute'. See Panel Report, *Argentina – Poultry Anti-dumping Duties*, para. 7.41 and Appellate Body Report, *Peru – Agricultural Products*, para. 5.101.

as between the territories of contracting parties, the formation of a customs union or of a free trade area or the adoption of an interim agreement necessary for the formation of a customs union or of a free trade area.'

In that case, the Appellate Body delivered the following conclusions as regards the functioning of Article XXIV GATT. First, the chapeau makes it clear that Article XXIV may, under certain conditions, justify the adoption of a measure that is inconsistent with certain other GATT provisions and may be invoked as a possible 'defence' to a finding of inconsistency.[32] Second, Article XXIV can justify the adoption of a measure that is inconsistent with certain other GATT provisions only if the measure is introduced upon the formation of a customs union, and only to the extent that the formation of the customs union would be prevented if the introduction of the measure were not allowed.[33] At this juncture, it has to be noted that the measure at stake concerns solely the benefits and rights of third countries, and the regime of the RTA itself should be affected.

Such use of Article XXIV GATT in the case of obligation conflict was once again highlighted by the Appellate Body in *Peru – Agricultural Products*. In this regard, the Appellate Body made its position rather clear: '[W]e consider that the proper routes to assess whether a provision in a regional trade agreement that may depart from certain WTO rules is nevertheless consistent with the covered agreements are the WTO provisions that permit the formation of regional trade agreements – namely: Article XXIV of the GATT 1994, or the Enabling Clause as far as agreements between developing countries are concerned, in respect of trade in goods; and Article V of the GATS in respect of trade in services.'[34]

In addition to the use of the Article XXIV exception clause dedicated specifically to RTAs, general exceptions enclosed under Article XX GATT have also been invoked insofar as RTAs are concerned. In *Mexico – Taxes on Soft Drinks*, Mexico invoked Article XX(d) and argued that the disputed measures are 'necessary to secure compliance' by the United States with its obligations under the NAFTA.[35] The central issue was thus whether the terms 'to secure compliance with laws or regulations' in Article XX(d)

[32] Appellate Body Report, *Turkey – Restrictions on Imports of Textile and Clothing Products*, WT/DS34/AB/R, adopted 19 November 1999, DSR 1999:VI, p. 2345, para. 45.

[33] Ibid., para. 46. [34] Appellate Body Report, *Peru – Agricultural Products*, para. 5.113.

[35] Appellate Body Report, *Mexico – Taxes on Soft Drinks*, para. 59.

GATT encompass WTO-inconsistent measures applied by a WTO member to secure compliance with another WTO member's obligations under an international agreement. The Appellate Body held that the terms 'laws or regulations' refer to rules that form part of the domestic legal system of a WTO member, and thus, the 'laws or regulations' with which the member invoking Article XX(d) may seek to secure compliance do not include obligations of *another* WTO member under an international agreement.[36]

Later on, in *Brazil – Retreaded Tyres*, the European Community challenged the WTO-consistency of Brazil's import regime in retreaded tyres. Brazil had imposed an import ban on retreaded tyres with the exemption for imports from MERCOSUR countries. The European Community took issue with the MERCOSUR exemption, pointing to its resulting discriminatory treatment between MERCOSUR countries and other WTO members. In fact, the original import ban did not have such an exemption, which was later introduced by Brazil as a result of a ruling issued by a MERCOSUR arbitral tribunal. In particular, the MERCOSUR tribunal had found Brazil's restrictions on the importation of remoulded tyres to be a violation of its obligations under MERCOSUR. According to Brazil, because the MERCOSUR exemption is based upon the decision of the MERCOSUR tribunal, it is thus justified under Article XX, particularly under Article XX(b), which offers immunity for domestic measures 'necessary to protect human, animal or plant life or health'.

The Appellate Body disagreed. The Appellate Body was of the view that 'the ruling issued by the MERCOSUR arbitral tribunal is not an acceptable rationale for the discrimination because it bears no relationship to the legitimate objective pursued by the Import Ban that falls within the purview of Article XX(b), and even goes against this objective. It does not necessarily mean that acts implementing a decision of a judicial or quasi-judicial body — such as the MERCOSUR arbitral tribunal — can be characterised as a decision that is "capricious" or "random"; however, discrimination can result from a rational decision or behaviour and still be "arbitrary or unjustifiable".'[37] The conclusion therefore is that the MERCOSUR exemption has resulted in the import ban being applied in a manner that constitutes arbitrary or unjustifiable

[36] Ibid., para. 69.

[37] Appellate Body Report, *Brazil – Measures Affecting Imports of Retreaded Tyres*, WT/DS332/AB/R, adopted 17 December 2007, DSR 2007:IV, p. 1527, para. 232.

discrimination within the meaning of and prohibited by the chapeau of Article XX.[38]

As shown earlier, when dealing with obligation conflict between the WTO and the RTA, the Appellate Body has mainly, if not exclusively, developed its legal reasoning and resolution on the basis of the exception clauses under Article XXIV and Article XX GATT. For the conflicting RTA obligation to prevail, or to justify the established WTO violation, such obligation has to qualify the requirements and criteria stipulated in the relevant WTO provisions on exceptions. However, no successful instance has been made so far.

4 Legitimacy Assessment

The first concern refers to the policy space that WTO adjudicators allow for members to deal with inconsistent, or even conflicting, commitments between the RTA and the WTO. While RTAs are in general permitted under Article XXIV GATT as exceptions to the WTO legal system, their existence, operation, as well as interaction with the WTO, are not without controversy as a result of the conditions and criteria stipulated in the Article, together with the interpretation thereof offered by the Appellate Body. Given the substantial and continuing rise of RTAs, interaction on the part of the WTO and its adjudicators with the coexisting trade regimes plays a significant role in global trade regulation: against the background of 'fragmented' bilateral, regional and multilateral regimes, the way of interaction between regimes and adjudicators will either deteriorate or ameliorate the fragmentation of trade policies and their enforcement.

At first glance, the current approach of WTO panels and the Appellate Body appears rather 'RTA unfriendly'. They follow a passive approach, only making reference when parties to the dispute have so argued; they rarely, in their adjudicating practice, consider RTAs and their judicial decisions as sources of authority or inspiration. Also, in the WTO disputes discussed earlier, most claims made on the basis of relevant RTA provisions and adjudicatory decisions have been rejected, although to a varying extent. However, rather than arguing that the WTO takes a hostile approach toward RTAs, a thorough survey of the existing case law indicates a slightly different picture. To date, there are no genuine 'WTO-

[38] Ibid., para. 228.

RTA' conflicts emerging in practice as almost all the alleged conflicts bear certain inherent 'birth defects'. In *Peru – Agricultural Products*, the disputed FTA was not yet ratified by Peru during the proceedings; in *Argentina – Poultry Anti-dumping Duties* and insofar as the jurisdiction conflict is concerned, the critical 'fork-in-the-road' clause was only added into the relevant MERCOSUR treaty after the completion of the arbitral proceedings; and in *Brazil – Retreaded Tyres*, the relevant MERCOSUR provision on the protection of human, animal and plant health, as well as the fact that Brazil might have raised this defence in the MERCOSUR arbitral proceedings, show that the discrimination associated with the MERCOSUR exemption does not necessarily result from a conflict between provisions under MERCOSUR and the GATT 1994.[39]

Furthermore, insofar as the WTO-RTA relationship is concerned, a number of critical questions remain unanswered, and before these questions are properly resolved, any conclusion on the WTO approach toward RTAs and their adjudicators would be impulsive. First of all, the approach of WTO adjudicators in dealing with RTA courts and tribunals stands in stark contrast with their approach toward the 'global' or 'general' international courts, such as the Permanent Court of International Justice (PCIJ) and International Court of Justice (ICJ). On the one hand, WTO adjudicators have proactively engaged with the PCIJ and ICJ in relation to a range of legal issues, relying upon their judgements and practice when searching for authority and inspiration in their legal reasoning. On many occasions, WTO adjudicators made reference to the PICJ and ICJ with the purpose of gap-filling, or bolstering their own conclusions. In *India – Patents (US)*, the Appellate Body quoted the judgement of PCIJ in *Certain German Interests in Polish Upper Silesia* with respect to the treatment of municipal law.[40] In *US – Wool Shirts and Blouses* and when dealing with the issue of burden of proof, the Appellate Body stated that 'various international tribunals, including the International Court of Justice, have generally and consistently accepted and applied the rule that the party who asserts a fact, whether the claimant or the respondent, is responsible for providing proof thereof.'[41] Similar

[39] Ibid., para. 234.

[40] Appellate Body Report, *India – Patent Protection for Pharmaceutical and Agricultural Chemical Products*, WT/DS50/AB/R, adopted 16 January 1998, DSR 1998:I, p. 9, paras. 65–6.

[41] Appellate Body Report, *United States – Measure Affecting Imports of Woven Wool Shirts and Blouses from India*, WT/DS33/AB/R, adopted 23 May 1997, and Corr.1, DSR 1997:I, p. 323, p. 14.

reference can be also found in *EC – Bananas III (Article 21.5), Turkey – Textiles US – 1916 Act* and *Korea – Procurement* in relation to both procedural and substantive issues.[42]

On the other hand, however, WTO adjudicators have been highly prudent when dealing with RTA adjudicators, the rulings of which have been mainly considered as part of the evidence and arguments of the disputing parties and thus subject to restrictive judicial scrutiny. Is there any plausible explanation for such diverging approaches of the WTO adjudicators? What are the relevant reasons for distinct treatment for different departments of public international law? It has been argued that the WTO may have found its place as part of the broader international law family; it is nevertheless still struggling to learn from and find its place vis-a-vis other subbranches of international law, including subbranches within its own field of international trade law, e.g. RTAs.[43]

The second legitimacy-related issue arises from the approach of WTO panels and the Appellate Body in dealing with their jurisdiction and the admissibility of the pending dispute. To a certain extent, it responds to

[42] In *EC – Bananas III (Article 21.5)*, the Appellate Body made reference to the ICJ's approach in addressing the interpretation of declarations of acceptance of the compulsory jurisdiction of the Court, in order to buttress its position that 'the relinquishment of rights granted by the DSU cannot be lightly assumed' (Appellate Body Report, *European Communities – Regime for the Importation, Sale and Distribution of Bananas*, WT/DS27/AB/R, adopted 25 September 1997, DSR 1997:II, p. 591, para. 217). In *Turkey – Textiles*, the Panel found that it did not have the authority to find that a claim was inadmissible because of the missing participation of a WTO member. The finding is essentially based upon a series of relevant ICJ judgements that dismiss the 'indispensable parties' rule (Panel Report, *Turkey – Restrictions on Imports of Textile and Clothing Products*, WT/DS34/R, adopted 19 November 1999, as modified by Appellate Body Report WT/DS34/AB/R, DSR 1999:VI, p. 2363, paras. 9.8–9.10). In *US – 1916 Act* and on the basis of several cases of PCIJ and ICJ, the Appellate Body noted that 'it is a widely accepted rule that an international tribunal is entitled to consider the issue of its own jurisdiction on its own initiative, and to satisfy itself that it has jurisdiction in any case that comes before it' (Appellate Body Report, *United States – Anti-Dumping Act of 1916*, WT/DS136/AB/R, WT/DS162/AB/R, adopted 26 September 2000, DSR 2000:X, p. 4793, Footnote 30). In *Korea – Procurement*, the Panel opined that error in respect of a treaty is a concept that has developed in customary international law through the case law of the PICJ and of the ICJ. By means of footnote, the Panel named the PICJ case on Legal Status of Eastern Greenland and the ICL case concerning the Temple of Preah Vihear (Panel Report, *Korea – Measures Affecting Government Procurement*, WT/DS163/R, adopted 19 June 2000, DSR 2000:VIII, p. 3541, para. 7.123).

[43] J. Pauwelyn, 'Interplay between the WTO Treaty and Other International Legal Instruments and Tribunals: Evolution after 20 Years of WTO Jurisprudence' (February 10, 2016). Available at SSRN: http://ssrn.com/abstract=2731144 or http://dx.doi.org/10.2139/ssrn.2731144.

the phenomenon and ongoing discourse of forum shopping in international trade adjudication. On the one hand, the exclusive nature of WTO jurisdiction is unambiguously spelt out in the DSU and confirmed by the Appellate Body. Pursuant to Article 23.1 DSU, a complaining member is obliged to bring any dispute arising under the WTO agreements to the WTO dispute settlement system. Article 23.1 DSU thus ensures the exclusivity of the WTO vis-a-vis other international fora at least in the sense that, for example, a 'fork-in-the-road' clause in RTA cannot take away the exclusive jurisdiction of the WTO panel, which is the only adjudicator for disputes over WTO rights and obligations.[44] As the Panel observed in *US – FSC*, 'a member has the right to resort to WTO dispute settlement at any time . . . this fundamental right to resort to dispute settlement is a core element of the WTO system. Accordingly, we believe that a panel should not lightly infer a restriction on this right . . .; rather there should be a clear and unambiguous basis in the relevant legal instrument for concluding that such a restriction exists.'[45]

On the other hand, the Appellate Body has clearly acknowledged that there may be 'legal impediment to the exercise of a panel's jurisdiction'. What is unclear is what can constitute such impediment and, when the existence of impediment is confirmed, to what extent it can affect the exercise of the WTO jurisdiction. What emerges from *Argentina – Poultry Anti-dumping Duties* and *Mexico – Taxes on Soft Drinks* is that WTO adjudicators will go through thorough and highly technical judicial scrutiny over any objection against their jurisdiction, rendering the term 'legal impediment' with a complex threshold. With this evident safeguarding approach from the WTO adjudicators toward their jurisdiction, it would be interesting to see under what circumstances a 'legal impediment' can be properly established.

Third, insofar as interpretation is concerned, the recent Appellate Body Report in *Peru – Agricultural Products* seems to have closed the door to the RTAs on the ground that the general rule of interpretation in VCLT is aimed at reflecting the *common intention* of the parties to the treaty, as opposed to the intentions of some parties only. In particular, the Appellate Body expressed the view that 'with multilateral treaties

44 The 'fork-in-the-road' clause might turn the dispute to the RTA forum for resolution, but in that case, the applicable law is the relevant RTA provisions, rather than the WTO rules.

45 Panel Report, *United States – Tax Treatment for "Foreign Sales Corporations"*, WT/DS108/R, adopted 20 March 2000, as modified by Appellate Body Report WT/DS108/AB/R, DSR 2000:IV, p. 1675, para. 7.17.

such as the WTO covered agreements, the "general rule of interpretation" in Article 31 of the Vienna Convention is aimed at establishing the ordinary meaning of treaty terms reflecting the common intention of the parties to the treaty, and not just the intentions of some of the parties. While an interpretation of the treaty may in practice apply to the parties to a dispute, it must serve to establish the common intentions of the parties to the treaty being interpreted.'[46] As it is highly doubtful whether a RTA could ever qualify to reflect 'common intention' of the entire WTO membership, its role in interpreting relevant WTO obligations thus seems very limited.

However, it might be argued that the Appellate Body has been quite open to non-WTO international law and agreements when interpreting the meaning of relevant WTO rules. This proposition was first launched in *US – Shrimp*, by adopting the 'evolutional interpretation' for 'exhaustible natural resources' under Article XX(g) GATT and taking into account the modern international conventions and declarations, i.e. United Nations Convention on the Law of the Sea and the Resolution on Assistance to Developing Countries adopted in conjunction with the Convention on the Conservation of Migratory Species of Wild Animals, during its interpretative exercise.[47]

Even for the international agreements that are not signed up by the entire WTO membership, the Appellate Body did not completely sweep away their potential involvement in its interpretative exercise of the WTO law. In *EC and certain member States – Large Civil Aircraft*, the EC argued that the bilateral agreement between the EC and the United States (the 1992 Agreement) ought to be treated as a 'relevant rule of international law' under Article 31(3)(c) in interpreting relevant rules of the *Agreement on Subsidies and Countervailing Measures* (SCM Agreement) of the WTO. Admittedly, different from RTAs and from the perspective of WTO law, the 1992 agreement does not fall into any exception clauses as permitted under the WTO agreements. On the one hand, this distinction is of significant importance where alleged WTO violation has been properly established and confirmed by the panel. In this case, the defendant can invoke the RTA-specific exception clause, which is not available for other types of international agreements, in justifying the established violation. On the other hand, however, the same

46 Appellate Body Report, *Peru – Agricultural Products*, para. 5.95.

47 Appellate Body Report, *United States – Import Prohibition of Certain Shrimp and Shrimp Products*, WT/DS58/AB/R, adopted 6 November 1998, DSR 1998:VII, p. 2755, para. 130.

distinction does not weigh the same or hold similar importance during the interpretative exercise, which is overwhelmingly guided by Articles 31 and 32 of the VCLT. In other words, what matters for the Appellate Body in understanding the meaning of the WTO rules under dispute is whether such non-WTO international law qualifies the elements and criteria embodied in the VCLT.

In *EC and certain member States – Large Civil Aircraft*, the Appellate Body, while suggesting 'one must exercise caution in drawing from an international agreement to which not all WTO Members are party', nevertheless took into account the 'principle of systemic integration' that seeks to ensure that 'international obligations are interpreted by reference to their normative environment' in a manner that gives 'coherence and meaningfulness' to the process of legal interpretation. As a conclusion, the Appellate Body made the following observation: '[I]n a multilateral context such as the WTO, when recourse is had to a non-WTO rule for the purposes of interpreting provisions of the WTO agreements, a delicate balance must be struck between, on the one hand, taking due account of an individual WTO member's international obligations and, on the other hand, ensuring a consistent and harmonious approach to the interpretation of WTO law among all WTO members.'[48] Undoubtedly, any RTA commitment will naturally fall into 'an individual WTO Member's international obligations' and thus, following the preceding reasoning of the Appellate Body, should be considered as one end of the equilibrium in interpreting provisions of the WTO agreements. Thus, there is definitely space for clarification between the Appellate Body's emphasis on 'common intention' in *Peru – Agricultural Products* and on 'delicate balance' established in *EC and certain member States – Large Civil Aircraft*. While the former by and large renders the involvement of RTAs close to irrelevant, the latter highlights the need for attention being paid to a member's international obligations in general, inter alia, its RTA commitments.

In sum, the judicial interaction by WTO adjudicators so far certainly shows a passive approach, which leads to the outcome that the practice and decisions of RTA adjudicators are generally not among the judicial externalities that will be quoted at the WTO as sources of authority and inspiration. The Appellate Body's attempt trying to maintain 'clinic isolation' from RTAs and other trade fora stands in stark contrast to its

[48] Appellate Body Report, *EC and certain member States – Large Civil Aircraft*, para. 845.

general openness and resistance to fragmentation toward public international law.[49] To a certain extent, the current 'clinic isolation' between the WTO and RTAs is normatively plausible in that the latter falls into the category of 'exceptions' to the former and logically, should be interpreted in a restrictive manner. It also has to be noted the 'birth defects' stemming from the factual backgrounds of each dispute. Therefore, it remains to be seen what would be the response from WTO adjudicators in the case of a typical WTO-RTA dilemma or a 'perfect' conflict between the multilateral and regional regimes.

5 Concluding Remarks

To date, judicial practice and existing jurisprudence present a WTO-centric network of interaction in international trade adjudication. While non-WTO adjudicators are making proactive input in the judicial exercise of cross-fertilisation, particularly in the form of intense references to specific rulings of WTO disputes, WTO panels and the Appellate Body have not disclosed equally strong will in their participation.

WTO adjudicators have so far interacted with RTA courts and tribunals mainly in a passive fashion: references are made to their practice and decisions only under the circumstance where parties to the dispute invoke them as part of the arguments. That is to say, the panels and the Appellate Body are 'requested' or 'obliged' to deal with such judicial externality.

Legitimacy enquiries arising from the judicial interaction conducted by WTO adjudicators evolve around the policy margin of the WTO members when dealing with WTO-RTA conflicts in areas such as jurisdiction, admissibility, legal interpretation and obligation clashes. It is still far-fetched to argue for a 'RTA unfriendly' attitude of the WTO solely on the basis of the passive interacting approach and the fact that most RTA-related arguments have been so far unsuccessful.

The relationship between the WTO dispute settlement system and other trade courts and tribunals is under ongoing debates, and the adjudicators involved have shown considerable caution when dealing with questions as such. Although a number of critical questions remain unsolved, clear response from WTO adjudicators is of significant importance, not only because it relates to the empirical constraints upon the

[49] R. Howse, 'The World Trade Organization 20 years on: Global governance by judiciary', *European Journal of International Law*, 27 (2016), 9–77 at 72.

state's discretion in dealing with a WTO-RTA dilemma, but also because it is inextricably linked to many legitimacy challenges, e.g. forum shopping and conflicting adjudicatory decisions.

Arguably, judicial interaction can either enhance or diminish the legitimacy of international trade adjudication. Deliberation and willing for communication on the part of adjudicators will not only reduce irrational dissonance among them, but also foster a process of collective judicial deliberation on a set of common problems and lift the overall quality of their decisions, as well as the perceived credibility of the adjudication system they are embedded in. Therefore, adjudicators involved should deal with cross-regime interaction with great caution and necessarily, a comprehensive systemic vision.

15

Access to Trade Tribunals – Comparative Perspectives

OLE KRISTIAN FAUCHALD

1 Introduction

This chapter examines access to trade tribunals in the sense of who can initiate cases. The extent to which various actors have access to international trade tribunals has significant implications for the legitimacy of the tribunals in at least two senses. First, to the extent that international trade rules establish or define rights and duties, the legitimacy of trade tribunals may vary according to the degree to which rights-holders and others who have their essential interests protected by the international rules have formal and real opportunities to bring their cases to the tribunals. In other words, it is of interest to explore whether the formal and real access to the tribunal corresponds to the jurisdiction of the tribunals and the effects of their decisions for rights and duties of various actors.

Second, to the extent that trade disputes significantly affect the interests of third parties (i.e. parties that are not taking part directly in the dispute), trade tribunals' legitimacy may depend on the degree to which third parties have formal and real opportunities to present factual and legal arguments in favour of such interests. Such access to the courts can influence their legitimacy in various ways. It may, for example, contribute to legitimacy by improving the quality of the reasoning and ensure that the courts' conclusions have broad support. It may also undermine the legitimacy by increasing the costs of cases in terms of time, economic and human resources, or by opening up for allegations that the courts are too accommodating to special interests or that they become biased in favour of the interests of resourceful third parties.[1]

[1] See, in this direction, Eric A. Posner and John C. Yoo, 'Judicial independence in international tribunals', *California Law Review*, 93 (2005), 28, where they emphasise that judicial independence is likely to undermine the effectiveness of courts because they 'are

Therefore, it should not be assumed that increased access leads to increased legitimacy. Issues of legitimacy will be discussed by asking whether and under what conditions the various forms of accessibility are likely to increase or decrease the courts' legitimacy in the eyes of key stakeholders. Rights-holders and duty-bearers under the free trade agreements (FTAs) are key stakeholders. In addition, those who have significant interests at stake in the trade disputes will be regarded as key stakeholders for this purpose.[2] However, it remains difficult to draw a line between 'significant interests' and other interests. Some key interests have been highlighted in trade treaties as potentially sufficient to justify general exceptions from the trade rules (e.g. public order, balance of payment, exhaustible natural resources and health issues). Such exceptions are indicative of stakeholder groups whose interests may qualify as significant.

Historically, the general perception has been that disputes concerning interstate trade have concerned interests that best can be defended by states. The interests of states essentially corresponded to the interests of traders in access to foreign markets and to the interests of domestic industries in protection against increased imports. This logic was convincing as long as disputes essentially concerned border measures, such as tariffs, quantitative restrictions, and discriminatory internal taxes and regulations based on country of origin. Commitments regarding border measures are based on negotiations and reciprocity among states, and there are consequently strong arguments in favour of resolving disputes regarding tariffs, quantitative restrictions, and origin-based discrimination through adjudication between states. Such disputes were, with some exceptions, predominant in the WTO until the 1980s.

Increased application of international trade rules in other contexts has challenged this starting point. First, trade rules have increasingly been applied to internal policy measures. This has been the case for nondiscrimination rules all the way back to GATT 1947. But despite a handful of cases concerning origin neutral differential treatment,[3] the extensive

less likely to issue decisions that are satisfactory to all state parties to a dispute'. See also the discussion of this claim by Y. Shany, 'Assessing the effectiveness of international courts: A goal-based approach', *The American Journal of International Law*, 106 (2012), 257–61.

2 See, in the same direction, the discussion of 'goal setters' and legitimacy in Y. Shany, ibid., 242 and 266–7.

3 See, in particular, *Treatment by Germany of imports of sardines* (BISD 1S/53), *Japan – Customs duties, taxes and labelling practices on imported wines and alcoholic beverages*

application of nondiscrimination rules to origin neutral discrimination in the case law of recent years has marked a significant shift of focus from border measures to internal measures. Second, similar developments have occurred since the 1980s as regards 'technical barriers' to trade, a milestone being the adoption of the Agreement on Technical Barriers to Trade at the end of the Tokyo Round in 1979. Third, international rules to 'level the playing field' of market actors have been gradually strengthened, in particular through limiting subsidies and unfair competition among market actors. These and other developments have broadened the range of stakeholders having significant interests in the application of international trade rules and made the relationship between state interests and the interests of private parties more complex. The strengthened focus on internal policy measures also means that the links between international trade disputes and the domestic judiciary are multiplying and becoming stronger.

This chapter will focus on disputes concerning trade issues. However, there is no clear distinction between trade law and other areas of law. Many FTAs go beyond traditional trade topics and address other issues, such as competition, government procurement, intellectual property rights, protection of investment, human rights, migration, labour law and environmental protection. This chapter will use the WTO Agreement as the starting point and benchmark when determining the scope of the analysis of the case law of regional FTA courts. The focus in the following will consequently be on issues that are regulated by the WTO Agreement as well as disciplines that are or have been negotiated under the WTO.

Because regional FTAs in general contain more far-reaching trade liberalization than the WTO, including broader regulation of internal policy measures, they will more extensively affect rights, duties, and interests of a broader range of stakeholders. We should therefore expect more comprehensive formal and real access to tribunals under regional FTAs than under the WTO. However, there may be important factors that prevent regional FTAs from providing more comprehensive access to tribunals in trade disputes. Such factors may, for example, include preferences for the WTO Dispute Settlement Mechanism (DSM) due to predictability, compliance, and fear of fragmentation, as well as preferences for

(BISD 34S/83), *United States – Measures affecting alcoholic and malt beverages* (BISD 39S/206), and *Canadian import, distribution and sale of certain alcoholic drinks by provincial marketing agencies* (BISD 39S/27).

alternative means of resolving disputes in regional contexts. It is therefore not a matter of course that regional FTA courts should be more accessible than the WTO DSM. The design and role of courts under regional FTAs can for these and other reasons be expected to differ significantly.

The first main aim of this chapter is to identify the degrees of discrepancy between substantive rules and the ability to initiate cases, with a focus on whether rights-holders, duty-bearers and those with significant interests can bring cases to courts. The assessment of the degree of discrepancy must be carried out at a general level; space does not permit venturing into the details of the substantive scope of the various regimes. The assessment will start out by providing an overview of who can initiate cases, and thereafter consider whether important groups of rights-holders, duty-bearers or significantly interested parties lack the possibility of bringing cases. The second main aim is to explore reasons why the regional FTAs follow different development trajectories in terms of which groups of stakeholders bring cases and the kinds of substantive issues that are brought before them.

Accordingly, this chapter will first consider access in terms of who has formal opportunity to initiate cases (Section 2). It thereafter proceeds to consider the actual recourse to regional FTAs by those given formal access (Section 3). Finally, it considers discrepancies between stakeholders' rights, duties, and interests under the FTAs and their access to the FTA courts, as well as potential reasons for variations in the development trajectories of the courts (Section 4). The chapter will be limited to and draw on information and analyses regarding the tribunals considered elsewhere in this book, i.e. the WTO DSM, the Andean Court of Justice, the Permanent Review Court of Mercosur, the ASEAN Dispute Settlement Mechanism, the Economic Court of the Commonwealth of Independent States (CIS), the Court of Justice of the Common Market for Eastern and Southern Africa (COMESA), the Court of Justice of the West African Economic and Monetary Union (WAEMU), the European Free Trade Association (EFTA) Court, and the Court of Justice of the European Union (CJEU).

2 Formal Access to Courts

2.1 The WTO Dispute Settlement Mechanism

When considering who can bring cases to trade tribunals, major distinctions can be drawn between tribunals that are open only to disputes among members of the FTA (including in some cases customs territories), those that can deal with cases initiated by or against international institutions and those in which private parties may be directly or indirectly involved. A somewhat different distinction can be drawn between tribunals that only have an adjudicatory role and those that also have advisory functions. The latter is particularly relevant in relation to domestic courts. In terms of these two distinctions, the WTO DSM is placed in the category of tribunals that are open to disputes between members, and it does not have any advisory functions. Although formal access to the WTO DSM is broad in the sense that members can challenge mandatory legislation as such regardless of whether the legislation has been applied or not[4] and bring cases regarding nullification and impairment of benefits,[5] the real access to bring cases may be questioned. Bringing cases is resource demanding and may be politically sensitive. Despite initiatives to provide assistance to developing countries to bring and defend cases,[6] there are significant concerns that real access to the WTO DSM remains limited.[7]

On the one hand, when significant interests (including effects on rights and duties) of private parties are involved, the starting point is that WTO members are free as to whether to initiate disputes. Possibilities for private parties to influence state behaviour in this regard depend on domestic legislation and administrative practices, and they vary significantly among states. Some states allow private parties to make petitions and thereby force the states to consider whether to initiate cases.[8] I am not aware that any state has passed legislation that allows private parties to force the state to initiate cases.[9] On the other hand, there are some WTO rules that prohibit

[4] See Appellate Body report, *United States –1916 Act*, paras. 60–1.

[5] See Article XXIII of GATT.

[6] In particular through the Advisory Centre on WTO Law, see www.acwl.ch.

[7] See J. A. Laker, *African Participation at the World Trade Organization: Legal and Institutional Aspects, 1995 – 2010* (Leiden: Brill and Nijhoff, 2013), p. 219–23; and G. C. Shaffer and R. Meléndez-Ortiz (eds.), *Dispute Settlement at the WTO: The Developing Country Experience* (Cambridge University Press, 2010), pp. 342–3.

[8] See, inter alia, for the United States: 19 USC 2412, and for the European Union: Council Regulation (EC) No 3286/94 of 22 December 1994 laying down Community procedures in the field of the common commercial policy in order to ensure the exercise of the Community's rights under international trade rules, in particular those established under the auspices of the World Trade Organization (Trade Barriers Regulation).

[9] The closest one comes to such an arrangement seems to be the European Union. The European Court of First Instance has found that a complainant under the EU Trade Barriers Regulation has the 'right to submit for review by the Court any decision of the Commission terminating an examination procedure initiated as a result of his complaint',

states from taking certain measures in the absence of initiatives of private parties. Article 5 of the Anti-Dumping Agreement and Article 11 of the Agreement on Subsidies and Countervailing Measures state that, as the general rule, antidumping and countervailing duties cannot be imposed unless they have been initiated upon a written application by or on behalf of the domestic industry. Hence, the existence of such applications and the subsequent withdrawal may have significant impact on disputes, but such applications and withdrawals cannot force countries to initiate or abandon cases at the WTO DSM.

It has in general been considered that obligations under the WTO Agreement do not have 'direct effect'. One reason for such a conclusion (but certainly not the only) would be that the WTO only defines rights and duties of states and not of private parties.[10] Nevertheless, WTO rules may have significant implications for the rights, duties, and interests of private parties.[11] It is clear that certain rules of the WTO do indirectly affect rights of private parties, for example the WTO members' duty under the WTO Agreement on Trade-related Aspects of Intellectual Property Rights to protect intellectual property rights.

In conclusion, the WTO Agreement does not directly provide rights and duties of private parties. However, such rights and duties are indirectly affected. Moreover, the WTO Agreement may seriously affect significant interests of private parties. Against this background, it can be concluded that there are 'tensions' within the WTO regime between the effects that the WTO Agreement may have for private parties' rights, duties, and significant interests, and the lack of formal access of private

see Case T-317/02 (2004), para. 41. As regards the discretionary power of the Commission to terminate the procedure under Article 11(1) of the Trade Barriers Regulation, the Court found: 'The question whether the interests of the Community require that action be taken involves appraisal of complex economic situations, and judicial review of such an appraisal must be limited to verifying that the relevant procedural rules have been complied with, that the facts on which the choice is based have been accurately stated and that there has not been a manifest error of assessment of those facts or a misuse of powers' (para. 94). The Court also stated: 'Article 12(1) of Regulation No 3286/94 does not enable the regulation to be relied on by a complainant to urge the Community to take action in defence of the general interests of the Community, if the complainant has not itself suffered adverse trade effects. In any event, even if it has, it is not sufficient to hold that such an adverse trade effect exists for the Community to be required to act under Regulation No 3286/94, as the Commission has a wide discretion when assessing the commercial interests of the Community, seen as a whole' (para. 122).

10 Panel report, *United States – Sections 301 Trade Act*, paras. 7.72–7.79.

11 See, inter alia, H. R. Fabri, 'Is there a case – legally and politically – for direct effect of WTO obligations?', *The European Journal of International Law*, 25, 1, (2014), 154–60.

parties to the WTO DSM. Such tensions may constitute a challenge in terms of the legitimacy of the WTO DSM in the eyes of private parties.

2.2 *Formal Access to Regional Courts*

In line with Article XXIV of GATT, we can assume that regional FTAs reduce trade barriers and facilitate trade within the region. Many FTAs go beyond trade facilitation to other fields of cooperation. The starting point is therefore that regional FTAs contain rules that define rights, duties, and significant interests more comprehensively for a broader range of subjects than does the WTO. We may therefore expect regional FTAs to provide additional opportunities for access to courts when compared to the WTO.

The regional FTAs studied in this book fall into two main groups. The first group is those that mainly follow the model of the WTO and essentially provide for state–state dispute settlement. The second group of FTAs includes those that extend access to the FTA courts to institutions of the FTAs, courts of member states, and/or private parties. ASEAN clearly belongs to the first group. One important exception, however, has been the ASEAN rules on investment. Starting out with the 1987 ASEAN Agreement for the Promotion and Protection of Investments, followed up by the 1998 Framework Agreement on the ASEAN Investment Area, and updated by the 2009 ASEAN Comprehensive Investment Agreement (in force 2012), ASEAN has had in place investment treaties that include investor–state dispute settlement since the 1987 Agreement. However, so far we know of only two disputes under these agreements.[12] As will be further elaborated later, the courts of the Andean Community, COMESA, EFTA, European Union and WAEMU belong to the second group.

The Mercosur was initially based on an ad hoc 'Arbitration Court' and has subsequently included the possibility of review of the Arbitration Court's decisions by the Permanent Review Court.[13] This Court is in essence limited to state–state disputes and should therefore be placed in the first group. However, there are two modifications to this starting

[12] *Cemex Asia Holdings Ltd. v. Republic of Indonesia*, ICSID Case No. ARB/04/3 (based on the 1987 Agreement, the case was settled), and *Yaung Chi Oo Trading Pte. Ltd. v. Government of the Union of Myanmar*, ASEAN I.D. Case No. ARB/01/1 (based on the 1987 Agreement and the 1998 Framework Agreement, the tribunal concluded that it lacked jurisdiction).

[13] Chapters VI and VII of the Olivos Protocol for the Settlement of Disputes in MERCOSUR, Olivos, 18 February 2002, in force 10 February 2004, 42 ILM 2 (2003).

point. First, Mercosur allows private parties to bring forward disputes concerning legal or administrative measures having a restrictive, discriminatory or unfair competition effect in violation of Mercosur instruments. The procedure that has been set up for such disputes does not directly involve the Mercosur courts, and private parties are not accorded any significant roles during subsequent state-based proceedings.[14] Second, and more important for our purposes, Mercosur has adopted decisions that allow domestic courts to request advisory opinions from the Permanent Review Court.[15]

The Economic Court of the CIS may also arguably belong to the first group because it started out as a state–state court and has essentially remained as such. However, the institutions of the CIS may bring cases to the Court, and the court has functions in relation to domestic courts and thus indirectly also for private parties.[16]

In light of this, the Mercosur and CIS courts will be considered in more detail together with the second group of courts. Table 15.1 provides an overview of how the FTAs extend access to the courts beyond states. The following discussion will consider four topics: (1) the FTA institutions' access to the courts, (2) domestic courts' access to FTA courts, (3) private parties' access to FTA courts, and (4) access to FTA courts by employees of the FTA institutions.

(1) According to the first row of Table 15.1, all but one of the FTAs allow institutions of the FTAs to initiate court proceedings when they consider states to be in noncompliance with FTA provisions (often referred to as infringement proceedings). The particular significance of this avenue for dispute settlement in the context of this chapter is that it allows private parties to present their concerns to institutions of the FTAs, and these institutions can proceed with cases 'on behalf of' the private parties. However, private parties do only indirectly benefit from the FTA institutions bringing such cases because the private parties are not themselves parties to the disputes.

[14] Chapter IX of the Olivos Protocol. The procedure was originally established under the Protocol of Brasilia, see Raúl Emilio Vinuesa, 'Enforcement of Mercosur arbitration awards within the domestic legal orders of member states', *Texas International Law Journal*, 40 (2005), 429.

[15] This opportunity was established subsequent to the establishment of the Court, see MERCOSUR/CMC/DEC 02/07, and has taken effect depending on the establishment of national procedures for requests for such opinions.

[16] See Statute of the Economic Court of the Commonwealth of Independent States, paras. 3 and 5.

Table 15.1 *Access to courts in selected regional FTAs*

	Andean[1]	CIS[2]	COMESA[3]	EEA[4]	EU[5]	Mercosur[6]	WAEMU[7]
FTA institutions	Arts. 17, 23(2), 24(2), 37	Para. 3	Arts. 25, 32	Art. 31	Art. 258		Arts. 15(1), (2), (7)
Domestic courts	Arts. 20(3), 33	Para. 5	Art. 30	Art. 34	Art. 267	Art. 2, 4	Art. 15(6)
Private vs. states	Art. 25		Art. 26				
Private vs. institution	Arts. 17, 19, 37		Art. 26	Arts. 36, 37, 39	Arts. 263(4), 265(3), 268, 340		Arts. 15(2), (3), (5)
Employees	Art. 40		Art. 27		Art. 270		Art. 15(4)

1 References in the table and in the footnotes below are to the Cochabamba Protocol (1996).

2 References in the table and in the footnotes below are to the Statute of the Economic Court of the Commonwealth of Independent States, as confirmed by the Agreement of the Council of the Heads of States of the CIS, 6 July 1992.

3 References in the table and in the footnotes below are to the Treaty Establishing the Common Market of Eastern and Southern Africa (1993), Kampala, 5 November 1993, in force 8 December 1994, 33 ILM 1067 (1994).

4 References in the table and in the footnotes below are to the Agreement between the EFTA States on the Establishment of a Surveillance Authority and a Court of Justice (1992).

5 References in the table and in the footnotes below are to the Treaty on the Functioning of the European Union, OJ C 326, 26 October 2012, p. 47–390.

6 References in the table and in the footnotes below are to the Reglamento del Protocolo de Olivos para la solución de controversias en el Mercosur, MERCOSUR/CMC/DEC 37/03.

7 References in the table and in the footnotes below are to the Règlement n° 01/1996 portant règlement des procédures de la Cour de Justice de l'UEMOA.

The policies and procedures of the FTA institutions differ significantly in how they initiate infringement cases, ranging from the CIS institutions, which have only asked the court to interpret provisions,[17] to the European Commission and the EFTA Surveillance Authority, which have launched a high number of significant infringement proceedings against states as follow-up of complaints from private parties.[18] Two of the FTAs even impose a duty upon the institutions to initiate cases where their assessment concludes that there is a violation of the FTAs.[19]

In addition, some FTAs also allow institutions to initiate cases concerning the validity of decisions and/or omissions of other institutions of the FTAs.[20] Finally, four FTAs allow institutions to seek advisory opinions from the courts.[21] Such proceedings and advisory opinions may be of some interest in the context of this chapter to the extent that they can be used to safeguard the interests of other stakeholders.

(2) According to the second row of Table 15.1, all the FTA courts shall support domestic courts in their interpretation and application of the FTA rules. However, the relationships between FTA courts and domestic courts vary significantly. First, as regards the duty to bring questions concerning the interpretation of the FTAs to the courts of the FTAs the rules fall into two categories: those where the request for interpretation is mandatory in all cases where the domestic court considers that an interpretation is required for it to be able to decide the case,[22] and those that only allow domestic courts to ask for advisory opinions.[23] Second, where the FTA courts have provided interpretations, it would generally be extraordinary for domestic courts not to respect and apply the

[17] See Chapter 9. [18] See Chapters 3 and 4.

[19] Andean (Article 23 second para.) and COMESA (Article 25.3).

[20] This is the case for Andean (Articles 17 – validity, and 37 – omissions) and WAEMU (Article 15(2) – validity).

[21] Table 15.1 does not include provisions on the right of institutions to seek advisory opinions. The relevant provisions are: CIS (para. 5), COMESA (Article 32), Mercosur (Articles 2 and 3) and WAEMU (Article 15(7)).

[22] Andean (Article 20 in cases where litigants claim invalidity of a decision by an institution, Article 33 in cases concerning interpretation), COMESA (Article 30), EU (Article 267) and WAEMU (Article 15(6)). According to these FTAs, requests are only mandatory where the decisions of the domestic courts in question cannot be appealed.

[23] EEA (Article 34 – this provision even states that an 'EFTA State may in its internal legislation limit the right to request such an advisory opinion to courts and tribunals against whose decisions there is no judicial remedy under national law'), Mercosur (Article 3), and CIS (para. 5).

interpretation.[24] Nevertheless, although some FTAs make compliance with the interpretations of FTA courts mandatory for domestic courts,[25] other FTAs seem to leave some discretion to the domestic courts.[26]

(3) The third and fourth rows of Table 15.1 touch on the most complex issue regarding access to FTA courts: the access of private parties. We may distinguish between the following three forms of such access:

(a) While we have seen that most FTAs require or allow institutions of the FTAs to raise infringement cases before the FTA courts where seized to do so by private parties, two of the FTAs also allow private parties to initiate cases concerning states' noncompliance with duties under the FTAs.[27] At least formally, the availability of such procedures strengthens the position of private parties in situations of states' noncompliance. However, such access to regional FTA courts remains rare. Hence, the opportunities private parties have to initiate cases through FTA institutions and by presenting arguments to domestic courts remain essential to their possibility of compelling states to comply with their duties under FTAs.
(b) The FTA institutions may in some cases adopt decisions that are directly binding upon private parties, in particular decisions regarding the lawfulness of subsidies, the lawfulness of anticompetitive practices of private parties and intellectual property rights. Where the FTAs provide for such decisions, private parties are generally allowed to bring cases concerning their validity directly to the FTA courts.[28] Three of the FTAs explicitly allow private parties to seek compensation through

24 However, as indicated in Chapter 7, national courts do not always follow the advice of the regional FTA courts.

25 Andean (Articles 35 and 36), COMESA (Articles 29.2 and 34.2) and EU (Articles 267 – implicitly).

26 CIS (para. 5, indicative but is inconclusive on the issue), EEA (Article 34 refers to the interpretations as 'advisory'), Mercosur (Articles 2 and 4) and WAEMU (Articles 15(6) and 84, indicative but are inconclusive on the issue).

27 Andean (Article 24, the case must be brought through the General Secretariat) and COMESA (Article 26, requires prior exhaustion of domestic remedies). In this context, we may note the special infringement procedure provided under Mercosur, which does not involve the FTA courts (chapter XI), as well as the availability of investor–state dispute settlement in the ASEAN investment agreements and the Investment Agreement for the COMESA Common Investment Area (not yet in force).

28 Andean (Articles 17 and 19), COMESA (Article 26), EEA (Article 36, the provision extends the opportunity to bring a case to 'a decision addressed to another person, if it is of direct and individual concern' to the private party bringing the case), EU (Article 263.4) and WAEMU (Article 15(2)).

FTA courts where such decisions have caused economic damage.[29] Such damages may also be available under other FTAs despite their silence on the issue. Three of the FTAs extend the possibility of private claims far beyond decisions directed at the private party bringing the case.[30] Four of the FTAs allow private parties to initiate cases where an FTA institution has failed to act despite a duty to do so.[31]

(c) Finally, only one of the FTAs implicitly allows private parties to request advisory opinions directly from the FTA court. Such requests are normally limited to states and institutions of the FTA. As a starting point, this was also the case for the CIS. However, the Economic Court of the CIS has interpreted broadly the range of institutions allowed to initiate advisory opinion cases.[32]

(4) The final row of Table 15.1 concerns the relationship between the FTA courts and the employees of the FTA institutions. Among the FTA courts, four explicitly provide for the FTA courts to deal with employment disputes.[33] While seeming to constitute a minor issue in terms of the general legitimacy of the FTA courts, it has nevertheless turned out to become an issue of particular interest to at least two of the courts; the COMESA and the WAEMU courts have to a large extent become employment courts.[34] From a legitimacy perspective, it is relevant to explore why these courts have followed such development trajectories.

Based on the preceding findings, we may provide a relatively nuanced comparative assessment of formal access to the FTA courts. The assessment is carried out by evaluating the extent of access on a scale from 0 to 3 within four categories of access; including the three first categories of access, of which the access of private parties has been split into two (private parties vs. states and private parties vs. institutions). We have not taken

[29] EEA (Article 39), EU (Articles 268 and 340) and WAEMU (Article 15(5)).

[30] Andean (Article 19 extends the court's jurisdiction to decisions that 'affect' the 'subjective rights' or the 'legitimate interests' of private parties), COMESA (Article 26 extends the court's jurisdiction to the lawfulness of decisions of the Council regardless of whether the decision in question affects the rights or interests of the private parties), and WAEMU (Article 15(2) extends the court's jurisdiction to the lawfulness of any decision that causes 'grief' to the private parties).

[31] Andean (Article 37), EEA (Article 37), EU (Article 37) and WAEMU (Article 15(3) – limited scope in competition cases).

[32] See Chapter 9.

[33] Andean (Article 40), COMESA (Article 27), EU (Article 270 – appeals from the European Union Civil Service Tribunal), WAEMU (Article 15(4)).

[34] See Section 3.2.

Table 15.2 *Scoring of formal access, ranked according to access*

	Inst. vs. states	Domestic courts	Private vs. states	Private vs. inst.	Score
Andean	3	3	2	2	10
COMESA	2	3	2	1	8
EU	2	2	0	3	7
WAEMU	2	1	0	3	6
EEA	2	1	0	3	6
CIS	2	1	0	0	3
Mercosur	0	1	0	0	1
ASEAN	0	0	0	0	0

into account the access provided to employees of the FTA institutions because such access is considered to be insignificant for the general legitimacy of the courts. The WTO DSM provides for only state–state disputes and constitutes the 'baseline' (score 0 on all four categories). The scores in Table 15.2 thus indicate the extent to which the regional FTA courts provide formal access beyond that of the WTO. The scores reflect the formal access to the FTA courts according to the rules as analysed earlier. There has been some discretion involved in assigning the scores.

This ranking indicates the extent to which states have delegated dispute resolution to the FTA courts, i.e. the states' willingness to be subject to the courts' jurisdiction. It can be used as a proxy for the degree of states' trust in the courts.[35] It does also provide an indication of how states perceive the relationship between the rights and duties provided for in the treaties and the rights-holders and duty-bearers. Moreover, it indicates the states' perception of the importance of courts in terms of resolving disagreements regarding rights and duties as compared to alternative means of dispute resolution. These scores can be expected to influence the degree to which the courts are likely to be used by stakeholders. Hence, courts on the high end of the scale could be expected to be busier than the courts at the lower end of the scale.[36] The next section considers other factors that affect the use of FTA courts.

35 For a more detailed discussion on this point, see L. R. Helfer and A.-M. Slaughter, 'Why states create international tribunals: A response to Professors Posner and Yoo', *California Law Review*, 93 (2005), 931–40.

36 The importance of access as a factor influencing usage of courts was emphasised by L. R. Helfer and A.-M. Slaughter, ibid., 928–9.

2.3 *Factors Affecting the Use of Regional FTA Courts*

One key factor when considering the opportunity to make use of regional FTA courts and their potential for dispute resolution is their time of operation. The courts differ significantly in this regard. Table 15.3 sets out the years of establishment (i.e. the adoption of the treaty establishing the court), the years when the courts became operational (i.e. when required infrastructure had been established and judges appointed), and the years of the first rulings of the courts. Some courts were preceded by other means of dispute settlement, including ad hoc arbitration. The years provided in the table refer to the activities of the current FTA courts and do not take into account previous arbitration arrangements.

The CJEU has by far the longest history of these courts, having rendered its first ruling more than three decades before the next in line, the Andean Court of Justice. As has been pointed out elsewhere in this book, the CJEU has also been a significant model for many other regional courts. All the other regional FTA courts considered here have been established since the beginning of the 1990s, and their time of operation has been less than twenty-five years. Given the time that it takes for an international court to attain acceptance and trust among key stakeholders, we may observe that one court is 'unborn' (ASEAN), two courts are still in their 'infancy' (Mercosur and COMESA), three courts are in their 'adolescence' (WAEMU, CIS and EEA), and two courts can be considered as 'grown-ups' (Andean and CJEU). In addition, it should be taken into account that the Economic Court of the CIS seems to be moving toward an early retirement.[37]

Table 15.3 *Time of operation, ranked according to year of establishment*

	Establishment	Operational	First ruling
EU	1952	1952	1954
Andean	1979	1984	1985
EEA	1992	1994	1994
CIS	1992	1994	1997
WAEMU	1994	1995	1996
COMESA	1994	1998	2001
Mercosur	2002	2004	2005
ASEAN	2004	Not operational	No ruling

[37] See Chapter 9.

It is also of interest to note the differences in the time that it took from the decision to establish the courts to their first rulings, ranging from two years for the EU, EEA, and WAEMU to eleven years and counting for ASEAN. Except for expediency of the Western European courts and the slowness of the ASEAN dispute settlement mechanism, there does not seem to be any clear regional pattern (the two African courts took two and seven years, and the two Latin American courts took three and six years). However, it is of interest that the two highest ranking courts in Table 15.2 were among the courts that took the longest to become operational – five (Andean) and four (COMESA) years, and provide their first rulings – six (Andean) and seven (COMESA) years. One possible explanation could be the fact that these FTAs provide access for private parties to bring cases directly against member states before the courts.

In addition to the time that the courts have been in operation, the context in which they operate is likely to affect their level of activity. Table 15.4 looks closer at four such factors, namely the geographical scope of the courts' jurisdiction (measured as the number of member countries of the FTAs), the size of the economies covered by the FTA (measured as GDP of the member countries), the population of the member countries, and the trade among the member countries of the FTAs (both import from and export to other member countries). These factors are considered likely to affect the caseload of FTA courts in the sense that courts covering many member countries with a high GDP, significant trade among them and a high population are expected to be busier than FTA courts covering few member countries with a low GDP, limited trade and a low population.[38] In order to facilitate comparison with other factors affecting the use of FTA courts, each of the four factors considered here have been assigned a value between 1 and 3 as a proxy for the expected effect on the caseload of FTA courts (the values are provided within parentheses). These are relatively crude measures, but will nevertheless serve as a useful point of reference for comparing the performance of the regional FTA courts.

The figures in Table 15.4 show that the regional FTA courts serve very heterogeneous groups of countries, ranging from three small countries with one dominant economy (EEA) to two of the world's largest regional

[38] E. A. Posner and J. C. Yoo, 'Judicial independence in international tribunals', *California Law Review*, 93, 1, (2005), 46–8, uses similar factors when comparing the effectiveness of dispute settlement under GATT and the WTO.

Table 15.4 *Basic characteristics of FTAs, ranked according to GDP*

	Member countries	GDP (2013, USD)[39]	Population (2014)	Intra-FTA trade goods (2008, USD) import/export	
EU	28 (3)	17 736 bill. (3)	495 mill. (3)	3655.2 bill.	3873.9 bill. (3)
Mercosur	6 (1)	3 342 bill. (2)	297 mill. (2)	50.7 bill.[40]	50.5 bill. (1)
CIS	10[41] (2)	2 600 bill. (2)	235 mill.[42] (2)	123.3 bill.	123.1 bill. (2)
ASEAN	10 (2)	2 445 bill. (2)	621 mill.[43] (3)	222.3 bill.	244.3 bill. (2)
Andean	4 (1)	704 bill. (1)	105 mill. (1)	7.8 bill.	7.0 bill. (1)
COMESA	19 (3)	628 bill. (1)	393 mill.[44] (2)	5.2 bill.	5.8 bill. (1)
EEA	3 (1)	543 bill. (1)	5 mill. (1)	2.5 bill.	2.9 bill. (1)
WAEMU	8 (2)	88 bill. (1)	101 mill.[45] (1)	n.a.	n.a. (1)

Sources: UN Statistics Division (December 2015) and WTO World Trade Report 2011 pp. 199–200.

FTAs (EU in terms of members, GDP, and internal trade in goods, and ASEAN in terms of population).

By combining the assessments made in Tables 15.2–15.4, we should have a good basis for predicting the actual use of regional FTA courts. Table 15.5 repeats the ranking of Table 15.2. Moreover, it ranks the FTAs on a scale from 0 to 12 as regards their time of operation (two points per decade) and adjusts these scores by assigning the time it took for the courts to become operational a score of +1, 0 or −1 (based on the time between establishment and first judgement). The reason for adjusting according to the time it took for the courts to become effective is that this is a likely proxy for the willingness of FTA member countries to submit

[39] At current prices. [40] Including Venezuela.

[41] The figures are based on the following countries: CIS-based jurisdiction: Belarus, Kazakhstan, Kyrgyzstan, Moldova, Russia, Tajikistan and Uzbekistan. Economic Union-based jurisdiction: Armenia, Azerbaijan and Turkmenistan.

[42] The following country lacked updated numbers: Turkmenistan – 1995 (the year of the most recent number).

[43] The following country lacked updated numbers: Brunei Darussalam – 2011.

[44] The following countries lacked updated numbers: Comores – 2003, DR Congo – 1984, Djibouti – 2009, Eritrea – 1984, Ethiopia – 2007, Madagascar – 1993, Malawi – 2008, Zimbabwe – 2012.

[45] The following countries lacked updated numbers: Burkina Faso – 2006, Guinea-Bissau – 2009, Mali – 2009, Togo – 2010.

Table 15.5 *Expected use of courts*

	Formal access (from Table 15.2)	Time of operation (from Table 15.3)	Characteristics FTAs (from Table 15.4)	Total score
EU	7	13 (12+1)	12	32
Andean	10	5 (6−1)	4	19
COMESA	8	3 (4−1)	7	18
WAEMU	6	5 (4+1)	5	16
EEA	6	5 (4+1)	4	15
CIS	3	4	8	15
Mercosur	1	2	6	9
ASEAN	0	0	9	9

disputes to the courts. Finally, it adds the scores assigned according to the four characteristics of FTAs as presented in Table 15.4.

The fact that the CJEU is by far the most well-established and active regional FTA court is not surprising in light of the preceding findings. However, as will be elaborated in Section 3, the overall scores do not correspond well with the actual use of the other courts. This indicates that other aspects of the regional FTA courts may be essential for how they perform in practice. Such aspects will be further explored in Section 4.

3 Real Access to the FTA Courts

It can be argued that, from a legitimacy perspective, it is of more interest to study the outcomes of courts' activities than the output of courts in terms of judgements.[46] However, this chapter focuses on one particular aspect of legitimacy: the degrees of discrepancy between substantive rules and the ability of key stakeholders to initiate cases. When assessing access to courts, it is essential not only to focus on formal access, but also to consider real access. The real access to courts can best be assessed by considering their output, as this reflects the actual use of the courts by key stakeholders. The outputs of regional FTA courts have developed along different trajectories in two main dimensions: the extent to which

[46] The arguments in this direction are parallel to those that have been made in discussions about the effectiveness of international courts, see Y. Shany, 'Assessing the effectiveness of international courts', *The American Journal of International Law*, 106 (2012), 248–9.

they are used, and the subject matter that is brought before them. Section 3.1 will be based on of the analyses of the FTA courts elsewhere in this book, consider the extent to which key stakeholders have used the courts. Thereafter, Section 3.2 will compare the FTA courts as to the subject matters that have been brought before them, with the aim of comparing and explaining the extent to which they have been used to resolve trade disputes.

3.1 *Extent of Use of the Courts by Key Stakeholders*

3.1.1 States

In the WTO, states are the only stakeholders able to bring trade disputes to the dispute settlement mechanism. As a contrast, the chapters of this book show that states as such are in general – with a few exceptions – not active initiators of cases before the regional FTA courts. The exceptions include Mercosur,[47] the CIS[48] and COMESA.[49] However, even these courts have significant additional functions that differ from those of the WTO DSM, and which have been essential in practice.[50] One major puzzle is consequently why many regional FTA courts, which are set up to deal with interstate trade disputes, remain essentially unused for such purposes.

States are frequently actively involved in disputes in some regional FTA courts in roles that differ from those in the WTO. First, they can bring cases against the institutions of the FTAs, claiming that the acts of the institutions are unlawful.[51] They can also in some cases request advisory opinions regarding the interpretation of the FTAs.[52] And, as

[47] Altogether fourteen cases, of which four were under the Olivos Protocol (in relation to which the Permanent Review Court has made six decisions) and ten under the Brasilia Protocol (i.e. only subject to arbitration because they were decided prior to the establishment of the Permanent Review Court).

[48] Eight cases of which only two relate to market-based trade relations.

[49] Only one case between Ethiopia and Eritrea, which was subsequently withdrawn.

[50] For example, the Permanent Review Court of Mercosur provides advisory opinions to domestic courts, the Court of the CIS has important functions in commercial disputes, and the COMESA Court is important as an employment tribunal.

[51] One example is the EFTA Court, which has dealt with more than fifty actions for nullity against decisions of the EFTA Surveillance Authority, most of them brought by an affected state. Such cases are also common at the CJEU.

[52] This is the case for the Economic Court of the CIS, which has been more active as an advisory than as an adjudicatory institution, and which has to a large extent dealt with requests for advisory opinions from states. However, the normal approach is to allow only domestic courts to request the advisory opinion of the courts.

will be further elaborated later, states are frequently defendants in cases brought by FTA institutions or private parties. Hence, even if regional FTAs offer states broad opportunities to bring cases against other states, the tendency is rather that states take on other roles in relation to the courts of regional FTAs.

3.1.2 Domestic Courts

One group of stakeholders that is closely associated with states, but which is kept separate for our purposes here, are domestic courts. Table 15.2 shows that the regional FTAs differ significantly as to domestic courts' ability and duty to bring cases, as well as the effects of the FTA courts' decisions for domestic courts. In practice, requests for advisory opinions constitute a major element of the activities of the courts within five FTAs (Andean, CIS, EEA, EU and Mercosur).[53] The Andean Court stands out from the other courts as requests for interpretation amount to more than 90 per cent of its caseload. This court has also promoted requests for advisory opinions by accepting submissions from domestic institutions with a mix of administrative and judicial functions that operate outside the ordinary system of courts.[54] Advisory opinions are also the major group of cases before the EFTA Court, constituting approximately 40 per cent of its caseload. The extent to which requests for advisory opinions are submitted by the highest courts or lower courts is an issue of interest, as this can be an indicator of the extent to which the higher courts accept the authority of the FTA courts. Although such requests to the Andean Court are essentially made by courts whose judgements cannot be appealed, indicating a high degree of deference to the Andean Court, requests to the EFTA Court are made mostly by the lower courts, indicating a low degree of deference by the highest courts to the EFTA Court.

The extent to which advisory opinions constitute an important element of the caseload of the FTA courts does not clearly correspond to the extent to which the FTAs allow and promote such requests. Table 15.2 indicates that Andean and COMESA most clearly promote advisory opinions, while CIS, EEA, Mercosur and WAEMU are at the other end

[53] The Mercosur differs from the other FTAs in the sense that it was up to national supreme courts to specify the formal requirements relating to submission of requests for advisory opinions; see MERCOSUR/CMC/DEC 37/03 and 02/07.

[54] As indicated in Chapter 8, some of the reasons for increases in caseload have been the networking by Andean judges to former colleagues in national courts and self-promotion by the Andean Court.

of the scale. Yet, in the practice of the courts under these FTAs, we find very limited use of advisory opinions initiated by domestic courts in the caseload of the Court of Justice of the COMESA, and a significant portion of such cases in the caseload of the courts of the EEA, CIS and Mercosur.[55] Moreover, as is particularly evident in the European Union, domestic courts' recourse to advisory opinions varies significantly among the member states of the FTAs. Against this background, it seems that the ability of the regional FTA courts to gain the trust of domestic courts and lawyers is essential to promote their recourse to the FTA courts for advisory opinions.

3.1.3 Institutions of the Regional FTAs

Table 15.2 shows that, with two exceptions (Mercosur and ASEAN), institutions of the regional FTAs have significant opportunities to bring cases against member states. However, only two FTAs have institutions that actively initiate such infringement proceedings (the EU and EFTA). Such cases have been very significant in the caseload of these courts, but are almost entirely absent in the caseload of the remaining FTAs (Andean, CIS, COMESA and WAEMU). Although many factors may contribute to this situation, including the possibility of requesting advisory opinions,[56] it seems reasonable to assume that the use of infringement proceedings depends on the independence of and the resources available to the FTA institutions.

3.1.4 Private Parties

There are two main options for private parties to initiate cases in regional FTA courts: against states and against institutions of the FTA. Only two of the FTAs, Andean and COMESA, allow private parties to bring cases directly against states. The major difference between these two FTAs is that Andean makes it compulsory to bring the case to the General Secretariat before it can be brought to the Court, while COMESA

[55] Although more than 90 per cent of the caseload of CIS is advisory opinions, it should be noted that most of the requests are made by state organs and not by domestic courts. Although only three requests for advisory opinions have been submitted in Mercosur, these nevertheless constitute a significant portion of the caseload of the Permanent Review Court.

[56] This seems to be a major factor in the context of CIS and WAEMU, see Chapters 9 and 11. The extent to which the EFTA Surveillance Authority raises infringement proceedings is closely linked to the policy of the Commission of the European Union in this regard, see Chapter 4.

requires private parties to exhaust domestic remedies before bringing the case to the COMESA Court. Whether these requirements have been major reasons why we have seen very limited use of the courts by private parties for these purposes remains unclear. As has been pointed out in other chapters of this book, recent developments indicate that we may see increased use of the Andean Court of Justice but that we are less likely to see such developments for the Court of Justice of the COMESA.[57] The main reason seems to be that the former actively promotes private parties' use of the court, while the latter has adopted a restrictive approach to interpretation (e.g. when interpreting the duty to exhaust domestic remedies) and has had few outreach activities. It should also be taken into account that within Andean and COMESA it is under certain circumstances mandatory for domestic courts to request advisory opinions from the FTA courts. This represents an indirect opportunity for private parties to bring cases against states to these courts.

The majority of the FTAs allow private parties to bring cases against institutions of the FTAs. As indicated in Table 15.2, this option is most extensively developed in the EEA, European Union and WAEMU, and less so in Andean and COMESA. There are no such options in ASEAN, the CIS and Mercosur. Obviously, the extent to which such cases should be allowed and are likely to occur depends on the extent to which the FTA institutions adopt decisions that have direct consequences for the rights and duties of private parties. Examples include decisions concerning intellectual property rights, countervailing and antidumping duties, government procurement, state trading enterprises, monopolies, and anticompetitive practices. The extent to which the FTA institutions are allowed to and actually make decisions that affect rights and duties in these contexts varies significantly among the FTAs. All the four courts that come out on top as regards formal access to bring such cases also see such cases as a major share of their caseload (EEA, EU and WAEMU). There are few cases against institutions in the case law of Andean. The reason may be the opportunity to ask domestic courts to request advisory opinions.[58] For the African courts, the relevant cases are mostly initiated by employees against the institutions as employers, and not as decision makers based on authority provided by the FTAs. Hence, cases initiated to challenge the decisions of the FTA institutions essentially occur before the European courts. This situation may

[57] Chapters 8 and 10.

[58] See Chapter 8. Mercosur also allows private parties significant opportunities to request advisory opinions, see Chapter 7.

possibly be linked to the long traditions for recourse to courts to seek remedies against decisions of domestic institutions in the European context.

In conclusion, there seems to be a lack of correspondence between the formal access to bring cases to the courts and the actual use of the courts by key stakeholders. This implies that the reasons for the significant variation in number of cases among the FTA courts must be sought in other factors than the formal access to bring cases. Some such factors have been suggested earlier, including in particular the maturity of the regional FTA court. The maturity seems to explain the differences that we see between the CJEU and the Andean Court of Justice, as being clearly the most widely used courts, and the rest. The close link between the CJEU and the EFTA Court may explain the relative success of the latter when compared to other regional FTA courts of similar total score in Table 15.5. In addition, other factors have been suggested in relation to specific courts elsewhere in this book, such as the extent of overlap with the jurisdiction of other regional FTA courts (WAEMU),[59] the problem that countries fail to appoint judges (CIS),[60] the lack of knowledge of the FTAs among domestic lawyers and judges (e.g. Mercosur)[61] and the lack of political will to make regional courts available (ASEAN).[62]

3.2 *The Subject-Matter Dealt with by the Courts*

We have seen in Section 3.1 that the stakeholders using the regional FTA courts vary significantly and that there is limited correspondence between their formal access to the courts and their actual use of the courts. One essential factor that has not been addressed so far is the substantive jurisdiction of the courts. Obviously, one would expect that actual use of the courts would depend not only on whether the courts are formally accessible to the stakeholders, but also on the extent to which the courts can serve as a tool to realize the stakeholders' rights or interests. Hence, stakeholders' use of the courts would depend on the extent to which the substantive rules of the FTAs provide them with rights or benefits, and the extent to which the institutions of the FTAs can make decisions that affect (i.e. that add to or diminish) their rights, duties, or interests.

Given that the regional FTA courts start out as courts that shall facilitate and ensure implementation of and compliance with FTAs, one would expect that, regardless of maturity of the courts, their starting point would

[59] See Chapter 11. [60] See Chapter 9. [61] See Chapter 7. [62] See Chapter 12.

be resolution of trade disputes and that they may subsequently expand into other associated fields depending on the scope of the FTA. However, there are several reasons why this starting point may not hold. For example, states may be accustomed, or it may be more politically attractive for them, to use other means of resolving trade disputes than the regional FTA courts. Moreover, those regional FTA courts that have been used infrequently are likely to search for opportunities to be useful to key stakeholders, and such opportunities may appear in subject areas that are quite far removed from international trade in goods or services.

To compare the regional FTAs as to the extent of jurisdiction of their courts is complex, and the accuracy of such comparisons can be challenged from various perspectives. Nevertheless, in general terms we can observe that all the regional FTAs cover trade in goods, and that most of them establish customs unions (ASEAN being the only exception).[63] However, the extent of product coverage varies somewhat (an example being the exclusion of agricultural products under the EEA). We find greater variation in the extent to which the FTAs cover trade in services, from FTAs that have broad scope and extensive liberalization (EU, EEA and WAEMU) to FTAs that include very limited commitments (CIS and COMESA). The extent to which technical standards and regulations pertaining to goods and services are harmonised is a further issue where the FTAs differ significantly, but where all the FTAs have relevant activities (the EU and EEA being frontrunners).

We may also consider the FTAs in terms of their expansion into other policy areas than those closely related to trade in goods and services. While all the FTAs expand into such policy areas, the extent to which they do so and the extent to which such policies are subject to the jurisdiction of the FTA courts vary significantly and are very difficult to measure. Moreover, these are areas in which the courts themselves may play a very important role in determining the extent of their jurisdiction. In any case, the European Union stands out as the FTA that has expanded most extensively into such policy areas.

In sum, while the regional FTA courts differ significantly in terms of their substantive jurisdiction, the core of their jurisdiction – being interstate trade in goods and services – remains comparable across the courts. Against this background and taking into account that the courts offer similar formal opportunities to bring relevant disputes, we should expect there to be basic similarities in the profile of their cases. However, based on the chapters of this book, we may distinguish between three groups of

63 Arguably, the Economic Court of the CIS is also an exception. However, its jurisdiction does extend beyond the CIS to customs unions.

regional FTA courts. First, there are regional FTA courts that have essentially fulfilled their mandates by focusing on trade-related disputes and associated advisory opinions. These include the CJEU, the Economic Court of the CIS and the EFTA Court. However, these courts have only to a limited extent resolved disputes that could have been resolved by the WTO DSM in the sense of being interstate trade disputes.

Second, some of the regional FTA courts have tended to become 'single-issue' courts in the sense that they have specialized in certain disputes. The Andean Court of Justice has been described as an 'intellectual property tribunal',[64] the Court of Justice of the COMESA as an 'employment' court[65] and the Court of Justice of the WAEMU as an 'administrative tribunal' and 'legal counsel'.[66] However, it has been indicated that all these courts seem to be in the process of diversifying their substantive profile.

Finally, some regional FTA courts have essentially remained marginal or inactive. These include ASEAN and Mercosur. While the ASEAN dispute settlement mechanism remains unimplemented, the Permanent Review Court of Mercosur has been operational only since 2004. Despite the low level of activity of the latter, it is remarkable that it is the one regional FTA court that has had interstate trade as the most important part of its case law. Moreover, together with the CJEU it remains the court that has most clearly interacted with the WTO DSM.

Even if it can be argued that the regional FTA courts can be placed in three distinct categories in terms of the subject matters (or lack thereof) that are brought before them, there are trends indicating that their focus and roles might be converging. For all the 'single-issue' courts, there are recent developments that point in the direction of diversification, and the recent facilitation of advisory opinions in Mercosur may indicate increasing activities of this court.

4 Concluding Remarks

One main aim of this chapter has been to identify the degree of discrepancy between substantive rules and stakeholders' ability to initiate cases with the WTO DSM and regional FTA courts. With the exception of the WTO DSM, the preceding analysis indicates a low degree of discrepancy between the substantive rules relating to interstate trade and stakeholders' formal rights of access to the tribunals. However, there seems to be significant discrepancy

[64] See Chapter 8. [65] See Chapter 10. [66] See Chapter 11.

between the substantive rules and stakeholders' actual use of the regional FTA courts. Such discrepancies are indicative of legitimacy problems for these courts because they may not be fulfilling their functions in relation to these stakeholders.

The second aim has been to explore reasons why the FTAs follow different development trajectories in terms of which stakeholders bring cases and the substantive issues brought before them. It has been shown that formal access to the tribunals, their time of operation, and certain basic characteristics of the member countries of FTAs cannot explain why the regional FTA courts receive so few interstate trade disputes. More probable explanatory factors seem to be that states trust the WTO DSM, that alternative dispute resolution mechanisms under the FTAs may be more convenient and the courts' degree of independence from states and FTA institutions.[67]

The significant differences among regional FTAs as to the extent to which domestic courts request advisory opinions does only to a limited degree seem to relate to their formal access to or duty to make use of such remedies. Other factors seem to be at play in this context, in particular the degree of interaction between the regional FTA courts and domestic courts, for example in terms of exchange of judges, exchange of information between the courts, and the organization of formal and informal meetings. Moreover, national lawyers' knowledge of and familiarity with the regional FTA courts seem to be an important factor.

It remains hard to explain why certain courts have developed into 'single-issue' courts. The main reason may have been that they have filled a lacuna in one or more national judiciaries. Another reason could be that the courts have actively sought tasks, and that they have been successful in doing so only for some groups of cases. Such development trajectories may also be the result of evolving relationships between the regional FTA courts and certain groups of national stakeholders.

A general lesson learned seems to be that countries do only to a limited extent determine the development trajectories of regional FTA courts through their decisions on the mandates of the courts. The factors that influence the development trajectories of the courts are multiple and hard to control. Moreover, the extent to which the case law of regional FTA courts differs from the WTO DSM is remarkable. There seems to be no reason to believe that regional FTA courts would constitute any significant alternative to the WTO DSM in the foreseeable future.

[67] See Chapter 13.

16

Toward a More Just WTO: Which Justice, Whose Interpretation?[1]

ANDREAS FOLLESDAL

1 Introduction

Recurring protests against the WTO trading system are vocal and vivid indications that many individuals and NGOs regard these trade agreements and their way of settling disputes as grossly illegitimate. Trade liberalization not only seems to be WTO's *grundnorm*[2] but is also said to trump respect for human rights,[3] the environment[4] and global distributive justice. Thus several authors, civil society organizations and states regard the WTO system as a central cause and culprit of the world's present vast income disparities. Joseph Stiglitz underscores that 'the IMF, World Bank and WTO . . . set the rules of the game . . . in ways that, all too often, have served the interests of the more advanced industrialized countries – and particular interests within those countries – rather than those of the developing world.'[5]

Many critics and defenders of the WTO system agree that it must be understood, assessed and possibly reformed *in context*. Diagnoses and proposed prescriptions require an understanding of how the treaties and the bodies of the WTO are but important parts of a tangled web of

[1] This article was written under the auspices of ERC Advanced Grant 269841 MultiRights – on the Legitimacy of Multi-Level Human Rights Judiciary; and partly supported by the Research Council of Norway through its Centres of Excellence Funding Scheme, project number 223274 – PluriCourts The Legitimacy of the International Judiciary. I am very grateful to the editors for constructive comments on several earlier drafts.

[2] C. Carmody, F. Garcia, and J. Linarelli, 'Introduction' in C. Carmody, F. J. Garcia and J. Linarelli (eds.), *Global Justice and International Economic Law: Opportunities and Prospects* (Cambridge University Press, 2012), pp. 1–26, at p. 2.

[3] S. Joseph, 'Trade law and investment law' in D. Shelton (ed.), *The Oxford Handbook of International Human Rights Law* (Oxford University Press, 2013), pp. 841–70.

[4] K. Kulovesi, *The WTO Dispute Settlement System: Challenges of the Environment, Legitimacy and Fragmentation* (Alphen aan den Rijn: Kluwer Law International, 2011).

[5] J. Stiglitz, *Globalization and Its Discontents* (New York: Norton, 2002), p. 214.

domestic and international institutions and actors. This 'global basic structure' ('GBS') consists of institutions, rules and practices in complex interdependence, including states, treaties and their courts and treaty bodies. It is the overall impact of the GBS that creates such injustice as there is, and reforms must consider the complex interdependence between the WTO system and other central actors, not least states.

Thus constructive critics demand better government of this GBS as a whole, and of the WTO system in particular. The former objective is to be secured by global democratic arrangements,[6] by international legal primacy of international human rights obligations[7] or both – with careful assessment of conflicts between these normative standards.[8] Hotly contested proposals for improving the WTO system range from fundamental revision of the treaties enforced by the WTO, over proposals to make rights to trade conditional on human rights protection and to prohibit unfair gains from trade,[9] to increased transparency and accountability of the WTO dispute settlement mechanism, e.g. toward NGOs.[10]

Critics of such protests may first dismiss the objections as 'category mistakes', holding that standards of justice cannot apply to entities such as the WTO system. A second line of response would be that even granting that there are such risks, several reform proposals are ill-founded. To alleviate whatever injustice the WTO system is complicit in, less radical changes than fundamental treaty changes may suffice.

This chapter challenges the first of these counterarguments and supports the second, as regards WTO and global distribute justice. The chapter leaves urgent issues of the environment and many human rights concerns aside – though some of the arguments are also relevant for some of these issues. The focus is on the WTO dispute settlement mechanism (DSM, 'Mechanism'), especially the adjudicatory panels and the Appellate Body ('AB'). They serve central roles within the global

6 D. Archibugi, D. Held, and M. Kohler, (eds.), *Re-Imagining Political Community: Studies in Cosmopolitan Democracy* (Oxford: Polity Press, 1998).

7 T. W. Pogge, *World Poverty and Human Rights*, 2nd ed. (Oxford: Polity Press, 2008); S. Caney, *Justice beyond Borders* (Oxford University Press, 2005).

8 C. C. Gould, *Globalizing Democracy and Human Rights* (Cambridge University Press, 2004); M. Goodhart, 'Human rights and global democracy', *Ethics and International Affairs*, 22 (2008), 395–420.

9 M. Risse, *On Global Justice* (Princeton University Press, 2012) pp. 281–360.

10 A. S. Chilton and R. W. Davis, 'Equality, procedural justice, and the World Trade Organization', *Intercultural Human Rights Law Review*, 7 (2012), 101–51.

trade regimes and have been a model for other dispute settlement regimes such as the ASEAN Enhanced Dispute Settlement Mechanism.[11]

This article has three main objectives. It first defends the diagnoses that the WTO system contributes to global distributive injustice, against some potentially devastating criticisms. The substantive contents of the principles of global justice are not central to the arguments, but to fix ideas the next section of this introduction sketches the contours of such principles. Section 1 briefly explains why the GBS is a subject that merits particular normative concern. Section 2 rebuts one strand of the 'category mistake' criticism, namely that there is no such GBS. Section 3 challenges a second criticism, that the WTO system is not part of our present GBS.

The second objective is to challenge the prescriptions many critics hitherto have promoted, for two main reasons. Section 4 argues that principles of global justice for the GBS as a whole drastically underdetermine reform proposals for the Mechanism. Furthermore, many critics underestimate the scope of discretion international judges and panel members enjoy in interpreting and specifying treaties.[12] The upshot is that broad scale reforms may be neither possible nor effective – but also not necessary. Radical treaty changes are unlikely because many of them require consensus among states. Instead, the AB may change its interpretative practice to make significant moves toward a more just WTO system. The third contribution, in Sections 5 and 6, is to start to explore ways that the existing WTO system may become more just if members of the panels and of the AB develop their interpretive standards in one or more of four ways.

These observations also illustrate the mutual contributions of political theory and legal scholarship. They show how normative political arguments may help structure and sometimes lay to rest current controversies. They also contribute to enhance normative political theory, insisting that their research agenda must include the interpretive practices of judges and arbitrators. Indeed, I argue that these practices are part of the (global) basic structure. Members of the AB and of the panels may therefore have to be more attentive to and transparent concerning how

[11] R. Beckman, et al., *Promoting Compliance: The Role of Dispute Settlement and Monitoring Mechanisms in ASEAN Instruments* (Cambridge University Press, 2016).

[12] Extending the perceptive arguments from the area of international human rights found in C. McCrudden, 'Human Rights: Law, Politics and Philosophy' (2014) available at: https://www.wzb.eu/sites/default/files/u32/chr_mccrudden_human_rights_law_politics_and_philosophy.pdf.

normative considerations already affect these legal practices, and where considerations of global distributive justice might be appropriate.

This introduction concludes with some brief background information about the nature of principles of global distributive justice. Of particular interest are aspects of their interpretative techniques noted in the introduction to this volume: the role of precedence, reference to other tribunals and other areas of law and the discretion these bodies accord domestic authorities.

1.1 *Principles of Global Distributive Justice*

For purposes of these arguments the currently best defended principles of global distributive justice need not be specified in detail, though some components need mention to indicate some salient points of agreement and disagreement. Citizens and foreigners may have sound normative claims on the set of global institutions as a whole that it satisfies the minimum vital needs of all, e.g. in the form of international obligations to secure certain human rights or to otherwise reduce or remove extreme global poverty. Such claims have been defended by several prominent authors.[13] Beyond this minimum, several authors posit that global distributive justice requires some constraints on permissible inequalities, possibly even defending a requirement of equal shares of income and wealth among individuals. On such views the standards of global distributive justice are 'comparative principles concerned not merely with how individuals fare or are treated in absolute terms, but also in comparison with others'.[14] Such principles might, for instance, address the distribution of the benefits of international trade, in the form of equitable returns to all parties to the transaction. The relevant point here is that any such claims beyond a minimum floor concerning human rights are principles of *global distributive justice*. Some critics deny that such principles apply to the WTO and its mechanism at all.

[13] J. Rawls, *The Law of Peoples* (Cambridge, MA: Harvard University Press, 1999), pp. 38 and 105; S. Freeman, 'Distributive justice and the law of peoples' in R. Martin and D. Reidy (eds.), *Rawls's Law of Peoples: A Realistic Utopia?* (Oxford: Blackwell, 2006), pp. 243–60; M. Blake, 'Distributive justice, state coercion, and autonomy', *Philosophy and Public Affairs*, 30 (2001), 257–96; T. Nagel, 'The problem of global justice', (2005) 33 *Philosophy and Public Affairs*, 113–47; cf C. Barry and L. Valentini, 'Egalitarian challenges to global egalitarianism: A critique', *Review of International Studies*, 35 (2009), 485–512.

[14] A. Abizadeh, 'Cooperation, pervasive impact, and coercion: On the scope (not site) of distributive justice', *Philosophy and Public Affairs*, 35 (2007), 318–58.

1.2 *The World Trade Organization Dispute Settlement Mechanism*

Many critics of the WTO system will agree that liberalized trade can be an important means to secure and promote the vital interests and human rights of many individuals.[15] A central strand of criticism, also voiced by Director General of the WTO Pascal Lamy, concerns the design of the present WTO system: its treaties, rules and procedures, and how the WTO DSM appears to give undue priority to the objective of more open markets for goods and services.[16] The WTO mechanism may thus give too little weight to arguably more important values such as human rights constraints or environmental concerns[17] – or considerations of global distributive justice.[18] The trade policies promoted by the WTO system are claimed to have several potential weaknesses: they 'risk undermining human rights and policy coherence at home and abroad'.[19] For instance, the WTO system disfavours many developing states who complain that the WTO system permits high tariffs – 'tariff peaks'[20] – on their products in important markets. The 2013 Bali agreement improved some aspects for the world's poorest countries as regards duty-free access for their goods to other states, granted them some greater scope for farm subsidies and provided administrative assistance to handle the procedures.[21] Critics hold that these measures did not go far enough.

Is the WTO mechanism part of an unjust 'global basic structure' (GBS), and if so: what are the implications for what the WTO panels and AB should do?

[15] F. Teson and J. Klick, 'Global justice and trade' in C. Carmody, F. J. Garcia and J. Linarelly (eds.), *Global Justice and International Economic Law: Opportunities and Prospects* (Cambridge University Press, 2012), pp. 2017–260.

[16] P. Lamy, 'The Place and Role of the WTO (WTO Law) in the International Legal Order', *WTO* (2006), available at: https://www.wto.org/english/news_e/sppl_e/sppl94_e.htm.

[17] J. Lagomarsino, 'WTO dispute settlement and sustainable development: Legitimacy Through holistic treaty interpretation', *Pace Environmental Law Review*, 28 (2011), 545–67; discussed by C. D. Creamer and Z. Godzimirska, '(De-)legitimation at the WTO dispute settlement mechanism', *Vanderbilt Journal of Transnational Law*, 49 (2016), 1–38, at 2.

[18] E.-U. Petersmann, 'Time for a United Nations "global compact" for integrating human rights into the law of worldwide organizations: Lessons from European integration', *European Journal of International Law*, 13 (2002), 621–50.

[19] Ibid., 625. [20] https://www.wto.org/english/thewto_e/whatis_e/tif_e/dev4_e.htm.

[21] Ministerial Conference, 'Agreement on Trade Facilitation, 7 December 2013 (the Bali Agreement)' WT/MIN(13)/36, WT/L/911 (2013).

2 Why the 'Basic Structure' Merits Particular Principles of Distributive Justice

This section lays out salient aspects of the domestic and global 'basic structure'. Many present-day discussions about political justice take the subject matter to be 'basic structure of society' ('BS'), a term of art forged by the philosopher John Rawls. It includes 'the political constitution and the principal economic and social arrangements' and other rule-regulated practices that affect what people chose to do.[22] Rawls held that special principles of distributive justice apply to this topic. When subjects live their lives within the same BS, this affects the substantive normative claims they have on it and thus on one another. There are several reasons why the BS is subject to such special principles of justice, reasons that merit consideration to determine whether they also hold for subjects of a *global* basic structure ('GBS') – possibly including the WTO system.

First, the direct impact on individuals' lives of the distribution of benefits of the BS is drastic. Consider the effects of career opportunities, income and wealth, and legal powers of property, which Rawls labels 'social primary goods' (SPGs). Second, the BS provides stable expectations about others' future behaviour, structures that shape individuals' life plans and aspirations. Third, these SPGs are social constructs, constituted by individuals' institutionalized cooperation within the BS. These goods are thus constituted by subjects' patterned, rule-regulated behaviour. A fourth reason to regard the BS as a special topic of justice is that it allows a certain institutional division of labour, between the BS itself, and the rules individuals follow in particular interactions.[23] The BS should be set up to ensure domestic distributive justice, a requirement that is too complex for individuals to pursue given the indirect and systemic impact of their private actions. A final reason the BS should be assessed by particular principles of distributive justice is that the state maintains it on threat of coercion, with subjects who cannot escape. The upshot of these arguments within Rawls's theory is that the BS of a society should be held to particular standards of justice, which take as a baseline equal shares among citizens.

22 J. Rawls, 'The basic structure as subject' in J. Rawls (ed.), *Political Liberalism* (New York: Columbia, 1993), pp. 257–88.

23 S. Scheffler, 'Is the basic structure basic?' in C. Sypnowich (ed.), *The Egalitarian Conscience: Essays in Honour of G. A. Cohen* (Oxford University Press, 2006), pp. 102–30, 268–9, cf.

Do similar arguments apply to the GBS – possibly including the WTO system – in support of special principles of global distributive justice?

3 'There Is No Global Basic Structure'

This section defends the view that there is a global basic structure (GBS) of which the WTO system is a part, against several objections. For clarification let us talk of a possible GBS as rules, practices and institutions that structure individuals' actions and shared practices, and otherwise serves the functions of the domestic BS as discussed earlier – wherever on the globe the individuals are.

If it exists in our present world order, a GBS thus includes domestic BSes, as well as an international basic structure. The latter includes a wide range of international law and international institutions and organizations. These include international rules about sovereignty to 'background' rules and institutions that enable states and private parties to agree on issues including trade, investment, currency exchange and travel. These international rules and practices, together with domestic BSes, combine to have large effects on individuals.

Note that the set of rule-governed practices of the GBS share several of the normatively salient features of domestic BSes. They impact fundamentally on individuals' starting points, life chances and preference formation – though often mediated by states, which enjoy rights and immunities due to international rules and practices of state sovereignty.

Several scholars object that the present international institutions are not part of a GBS of a kind that can ground claims of distributive justice among its subjects. If they are right, those who criticize the injustice of the WTO system may be dismissed as fundamentally confused. The critics are making a 'category mistake' because the WTO system is not the sort of entity to which standards of distributive justice can apply.[24] What are we to make of objections of the kind that the impact, source, means or objectives of such international laws, international institutions and other international public practices are so different in kind from domestic institutions as to make principles of distributive justice inapplicable?[25]

[24] G. Ryle, *The Concept of Mind* (Chicago: University of Chicago Press, 1949), pp. 16–17.

[25] For further objections and discussion, cf. A. Follesdal, 'The distributive justice of a global basic structure: A category mistake?' *Politics, Philosophy and Economics*, 10 (2011), 46–65.

Some hold that any impact of international law is both caused by and mediated by domestic political choices. Any distributive claims of justice therefore have domestic BS as their subject. International norms and institutions are 'secondary':

> [T]here may be trade and other agreements among governments specifying original norms, and procedures for making norms, that are independent of any particular people's legal system. But these original global norms ... are supervenient upon peoples' existing property, economic, and political systems – the basic social institutions that structure and regulate their everyday life. Moreover, whatever jurisdiction global regulators and courts have, they have been granted and continue to enjoy only by virtue of the political acts of different peoples.[26]

In response, consider first that the authority, powers and immunities of states are themselves partly defined by international law and institutions. Second, states' opportunity spaces and relative bargaining power vis-à-vis multinationals and other states are profoundly affected by the GBS, for instance when agricultural subsidies in rich countries are protected against countervailing measures by the rules of the WTO system. Important decisions are made at the domestic level, and much harm may be wrought by domestic authorities.[27] But their power and decisions are often framed by international rules, for instance those that allow authoritarian states access to international markets and thus to maintain their power. Other international rules could have refused to recognize dictators' claims to their country's resources or right to international lending.

Third, the WTO is a gatekeeper of great importance to very many states, so much so that many governments have few de facto political options but to join this regime. These factors are exacerbated by the dynamic development of many treaties, including those enforced by the WTO system. Philippe Sands expresses the point thus:

> [T]he rules, once adopted, take on a logic and a life of their own. They do not stay within the neat boundaries that states thought they were creating when they were negotiated. You can see that most clearly in the rules on free trade and foreign investment.[28]

[26] Freeman, 'Distributive justice and the law of peoples', p. 18.

[27] M. Risse, 'How does the global order harm the poor?', *Philosophy and Public Affairs*, 33 (2005), 349–76, 356–79.

[28] P. Sands, *Lawless World* (London: Allen Lane, 2005), p. 8.

The upshot is that although states remain the primary political organizations of our global order, this does not detract from the claim that the GBS in principle can be subject to principles of global distributive justice. Its impact on individuals is sufficiently similar in kind to that of domestic basic structures. If the WTO system is part of the global basic structure, it may thus be subject to such normative assessment.

4 There Is a Global Basic Structure – but the WTO Is Not Part of It

This section explores and rejects the claim that the WTO system is somehow 'outside' the scope of the GBS and hence beyond the domain to be assessed by principles of global distributive justice. The upshot is that the WTO system should be assessed according to how well it contributes to promote and maintain global distributive justice.

Some authors may agree that there is a GBS whose distributive justice may be assessed, but deny that international trade agreements and their bodies are part of it. Such a claim might seem to support various attempts to insulate the WTO system from normative criticism, e.g. defending the position that

> WTO Members remain responsible and liable for their human rights violations, but their responsibility cannot be pursued or enforced before WTO adjudicating bodies . . . In situations of conflict between the system of human rights law and that of WTO law, it may be best considered as a matter for states to decide, rather than for WTO adjudicating bodies.[29]

Consider one line of defence of this position:

> International trade law is founded on the primary value of promoting individual economic exchanges, about the value of specialization and the economic welfare that results from specialization and exchange. Rather than focusing on the independence of States, international trade law highlights the concept of interdependence. In fact, when we talk of international trade law and of international law we are dealing with two regimes, with two systems that in quite a fundamental way are talking about different things.[30]

One defence of this view may hold that just as the law of contract regulating voluntary agreements is outside the domestic BS, voluntary

[29] Expressed in – though not necessarily shared by – G. Marceau, 'WTO dispute settlement and human rights', *European Journal of International Law*, 13 (2002), 753–814 at 814.

[30] D. McRae, 'The contribution of international trade law to the development of international law', *Recuil des Cours*, 260 (1996), 116–17.

international trade agreements are not part of the GBS. However, two rebuttals are appropriate.

First, one may deny the first premise and argue that the domestic law of contract *is* part of the BS, because it is

> a perfect fit for the institutional division of labour Rawls has in mind, as it 'allows us to abstract from the enormous complexities of the innumerable transactions of daily life and frees us from having to keep track of the changing relative positions of particular individuals'.[31]

Second, the arguments canvassed above entail that the WTO system has an impact that merits inclusion in the GBS. The treaties enforced by the WTO system provide precisely such background structures that have a large distributive impact:

> If leaving certain areas of interaction unregulated will heavily distort the 'division of advantages that arises from social cooperation over time', there is a case for saying that some phenomena are not, but ought to be, regulated or at least shaped and informed by the influence of the basic structure. Consider, for instance, the case of international agreements and 'chosen behaviour' between global actors.[32]

The upshot is that the WTO system is part of the GBS, the distributive impact of which should be assessed by appropriate principles of global distributive justice.

We now turn to consider implications for how the design and decisions of the WTO mechanism may be guided by such principles of justice.

5 How Should Principles of Global Distributive Justice Apply to the WTO System?

Considerations of global distributive justice should be brought to bear on the WTO system, but how, and by whom? The masters of the treaties must clearly take responsibility to ensure that these treaties satisfy or promote principles of distributive justice. The difficulties of formal treaty change may also require other actors to heed such principles, including

[31] J. Klijnsma, 'Contract law as fairness', *Ratio Juris*, 28 (2012), 68–8 at 77, citing J. Rawls, *Justice as Fairness: A Restatement* (Cambridge, MA: Harvard University Press, 2001), p. 51.

[32] M. Ronzoni, 'Two concepts of basic structure, and their relevance to global justice', *Global Justice: Theory Practice Rhetoric*, 1 (2008), 68–85 at 80.

judges and panel members with some discretion. Such good faith efforts to realize principles of distributive justice within institutions that are parts of the GBS face several challenges. Consider three forms of 'underdetermination' by principles of (global) distributive justice.

First, the normative tradition of political philosophy presented earlier argues about standards for the *comparative assessment of alternative sets of institutions and practices.* Thus the claim that the present GBS is unjust implies that there could be another, stable GBS that would be less unjust, e.g. one with other rules upheld by the WTO system. Such counterfactual statements are problematic in general, and especially in these cases. Consider that while suffering endured under the present GBS may be massive, this GBS may still be better than any politically and practically feasible alternative. Against this 'Panglossian' objection, some hold first that counterfactuals are no more problematic for normative arguments than, e.g. in economics. Moreover, changes in certain features of the GBS would arguably be very likely to improve the situation for some without engendering worse outcomes for others. Such suggestions might include to remove rich and powerful states' current ability to protect their markets from developing countries' products.[33] Critics may still maintain that our conditions of complex interdependence make it very difficult to discern which changes to the present regimes would plausibly make for a more just system.[34]

A second underdetermination stems from the broad subject matter of a GBS. Principles of distributive justice do not indicate on their own which of several possible changes should be undertaken to enhance the distributive justice of the GBS. Quite different alternative changes to the GBS may be equal from the point of view of justice, as long as the effects render the system as a whole more just to the same extent. Philosophical considerations on their own neither aspire to nor can overcome a 'limited knowledge of remedies'.[35] To illustrate, consider two very different changes to the GBS. The WTO system could remove tariffs for agricultural products from the

[33] T. W. Pogge, 'The role of international law in reproducing massive poverty' in S. Besson and J. Tasioulas (eds.), *The Philosophy of International Law* (Oxford University Press, 2010), pp. 417–36.

[34] R. L. Howse and R. Teitel, 'Global justice, poverty and the international economic order' in S. Besson and J. Tasioulas (eds.), *The Philosophy of International Law* (Oxford University Press, 2010), pp. 437–49.

[35] J. P. Trachtman, 'Doing justice: The economics and politics of international distributive justice' in Chi Carmody, F. J. Garcia and J. Linarelly (eds.), *Global Justice and International Economic Law: Opportunities and Prospects* (Cambridge University Press, 2012), pp. 273–86, at pp. 273 and 277.

least developing countries, or appropriate international bodies could impose a tax on financial transactions to the benefit of developing countries.[36] If either of these very different alternative changes improve the distributive justice of the GBS overall, the normative theory does not indicate which change should occur. Indeed, Ratner observes that:

> perhaps trade law is not the proper place to fix the problems of global poverty or deprivations of basic human rights of the economic kind. Rather, other measures, for example more development assistance outside the trade context, or sanctions against violators, would be more efficient (economically) or effective (politically).[37]

Such underdetermination is especially unfortunate when seeking to alleviate present injustice, where each suboptimal alternative entails difficult trade-offs and continued injustice inflicting harm on some.[38] In response, I submit that it is no objection that normative political philosophy on its own underdetermines alternatives. This rather underscores the need for multidisciplinary insights concerning empirical impact and feasibility, to inform political prudence and democratic decision making about which improvements to implement.

For our purposes, an important, third form of underdetermination stems from the loose links between institutions and the particular practices that they engender. The same formal set of legal rules and allocation of legal powers to various bodies may contribute to widely diverse sets of actual practices.

In particular, the same rules for market transaction and property may be used by actors to yield strikingly different patterns of final distributions of material goods and services. We return to this later; note here that this is a challenge to the normative theories' apparent focus on sets of institutions regarded as formal rules. The BS or the GBS might be assessed by counterfactual assessment of which practices they are most likely to give rise to, or by counterfactual assessment of which of them are most likely to avoid the normatively worst distribution.

A further, related challenge is that it sometimes is difficult to maintain a strict distinction between background structure and decisions by actors

[36] J. M. Keynes, *The General Theory of Employment, Interest, and Money* (San Diego: Harcourt Brace Jovanovich, 1953), pp. 147–164; J. Tobin, 'A proposal for international monetary reform', *Eastern Economic Journal*, 4 (1978), 153–59.

[37] S. R. Ratner, *The Thin Justice of International Law: A Moral Reckoning of the Law of Nations* (Oxford University Press, 2015), p. 346.

[38] Ronzoni, 'Two concepts of basic structure', 83.

who manoeuvre against that backdrop. In particular, for our topic it is important to keep in mind that treaties are often less precise than domestic legislation, leaving international courts and tribunals more interpretative discretion than their domestic counterparts. Thus the DSM of the WTO system is unavoidably required to engage in treaty interpretation. And 'dynamic' treaty interpretation also becomes more necessary over time to adjust to changing circumstances, especially when sufficient consensus about treaty change is difficult to secure.

The combination of these forms of underdetermination cautions against reliance only on normative arguments in favour of particular reform proposals: such proposals would also need to be supported by arguments that such proposals are required, politically more feasible, etc. Thus Robert Howse and Ruti Teitel observe against Thomas Pogge's concrete suggestions for WTO reform that

> the effects of rules are not really *foreseeable* without considering how they are interpreted and by whom, and so this is an issue that is crucial to the very argument that Pogge makes in his essay.[39]

Presumably, Howse and Teitel would agree that different rules do affect the discretionary space for interpretation – otherwise it is difficult to explain why states mistakenly spend resources negotiating treaty texts. This caveat notwithstanding, they seem correct in noting that

> the TRIPs agreement, which contains significant limitation or balancing clauses, need not have negative effects on the well-being of people in poor countries. However, certain narrow developed country interests managed to largely capture the interpretative space with respect to TRIPs ... it is far from clear that more poverty would be eliminated through these new rules, given existing interpretative practices, than would be eliminated through changing the interpretative practices and culture surrounding the existing rules, and especially integrating existing positive international human rights law into the interpretation of the economic rules.[40]

In partial response, note that the GBS as defined here includes not only institutions, but also rules and practices that shape actors' expectations and plans.[41] Thus the GBS includes not only treaty texts, but also established practices of authoritative interpretation. The justice of 'trade

[39] Howse and Teitel, 'Global justice', pp. 446–7. [40] Ibid., p. 447.

[41] T. W. Pogge, 'The role of international law in reproducing massive poverty' in S. Besson and J. Tasioulas (eds.), *The Philosophy of International Law* (Oxford University Press, 2010), pp. 417–36 at p. 417.

law' cannot be assessed independent of how it is interpreted and applied. To illustrate: Ratner observes that some criticisms against international trade law are overdrawn because

> the actual workings of the law undercut simple conclusions regarding trade law's justice. Trade law can be interpreted to deny a state policy space to protect human rights, but on two core issues – conflict diamonds and HIV medicines – states avoided a direct conflict.[42]

This has at least two implications for discussions about the justice of the WTO system and strategies to render the international courts and tribunals more just. On the one hand, the 'good news' may be that treaty changes may not be required, insofar as the outcomes also depend on interpretation of the written rules. On the other hand, insofar as much hinges on interpretation and discretion, the risks remain. The bad news is that just outcomes appear to depend completely on the goodwill of the interpreters: 'The decision-makers will need to accept the priority of basic human rights in their interpretations of the texts.'[43]

What conclusions may be drawn from these various forms of underdetermination for strategies to reduce any present injustice of the WTO system? For our purposes, two modest premises seem plausible to draw on.

First, other things equal, changes should be *incremental* rather than drastic. A risk of this prudential approach is certainly that abhorrent institutions are kept with only cosmetic improvements – resulting in piecemeal 'local' improvements at the cost of forsaking 'global' improvements.[44] However, the effects of large-ale or revolutionary changes to a BS and a GBS are extremely difficult to predict.

Secondly, we might prefer that new institutions or practices should be such that they can remain in place also under later reforms, rather than be temporary arrangements that must later be dismantled. Such strategies may better promote stability and predictability.

6 Four Paths of Changes to Interpretation of the WTO System

One conclusion from these forms of underdetermination is that the distributive justice of the GBS, and of the WTO system in particular,

[42] Ratner, *The Thin Justice of International Law*, p. 347. [43] Ibid., p. 337.

[44] E. J. Elster, 'Arguments for constitutional choice: Reflections on the transition to socialism' in J. Elster and R. Slagstad (eds.), *Constitutionalism and Democracy* (Cambridge University Press, 1988), pp. 303–26 at p. 306.

might not require drastic changes to the rules of the system. Such drastic changes appear neither required nor effective. This is not to deny that other important relevant normative standards may counsel more thoroughgoing reforms, such as standards of international rule of law, or transparency may require very different procedures for selection of panel members. The concern in the present discussion is limited to the requirements of global distributive justice.

It would appear very difficult to secure the requisite consensus among the states for treaty changes to explicitly include reference to standards of global distributive justice or international obligations pertaining to minimum human rights. However, several authors note that there is wide room for interpreting trade treaties and agreements when the judges and arbitrators are engaged in dispute resolution. This may improve the distributive justice of the WTO system drastically.

To exemplify some such changes to the interpretative practices of judges and panel members, the following section sketches some of the interpretative practices that the WTO DSM might develop more fully. The claim is not that such interpretational shifts are likely to occur, but that the DSM has a wide scope of discretion. Four interrelated features show how trade dispute resolution bodies have engaged in systemic interpretation to include a variety of international law sources, and that this practice may also come to include further considerations of distributive justice and human rights concerns. The four features are those indicated by the editors in their introduction, albeit in a different order. Some final reflections consider how the judges and arbitrators may be moved or nudged toward such changes.

6.1 *Authority to Specify the Contents of Non-Trade Exemption Clauses*

Several treaties allow states derogations, e.g. on the basis of emergencies, public order, etc. Similarly, the General Agreement on Tariffs and Trade (GATT)[45] and the General Agreement on Trade in Services (GATS)[46] allow states to act on such concerns. GATT Article XX and GATS XIV on General Exceptions lay out several specific instances where members may be exempted from GATT or GATS rules – as long as 'such measures are

[45] General Agreement on Tariffs and Trade, Marrakesh, 15 April 1994, in force 1 January 1995, 1867 UNTS 187; 33 ILM 1153 (1994).

[46] General Agreement on Trade in Services, Marrakesh, 15 April 1994, in force 1 January 1995, 1869 UNTS 183; 33 ILM 1167 (1994).

not applied in a manner which would constitute a means of arbitrary or unjustifiable discrimination between countries where the same conditions prevail, or a disguised restriction on international trade' (GATT XX).

Exceptions are allowed if necessary to protect 'public morals' as it is stated in the treaty[47] – and this has been interpreted to include concerns about seal welfare;[48] to protect human, animal or plant life or health;[49] or to conserve exhaustible natural resources.[50] GATS has similar clauses.[51] Several authors argue that these exemptions should include international human rights law.[52]

The burden of argument for states defending an exemption varies among the international courts and tribunals. There is some disagreement as to how much discretion states enjoy when claiming the right to derogate, but the Panel adjudicating *China-Audio-visual Products* acknowledged some 'margin of appreciation' to the member state to apply the term 'public morals' 'according to their own systems and scales of values'.[53] As regards moral or cultural factors, or precautionary measures, several international courts and tribunals have a low standard of proof; an example is the EFTA Court case on the Norwegian monopoly on gaming machines[54] and the *Philip Morris* case.[55] The EFTA Court refrains from detailed review about the plausibility of benefits to morals or health from national measures.

Some argue that the WTO judges do and should defer on the basis of the principle *dubio mitius* which

[47] GATT XX:a.

[48] Appellate Body Reports, EC –Seal Products; A. E. Appleton, 'PIL and IEL: Will seal deaths resurrect the dream of international legal coherence?', *Questions of International Law*, 1 (2014). Available at: http://qil-qdi.org/pil-iel-will-seal-deaths-resurrect-dream-international-legal-coherence/.

[49] GATT XX:b. [50] GATT XX:g. [51] GATS XIVa.

[52] S. H. Cleveland, 'Human rights sanctions and international trade: A theory of compatibility', *Journal of International Economic Law*, 5 (2002), 162–3; Petersmann, 'Time for a United Nations 'global compact' for integrating human rights', 625; M. J. Trebilcock and R. L. Howse, 'Trade policy and labour standards', *Minnesota Journal of Global Trade*, 14 (2005), 261; further references in M. Wu, 'Free trade and the protection of public morals: An analysis of the newly emerging public morals clause doctrine', *The Yale Journal of International Law*, 33 (2008), 215–51.

[53] Panel Report, *China – Publications and Audiovisual Products*, para. 7.759; see also Chapter 2 of this volume.

[54] Case E-1/06, *EFTA Surveillance Authority v. Norway* [2007] EFTA Court Report 8, paras. 29 and 51.

[55] Ref Case E-16/10, *Philip Morris* [2011] EFTA Court Report 330, para. 82.

> requires that where there are two plausible approaches to the interpretation of a treaty provision, the treaty interpreter adopt the interpretation that is less restrictive of the sovereignty of the state or states undertaking the obligation in question.[56]

The WTO panels may hitherto be less willing to defer to states' defences, but this is a matter of interpretation of the treaties and could change without requiring a treaty change.

As to the application of the exemption clauses of GATT XX, the AB has relied on a 'principle of effectiveness' to grant WTO members the right to invoke nontrade concerns, as 'equal in value and importance to the market access rights of WTO Members'. The domain of exemptions seems underspecified, and the AB appears to allow states great discretion about the objectives they appeal to. For instance, it would not seem to require a change in the treaty text for the AB to allow 'public morals' to include international human rights obligations or global distributive justice norms, which are widely shared among states – e.g. as expressed in the Millennium Development Goals, or in core labour standards.

6.2 *Evolutionary Interpretation*

The ICTs enjoy little de jure authority to engage in dynamic or evolutive interpretation beyond that stated by the object and purpose of the treaty.[57] To the contrary, the Marrakesh Agreement insists that the political organs (Ministerial Conference and General Council) retain the power of authoritative interpretation of the WTO covered agreements.[58]

As a matter of actual practice, the WTO panels have allowed amicus submissions without any bases in the relevant treaties. Although there may be a grey area between specification of a treaty norm and evolutionary interpretation, many scholars point to several cases as evidence of evolutionary interpretation by WTO bodies, starting with how 'exhaustible natural resources' was defined in *US Shrimp* to include endangered species.[59]

[56] Trebilcock and Howse, 'Trade policy and labour standards', 261.

[57] Vienna Convention on the Law of Treaties, Vienna, 23 May 1969, in force 27 January 1980, 1155 UNTS 331; (1969) 8 ILM 679; UKTS (1980) 58, Articles31.1 and 31.3.c.

[58] Agreement Establishing the World Trade Organization, Marrakesh, 15 April 1994, in force 1 January 1995, 1867 UNTS 154; 33 ILM 1144 (1994).

[59] See Chapter 2.

One way such dynamic interpretation may occur is through perceived consensus among states. Thus the AB members appear to rely on such perceptions in some decisions:

> the dicta in Korea – Beef – stating that the more state measures are designed to pursue 'common interests or values' (rather than narrow national interests), the more likely they will be accepted by the AB as necessary to achieve state objectives under article XX – are now routinely cited and its terms debated throughout the proceedings.[60]

One source of such consensus may be the 'common constitutional traditions' of the member states. In the European region, the Court of Justice of the European Union, the EFTA Court and the European Court of Human Rights invoke constitutional and other traditions common to the member states to interpret – dynamically – human rights norms.[61] The Canadian Supreme Court has stated that values reflected in international human rights law may help inform the contextual approach to statutory interpretation and judicial review'[62] – even unimplemented treaties. Some human rights treaties that enjoy very close to universal state consent may be taken to express such a consensus, arguably appropriate for the GATT exception clauses.[63]

As for standards of distributive justice, universal consensus is currently less plausible. At the regional level, possible sources may include EU treaties that commit the member states to 'economic, social and territorial cohesion, and solidarity among Member States'.[64]

6.3 *Increased Significance of Case Law*

One significant shift not only in its interpretational tradition but also in the role of the WTO system is due to the development of a tradition of

[60] A. S. Sweet and T. L. Brunell, 'Trustee courts and the judicialization of international regimes: The politics of majoritarian activism in the European Convention on Human Rights, the European Union, and the World Trade Organization', *Journal of Law and Courts*, 1 (2013), 61–88 at 85.

[61] A. Williams, *EU Human Rights Policies: A Study in Irony* (Oxford University Press, 2004), 13–14.

[62] See Chapter 6.

[63] Office of the United Nations High Commissioner for Human Rights, 'Human Rights and World Trade Agreements: Using General Exception Clauses to Protect Human Rights', (2005) *HR/PUB/05/5*.

[64] European Council, 'Treaty of Lisbon Amending the Treaty on European Union and the Treaty Establishing the European Community, Signed at Lisbon, 13 December 2007', *Official Journal of the European Union*, 50 (2007), Article3.

precedent, which is not mentioned in the founding WTO documents. The role of the panels and the AB has for a long time gone beyond primarily adjudicating individual cases by applying rules in single disputes, in the direction of becoming mechanisms that shape and stabilize the actors' expectations by making rules. Such developments are widely recognized, and one might argue that the system should also explicitly acknowledge that the AB is in fact creating law. Such statements may contribute to increase the appropriate discussions about the legitimacy of the AB. This function is strictly speaking beyond the immediate objectives the parties may have had in setting up the WTO system, yet merits detailed study and assessment. Note that such a movement also leads the WTO panels and the AB in particular to take a more 'constitutional' perspective, in the sense of considering the longer-term effects of one-shot decisions, and the division of labour among them and other institutions and actors. Such a constitutional turn may increase the salience among the AB members of human rights constraints and considerations of global distributive justice – and may increase the pressure on the AB by NGOs to do so.

Such developments toward a practice of stabilizing norms have occurred – to some extent – as regards the consideration of environmental concerns. Similar developments may arise as regards human rights or other global distributive justice issues. Note that this is just intended as an example of a change that *may* give more room for considerations of human rights or global distributive justice; precedents may also emerge that are completely dismissive of such concerns.

6.4 *Systemic Interpretation*

The WTO system may develop a more consistent practice for how to include other treaties in the interpretation. Article 3.2 of the DSU holds that the recommendations and rulings of the Dispute Settlement Bodies – presumably including the interpretations – cannot add to or diminish the rights and obligations of the WTO members provided in the WTO covered agreements. However, a completely insular interpretational practice of WTO law as a 'self-contained regime' has never been maintained. Thus the AB maintained that WTO covered agreements cannot be interpreted 'in clinical isolation from public international law'.[65] Many scholars note that there is pressure on the WTO mechanism toward

[65] Appellate Body Report, *US – Gasoline*, p. 16.

more systemic interpretation to incorporate international public law.[66] Several argue that there are no formal hindrances against this, though its scope is contested. Some thus hold that the WTO covered agreements should be interpreted in accordance with international human rights law:

> a good faith interpretation of the provisions of the WTO, including its exception provisions, should lead to a reading and application of WTO law consistent with human rights. The recent Doha Declaration on TRIPS and Public Health is a good example of such a possible coherent reading of WTO provisions taking into account potentially relevant human rights law.[67]

Similarly, Margot Salomon and others argue that present international human rights law – including protections against abject poverty – has implications for interpreting and applying international economic law.[68] This is not to deny that such more expansive attempts by members of a WTO body to include human rights considerations or other concerns of global distributive justice may violate current interpretations of WTO rules. The point is rather that there seems to be room for changes in these interpretations.

These sketches of four paths of changes to interpretational practices of ICTs have had a limited objective, namely to indicate how such shifts may include much – if not all – of what global distributive justice may require.

Note that several of these changes may be characterised as 'constitutionalization' of international trade law, in that they nudge the arbitrators and members of the AB to consider their particular judgements as important but limited parts of a Global Basic Structure, with precedential effects, based on systemic and evolutionary interpretations. This is not to argue that the four paths imply that the WTO system should be 'constitutionalized' in whatever way possible. Several scholars point out that such developments risk that private economic interests are given priority over other more weighty societal concerns. Moreover, neither the panels

[66] S. Hindelang and M. Krajewski, *Shifting Paradigms in International Investment Law: More Balanced, Less Isolated, Increasingly Diversified* (Oxford University Press, 2016).

[67] Marceau, 'WTO dispute settlement and human rights', 753; cf Appleton, 'PIL and IEL' 9.

[68] M. E. Salomon, *Global Responsibility for Human Rights: World Poverty and the Development of International Law* (Oxford University Press, 2008); R. G. Teitel, *Humanity's Law* (New York: Oxford University Press, 2011); K. N. Schefer, (ed.), *Poverty and the International Economic Legal System: Duties to the World's Poor* (Cambridge University Press, 2013).

nor the AB are selected or well positioned to address all such conflicts.[69] Rather, the upshot is that formal treaty reforms may not be what global distributive justice requires, but rather changes in interpretive practices by the WTO system.

Are such changes in interpretative practices possible, and if so what might be suitable strategies? In conclusion, I indicate some examples drawing on the comparisons available in this volume to illustrate how such changes may come about.

7 How Might Desirable Interpretational Changes Come About?

In conclusion, some lessons might be gathered about how to promote the appropriate 'judicial ethos' among the panellists and AB members of the WTO system, so that they include considerations of human rights and global distributive justice in their interpretational practice.

Two background observations are relevant. First, it has been a long-standing concern that ad hoc judges (and thus ad hoc panels) are more likely than permanent courts or tribunals to be partial to the state that appoints them.[70] Thus permanent courts may be expected to give more consideration to the longer-term effects and indirect effects of their judgements beyond the particular case. They may be somewhat more likely to take on such 'constitutional' perspectives, including attention to their impact on the expectations of the parties, the value of predictability and their need to maintain social legitimacy under conditions of complex interdependence on other actors including treaty bodies, states, domestic courts and NGOs. Thus the AB members may be more appropriate subjects for such considerations than WTO panel members, who may in turn be guided by the practices of the AB.

Second, several observers note that some of these shifts – toward precedent, systemic interpretation, etc. – involve a trade-off in support for the WTO system from the 'insiders' to the particular dispute to the

[69] R. L. Howse and C. Nicolaidis, 'Enhancing WTO legitimacy: Constitutionalization or global subsidiarity?', *Governance*, 16 (2003), 73–94; A. v. Bogdandy, 'Law and politics in the WTO – Strategies to cope with a deficient relationship' in J. A. Frowein and R. Wolfrum (eds.), *Max Planck Yearbook of United Nations Law* (Dordrecht: Kluwer, 2001), pp. 609–74.

[70] Lauterpacht, *The Function of Law in the International Community* (Oxford: Clarendon Press, 1933), p. 233; cited by M. S. McDougal, H. H. D. Lasswell and J. C. Miller, *The Interpretation of International Agreements and World Public Order* (New Haven, CT: New Haven Press, 1994), p. 358.

'outsiders' – including other parties, both potential litigants and the general public. Thus Malacrida and Marceau and note that

> The WTO-DSM bodies seem to have enhanced the legitimacy of their decisions for the insiders (WTO Members) by grounding the decisions in the text of the treaty, as the text gives way to the intentions of the Parties, but the same approach has drawn flak from the outsiders on account of not being as integrative as envisaged by the VCLT.[71]

These findings suggest that strategies to change interpretative practices should seek to enhance the self-perception of AB members and panel arbitrators as being part of a profession with a constitutional perspective. Furthermore, it is strategically important that AB members and panel arbitrators are aware of how third parties perceive the legitimacy of the AB and panels.

Consider two ways to increase the ICTs' concern to maintain their social legitimacy among third parties to the particular disputes they address, by modifying their interpretational practices so as to incorporate more concerns about global distributive justice.

7.1 Solange Judgements on Behalf of International Human Rights and Distributive Justice

One strategy for reforming interpretational practices may be a particular form of *judicial 'dialogue'*, by which other courts and tribunals, domestic, regional or international, exercise pressure on the WTO system. An example as regards human rights may be found in the European Union: the German Constitutional Court made clear in several 'Solange' judgements that its deference to the European Court of Justice (ECJ, now the Court of Justice of the European Union) was contingent upon the ECJ's respect for human rights.[72] The ECJ responded inter alia by a dynamic interpretation of the EU treaties, so as to include human rights into the EU treaties. Similar strategies may be contemplated by other domestic, regional and international courts and tribunals vis-à-vis the WTO system.

[71] See Section 5.4 of Chapter 2 in this volume.

[72] Bundesverfassungsgericht, 'Solange I: Internationale Handelsgesellschaft v. Einfuhr Und Vorratsstelle Für Getreide Und Futtermittel' *BVerfGE 37, 271* (1974); Bundesverfassungsgericht, 'Solange II: Wuensche Handelsgesellschaft' (1986); J. Frowein, 'Solange Ii', *Common Market Law Review*, 25 (1988), 201.

7.2 *Public Pressure*

Several scholars have noted that international courts and tribunals are sensitive to informal pressure from third parties, such as NGOs and civil society more broadly. Thus Jagdish Bhagwati was (unpleasantly) astounded

> that the appellate court, in effect, reversed long-standing jurisprudence on process and production methods in the Shrimp/Turtle case. I have little doubt that the jurists were reflecting the political pressures brought by the rich-country environmental NGOs and essentially made law that affected the developing countries adversely.[73]

As Bhagwati claimed, there is, of course, no reason to believe that such pressure will always be toward normatively preferable changes. Not all civil society bodies are particularly civil, responsive to all affected parties or particularly prescient. Those risks notwithstanding, one intriguing research challenge is to understand better why and how individual judges and arbitrators in general, and in the WTO system in particular, may be affected by public 'diffuse' support or lack thereof.

8 Conclusion

Several authors, civil society organizations and states criticize the 'global basic structure' – our tangled web of domestic and international institutions, rules and practices – as drastically unjust. The WTO system is often singled out as a major culprit because their rulings serve to maintain such distributive injustice. This chapter offers some support for this diagnosis, in particular rebutting claims that the WTO system should be exempt from criticisms that it promotes global injustice. The chapter also counsels a more cautious assessment of possible prescriptions than several critics have promoted. Improvements must heed several challenges, in particular that normative standards underdetermine reform proposals, suggesting that broad scale reforms may be not possible, effective or necessary. The final sections of the chapter thus explored ways that the existing WTO system may become more just by developing the interpretive standards of the members of the AB and the panel members in one or more of four ways. This neither assumes nor entails that there are no, or should not be any, limits to interpretative practices.

[73] J. Bhagwati, 'After Seattle: Free trade and the WTO' in R. Porter, P. Sauve, A. Subramanian, and A. Zampetti (eds.), *Equity, Efficiency and Legitimacy: The Multilateral System at the Millennium* (Washington, DC: Brookings Institution Press, 2001), p. 225.

But the legitimate limits of such practices for the WTO system remain to be determined. The chapter contributes to normative political theory by insisting on the need to understand better the importance of interpretive practices of judges and arbitrators and to research on the international judiciary by pointing out where and how normative considerations already affect the legal practice.

This is not to ignore warnings that the members of the AB and panels of the WTO system may be ill-equipped to promote global distributive justice. They may lack a clear sense of the implications of such decisions and their precedential effects. There may be little reason to believe that they can assess overall impact, and identify how to best adjust.[74] It is also important to insist that there are several ways to secure more harmony among the treaties, where some may be worse than the present fragmentation.[75] However, the members of panels and the AB cannot refrain from interpretation: that is not an alternative. And given the nature of the state system, it is not clear that any other institutions are better situated than our current crop of international courts, tribunals and adjudicative bodies to move toward a less unjust world order.

The judges and members of these treaty bodies have the legal authority to interpret the existing rules, and cannot avoid interpreting – in ways that are informed by, or which support, some such considerations. Three contributions of scholarship may be to first remind them of that responsibility. Second, scholars may remind members of the WTO mechanism that to ignore the distributive consequences of their decisions is also to rely on normative theories of distributive justice:

> Practical men, who believe themselves to be quite exempt from any intellectual influences, are usually the slaves of some defunct economist.[76]

Third, faced with the fact that some principles of global distributive justice are vague and contested, one lesson may still be that in this as in many other matters, '[i]t is better to be vaguely right than exactly wrong.'[77]

[74] R. L. Howse and R. Teitel, 'Beyond compliance: Rethinking why international law really matters', *Global Policy Journal*, 1 (2010), 127–36.

[75] J. Alvarez, 'How not to link: Institutional conundrums of an expanded trade regime', *Widener Law Symposium Journal*, 7 (2001), 1–20; J. Alvarez, 'Beware boundary crossing', in T. Kahana and A. Scolnicov (eds.), *Boundaries of Rights, Boundaries of State* (Cambridge University Press) 2016.

[76] Keynes, *The General Theory of Employment, Interest, and Money*, 383.

[77] C. Read, *Logic: Deductive and Inductive* (London: Simpkin, Marshall, Hamilton, Kent & Co., 1914), p. 272.

17

Conclusions

ROBERT HOWSE, HÉLÈNE RUIZ-FABRI, GEIR ULFSTEIN AND MICHELLE Q. ZANG

International trade regimes are characterised by a high number of courts and tribunals (ITCs). Dispute settlement mechanisms (DSMs) established under multilateral, regional and bilateral trade agreements have increasingly shifted from politically oriented procedures, to more sophisticated, legalistic mechanisms. Two institutional models of ITCs have been widely adopted, namely, the quasi-judicial WTO model and the Court of Justice of the European Union (CJEU) judicial model. One explanation for the choice of model may be that if the purpose of the regime is to achieve substantive economic integration and create strong intraregional connections, the judicial model is preferred, due to its advantages in institutional permanence and broader access for stakeholders.

Sixty-five per cent of the existing ITCs have adopted the quasi-judicial model. Under this model, the adjudicating body is established for the purpose of resolving a specific dispute and dissolved once it has issued a decision. Under this category, we also include the small group of DSMs that combine an ad hoc, first instance adjudicative body, together with a standing body at the appellate stage, such as the WTO, the ASEAN system and MERCOSUR. However, the vast majority of the quasi-judicial mechanisms only provide for a single instance of third-party adjudication.

The minority of ITCs that has adopted the judicial model share a defining characteristic with the quasi-judicial model on the right of the states parties to refer disputes, but they also offer a greater degree of independence and court-like procedures. The judicial model ITCs are witnessed in the Andean Community, the EFTA and most African subregional regimes. As a rule, they have followed the institutional structure and arrangement of the CJEU. The judicial model has a clearer emphasis on private rights and participation, allowing direct access for individuals. Furthermore, although being established as economic courts, ITCs of the judicial model are usually bestowed with jurisdiction that goes beyond trade disputes and may extend into areas such as human rights and administrative cases.

This book discusses the seven research questions put forward in the introduction with respect to 11 ITCs both on the global level (WTO) and in different regions of the world: Europe, Latin America, Africa and Asia. These questions cover legitimacy issues relating to institutional arrangement, procedure-related aspects, interpretative approaches and implementation of findings by domestic courts.

1 Independence

One of the most essential requirements for the legitimacy of courts is their independence. The selection and composition of the adjudicators depend mainly on the chosen institutional model of the ITC, respectively the judicial and the quasi-judicial model. When the ITC is established in the form of a permanent body or court, e.g. the WTO Appellate Body, the Economic Court of Commonwealth of Independent States (ECCIS) and the Common Market for Eastern and Southern Africa (COMESA) Court of Justice, the adjudicators are selected by the states members with a fixed term of office. In the quasi-judicial model, i.e. ad hoc panels, the WTO practice on panellist selection has been widely used among the ITCs, e.g. the MERCOSUR and the ASEAN. The disputing states parties propose the panellist or arbitrator from an indicative list with assistance from the administrative organ, which might intervene in the case of disagreement.

As Squatrito shows, different regional trade courts display varying degrees of independence.[1] She finds that on average African courts score lower in their formal independence than those from Europe and the Americas. One example is the ECCIS Court, where, according to Dragneva-Lewers, each state can recall its judge.[2] We also see infringements of the courts' independence in practice. Illy mentions that all the judges, except for one, of the Court of Justice of the West African Economic and Monetary Union (the WAEMU Court) have, without a legal basis, been dismissed by the member states.[3]

But how to ensure independence while accommodating accountability is a persistent dilemma for trade courts – like any other international court. As shown in the recent experience at the WTO Appellate Body, timely appointments of members are not guaranteed owing to the positive consensus requirement across the membership, while reappointments of incumbent members seeking a second term might also be

[1] See Chapter 12. [2] See Chapter 6. [3] See Chapter 8.

hindered by the veto right of his or her own government or any other member state. As stated by Malacrida and Marceau, the uncertainty surrounding reappointment could detract from the independence of adjudicators.[4] The reappointment of judges has, according to Kuijper, also been seen as a weak point for the independence of the European Court.[5] And Haukeland Fredriksen refers to a recent dispute about reappointment of the Norwegian to the EFTA Court.[6]

2 Procedural Legitimacy

The procedural legitimacy issues of ITCs include their accessibility and the transparency of the proceedings. Like the independence of the judiciary, access to the courts covered by this book varies to a considerable extent, as demonstrated by Fauchald.[7]

Access to the ITCs covers issues relating to the standing of states and private parties directly affected by a measure (*locus standi*), third-party participation and amicus curiae submissions. While the judicial model typically allows some role by private parties, most ad hoc ITCs are limited to participation by states parties. For the WTO and the MERCOSUR, a major access-related problem is the participation of third parties, i.e. the rights of access by nondisputing members with substantial interest in the dispute.

Amicus curiae submissions from individuals or other nongovernmental entities have created controversies both in the judicial and quasi-judicial models. The CJEU does not allow such submissions, while the WTO Appellate Body has held that panels have 'the authority either to accept and consider or to reject information submitted to it, whether requested by a party or not'. This stance prompted a conflict with the WTO's highest body, the General Council.

Discussion on procedural transparency is not limited to the openness of hearings and disclosure of documents; it further touches upon issues such as the confidentiality of judicial proceedings. There are distinct approaches between judicial and quasi-judicial ITCs: while the former is generally open for public hearing and the availability of documents, the fact that the latter in most cases hold the hearing behind closed doors and that submissions of parties are treated as confidential, attracts legitimacy critique. Panels and the Appellate Body of the WTO have allowed public

[4] See Chapter 1. [5] See Chapter 2. [6] See Chapter 3. [7] See Chapter 14.

observation of the proceedings if accepted by the disputing parties. However, what the two models share is the secrecy of the deliberation of the adjudicators.

3 Fact-Finding, Burden of Proof, etc.

The ITCs also raise issues of fact-finding, burden of proof, rules of evidence and standards of review. A debated legitimacy matter refers to the standard of review when examining measures taken at the national level. This matter is embedded in the broader issue of the regulatory space and sovereignty reserved for the national authority in economic matters discussed later. For cases referred by national courts to the EFTA Court and CJEU, it is for the referring national court to ascertain the facts that have given rise to the dispute. At the WTO, depending on the role of the panel either as the initial tester of facts or a reviewer of fact-based determination made by domestic authorities, different standard of scrutiny applies with varying degree of deference to the decisions made domestically. In the domestic context, Pogue shows that the U.S. Court of International Trade (USCIT) follows the statutory standards established for judicial review. According to these standards, de novo review is applicable only to customs cases while a more deferential standard prevails among most trade cases.[8]

4 Styles of Interpretation

Another element that affects the legitimacy is the ITC's interpretative techniques. Only the most established ITCs have developed consistent interpretative approaches, i.e. the WTO DSM, the CJEU and the EFTA Court. These courts embrace the rules of interpretation as reflected in the Vienna Convention on the Law of Treaties as a legal framework. But these rules are not necessarily explicitly referred to. The President of the EFTA Court has even stated that his Court should not be limited to what he sees as the 'conservative' components of the Convention.

However, some interpretational techniques attract criticisms. For example, controversial interpretative issues at the WTO include the (former) strictly text-based approach and the strong persuasive power granted to the previous decisions. A problem for the EFTA Court has been its mandate to facilitate harmonization between EU and EFTA law

[8] See Chapter 10.

when the EEA treaty, unlike its EU counterpart, has not been updated since it was concluded in 1992.

The interpretative approach of the adjudicator is also of significance when ITCs deal with conflicts between trade and other societal policies, such as environment protection and human rights enhancement. The CJEU has been able to include respect for human rights in its interpretation even before the EU treaty explicitly referred to such rights. The WTO Appellate Body has, through dynamic interpretation of the GATT exception clauses, been able to protect environmental interests. Follesdal concludes that the WTO DSB has considerable room through interpretational techniques to take into account aspects of global justice.[9]

It is also interesting to note that both the WTO Appellate Body and the CJEU seem sensitive to their political context. While Malacrida and Marceau state that '[t]here is a tacit understanding that the resolution of disputes at the WTO demands sensitivity to the broader political context', Kuijper remarks that the CJEU 'knows who won the last elections'.

5 Interaction between ITCs

Overlap of jurisdiction among different ITCs, or between ITCs and other adjudicators, may lead to forum shopping, parallel litigations and contradicting and inconsistent jurisprudence. Some jurisdictional conflicts have appeared in practice, i.e. between the WTO DSB on the one hand and, respectively, MERCOSUR and NAFTA on the other. As shown by Zang, neither of the conflicts prevented the WTO DSB from dealing with the cases.[10] The limited activity of the regional ITCs means that there have only been a few clashes between the courts and tribunals. But there is a potential for more conflicts in the future.

Elements that may be taken into account by the complaining party in choosing between ITCs include the economic and political costs, the chance of success, the applicable law, the duration of the proceedings and the subsequent implementation mechanism. Ewing-Chow and Yusran demonstrate that ASEAN states prefer the WTO DSB rather than the regional mechanism.

It is also interesting that, according to Zang, regional trade adjudicators heavily refer to WTO practice, whereas the WTO DSB is rater restrictive in referring the other way. In contrast, the WTO DSB is

[9] See Chapter 15. [10] See Chapter 13.

concerned with ensuring consistency between WTO law and general international law. The EFTA Court is special in the sense that a main purpose is to ensure harmony between EU law and EFTA law.

For the difficulties arising from jurisdictional conflicts, solutions can be sought in two directions. Not only should the agreement upon which the ITC is established include a forum selection clause in dispute resolution, but also the ITCs themselves should also exercise prudence in accommodating a mutually constructive relationship.

6 ITCs and the Domestic Level

Trade rules and the findings by ITCs are increasingly limiting national regulatory freedom, while their effectiveness is dependent on national implementation. Therefore, the interaction between the international and national level is of increasing importance. It is also essential for the legitimacy of ITCs that they resolve trade disputes without interfering too much with decision making by national constitutional organs.

First, it is interesting to examine to what extent ITCs allow discretion to the national level. The exception for 'public morals' in Article XX(a) of the GATT 1994 has, as highlighted by Malacrida and Marceau, been interpreted to allow each member state a certain freedom to determine their specific needs based on their own values. Kuijper states that the CJEU normally does not leave member states any margin of discretion. But EU decisions in the form of directives allow a certain choice of means for implementation. Furthermore, exception clauses may also allow certain discretion for member states, in particular in respect of public morality.

On the national level, findings by ITCs may have different legal status in different states. Malacrida and Marceau say that certain member states have been reluctant to give direct effect to WTO DSB rulings in the national legal system. This may be due to several reasons. First, the DSB may partly be seen to have a diplomatic character; second, a direct effect may be seen to place the relevant state at a competitive disadvantage compared to other member states; and, finally, such effect could jeopardize the domestic legal order. Kuijper states that the CJEU never has admitted that panel or Appellate Body reports are binding in the EU legal order. As shown by Pogue and Irish in, respectively, the US and Canadian contexts, WTO DSB findings may, however, be taken into account by interpreting domestic law to ensure consistency with international obligations.

But the relationship between the international and national level may not only be unidirectional. Kuijper refers to the changes in the CJEU's practice to respect human rights as part of the EU legal order, as a response to the German Constitutional Court's *solange* doctrine. Irish points to the role of domestic courts in the elaboration of the law. Domestic judgments can serve as evidence of state practice and of subsequent treaty interpretation, as well as being a subsidiary source of international law pursuant to Article 38 (1) (d) of the Statute of the International Court of Justice.

7 Underuse and Diverted Use of ITCs

The underuse of a number of quasi-judicial ITCs or diverted use of certain judicial ITCs to nontrade disputes is a striking feature of the regional trade mechanisms in Latin America, Africa and Asia. For example, the DSM established under the ASEAN has never been used since its establishment in 2008; the Andean Community Court of Justice and most subregional courts in Africa have been used in areas other than trade. Most African ITCs have overwhelmingly decided cases in human rights and administrative employment, and the Andean Community Court of Justice has become a de facto judiciary specialised in intellectual property rights. Such use of ITCs for nontrade cases raises doubts about their ability to fulfill their mandates. It can indicate legitimacy deficits by the relevant trade courts and tribunals – but it can also be a result of the political context in which they are situated.

The usage of ITCs may be linked to the access opportunities they offer to the stakeholders. But Fauchald finds no correspondence between formal access to the ITCs and the use of these mechanisms. The chapters in this book have shown specific deficits in structure, procedure and practice of individual ITCs. It is, however, difficult to find common design features of the ITCs and their practice, which could account for the reluctance to use them or for their transformation to nontrade courts. As for their transformation, two reasons may be identified: the ITC might have filled a lacuna in one or more national judiciaries; alternatively, the ITC might have been actively seeking tasks and been successful in doing so only for certain category of cases.

Political explanations of the limited use of regional ITCs outside Europe – and to a certain extent the MERCOSUR – include that the intraregional trade flow may be comparatively low and therefore very few trade-related disputes have emerged in practice. In Africa, only around 10–12 per cent of trade takes place between African countries, while around 40 per cent of North American and 63 per cent of Western European is intraregional.

Political asymmetries in the relevant region may also be of significance. Dragneva-Lewers refers to the importance of the regional hegemon Russia as an important factor for preferring consensual mechanisms, rather than binding third -party dispute settlement through the Economic Court of the Commonwealth of Independent States.

There may also be combinations between legal and political factors behind the nonuse of regional courts for trade purposes. Gathii explains that the restricted number of trade disputes before the COMESA Court probably can be explained by: the failure by the Court to mobilize local constituencies; starting of the Court's work at a time where the member states were hostile to judicial review; the limited accessibility of the location of the Court in Khartoum; and, finally, its restrictive and formalistic interpretation when it comes to access to the Court.

It may also be asked whether a local culture that is hesitant to accept settlement of disputes by international courts may explain the limited use of regional ITCs. For example, one explanation for the nonutilization of the ASEAN DSM has been the states' persistent practice of dispute management through the 'ASEAN Way' of diplomacy. But Ewing-Chow and Yusran show that the ASEAN States have used other international courts than the ASEAN mechanism in disputes over territorial sovereignty as well as trade. The first trade dispute before the WTO was, in fact, between two ASEAN member states, Malaysia and Singapore in 1995. The authors also refer to imperfections of the ASEAN DSM, for example, in terms of time limits and lack of capacity. This means that the WTO DSM has a comparative advantage – and not necessarily that ASEAN is reluctant to use the regional ICT.

This means that the use – or nonuse – of ICTs may depend on a complex interdependence between: legal design features and practice of these mechanisms, which could induce or reduce their legitimacy among relevant stakeholders; political factors that are specific to the relevant region, including the trade relations between the member states; and the availability of alternative mechanisms, whether it is the WTO or political channels for resolving trade disputes. This also means that changes in these factors may have implications of the legitimacy and use of the ICTs. Finally, the availability, legitimacy and use of ICTs will be influenced by regional and global general attitudes toward international courts and tribunals – will we see a reversal in the recent rise of the regional and global judiciary?

INDEX

AB members. *See* appellate body members
access to courts
CJEU, 89–95
for third-parties, 89–91
EFTA Court, 150–54
for EFTA Member States, 150–51
for individuals, 151–52
through national courts, 152
for third-parties, 150–51, 154
USCIT, 187–90
WAEMU Court of Justice, 360–61
access to trade tribunals, 457–70
legitimacy through, 454
regional FTA courts
formal, 460–66
real access, 470–77
through WTO DSM, 457–60
accountability, of courts
USCIT, 187
CAFC and, 186
ACIA. *See* ASEAN Comprehensive Investment Agreement
ACWL. *See* Advisory Centre on WTO Law
ad hoc tribunals, 237–38
ADA. *See* Anti-Dumping Agreement
adjudicating bodies, of WTO, 68–69
duration of proceedings, 57
ICJ and, 447–48
independence of, 24–25
in judicial interactions, 438–46
legitimacy of, 446–52
AB Members and, 448–52
panelists in, election of, 22–25
PCIJ and, 447–48
RTAs and, 438–46
admissibility, 441
under GATT, 443–46
jurisdiction conflicts between, 439–41
legal interpretation of, 441–43
in MERCOSUR, 443, 445–46
obligation conflicts between, 443–46
under VCLT, 438–39
scope of, 22, 52–53
selection of, 22–28
administrative law, USCIT and, 200–1
adversarial principle, 98
Advisory Centre on WTO Law (ACWL), 56
advisory jurisdiction, of WAEMU Court of Justice Court, 359
Advocates-General (AGs), in CJEU
in CoJ, 71–75
functions of, 84–85
GC and, 71–75
influence of, 85
AEM. *See* ASEAN Economic Minister Meeting
African Charter on Human and Peoples' Rights, 339–40
African Court of Human and Peoples' Rights, 338–39
African courts and tribunals. *See also* Common Market for Eastern and Southern Africa Court of Justice; Western African Economic and Monetary Union Court of Justice
African Union Advisory Board on Corruption, 338–39
civil society movements in, 337

African courts and tribunals. (cont.)
EACJ and, 315–16, 322, 328, 340–41
COMESA Court of Justice compared to, 336–38, 348
exhaustion of domestic remedies and, 332
expansion of jurisdiction for, 339–42
human rights cases at, 333, 337, 339
ECOWAS Court of Justice, 315–16
COMESA Court of Justice compared to, 336
jurisdictional power of, 328
legitimacy of, 316
expansion of jurisdictions for, 342–43
International Criminal Court for Rwanda, 338–39
Mixed International Criminal Tribunal, 338–39
NGOs and, 338–39
SADC, 322, 328
COMESA Court of Justice compared to, 336
human rights cases at, 339
sub-regional ICs, 314–15
African Institute of International Law, 338–39
African Union Advisory Board on Corruption, 338–39
AFSJ. *See* Area of Freedom and, Security and Justice
Agreement on Sanitary or Phytosanitary Measures (SPS Agreement), 39
Agreement on Subsidies and Countervailing Measures (ASCM), 46–47, 450, 459
Agreement on Technical Barriers to Trade (TBT), 442–43, 456
Agreement on Trade-related Aspects of Intellectual Property Rights (TRIPS), 111–12, 459, 491
AGs. *See* Advocates-General
Andean Community Court of Justice. *See also* judges
annual budget for, 266–67
Bolivia and, 281
CA and, 255–58
establishment of, 258–59
caseload of, 275–77
Cochabamba Protocol and, 260
Colombia and, 281–82
confidentiality of, 274
Ecuador and, 282
establishment of, 255–56, 258–59
through Andean legal systems, 261–62, 270
historical background for, 256–62
through revamp of integration systems, 259–60
European influences on, 256–62
fact-finding by, 277–78
forum shopping and, 280–81
implementation of judgments, 281–82
intellectual property cases, 283
interpretative approaches by, 278–80
under integration law, 278–79
judicial independence in, 262–68
jurisdiction of, 268–74
for labour disputes, 273–74
through prejudgment interpretations, 271–72
legitimacy of, 282–84
under procedural rules, 274–75
MERCOSUR and, 243, 246
national and domestic courts and, interactions with, 249–52, 281–82
prejudgment interpretations by, 271–72
NGOs and, 275–77
outreach activities of, 276–77
Pacific Alliance and, 280
Peru and, 282
private parties and, 275–77
procedural rules for, 268–77
for annulments, 269–70
for arbitration, 274
legitimacy under, 274–75
for non-compliance requests, 270
for omissions, 273
purpose and function of, 12–13
re-engineering process of, 284

regional FTA courts and, 471
as single-issue court, 477
Trujillo Protocol and, 260
Venezuelan withdrawal from, 262, 281, 285
WTO and, 280
Andean legal systems, 261–62, 270, 283
annulment procedures, 269–70
arbitration procedures, 274
Anti-Dumping Agreement (ADA), 41–43, 127–28, 459
anti-dumping cases, 231
appeals, of judgments
of Federal Courts of Canada, 205–6
USCIT, 201
appellate body (AB) members, in WTO, 22
hearings by, 32–33
interpretation of provisions by, 50–51
legitimacy assessment of, 448–52
provisions reports, 50–51
selection of, 25–27
Chinese Taipei response to, 26
standards of review by, 39–42
arbitrators, for MERCOSUR, 236–40
independence of, 240–42
nominations for, 236–40
qualifications of, 240–42
Area of Freedom and, Security and Justice (AFSJ), CJEU, 90
Argentina, MERCOSUR and, 231–32
Article 21.5, DSU, 60–61
ASCM. *See* Agreement on Subsidies and Countervailing Measures
ASEAN. *See* Association of Southeast Asian Nations
ASEAN Agreement for the Promotion and Protection of Investment Area, 460
ASEAN Comprehensive Investment Agreement (ACIA), 401–2
ASEAN Dispute Settlement Mechanisms. *See also* Enhanced Dispute Settlement Mechanism
in Cambodia, 394
DSMP and, 377–79, 383
establishment of, 365–66
functions of, 397–401
future of, 401–2
implementation of ASEAN instruments and, 392–93
in Indonesia, 389–92, 396–97
lack of capacity of, 397–401
lack of usage of, 366–79, 384–401
ASEAN Way of diplomacy as factor in, 387–93
through interpretative approaches, 392–93
third-party dispute alternatives as factor in, 384–85, 393–97
legitimacy of, 380–84
comparative benefits as condition of, 381
institutional integrity as condition of, 381–83
minimum moral acceptability as condition of, 380–81
in Malaysia, 388–91, 396–97
non-compliance with, 379
in the Philippines, 391–92, 394
political context for, 396–97
Secretariat's role in, 397–99
in Thailand, 391–92, 394
for trade agreement issues, 395–96
LSAD and, 399
unresolved disputes and, 379
ASEAN Economic Minister Meeting (AEM), 370
ASEAN Way, of diplomacy, 387–93
for intra-ASEAN disputes, 387–92
Asia, trade courts and tribunals in. *See* Association of Southeast Asian Nations
Association of Southeast Asian Nations (ASEAN), 3–4. *See also* ASEAN Dispute Settlement Mechanisms; ASEAN Way
Agreement for the Promotion and Protection of Investment Area, 460
CEPT-AFTA and, 368
dispute settlement system of, 12
establishment of, 365–66
purpose and function of, 12
Secretariat's role in, 397–99
TAC in Southeast Asia and, 12, 365–67

Baudenbacher, Carl, 130, 142–43
Belarus, 11–12, 286, 293
bindingness, of judgments
for ECCIS, 309
for USCIT, 199–200
Bolivia, 281
bounded discretion, of ITCs, 410
Brasilia Protocol, 227–28, 233, 245–46, 471
Brazil, MERCOSUR and, 231–33
burden of proof. *See also* standards of proof
for ITCs, 506
in WTO, 36–38
Burundi, 331

CA. *See* Cartagena Agreement
CAFC. *See* Court of Appeals for the Federal Circuit
Cambodia, 394
Canada
Charter of Rights and Freedom, 221
Custom Tariff Act, 223
Federal Court of Appeal in, 210–13, 217, 224–25
Supreme Court of Canada, 210–11, 217, 219–20
trade courts and tribunals in. *See* Federal Courts of Canada; North American Free Trade Agreement
Canada–United States Free Trade Agreement, 211–12
Canadian Border Services Agency (CBSA), 205–6
Canadian Charter of Rights and Freedom, 221
Canadian International Trade Tribunal (CITT), 203–6
jurisdiction of, 204–5
public hearings for, 206–7
review of judgments, 211–12
Caribbean Court of Justice (CCJ), 413
Cartagena Agreement (CA), 13
Andean Community Court of Justice and, 255–58
Chile's withdrawal from, 257
establishment of, 258–59
CBSA. *See* Canadian Border Services Agency
CCJ. *See* Caribbean Court of Justice
CEEU. *See* Court of the Eurasian Economic Union
CEPT-AFTA. *See* Common Effective Preferential Tariff Scheme for ASEAN Free Trade Area
CFSP. *See* Common Foreign and Security Policy
Charming Betsy doctrine, 199
Chevron doctrine, 193
Chief Judges, in USCIT, 182
Chile, withdrawal from CA, 257
CIS. *See* Commonwealth of Independent States
CIT. *See* U.S. Court of International Trade
CITBA. *See* Customs and International Trade Bar Association
Citizenship Directive, 167–68
CITT. *See* Canadian International Trade Tribunal
civil society movements, in East Africa, 337
CJEU. *See* Court of Justice of the European Union
CMC. *See* Common Market Council
CMG. *See* Common Market Group
Cochabamba Protocol, 260
CoJ. *See* Court of Justice
Colombia, 281–82
COMESA Court of Justice. *See* Common Market for Eastern and Southern Africa Court of Justice
Common Effective Preferential Tariff Scheme for ASEAN Free Trade Area (CEPT-AFTA), 368
Common Foreign and Security Policy (CFSP), 90–91
Common Market Council (CMC), 227, 241, 250
Common Market for Eastern and Southern Africa (COMESA) Court of Justice
Burundi and, 331

caseload for, nature of cases, 323
EACJ compared to, 336–38, 348
ECOWAS Court of Justice compared to, 336
establishment of, 13–14, 316–20
future trajectory of, 315–16
goals of, 346–47
interim orders through, 320
judges for, 318
jurisdiction of, 317–20, 322
over COMESA employee conduct, 327–28
over employment disputes, 321–27
legal diplomacy and, through judgments, 331
legitimacy of, 316, 333–35
assessment of, 334
human rights cases and, 333–34
limitations for development of, 335–42
cases and, types of, 335–38
local political contexts for, 336–37, 347–48
location of court as factor in, 338–39, 343–44
restrictive interpretative approach and, 339–42, 345
national and domestic courts, interactions with, 319
NGOs and, 315–16
PTA and, 13–14
PTA Bank case, 324–26
purpose and function of, 13–14, 314–15, 346–47
Republic of Mauritius v. Polytol Paints and Adhesives Manufacturers Co. Ltd., 329, 332–33, 340, 346
SADC compared to, 336
as single-issue court, 477
Treaty for the Establishment of COMESA, 321–23
exhaustion of domestic remedies under, 328–32
VCLT and, 333
Common Market Group (CMG), 227, 241–42
Commonwealth of Independent States (CIS), 288–90. *See also* Economic Court of the Commonwealth of Independent States
economic integration strategies by, 291–95
Russian Federation and, 293–95
comparative benefits condition, for legitimacy, 381
compensatory measures mechanism, 235
competition law, 356
in EFTA Courts, 151, 159
compliance. *See also* non-compliance requests
through EDSM, 370–72
WTO rulings and, review for, 60–61
confidentiality, principle of
Andean Community Court of Justice and, 274
judicial independence and, 418
WTO and, 32
Constitution, U.S., USCIT influenced by, 184–87, 190–91
constrained independence, of ITCs, 410
Co-operation Council for the Arab States of the Gulf, 169
Corruption Perception Index, 383
Court French, in CJEU, 85–87
Court of Appeals for the Federal Circuit (CAFC), 186
Court of Justice (CoJ), CJEU, 71
AGs and, 71–75
international law and, 111–12
interpretation of EU Law, 118
judges in, 71–75
organization and functioning of, 81–89
WTO members and, 126–29
Court of Justice of the European Union (CJEU). *See also* judges, in CJEU
access to, 89–95
CFSP and, 90–91
preliminary issues, 89–91

Court of Justice of the European Union (CJEU). (cont.)
administrative structure of, 71
AFSJ and, 90
AGs in
in CoJ, 71–75
functions of, 84–85
GC and, 71–75
influence of, 85
under ECHR, 133–35
ECtHR and, 132–35
EU Charter of Fundamental Rights, 132–33
EFTA Court and, 129–32
ESM and, 104
establishment of, 4–11
EUCST in, 71
creation of, 72
judges in, 75–76
organization and functioning of, 82–83, 88–89
fact-finding by, 95–102
adversarial principle and, 98
ascertainment of facts, 95–100
infringement procedures, 95–97
measures of inquiry, 99–100
measures of organization of the procedure and, 99
fixed price mechanism and, 101
GATT and, 103–4
GC in, 71
AGs and, 71–75
judges in, 71–75
organization and functioning of, 81–89
WTO members and, 126–29
ICJ and, 124–25
implementation of judgments, by Member States, 113–23
in domestic Member State courts, 117–22
infringement procedures, 113–17
practical measures in, 120–22
preliminary question procedures, 117–22
internal organization of, 81–89
international law and, 108–13
CoJ and, 111–12
direct effect and, 110–13
as EU Law, 108–10
harmonious interpretation and, 110–13
interpretative approaches by, 102–13
direct effect approach, 110–13
harmonious interpretation approach, 110–13
of international law, 108–13
of secondary law, 105–6
of unwritten European Union law, 106–8
of Vienna Convention on the Law of Treaties, 102–5
ITLOS and, 125–26
judicial independence of, 78, 411
judicial protections in, 91–93
juriconsult of recognized competence and, 73
language regime in, 85–87
legacy of, 135–37
legitimacy of, 81, 87, 135–37
in national and domestic courts
enforcement of ECJ judgments in, 122–23
in France, 121
in Germany, 121–22
in Italy, 96, 117, 121
in the Netherlands, 108, 123
in Spain, 117
OECD Agreement and, 103–4
primary law and, 136
purpose and functions of, 4–11, 70–89
Rome Treaty and, 103–4, 108–9
secondary law and, 136
standards of review, 95–102
TEU and, 70, 97
TFEU and, 70–71, 93
transparency of, 105
Treaty of Lisbon and, 93, 113, 115
UNCLOS and, 112, 126
WAEMU Court of Justice compared to, 355
weaknesses of, 135–36
WTO members and, 126–29
Court of the Eurasian Economic Union (CEEU), 295

Custom Tariff Act (1997), Canada, 223
Customs and International Trade Bar Association (CITBA), 187
Customs Court Act (1980), U.S., 184, 191. *See also* U.S. Court of International Trade
Customs Union Agreement, 286

de facto independence, 407
decision-making processes, in MERCOSUR, 242–52
  legal precedents as factor in, 243–49
  other tribunals as influence on, 243–49
Declaration on the Zone of Peace, Freedom and Neutrality, 12
democratic legitimacy, 229
diplomatic privileges, judicial independence through, 419–21
direct effect approach, 110–13, 459
Dispute Settlement Body (DSB). *See* Dispute Settlement Understanding
dispute settlement mechanisms (DSM), 10. *See also* ASEAN Dispute Settlement Mechanisms
  MERCOSUR, 230–36, 252–53
    compensatory measures, 235
    individual access to, 233–34
    WTO as influence on, 234–35
  RTA-DSM, 57–58
  for WTO, 20–21, 483
    access to trade tribunals through, 457–60
    treaty interpretation by, 491
Dispute Settlement Understanding (DSU), 22
  Article 21.5, 60–61
  procedural protections and, 33–34
  right to complain and, 29
  surveillance of implementation of, 59–60
  third-party participation under, 29–30
  time-frames for, 59
diversity, of CJEU judges, 80–81
document disclosure, by WTO, 32
domestic courts. *See* national and domestic courts
DSB. *See* Dispute Settlement Understanding
DSM. *See* dispute settlement mechanism
DSMP. *See* Protocol to the ASEAN Charter on Dispute Settlement Mechanisms
DSU. *See* Dispute Settlement Understanding

EACJ. *See* East African Court of Justice
East African Civil Society Organization's Forum, 338
East African Court of Justice (EACJ), 315–16, 322, 328, 340–41
  COMESA Court of Justice compared to, 336–38, 348
  exhaustion of domestic remedies and, 332
  expansion of jurisdiction for, 339–42
  human rights cases at, 333, 337, 339
East African Law Society, 337–38
ECCIS. *See* Economic Court of the Commonwealth of Independent States
ECHR. *See* European Convention on Human Rights
ECJ. *See* European Court of Justice
Economic Community of West Africa (ECOWAS), 361–62
Economic Community of West Africa (ECOWAS) Court of Justice, 315–16
  COMESA Court of Justice compared to, 336
  composition of, 351
  jurisdictional power of, 328
  legitimacy of, 316
Economic Court of the Commonwealth of Independent States (ECCIS)
  adjudication disputes, 310–12
  Belarus and, 11–12
  bindingness of judgments, 309
  CIS and, 288–90
  coercion issues for, 310–12
  consensus disputes for, 310–12

Economic Court of the Commonwealth of Independent States (ECCIS) (cont.)
economic integration strategies and, 291–95
EEC and, 293–94
Free Trade Agreement and, 291–92
inter-state disputes and, 297
in post-Soviet region, 307
under TEU, 291–92
establishment of, 11–12, 286–87
fact-finding procedures of, 303–4
forum shopping and, 305–8
through EEU, 307–8
under international law, 306–8
under TEU, 305–6
through WTO, 308
Free Trade Agreement and, 291–92, 298, 304–5, 308
free trade areas and, 298
as FTA, 461
GATT provisions and, 304–5
historical legacy of, 286
ICJ and, 306
institutional setting for, 286–98
legal basis for, 298
International Centre for Dispute Resolution and, 295–96
interpretative approaches for, 304–5
judges for, 299–301
judicial independence of, 299–301
jurisdiction for, 287–90
limits for, 302
legal basis of, 287–90
legitimacy issues for, 299–312
long-term legacy of, 312–13
national and domestic courts, interactions with, 309–10
operational status of, 296–98
procedural rules for, 302–3
transparency of, 303
purpose and function of, 11–12, 286
regional FTA courts and, 471
regional integration context for, 286–98
Russian Federation and, 11–12, 286, 291–92, 311–12
socioeconomic rights and, judgments influenced by, 297–98
TEU and, 291–92, 305–6, 309
third-party involvement in, 302
Ukraine and, 11–12
VCLT and, 304–5
WTO and, 304–5, 308
economic integration strategies, of ECCIS, 291–95
EEC and, 293–94
FTA and, 291–92
inter-state disputes and, 297
in post-Soviet region, 307
under TEU, 291–92
ECOWAS. *See* Economic Community of West Africa
ECOWAS Court of Justice. *See* Economic Community of West Africa Court of Justice
ECtHR. *See* European Court of Human Rights
Ecuador, 282
EDSM. *See* Enhanced Dispute Settlement Mechanism
EEA Agreement. *See* European Economic Area Agreement
EEC. *See* Eurasian Economic Community
EEU. *See* Eurasian Economic Union
effectiveness principle, 45, 495
EFTA. *See* European Free Trade Association
EFTA Court. *See* European Free Trade Association Court
EFTA Surveillance Authority, 149–50, 172, 174–78
employment dispute cases, 321–27, 351
energy trading scheme (ETS), 111
Enhanced Dispute Settlement Mechanism (EDSM), 365–66, 368–77
adjudication through, 368–70
time-frame limitations for, 374–75
for trade disputes, 373–74
administrative structure of, 372–73
AEM and, 370
appellate body members for, 372
CEPT-AFTA and, 368

compliance phase of, 370–72
functions of, 383–84
funding of, 372–73, 375–77
legitimacy of, 380–84
comparative benefits as condition of, 381
institutional integrity as condition of, 381–83
minimum moral acceptability as condition of, 380–81
negative consensus in, 368–69
operation costs of, 372–73
panelist selection for, 372
SEOM and, 368–70, 374–75, 400–1
WTO as model for, 368, 371–72, 382–83, 401–2
ESM. *See* European Stability Mechanism
ETS. *See* energy trading scheme
EU Charter of Fundamental Rights, 132–33
EU citizenship
EFTA Court and, 167–68
under EU law, 167
EU Civil Service Tribunal (EUCST), CJEU, 71
creation of, 72
judges in, 75–76
organization and functioning of, 82–83, 88–89
EU Law. *See* European Union Law
EUCST. *See* EU Civil Service Tribunal
Eurasian Economic Community (EEC), 293
ECCIS and, 293–94
Eurasian Economic Union (EEU), 295
ECCIS and, 307–8
European Convention on Human Rights (ECHR)
CJEU and, 133–35
in ECtHR case law, 134
EFTA Court and, 148, 152–53
European Court of First Instance, 458–59
European Court of Human Rights (ECtHR)
CJEU and, 132–35
EU Charter of Fundamental Rights, 132–33
ECHR interpreted by, 134
judicial independence, eligibility criteria for, 415–16
as regional court, 124
European Court of Justice (ECJ)
CJEU judgments and, 122–23
EEA Agreement and, 170, 172
EFTA Court and, 140, 154–56
procedural rules of, 147–48
interpretative approaches in, EFTA compared to, 160–61
MERCOSUR and, 243, 246–49
Solange judgments and, 500
European Economic Area (EEA) Agreement, 11, 148–50. *See also* European Free Trade Association Court
ECJ judgments and, 170, 172
EU law in conflict with, 164–67, 172
law of, 161–64
procedural rules, 160–61
treaty amendment and, 165
European Free Trade Association (EFTA), 138
non-trade exemption clauses and, 494
European Free Trade Association (EFTA) Court, of EEA. *See also* judges
challenges for, 139–40
Citizenship Directive and, 167–68
CJEU and, 129–32
competition law and, 151, 159
ECHR and, 148, 152–53
ECJ and, 140, 154–56
procedural rules influenced by, 147–48
establishment of, 11, 138–39
Extended Court in, 142
fact-finding procedures, 157–59
assessment of facts, 157–58
standards of proof in, 158–59
forum shopping and, 169–74
by national courts, 174
implementation procedures for, 174–79

European Free Trade Association (EFTA) Court, of EEA. (cont.)
for advisory opinions, 176–79
for judgments, 174–76
infringement procedures and, 113, 175–76
interpretative approaches in, 160–68
ECJ approaches compared to, 160–61
EEA law as influence on, 161–64
for EU citizenship, 167–68
EU law and, conflicts with, 164–67
methodology in, 160–61
legitimacy of, 166–67, 180–81
national and domestic courts and, 140–41
access through, 152
forum shopping by, 174
interactions with, 179–80
principle of procedural homogeneity and, 148
procedural rules, 147–56
for access to court, 150–54
case categorization and, 148–50
ECJ model as influence on, 147–48
for transparency, 154–56
purpose and functions of, 11
as regional court, 124
regional FTA courts and, 471
Surveillance and Court Agreement and, 130
Surveillance Authority, 149–50, 172, 174–78
Switzerland and, 138
European Stability Mechanism (ESM), 104
European Union, trade courts and tribunals in. *See specific trade courts*; *specific tribunals*
European Union (EU) Law
CJEU and, 95, 106–8
CoJ and, 118
international law and, 108–10
in Dutch systems, 108
EEA Agreement in conflict with, 164–67, 172
in German systems, 108
principle of proportionality and, 107
Union Citizenship concept under, 167
unwritten, 106–8
evidence, rules of
for USCIT
through judicial review, 192–94
in procedural rules, 190–91
in WTO fact-finding procedures, 38
evolutionary interpretation principle, 49–50
exhaustion of domestic remedies, 328–32
Extended Court, in EFTA, 142
external legitimacy, of ITCs, 6
external transparency, 32–35

fact-finding procedures
for Andean Community Court of Justice, 277–78
by CJEU, 95–102
adversarial principle and, 98
ascertainment of facts, 95–100
infringement procedures, 95–97
measures of inquiry, 99–100
measures of organization of the procedure and, 99
in EFTA Court, 157–59
assessment of facts, 157–58
standards of proof in, 158–59
in Federal Courts of Canada, 207
by ITCs, 506
by WAEMU Court of Justice, 361
of WTO, 38
allocation of, 35
burden of proof and, 36–38
rules of evidence as part of, 38
Federal Court of Appeal, Canada, 210–13, 217, 224–25
Federal Courts of Canada, 14
appeals process, 205–6
Canadian Charter of Rights and Freedom, 221
Canadian Import Tribunal and, 208
CBSA and, 205–6
CITT and, 203–6
jurisdiction of, 204–5
public hearings for, 206–7
review of judgments, 211–12

establishment of, 202–3
fact-finding by, 207
forum shopping and, 212–16
by NAFTA countries, 213–16
international courts and, interaction with, 217–23
dualist approach to treaty law in, 220
ICJ, 217–18
International Trade Commission and, 213–15
interpretative approaches by, 208–12
for judicial review, 208–9
for standards of review, 210–12
legitimacy of, 224–25
mandates of, 202–6
national and domestic courts, interaction with, 217–23
dualist approach to treaty law in, 220
procedural rules for, 206–7
purpose and functions of, 203–6
WTO and, 213–16
fixed price mechanism, 101
Fontoura Nogueira, Jorge Luiz, 241
formal judicial independence, 407, 422–24
forum shopping, 8
Andean Community Court of Justice and, 280–81
EFTA Court and, 169–74
by national courts, 174
Federal Courts of Canada and, 212–16
by NAFTA countries, 213–16
WAEMU Court of Justice and, 361–62
WTO and, 53–58
through jurisdictional conflict, 53
RTAs and, 53–56
France, CJEU judgments in, 121
Free Trade Agreement, ECCIS and, 291–92, 298, 304–5, 308
free trade agreements (FTAs). *See also* access to trade tribunals; regional FTA courts
under ASEAN Agreement for the Promotion and Protection of Investment Area, 460
ECCIS as, 461
expansion of, 3
key stakeholders in, 455
MERCOSUR as, 460–61
plurilateral negotiations of, 3
procedural rules for, 463
types of, 460
free trade areas, 298
FTAs. *See* free trade agreements

GATS. *See* General Agreement on Trade in Services
GATT. *See* General Agreement on Tariffs and Trade
GBS. *See* global basic structure
GC. *See* General Court
gender, of CJEU judges, 80–81
General Agreement on Tariffs and Trade (GATT)
CJEU and, 103–4
ECCIS and, 304–5
non-trade exemption clauses, 493–94
reverse consensus and, 64–65
RTAs and, 3
WTO-RTA interactions under, 443–46
General Agreement on Trade in Services (GATS), 493–94
General Court (GC), CJEU, 71
AGs and, 71–75
judges in, 71–75
organization and functioning of, 81–89
WTO members and, 126–29
Germany, CJEU judgments in, 108, 122
global basic structure (GBS), of WTO
arguments against, 485–87
components of, 480
conceptual development of, 484–85
as separate from WTO, 487–88
SPGs and, 484
global distributive justice, 482
principles of, 484–85
WTO system and, 488–92, 502

harmonious interpretation principle, 46–47
of international law, 110–13

human rights cases, in African courts and tribunals, 343
at COMESA, 333–34
at EACJ, 333, 337, 339
at SADC, 339

Iceland, 153–54. *See also* European Free Trade Association Court
ICJ. *See* International Court of Justice
immunity, judicial independence through, 419–21
impartiality, of CJEU judges, 78
Implementation Act, 189
implementation of judgments. *See* interpretative approaches; *specific courts and tribunals*
IMS procedure. *See* Internal Market Scoreboard procedure
in dubio mitius principle, 494–95
WTO and, 47–48
inactive regional FTA courts, 477
independence. *See also* judicial independence
of MERCOSUR arbitrators, 240–42
Indonesia, 389–92, 396–97
informal judicial independence, 407
infringement procedures
CJEU and, 95–97
in implementation of judgments, 113–17
for EFTA Court, 113, 175–76
insider-outsider model, for WTO, 20–22
institutional integrity condition, for legitimacy, 381–83
INTAL. *See* Integration of Latin America and the Caribbean
integration law, 278–79
Integration of Latin America and the Caribbean (INTAL), 257–58
intellectual property cases, Andean Community Court of Justice and, 283
interim relief
through COMESA Court of Justice, 320
WTO rulings, 66–67
interim review, WTO, 66
internal legitimacy, of ITCs, 6
Internal Market Scoreboard (IMS) procedure, 116
internal transparency, 32–35
International Centre for Dispute Resolution, 295–96
International Court of Justice (ICJ)
CJEU and, 124–25
ECCIS and, 306
Federal Courts of Canada and, 217–18
MERCOSUR and, 232, 243, 245
WTO adjudicating bodies and, 447–48
International Criminal Court for Rwanda, 338–39
international law
CJEU and
CoJ and, 111–12
direct effect and, 110–13
EU Law and, 108–10
harmonious interpretation and, 110–13
interpretative approaches by, 108–13
under TFEU, 110
International Trade Commission, 213–15
international trade courts (ITCs). *See also specific courts and tribunals*
adjudication structure of, 432
bounded discretion of, 410
burden of proof for, 506
constrained independence of, 410
diverted use of, 509–10
embedding of, 9
fact-finding by, 506
implementation of, 9
interactions between, 507–8
interpretative approaches by, 506–7
judicial independence of, 406–9, 427–31, 504–5
assessment of, 409–12
evaluation of, 421–27
measurement criteria for, 412–21
judicial model for, 503
legitimacy of, 4–7

through consent of sovereign states, 5
external, 6
internal, 6
judgment output as factor for, 6
legal procedures and practices and, 6, 505–6
national and domestic courts and, interactions with, 9, 508–9
local cultural context as influence on, 510
procedural legitimacy of, 505–6
research methodology for, 7–9
through selection of trade courts, 9–14
under-use of, 509–10
International Tribunal for the Law of the Sea (ITLOS), 125–26
interpretative approaches, for judgments
by Andean Community Court of Justice, 278–80
under integration law, 278–79
in ASEAN Dispute Settlement Mechanisms, 392–93
by CJEU, 102–13
direct effect approach, 110–13
harmonious interpretation approach, 110–13
of international law, 108–13
of secondary law, 105–6
of unwritten European Union law, 106–8
of Vienna Convention on the Law of Treaties, 102–5
by COMESA Court of Justice, 339–42, 345
for ECCIS, 304–5
in EFTA Court, 160–68
ECJ approaches compared to, 160–61
EEA law as influence on, 161–64
for EU citizenship, 167–68
EU law and, conflicts with, 164–67
methodology in, 160–61
by Federal Courts of Canada, 208–12
for judicial review, 208–9
for standards of review, 210–12
by ITCs, 506–7
by regional FTA courts, 463–64
Italy, CJEU judgments and, 96, 117, 121
ITCs. *See* international trade courts
ITLOS. *See* International Tribunal for the Law of the Sea

judges. *See also* tenure of judges
active, 182
in Andean Community Court of Justice, 262–68
composition of, 262–64
conflicts of interest for, 266
immunity for, 265–66
nomination of, 264–65
oath of office for, 264–65
removal of, 265–66
requirement criteria for, 263
selection of, 264–65
in CCJ, 413
Chief Judges, 182
in CJEU
CoJ, 71–75
composition of, 71–81
diversity of, 80–81
in EUCST, 75–76
GC, 71–75
gender of, 80–81
impartiality of, 78
independence of, 78
length of mandate for, 71–81
qualifications of, 71–81
for COMESA Court of Justice, 318
for ECCIS, 299–301
in EFTA Court, 141–47
independence of, 146–47
length of tenure for, 143–44
nomination process in, 143
number of judges, 141
qualification criteria for, 145–46
reappointment of, 146
in Federal Courts of Canada, 203
selection of, 202–6
in USCIT
appointment of, 183
purpose and function of, 182
for WAEMU Court of Justice, 352
independence of, 353–54

judicial dialogue, 433
judicial independence
activity limitations and, 417–18
of Andean Community Court of Justice, 262–68
of CJEU, 78, 411
confidentiality of deliberations and, 418
court resources for, 416–17
through diplomatic privileges, 419–21
of ECCIS, 299–301
of ECtHR, eligibility criteria for, 415–16
in EFTA Court, 146–47
eligibility criteria as factor for, 415–16
formal, 407, 422–24
through immunity, 419–21
informal, 407
of ITCs, 406–9, 427–31, 504–5
assessment of, 409–12
evaluation of, 421–27
measurement criteria for, 412–21
as legal concept, 405–6
legitimacy and, as significant factor for, 406–9
through oaths, 418–19
recusal mechanisms as factor for, 417–18
rules of procedure as influence on, 417
selection of judges as factor in, 413–15
tenure of judges as factor in, 413–15
in USCIT, 184–87
in WAEMU Court of Justice, 353–54
of WTO adjudicating bodies, 24–25
judicial interactions, between international trade courts and tribunals, 507–8. *See also specific courts*
definitions of, 433–34
judicial dialogue as distinct from, 433
NAFTA and, 437
overlapping jurisdictions as influence on, 434–35
preconditions for, 434
scope of, 432–35
typology of, 435–38
passive interactions, 436
proactive interactions, 435–36
of WTO adjudicators, 438–46. *See also* adjudicating bodies, of WTO
assessment of legitimacy for, 446–52
judicial review
by Federal Courts of Canada, 208–9
through USCIT, 191–95, 506
for discretionary standards, 194
for evidentiary standards, 192–94
for trade cases, 192
jurisconsult of recognized competence, 73
jurisdiction
for African courts and tribunals, expansion of, 342–43
of Andean Community Court of Justice, 268–74
for labour disputes, 273–74
through prejudgment interpretations, 271–72
of CITT, 204–5
of COMESA Court of Justice, 317–20, 322
over COMESA employee conduct, 327–28
over employment disputes, 321–27
for EACJ, expansion of, 339–42
for ECCIS, 287–90
limits for, 302
for ECOWAS Court of Justice, 328
forum shopping and, 53
judicial interactions influenced by, 434–35
of regional FTA courts, 475–77
of USCIT, 188–90
limitations of, 188
of WAEMU Court of Justice
for annulment of Union acts, 355–56
of WAEMU Court of Justice Court, 354–57
advisory, 359

for compensation payments, 357
for competition law, 356
for contractual liability, 357
for employee dispute cases, 356–57
for infringement actions, 354–55
of WTO, conflicts surrounding, 53
justice. *See* global distributive justice

Kazakhstan, 286, 293
Kituo Cha Kitaba, 338
Kyrgyzstan, 293

labour dispute cases, 273–74
Lamy, Pascal, 483
language regime, in CJEU, 85–87
Latin America, trade courts and tribunals in. *See* Andean Community Court of Justice; Southern Common Market in Latin America
Latin American Free Trade Association, 257
law. *See specific topics*
least developed countries (LDCs), WTO and, 29
legal diplomacy, 331
Legal Services and Agreements Division (LSAD), 399
legitimacy
through access to trade tribunals, 454
of ASEAN Dispute Settlement Mechanisms, 380–84
comparative benefits as condition of, 381
institutional integrity as condition of, 381–83
minimum moral acceptability as condition of, 380–81
of CJEU, 81, 87, 135–37
of COMESA Court of Justice, 316, 333–35
assessment of, 334
human rights cases and, 333–34
defined, 5, 228–29
democratic, 229
of ECCIS, 299–312
of ECOWAS Court of Justice, 316
of EDSM, 380–84
comparative benefits as condition of, 381
institutional integrity as condition of, 381–83
minimum moral acceptability as condition of, 380–81
of EFTA Court, 166–67, 180–81
of Federal Courts of Canada, 224–25
of ITCs, 4–7
through consent of sovereign states, 5
external, 6
internal, 6
judgment output as factor for, 6
legal procedures and practices and, 6, 505–6
of MERCOSUR, 230–36
through absence of institutionalised sanction mechanism, 234–36
forum choice as factor in, 230–33
through individual access to tribunals, 233–34
normative, 408–9
normative conception of, 229
sociological, 408
of USCIT, 200–1
of WTO, 20–22, 64–68
of DSM, 20–21
insider-outsider model, 20–22
of RTA-DSMs, 57–58
of WTO adjudicators, 446–52
AB Members and, 448–52
lex specialis principle, 48–49
Liechtenstein. *See* European Free Trade Association Court
Lisbon Treaty. *See* Treaty of Lisbon
LSAD. *See* Legal Services and Agreements Division

Malaysia, 388–91, 396–97
marginal regional FTA courts, 477
MarPol Convention, 112
Marrakesh Agreement, 495
MERCOSUR. *See* Southern Common Market in Latin America
Mike Campbell case, 330

minimum moral acceptability condition, for legitimacy, 380–81
Mixed International Criminal Tribunal, 338–39
Multilateral Surveillance Mechanism, 355

NAFTA. *See* North American Free Trade Agreement
national and domestic courts
Andean Community Court of Justice and, interactions with, 249–52, 281–82
prejudgment interpretations by, 271–72
CJEU and
enforcement of ECJ judgments in, 122–23
in France, 121
in Germany, 121–22
in Italy, 96, 117, 121
in the Netherlands, 123
in Spain, 117
COMESA Court of Justice and, 319
ECCIS and, interactions with, 309–10
EFTA Court and, 140–41
access for, 152
forum shopping and, 174
interactions between, 179–80
Federal Courts of Canada and, interaction with, 217–23
dualist approach to treaty law in, 220
ITCs and, interactions with, 9, 508–9
local cultural context as influence on, 510
MERCOSUR and, interactions with, 234
through advisory opinions, 250–52
regional FTA courts and, 472–73
WAEMU and, interactions with, 362–63
WTO rulings and, 59–63
compensation mechanisms, 61–62
compliance review for, 60–61
implementation framework for, 59, 62–63
surveillance of, 59–60
time-frame for, 59
negative consensus, 368–69
the Netherlands, CJEU judgments in, 108, 123
NGOs. *See* non-governmental organizations
non-compliance requests, 270
ASEAN Dispute Settlement Mechanisms and, 379
non-contractual liability, 357
non-governmental organizations (NGOs)
Andean Community Court of Justice and, 275–77
COMESA Court of Justice and, 315–16
in East Africa, 338–39
in WTO, 20–40
non-trade exemption clauses
EFTA Courts and, 494
GATS and, 493–94
GATT and, 493–94
WTO and, 493–95
normative legitimacy, 229, 408–9
North American Free Trade Agreement (NAFTA), 189, 196–97, 434
forum shopping and, 213–16
Norway, 153–54. *See also* European Free Trade Association Court
EEA law in, 161–64

oaths, for judicial independence, 418–19
OECD Agreement. *See* Organisation for Economic Co-operation and Development Agreement
Ogang, Martin, 324–26
Olivos Protocol, 227–28, 233, 238–41, 253, 471
omissions procedures, 273
Organisation for Economic Co-operation and Development (OECD) Agreement, 103–4
outreach activities, of Andean Community Court of Justice, 276–77

Pacific Alliance, 3, 280
PCIJ. *See* Permanent Court of International Justice
Permanent Court of Arbitration, 306
Permanent Court of International Justice (PCIJ)
  MERCOSUR and, 243, 245
  WTO adjudicating bodies and, 447–48
Permanent Review Court (PRC), MERCOSUR, 228, 238–40, 249–51
Permanent Review Tribunal (PRT), MERCOSUR, 423–24
Perotti, Alejandro, 237, 241–42
Peru, 282
Philippines, 391–92, 394
plurilateral negotiations
  for FTAs, 3
  for Pacific Alliance, 3
  for Regional Comprehensive Partnership Agreement in Asia, 3
  for TPP Agreement, 3
  for Tripartite Agreement, 3
  for TTIP Agreement, 3
Pogge, Thomas, 491
political sensitiveness, 65
PRC. *See* Permanent Review Court
Preferential Trade Area (PTA), for Eastern and Southern Africa, 13–14
Preferential Trade Area (PTA) Bank, 324–26
  Burundi and, 331
prejudgment interpretations, 271–72
primary law
  CJEU and, 136
  MERCOSUR and, 228
principle of effectiveness. *See* effectiveness principle
principle of procedural homogeneity. *See* procedural homogeneity
private parties
  Andean Community Court of Justice and, 275–77
  in regional FTA courts, 473–75
procedural homogeneity, principle of, 148
procedural rules. *See also* fact-finding procedures; infringement procedures
  for Andean Community Court of Justice, 268–77
    for annulments, 269–70
    for arbitration, 274
    legitimacy under, 274–75
    for non-compliance requests, 270
    for omissions, 273
  for ECCIS, 302–3
    transparency of, 303
  under EEA Agreement, 160–61
  for EFTA Court, 147–56
    for access to court, 150–54
    case categorization and, 148–50
    ECJ model as influence on, 147–48
    for transparency, 154–56
  for Federal Courts of Canada, 206–7
  for FTAs, 463
  for TAC in Southeast Asia, 367
  for USCIT, 191
    for documentation, 190
    for evidence, 190–91
    for transparency, 190–91
  for WAEMU Court of Justice, 354–61
    for access to courts, 360–61
  WTO, 28–35
    for *amicus curiae* submissions, 30–31
    for participation in proceedings, 28–35
    right to complain, 28–29
    for third-party participation in, 29–30
    for transparency, 32–35
proof. *See* burden of proof; standards of proof
proportionality principle, European Law and, 107
Protocol to the ASEAN Charter on Dispute Settlement Mechanisms (DSMP), 377–79, 383

provisions, of WTO, interpretation of, 43–53
AB reports in, 50–51
clarification compared to, 43–44
cross-referencing in, 50
effectiveness principle, 45, 495
evolutionary interpretation principle, 49–50
harmonious interpretation principle, 46–47
lex specialis principle, 48–49
in dubio mitius principle, 47–48, 494–95
prior panel reports in, 50–51
for treaties, 44–50
tribunal reports in, 51
PRT. *See* Permanent Review Tribunal
PTA. *See* Preferential Trade Area
PTA Bank. *See* Preferential Trade Area Bank

Rawls, John, 484
reasonable period of time (RPT), 59
RECs. *See* Regional Economic Communities
recusal, of judges, judicial independence and, 417–18
Regional Comprehensive Partnership Agreement in Asia, 3
Regional Economic Communities (RECs)
in Africa, 349
ECOWAS and, 361–62
WAEMU and, 349, 361–62
regional FTA courts, 460–77. *See also specific courts*
Andean Community Court of Justice and, 471
basic characteristics of, 469
development trajectories of, 478
ECCIS and, 471
EFTA Court and, 471
formal access to, 460–66
scoring of, 466
types of, 464–65
inactive, 477
institutions of, 473
interpretative approach by, 463–64
jurisdiction of, 475–77
marginal, 477
private parties in, 473–75
real access to, 470–77
by domestic courts, 472–73
by key stakeholders, 471–75
by states, 471–72
single-issue courts, 477
subject-matter for, 475–77
use of, factors for, 467–70
expected use, 470
length of operation of court, 467
timing of first ruling, 468
regional trade agreements (RTAs)
expansion of, 3, 432–33
interactions with WTO adjudication bodies, 438–46
admissibility of evidence issues in, 441
under GATT, 443–46
jurisdiction conflicts between, 439–41
legal interpretation of, 441–43
in MERCOSUR, 443, 445–46
obligation conflicts between, 443–46
under VCLT, 438–39
RTA-DSM, 57–58
WTO and
dispute resolution under, 53–56
economic costs of, 56
forum shopping and, 53–56
legitimacy of DSMs, 57–58
political costs of, 56
reports. *See* tribunal reports
Republic of Mauritius v. Polytol Paints and Adhesives Manufacturers Co. Ltd., 329, 332–33, 340, 346
reverse consensus, 64–65
right to complain, 28–29
Rome Treaty, CJEU and, 103–4, 108–9
RPT. *See* reasonable period of time
RTAs. *See* regional trade agreements
Russian Federation. *See also* Free Trade Agreement
CIS and, 293–95
Customs Union Agreement and, 286

ECCIS and, 11–12, 286, 291–92, 311–12
SACU. *See* States of the Southern African Custom Union
SADC. *See* Southern African Development Tribunal
secondary law, 105–6
CJEU and, 136
MERCOSUR and, 228
selection, of judges
in Andean Community Court of Justice, 264–65
in Federal Courts of Canada, 202–6
judicial independence influenced by, 413–15
in WTO adjudicating bodies, 22–28
Senior Economic Officials Meeting (SEOM), of EDSM, 368–70, 374–75, 400–1
separation of powers doctrine, 184–85
single-issue courts, 477
social primary goods (SPGs), 484
socioeconomic rights, 297–98
sociological legitimacy, 408
Solange judgments, 500
SOLVIT procedure, 116
Southern African Development Tribunal (SADC), 322, 328
COMESA Court of Justice compared to, 336
human rights cases at, 339
Southern Common Market in Latin America (MERCOSUR), 3–4
Andean Community Court of Justice and, 243, 246
anti-dumping cases and, 231
arbitrators for, 236–40
independence of, 240–42
nominations for, 236–40
qualifications of, 240–42
Argentina and, 231–32
Brasilia Protocol and, 227–28, 233, 245–46, 471
Brazil and, 231–33
CA and, 13
CMC in, 227, 241, 250
CMG in, 227, 241–42
dispute settlement mechanisms, 230–36, 252–53
compensatory measures, 235
individual access to, 233–34
WTO as influence on, 234–35
ECJ case law and, 243, 246–49
establishment of, 12–13, 227
FTAs and, 460–61
ICJ case law and, 232, 243, 245
judicial decision-making processes, 242–52
legal precedents as factor in, 243–49
other tribunals as influence on, 243–49
legitimacy of, 230–36
through absence of institutionalised sanction mechanism, 234–36
forum choice as factor in, 230–33
through individual access to tribunals, 233–34
national and domestic courts and, interactions with, 234
through advisory opinions, 250–52
Olivos Protocol and, 227–28, 233, 238–41, 253, 471
PCIJ case law and, 243, 245
primary law and, 228
PRT, 423–24
purpose and function of, 12–13, 227–30
secondary law and, 228
Treaty of Asunción and, 227
tribunals for, 236–40
ad hoc, 237–38
composition of, 236–40
nominations for, 236–40
PRC in, 228, 238–40, 249–51
VCLT and, 243–44
WTO law and, 234–35, 245–46
WTO-RTA interactions, 443, 445–46
Spain, CJEU and, 117
SPGs. *See* social primary goods
SPS Agreement. *See* Agreement on Sanitary or Phytosanitary Measures

standards of proof, in EFTA Court, 158–59
standards of review
by AB members, in WTO, 39–42
for CJEU, 95–102
by Federal Courts of Canada, 210–12
States of the Southern African Custom Union (SACU), 169
Stiglitz, Joseph, 479
Supreme Court of Canada, 210–11, 217, 219–20
Surveillance and Court Agreement, 130
Switzerland, EFTA Court and, 138

TAC. *See* Treaty of Amity and Cooperation in Southeast Asia
Tajikistan, 293
TBT. *See* Agreement on Technical Barriers to Trade
tenure of judges
in CJEU, 71–81
judicial independence influenced by, 413–15
TEU. *See* Treaty on European Union
TFEU. *See* Treaty on the Functioning of the European Union
Thailand, 391–92, 394
third-parties
as alternative to ASEAN Dispute Settlement Mechanisms, 384–85, 393–97
DSU participation by, 29–30
in ECCIS cases, 302
in EFTA Court, 154
under TFEU, 94–95
amicus curiae and, 94–95
TPP Agreement. *See* Trans-Pacific Partnership Agreement
trade agreement disputes. *See also* access to trade tribunals; international trade courts
ASEAN Dispute Settlement Mechanisms and, 395–96
LSAD and, 399
historical approach to, 455–56
under TBT, 456
trade courts and tribunals, 9–14. *See also* international trade courts; *specific courts*; *specific tribunals*
Federal Courts of Canada and, interaction with, 217–23
dualist approach to treaty law in, 220
ICJ and, 217–18
for MERCOSUR, 236–40
ad hoc tribunals, 237–38
composition of, 236–40
nominations for, 236–40
PRC in, 228, 238–40, 249–51
Transatlantic Trade Investment Partnership (TTIP) Agreement, plurilateral negotiations for, 3
Trans-Pacific Partnership (TPP) Agreement, plurilateral negotiations for, 3
transparency
of CJEU, 105
in ECCIS procedural rules, 303
of EFTA Court, 154–56
external, 32–35
internal, 32–35
of USCIT
Constitutional roots of, 190–91
procedural rules for, 190–91
of WTO adjudication, 32–35
treaties. *See also specific treaties*
dualist approach to, 220
WTO interpretation of, 44–50
through DSMs, 491
Treaty for the Establishment of COMESA, 321–23
exhaustion of domestic remedies under, 328–32
Treaty for the Establishment of the East African Union, 339–40
Treaty of Amity and Cooperation (TAC) in Southeast Asia, 12, 365–67
procedural rules for, 367
Treaty of Amsterdam, 165
Treaty of Asunción, 227
Treaty of Lisbon, 165
CJEU and, 93, 113, 115
Treaty of Maastricht, 165
Treaty of Nice, 165
Treaty on European Union (TEU)
CJEU and, 70, 97
ECCIS and, 291–92, 305–6, 309

Treaty on the Free Trade Area, 295
Treaty on the Functioning of the European Union (TFEU)
  CJEU and, 70–71, 93
  failure to act under, 361
  under international law, 110
  third-party interventions in, 94–95
    amicus curiae, 94–95
tribunal reports, by WTO, 51
tribunals. *See* international trade courts; trade courts and tribunals; *specific tribunals*
Tripartite Agreement, 3
TRIPS. *See* Agreement on Trade-related Aspects of Intellectual Property Rights
Trujillo Protocol, 260
TTIP Agreement. *See* Transatlantic Trade Investment Partnership Agreement

Ukraine, 11–12
UN Convention on the Law of the Sea (UNCLOS), 112, 126
uniformity requirement, 183
United States (U.S.). *See also* Constitution, U.S.; North American Free Trade Agreement
  Canada–United States Free Trade Agreement, 211–12
  Customs Court Act, 184
  International Trade Commission, 213–15
  trade courts and tribunals in. *See* U.S. Court of International Trade
Uruguay Round Agreements Act (URAA), 189, 198
U.S. *See* United States
U.S. Court of International Trade (USCIT), 14. *See also* judges
  access to, 187–90
  accountability of, 187
    CAFC and, 186
  administrative law and, 200–1
  appeals of judgments, 201
  bindingness of judgments, 199–200
  Charming Betsy doctrine and, 199
  Chief Judges in, 182
  CITBA and, 187
  Constitutional framework for, 184–87
  historical background of, 183–84
  Implementation Act and, 189
  judicial independence of, 184–87
  judicial review through, 191–95, 506
    for discretionary standards, 194
    for evidentiary standards, 192–94
    for trade cases, 192
  jurisdiction of, 188–90
    limitations of, 188
  legitimacy of, 200–1
  NAFTA and, 189, 196–97
  procedural rules for, 191
    for documentation, 190
    for evidence, 190–91
    for transparency, 190–91
  purpose and function of, 182
  separation of powers doctrine and, 184–85
  transparency of
    Constitutional roots of, 190–91
    procedural rules for, 190–91
  uniformity requirement for, 183
  URAA and, 189, 198
  WTO and, 197–200
U.S. Customs Court, 184
USCIT. *See* U.S. Court of International Trade

VCLT. *See* Vienna Convention on the Law of Treaties
Venezuela, withdrawal from Andean Community Court of Justice, 262, 281, 285
Vienna Convention on the Law of Treaties (VCLT), 102–5
  COMESA Court of Justice and, 333
  ECCIS and, 304–5
  MERCOSUR and, 243–44
  WTO-RTA interactions under, 438–39

WAEMU. *See* Western African Economic and Monetary Union
WAEMU Court of Justice. *See* Western African Economic and Monetary Union Court of Justice

Western African Economic and Monetary Union (WAEMU)
establishment of, 349
purpose and function of, 349–50
RECs and, 349, 361–62
Treaty of Dakar and, 349
Western African Economic and Monetary Union (WAEMU) Court of Justice
annulment procedure, 355–56
as arbitration tribunal, 358
cases before, types of, 357
CJEU compared to, 355
employee dispute cases at, 351, 356–57
establishment of, 13–14, 350
fact-finding by, 361
forum shopping and, 361–62
judges for, 352
independence of, 353–54
jurisdiction of, 354–57
advisory, 359
for annulment of Union acts, 355–56
for compensation payments, 357
for competition law, 356
for contractual liability, 357
for employee dispute cases, 356–57
for infringement actions, 354–55
limitations of, 350–51
long-term implications for, 363–64
members of, 352–54
composition of, 352
selection process for, 352
Multilateral Surveillance Mechanism, 355
national and domestic courts and, interactions with, 362–63
procedural rules for, 354–61
for access to courts, 360–61
purpose and function of, 13–14
references for preliminary rulings, 358
as single-issue court, 477
WTO and, 352
women, as CJEU judges, 80–81
World Trade Organization (WTO). *See also* adjudicating bodies, of WTO; dispute settlement mechanisms
AB members, 22, 25–27
assessment of legitimacy for, 448–52
hearings by, 32–33
interpretation of provisions by, 50–51
reports on provisions, 50–51
standards of review by, 39–42
ACWL, 56
ADA, 127–28, 459
Andean Community Court of Justice and, 280
CJEU and, 126–29
confidentiality and, 32
critics of, 479–80
defenders of, 479–80
document disclosure, 32
DSMs, 10, 483
access to trade tribunals through, 457–60
legitimacy of, 20–21
of RTA-DSMs, 57–58
treaty interpretation through, 491
DSU, 22
Article 21.5, 60–61
procedural protections and, 33–34
right to complain and, 29
surveillance of implementation of, 59–60
third-party participation under, 29–30
time-frames for, 59
ECCIS and, 304–5, 308
EDSM influenced by, 368, 371–72, 382–83, 401–2
external transparency of, 32–35
fact-finding power of, 38
allocation of, 35
burden of proof and, 36–38
rules of evidence as part of, 38
Federal Courts of Canada and, 213–16
forum shopping and, 53–58
through jurisdictional conflict, 53
RTAs and, 53–56
GBS of
arguments against, 485–87

components of, 480
conceptual development of, 484–85
as separate from WTO, 487–88
SPGs and, 484
GC and, 126–29
global distributive justice and, 488–92, 502
institutional structure, 64–65
nomenclature in, 64
reverse consensus, 64–65
internal transparency of, 32–35
interpretation of, 492–501. *See also* provisions
through case law, 496–97
changes in, promotion strategies for, 499–501
evolutionary, 495–96
through non-trade exemption clauses, 493–95
public pressure as influence on, 501
Solange judgments and, 500
systemic, 497–99
LDCs and, 29
legitimacy of, 20–22, 64–68
of DSMs, 20–21
insider-outsider model, 20–22
of RTA-DSMs, 57–58
MERCOSUR and, 234–35, 245–46
national courts, interactions with, 59–63
compensation mechanisms, 61–62
compliance review for, 60–61
implementation framework for, 59, 62–63
surveillance of, 59–60
time-frame for, 59
NGOs and, 20–40
panel meetings and, 32–33
political sensitiveness, 65
procedural proceedings, 66–68
for interim relief, 66–67
for interim review, 66
for preliminary rulings, 66
for provisional measures, 66–67
procedural rules, 28
for *amicus curiae* submissions, 30–31
for participation in proceedings, 28–35
right to complain, 28–29
for third-party participation in, 29–30
for transparency, 32–35
RTAs
dispute resolution under, 53–56
economic costs of, 56
forum shopping and, 53–56
legitimacy of DSMs, 57–58
political costs of, 56
standards of review, 39–42
USCIT and, 197–200
WAEMU Court of Justice and, 352

Yayi case, 362–63